I0592270

Bernhard von Cotta, Philip Henry Lawrence

Rocks classified and described

A Treatise on Lithology

Bernhard von Cotta, Philip Henry Lawrence

Rocks classified and described
A Treatise on Lithology

ISBN/EAN: 9783337177027

Printed in Europe, USA, Canada, Australia, Japan

Cover: Foto ©ninafisch / pixelio.de

More available books at **www.hansebooks.com**

LITHOLOGY.

LONDON
PRINTED BY SPOTTISWOODE AND CO.
NEW-STREET SQUARE

ROCKS

CLASSIFIED AND DESCRIBED.

A Treatise on Lithology.

BY BERNHARD VON COTTA.

AN ENGLISH EDITION

BY

PHILIP HENRY LAWRENCE.

WITH ENGLISH, GERMAN, AND FRENCH SYNONYMS.

REVISED BY THE AUTHOR.

LONDON:

LONGMANS, GREEN, AND CO.

1866.

LITHOLOGY, or a Classified Synopsis of the
Names of Rocks and Minerals, also by Mr. LAWRENCE,
adapted to the present work, may be had, price 5s. or
printed on one side only (interpaged blank) for use in
Cabinets, price 7s.

TRANSLATOR'S PREFACE.

In presenting this work to English readers, I wish to acknowledge the kind assistance I have received from Professor Jukes and Mr. Bristow in my own country, from M. Daubrée and M. Guyerdet in France, and last, but not least, from the distinguished author, Professor Cotta himself, and from Mr. Stelzner, of Freiberg, to whose valuable assistance I owe most of what is good in the new arrangement of the Mineralogical part of the work. For the many imperfections which, in spite of much care, will probably be found, I am alone responsible. Nevertheless, I hope that this work may in some measure supply a want which has been long felt in our geological literature.

I trust that allowance will be made for the difficulties of a translator if, in some instances, terms have been used in this work in a slightly extended or even different sense from that of some English authors. This has never been done without much consideration, and what appeared to me absolute necessity in rendering the meaning of my author, and in the absence of an exact equivalent for the German term in our accepted geological language.

The juxtaposition of the English, German, and French equivalent names for each rock, although frequently presenting doubts and difficulties, will, I trust, in the main meet with acceptance, in which case it cannot fail to prove useful.

Scientific names are the coin in which enquirers must exchange their ideas; and if they can be made to correspond in different countries, the gain to science will be great. Such correspondence is as important in its way as the assimilation of currency for the operations of commerce. Should this object have been in any way promoted by the present work, my most sanguine expectations will have been fulfilled.

I may here mention that, in furtherance of the same object, I have published, separately, a catalogue of the names of Rocks in the three languages. This catalogue, which is an outline of this work, may, perhaps, prove useful to collectors.

P. H. LAWRENCE.

London: *January* 1866.

AUTHOR'S PREFACE

TO THIS EDITION.

BEFORE my friend the Translator undertook the translation of this work, I had collected materials and made certain alterations with a view to a third edition.

The Translator himself, in the course of his labour, proposed certain alterations, which were adopted with my entire concurrence.

As far as my knowledge of the language enables me to judge, after a careful perusal, the translation appears to me to be very accurate.

This English edition may therefore be considered as the third edition of my original work, although, if the appearance of a third German edition should be delayed for some time longer, there will doubtless be new matter and fresh alterations to be introduced; for Science marches with uninterrupted steps towards new fields of discovery, and every year alters its aspect.

In a system of Lithology, however, most of the names

which are in use will probably remain, and one chief object of this book is to define these so as to render intelligible the ideas which each name should convey; and both Author and Translator are actuated by the desire and ambition of arriving, as far as may be possible, at a common ground for all nations in respect of the important matter of rock-nomenclature.

B. COTTA.

FREIBERG : *January* 1866.

CONTENTS.

PART I.

CHAPTER I.

CHAPTER II.

CHAPTER III.

CHAPTER IV.

CHAPTER V.

PART II.—The Rocks.

INTRODUCTORY CHAPTER.

CHAPTER IV.

CHAPTER V.

PART III.

LITHOLOGY.

PART I.

CHAPTER I.

MINERALS.

THE SEVERAL SUBSTANCES which form the materials of the earth's crust are termed 'Rocks,' the idea of a solid rocky substance not being necessarily implied. Most of what we call rocks are no doubt of a firm and solid character, but some consist only of soft or loose aggregates or accumulations of their component parts.

These component parts are always minerals; that is to say, all rocks are mineral aggregates, consisting of minute mineral parts more or less solid and more or less intimately and firmly united, knit, or cemented together. By this definition it will be seen that we exclude the animal and vegetable kingdoms; it may therefore be well to add that under the term mineral we include all mineralised remains of organic bodies.

Most rocks are made up of parts of two or more different minerals, in which case they are termed *composite*. Some rocks, however, consist essentially of particles of one mineral only, such for instance as limestone; these, in contradistinction to the composite, are termed *simple* rocks.

The composite as well as the simple rocks not unfrequently contain subordinate ingredients, besides those which are essential to their character. These subordinate ingredients are termed *accessory* or *non-essential*. In most cases they are inconsiderable in quantity, or they only occur locally and do not appreciably alter the nature

B

of the rock; but sometimes these accessory ingredients impart a special character to it, and so to a certain extent pass into essentials. Their presence creates the varieties of species.

The constituent minerals (whether accessory or essential) of any given rock either occur in separate crystals or particles distinguishable by the naked eye, or they consist of small finely divided particles so intimately blended together as apparently to form a homogeneous mass; nevertheless, in the latter case, their separate existence may be generally recognised by magnifying power.

The first and principal requisite for the student of Lithology is to be able to recognise and determine the minerals of which a given rock consists. This is in many cases no easy task; he must therefore have a competent knowledge of mineralogy. Not with a view adequately to supply the want of such knowledge, but by way of introduction to our subject, and for the purpose of reference in the absence of more comprehensive works, we propose to give in this chapter a brief notice of the principal minerals with which we have to do in examining the structure of rocks, adding such particulars as are more especially useful for our present purpose.

The number of these principal minerals is relatively very small. They may be classed under the following comprehensive names: — FELSPAR, QUARTZ, MICA, HORNBLENDE (Amphibole), PYROXENE (Augite), CALCSPAR, and DOLOMITE. The following occur less frequently :—CHLORITE, TALC, LEUCITE, NEPHELINE, OLIVINE, TOURMALINE, GARNET, GYPSUM, COAL, some SULPHURETS, and some IRON ORES.

The number of the accessory ingredients is very much greater, and indeed almost unlimited; that is to say, under certain circumstances almost every known mineral may occur as an accessory in any rock, and the essential ingredients of one rock frequently occur as accessories in another rock. But although we may say with truth that the number of the accessory minerals is without limit, yet in fact only about a quarter of the number of hitherto known minerals occur in rocks so abundantly and frequently as to be specially noticed in a treatise of Lithology.

One consideration is particularly deserving the atten-

tion of the scientific observer of rocks; we refer to what
is termed by Breithaupt the ' Paragenesis ' of minerals.
By this is meant the law of mutual association or repulsion
of certain minerals. It is well known to mineralogists
that the presence of one mineral very frequently denotes
the neighbourhood of another, and, *vice versâ*, that the
presence of some minerals forbids the simultaneous presence of certain others.

In 1849 Breithaupt first treated this subject, and published in his ' Paragenesis der Mineralien ' a great number
of remarkable instances of this law. We may, for the sake
of illustration only, select the following as examples : —

1. Minerals which are usually associated together :—
   Quartz and mica; orthoclase, quartz, and mica ; orthoclase and oligoclase ; labradorite and augite ; orthoclase
   or oligoclase and hornblende ; hornblende and epidote.
2. On the other hand, quartz and augite appear each to
   exclude the presence of each other; also (according to
   Roth) labradorite and hornblende (?).

We are unable to pursue this important subject in this
place ; we have been compelled to confine ourselves, in
the following notice, to appending a few of the more important instances of paragenesis to the description of
some of the principal mineral classes.

As to the much-debated question of classification of the
minerals, we have adopted one which appeared to us best
suited for our present purpose; it is not exactly that of
any one author. We have placed a few of those minerals
first which are of the most frequent occurrence ; otherwise,
the arrangement adopted will be found to correspond in
several respects with Dana's ' System of Mineralogy.'

The following are the abbreviations we have used :—
H. for *hardness*; S.G. for *specific gravity*; Cp. for
chemical composition ; Bp. for *before the blowpipe*. The
quantities of the chemical elements we have given in
round numbers, as being sufficient for our present purpose. In the chemical formulæ we have, for the sake of
convenience, adopted the abbreviations usual on the Continent, of expressing the oxygen atoms by dots, and a
stroke to denote a double atom; thus, Fe^2O^3 is written
$\ddot{Fe}$. We subjoin the following list of formulæ for the
elementary bodies and their simple compounds :—

CHEMICAL SYMBOLS.

Al	Aluminum, Aluminium	Li	Lithium
Äl	Alumina	L̇i	Lithia
Ag⁻	Silver	Mg	Magnesium
As	Arsenic	Ṁg	Magnesia
Äs	Arsenic Acid	Mn	Manganese
Au	Gold	Ṁn	Protoxide of Manganese
Ba	Barium	M̈n	Sesquioxide of Manganese
Ḃa	Baryta	Na	Sodium
B	Boron	Ṅa	Soda
B̈	Boracic Acid	Ni	Nickel
Ca	Calcium	Ṅi	Protoxide of Nickel
Ċa	Lime	N	Nitrogen
C	Carbon	N̈	Nitric Acid
C̈	Carbonic Acid	O⁻	Oxygen
Cb	Columbium, Niobium	P	Phosphorus
C̈b	Columbic Acid	P̈	Phosphoric Acid
Ce	Cerium	Pb	Lead
Ċe	Protoxide of Cerium	Ṗb	Oxide of Lead
Cl	Chlorine	Se	Selenium
HCl	Hydrochloric Acid	Si	Silicon
Cr	Chromium	S̈i	Silica
C̈r	Oxide of Chromium	Sn	Tin
C̄r	Chromic Acid	Ṡn	Oxide of Tin
Co	Cobalt	Sr	Strontium
Ċo	Oxide of Cobalt	Ṡr	Strontia
Cu	Copper	S	Sulphur
Ċu	Oxide of Copper	S̈	Sulphuric Acid
Fe	Iron	Ta	Tantalum
Ḟe	Protoxide of Iron	Ṫa	Tantalic Acid
F̈e	Peroxide of Iron	Ti	Titanium
F⁻	Fluorine	Ṫi	Oxide of Titanium
HF	Hydrofluoric Acid	T̄i	Titanic Acid
G	Beryllium or Glucinum	V	Vanadium
G̈	Glucina	Y	Yttrium
Hg⁻	Mercury	Ẏ	Yttria
H	Hydrogen	Zn	Zinc
Ḣ	Water	Żn	Oxide of Zinc
K⁻	Potassium	Zr	Zirconium
K̇	Potassa	Z̈r	Zirconia
La	Lanthanum		
Lȧ	Protoxide of Lanthanum		

I. Oxygen Compounds.

A. OXIDES OF SILICON AND ALUMINUM (EARTHS).

1. *Quartz.*—Rhombohedral crystals, usually combinations of two rhombohedrons and hexagonal prism. Cleavage according to the planes of one rhombohedron, but imperfect. Fracture conchoidal to uneven and splintery. H.=7. S.G.=2·5— 2·8. Colourless and limpid, or variously coloured, forming many varieties. Lustre vitreous, sometimes resinous, especially on the surfaces of fracture. Cp.=S̈i, with admixture of minute particles of colouring oxides. Two modifications of chemical composition are distinguished by their different degrees of solubility. The one is insoluble in water and in every acid, except hydrofluoric acid; the other is soluble in water at high temperatures, especially in the presence of other acids and alkalies. The insoluble variety of quartz may, in process of time, become converted into the soluble by the contact-influence of infiltrated moisture. The soluble variety of quartz, in small proportions, is found in many waters of springs and rivers, and in the sea, e. g., at the Geysers in Iceland, up to $\frac{1}{18400}$ per cent. and in sea-water to $\frac{3}{100000}$ per cent. Bp. infusible; with soda fusible to a clear glass with effervescence. Not affected by phosphoric acid.

(*a*) *Common Quartz*, the most abundant of all minerals. It is found :—

(*a*) As an independent rock. (See *post.*)

(*β*) As essential ingredient of many crystalline rocks, especially the plutonic. In most kinds of granite, in greisen, and in the crystalline schists it is found in crystalline grains. In quartz-porphyry, rhyolite, and, exceptionally, in some kinds of granite (e.g. St. Austell, Cornwall), it is perfectly crystallised.

(γ) As accessory constituent mass of some rocks (such as crystalline schists), in form of veins and swellings, or clothing the interior of geodes in other rocks (e.g. in the granites of Switzerland, Carrara marble, the variegated sandstone of the Schwarzwald, &c.) The quartz of the geodes is frequently in the form of transparent crystals (rock crystal), or in greyish-brown to black crystals (smoky quartz, false topaz).

(δ) As principal ingredient of many fragmental rocks (sandstones, conglomerates). As sand and gravel in beds of deposit.

(b) *Amethyst.*—Violet, coloured by the oxide of manganese.

(c) *Chalcedony.*—An intimate admixture of crystalline and amorphous silica.

(d) *Agate.*—A variegated combination of common quartz, amethyst, jasper, carnelian, and other varieties of quartz, arranged in alternate stripes or layers, or irregularly mixed together.

[*b, c,* and *d* chiefly occur in the geodes of volcanic rocks (in Iceland, Faroe Islands, the Brazils, &c.), or in metallic veins (e.g. in Saxony).]

(e) *Jasper.*—Very frequently in globular masses (ball-jasper) coloured red by the peroxide of iron; found in the bog iron-ore of Briesgau, in Germany, and elsewhere, or coloured yellowish-brown by the hydrated oxide of iron. (Occurs in form of pebbles, e.g. in the sand of the Nile and Desert.) Jasper sometimes forms subordinate layers in other rocks.

(f) *Flint.*—Coloured greyish-blue, or black, by presence of carbon. Occurs as a concretionary formation in sedimentary limestone rocks, e.g. in the Chalk of England and France, in the Upper White Jurassic of the Franconian Switzerland in Bavaria.

(*g*) *Chert, Hornstone* is distinguished from flint by its more splintery fracture, by its transparency, and colour, which is grey, yellow, green, red, or brown, resembling jasper. It frequently furnishes the material of fossils, especially of fossil wood (woodstone).

There are at least three different processes in nature which have contributed to the formation of quartz.

Quartz has been formed:—1. *By organic agency.* The siliceous needles (spiculæ) of sea-sponges, the siliceous shields of certain Protozoa (kieselguhr, tripoli), and many plants (especially grasses) either contain quartz, or consist entirely of quartz. 2. *By agency of water.* The concretionary formations of flint, jasper, &c., the crystals and amorphous quartz contained in geodes, and many formations at springs which consist of pure quartz, and are termed freshwater quartz. 3. *By hydroplutonic agency.* Daubrée has actually produced quartz, by way of experiment, through the agency of steam on chloride and fluoride of silicon. Many kinds of quartz have no doubt been produced by pure plutonic agency.

2. *Opal.*—Amorphous, massive. Fracture conchoidal to uneven; friable. H.=5·5—6·5. S.G.=1·9—2·3. Colourless or variegated with rich play of colours. Transparent to opaque. Lustre vitreous, also resinous. Possesses many varieties, distinguished by their different colours and degrees of transparency. Cp. *amorphous* $\ddot{\text{S}}\text{i}$ *combined with water*, in varying proportion (up to 13 per cent.), and small quantities of colouring matter. It is distinguishable from quartz by being almost entirely soluble in potash ley, in matrass yields water. Bp. most kinds of opal decrepitate ; otherwise behaviour like quartz.

Occurrence and Mode of Formation.—Opal is never an essential ingredient of rocks, but is of very frequent occurrence as a secondary product, furnishing the interior of small nests, and filling vesicular cavities in volcanic rocks, or clothing the surfaces of clefts in the same rocks. In these and similar cases the opal is a product of exfiltration from the rock in or near which it occurs. Thus, the precious opal found in the trachytic rocks of Hungary, the colourless hyalite in clefts of basalt and lava (Bohemia, Auvergne). In rare cases, however, opal forms independent layers of small extent (riband opal) in siliceous rocks, e. g. in the tripoli of Bilin. The variety known as menilite occurs in knobs and layers embedded in the adhesive slate of Menil Montant, Paris.

3. *Corundum.*—Occurs in rhombohedral crystals, or granular aggregates (emery). Cleavage basal, also rhombohedral in various degrees of perfection. Fracture conchoidal to uneven and splintery. H.$=9$. S.G.$=3.9$—4.2. Colourless or coloured blue (sapphire), red (ruby), or cloudy (corundum). Lustre vitreous, and frequently, on the basal cleavage surface, mother-of-pearl lustre. Transparent to translucent. Cp.$=\overline{\ddot{A}l}$, with small quantities of $\dot{M}g$, $\dot{C}a$, $\ddot{S}i$. Bp. infusible when alone, perfectly fusible with borax, but not without difficulty; not affected by acids. Occurs as an original product accessorily in many rocks (granite of Silesia, basaltic lava of Niedermendig on the Rhine, dolomite of the St. Gotthard). The precious varieties are chiefly found in alluvial beds (Ceylon, China). Emery forms separate masses of deposit in the talcose schist (Naxos, Saxony).

B. SILICATES.

(*a*) FELSPAR SECTION.

The felspars are, after quartz, the most important of all ingredients of rocks. We distinguish two principal kinds of felspar, the orthoclastic (monoclinic), the two most perfect cleavage planes forming an angle of 90°, and the plagioclastic (triclinic) with an angle of less than 90°. All felspars have a great tendency to form twin crystals, and this duplication occurs in them in a very marked manner, and according to six different laws.

Orthoclastic Felspars.

4. *Orthoclase.*—Monoclinic. Cleavage basal and clinodiagonal, very perfect in both directions, hemiprismatic, imperfect. Fracture conchoidal to uneven and splintery. H.=6. S.G.=2·4—2·62. Colourless, sometimes limpid, more frequently coloured, especially reddish, yellowish, rarely green (amazon stone coloured by copper). Lustre vitreous, frequently with mother-of-pearl lustre on the most perfect cleavage surfaces. Possesses every degree of transparency, sometimes with iridescence or play of colours. Cp.$=\ddot{\mathrm{K}}\ddot{\mathrm{S}}\mathrm{i}+$ $\ddot{\mathrm{A}}\mathrm{l}\ddot{\mathrm{S}}\mathrm{i}^3$ with 65$\ddot{\mathrm{S}}$i, 18$\ddot{\mathrm{A}}$l, and 17$\dot{\mathrm{K}}$. A portion of the $\ddot{\mathrm{A}}$l is frequently replaced by $\ddot{\mathrm{F}}$e,·or $\dddot{\mathrm{M}}$n, and a portion of the $\dot{\mathrm{K}}$ is sometimes replaced by $\dot{\mathrm{N}}$a or $\dot{\mathrm{C}}$a. Bp. fusible with difficulty, and only at the edges, where it forms a dull porous glass. The varieties which contain soda colour the flame yellow. In microcosmic salt it is only soluble with difficulty, leaving behind a skeleton of silica. With cobalt solution the fused edges are coloured blue. Not susceptible to the action of acids.

Varieties of Colour and Lustre.

(a) *Adularia.*—Colourless, or only slightly coloured, with bright lustre, transparent to semi-transparent. Essential ingredient of the adularia-granite and adularia-gneiss abundant in the Alps, also frequently found in the geodic cavities of granitic rocks (St. Gotthard).

(b) *Common Felspar (Pegmatolite, Microcline).*—Variously coloured, less lustrous than adularia, translucent to opaque. A characteristic ingredient of very many rocks, especially amongst the plutonic, such as granite, .gneiss, syenite, porphyry. Frequently large felspar crystals (such as the so-called Carlsbad twins) occur porphyritically embedded in an otherwise regularly constituted rock (e.g. in the granite of Carlsbad in Bohemia, and of Cornwall, porphyry of Ilmenau), or larger crystals clothe the sides of geodes (as in the granite of Baveno and the rocks of the Mourne Mountains, in Ireland).

(c) *Sanidine.*—Colour greyish- and yellowish-white, also grey. Lustre vitreous, very bright, transparent, translucent. The crystals are very often split and creviced. It forms a very characteristic ingredient of genuine volcanic rocks, and only occurs in these. Thus it is found in phonolites, trachytes, pitchstones, obsidian, and lavas. Sometimes it occurs porphyritically in large tabular crystals, as in the trachyte of Drachenfels.

Plagioclastic Felspars.

All plagioclastic felspars are triclinic ; they cleave perfectly according to the base and the brachydiagonal, imperfectly according to the hemiprism.

5. *Albite.*—Fracture uneven. H.$=6$—$6·5$. S.G. $= 2·59$—$2·65$. Colourless or light red, yellow, green, or brown. Lustre vitreous ; mother-of-pearl lustre on the basal cleavage surfaces. Transparent, translucent. A white and usually semi-opaque variety termed pericline, is distinguished by its constant crystallographic habitus. Cp.$=\ddot{N}a\ddot{S}i+\ddot{A}l\ddot{S}i^3=69\ddot{S}i+19\ddot{A}l+12\dot{N}a$. The $\dot{N}a$ is frequently in part replaced by $\dot{C}a$, $\dot{K}$, or $\dot{M}g$. Bp. it fuses with difficulty, colouring the flame yellow. It is scarcely affected by acids. Albite is

frequently found associated in parallel growth with ortho. clase. It is likewise a characteristic ingredient of many diorites and granites. Exceptionally crystals of albite are found in compact limestone (Col du Bonhomme).

6. *Oligoclase.*—Fracture uneven. H.=6. S. G.=2·58—2·69. Colour greyish, yellowish, or greenish. Lustre upon the principal cleavage surface vitreous, otherwise resinous. Usually is much weathered, and in that state dull; in its fresh state translucent at the edges. Cp. $= \dot{N}a\ddot{S}i + \overset{\cdots}{A}l\ddot{S}i^2 =$ $62\ddot{S}i + 24\overset{\cdots}{\underline{A}l} + 14\dot{N}a.$ The $\dot{N}a$ replaced in part (up to 6 per cent.) by $\dot{C}a$, $\dot{K}$ and small quantities of $\dot{F}e$ or $\dot{M}n$. Bp. fuses much more easily than orthoclase and albite, forming a clear glass. Little attacked by acids. Oligoclase is an essential constituent of diabase, diorite, and kersantite; it is frequently associated with orthoclastic felspars as a constituent of many kinds of granite (Stockholm), syenite (Dresden), porphyry (Southern Tyrol), and trachytes (Hungary).

Andesine may be considered as an oligoclase rich in lime. It has much the outward appearance of albite. It is an ingredient of many trachytic rocks of the Andes, and likewise of many crystalline rocks of the Vosges.

7. *Labradorite.*—H. = 6. S.G. = 2·67—2·76. Rarely colourless, usually grey, reddish, bluish or otherwise coloured; usually displays a rich play of colours. Lustre vitreous, sometimes resinous; translucent, but usually only at the edges. Cp.$= \dot{R}\overset{\cdots}{S}i + \overset{\cdots}{A}l\ddot{S}i = 53\ddot{S}i + 30\underline{Al} + 12\dot{C}a + 5\dot{N}a.$ Bp. fuses somewhat more readily than oligoclase to a colourless glass. Unlike other felspars, its powder is thoroughly soluble in heated muriatic acid. Labradorite is an essential constituent of many, and especially of the augitic, rocks, e. g. dolerite, basalt, gabbro (Isle of Skye), hypersthenite, and many lavas of Etna.

Saussurite (jade) is probably only an impure labradorite,

bearing somewhat the same relation to it as felstone to orthoclase. It remains unchanged by acids, occurs only in compact or finely granular masses, and forms an essential constituent of many kinds of gabbro and greenstones.

8. *Anorthite.*—H.= 6—7. S. G. = 2·66 — 2·78. Colourless, white. Lustre, mother-of-pearl on the cleavage surfaces, otherwise vitreous; transparent to translucent. Cp.= $\dot{R}^3\ddot{S}i$ $+3\ddot{A}l\ddot{S}i = 43\ddot{S}i+37\underline{\ddot{A}l}+20\dot{C}a$. The $\dot{C}a$ replaced by $\dot{M}g$, $\dot{K}$, and $\dot{N}a$ to the extent of 5 per cent. Anorthite is completely soluble by concentrated muriatic acid, without *gelatinising*, but is distinguished from labradorite by its being more difficult of fusion. It is an essential constituent of the orbicular diorite (Kugeldiorit) of Corsica and of many ancient lavas (Monte Somma). It is also found in meteoric stones.

Some Aids for distinguishing the Felspar Species.

(a) *Crystallographic Signs.*—When the light is brought to play on the basal cleavage plane of the orthoclastic felspars it presents an unbroken surface, or in case of twin crystals (according to the Carlsbad law) is double; whereas in the case of the plagioclastic felspars a fine parallel striping is usually observed, occasioned by the parallel growth of numberless individual crystals as thin as leaves of paper. This striping, when observable, is a very characteristic sign, but its absence is not equally so.

(β) *Signs of Paragenesis.*—The following minerals are frequently found in comparing: Orthoclase with oligoclase; orthoclase and oligoclase with hornblende; labradorite with pyroxene.

On the other hand, we seldom or never find together:— the alkali felspars (Nos. 4. 5, 6) and the calcareous felspars (Nos. 7, 8); or orthoclase with pyroxene; oligoclase with leucite and nepheline; labradorite with

hornblende; labradorite or anorthite with quartz or
leucite. ·

(γ) The weathering of felspars is noteworthy, and is particularly useful for purposes of distinction where two
species are found together in one rock. Labradorite
and oligoclase weather more readily than orthoclase,
orthoclase more readily than albite. Bearing this law
in mind, if we have determined the species of the unchanged felspar, we may usually determine the other
with a high degree of probability.

(δ) The chemical and physical characteristics of felspars
have been already noted as above.

As regards the origin of felspars :—

They are sometimes clearly the result of wet process ;
evidence of which is their appearance in veins and
clefts, also the pseudomorphs which we find after
leucite, analcime, laumontite, &c.

Sometimes metamorphic, for Daubrée succeeded in producing sanidine-like crystals by subjecting obsidian to
the influence of overheated steam.

And sometimes plutonic, as is proved by the presence of
felspars in lavas and many other rocks of undoubted
igneous origin, as also in the slags of smelting furnaces.

Finally, some are the result of process of sublimation.
Thus, crystals of felspar have been found in blown-out
furnaces, and, reasoning from analogy, we may suppose
the same process to have taken place in nature.

9. *Kaolin* may be put as an appendix to the felspar group,
as it is a product of the disintegration of orthoclase, albite,
and other felspars. Its chemical formula may be stated
as $\ddot{A}l\ddot{S}i + 2\dot{H}$ or $\ddot{A}l^3\ddot{S}i^4 + 6\dot{H}$. Occasionally kaolin is the
result of the decomposition of whole rock masses (granite
of St. Stephen's in Cornwall, gneiss of St. Yrieux, near

Limoges, granulite near Passau). It occurs only in primary formations. On the other hand, the clays (which, in a chemical point of view, may be called impure kaolin) always occur in secondary formations.

More or less allied to kaolin are the following minerals, all of whose composition is, however, more or less indefinite, viz. *lithomarge, myelin, halloysite, bole* or *bolus, rocksoap,* and *agalmatolite.* These sometimes occur as separate independent mineral deposits, but principally are found filling cavities and nests in various rocks, in which latter case they are to be regarded as products of exfiltration from those rocks. Chemically they are all hydrous aluminous silicates, and in appearance may easily be mistaken for soapstone, talc, &c.

Leucite and Nepheline Group.

The minerals of this group, which in many respects are closely allied to the felspars, are without doubt of contemporaneous origin with the volcanic (or plutonic) rocks, in which they occur as essential constituents. They are, therefore, almost always, if not always, igneous products. We do not, however, mean to dispute the possibility of some having arisen by wet process. The most questionable of all in respect of origin is probably lapis lazuli.

10. *Sodalite.*—Monometric in dodecahedrons; cleavage, accordingly, also massive. Fracture conchoidal to uneven. H. $= 5\cdot5 - 6$.   S.G. $= 2\cdot26$.   Colour yellowish, greenish-white, greenish-grey, and blue.   Lustre on crystal surfaces vitreous; on fracture surfaces resinous.   Translucent. Cp. $= \ddot{N}a^3\ddot{S}i + 3\underline{\ddot{A}^l}\ddot{S}i + NaCl$.   Bp. fuses, with more or less difficulty, to a colourless glass, sometimes with intumescence. Gelatinises with muriatic and nitric acids.   Sodalite is an essential constituent of miascite, and an accessory in other igneous rocks (dolerite at the Kaiserstuhl).

11. *Lapis lazuli (ultramarine).*—Monometric in dodecahedrons; cleavage accordingly, usually massive. H. = 5·5. S. G. = 2·4. Colour azure-blue. Lustre glassy, resinous. Translucent at the edges to opaque. Cp. a silicate of $\ddot{\text{Al}}$ with $\dot{\text{Na}}$ and $\dot{\text{Ca}}$, containing also NaS. Bp. loses its colour and fuses to a white vesicular glass. Gelatinises with muriatic acid, and evolves HS. Lapis lazuli is found as an accessory in granite, limestone, and dolomite.

12. *Haüyne.*—Monometric in dodecahedrons; cleavage, accordingly, usually in crystalline grains. H. = 5·5. S. G. = 2·4—2·5. Colour blue, rarely green or red. Lustre vitreous to resinous; semi-transparent to translucent. Cp.= $\dot{\text{Na}}^3\ddot{\text{Si}}+3\ddot{\text{Al}}\ddot{\text{Si}}+2\dot{\text{Ca}}\ddot{\text{S}}$. Bp. decrepitates violently, and fuses to a blue-green vesicular glass. Gelatinises with muriatic acid. It occurs in single crystals imbedded in the lavas of active volcanoes (Volturara, near Melfi), or in the basaltic lavas of extinct volcanoes (Niedermendig, on the Rhine), in which latter it is characteristic as an accessory mineral, and occasionally occurs in such quantity as to have given rise to the name of Hauynophyre for those rocks.

Nosean is very similar to haüyne in its mineralogical character and geological habitat, usually yellowish-grey or greyish-white. In Brava, one of the Cape Verde Islands, there occurs a porphyry rock, consisting of very numerous small crystals of nosean in a felsitic mass. Cp. = $\dot{\text{Na}}^3\ddot{\text{Si}}+3\ddot{\text{Al}}\ddot{\text{Si}}+\dot{\text{Na}}\ddot{\text{S}}$.

13. *Leucite.*—Monometric, only known in trapezohedrons (embedded). Cleavage cubic, imperfect. Fracture conchoidal. H. = 5·5—6. S. G. = 2·48. Colour greyish or reddish-white, also ashen-grey. Lustre vitreous, in fracture resinous. Semi-transparent to translucent only at the edges; brittle. Cp. = $\dot{\text{K}}^3\ddot{\text{Si}}^2+3\ddot{\text{Al}}\ddot{\text{Si}}^2$. Bp. unchanged; with cobalt solution coloured a beautiful blue; with borax melts to a

clear glass. Gelatinises with muriatic' acid. Leucite is a frequent and very characteristic constituent of recent igneous rocks, in which it appears to some extent to be a substitute for felspar. It is especially frequent in basaltic lavas (leucitophyre), in which it always appears porphyritically imbedded. In the older rocks leucite is unknown.

14. *Nepheline (Davyne, Elæolite)*.—Hexagonal. Crystals with imperfect basal and prismatic cleavage, or massive. Fracture conchoidal to uneven. H. $= 5\cdot5$—6. S. G. $= 2\cdot5$ —2·64. Colourless, white and usually crystallised (nepheline), or green, red, brown, and then massive (elæolite). Lustre on crystal surfaces vitreous; on fracture surfaces pre-eminently resinous. Transparent to translucent at the edges. Cp. $= (\dot{N}a\dot{K})^2\ddot{S}i + 2\ddot{A}l\ddot{S}i = 44\ddot{S}i + 33\ddot{A}l + 16\dot{N}a + 5\dot{K}$ (with small quantities of $\ddot{F}e$ and $\dot{C}a$). Davyne, which is very similar, both chemically and mineralogically, contains, in addition to the above, some Cl and $\ddot{C}$. Bp. nepheline fuses with difficulty, and elæolite readily to a vesicular glass. Slowly dissolved in borax and phosphor-salt. The fused edges are coloured blue in cobalt solution. Gelatinises with muriatic acid. It occurs in *geodic* cavities of lavas, and as an accessory constituent of dolerite and basalt. In these rocks it sometimes forms a complete substitute for the felspar, producing nepheline rock. Finally it appears as an essential constituent of some of the older plutonic rocks (miascite, zirconsyenite). In dolerite it may be recognised by its forming short thick columns, whilst the apatite, which is associated with it in those rocks, assumes the form of acicular hexagonal columns.

(b) AUGITE SECTION.

15. *Hornblende (Amphibole)*.—Monoclinic. Crystallised or massive, in stalklike or granular aggregates. Cleavage pris-

matic, very perfect; in other directions imperfect. Fracture uneven. H. = 5—6. S.G. = 2·9—3·4. Colour passing from white through various shades of green and brown to black. Streak either colourless or lighter than the colour of the mineral. Lustre vitreous, on cleavage surfaces mother-of-pearl; the fibrous varieties silky. All degrees of transparency to the opaque. Cp. variable. We may give as a normal formula, $\dot{R}^3\ddot{S}i^2 + \dot{R}\ddot{S}i$, in which $\dot{R} = \dot{M}g$, $\dot{C}a$, and $\dot{F}e$, and $\ddot{S}i$ is sometimes partially replaced by $\underset{\cdots}{Al}$. Bp. these minerals usually fuse, with intumescence, to a grey, greenish, or black glass, and the more readily the more iron they contain. The varieties richest in iron are partially decomposed by muriatic acid; other varieties are little affected by that acid.

(a) *Tremolite* (*Grammatite, Calamite*). — Of light colour, semi-translucent. Iron not an essential ingredient. $Cp. = \dot{M}g^3\ddot{S}i^2 + \dot{C}a\ddot{S}i = 60\ddot{S}i + 27\dot{M}g + 12\dot{C}a$. Usually imbedded in granular limestones and dolomites, in the form of long columnar crystals, or long stalklike or fibrous masses.

(b) *Actinolite* (*Strahlstein, Glassy Actinolite*).—Colour green. Cp. like tremolite. Occurs as an accessory in talc-schist, chlorite-schist, &c. also as an independent rock (actinolite-schist).

(c) *Hornblende* (*proper*). — Colour dark-green or black; opaque. Cp. rich in iron and alumina. Forms an independent rock of itself, or occurs as an essential constituent of many compound rocks (syenite, diorite, many kinds of gneiss and porphyry). Occurs in the form of very perfect brownish-black crystals, imbedded in basaltic and trachytic rocks. A variety of the mineral is termed gamsigradite, and forms an essential constituent of the rock timazite.

C

(*d*) *Uralite* has the same cleavage, structure, and composition as hornblende, but the exterior form of augite. Crystals of this mineral occur in many greenstones (uralite-porphyries). —(Predazzo.)

(*e*) *Asbestus* and *amianthus* are fibrous varieties of tremolite and actinolite. In the variety known as *Mountain leather* the fibres are closely interlaced, or woven like felt. These minerals fill cavities and clefts in limestone and serpentine.

(*f*) *Nephrite* and *Jade* may be here added. They consist of a compact white or light-green translucent mass, with splintery fracture. Cp. very variable, sometimes that of tremolite. It is not a rigidly-defined mineral; forms independent layers as deposits between talcose rocks (in Turkey, New Zealand, &c.).

16. *Pyroxene* (*Augite*).—Monoclinic. In crystals imbedded or attached, or in stalklike, scaly, or granular masses. Cleavage prismatic, but usually less perfect than hornblende. Fracture conchoidal to uneven. H.$=$5—6. S.G.$=3\cdot2$—$3\cdot5$. Rarely colourless. Colour usually grey, green, or black. Lustre vitreous, sometimes mother-of-pearl. All degrees of transparency. Cp.$=\ddot{R}^3\ddot{S}i^2$, but very variable. $\ddot{S}i$ partly replaced by $\ddot{A}l$; $\dot{R}=\dot{C}a$, $\dot{M}g$, $\dot{F}e$, $\dot{M}n$. Bp. the pyroxenes fuse (some quietly, others with some effervescence) to a white, grey, green, or black glass. Usually they are with difficulty reducible by microcosmic salt; those that contain $\ddot{A}l$ almost not at all. Almost all exhibit the reaction for iron, the white and light-coloured varieties manganese. Imperfectly decomposed by acids. The following mineralogical varieties are distinguished:—

(*a*) *Diopside.*—Light-coloured, transparent and translucent varieties, and

(*b*) *Salite.*—Green, translucent only at the edges; usually foliated. This and the last are without much geological importance. A sahlite, termed *malakolite*, is however found separately imbedded in the granular limestone.

(c) *Augite.*—Green to black, opaque. Occurs as an essential ingredient in basalt, dolerite, diabase, and many lavas. Frequently in the form of perfect crystals porphyritically imbedded. Also found in meteoric stones.

(d) *Omphazite.*—Grass-green, always accompanied by garnet, and together with it forming eklogite.

(e) *Hypersthene (Paulite).*—Reddish-brown, greenish-black, or black, with metallic mother-of-pearl lustre on the faces of most perfect cleavage, and sometimes a change of colours showing a copper-red tinge. Lustre otherwise vitreous or resinous. In thin lamellæ translucent. Cp. very poor in lime, rich in iron and manganese. Hypersthene is an essential constituent of the rock hypersthenite (Penig in Saxony, Isle of Skye, Southern Tyrol). Otherwise it is usually an accessory, and is especially frequent in gabbro.

Appendix to Pyroxene.

Diallage (Smaragdite), which is an essential constituent of many gabbro rocks, is only a peculiar variety of pyroxene or hornblende, or perhaps a mixture of both.

The following are hydrous products of the decomposition of pyroxene :—

Schillerspar.—An essential constituent of schiller rock (Baste, in the Harz), accessory in serpentine.

Palagonite.—The principal ingredient of the tufa of that name (Sicily, Nassau).

Green Earth.—Frequent in vesicular cavities of amygdaloids and in basaltic tufas.

c 2

The distinction between hornblende and pyroxene is extremely important lithologically, but is often attended with considerable difficulty. Some assistance may be derived from the following remarks :—

(α) *As to Crystallographic Differences.*—Only recognisable in cases of granular texture, where the crystals are tolerably perfect. One of the most essential and best-marked differences consists in the different angles of the cleavage prisms of the two minerals (and those are usually identical with the angles of the exterior faces of the crystal.) In hornblende the larger angle of the prism is 124° 30' (giving a complement of 55° 30') ; in pyroxene the angles are 87° 5' to 92° 55'.

(β) *Differences of Paragenesis.*—Rocks containing free quartz, felspars rich in silica (such as orthoclase and albite), or potash-mica as essential constituents, seldom likewise contain augitic minerals, but if the latter occur, they are almost invariably hornblende, and not pyroxene. In pyroxenic rocks, quartz especially is very rarely found, and if present is only accessory (eklogite, hypersthenite). On the other hand, labradorite and magnesian micas are very frequent in such rocks, though not exclusively there found.

Pistacite and pyrites are more frequent accessories in hornblendic than pyroxenic rocks. The pistacite is found adhering to the surfaces of clefts, or in geodic cavities, and would appear in most cases to be a product of the decomposition of amphibolite.

Leucite and olivine are characteristic as accessory minerals in pyroxenic rocks.

As a very general rule, we may characterise hornblende as the constituent of the plutonic, pyroxene as that of the volcanic igneous rocks. Nevertheless, sometimes both are found together in the same rock (basalt, omphacite, trachyte of Etna). In this latter case the pyroxene is the older formation of the two, i.e. it has cooled and become solid more rapidly than the hornblende.

(γ) *The chemical differences* between pyroxene and hornblende are not marked. It would appear as if one or the other might have resulted ̣from the same identical mass according to the conditions under which it cooled and solidified. The origin both of hornblende and of pyroxene may be of various kinds.

The possibility of their formation by wet process during the development or the transmutation of a rock's mass has been proved by Daubrée, who actually produced diopside by subjecting glass to the influence of the thermal waters of Plombières.

Many of the crystals which are found disseminated in limestone rocks would appear to be the result of metamorphosis (Pargas, Tyrol).

Again, both these minerals may be products of sublimation (Elie de Beaumont, Sacchi), or they may be simple products of igneous action, since we find in the slags of smelting furnaces products of precisely similar form and composition.

17. *Spodumene (Triphane)*.—Monoclinic, isomorphous with pyroxene ; crystallised or massive in broad fibrous or scaly masses. Cleavage orthodiagonal and prismatic. Fracture uneven. H.$= 6 \cdot 5 — 7$ S.G.$= 3 \cdot 1 — 3 \cdot 2$. Lustre vitreous, with mother-of-pearl lustre on the cleavage surfaces. Colour greenish-grey to apple-green. Translucent, but frequently only at the edges. Cp.$= \dot{L}i^3 \ddot{S}i^3 + 4 \ddot{A}l \ddot{S}i^2$ frequently with some $\dot{N}a$, $\dot{K}$, or $\dot{C}a$. Bp. intumescent ; colours the flame red, but

weakly and transitorily. Fuses easily to a clear glass. When mixed with Ca F and $\ddot{K}\ddot{S}^2$, it gives a purple-red flame. Is not affected by acids. Spodumene is found imbedded in granite (Utö in Sweden; Killiney Bay, Ireland; Peterhead, Scotland). It also occurs in the quartz veins of mica-schist (Massachusetts).

Killinite is a product of the weathering or decomposition of spodumene.

(c) MICA SECTION.

This is a section of minerals distinguished by their pre-eminent foliation (basal cleavage) to a degree not known in any other mineral. As regards origin, they are in part purely plutonic, being found even in the most recent igneous rocks. In part however, they are products of wet processes, and we find pseudomorphs after felspar, tourmaline, and other minerals.

18. *Potash-Mica (Phengite, Muscovite, Binaxial Mica)*.— Trimetric with monoclinic aspect. The crystals usually appear as rhombic or hexagonal plates. Sectile, and its thin laminæ elastic. H.=2—2·5. S.G.=2·75—3·1. Colourless, frequently white, and various shades of yellow, green, or red. Light colours are characteristic. Metallic mother-of-pearl lustre. Transparent to translucent. Optically very distinctly binaxial; the angle of the optical axes=45°—75°. Cp. variable—average formula=$m\ddot{A}l\ddot{S}i + \dot{K}\ddot{S}i$; in which formula m=2, 3 or 4. A portion of the $\ddot{A}l$ may be replaced by $\ddot{F}e$, $\ddot{M}n$, $\ddot{C}r$; a portion of the $\dot{K}$ by $\dot{F}e$ and $\dot{M}n$. Strange to say no $\dot{C}a$ is to be found in any species of mica. The $\dot{K}$ is usually=8—9 per cent. There is usually from 1—5 per cent. of water and some fluorine.

Bp. fuses, with more or less readiness, to a cloudy glass or a white enamel. Not affected by muriatic or sulphuric acid.

Potash-mica is an essential ingredient of many rocks, and especially characteristic for the older plutonic or metamorphic rocks, thus for many kinds of granite, gneiss, and mica-schist.

Damourite, Margarodite, and other similar minerals of very limited frequency, are, in part at least, products of transmutation of potash-mica. They occasion a transition to the chlorites. The same may be said of *Sericite*, a green mineral, of silky lustre, which is said to form the base of several crystalline schists and clay-slates; but it is not .yet free from doubt whether or not sericite is entitled to be regarded as an independent mineral. *List* gives the following account of sericite—H.=1. S.G.=2·89. Foliated in one direction; planes undulated. Lustre silky. Colour greenish or yellowish-white.

19. *Lithia-Mica* (*Lepidolite, Lithionite*).—Trimetric, corresponds with potash-mica in many crystallographic and physical properties, except that its colour is frequently red. H.=2·5—4. S.G.=2·84—3. The angle of the optical axes =70°—78°.

Cp. very variable, may be generally expressed by the formula $m\ddot{R}\ddot{S}i + n\ddot{R}\ddot{S}i$; $m=n=1$; or $m=2$, $n=3$; or sometimes $m=3, n=2$. Again, a part of the bases, as well as of the acids, are compounds of fluorine, not oxygen. The content of lithia is usually 2—5 per cent., and of fluorine 2—10. Bp. fuses very readily, with efflorescence to a colourless, brown, or black glass. The flame is coloured purple-red; with acids it is imperfectly soluble, but completely decomposed.

Lithia-mica is an essential ingredient of *Greisen*, very frequent in some kinds of granite, and in metalliferous veins, especially those of tin. In all these cases this mineral is usually associated with other fluorides, such as topaz, tourmaline, apatite, &c.

20. *Magnesia-Mica* (*Biotite, Hexagonal or Uniaxial Mica*). —The name of uniaxial mica is now found to be incorrect, as

all magnesia-mica is binaxial, if only slightly. The angle of the two axes is for the most part less than 5°. Trimetric (?) crystals, usually tabular; usually sectile, and in thin plates, elastic. H.$=2\cdot5$—3. S.G. $= 2\cdot7$—$3\cdot1$. Green, brown, black, in general colours usually dark. Metallic mother-of-pearl lustre. Translucent to opaque. Cp. very variable; chiefly $= \ddot{\text{A}}\text{l}\ddot{\text{S}}\text{i} + \dot{\text{R}}^3\ddot{\text{S}}\text{i}$, in which $\ddot{\underline{\text{A}}}\text{l}$ is in part replaced by $\ddot{\text{F}}\text{e}$, and $\dot{\text{R}} \dot{=} \underline{\dot{\text{M}}}\text{g}, \dot{\text{K}}$, $\dot{\text{F}}\text{e}$. The $\dot{\text{M}}\text{g}=9$—25 per cent. Some fluorine, chlorine, and water likewise enter into the composition. Bp. fuses with greater difficulty than the before-mentioned species of mica, to a grey or black glass. It is little attacked by muriatic acid; on the other hand, unlike potash-mica, it is completely decomposed by concentrated sulphuric acid, leaving a white residue of silica.

The geological area of biotite is far more extensive than that of potash-mica, for it is not only found in the older plutonic rocks and crystalline schists (granite, porphyry, gneiss), but also in more recent and the most recent volcanic products (trachyte, basalt, and the corresponding lavas).

Rubellan and *Phlogopite* are minerals closely allied to magnesia-mica, of which rubellan is perhaps only a transformed product.

(d) HYDROUS MAGNESIAN SILICATES (TALC SECTION).

These have many characteristics and properties in common. Some minerals which contain $\ddot{\text{F}}\text{e}$ instead of $\dot{\text{M}}\text{g}$ belong to the same group. We may make three principal divisions: the Chlorites (21), the Serpentines (22—25), and the Talcs (26,27). The chlorites under certain circumstances may be regarded as hydrous mica; the serpentines and talcs appear chiefly to be products of metamorphosis, perhaps occasioned by percolating water. The most important species are:—

21. *Chlorite* (*Ripidolite*). — Rhombohedral; the crystals

grouped in the form of comb or botryoidal shape, usually in massive, foliated, or scaly aggregates. Cleavage basal, very perfect; sectile. Its thin lamellæ flexible, but not elastic. H.$=1$—1.5. S.G.$=2.65$ to 2.85. Colour green, in various shades. Its crystals are frequently translucent, and of red colour when regarded in the direction of the principal axis. Streak greenish-grey. Lustre mother-of-pearl. Thin laminæ transparent to translucent. Cp.$=3\ddot{R}^3\ddot{S}i+\ddot{R}^3\ddot{S}i+12\ddot{H}=30$—$31\ \ddot{S}i+14$—$19\ \underline{\ddot{A}l}+32$—$37\ \dot{M}g+5$—$6\ \dot{F}e$. In matrass it gives out water. Bp. fuses on charcoal; with borax it melts and shows the reaction of iron. Thin laminæ are decomposed by concentrated sulphuric acid.

Chlorite forms the most important and essential elements of chlorite-schist, also of chlorite mica-schist, both frequent in the Alps. In the protogine-granite and protogine-gneiss it is a substitute for mica. It is also a characteristic constituent of diabase, and many kinds of syenite-porphyry (Altenberg in Saxony).

Delessite is a mineral closely allied to chlorite, but richer in iron. It is frequent in vesicular cavities of melaphyres.

Pennine, Ripidolite, and *Clinochlore* are minerals resembling chlorite, but not yet accurately defined. They are of frequent occurrence in chloritic schists as essential ingredients.

Some of the minerals which we have already noticed as having arisen from transmutation of augite, such as schiller spar, green earth, &c., are externally very similar to chlorite.

22. *Saponite* (*Soapstone*).—Massive, sectile, and very soft. S.G.$=2.26$. Colour white or light grey, yellow or reddish brown, dull, with lustrous streak. Greasy feel, not adhesive to the tongue. Cp.$=2\dot{M}g^3\ddot{S}i^2+\underline{\ddot{A}l}\ \ddot{S}i+10\dot{H}$. In the matrass it gives out water and becomes black. Thin laminæ melt with difficulty at the edges. It is readily and completely decomposed with sulphuric acid.

Saponite occurs in fissures of serpentine rock (Lizard's Point, Cornwall).

23. *Serpentine.*—Usually compact, sometimes granular or fibrous; in the latter case it is called chrysolite or serpentine-asbestus. Fracture conchoidal, flat, or uneven, splintery, fine-grained, or of twisted fibres. H.$=3$—4, rarely 5; S.G.$=2\cdot2$—$2\cdot6$. Bright coloured and translucent varieties are termed precious serpentines to distinguish them from the ordinary serpentine, which is usually of dark colour — green, red, or brown. Cp.$=$the general formula $\dot{M}g^9\ddot{S}i^4\dot{H}^6=43\ \ddot{S}i+42\ \dot{M}g+12\ \dot{H}$, with a trifling percentage of $\ddot{A}l$ and $\ddot{F}e$. In matrass gives out water and becomes darker in colour. Bp. almost infusible, exhibits the reaction of iron; easily soluble in borax, in microcosmic salt with effervescence. When powdered, soluble in muriatic acid, and still more readily in sulphuric acid.

Serpentine is found disseminated in rocks, usually massive, sometimes in broken masses, plates, and veins. It likewise forms a rock of itself.

The right of serpentine to the character of an independent mineral is open to doubt, as it frequently appears to be only a pseudomorph of other minerals, e. g. hornblende, augite, garnet, spinel, &c. The rock serpentine also appears to be usually, if not always, a product of transmutation derived from other rocks, such as granite, gneiss, gabbro, chlorite-schist, &c.; and only to resemble the mineral, not to constitute, strictly speaking, an aggregate of it. (Vide post, p. 314.)

24. *Ottrelite.*—In small thin hexagonal or rounded laminæ; cleavage parallel to the lateral faces. Hard; is capable of scratching glass. S.G.$=4\cdot4$. Greenish grey to blackish-green. Lustre vitreous; translucent. Cp.$=(\dot{F}e,\dot{M}n)^3\ddot{S}i^2+2\ddot{A}l\ddot{S}i+3\dot{H}$. In matrass gives out water. Bp. fuses with difficulty

at the edges to a black magnetic globule ; with borax, iron reaction ; with soda, that of manganese.

Ottrelite is found disseminated in various kinds of clay-slate, which have received the name of Ottrelite Slate (Lux-embourg).

25. *Glauconite.*—Small, round, dark-green grains, which when recently exposed are frequently very soft, but in time assume about the hardness of gypsum. S.G.$=2\cdot29$—$2\cdot35$. Cp.$=$a hydrous silicate of $\dot{F}e$ and $\dot{K}$ (5—10 per cent. $\dot{K}$), moreover $\ddot{A}l$ and small quantities of $\dot{C}a$ and $\dot{M}g$.

Glauconite is found in the form of grains or nuclei of minute fossils (Foraminifera) imbedded in clay-marl and sandstone rocks. Very characteristic for rocks of the Chalk formation (Upper Greensand, Isle of Wight; Chalk of Calais). Occurs also in other sedimentary formations (Muschelkalk of Berlin ; Calcaire grossier, Paris ; Browncoal Sandstone of the North-eastern Alps).

26. *Talc.*—Trimetric (?) ; rarely crystallised, usually mas-sive, in granular, foliated or scaly aggregates. Cleavage basal, very perfect. Very sectile with greasy feel. Thin laminæ flexible, but not elastic. H.$=1$—$1\cdot5$. S.G.$=2\cdot56$—$2\cdot8$. Colour white, grey, and green, in various shades. Lustre mother-of-pearl, or resinous. Translucent to opaque. Opti-cally binaxial. Cp.$=\dot{M}g^6\ddot{S}i^5+2\dot{H}=62\ \ddot{S}i+32\cdot9\ \dot{M}g+4\cdot9\ \dot{H}$. The $\dot{M}g$ is partly replaced by $\dot{F}e$. Bp. shines brightly and loses its colour ; exfoliates ; becomes hard ; does not fuse. If heated with cobalt solution, becomes pale-red. Is not at-tacked by acids.

Varieties especially noticeable are :—

(*a*) *Foliated Talc.*—The purest crystalline talc.

(*b*) *Steatite.*—Amorphous. Frequently pseudomorphous after other minerals. Decomposes with boiling sulphuric acid.

Talc is a very widely diffused mineral. Talc-schist and many beds of rock in the regions of crystalline schists consist almost exclusively of this mineral. Talc-mica-schist, protogine, and some sandstones contain it as an essential ingredient.

27. *Meerschaum.*—Massive and in nodules. Fracture flat conchoidal, and fine-grained, earthy ; sectile. $H. = 2 — 2 \cdot 5$. $S.G. = 0 \cdot 8 — 1$. Colour yellowish or greyish-white, dull. Streak little lustrous. Opaque. Greasy feel ; adhering strongly to the tongue. Cp. (probably) $\dot{M}g\ddot{S}i + \dot{H}$, usually with some $\ddot{C}$. Bp. contracts, becomes hard, and fuses at the edges to a white enamel.

Forms separate beds, which are the result of a process of transmutation, probably of Magnesite.

(e) ZEOLITE SECTION (NON-MAGNESIAN HYDROUS SILICATES.)

The minerals which are grouped under the name of Zeolites are an extensive family of the silicates, having both as to chemical composition and crystallographic form much in common with the Felspar group, as well as with the Augite and the Andalusite groups—but their chief distinguishing feature is that they invariably contain a large proportion of water, varying from 4—22 per cent.

The following properties are common to all zeolites. Before the blowpipe they froth up and melt to a glass, which owing to the many bubbles never becomes very clear or transparent. They are all decomposed by muriatic acid, under which process the $\ddot{S}i$ is precipitated to a gelatinous or slimy mass. Again, they all have a colourless streak, which circumstance is owing to the small proportion of colouring oxides (not above 2 per cent.) which they contain.

The geological character of the zeolites is very uniform. They are principally found in the volcanic rocks. They are either found in the vesicular cavities, veins and fissures of those rocks in the form of crystals and foliated and radiated masses, or they sometimes form an essential ingredient of the rock's mass (in basalt, phonolite). In either case they are not original products, i. e. not of contemporaneous formation with the rock in which they are found; they are products of exfiltration or of the internal decomposition and transmutation of the mother rock. It is interesting to notice with reference to those zeolites which are the products of what we have termed exfiltration, that Daubrée has shown them not to be simple deposits of substances held in solution by the percolated water to which they owe their origin, but rather products of the chemical action of that water at a high degree of temperature on a portion of the rock's mass which had already oozed out; and thus that the same rill of water percolating through different rocks will produce different species of zeolite. As regards zeolite forming part of the composition of the rock's mass, this is so frequently the case in basalt, that it has recently been put forth as a universal rule that no rock can be a genuine basalt without zeolite. Nevertheless we think this assertion too general, and it is possible that nepheline, which enters largely into the composition of basalts, may by reason of its great solubility in muriatic acid, have been sometimes mistaken for zeolite. Zeolites are seldom found in metalliferous veins, or in the fissures of the older plutonic rocks.

The most convenient arrangement of the individual species for our present purpose will be the crystallographic. We begin with—

The Monometric Zeolites.

28. *Analcime.*—Usually in trapezohedrons ; more rarely a combination of these with the cube. The crystals usually

found grouped together in geodic cavities. Sometimes massive, granular. Cleavage cubal, imperfect. Fracture uneven. H.$=5\cdot5$. S.G.$=2\cdot1$. Colourless, white to grey, or flesh-red. Lustre vitreous. Transparent to translucent at the edges only. Cp.$=\dot{N}a^3\ddot{S}i^2 + 3\ddot{A}l\ddot{S}i^2 + 6\dot{H}$.

Analcime is found in geodic cavities of basaltic rocks (Giant's Causeway, Ireland; Dumbartonshire; Seisser Alp); in metalliferous veins (Kongsberg; Andreasberg in the Harz); and as a recent formation at the mouth of springs (Plombières). It is especially frequent in the old dolomitic lavas of the Cyclopean Islands near Sicily, and those have been named Analcymite accordingly. The observer must avoid confounding the crystals of analcime with those of leucite.

29. *Apophyllite (Ichthyophthalmite, Albine).*—Crystals pyramidal, columnar, or tabular. Usually grouped together in geodes; occasionally in scaly aggregates. Cleavage basal, perfect. Fracture uneven. H.$=4\cdot5$—5. S.G.$=2\cdot33$. Colourless, or yellow, greyish, or reddish-white. Lustre vitreous, on the cleavage surfaces mother-of-pearl. Transparent to translucent at the edges. Cp.$=8\dot{C}a\ddot{S}i + \dot{K}\ddot{S}i^2 + 16\dot{H}$, with sometimes 1 per cent. of fluorine.

Apophyllite is found in the geodic cavities of volcanic rocks (Iceland, Faroö, Fassa Thal) in metalliferous veins (at Utoe in Sweden, at Andreasberg, and in the Bannat associated with wollastonite). In the Tertiary limestone near intruded basaltic rocks at Puy de la Piquette, in Auvergne. Finally as a recent deposit from spring water at Plombières.

Hexagonal Zeolites.

30. *Chabasite (Phacolite).*—Rhombohedral. Crystals often of twin growth. Cleavage rhombohedral. Fracture uneven. H.$=4$—$4\cdot5$ S.G.$=2\cdot08$—$2\cdot17$. Colourless, white, or red-

dish. Lustre vitreous. Transparent to translucent. Cp. =
$(\dot{C}a,\dot{N}a,\dot{K})^3\ddot{\ddot{S}}i^2 + 3\underline{\ddot{A}l}\ddot{S}i^2 + 18\dot{H}.$
It occurs in geodes of volcanic rocks (Faroë, Fassa Thal,
Giant's Causeway) ; in syenite (Massachusetts) ; in gneiss
(Connecticut).

Trimetric Zeolites.

31. *Prehnite.*—Crystals tabular or short columnar. Grouped
in geodes in fan-shaped or spheroidal aggregates. Cleavage
basal, perfect. H. = 6—6·7. S.G. = 2·8—2·95. Rarely colourless, usually green. Lustre vitreous ; on the cleavage surfaces,
mother-of-pearl lustre. Transparent to translucent at edges
only. Cp. = $\dot{C}a^2\ddot{\ddot{S}}i + \underline{\ddot{A}l}\ddot{S}i + \dot{H}$, frequently with some $\dot{F}e$.
Occurs in basaltic amygdaloids (Fassa Thal) ; in the trap
rocks of Dumbarton.

32. *Thomsonite (Comptonite).*—In geodes, the crystals in
sheaves or fan-shaped groups, or in fibrous aggregates. Cleavage, according to the brachy- and macro-diagonal, almost
equally perfect. Fracture uneven. H. = 5—5·5. S.G. = 2·35
—2·38. Colour white. Lustre vitreous, sometimes mother-of-
pearl. Translucent, but usually clouded. Cp. = $(\dot{C}a,\dot{N}a)^3\ddot{\ddot{S}}i +$
$3\underline{\ddot{A}l}\ddot{S}i + 7\dot{H}.$
Thomsonite occurs in amygdaloids at Kilpatrick, in Dumbartonshire, and Lochwinnock, in Renfrewshire, in the
vesicular cavities of Vesuvian lavas, in the analcimite and
phonolite of Bohemia.

33. *Natrolite (Soda-Mesotype).*—Crystals usually thin, columnar, acicular, or capillary. In geodes, also in bunches or
reniform masses. Cleavage prismatic, perfect. H. = 5—5·5.
S.G. = 2·17—2·24. Colourless, greyish-yellow or reddish-
white. Lustre vitreous, occasionally mother-of-pearl. Trans-
lucent, or only at the edges. Cp. = $\dot{N}a\ddot{\ddot{S}}i · \underline{\ddot{A}l}\ddot{S}i + 2\dot{H}$, occasionally a small quantity of $\dot{F}e$.

Natrolite occurs in vesicular cavities of basaltic and phonolite rocks (Kilmalcolm in Renfrewshire, Aussig in Bohemia).

34. *Phillipsite* (*Lime-Harmotome*). — Columnar crystals,
sometimes long and sometimes short, frequently twin, growth
cross-shaped. Cleavage brachy- and macro-diagonal. H.=
4—4·5. S.G.=2·2. Colourless, white, yellowish or reddish.
Lustre vitreous. Transparent to translucent at the edges
only. $Cp. = (\dot{C}a, \dot{K})\ddot{S}i + \underline{\ddot{A}l}\ddot{S}i^2 + 5\dot{H}$.

Phillipsite is found in the basaltic lavas of Capo di Bove
near Rome, County Antrim, in Ireland, &c.

35. *Harmotome* (*Baryt-harmotome*). — Columnar crystals
almost always twins, shaped in form of a cross. Cleavage imperfect, the brachydiagonal more perfect than the
macrodiagonal. H.=4·5. S.G.=2·39—2·5. Colourless, or
different shades of white. Lustre vitreous, little translucent.
$Cp. = \dot{B}a\ddot{S}i + \underline{\ddot{A}l}\ddot{S}i^2 + 5\dot{H}$, with some $\dot{K}$ and $\dot{C}a$.

Harmotome occurs in the metalliferous veins of Andreasberg, in nodules of agate from the melaphyre of Oberstein,
Zweibrucken, under like circumstances in Dumbartonshire,
where its crystals are simple.

Monoclinic Zeolites.

36. *Laumontite* (*Laumonite*).—The crystals usually in columnar combinations, also in granular and fibrous masses. Cleavage prismatic, perfect; very friable and brittle. H.=3·5—4.
S.G.=2·29—2·36. Colour yellowish, or greyish-white, also
reddish. Lustre vitreous, on the cleavage surfaces mother-of-
pearl. Transparent to translucent on the edges only. $Cp. =$
$\dot{C}a^3\ddot{S}i^2 + 3\underline{\ddot{A}l}\ddot{S}i^2 + 12\dot{H}$. It loses a portion of its water very
quickly on exposure, and then falls to powder.

Laumontite is found in vesicular cavities of basaltic rocks
(Dumbartonshire, Faroë), in clefts and fissures of syenite
(Dresden), or quartz-porphyry (Botzen).

37. *Scolecite* (*Lime-Mesotype*).—Crystals long or short prisms or acicular; also massive, radiated, and fibrous. Cleavage prismatic, tolerably perfect. H. = 5—5·5. S.G.=2·2—2·7. Colourless, greyish, yellowish, or reddish-white. Lustre vitreous, the fibrous clusters silky. Transparent to translucent at the edges only. Cp. = $\ddot{C}a\ddot{S}i + \ddot{A}l\ddot{S}i + 3\dot{H}$.

Scolecite occurs in the vesicular cavities of basaltic rocks (Auvergne, Staffa), or in the fissures of the same rocks (Kil patrick hills). •

38. *Heulandite* (*Foliated Zeolite, Stilbite*, in part).—Crystals usually tabular, rarely prismatic, either single or clustered in geodes, also massive, in radiated, foliated, or globular aggregates. Cleavage clinodiagonal, very perfect. H.=3·5—4. S.G.=2·2. Colourless, white, usually red to brown. Lustre vitreous, on the cleavage surfaces, mother-of-pearl. Transparent to translucent at the edges only. Cp.=$\dot{C}a\ddot{S}i + \ddot{A}l\ddot{S}i^3 + 5\dot{H}$.

Heulandite occurs frequently in the vesicular cavities of basaltic rocks (Faroë, Iceland, Skye, Fassa Valley); rare in metalliferous veins (Andreasberg).

39. *Stilbite* (*Desmine, Radiated Zeolite*).—Its monoclinic character is questionable. The crystals are broad prisms, frequently clustered into sheaves or bundles; also massive and fibrous aggregates. Cleavage brachydiagonal, very perfect, macrodiagonal imperfect. H.=3·5—4. S.G. = 2·1—2·2. Colourless, white, grey, yellow, or red. Lustre vitreous, on the most perfect cleavage surfaces, mother-of-pearl lustre. Translucent, perfect or only on the edges. Cp. = $\dot{C}a\ddot{S}i + \ddot{A}l\ddot{S}i^3 + 6\dot{H}$.

Stilbite is a frequent inhabitant of vesicular cavities or fissures of volcanic rocks (Fassa-Thal, Faroë, Iceland) also occurs in metalliferous veins (Andreasberg, Kongsberg).

40. *Smithsonite* (*Hydrous Silicate of Zinc, Galmey*, in part) may be added here by way of appendix, although geologically it is very far removed from the zeolites, since chemically it

D

agrees with them in being a hydrous silicate free from magnesia.

It crystallises trimetrically, hemimorph. The crystals are usually small, tabular, and prismatic, independent or in geodes, frequently grouped in fan-like, grape-like, botryoidal, or reniform clusters; also fine fibrous to felt-like varieties occur. Cleavage prismatic, very perfect, macro-domatic perfect. Fracture uneven. H.$=$4·5—5. S.G. $= 3·16$—3·9. Colourless, white and variously coloured (but always ·light coloured). Lustre on crystal surfaces vitreous. Semi-transparent to opaque. Cp.$=2\dot{Z}n^3\ddot{S}i+3\dot{H}$. When heated in matrass gives out water. Bp. decrepitates a little, shows green phosphorescent light, but does not melt. Gelatinises with acid.

Smithsonite takes no essential part in the composition of rocks, but both alone and with other zinc-ores and galena forms separate beds of ore of considerable extent. These ores are usually associated with dolomites and limestones (Raibl and Bleiberg in Carinthia, Aachen, Tarnowitz in Silesia, Mendip hills). Smithsonite occurs in veins of lead-ore at Matlock in Derbyshire, and many other English localities.

(ƒ) ANDALUSITE SECTION.

With respect to the minerals grouped under this head, we must remark that they are allied together more by their chemical and physical properties than their geological affinities.

41. *Andalusite* (*Chiastolite, Hohlspath*).—Trimetric. The crystals are usually combinations of the prism and base, hence columnar, attached, also imbedded; also in radiated, fibrous, and granular clusters. Cleavage prismatic, imperfect. Fracture uneven and splintery. H. $= 7·5$. S.G. $= 3·1$—3·2. Colour grey, greenish, or reddish-grey. Lustre vitreous, usually weak. Rarely transparent, and in that case showing trichroism;

usually translucent, or translucent only at the edges. [The variety chiastolite fluctuates in hardness between 3 and 7·5. This difference is attributable to foreign substances contained in its crystals. These foreign substances are arranged in some sort symmetrically about the edges and axis so as to give a tesselated appearance in the section. The crystals are mostly twins or fourfold.] Cp. = $\ddot{A}l^3\ddot{S}i^2$, sometimes $\ddot{A}l^4\ddot{S}i^3$, usually with some $\dot{F}e$ and $\ddot{M}n$. Bp. infusible. When reduced to powder, fuses with difficulty in borax to a transparent colourless glass; with cobalt solution coloured blue. Not affected by acids.

Andalusite occurs as an accessory in granite and crystalline schists (gneiss, mica-schist), Devonshire and Aberdeenshire. The variety chiastolite occurs exclusively in clay-slate, and usually in the neighbourhood of granites or other igneous rocks. It probably is the product of a metamorphosis resulting from percolated water.

42. *Topaz.*—Trimetric. Crystals sometimes hemimorphous, always prismatic. Single crystals attached or imbedded, or clusters incrusted in geodes; also coarse or fine-grained masses. Cleavage basal, very perfect. Fracture conchoidal to uneven. H.=8. S.G.=3·4—3·6. Colourless and transparent, but usually yellow, red, or blue. Lustre vitreous. Transparent to translucent at the edges only. Cp.=$5\ddot{A}l^3\ddot{S}i^2+$ ($3\ddot{A}lF^3+2SiF^3$) shows reaction of fluorine. Bp. infusible, but soluble in microcosmic salt, leaving a skeleton of silica. Not affected by muriatic acid. With sulphuric acid, some hydrofluoric acid is formed.

Pycnite is a fibrous variety of topaz.

Topaz is an essential constituent of topaz-rock, an accessory of granite (imbedded, or incrusting geodic cavities): Mourne in Ireland, Mursinsk in Siberia, Greifenstein in Saxony. Very frequently associated with other minerals which contain fluorine, and with beryl and tin ore. Also in separate localities, associated with the like minerals (Cornwall, Saxony).

Although the topaz crystals which are found imbedded in granite appear to be of simultaneous formation with that rock, and therefore of plutonic origin, Daubrée has succeeded in producing topaz by subjecting alumina to the action of fluoride of silicon.

43. *Staurotide (Staurolite).* — Trimetric. Crystals always imbedded, prismatic, frequently cruciform. Cleavage brachydiagonal, perfect. Fracture conchoidal to uneven. H. = 7—7·5. S.G.=3·5—3·7. Deep red to blackish-brown. Lustre vitreous. Translucent to opaque. Cp. variable=$(\ddot{A}l\ddot{F}e)^2\ddot{S}i$, or $\ddot{R}^3\ddot{S}i^2$, or $\ddot{R}^5\ddot{S}i^4$. Bp. infusible. With difficulty soluble in borax and microcosmic salt. Not affected by muriatic acid.

Staurotide occurs in association, sometimes twin growth, with the next named species; accessory in mica-schist and gneiss (Switzerland, Tyrol, Brittany).

44. *Kyanite (Disthene, Rhœtizite).*—Triclinic. Crystals usually long and broad-shaped (bladed), without terminal faces, frequently in twins; imbedded singly or grouped in fibrous masses. Cleavage prismatic, very perfect, brittle. H.=6—7·2. S.G.=3·56—3·67. Colourless or common blue. Lustre vitreous, on the most perfect cleavage planes, mother-of-pearl. Transparent to translucent on the edges only. Cp.=$\ddot{A}l^3\ddot{S}i^2$, with little $\ddot{F}e$. Bp. infusible; dark blue if heated with cobalt solution. Not affected by acids.

Kyanite occurs as an accessory ingredient in granulite, also in gneiss and mica-schist similarly to staurotide.

45. *Lievrite (Ilvaite, Jenite).*—Trimetric. Crystals long prisms. Crystals attached or incrusting geodic cavities; also massive, usually in fibrous, rarely in granular aggregates. The crystals usually coated with brown iron-ochre. Cleavage indistinct. Fracture conchoidal to uneven. Brittle. H.=5·5—6. S.G.=

3·8—4·2. Colour brownish to greenish-black. Streak black. Lustre resinous. Opaque. Cp.=2$\ddot{\text{F}}$c³S̈i + Ca³S̈i + $\ddot{\text{F}}$e²S̈i. Bp. fusible to a black magnetic globule; with microcosmic salt shows the reaction of iron, and leaves a skeleton of silica. With muriatic acid gelatinises.

Lievrite is found associated with pyroxene in subordinate masses in the mica-schist of Elba, also (according to Dana) in the granite of Predazzo in Tyrol.

46. *Tourmaline (Schorl).*—Rhombohedral, eminently hemimorphous. Crystals mostly columnar, imbedded or attached, also massive, fibrous, or granular aggregates. Cleavage rhombohedral, very imperfect. H. = 7—7·5. S.G. = 2·94—3·3. Colourless, seldom transparent, most usually black, also brown, red, blue, green, &c. Lustre vitreous. Every degree of pellucidity from transparent to opaque. Very eminently polar electric. Cp.=very various and complicated. The following ingredients take part in its composition :—S̈i, B̈, P̈, F, K̇, Ṅa, L̇i, Ċa, Ṁg, $\dot{\text{F}}$e, Ṁn, Ä̤l, $\ddot{\text{F}}$e, Ṁn. The oxygen ratio of all the bases in this compound (including boracic acid as a base) to the silica is constant, and is=4 : 3. Bp. very variable, in part fusible (in different degrees), in part intumescent, and in part not. All kinds of tourmaline, when mixed with fluor-spar and sulphate of potash, exhibit the reaction for boron. Not affected by muriatic acid. Sulphuric acid almost completely decomposes the powder of fused tourmaline after lengthened digestion.

Tourmaline is of very frequent occurrence; but is almost exclusively confined to the plutonic-igneous and the metamorphic rocks. It is an essential constituent of schorl rock; accessory in granite, granulite, mica-schist, topaz-rock, and it sometimes appears in such quantity in these rocks as to cause varieties to be specially named after it. [See post.] It is unknown in augitic and volcanic rocks. In dolomite it appears exceptionally (Capo Longo, south of St. Gotthard); also in sandstone, but only in neighbourhood of intruded plutonic rocks.

The origin of tourmaline is sometimes contemporaneous with that of the mother rock, sometimes it is a secondary product occasioned by metamorphism (percolation of fresh-water springs?). It has not yet been artificially produced.

Tourmaline is also known in pseudomorphs after felspar (in the granite of Trevalgan, Cornwall), and on the other hand pseudomorphs of mica, chlorite, and steatite after tourmaline, occur in many places.

(g) GARNET SECTION.

The affinity of the different minerals of this section to each other consists in their containing the like ratio of oxygen between the acids and bases.

47. *Chrysolite (Olivine, Peridot).*—Trimetric. The crystals usually columnar and imbedded (chrysolite), but very often massive, in granular aggregates, and disseminated (olivine). Cleavage brachydiagonal, tolerably distinct. Fracture conchoidal. H.=6—7. S.G. = 3·3—3·5. Lustre vitreous. Colour green, asparagus-green, olive-green, also yellow and brown. Transparent to translucent. (Chrysolite usually includes the transparent crystals of paler colour, while olivine, so called from the olive-green tint, is applied to imbedded masses and grains of inferior colour and clearness.—*Dana.*) Cp. = $(\dot{M}g,\dot{Fe})^3\ddot{S}i$, with some $\dot{M}n$, $\dot{C}a$, $\ddot{T}i$, and $\dot{H}$. Bp. only the varieties containing much iron are fusible. All varieties are easily decomposed by sulphuric acid.

The most beautiful crystals of chrysolite are said to come from granitic rocks of Upper Egypt. Fayalite, a variety very rich in iron, is found in granite of Mourne Mountains. Otherwise this mineral is known as essential ingredient of the rock called eulisite. It is an accessory constituent of hypersthene rock (Elfdalen) in talc-schist (Katherinenburg). All these occurrences are insignificant compared with the abundance and frequency in which both grains and crystals of olivine occur in basalts and lavas. In basalt, olivine is almost an essential constituent. It is also found in meteoric stones.

Olivine is, doubtless, usually a purely igneous product. If additional proof of this were wanted, it may be found in the crystals of an olivine rich in iron which occur in the slags of smelting furnaces.

A rock of New Zealand, which has been called *Dunite*, consists of granular olivine.

48. *Beryl* (*Emerald, Smaragd*).—Hexagonal. Crystals columnar, either singly attached or imbedded, or clustered in geodes; also fibrous aggregates. Cleavage basal, tolerably perfect. Fracture conchoidal to uneven. H. = 7·5—8. S.G. = 2·68—2·73. Colourless, limpid, but usually green or blue. Lustre vitreous. Transparent to translucent at the edges only. Cp. = $\ddot{G}\ddot{S}i^2 + \ddot{A}l\ddot{S}i^2$, with some $\ddot{F}e$ and $\ddot{C}r$. Bp. fuses with difficulty at the edges to a clouded scoriated glass, completely soluble in microcosmic salt. Not affected by acids.

Beryl occurs as an accessory in mica-schist (Salzburg), in granite (Mourne Mountains, Bodenmais in Bavaria), in black limestone (Muzo in Columbia), and with tin-ore (Saxony).

Phenakite or *Phenacite*.—Cp. $\ddot{G}\ddot{S}i$. Rhombohedral crystals, and occurs under precisely similar conditions to beryl.

49. *Garnet.*—Monometric, in rhombic dodecahedrons or trapezohedrons or in combinations of both. Crystals singly attached or imbedded or clustered in geodes, also massive, in granular to compact aggregates. Cleavage indistinct, dodecahedric. Fracture conchoidal, or uneven and splintery. H. = 6·5—7·5. S.G. = 3·15—4·3. Seldom colourless, usually green, yellow, red, brown or black. Lustre vitreous to

resinous. Transparent, translucent, opaque. Cp. extremely manifold, so that six groups may be distinguished of essentially different composition, passing over, however, one into the other. The common formula may be thus given : $\dot{R}^3\overset{...}{Si}+$ $\overset{...}{R}\overset{.}{Si}$, in which formula $\dot{R}=(\dot{C}a,\ \dot{F}e,\ \dot{M}n,\ \dot{M}g)$, and $\overset{...}{R}=(\overset{..}{A}l,$ $\overset{...}{F}e,\ \overset{..}{C}r)$. Bp. fuses with considerable ease to a green, brown, or black glass, which is frequently magnetic. With phosphor-salt gives a siliceous skeleton, otherwise iron and manganese reaction. In raw state little affected by muriatic acid, but after fusion easily and completely decomposed by that acid, with a gelatinous precipitate of silica.

Almandine, Grossularite, Essonite, Common or *Aplome Garnet, Colophonite* and *Melanite* are varieties chiefly distinguished by their colour and different degrees of transparency.

Garnet occurs as an essential, and sometimes sole ingredient of the following rocks : garnet rock, eklogite, eulisite, kinzigite. It likewise is a very frequent accessory in granite, granulite, vitreous trachyte and perlite (in which it would appear to be a contemporaneous formation with the mother-rock), and in metamorphic rocks (e.g. chlorite-schist, mica-schist), where it is probably a product of the very process of metamorphism. In limestone and sandstone rocks (Killan and Wexford in Ireland), and in lavas of Vesuvius.

50. *Pyrope.*—Monoclinic, crystals almost always rounded off at the edges, imbedded, or scattered loose in alluvial soil. ,Fracture conchoidal. H.=7·5. S.G.=3·69—3·8. Colour deep hyacinth to blood-red. Lustre vitreous. Transparent or very translucent. Cp. a magnesian alumina-garnet, with a considerable portion of the magnesia replaced by $\dot{F}e$ and $\dot{C}r$. Bp. becomes black and opaque at a red heat, but resumes its transparency and red colour on cooling. With borax, gives the reaction of chromium. Not affected by acids unless previously fused.

Pyrope is a very characteristic accessory constituent of many kinds of serpentine (Saxony), and of the opal-rock termed vitrite (Bohemia).

51. *Zircon* (*Hyacinth*).—Dimetric. Crystals columnar or pyramidal, singly imbedded or attached. Cleavage pyramidal and prismatic, imperfect. Fracture conchoidal to uneven. H.=7·5. S.G.=4—4·7. Colourless, rarely white, usually coloured yellow, red or brown. Lustre adamantine, vitreous. Every degree of transparency. $Cp. = \ddot{Z}r\ddot{S}i$, with little $\ddot{F}e$. Bp. infusible, only soluble with borax. Partially decomposed in sulphuric acid after long digestion. Not affected by any other acid.

Zircon occurs in many rocks (more or less abundantly), usually as an accessory ingredient only, viz. in zirconsyenite (Norway, Ural); in granite (Criffel, Kircudbright and New Jersey); in basaltic lavas of extinct volcanoes (Rhenish Prussia); and in volcanic tufa (Auvergne); in granular limestone (Hammond).

52. *Idocrase* (*Vesuvian, Egeran, Wiluit*).—Dimetric. Crystals usually columnar or pyramidal, imbedded and attached; also massive in fibrous and compact aggregates. Cleavage prismatic, imperfect. Fracture uneven and splintery. H.= 6·5. S.G.=3·45. Colour yellow, green or brown. Lustre vitreous or resinous. Transparent, translucent, opaque. $Cp. = \dot{R}^3Si + R\ddot{S}i$, and $\dot{R}$=principally $\dot{C}a$, $\dot{F}e$, $\dot{M}g$, with $\dot{H}$ up to 3 per cent. $\ddot{R}=\ddot{A}l$, $\ddot{F}e$. Bp. fuses easily, with effervescence, to a yellowish-green or brownish glass. With microcosmic salt it produces the reaction of iron and a siliceous skeleton. In raw state, imperfectly decomposed by muriatic acid, but after fusion, completely decomposed with a gelatinous precipitate of silica.

Idocrase occurs as an accessory in old lavas of Vesuvius; in serpentine (Mussa Alp, Piedmont); in dolomite (Fassa Thal, where it is an unmistakable product of metamorphism); and in metalliferous veins (Swarzenberg, Saxony).

Its igneous origin, at least in part, is proved by the appearance of similar products in slags of furnaces.

53. *Scapolite* (*Wernerite*).—Dimetric. The crystals columnar, attached and imbedded, also clustered in geodes, or massive and granular. Cleavage prismatic, tolerably perfect. H. = 5—5·5. S.G. = 2·6—2·7. Colourless, or coloured pale green, green, or reddish. Lustre vitreous to resinous. Semi-transparent to opaque. Cp. very fluctuating, in part answering to the formula: $\dot{R}^3\ddot{S}i^2 + 2\ddot{A}l\ddot{S}i$, with $\dot{C}a$, $\dot{N}a$, some $\dot{H}$ and $\ddot{F}e$.

Scapolite is an essential constituent of wernerite rock; it also occurs as an accessory in granite and other crystalline rocks, likewise in limestone, but in that case usually near the margin of intruded granites. Finally in veins of ore (Arendal).

Meionite and *Mellilite*.—Limpid crystals found in the marble blocks of Somma, and *Mellilite*, dirty yellow, found in nepheline rocks at Capo di Bove near Rome, are two minerals very closely allied to scapolite.

54. *Epidote* (*Pistacite*, *Zoisite*).—Monoclinic. Crystals columnar, extended in the direction of their horizontal axis, usually in geodes, also massive and in fibrous, granular, or compact aggregates. Cleavage orthodiagonal, very perfect, hemidomatic perfect. Fracture conchoidal to uneven. H. = 6—7. S.G. = 3·2—3·5. Almost always coloured, viz. green, yellow or grey. Lustre vitreous, and on the cleavage surfaces adamantine. Transparent to opaque. Cp. = $\dot{R}^3\ddot{S}i + 2\ddot{R}\ddot{S}i$, in which formula $\dot{R} = \dot{C}a$, with some $\dot{M}g$ and up to 2 per cent $\ddot{H}$; $\ddot{R} = \ddot{A}l$, $\ddot{F}e$. Bp. variable; after being subjected to strong heat or melted, all varieties may be decomposed by muriatic acid and they become gelatinised.

Zoisite is grey, with $\dot{C}a$ and $\ddot{A}l$; it occurs as an accessory in granular limestone and granite (Fichtelgebirge).

Pistacite is green and rich in $\overset{...}{\text{Fe}}$. It occurs as an accessory and very frequently in hornblende rocks, and is probably the product of decomposition of hornblende. It also occurs in beds of iron-ore (Arendal).

55. *Orthite* (*Allanite, Cerine*). — Monoclinic, isomorphous with epidote, but seldom occurs in distinct crystals. More usually massive, in granular and short fibrous aggregates. Fracture conchoidal to uneven. H. = 5—5·6. S.G. = 3·3—4·2. Colour, pitch-brown to black. Streak greyish or greenish. Lustre imperfect, metallic to vitreous and resinous. Translucent at the edges to opaque. Cp. variable. In part, $\overset{...}{\text{R}}{}^3\overset{.}{\text{Si}}+$ $\overset{..}{\text{R}}\overset{.}{\text{Si}}$, in which $\overset{..}{\text{R}}=\overset{..}{\text{Al}}$ and $\overset{..}{\text{R}}=\overset{.}{\text{Ce}}$, $\overset{.}{\text{Ca}}$, $\overset{.}{\text{Mg}}$, with little $\overset{.}{\text{La}}$ and $\overset{.}{\text{H}}$, and in the variety orthite, $\overset{.}{\text{Y}}$. Bp. on charcoal, puffs up slightly and fuses to a black glass; with borax fuses easily and makes with oxidising flame a bead of blood-red colour in the heat and yellow on cooling; with the reduction flame the bead is green.

Orthite occurs as an accessory in granite, especially in certain narrow dykes of granite, rich in felspar, which traverse hornblendic rocks (Greenland, Dresden); in zirconsyenite (Hitteroë in Norway), where the crystals are a foot in height; sometimes in porphyries (Totun Fjeld in Norway).

56. *Gadolinite.*—Monoclinic, but seldom in crystals, usually massive and imbedded. Fracture conchoidal to uneven. H.= 6·5—7. S.G. = 4—4·3. Pitch- and raven-black. Streak greenish-grey. Lustre vitreous, resinous. Translucent at the edges to opaque. Cp. various, in general $\overset{...}{\text{R}}{}^3\overset{.}{\text{Si}}$; and $\overset{..}{\text{R}}=$ $\overset{.}{\text{Y}}$, $\overset{.}{\text{Ce}}$, $\overset{.}{\text{Fe}}$, $\overset{.}{\text{Ca}}$. Bp. puffs up slightly without fusing, glows vividly and burns to a light-grey colour. Gelatinises with muriatic acid.

Gadolinite occurs chiefly in granite, and as an accessory, imbedded (Fahlun in Sweden, Hitteroë in Norway).

57. *Axinite* (*Thumite*). — Triclinic. Crystals singly attached, or clustered in geodes, also massive, in scaly aggre-

gates. Cleavage indistinct. H.$=6\cdot5$—7. S.G.$=3\cdot3$. Colour clove-brown, grey, or plum-blue. Transparent to translucent at edges only. Exhibits trichroism in an eminent degree. Cp. very complicated $= \dot{R}^3\ddot{S}i + 2\ddot{R}\ddot{S}i + \frac{1}{4}\ddot{B}\ddot{S}i$; and $\dot{R} = \dot{C}a$, $\ddot{M}g$, $\dot{K}$; $\ddot{R} = \ddot{F}e$, $\ddot{M}n$. Bp. melts easily, and with intumescence, to a dark green glass, which becomes black in the oxidation flame; with fluor-spar and sulphate of potash gives the reaction of boracic acid. After fusion it gelatinises completely with muriatic acid. Axinite occurs in the geodes of granite (Oisans, St. Gotthard), or in metalliferous veins (Botallack in Cornwall; Kongsberg in Norway).

58. *Cordierite* (*Dichroite, Peliom, Iolite*).—Trimetric. Crystals usually columnar, hexagonal, also massive and disseminated. Cleavage brachydiagonal, tolerably perfect. Fracture conchoidal to uneven. H.$= 7$—$7\cdot5$. S.G.$= 2\cdot6$. Colourless, but usually coloured bluish-grey, violet-blue, or brownish. Lustre vitreous; in fracture eminently resinous. Transparent to translucent, beautiful trichroism. Cp.$= \dot{R}^3\ddot{S}i^2 + 3\ddot{A}l\ddot{S}i$; and $\dot{R} = \ddot{M}g$, $\dot{F}e$, $\ddot{M}n$ and $\dot{H}$. Bp. fuses with difficulty at the edges to a glass; dissolved with difficulty in borax. Little affected by acids.

Cordierite occurs as a substitute for quartz, and an essential ingredient in several granites and in metamorphic gneiss, under circumstances pointing to an igneous origin, or to an origin from contact with igneous masses (Saxony). It also occurs in beautiful crystals in metalliferous veins (Bodenmais in Bavaria).

Fahlunite and *Pinite* are products of transmutation from cordierite, or (according to some authors) from nepheline. They occur porphyritically in granite.

Liebnerite and *Oosite* are like products. They occur chiefly in porphyry rocks.

C. TANTALATES (OR COLUMBATES) TITANATES, VANADATES.

The minerals here grouped occur very frequently as accessory ingredients in plutonic and igneous rocks, and are for the most part of contemporaneous origin with the rocks in which they occur.

59. *Pyrochlore.*—Monometric, usually in octahedrons (crystals or grains imbedded.) Fracture conchoidal, brittle. H.= 5—5·5. S.G.=3·8—4·3. Colour dark reddish- and blackish-brown. Streak light brown. Lustre vitreous. Translucent at the edges to opaque. Cp.=($\dot{C}a,\dot{F}e,\dot{C}e,\dot{M}n$)($\ddot{C}b,\ddot{T}i$) with some NaF and $\overset{..}{\underset{-}{H}}$. Bp. becomes yellow and fuses with difficulty to a brown slag, previously (sometimes) emitting an intense light. When powdered, it is decomposed in concentrated sulphuric acid.

Pyrochlore occurs as an accessory in granite and syenite (imbedded), (Miask, Brevig in Norway), also in granular limestone (Kaiserstuhl in Baden).

60. *Perofskite.*—Monometric, usually in cubes or octahedrons. Crystals attached or imbedded, also massive. Cleavage cubal. H.=5·5. S.G.=4. Colour greyish- to iron-black, or reddish-brown. Streak greyish-white. Lustre metallic-adamantine. Opaque. Cp.=$\dot{C}a\ddot{T}i$, with small quantity of $\dot{F}e$. Bp. infusible. Scarcely affected by acids.

Perofskite occurs as an accessory in chlorite schist (Slatoust, in the Ural) in talc schist (Zermatt), and in granular limestone (Kaiserstuhl).

61. *Tantalite.*—Trimetric. Crystals usually columnar, also massive and disseminated. Fracture conchoidal to uneven. H.=6—6·5. S.G.=7·1—7·9. Colour iron-black. Streak brown. Lustre adamantine metallic. Opaque. Cp. = ($\dot{F}e,\dot{M}n$)($\ddot{T}a,\ddot{C}b^2$), with sometimes some $\dot{C}a$ and up to 16 per

cent. of $\ddot{\text{S}}$n. Bp. unchanged. Not affected, or very little affected, by acids.

Tantalite occurs as an accessory in granite, imbedded, and is usually associated with beryl and tourmaline (Finland, Sweden).

62. *Columbite (Niobite)*.—Trimetric, usually in thick tabular or broad columnar crystals. Cleavage macrodiagonal, very distinct, brachydiagonal distinct. Fracture conchoidal to uneven. H.=6. S.G. = 5·4.—6·4. Colour brownish-black to iron-black. Streak reddish-brown to black. Lustre metallic adamantine. Opaque. Cp. = $(\dot{\text{F}}\text{e},\dot{\text{M}}\text{n})^3\ddot{\text{C}}\text{b}^2$, with little $\dot{\text{C}}$a and $\ddot{\text{S}}$n. Bp. infusible, unchanged. Not affected by acids.

Columbite occurs as an accessory in granite, associated with beryl and tourmaline (Bodenmais in Bavaria, Connecticut and Massachusetts), also imbedded in cryolite (Greenland).

63. *Wöhlerite*.—Trimetric. Distinct crystals very rare, usually massive and disseminated. Fracture conchoidal. H.= 5·5. S.G. $=$ 3·4, Colour wine-yellow to honey-yellow, or yellowish-brown. Lustre resinous in the fracture. Translucent. Cp.=a silicate of $\dot{\text{C}}$a, $\dot{\text{N}}$a, $\ddot{\text{T}}$a, $\underline{\ddot{\text{Z}}\text{r}}$. Bp. at first unchanged, after some time fuses to a yellow glass. Decomposes in concentrated muriatic acid.

Wöhlerite occurs as an accessory in zirconsyenite (Brevig in Norway), in syenite and miascite (Ditro in Transylvania).

64. *Titanite (Sphene, Menochine ore)*.—Monoclinic, frequently crystallised, prisms and tabular, imbedded and attached, twins frequent, also massive and in scaly aggregates. Cleavage indistinct. H.=5—5·5. S.G.=3·4—3·56. Colour grey or brown. Lustre adamantine, often resinous. Semi-transparent to opaque. Cp.=$2\dot{\text{C}}\text{a}\ddot{\text{S}}\text{i}=\dot{\text{C}}\text{a}\ddot{\text{T}}\text{i}^3$. Bp. fusible only at the edges. With microcosmic salt and metallic tin gives the reaction of titanium in the reduction flame. Incompletely decomposed by muriatic acid; completely decomposed by sulphuric acid, gypsum being formed.

Greenovite is red-coloured titanite containing M̈n.

Titanite occurs as an accessory in the mica-schist of the Alps, and there usually in cruciform twin crystals, in gneiss (Massachusetts), in granite (Greenland), in syenite and zirconsyenite (Strontian, Argyleshire ; Arendal), in volcanic rocks, rich in felspàr (Laachersee, Andernach on the Rhine), in phonolite (Bohemian Mittelgebirge), in beds of iron-ore (with pyroxene in Arendal), finally in granular limestone (in many localities in North America).

65. *Volborthite.*—Hexagonal. Crystals are small, often only scaly particles on an earthy incrustation. H.=3—3·5. S.G.= 3·45—3·86. Colour olive- or grass-green, also yellow. Streak almost yellow. Lustre mother-of-pearl, vitreous. Translucent in thin plates. Cp. = (Ċu,Ċa)⁴V̈+Ḣ. When heated in glass tube gives out water. Bp. fuses easily on charcoal, and at a higher temperature consolidates to a slag, resembling graphite, which slag contains grains of metallic copper. It is soluble in muriatic acid.

Volborthite occurs as an accessory ingredient in many sandstones of the Permian formation of Russia, or as incrustation on the walls of clefts in the same rocks.

D. SULPHATES.

(a) ANHYDROUS SULPHATES.

66. *Barytes (Heavy Spar).*—Trimetric. Crystals tabular or columnar, very various; also lamellar, fibrous, granular, or compact. Cleavage perfect in the planes of the brachy- and macro-diagonals. H.=2·5—3·5. S.G. = 4·3—4·7. Colourless, limpid, or variously coloured, white, yellow, brown, or red. Lustre vitreous or resinous. Transparent, translucent, opaque. Cp.=BaS̈, with admixture, in small quantities, of other bases, such as Ċa, S̈r, and Ḟe. Bp. decrepitates, and fuses

with difficulty.   Colours the flame yellowish-green.   Not
affected by acids.

Barytes seldom occurs as an independent rock.   It occurs
as an accessory in the form of lamellar nodules in the clay
strata of Monte Paterno near Bologna, where it is called
Bologna-spar or Bolognese stone.   It also occurs in the
cavities of fossils in the Swabian Jurassic formation ; also very
frequent in veins of ore.

67. *Celestine.*—Trimetric, isomorphous with barytes, also
the same cleavage, frequently fibrous, granular, or compact.
H.=3—3·5.   S.G. = 3·9.   Colourless, limpid, but usually
white, rarely blue.   Lustre vitreous to resinous.   Transparent,
translucent.   Cp.=$\dot{S}r\ddot{S}$.   Bp. decrepitates and fuses without
difficulty to a milk-white bead.   If moistened with muriatic
acid, it colours the flame carmine-red.   It is only slightly
affected by acids.

Celestine only occurs as an accessory constituent in rocks.
Sometimes it is found in layers of a fibrous texture imbedded
in marly limestone (Jena), in lamellar or radiated nodules in
dolomite (Seisser Alps), or in fossils (Swabia), also in many
metalliferous veins.

68. *Anhydrite (Muriacite, Karstenite).*—Trimetric.   Crystals
thick, tabular, but rare ; usually massive, in granular or compact aggregates.   Cleavage macro- and brachy-diagonal, very
perfect, basal perfect.   H. = 3—3·5.   S.G. = 2·8—3.   Colourless, white, but most frequently light bluish-grey or reddish-
grey.   Lustre vitreous, on the faces of basal cleavage, resinous.
Cp. = $\dot{C}a\ddot{S}$.   Bp. fuses with difficulty to a white enamel; with
borax effervesces, and fuses to a transparent glass, which on
cooling becomes yellowish.   Little soluble in acids.

Anhydrite occurs as an independent rock, associated with
gypsum and rock-salt (frequent in the Alps).   It also occurs
in metalliferous veins (Andreasberg).

69. *Glauberite.*—Monoclinic, also massive, in thin lamellar aggregates. Cleavage basal perfect. H.=2·5—3. S.G.= 2·6—2·8. Colourless and coloured, greenish, yellowish or reddish-white. Lustre vitreous to resinous. Translucent. Taste salt and bitter. Cp. $= \ddot{Na}\ddot{S} + Ca\ddot{S}$. Bp. decrepitates violently, and fuses readily to a transparent glass. Colours the flame reddish-yellow.

Glauberite occurs as an accessory in rock-salt (Villa Rubia in Spain, Berchtesgaden in Bavaria, Tarapaca in Peru).

(b) HYDROUS SULPHATES.

70. *Gypsum (Alabaster, Selenite).*—Monoclinic. Crystals prismatic and tabular, various, frequently twins, also massive, fibrous, lamellar, granular, or compact. Cleavage clinodiagonal, very perfect, hemipyramidal less perfect. Sectile. In thin plates flexible. H. = 1·5—2. S.G. = 2·3. Colourless, limpid, or white, sometimes variously coloured grey, flesh-red, yellow, &c. Lustre mother-of-pearl on the faces of most perfect cleavage, silky on the hemi-pyramidal faces, otherwise vitreous. Transparent, translucent, opaque. Cp. $= Ca\ddot{S} = 2\dot{H}$. In matrass yields much water. Bp. becomes dull and white, exfoliates and fuses with difficulty to a · white enamel, which has an alkaline reaction. Soluble in 460 parts of water, in acids somewhat more easily.

Gypsum occurs as an independent rock in sedimentary formations, or in metamorphic schists (mica-schist of the Alps). It occurs accessorily in the form of crystals or nodules in clay-marls, rarely in metalliferous veins or dykes; sometimes, however, in mines as a recent product.

The origin of gypsum may be either by wet or dry process, or by metamorphism. It is formed (1) in volcanic districts by fumes of sulphuric acid and sulphuretted hydrogen issuing from cracks or other openings in the ground, and acting upon

E

lavas previously containing pyroxene and labradorite; (2) by
wet process, where pyrites is decomposed in the neighbourhood of lime, or as a sediment from the evaporation of sea-
water. The latter process may be observed taking place artificially in salt pans; (3) by metamorphism from anhydrite by
simple absorption of water.

71. *Alunogen (Hair Salt).*—Occurs in capillary or acicular
crystals or crystalline masses of irregular form, usually in
crystalline crusts or reniform aggregates of fibrous structure.
H.=1·5—2. S.G.=1·6—1·8. Colour white and yellowish,
or greenish. Lustre silky. Cp.=$\ddot{A}l\ddot{S}^3+18\dot{H}$. Easily soluble
in water. If heated in test tube, it intumesces and gives out
water.

Alunogen is sometimes the product of volcanic action (volcano of Pasto, Milo Isle), sometimes a result of the decomposition of pyrites in coal districts, and in alum-shales (Bonn,
Dresden); sometimes is found as an efflorescence in numerous
places in the United States.

72. *Native Alum.*—Chemically speaking there are several
subspecies. Crystallographically all monometric, and usually
in octahedrons; also occurs in fibrous masses. Fracture conchoidal. H.=2—2·5. S.G.=1·6—1·9. Soluble in water.
Taste sweet-astringent. Cp.=$\dot{R}\ddot{S}+\ddot{A}l\ddot{S}^3+24\dot{H}$. According
to the various bases, different species are distinguished, viz.:—
Potash-alum, soda-alum, magnesia-alum, iron-alum, manganese-
alum, and ammonia-alum. Bp. on charcoal, efflorescence;
with cobalt solution blue.

Alum is found in the vicinity of the crater of Ætna, filling
clefts in the Coal and Browncoal formations, especially in
pyritous shales (Saarbrucken, Bohemia), and as an efflorescence
on other minerals or rocks. In fresh alum-slate no alum is
contained, but the latter is only developed in that rock by
weathering and the consequent decomposition of the pyrites
contained in it.

73. *Epsomite* (*Epsom Salt*).—Trimetric. Crystals columnar, usually in granular, fibrous, or earthy aggregates. Cleavage brachydiagonal. H. = 2·25. S.G.=1·75. Colourless. Transparent. Taste saline bitter. Cp.=2$\ddot{\mathrm{M}}\mathrm{g}\ddot{\mathrm{S}}$+7$\dot{\mathrm{H}}$. Easily soluble in water. Bp. if heated in test tube gives water, fuses, and then remains unchanged. On charcoal it effervesces violently, and shows alkaline reaction; if heated with cobalt solution, becomes rose-pink.

Epsomite occurs as an efflorescence from marshy ground (Steppes of Siberia), and from many kinds of rock (gneiss near Freiberg, alum-slate at Idria), also in solution in spring waters (Epsom, Saidschutz in Bohemia).

74. *Glaubersalt* (*Mirabilite*).—Monoclinic, usually incrusted. H.=1·5—2. S.G. = 1·48. Colourless, transparent. Taste cooling, and saline bitter. Cp.=$\dot{\mathrm{N}}\mathrm{a}\ddot{\mathrm{S}}$+10$\dot{\mathrm{H}}$. Easily soluble in water, quickly decomposing, and falling to powder in the atmosphere. Bp. in test tube it melts in its water of crystallisation. It colours the flame reddish-yellow.

Glaubersalt occurs as an independent rock (Guipuscoa in Spain), accessory in rock-salt strata (Berchtesgaden); also in mineral springs (Carlsbad in Bohemia), and salt lakes.

75. *Alunite* (*Alumstone*).—Rhombohedral. The crystals mostly very small, and clustered in geodes. Usually massive, in granular, earthy, and compact aggregates. It occurs mixed and interlaced with quartz, hornstein, and felsite. Cleavage basal. H.=3·5—4. S.G. = 2·6—2·7. Colourless, white, yellow, or reddish. Lustre vitreous, with mother-of-pearl lustre on the basal cleavage faces. Translucent. Cp.=$\dot{\mathrm{K}}\ddot{\mathrm{S}}$+3$\ddot{\underline{\mathrm{Al}}}\ddot{\mathrm{S}}$+ 6$\dot{\mathrm{H}}$. In test tube gives out water. Bp. decrepitates violently and is infusible. Not affected by muriatic acid; soluble in heated concentrated sulphuric acid. Alum is manufactured from this mineral by heating and adding water to it.

Alunite is met with in the largest known quantities at La

Tolfa near Rome, where it occurs in small geodes in decomposed trachytic rocks, and owes its origin to the action of
sulphuric acid (a product of volcanic agency) upon the rock
during long periods of time (Muzay, Hungary; Montdore,
Auvergne).

E. BORATES.

76. *Boracite.*—Monometric, tetrahedral. The crystals sometimes show combinations of the cube, the rhombic dodecahedron, and tetrahedron. Always porphyritically imbedded.
Cleavage imperfect. Fracture conchoidal. Brittle. H.=7.
S.G.=2·97. Colourless, white or greyish, yellowish, greenish.
Lustre vitreous to adamantine. Transparent to translucent at
edges only. Cp.=$\dot{M}g^3\ddot{B}^4$. Bp. intumesces, fuses with difficulty, forming a pearl which, whilst hot, is transparent and
yellowish, and when cooled is white and crystalline, acicular.
It colours the flame green when fused with sulphate of soda
and fluor spar. In muriatic acid it is perfectly soluble.

Boracite occurs, as an accessory only, in gypsum, anhydrite,
or rock-salt (Lüneburg in Hanover, Seegeberg in Holstein,
Luneville in France; in the last place in radiated fibrous
masses). A fine-grained to compact rock, which occurs in
subordinate masses in the salt mountains of Stassfurt near
Magdeburg, consists essentially of boracite with some chloride
of magnesium. It is called stassfurtite.

77. *Borax (Tinkal).*—Monoclinic, isomorphous with pyroxene. The crystals usually broad and short, columnar. Cleavage
clinodiagonal and prismatic. Fracture conchoidal. H.=
2—2·5. S.G.=1·72. Colourless, or more usually yellowish
and greyish-white. Lustre resinous. Translucent. Cp.=
$\dot{N}a\ddot{B}^2+10\dot{H}$; usually impure. Bp. decrepitates with rapid
heating, puffs up violently, becomes black, and finally melts to
a transparent colourless powder. It tinges the flame reddish-

yellow. If moistened with sulphuric acid, it tinges the flame green.

Borax is met with in loose crystals and crystalline grains or incrustations, associated with rock-salt, on the shores of several lakes in Thibet, where it is a recent formation. Clear lake in California, in crystals several inches long.

F. PHOSPHATES.

(a) ANHYDROUS PHOSPHATES.

78. *Apatite (Spargelstein, Phosphorite).*—Hemihedral hexagonal. The crystals short, columnar, or tabular; also massive, in granular, fibrous, or compact masses (phosphorite). Cleavage prismatic and basic. Fracture conchoidal to uneven, and splintery. Brittle. H.=5. S.G.=3·25. Colourless, white, but more usually light green, blue, or grey. Lustre vitreous on crystal faces; resinous on fracture or cleavage surfaces. $Cp.=3\dot{C}a^3\dddot{P}+\frac{1}{3}Ca(Cl,F)$, with sometimes $\dot{M}g$ and $\dot{F}e$. Bp. only fusible in thin laminæ. If moistened with sulphuric acid, colours the flame bluish-green. Soluble in muriatic and in nitric acids.

Apatite is met with—(1) as an independent rock or in concretions, principally in strata of the Browncoal formation, more rarely in the Chalk formations, always massive (phosphorite); frequent in the Oberpfalz of Bavaria: (2) as an accessory constituent of rocks, especially the volcanic (nepheline-dolerite at Löbau in Saxony; basalt in Bohemia; volcanic rocks of Tumilla and in meteorites); in talc-schist (Zillerthal), and in limestone (Gouverneur in North America, Arendal, Pargas); (3) very frequent in veins of tin-ore.

It will be therefore seen that apatite in many cases must be a formation by wet process, and in others a plutonic product. Daubrée has succeeded in producing artificial crystals of apatite by conducting fumes of chloride of phosphorus over heated quicklime.

79. *Turquois* (*Calaite*).—Amorphous in cavities and veins, reniform or stalactitic. Fracture conchoidal to uneven. H. = 6. S.G. = 2·6—2·8. Colour sky-blue to verdigris-green. Streak greenish-white. Lustre feeble. Translucent at the edges to opaque. Cp. = $\overset{..}{\text{Al}}{}^2\overset{...}{\text{P}}+5\overset{.}{\text{H}}$, with some $\overset{.}{\text{Cu}}$ up to 3 per cent. If heated in test tube, it gives water, decrepitates violently, and becomes black. Bp. infusible; tinges the flame green. Soluble in acids.

Turquois is met with as an incrustation in the fissures of Lydian stone ; very precious varieties in Persia. Also occurs in sandstone in Arabia.

(*b*) HYDROUS PHOSPHATES.

80. *Vivianite* (*Blue Iron-Earth*).—Monoclinic. The crystals usually single, attached, also fibrous, divergent, earthy. Cleavage clinodiagonal, very perfect; in thin laminæ, flexible. H. = 1·5—2. S.G. = 2·66. Colour indigo-blue to blackish-green, sometimes white, and becoming blue by exposure. Lustre on cleavage surfaces, mother-of-pearl. Translucent. Cp. = $\overset{.}{\text{Fe}}{}^3\overset{...}{\text{P}}+$ 8$\overset{.}{\text{H}}$. Bp. in matrass gives out much water, puffs up, and becomes particoloured grey and red ; on charcoal burns and becomes red, and then fuses to grey, lustrous, and magnetic globule. Readily soluble in muriatic and nitric acids.

Vivianite is usually a product of decomposition from magnetic pyrites, in veins traversing the clay slate (St. Agnes, Cornwall), or in granite (Bodenmais in Bavaria). The earthy variety is very frequent as an accessory constituent of turf mosses and Tertiary clays. Pseudomorphous in form of oysters and belemnites in New Jersey, U. S.

81. *Wavellite* (*Lasionite*).—Trimetric. The crystals usually small, acicular, and clustered to reniform aggregates of radiated

structure. H.$=3\cdot25$—4. S.G.$=2\cdot34$. Colourless, white, or coloured greyish, or a beautiful green or blue. Lustre vitreous. Cp.$=(\ddot{A}l^3\dot{\ddot{P}}+18\dot{H})+\frac{1}{3}AlF$. Bp. in matrass gives out water and traces of hydrofluoric acid. In the forceps puffs up and tinges the flame bluish-green, especially if moistened with sulphuric acid.

Wavellite is met with as an accessory and a secondary product in fissures of a soft clay-slate at Barnstaple in Devonshire; in Lydian stone at Langenstriegis, near Freiberg; and in Devonian sandstone at Zbirow in Bohemia.

G. NITRATES.

82. *Nitre (Saltpetre).*—Trimetric. The crystals prismatic, isomorphous with aragonite, but usually only very thin, capillary, and acicular. Fracture conchoidal. H.$=2$. S.G. $=1\cdot9$. Colourless, white and grey. Lustre vitreous. Taste saline, cooling. Cp.$=\dot{K}\ddot{N}$. Readily soluble in water; deflagrates vividly on glowing charcoal. Bp. fuses easily on platinum wire, tinging the flame violet.

Nitre occurs as a separate formation in the caverns of several limestone mountains (Ceylon, Calabria), as an efflorescence from the surface of the ground, especially in hot weather after rain (Aragon, Hungary, East India); also in springs.

83. *Nitratine (Chili saltpetre).*—Rhombohedric. In crystals, and crystalline grains; cleavage, rhombohedric. H.$=1\cdot5$—2. S.G.$=2\cdot1$—$2\cdot3$. Colourless or light coloured. Transparent to translucent. Taste saline, cooling. Cp.$=\dot{N}a\ddot{N}$. Soluble in water; deflagrates in glowing charcoal, but less vividly than saltpetre. Bp. fuses, tinging the flame yellow.

Nitratine is a marine product, found in grains mixed with the sand, and associated with gypsum, rock-salt, and glauber-salt, occurring at many parts of the coast of Chili.

H. CARBONATES.

(a) ANHYDROUS CARBONATES.

The most important of the carbonates are those comprised in the Calcite group. The calcspar and dolomites form whole mountain ranges (limestone and dolomite) as well as isolated mineral formations of minor extent in cliffs, fissures, and veins.

They are chiefly of neptunian origin, partly crystalline or compact precipitates; partly formed by springs; and partly the result of organic processes (chalk, coral). There are probably no limestone rocks of plutonic origin, although carbonate of lime under high pressure is capable of fusion without chemical decomposition. The minor mineral formations in clefts, veins, dykes, and geodes are doubtless, for the most part, the result of infiltration.

All calcites are rhombohedral in crystallisation. Calcspar alone presents great variety of form. Its crystals are grouped and interlaced in almost every conceivable shape and fashion, and the uncrystallised varieties are fibrous, granular, compact. The cleavage of the crystals is rhombohedral, very perfect. The angle of the cleavage rhombohedron is the most characteristic distinguishing feature of the different species, which can only be determined in many cases by an accurate measurement of that angle. Fracture conchoidal, but in the crystallised varieties it is somewhat difficult to obtain a genuine fracture. The colour is usually white, grey, yellowish, reddish, or brownish. Lustre vitreous, sometimes resinous. Calcspar and magnesite alone are sometimes perfectly transparent, the other calcites at most only attain translucence. The Cp. of all calcites comes under the general formulæ ṘC̈. .

The following are the principal species of this important group of minerals :—

84. *Calcspar* (*Calcareous Spar, Calcite*). — H. = 2·5—3·5. S.G. = 2·5—2·8. Cp. = $\dot{C}a\ddot{C}$, usually with small quantities of· $\dot{F}e$, $\dot{M}g$, $\dot{M}n$. Bp. infusible, but burns to quicklime with a bright light. Readily soluble in muriatic acid, even in large pieces, with effervescence, caused by the evolution of carbonic acid.

Limestone, marble, chalk, oolite, pisolite, coral, are some of the most important of the very numerous varieties which form independent rocks, and will be described hereafter as such. Marl is a mixture of clay and lime. Iceland spar is a pure transparent variety of calcspar. Anthraconite is coloured black by admixture of carbon. It would lead us too far to attempt to enumerate all the varieties of this very abundant mineral.

Calcspar stands next to quartz in importance, as constituting the mineral of the greatest frequency after it, and forming nearly as large a portion of the earth's crust.

85. *Magnesite* (*Talc-spar*). — H. = 3·5—4·5. S.G. = 2·8—3. Cp. = $\dot{M}g\ddot{C}$, usually also some $\dot{F}e$. Bp. becomes red if heated with cobalt solution. Soluble in acids, if powdered and heat applied.

86. *Dolomite* (*Bitter Spar, Brown Spar, Ankerite*).—H. = 3·5—4. S.G. = 2·85—2·92. Cp. = $\dot{C}a\ddot{C} + \dot{M}g\ddot{C}$, usually with admixtures of $\dot{F}e$ and $\dot{M}n$. Ankerite is particularly rich in iron. Bp. infusible, burns to caustic. Does not usually effervesce with muriatic acid, and is only soluble in that acid if powdered and heat applied.

87. *Breunnerite* (*Bitter and Brown Spar*, in part; *Mesitine Spar*).—Cp. = $\dot{F}e\ddot{C} + 2\dot{M}g\ddot{C}$. H. = 4·5. S.G. = 3—3·63.

88. *Spathic Iron* (*Sparry Iron-ore, Siderite*).—H. = 3·5—4·5. S.G. 3·7—3·9. Colour always yellowish-grey or yellowish-brown. Cp. $\dot{F}e\ddot{C}$, with some $\dot{M}n$, $\dot{M}g$, and $\dot{C}a$. In matrass decrepitates and gives out carbonic acid. Bp. infusible ; but

becomes black and magnetic. Soluble in acids without heat applied (effervescing).

In the compact state, or when occurring in reniform masses or concretions, this mineral is termed *Sphærosiderite*, and if, moreover, combined with clay, *Clay Ironstone*.

89. *Zinc Spar* (*Calamine*, *Galmey*, in part).—H. = 5. S.G. = 4—4·3. Cp. = $\dot{Z}n\ddot{C}$, with small quantities of $\dot{F}e$, $\dot{M}n$, $\dot{C}a$, $\dot{M}g$. Bp. loses its carbonic acid, and then shows reaction of oxide of zinc. Readily soluble in acids, with effervescence.

90. *Aragonite.*—Trimetric. Crystals usually columnar, with inclination to twin formations. Singly imbedded or clustered in geodes; also occurring in divergent and fibrous aggregates and stalk-like, coralloidal shapes (flos ferri), or in the form of peastone (pisolite). Cleavage brachydiagonal, distinct; prismatic, and brachydomatic, imperfect. Fracture, conchoidal to uneven. H. = 3·5—4. S.G. = 2·93. Colourless and coloured yellow, wine-yellow, reddish. Lustre vitreous. Transparent to translucent. Cp. = $\dot{C}a\ddot{C}$, very often with $\dot{S}r\ddot{C}$ (up to 2·4 per cent.), also some CaF. Bp. in matrass decrepitates violently, and falls to a white coarse powder; on charcoal burns to caustic lime; if containing strontian colours the flame carmine. Soluble both in muriatic and nitric acids, with effervescence.

Aragonite occurs as an accessory in clay and gypsum (Molina and Valencia in Aragon). In clefts and veins of vesicular cavities of basaltic rocks (Bilin, Bohemia). Flosferri is formed in great perfection in the Styrian iron mines. A fine fibrous variety called satinspar is found in thin silklike veins traversing the shale at Alston Moor. Peastone (sprudelor erbsenstein) occurs in great beauty at Carlsbad.

Aragonite is entirely a watery product. It is said that whereas cold springs can only produce calcspar, hot springs give birth to aragonite. Moreover, according to Becquerel, aragonite is formed by the action of a saturated solution of $\dot{N}a\ddot{C}^2$ on gypsum, but calcspar if the solution of $\dot{N}a\ddot{C}^2$ be much diluted.

(b) HYDROUS CARBONATES.

91. *Trona* (*Urao*).—Monoclinic. Crystals broad, columnar; in direction of horizontal axis, also in fibrous and divergent aggregates. Cleavage orthodiagonal, perfect. H. $=2\cdot5$—3. S.G. $=2\cdot1$. Colourless or grey. Lustre bright vitreous. Transparent. Cp. $=\dot{N}a^2\ddot{C}^3+4\dot{H}$. Sometimes with some NaCl. Does not alter by exposure in a dry atmosphere. Yields water in matrass. Soluble in dilute muriatic acid with brisk effervescence.

Trona forms an independent rock (Figzan, North Africa). It forms a crust on the ground on mountain slopes at Maracaibo in Peru; and occurs as an efflorescence near Sweetwater River, Rocky Mountains, mixed with sulphate of soda and common salt.

92. *Natron* (*Carbonate of Soda*). — Monoclinic. Is only known in nature in form of incrustation, or mealy efflorescence on the surface of the ground, or various rocks. H. $=1$—$1\cdot5$. S.G. $=1\cdot4$. Colourless, white or grey. Lustre vitreous, dull. Taste alkaline. Cp. $\dot{N}a\ddot{C}+10\dot{H}$. Unlike trona it weathers rapidly on exposure to the air. Liquifies at a moderate temperature, and dissolves in its own water of crystallisation; otherwise, however, has the same attributes as trona (Egypt, Hungary, Vesuvius).

93. *Malachite*.—Monoclinic. In aggregates composed of minute crystallisations, acicular and capillary, lamellar, botryoidal, and stalactitic, fibrous to compact. Cleavage when crystallised basal and clinodiagonal, very perfect. H. $=3\cdot5$—4. S.G $=3\cdot7$—4. Colour emerald- to verdigris-green. Streak verdigris- to apple-green. Lustre of crystals adamantine and vitreous; of aggregates silky to dull. Translucent to opaque. Cp. $=\dot{C}u^2\ddot{C}+\dot{H}$. In matrass yields water and blackens. Bp.

fuses on charcoal, and is finally reduced to copper. Soluble in acids, with effervescence.

Malachite occurs as an accessory in various rocks. It is doubtless usually, if not always, a product of the decomposition of copper-ores (Siberia; Chessy near Lyons; Cornwall). It very frequently is found in the form of a pseudomorph of azurite and red copper-ore.

94. *Azurite* (*Lasurite, Blue Copper-ore*).—Monoclinic. Crystals columnar or tabular, usually in clusters or geodes; also massive and earthy varieties. Cleavage clinodomatic, tolerably perfect. Fracture conchoidal to uneven, and splintery. H. = 3·5—4·25. S.G. = 3·5—3·8. Colour azure-blue, in earthy varieties smalt-blue. Lustre vitreous. Translucent, opaque. Cp. = $\dot{C}u^3\ddot{C}^2 + \dot{H}$. Bp. similar to malachite.

Azurite resembles malachite in the places where it is found in nature, and in the mode of its occurrence in other respects. The earthy variety of azurite may, from its outward appearance, be easily mistaken for vivianite.

I. OXIDES OF ELEMENTS OF THE HYDROGEN GROUP.

The oxides collected under this head properly speaking belong more justly to the family of earths (Nos. 1—3). We have, however, postponed their consideration in order to give place as far as possible to those minerals which are more important to the geologist.

(a) ANHYDROUS OXIDES.

95. *Spinel* (*Ceylonite, Pleonaste, Automolite, Gahnite*). — Monometric, usually octahedrons and rhombic dodecahedrons. Crystals singly imbedded and attached, seldom gathered into geodic clusters. Cleavage octahedral. Fracture conchoidal. H. = 8. S.G. = 3·5—4·9. Usually coloured, red-blue, green, yellow, brown, or black. Lustre vitreous, sometimes

resinous. Transparent, translucent, opaque. Cp.=$\ddot{\mathrm{R}}\ddot{\mathrm{A}}$l; R= ($\dot{\mathrm{M}}$g,$\dot{\mathrm{F}}$e,$\dot{\mathrm{C}}$a,$\dot{\mathrm{Z}}$n,$\dot{\mathrm{M}}$n), and a part of the $\ddot{\mathrm{A}}$l is sometimes replaced by $\ddot{\mathrm{F}}$o and a little $\ddot{\mathrm{C}}$r. The varying composition gives rise to distinguishable varieties of the mineral. Thus $\dot{\mathrm{M}}$g$\ddot{\mathrm{A}}$l, red, transparent, is spinel proper; ($\dot{\mathrm{M}}$g,$\dot{\mathrm{F}}$e)$\ddot{\mathrm{A}}$l, black, translucent at the edges, is pleonaste; $\dot{\mathrm{Z}}$n$\ddot{\mathrm{A}}$l, greenish-black, translucent at the edges, automolite. Bp. the red varieties infusible, but lose their colour; on cooling the colour returns. The black varieties fuse to a dark-green bead. The zinc-spinels with soda give oxide of zinc. Not affected by acids.

Spinel occurs as an accessory in granular limestone (pleonaste at Monzoni; blue spinel in North America in several places), in gneiss and talc-schist (the automolite of Fahlun); in the vesicular cavities of volcanic rocks (Somma), and in alluvium (Ceylon). Sometimes spinel is a product of metamorphosis, e.g. of the action of syenite on limestone, at Monzoni. Ebelmen has also succeeded in producing spinel artificially by igneous means.

96. *Magnetic Iron-ore (Magnetite, Oxydulated Iron)*.—Monometric, most usually in octahedrons and rhombic dodecahedrons. Crystals imbedded and attached, and clustered in geodes; very generally massive in granular or compact aggregates, also earthy (eisenmulm). Cleavage octahedral. Fracture conchoidal to uneven. Brittle. H.=5·5—6·5. S.G.= 4·9—5·2. Colour iron-black. Streak black. Lustre metallic. Opaque. Very strongly magnetic. Cp.=$\ddot{\mathrm{F}}$e$\ddot{\mathrm{F}}$e, sometimes with some $\dot{\mathrm{M}}$g. Bp. fuses with difficulty, and with borax gives iron reaction. The powder completely soluble in muriatic acid.

Magnetic iron-ore is found in separate beds (Arendal, Dannemora); it also occurs as an accessory in many rocks, especially in chlorite-chist, talc-schist, serpentine, granite, syenite, basalt, and limestone.

97. *Chromic Iron-ore* (*Chromite*). — Monometric in octa-hedrons, usually massive, in granular aggregates, and dispersed. Cleavage octahedral, imperfect. Fracture conchoidal to uneven. H.=5·5. S.G.=4·3. Colour brownish-black. Streak brown. Lustre semi-metallic. Opaque. Sometimes magnetic. Cp.=$\ddot{F}e\underline{\ddot{C}}r$, with some $\dot{F}e$ replaced by $\dot{M}g$ and some $\underline{\ddot{C}}r$ by $\underline{\ddot{A}}l$. Bp. infusible. With borax it fuses to a green globule. If fused with saltpetre and dissolved in water, it yields a yellow solution, which shows the reaction of chromic acid. Scarcely affected by acids.

Chromic iron very frequently occurs as an accessory in serpentine (Islands of Unst and Fetlar, Shetland), rarely in dolomite (Hoboken, New Jersey).

98. *Hematite* (*Specular Iron, Red Iron-ore*). — Rhombo-hedral; in rhombohedrons, pyramidal or tabular crystals, which are singly imbedded or attached in groups (*Specular Iron, Micaceous Iron*), or subcrystalline, frequently fibrous in botryoidal, reniform, or stalactitic masses ; also granular, lamellar, compact, and earthy textures (*Red Hematite, Fibrous Red Iron, Scaly Red Iron, Red Iron Froth, Reddle, or Red Chalk,* &c.) The crystallised varieties have :—Cleavage basal and rhombohedral, imperfect. H.=5·5—6·5. S.G. = 4·5—5·3. Fracture conchoidal to uneven. Colour iron-black to dark steel-grey. Streak cherry- or blood-red. Lustre metallic. The subcrystalline varieties have :—H.=3·5 only. S.G.= 4·5—4·9. Colour blood-red to brownish-red, sometimes passing over into steel-grey. Streak blood-red. Lustre dull. Cp.=$\ddot{F}e$, sometimes with some $\ddot{T}i$. Bp. both varieties become black and magnetic in the reducing flame. In acids but slowly soluble.

Specular iron (eisenglanz) includes the varieties with perfect metallic lustre ; red iron-ore the amorphous varieties. The sub-crystalline varieties of hematite frequently contain impurities,

siliceous, argillaceous, &c. Itabirite is a granular variety of
the same mineral containing quartz, jaspery clay-iron ; reddle,
argillaceous iron. Hematite forms independent rocks and
beds, sometimes horizontally imbedded between the strata of
other sedimentary rocks. It also forms an essential constituent
of micaceous iron-gneiss and micaceous iron-schist. It is likewise met with as an accessory in many other rocks. At Vesuvius
and Ætna it fills clefts in lava, or is found in vesicular cavities
of lava, where it is probably the result of the decomposition of
fumes of chloride of iron by the vapour of water (steam). In
other cases it is usually a product of metamorphism from
spathic iron and brown hematite. Again, it is sometimes possibly a direct hydrogenic formation (especially where it is
pseudomorphous of other minerals or dendritic on the surfaces
of rock clefts).

99. *Titaniferous Iron* (*Titanic Iron-ore, Ilmenite, Crichtonite*).
—Rhombohedral, isomorphous with specular iron. Crystals
imbedded singly, or attached in groups. Also massive, in
granular lamellar aggregates, or dispersed in grains. Cleavage
sometimes rhombohedral. Fracture conchoidal to uneven.
H.=5—6. S.G.=4·5—5. Colour iron-black to brown or
steel-grey. Streak black to brownish-red. Lustre semi-
metallic. Opaque. Cp.=$\ddot{\mathrm{Ti}}$ and $\dot{\mathrm{Fe}}$ in various and probably
indefinite proportions, sometimes with some $\dot{\mathrm{Mn}}$, or $\dot{\mathrm{Mg}}$. It
will be seen that this composition admits of a near approach to
that of hematite, and in truth the division between the two is
not very definitely marked. Bp. infusible, with fluxes gives
the reactions of iron and titanium. If heated in concentrated
sulphuric acid, it gives a blue colour. Soluble with difficulty
in muriatic or nitric acid, titanic acid being separated.

Titaniferous iron is an accessory ingredient in many rocks,
especially in basalts and dolerites, also in talc-mica-schist
(Gastein), miascite (Ilmensee near Miask), granite (Aschaf-

fenburg). Very frequent in river deposits (Menaccan in Cornwall).

100. *Braunite.*—Dimetric. Crystals usually small and in pyramids resembling the octahedron, clustered in geodes and in granular aggregates. Cleavage pyramidal, tolerably perfect. H. = 6—6·5. S.G. = 4·75—4·82. Colour iron-black to brownish-black. Streak black. Lustre metallic, resinous. Opaque. Cp. = $\dot{\text{M}}$n or Mn$\ddot{\text{M}}$n. Bp. infusible. With borax, phosphor-salt, or soda gives the reaction of manganese. Soluble in muriatic acid, chlorine being evolved in the process.

Braunite occurs sometimes as an accessory in other rocks, chiefly, however, in veins. (In the porphyry of Oehrenstock near Ilmenau, Elgersburg in Thuringia.) This mineral and similar manganese products very frequently form dendritic coatings to the faces of clefts in rocks. These dendritic formations are usually exfiltrations from the mother rock.

101. *Hausmannite* (*Braunstein*).—Dimetric. Crystals always pyramidal, grouped in geodes. Cleavage basal, tolerably perfect, pyramidal less distinct. H. = 5—5·5. S.G. = 4·7. Colour iron-black. Streak brown. Lustre bright metallic. Opaque. Cp. = Mn$\ddot{\text{M}}$n. Bp. like oxide of manganese. Soluble in muriatic acid, with disengagement of chlorine. In concentrated sulphuric acid, after a short time, assumes a bright red colour.

Hausmannite is usually found in separate beds (Ilmenau in Thuringia, Ihlefeld in the Harz), and would appear to be in almost all cases a hydrogenic product, $\dot{\text{M}}$n having been first dissolved in spring and other water, and having afterwards absorbed more oxygen from the air. Daubrée has, however, shown the possibility of producing hausmannite by the reaction of water in the state of steam upon chloride of manganese at a red heat.

102. *Polianite.*—Trimetric. Crystals usually in short prisms,

vertically striped. Also massive in granular aggregates. Cleavage brachydiagonal. H.=6·5—7. S.G.=4·84—4·88. Colour light steel-grey. Streak black. Lustre black metallic. Opaque. Cp.=M̈n. Bp. infusible; on charcoal changes to brown M̈nM̈n. Soluble in muriatic acid, with brisk effervescence of chlorine.

Pyrolusite is sometimes a modification of polianite, sometimes a product of the transmutation of manganite, a mineral which we shall presently notice. The manganite is a compound of M̈n and water, and it has a strong tendency to part with its water and absorb oxygen. Polianite is frequently found in beds of the manganese-ores (Platten in Bohemia, Johanngeorgenstadt, Saxony). Pyrolusite is found in the same localities, or associated with iron-ores (Siegen, in many parts of France).

103. *Cassiterite (Tin-ore, Tinstone).*—Dimetric. Crystals in short prisms or pyramids, very often twins, imbedded or attached ; also massive, granular, or fibrous (wood-tin). Cleavage prismatic, imperfect. Brittle. H.=6—7. S.G.=6·3—7·1. Colour usually yellowish-, reddish-, or blackish-brown; rarely colourless. Streak colourless or brownish. Lustre adamantine or resinous. Translucent to opaque. Cp.=S̈n, usually with some F̈e, M̈n, S̈i, and T̈a. Bp. unchangeable, on charcoal with carbonate of soda reducible to metallic tin. Not affected by acids.

Tin-ore is principally found in metalliferous veins, also as an accessory, and especially so in plutonic rocks (greissen, granite, and tourmaline rocks). Wolfram, tourmaline, beryl, and topaz are almost always associated with this mineral.

Tin-ore in nature is doubtless in many cases a product of wet processes (we find pseudomorphs after felspar in Cornwall) ; but Daubrée has also proved that crystallised oxide of tin may be formed by the action of steam on fumes of chloride of tin.

F

104. *Rutile (Nigrine).*—Dimetric. Crystals always columnar, frequently very thin, acicular and capillary, imbedded and attached, frequently twins; also massive, compact, or granular. Cleavage prismatic, perfect. Fracture conchoidal. H.=6—6·5. S.G.=4·18—4·25. Colour yellowish- or reddish-brown to black (nigrine). Streak yellowish-brown. Lustre metallic adamantine. Translucent to opaque. Cp.=T̈i, with small quantity of F̈e. Bp. unchangeable; with borax gives reaction of titanium. Not affected by acids.

Rutile occurs only as an accessory ingredient in rocks; chiefly in greenstones and diorites, rarely in granite (Warwick in America); gneiss and mica-schist (Barre and Shelburne in Massachusetts); or in granular limestone (Edenville in New York).

Daubrée has produced crystallised titanic acid by the action of steam upon fumes of chloride of titanium.

(b) HYDROUS OXIDES.

105. *Manganite.*—Trimetric, sometimes hemihedral. Crystals always columnar and distinctly marked with vertical stripings, frequently grouped in bundles or clustered in the form of geodes. Also massive in fibrous, divergent, rarely in granular aggregates. Cleavage, brachydomatic very perfect, basic and prismatic imperfect. Somewhat brittle. H.=4. S.G.=4·2—4·4. Colour dark steel-grey to nearly iron-black, frequently brownish-black. Streak brown. Lustre imperfectly metallic. Opaque. Cp.=M̈nḦ. Bp. in matrass yields water, with borax gives reaction of manganese. Perfectly soluble in concentrated muriatic acid, chlorine being disengaged. Slightly soluble in sulphuric acid, which colours it pale red.

Manganite is found in separate beds with other manganese-ores (Ihlefeld in the Harz, Ilmenau and Oehrenstock in

Thuringian Forest). We have already noticed the tendency of manganite to change into pyrolusite.

Psilomelane and *Wad* are two hydrous ores of manganese, occurring frequently with other manganese ores, or as accessories in rocks. They are crystalline, also amorphous, sometimes massive, in reniform, stalactitic, lamellar, and earthy varieties. Cp. (of psilomelane) $=\dot{R}\ddot{M}n^2+\dot{H}$, with $\dot{M}n$, $\dot{B}a$, $\dot{K}$; (of wad) very variable, so that it is hardly to be called an independent mineral: consists principally of $\dot{M}n$, $\ddot{M}n$, and $\dot{H}$, with variable proportions of $\dot{B}a$, $\dot{C}a$, $\dot{C}u$, $\dot{C}o$ (earthy cobalt or asbolan).

106. *Limonite* (*Brown Iron-ore, Brown Hematite*).—Subcrystalline. In fibrous masses of globular, reniform, or stalactitic shape. Also compact or earthy. H.$= 5$—$5\cdot5$. S.G.$=3\cdot6$—4. Colour, clove-brown to yellowish- or blackish-brown, black. Lustre silky, shining or dull. Opaque. Cp.$=Fe^2\dot{H}^3$. Bp. becomes black and magnetic, is fusible in thin laminæ. With borax it gives reaction of iron. Soluble in heated nitric acid.

Limonite is a very abundant mineral, sometimes in independent beds, sometimes as an accessory.

Göthite or *Stilpnosiderite* ($\ddot{F}e\dot{H}$) is a mineral very closely allied to limonite and frequently associated with it.

II. Fluorides and Chlorides.

107. *Common Salt* (*Rock-salt*). — Monometric. Crystals always cubic; usually in granular or fibrous aggregates or massive. Cleavage cubic, very perfect. Fracture conchoidal. Slightly brittle. H.$=2\cdot5$. S.G.$=2\cdot1$—$2\cdot2$. Colourless or grey, or yellowish, or reddish; rarely blue or green. Lustre vitreous. Transparent. Taste pure saline. Cp.$=NaCl$, very often impure, containing F, Br, KCl, MgCl, and other

salts. Soluble in 3·7 parts of water. Liquefies on exposure
to moist atmospheres. Bp. decrepitates in matrass; fuses on
charcoal and evaporates with strong heat; tinges the flame
reddish-yellow, and if combined with microcosmic salt and
oxide of copper, it gives a beautiful blue flame.

Rock-salt is frequently met with as an independent rock in
sedimentary formations of every age. It also occurs as an
accessory ingredient in clay marls of the salt mountains
(Berchtesgaden) where it is in the form of cubic crystals
porphyritically imbedded. In each case it is a neptunian
product. It is found in a state of solution in sea-water, which
contains about 2·5 per cent of salt. It occurs in the steppes,
in the sand of the Desert, in inland springs and lakes, and
finally as a sublimation at the craters of volcanos. We shall
have occasion to mention rock-salt again amongst the rocks.

108. *Sal-ammoniac.*—Monometric, usually in uncrystalline
crusts, stalactites, or as an earthy coating. The crystals have
conchoidal fracture. H.=1—1·5. S.G.=1·5. Colourless, or
coloured yellow or brownish. Taste saline and pungent. Cp.=
NH^4Cl. Easily soluble in water. Bp. in matrass evaporates
entirely; with soda emits a strong smell of ammonia. If
melted with phosphor-salt and oxide of copper, it colours the
flame a beautiful blue.

Sal-ammoniac occurs as a product of sublimation in the
clefts and fissures of volcanic rocks, and many lavas, also in
burnt seams of coal.

109. *Fluor (Fluor-spar).*—Monometric. Cubic form very
frequent. Crystals single or in groups, attached, also massive,
in coarse granular and radiated aggregates, or amorphous and
earthy. Cleavage octahedral, perfect, so that the conchoidal
fracture is seldom observable. Brittle. H. = 4. S.G.=
3·14—3·19. Colour blue, yellow, green, and various. Sometimes colourless and limpid. Lustre vitreous. Transparent,

translucent, opaque. Cp.=CaF. Bp. decrepitates violently, shows phosphorescence, and in thin laminæ fuses to a clouded mass, tinging the flame red. In a stronger flame the fused product becomes infusible, and acts like lime. Is completely decomposed by concentrated sulphuric acid, giving forth hydrofluoric acid.

Fluor-spar forms independent rocks of subordinate extent. It occurs most frequently in metalliferous veins, from which it has occasionally spread into the mother rock. In dolomite it sometimes occurs as an accessory (St. Gotthard), and in geodic cavities of the variegated sandstone at Waldshut. It is also met with as a recent deposit from springs of water (Plombières). The last mentioned case proves that fluor-spar may be produced by purely wet chemical process.

110. *Cryolite.*—Trimetric (?). Hitherto only known in amorphous single masses or thick crusts of coarse granular texture. Cleavage basal, tolerably perfect. Brittle. H.= 2·5. S.G.=2·9—3·0. Colourless, greyish-white, or reddish. Lustre vitreous, on the basal cleavage face mother-of-pearl. Translucent. Cp.=NaF+$\frac{1}{3}$Al²F³. Bp. very readily fuses to a white enamel, tinging the flame reddish-yellow. In glass tube gives the reaction of fluor; on charcoal also it fuses easily, but is decomposed, and leaves a deposit of alumina. In concentrated sulphuric acid it is perfectly soluble, giving forth hydrofluoric acid.

Cryolite occurs in a separate bed or layer in the gneiss of Arksutfiord in West Greenland.

III. Sulphurets. Arseniurets.

111. *Galena* (*Blue Lead-ore*).—Monometric. Very usual in cubes, more rarely in rhombic dodecahedrons, octahedrons, and other forms. Crystals usually attached, clustered in geodes, also botryoidal and reniform. Chiefly massive in coarse

and fine grained or compact aggregates. Cleavage cubic, very perfect. Sectile. H.=2·5—2·75. S.G.=7·25—7·7. Colour lead-grey, sometimes with tinge of reddish colour, sometimes iridescent on the surface. Streak greyish-black. Lustre metallic. Opaque. Cp.=PbS, with frequently a small quantity of silver, or also of Fe, Se, Sb. Bp in glass tube, evolves sulphur and a sublimate of $\dot{P}b\ddot{S}$. On charcoal decrepitates, fuses after the sublimation of the sulphur, and finally yields a lead globule and lead fumes. Soluble in nitric acid, with development of nitrous acid and precipitate of sulphur.

Galena is met with as an accessory in many rocks, e.g. sandstones (in the form of disseminated grains—Commern in the Eifel) ; in the argillaceous sphærosiderite of the Coal formation, and elsewhere. Very frequently in veins of ore (in the gneiss of Freiberg, in the Devonian strata of the Harz, in mountain limestone of Derbyshire and Cumberland, in granite of Linares) ; also in nests and irregular masses imbedded, which are usually met with in limestone or dolomite (Tarnowitz in Silesia, Bleiberg in Carinthia, Alpujarras in Spain).

Although galena may very frequently be of hydrogenic origin, it is not less certainly in many cases a product of sublimation ; artificially it is formed in the cracks of furnaces.

Galena has given rise to many secondary products, such as cerusite ($\dot{P}b\ddot{C}$) ; pyromorphite ($3\dot{P}b^3\ddot{\ddot{P}}+PbCl$) ; and mimetisite ($3\dot{P}b^3\ddot{\ddot{A}}s+PbCl$).

112. *Blende* (*Zincblende, Sphalerite*). — Monoclinic, tetrahedral. The crystals frequently irregularly twisted, sometimes twin growth ; often massive, in granular, rarely in fibrous or radiated aggregates. Cleavage very perfect according to the rhombic dodecahedron. Very brittle. H.= 3·5—4. S.G.=3·9—4·2. Colour, most frequently brown or

black, more rarely yellow-red, white or colourless.   Lustre
adamantine to resinous.   Semi-transparent to opaque.   Cp.=
ZnS, sometimes combined with considerable quantities of FeS
(up to 23 per cent) and a little cadmium.   Bp. decrepitates
violently, but is only fusible at the sharp edges.   On charcoal
in the oxidation flame gives zinc fumes.   Soluble in concentrated nitric acid, with precipitate of sulphur.

Its place and mode of occurrence in nature are similar to
those of galena, which is almost always associated with it.   It
has been likewise found in the cells of ammonites of the
brown Jura and Lias formations, a fact which proves its partial
formation by wet processes.

113. *Cinnabar.*—Rhombohedral.   Crystals in rhombohedrons
or thick tabular, small and in geodes.   Usually massive, in
granular, compact or earthy aggregates, dispersed or incrusting.   Cleavage prismatic.   Fracture uneven and splintery.
Sectile.   H.=2·25.   S.G.=8·99.   Colour cochineal-red and
scarlet ; streak scarlet.   Lustre adamantine.   Translucent ;
opaque.   Cp.=HgS.   Bp. in matrass burns black ; in open
tubes sulphur burns with a blue flame, and sublimes, yielding
fumes of sulphurous acid with black sublimate and a mirror
of metallic mercury.   Soluble in nitro-muriatic acid (aqua
regia).

Cinnabar forms independent beds, appears as impregnation
of bituminous shale, or in veins (Idria), also forms incrustation
on clefts of many kinds of rock (granite, clay-slate).

114. *Magnetic Pyrites.* — Hexagonal ;, rarely crystallised,
usually massive and disseminated, in lamellar, granular or
compact aggregates.   Cleavage basal, perfect ; prismatic imperfect.   Fracture conchoidal.   H.=3·5—4·5.   S.G.=4·4—
4·7.   Colour between bronze-yellow and copper-red ; streak
grey-black.   Magnetic.   Lustre metallic.   Opaque.   Cp.=
Fe^7S^8, sometimes contains Ni.   Bp. unchangeable in matrass ;

in glass tube gives out S̈, but no sublimate; on charcoal fuses
in reduction flame to a greyish black and highly magnetic
bead. Soluble in muriatic acid, sulphuretted hydrogen being
developed, and sulphur precipitated.

Magnetic pyrites occurs with metallic ores, also as an accessory ingredient in many igneous rocks, especially diorite, in
Vesuvian lavas and in meteorites.

115. *Pyrites (Iron Pyrites).*—Monometric, in various hemihedral combinations. Crystals singly imbedded, or combined
in geodes and various groups; also in globular and reniform
or fibrous aggregates, or massive. Cleavage cubic, imperfect.
Fracture conchoidal to uneven. Brittle. H.=6—6·5. S.G.=
4·8—5. Bronze-yellow to gold-yellow. Streak brownish-
black. Lustre metallic. Opaque. Cp.=FeS^2, with occasionally small quantities of Au or Ag. Bp. in matrass gives out
sulphur and sulphurous acid, and afterwards acts like magnetic
pyrites. Scarcely affected by muriatic acid. Soluble in nitric
acid, leaving a precipitate of sulphur.

Pyrites is found in independent beds. It is also an essential
constituent of the species of granite called beresite. It is a
very frequent accessory ingredient in many rocks; very frequent in the crystalline schists, in diorite, limestone, in clay
rocks, in coal. It is no less frequent in metalliferous veins.

Pyrites is sometimes formed by the action of a solution of
copperas on organic substances, and this will account for its
often being found in the form of fossils. Wöhler has produced
artificial pyrites by slowly heating oxide of iron, together with
sulphur and sal-ammoniac.

116. *Marcasite (White Iron Pyrites, Hydrous Pyrites).*—
Trimetric. Crystals tabular or columnar, usually clustered
into groups termed radiated pyrites, spear pyrites, hepatic
pyrites, cockscomb pyrites, cellular pyrites, according to varying texture. Cleavage prismatic, indistinct. Fracture uneven.

Brittle. H.=6—6·5. S.G.=4·6—4·8. Colour greyish bronze-yellow, inclined to green; tarnishes very readily. Streak dark greenish-grey. Lustre metallic. Opaque. Cp. like pyrites, but more prone to decompose and turn to vitriol. Bp. like pyrites.

Marcasite is found in separate beds, and as an accessory mineral (Browncoal formation of the Carlsbad region, dolomites of Tharandt in Saxony, and Cornwall).

117. *Leucopyrite.*—Trimetric, usually massive and disseminated, granular, or fibrous. Cleavage basal. Fracture uneven. Brittle. H.=5—5·5. S.G.=7—7·4. Colour silver-white, merging into steel-grey. Streak black. Lustre metallic. Opaque. Cp.=$FeAs^2$, almost always with some sulphur, owing to admixture of mispickel. Bp. in matrass yields sublimate of metallic arsenic; on charcoal strong smell of arsenic, and a black magnetic residuum. Soluble in nitric acid, with a separation of arsenious acid.

Leucopyrite is an accessory in many rocks, especially in serpentine (Reichenstein in Silesia), and in metalliferous veins.

118. *Mispickel (Arsenopyrite).*—Trimetric. Crystals usually short prisms, or tabular, singly imbedded, or attached in groups; also massive, in granular or fibrous aggregates. Cleavage prismatic, rather distinct. Fracture uneven. Brittle. H.=5·5—5·6. S.G.=6—6·4. Colour silver-white, inclining to steel-grey. Streak black. Lustre metallic. Opaque. Cp.= $FeS^2 + FeAs$. Several varieties contain Ag (Weisserz), Au, or Co (Kobalt-arsenkies). In matrass gives first a red, afterwards a brown sublimate of sulphuret of arsenic, finally a sublimate of metallic arsenic. On charcoal the arsenic is dissipated, and leaves a black magnetic bead, which acts like magnetic pyrites, and sometimes gives cobalt reaction. Soluble in nitric acid, with separation of arsenious acid and sulphur.

Mispickel is frequently met with in veins of ore, is also an accessory ingredient in many rocks, e.g. the crystalline schists (Kongsberg in Norway, Freiberg, Franconia in New Hampshire), and serpentine in various localities.

119. *Chalcopyrite (Copper Pyrites)*.—Dimetric. Tetrahedral. Crystals usually small, frequently of regular twin growth, often massive. Cleavage pyramidal, sometimes distinct. Fracture conchoidal to uneven. Unlike pyrites, is very little brittle. H.= 3·5—4. S.G.=4·1—4·3. Colour brass-yellow, sometimes with tarnish of gold colour and iridescence. Streak black. Lustre metallic. Opaque. Cp.= $Cu^2S + Fe^2S^3$. Bp. becomes black on cooling, red, and fuses at a strong heat to a magnetic bead of steel-grey colour; with borax and soda gives a copper bead; when moistened with muriatic acid tinges the flame a beautiful blue. Soluble in nitro-muriatic acid (aqua regia) with separation of sulphur.

Chalcopyrite is a very frequent associate of pyrites. Is accessory in many rocks, e.g. tourmaline-granite, Predazzo, Tyrol.

IV. Native Elements.

120. *Sulphur.* — Trimetric. Crystals usually pyramidal, singly attached, or clustered in geodes; also globular, reniform, stalactitic; with fibrous or compact structure. Cleavage basal and prismatic, imperfect. Fracture conchoidal to uneven, and splintery. Not very brittle. H.=1·5—2·5. S.G.=2. Colour sulphur-yellow to straw-colour, or yellowish-grey. Lustre resinous; on crystal surfaces adamantine. Transparent, translucent. Cp.=S, frequently mixed with clay or bitumen. Bp. sublimates in matrass; inflammable, and burns with blue flame to sulphurous acid gas.

Sulphur occurs as an accessory in rocks, and also as a separate formation in beds. It is formed by sublimation in the clefts of volcanoes, also in the neighbourhood of burning coal seams. Sometimes it is the product of the decomposition of metallic sulphurets, or of the sulphuretted hydrogen of some spring waters, which are decomposed by contact with the atmosphere, and form deposits of sulphur.

Artificial crystals of sulphur may be produced in great perfection by dissolving sulphur in sulphuret of carbon, and setting it to crystallise at ordinary temperature. Monoclinic crystals of sulphur, which have not as yet been observed in nature, are obtained on the cooling of melted sulphur.

121. *Graphite (Plumbago)*.—Hexagonal, rhombohedral, usually in six-sided, thin tabular or short prismatic crystals ; also massive, in radiated, lamellar, or compact aggregates. Cleavage basal, very perfect, prismatic imperfect. Very sectile, flexible in thin laminæ. Feel greasy. H.=1—2. S.G.= 2·09. Colour iron-black to grey. Streak black, with metallic lustre, soils paper, used for pencils to draw and write with. Opaque. Cp.=C, with some iron, and often containing impurities of $\ddot{S}i, \dot{C}a$, and $\ddot{A}l$. Bp. burns with difficulty. If heated with saltpetre, puffs up slightly.

Graphite is sometimes found in separate beds, and is then probably the final product of the transmutation of vegetable remains. It is, however, also found as an accessory ingredient in igneous rocks (in trap at Borrowdale, Cumberland, in porphyrite at Elbingerode in the Harz, in granite boulders, Greenland) ; in limestones (Lower Styria, Fichtelgebirge), or in metalliferous veins (Arendal) ; finally as an essential constituent of graphite-granite, graphite-gneiss, graphite-mica-schist. The igneous origin of some graphite may be inferred from its presence in furnace slags, where it sometimes occurs in the form of thin laminæ.

v. Resins. Organic Compounds.

122. *Amber (Yellow Mineral Resin).*—It is exclusively found
in rounded masses of the shape of drops or fluid substance,
and frequently insects and fragments of plants are enclosed in
it. Fracture perfectly conchoidal. Little brittle. H.=2—2·5.
S.G.=1·1.   Colour yellow or brown in various shades, frequently with flame-shaped pencillings. Lustre resinous. Transparent, translucent. When rubbed, becomes negatively electric.
Cp.=$C^{10}H^4O$.   Bp. fusible, burns with a clear flame, and
agreeable smell.

Amber is a fossil gum-resin, the product of coniferæ or ter-
tiary lignites.   It is found as an accessory in strata of the
Upper Chalk formation (Lemberg), the planercoal (Skutsch in
Bohemia), in pebbles in the diluvium and alluvium of North
Germany, on the coast of the Baltic, and of Yorkshire and
Essex.

123. *Bitumen (Asphalte, Naphtha, Petroleum, Mineral Pitch,
Mineral Oil).*

Under the term bitumen are included a whole series of olea-
ginous and pitch-like substances, of which the most important
are naphtha and asphalte.

(a) *Naphtha,* a volatile, and, when pure, colourless, oil with
    bituminous smell. S.G.=0·7—0·84. Cp.=C^6H^5, fre-
    quently mixed with paraffine, asphalte and the like.

(b) *Asphalte,* a hardened mineral pitch without oil; massive
    with perfect conchoidal fracture. Colour pitch-black.
    Lustre resinous. Opaque. When rubbed gives a
    strong bituminous smell. Cp.=C, O, and H in un-
    certain proportions. Easily ignited, burning with a
    bright flame and thick smoke.

Naphtha flows from the ground in considerable quantities

(Persia, Pennsylvania, Amiano in Parma, Canada, California, &c.).

Asphalte is found in many localities (e.g. at the Dead Sea; Trinidad, where there is a complete pitch-lake; at Poldice in Cornwall it occurs in granite).

An intermediate substance between naphtha and asphalte is elastic mineral pitch or *elaterite* (Castleton in Derbyshire).

All these bituminous substances are of vegetable or animal origin, partly products of distillation of organic remains. They frequently occur as admixtures in shales and other rocks, which have received the name of bituminous (Autun in France, Bonn, Markersdorf in Bohemia, &c.)

124. *Mellite* (*Mellilite, Honey Stone*).—Dimetric, usually in pyramidal crystals, singly imbedded. Cleavage pyramidal, very imperfect. Fracture usually conchoidal. Somewhat brittle. H.=2—2·5. S.G.=1·5—1·6. Colour honey-yellow to wax-yellow, seldom white. Lustre resinous. Semi-transparent to translucent. Cp.=$\ddot{\text{Al}}(C^4O^3)+18\dot{\text{H}}$. Bp. it carbonises with smell of burning; on charcoal burns to a white ash, which acts like pure alumina. It is readily and completely soluble in nitric acid.

Mellite occurs as an accessory ingredient in Browncoal (Artern in Thuringia, Luschitz in Bohemia).

CHAPTER II.

ANALYSIS OF ROCKS.

MICROSCOPIC ANALYSIS.

IT not unfrequently happens that the various mineral ingredients of a composite rock are so small and intimately blended together as to be entirely undistinguishable even to the practised eye unaided by magnifying power. A simple lens will often render great service in this respect, but the aid of magnifying power may be carried much further with the microscope. For the microscope very thin plates of a rock, so thin as to be somewhat transparent, are cemented on glass, and by the aid of a powerful instrument, textures apparently quite compact are frequently resolved into a web of minute crystals, or we find individual crystals become prominent (porphyritic) in an actually compact matrix. The form of these minute crystals is sometimes to be recognised, and so serves as a guide to the determination of the mineral in doubtful cases. If we further call in the assistance of polarised light, we are enabled to pronounce, with greater certainty, on the amorphous or crystalline character of the compact mass, and on the character of the crystals which by these means are brought to view.

Delicate investigations such as these no doubt require the assistance of complicated apparatus and demand time, so that they are quite out of the question for the geologist on his travels; but as we have said, much may be discovered by a simple lens, which for the practical geological purposes of the general inquirer is in most cases sufficient.

MAGNETIC ANALYSIS.

An admixture of magnetic iron-ore makes many rocks magnetic in their entirety, so as to affect the magnetic needle, or if the iron-ore be present in small quantities only, it may be discovered by abrasure with a sharp-edged magnet, the magnetic particles of the powder so formed clinging to the magnet like a beard. As, however, magnetic iron-ore occurs in many very different rocks, its discovery does not often afford much help to the geologist in determining the character of any given rock.

Fostemann and Delesse have made careful investigations of the magnetism of many different rocks. The former is of opinion that by means of careful magnetic experiments, we ought to be able to ascertain whether a rock be of volcanic or neptunian origin, whether it has been rendered metamorphic by heat, whether it has retained its original position or been subsequently displaced (vide Poggendorff's Annalen, 1859, vol. cvi. p. 106). Delesse had previously discovered that almost all igneous rocks were somewhat magnetic as well as many sedimentary and metamorphic rocks. (Annales des Mines, 1849, vol. xv. p. 1, and Bulletin de la Soc. Géol. de France, 1850, vol. viii. p. 108.)

CHEMICAL ANALYSIS.

The geological interest attaching to the chemical analysis of rocks is chiefly in respect of the nature of their origin.

In the early stages of the science the analysis of composite rocks was conducted by mechanically separating, as far as possible, their several mineral ingredients, and analysing each mineral species individually; and this method is still sometimes adopted where the parts are very distinct and easily to be separated. Compact rocks, such as basalt, were mostly considered as simple mineral substances, and so analysed. When, however, it came to be recognised that many apparently homogeneous rocks were but mechanical compounds of several minerals, chemical analysis was directed to the discovery of these mineral constituents too intimately mixed to be distinguished by the eye.

Gmelin introduced the method of treating a powdered mass of rock with muriatic or other acid, and so sepa-

rating it into a part soluble, and another part insoluble in
such acid.   These two parts he separately analysed, and
reduced the results into chemical formulæ.   The object
he had in view was chiefly to discover the mineral constituents of the rock.   But this mode of analysis is in-
adequate for the purpose, since few minerals are wholly
soluble, or wholly insoluble, in acids, and therefore, instead of the several minerals being separated from each
other, a part of each is dissolved and a part of each left,
and no definite result as to the original structure can be
attained.   It is found that even the elementary constituents cannot be successfully so divided; but that some
elementary substances are only partly dissolved and partly
precipitated by the process.   Nevertheless, as a rough
approximate, and somewhat empirical mode of suggesting
rather than proving the constituents of a rock, it is still
sometimes employed, and may in certain cases be of use.

As the chemical character of minerals came to be better
known, less reliance was placed on chemical analysis as
a means of ascertaining and distinguishing the mineral
ingredients of rocks.   A small number of elements are so
universal in their character that they enter into the composition of a very large proportion of the whole series of
mineral bodies, a very slight variation in their proportionate quantities or combination serving to produce entirely different minerals, or even the very same elements
in the same relative quantities wearing a totally different
mineral aspect according to slight differences in the conditions of their original formation.   Therefore it is that
chemical analyses have always hitherto failed, and it
would appear that they must always fail, to detect many
important mineral differences.

For instance, a rock containing 72 silica, 11 alumina,
2·8 oxide or protoxide of iron, 1 lime, 1·2 magnesia, 1·2
potash, 2 soda, and 0·4 water, may either be a granite, or
a gneiss, protogine, granulite, quartz-porphyry, felsite,
petrosilex, pitch-stone, trachyte-porphyry, obsidian, or
pearlstone; and if we take a wider margin for the proportion of silica, say from 62 to 72, increasing some of the
other ingredients in proportion, then a rock, such as we
have described, may be a trachyte, phonolite, or minette,
for in all the rocks we have named similar values of their

elementary constituents occur. Again, a rock, containing 49—50 silica, 12 alumina, 5—10 oxide or protoxide of iron, 5 lime, 2—3 magnesia, 1 potash, 2 soda, and 0—1 water might just as well be a dolerite as a basalt, or a nepheline rock, leucite rock, diabase, diorite, gabbro, hypersthenite, melaphyre, or porphyrite, for in like manner those values occur in all these rocks.

On the other hand rocks, the same in mineral composition, may vary in the values of their chemical or elementary ingredients 10, 20, or even 40 per cent.

The mineral character of rocks is therefore now sought to be determined in doubtful cases by microscopic rather than chemical analysis, or by tracing the different stages of a rock's transition from a compact into a distinctly composite state; for many rocks (as we shall later have occasion to show) are found to pass by gradual stages from an apparently homogeneous mass into states where their mineral ingredients become distinctly and separately developed so as to be readily recognised.

Whilst chemical analysis was thus found insufficient for determining the mineral character of a rock, it derived a new importance from the igneous theory of the constitution of the primary rocks, when these came to be considered as the products of the consolidation of a general molten mass once the sole material of the earth's structure. The different minerals then came to be regarded as of subordinate importance in inquiring into the origin of rocks, and their differing forms of crystallisation or structure to be regarded but as accidental consequences of slightly different circumstances attending the consolidation of the formerly fused mass.

In this view even the sum of a separate analysis (if it were possible) of all the minerals constituting a rock would fail to present a complete picture of its aggregate chemical character, unless the exact proportionate quantity of each mineral could be also ascertained, which is practically impossible, although it has been sometimes roughly attempted.

These considerations led to the present mode of analysis, which is now usually adopted in the case of all rocks indiscriminately, whether compact or granular, homogeneous or distinctly composite. This is what is termed

in German the ' Bausch analyse' (or collective average
analysis). It consists in pulverising a number of representative specimens carefully selected from various parts
of the rock, and in mixing the powder thus obtained so
thoroughly as to make the portion taken for the analysis
a fair average sample of the whole rock.

The results of these analyses are sometimes combined
into chemical formulæ such as those by which minerals
are described. For instance :—

$$3(\ddot{R})\overset{...}{Si} + 2\overset{...}{R}\overset{...}{Si},$$
$$\text{or } (\dot{R})^2\overset{...}{Si}^3 + \overset{...}{R}^2\overset{...}{Si}^9.$$

In such formulæ we need hardly say there is always
more or less of speculation or theory involved.

The idea is to arrive at a view of the chemical constitution of the original molten mass, and chiefly in the first
instance of the preponderance of the silica or other acid
in the compound. In other words, the object is to ascertain if the original compound forming the rock, when in
its previous molten state, were acidic or basic in its
chemical character. It has been sought to express the
same idea more simply by giving the proportion of the
oxygen contained in the acids to that contained in the
bases of the compound. Thus if, in a compound say of
silica, alumina, peroxide of iron, potash and soda, the
silica contain 3 parts of oxygen to 1 of silicon, and
the alumina and peroxide of iron $1\frac{1}{2}$ oxygen to 1 of
aluminum and iron respectively, the potash and soda 1 of
oxygen to 1 of potassium and sodium respectively, the
oxygen quotient in a neutral compound would be

$$3 : 1\frac{1}{2} : 1$$

(a proportion which has been actually found to obtain in
some rocks), and any variation of this proportion on either
side would cause the compound to assume an acidic or a
basic character ; thus,

$$5 : 1\frac{1}{2} : 1$$

would constitute an acidic compound, and

$$3 : 3 : 2$$

would constitute a basic compound.

Bunsen endeavoured to set up two typical rocks, to be

termed the *trachytic* and the *pyroxenic*, the former containing much silica (acidic), the latter a preponderance of bases (basic).

He endeavoured to bring all the igneous rocks under one or other of these two heads, but soon found many rocks of intermediate character. These he regarded as mixtures of the two, or rather as the result of a combination of the two kinds of original material which he believed to have existed at their formation.

He suggested the idea of the existence of two great furnaces in the interior of the globe, containing these two different mixtures in a molten state; an idea which has, however, not met with much general favour or acceptance.

Others have suggested, with more plausibility, that at the time when the whole earth was fluid, its component parts would be in some degree separated according to their specific gravity, and the silica being the lightest of the very abundant ingredients of the mass, would prevail in greatest quantity at and near the surface, so that the rocks which were first consolidated and the earlier volcanic rocks would be acidic, the next formed igneous rocks would be more basic, containing chiefly the lighter bases, such as alumina, potash, soda or lime; whilst the latest or most recent igneous rocks would contain the least silica, and principally the heavier bases, e.g. iron. It has also been suggested that the older igneous rocks, as having been formed nearer to the surface of the globe, would probably contain more water than those of later origin.

These, then, are the chief problems which have been suggested for solution by chemical means. The most simple and useful of the chemical differences is that of the varying proportion of silica. This quantity when ascertained forms a clue to the proportion of the other ingredients and general chemical character of the rock. Scheerer has lately proposed that all the igneous rocks should be divided into nine or ten classes, according to their quantity of silica, without regard to their mineral character.

He has pointed out an easy mode of ascertaining the proportion by fusing the portion of the powdered rock selected for analysis with a certain proportion of carbonate of potash or soda (about five times its weight). So much of the silica as is more than the proportion required for a neutral compound will combine with the potash or soda of the carbonate salt, and drive off a proportionate quantity of carbonic acid so that from the quantity of carbonic acid so driven off, the quantity of silica contained in the original rock may be calculated.

Without pronouncing on the correctness of any of the foregoing speculations*, we may however confidently say that for the purpose of lithological classification, an exclusively chemical grouping of rocks would be utterly impracticable. How should the geologist pursuing his labours in the field, or on the mountain, wait for the tedious and uncertain process of a chemical analysis before naming the rocks which come under his ken? We must, therefore, still adhere in the main to a mineralogical designation and nomenclature, and all the more, as in general we find the mineral characteristics of rocks very much coincide with geological phenomena.

We need not, however, on this account disregard the results of chemical analysis, which are doubtless of the highest geological interest, and must prove of still greater value when they shall have been more fully and extensively carried out.

We propose, moreover, to use these chemical properties for the purposes of our classification to the extent proposed by Bunsen of dividing the igneous rocks into two great classes, the *acidic* and the *basic*, merely warning our readers that there is, so far as our present knowledge extends, no rigid boundary between the two, and that the state of our analytical knowledge in general is still very imperfect.

With these remarks we present the reader with the following extract from the analyses of Roth, as given in his masterly work on this subject ('Gesteinsanalysen'). For the sake of brevity, the decimal figures have in some instances been omitted or shortened to one figure.

* See post, pp. 367 *et seq.*

TABLE.

ACIDIC ROCKS (partly Igneous, partly Metamorphic)

	Granite	Gneiss Red or Grey	Protogine	Granulite	Felsitic		Quartz-Porphyry		Pitch-stone
					Hälle-flinta	Petro-silex	Rich in Quartz	Poor in Quartz	
Silica	62·0—81	64·0—76	70·0—75	72·0—73	74·0—81	71·0—78	70—81	59·0—66	63·0—75
Alumina	10·0—17	3·0—12	11·0—14	8·0—16	9·0—13	11·0—15	8—16	11·0—18	9·0—12
Iron {Fe̤	7	7	2	1	2	1	5	2	6
Fe	5	8	2	6	...	3	4	14	3
Lime	1·0—2	0·2—4	1·0—2	1·0—2	0·4—2	1	0·2—2	0·1—2	0·7—1
Magnesia	0·1—2	0·1—2	1	0·6—4	0·1—1	0·7—2	0·1—7	1·0—2	0·1—1
Potash	0·4—5	1—5	2	1—7	0·3—5	1·0—2	1·0—7	13	0·5—4
Soda	1·0—5	0·4—3	3	2·0—7	0·1—5	3·0—4	5	2	1·0—7
Water	0·4—2	0·4—1	0·4—1	0·4	0·2—1	1·0—2	0·5—1	1·0—2	4·0—8

ACIDIC ROCKS (all Igneous)

	Trachyte		Trachytic		Pearlstone	Phonolite	Syenite, chiefly Syenitic Granite	Minette
	with Sani-dine	with Sani-dine and Oligoclase	Porphyry	Obsidian				
Silica	59·0—66	60·0—67	67·0—81	70·0—82	70·0—77	50·0—62	50·0—70	56—82
Alumina	12·0—21	15·0—21	10·0—13	6·0—12	12·0—15	15·0—24	13·0—20	12—16
Iron {Fe̤	4	6	4	6·0	1	5	5	2—7
Fe	12	8	2	10·0	2	9	14	...
Lime	1·0—3	0·4—3	0·2—4	1·0—4·0	1·0—3	0·1—14	0·5—10	1—4
Magnesia	0·1—2	0·1—1	0·1—3	0·7—1·0	0·7—1	-0·1—3	0·2—3	2—6
Potash	3·0—8	2—4	1—8	3·0—11·0	1·0—5	0·1—9	1·0—5	4
Soda	2·0—9	4—6	1—5		1·0—6	2·0—9	1·0—6	2
Water	1·0—2	0·6—1	0·2—13	0·2	1·0—3	0·6—8	1·0—1	1—1

TABLE.

BASIC ROCKS (all Igneous)

	Dolerite	Basalt	Nepheline Rock	Leucite Rock	Diabase	Diorite	Gabbro	Hyper-sthenite	Melaphyre	Porphyrite
Silica	41·0—57	36·0—55	41·0—52	44·0—54	42·0—56	46·0—63	43·0—49	45·0—51	54·0—62	59—64
Alumina	6·0—26	7·0—25	11·0—19	13·0—23	13·0—20	12·0—18	8·0—17	14·0—16	10·0—23	15—16
Iron $\ddot{Fe}$	17	28	13	17	12	2	17	16	14	8
Iron $\dot{Fe}$	16	21	13	11	15	16	15	15	12	7— 8
Lime	3·0—14	4·0—16	3·0—13	4·0—12	4·0— 8	5·0— 9	8·0—11	5·0—14	1·0—10	1— 6
Magnesia	0·5— 9	1·0—16	1·0— 8	1·0— 6	1·0— 6	3·0— 9	6·0—11	2·0—10	0·1— 6	1— 2
Potash	0·2— 3	0·4— 4	0·5— 3	0·2— 8	1·0— 2	2·0— 3	0·2— 1	0·2— 1	1·0— 3	1— 4
Soda	1·0— 5	0·1—10	2·0— 6	1·0— 8	1·0— 5	2·0— 7	1·0— 3	1·0— 5	6	2— 3
Water	0·4— 6	0·5— 4	0·7— 6	0·1— 2	1·0— 5	0·4— 1	0·5— 5	0·7— 2	1·0— 2	1— 3

METAMORPHIC AND SEDIMENTARY ROCKS

	Grey Gneiss	Mica-Schist	Chlorite-Schist	Talc-Schist	Hornblende-Schist	Argillaceous Mica-Schist	Sericite-Schist	Clay-Slate	Alum-Slate	Greywacké Sandstone
Silica	64—68	40·0—82	31—42·0	27—58	48·0—54	45·0—79	59·0—72	40·0—75	48·0—65·0	75·0—84·0
Alumina	12—14	9·0—35	3— 5·0	4—18	13·0—20	8·0—24	13·0—15	10·0—36	15·0—26·0	5·0— 5·0
Iron $\ddot{Fe}$	3	5	10·0	28	27	15	1	18	5·0	
Iron $\dot{Fe}$	6	6	26·0	4	14	10	5	12	6·0	6·0
Lime	2— 4	0·3— 2	1·0	1	0·5—11	0·1—11	0·4— 2	0·1—13	0·1— 3·0	0·1
Magnesia	1— 2	0·3— 1	17—41·0	22—23	1·0— 4	0·1—13	0·6— 4	0·2—11	1·0— 2·0	0·2— 1·0
Potash	2— 5	1·0— 4	0·1	...	0·5— 1	0·2— 6	2·0— 5	0·5— 7	0·1— 7·0	0·4— 1·0
Soda	1— 2	0·3— 8	0·1	...	1·0— 2	0·1— 4	1·0— 6	0·2— 2	0·2— 0·4	0·2— 0·3
Water	1— 1	0·5— 2	9—11·0	2— 6	0·2— 1	0·7— 4	2·0— 3	1·0— 7	2·0— 6·0	0·3— 2·0

CHAPTER III.

PHYSICAL STRUCTURE OF ROCKS.

TEXTURE.

By the term texture, as applied to rocks, we mean chiefly their physical structure, having regard to the size, shape, and mode of adhesion of their individual mineral particles. All rocks may be divided into two principal classes, in respect of the size of their component parts. Either the separate mineral particles of which they are composed are large enough to be recognised as such by the naked eye, or they are so small as not to be distinguishable in the general mass. In the former case rocks are termed *granular*, in the latter *compact*. The word granular is, however, usually only applied when the different mineral parts are all of a granular shape of nearly the same size, and are crystallised into each other. If on the other hand a rock consists only of grains, pebbles, or fragments mechanically cemented together, it is termed according to its character either a *sandstone* (arenaceous), a *conglomerate*, or a *breccia*, which terms we shall explain more at large hereafter.

The term *compact* is usually only applied to a rock when its particles adhere firmly and closely together (without being fused into one mass like glass). If the particles only lie loosely together so that the mass is friable, then that condition is called *earthy*; if they are intimately blended and fused into a homogeneous mass, then the state is termed *vitreous* or *opalescent*. The vitreous and opalescent conditions are indeed essentially different from the ordinary compact and earthy conditions, inasmuch as in the former no individual particles are found, whilst the latter at best are but very fine-grained. In extreme cases, however, this difference is only to be discovered with certainty by means of polarised light.

Using the terms granular and compact in their wider sense, so as to include, on the one hand, the sandstones, conglomerates, and breccias; and on the other the vitreous and opalescent rocks; we may say that every rock must necessarily either be granular or compact—that is to say, we either can, or cannot recognise their individual component parts. A rock, for instance, which is granular cannot at the same time, in the same part, be compact, and *vice versa*. These conditions are inconsistent with each other; although transitions occur from one state to the other, and although the same mineral combination may at one place be granular and at another compact.

In the case of composite crystalline rocks formed by the cooling of matter previously in a state of igneous fusion, the coarse-grained, fine-grained, compact, or vitreous state is probably the result only of a more or less speedy process of cooling. The slower the cooling process, the more time would be allowed for the mineral parts to form themselves into separate crystals, and the more coarsely granular would the rock become; the more speedy the process, the more compact the rock would be, or if the process were very rapid, then the rock might even become vitreous.

The latter condition is almost exclusively confined to those igneous rocks, which contain a large proportion of silica; in such as contain but little silica, the compact and the vesicular state seem to be substitutes for the vitreous. If individual mineral particles occur in the form of distinct crystals (porphyritically) in an otherwise compact mass; then we may regard this as a sort of intermediate state between the granular and compact—some of the mineral constituents, more prone to crystallisation than the rest, having developed themselves into crystals earlier and more vigorously than those. The very same differences of texture and condition may be frequently observed in the products of artificial melting at furnaces.

In the case of compact rocks it is often very difficult to determine whether the undistinguishable particles have grown together in process of crystallisation, or are only mechanically bound together; whether they consist only of one mineral substance or a combination of several.

We now proceed to consider the special kinds of texture, structure, or state.

The texture of a rock is termed PORPHYRITIC when distinct crystals or crystalline particles are distributed through an otherwise compact principal mass or matrix. The texture of the matrix or principal mass need not, however, always be compact; it may be crystalline-granular, or may exhibit many varieties of texture. Accordingly the porphyritic texture may be subdivided into—

(a) *Porphyritic with compact matrix.*—Rocks exhibiting this texture are called *porphyries*, independently of the character of their mineral ingredients.

(b) *Porphyritic with granular matrix.*—Rocks exhibiting this texture are not called *porphyries*, but only *porphyritic*; such for instance as many porphyritic granites, with large crystals of felspar in the granular matrix.

(c) *Porphyritic with shaly or schistose matrix.*—Mica-schist for instance, if it contains garnets, thereby becomes *porphyritic*.

The crystals thus porphyritically disseminated in a rock may either belong to its essential constituents or they may be accessories only.

SCHISTOSE (FOLIATED), SLATY (CLEAVED), SHALY (LAMINATED), FISSILE are terms expressive of different kinds of internal parallel texture of rocks. The German geologists have the one term ' *Schiefrig* ' for all these varieties of texture, the common element in all of which is their tendency to split in the direction of a given plane.

This tendency may, however, be the result of very different causes, viz : —

(a) By the parallel arrangement of certain minerals, such as mica, chlorite, talc, &c. eminently cleavable in one direction. Mica-schist is a rock of this character, and the texture is termed *schistose* or *foliated.*

(b) By some cause or causes, not to be discovered by mere

ocular observation, the invisibly small mineral constituents or particles of the rock are arranged so
as to produce a fissility or cleavage in the direction of a given plane, which very often cuts at a
considerable angle the plane or curved surfaces of
stratification. The rock itself has frequently a
compact appearance. The ordinary roofing slate
is an eminent instance of this texture, which is
termed *slaty texture* or *cleavage.*

(*c*) By very thin parallel superposition or lamination of
the fine particles of the rock. Thus a fissile texture is developed in mud deposits, whether of marl,
clay, or sand. This is in truth nothing but a kind
of stratification on a small scale. The thin layers
of the rock are not in themselves of a fissile texture. Ordinary flagstones are of this character.
Or a similar texture may be occasioned by the
parallel juxtaposition of thin plates or lenticular
particles of the ingredients of the rock, thus for instance the laminated texture of certain browncoals
may be traced to their construction from an accumulation of actual leáves of trees, and a similar
texture of certain amygdaloids is owing to the shape
and position of the amygdaloidal particles.

These and similar textures more or less originating in the act and mode of deposition, and all of
which have a tendency to split in the direction of
their bedding, are called *laminated* or *shaly,* the
rocks themselves *shales.*

(*d*) Occasionally two of the above descriptions of texture
occur together; *fissile* is a general term which
may be applied to all or any of the above-named
textures.*

---

* When we wish to be precise, we speak of the '*foliation of schist*,'
the '*cleavage of slate*,' and the '*lamination of shale.*'—*Jukes.*

See Jukes's Student's Manual of Geology (2nd edit.), pp. 265—277.

See also Phillips's Manual of Geology (1855), p. 43, and in Glossary,
under heads of *slate, schist, shale, laminated, flagstone, &c.*

See also Page's Advanced Text-Book, 3rd edit. pp. 74, 81; also in
Glossary under heads *slate, schist, fissile, laminated, flags, shale.*

See also Dana's Manual of Geology, pp. 71, 93, 95, 96, 100, 101,
218, 381, &c.

All the above-named authorities agree, with very trifling excep-

As respects the different causes of the above mentioned varieties of the fissile texture, we have seen that the thin stratification productive of the *laminated* texture is invariably the consequence of the original construction of the rock. But if rocks exhibit a *slaty* texture, which is not parallel to their bedding, this must have another origin than stratification.

According to the opinions of Sharpe, Haughton, Sorby, and Tyndall, slaty texture or cleavage, when not identical with stratification, has in most cases been caused by pressure in one direction (viz. at right angles to the cleavage plane), applied to the rock either during or subsequent to its formation—that is to say, during consolidation in the case of igneous rocks, during process of transmutation in the case of the crystalline schists, and after their deposition in the case of the sedimentary rocks, in which it therefore seldom coincides with the plane of stratification. (Vide Journ. Geol. Soc. of London, 1848–1849, and Phil. Mag., 1856.)

On the other hand, the conjecture of Poulet Scrope, that *lamination* and *cleavage* may have arisen from friction of some kind appears to us improbable. Nor can we subscribe to the view advocated by Sedgwick, in his otherwise masterly treatise on the structure of large mineral masses (Trans. Geol. Soc. 1835, vol. iii. p. 469), namely, that this texture is the result of a crystallising force, although his view has been partially adopted by Sharpe and Murchison. (Vide Siluria, edit. 1859, p. 34.)

Many rocks exhibit, variously developed, a marked texture, consisting of parallel fibrous lines or particles, with a parallel linear arrangement, called by Naumann, *Linear Parallelism.* This linear parallelism is of two kinds essentially differing from each other. It is either a delicate zig-zag pencilling of slaty or schistose rocks, or an elongation or extension of the particles or vesicular cavities in one direction.

The *linear foldings* or *pencilling* of frequent occurrence

tions, in the nomenclature as laid down by Jukes, and which is adopted in this translation throughout. It is *almost* identical with that first proposed by Sedgwick in 1835. See his ' Structure of Large Mineral Masses ' in Trans. of Geol. Soc. of London: 2nd series, vol. iii. p. 480.—TRANSLATOR.

in gneiss, mica-schist, and clay-slate have the appearance of having been occasioned by lateral pressure, although such an explanation of the phenomenon is open to great and various difficulties. Transitions are found from the most delicate pencilling to the coarsest foliation.

Linear elongation or *fibrous* texture consists of a kind of an apparent extension or elongation of individual parts, or of all the particles of a rock in one principal linear direction, by which a texture resembling the fibres of wood is sometimes occasioned; or else the vesicular cavities of a rock, either empty or filled (amygdaloids) are elongated in one prevailing direction. In the latter case, we may easily explain the origin of the texture by supposing the mass of the rock, during the period of its consolidation and whilst yet soft, to have been flowing in one direction. But it is much more difficult to ascribe a cause to the linear extension of the particles in other rocks, as, for instance, in some kinds of gneiss.

VESICULAR, SCORIACEOUS (or *Slaglike*), PUMICEOUS, are textures of rocks containing cellular cavities more or less rounded, and which are evidently the result of gas bubbles, developed whilst the rock was in a soft state either at the time of its original formation, or at a subsequent period. If these cavities are only few and isolated, then the rock is termed *vesicular*. If, however, they are so numerous as to occupy an equal space with the solid part of the rock, then the texture is *scoriaceous*, and if the hollow part predominates over the solid, then *pumiceous* (bimssteinartig). The shape of the cellular cavities is most usually irregular, but sometimes very regularly spherical, or pear-shaped, lenticular, and occasionally the cavities are uniformly elongated in a particular direction, as if stretched. All these differences of shape may be easily explained by the circumstances under which the vesicular mass attained its solid state, whether it was in a state of quiescence, or was subjected to pressure, or whether it was in motion, and whether such motion was flowing or irregular.

This vesicular condition is most frequently found in those igneous rocks which possess a compact, or at least a very fine-grained or porphyritic principal mass occasioned by rapid cooling. It never occurs in coarse-grained igneous rocks, probably because these being always subjected to a high pressure, crystallised very slowly. But even sedimentary and metamorphic rocks sometimes contain genuine vesicular cavities, in which case we must always infer the rock to have been in a soft state during the development of the gas which caused the bubbles.

Many rocks are *porous* without being vesicular, that is, they are penetrated with irregular and often even angular cavities, not the consequence of the development of gas, therefore not to be termed *vesicular*. The differences between porous and vesicular textures are sometimes very difficult to determine.

To a certain extent almost all rocks are porous, although not so to the naked eye, in the sense that they admit of the percolation of water, even if but slowly. Daubrée has made many experiments upon this kind of porosity, the result of which is communicated in the Bullet. de la Soc. Géol. de France, 1861, vol. xviii. p. 183, and Delesse has investigated the moist condition of rocks arising from this cause. (Ibid. vol. xix. p. 64.)

A rock is said to be AMYGDALOIDAL when the vesicular cavities are filled either wholly or in part with new mineral substance. The filling of these cavities is always a process subsequent to the formation of the rock. The material for this purpose appears, as a rule, to have been derived from the rock itself by a species of exfiltration, and usually consists of chalcedony or quartz, or different kinds of carbonic spars or zeolites, or sometimes of greenearth, varying according to the character of the rock itself. The arrangement of these mineral substances is often very interesting ; concentric or horizontal layers, stalactites, and stalagmites, are formed within the cavities, or we find a crystallised geode or a compact mass.

We infer from all the attendant circumstances that the formation of these amygdaloids must have been a very slow process, and therefore have occupied a considerable time in their completion. Hence, we may explain the fact that the most recent of all the igneous rocks, the lavas, although they are very often vesicular, are never amygdaloidal ; whereas the frequency and completeness of the filling up of the cavities increases almost in direct ratio with the age of the rock.

Such igneous rocks as are rich in silica are not only less frequently vesicular, but their cavities, when they occur, are less frequently amygdaloidal than those with little silica in their composition, which probably arises from their containing fewer soluble substances adapted to the formation of amygdaloids, in particular, less lime and magnesia.

There are some appearances which may be easily mistaken for the amygdaloidal texture, but which only arise from a concretion of separate mineral parts without previous cavities. We shall mention these below under the names of *spherulite, globuliferous, nodular,* and *variolitic.*

OOLITIC *texture* is only found in limestones and ironstones, and it consists either in the entire mass being composed of small globules, or a great number at all events of such being contained in the mass. The globules are very much of the size and shape of peas or grains of millet or lentils, and when broken exhibit a concentric or radiated structure. Sometimes many very small globules combine to form a larger ball. In the so-called *roestone* the globules are grey, and usually internally compact, or somewhat radial in the common *oolitic limestone* or *oolite.* They are more frequently white or yellowish, and sometimes formed of concentric layers, or they show an organic origin. In *pisolite* or *peastone* they sometimes contain a nucleus of foreign substance, covered with concentric layers or coatings of calc sinter, and these layers also show a fibrous radial structure, so that we may distinctly recognise the process of structure to have been a repeated coating of a grain of sand.

In oolitic ironstone the grains are partly spherical, partly lenticular. In bog-ore they exhibit a concentric structure, and sometimes attain considerable size, culminating in reniform iron-ore.

The origin of this texture is only to be recognised with certainty in the case of pisolite; in the other similar formations it is more or less wrapped in obscurity, and especially in the Great Oolite beds it is still very problematical. L. von Buch observed a kind of oolite formation on the shores of the Canary Isles very analogous in its apparent origin to the pisolite. Virlet d'Aoust found a species of oolite in the Gulf of Mexico produced by the coating of minute insects' eggs with lime (Comptes

Rendus, 1857, vol. xlv. p. 865). Some recently formed limestones, on the surface of coral reefs, are occasionally oolitic. Many oolites appear to be formed entirely of small and almost spherical shells (these are strictly speaking not genuine oolites). Deicke communicated a careful observation of the texture of roestone in the Zeitschrift f. d. ges. Naturw., 1853, p. 188, and more recently in the Transactions of the Lyons Academy, 1853. Fournet published a comprehensive treatise ' Sur la Formation des Oolites Calcaires.'

In many of these rocks it would appear that the round grains are, in fact, only the result of a peculiar concretion of the homogeneous mass.

SPHERULITIC, or GLOBULIFEROUS (Dana).—A texture so named, somewhat similar to the oolitic, occurs in some felsitic igneous rocks, most distinctly in pearlstone. The round grains consist of pearl-like globules, or simply of compact felsitic concretions.

Another variety of a similar texture sometimes occurs in basalt, dolerite, or phonolite, where it appears that the rock by a singular process of decay has resolved itself into grains of a tolerably round shape.

NODULAR texture is closely allied to the oolitic, or sometimes to the porphyritic, and consists in this—that the mass of the rock contains small rounded or lenticular or somewhat elongated concretions of a firmer and more compact substance than itself. Under certain circumstances this appearance is termed *spotted, variolitic,* or *pock-marked.*

There also occur in rocks, but in a very subordinate degree, those states which in minerals are termed SPARRY, FIBROUS, or ASBESTIFORM.

PARTICULAR STATES OF ROCKS.

There are certain states or conditions (in part identical with the above-mentioned textural phenomena) which, although they frequently alter the very nature and properties of the rock into which they enter, are nevertheless not always considered a sufficient reason for giving a distinct name. This is not a consistent mode of treatment, for there are many cases in which rocks of precisely the same essential mineral constituents

are called by different names, by reason only of a differing texture; and, again, in cases where a series
of rocks form a long but gradual chain of transition or
gradation between two extremes of different character, it
is the custom to give distinct names to many members
of the series arbitrarily selected, and which can only be
regarded as links in the chain.   Still more inconsistent is
it when the same conditions or properties are used in one
case as a reason for a distinction, and in another not.
But if we would avoid these and similar inconsistencies,
we should be compelled to throw over the existing nomenclature of rocks altogether, and substitute an entirely new
one, which would be more hazardous than the inconsistencies themselves.

We will now proceed to describe the most important of
these special states in rocks, only observing in the outset
that the terms used for defining the mere states are frequently also used more generally to designate the rocks
themselves, and they sometimes even embrace a number
of different rocks.

1.   *Lava* is not a definite rock, but is the name given to
     every rock which has been originally poured forth
     from a volcano in a state of igneous fusion.   Thus
     we distinguish dolerite-lava, basalt-lava, trachyte-
     lava, &c.

2.   *Wacké* is the name given to a somewhat decomposed
     state of igneous rocks poor in silica.   The mass
     has become more or less soft, almost earthy, of a
     yellowish or brown colour, and its mineralogical
     structure quite unrecognisable and only to be
     traced by transitions from the fresh state of the
     original rock.   In subsequent pages we shall have
     occasion to speak of dolerite-wacké, basalt-wacké,
     melaphyre-wacké, greenstone-wacké, &c., or we
     shall use the adjective '*wackenitic*'* to designate
     this state of those rocks (wackenitic dolerite, &c.)

3.   *Porphyry* is the general designation for all porphyritic
     rocks with compact main mass or matrix, whereas
     those with a granular matrix are only termed *por-*

---

* We have here been compelled to coin an adjective for the German '*wackenartig*,' an equivalent for which we have been unable to
find in English text-books.   In analogy to porphyritic, granitic, &c.,
we trust the term may meet with acceptance.—TRANSLATOR.

phyritic. Therefore we distinguish between quartz-porphyry, mica-porphyry, trachyte-porphyry, and porphyritic granite, trachyte, &c. The quartz- or felsite-porphyries however (with compact felsitic matrix) are frequently, *par excellence*, termed porphyries without further designation.

4. *Amygdaloid* (*Mandelstein*, Germ.) is the name given to every rock originally vesicular, whose cavities have in course of time become filled with mineral substance; hence there are basalt-amygdaloids, melaphyre-amygdaloids, &c.

5. *Scoria* or *Volcanic Slag*, *Scoriaceous*, *Slag-like*, are terms expressive of very open cellular states of basalt, trachyte, or other volcanic rock.

6. *Pumice, Pumice Stone, Pumiceous.*—These terms are, properly speaking, only expressive of the state or condition of certain rocks; but this state is, generally speaking, confined to three kinds of rock—trachyte, trachyte-porphyry, and obsidian, whose composition is essentially one and the same.

7. *Schist, Slate, Shale*, are general terms for rocks consisting of very different mineral ingredients. The individual rocks are distinguished accordingly, e. g. as mica-schist, chlorite-schist, &c., or clay-slate, &c., or bituminous shale, argillaceous shale, &c.; or the adjectives *schistose, slaty, shaly*, are used in conjunction with the mineralogical name of the rock.

8. *Sandstone, Arenaceous*, are general terms applied to rocks, consisting of a mechanical compound of small rounded or sometimes angular siliceous grains, usually quartz.

9. *Conglomerate* is the universal designation for rocks consisting of rounded stones or pebbles, mechanically bound or cemented together.

10. *Breccia* is a general term for rocks consisting of angular fragments, mechanically cemented together. *t*

11. *Tuff, Tufa.*—These terms doubtless in the first ^ instance were used to express a loose, or little adhesive state of rock.

Tufa is now principally used to denote an earthy compound of volcanic products of the most various kind, and

H

Tuff is chiefly applied to certain calcareous or siliceous deposits at the mouths of springs, very porous, and frequently very firm and tenacious; in which case they are termed travertine.

The four last states in the preceding list are also universally made use of as separate classes of rock in themselves, and as such they cannot indeed be well dispensed with, unless we would give separate names to each of the endless variety of rocks in each of those states; a task not easily possible, nor are the varieties of rocks themselves of sufficient importance to deserve such distinction.

CONCRETIONARY STRUCTURE.

A molecular arrangement quite distinct from crystallisation causes clusters of particles to segregate themselves round centres, or otherwise present various and singular appearances and shapes, which have received different names.

Spherical concretions, which are very different from conglomerates, are frequently found in sandstones, clay rocks, marls, limestones, dolomites, quartz-porphyries, pitchstones, and greenstones. This structure has given rise to various names—the oolite is an instance, so called from the egg-shape of the concretions; pisolite is so called from its pea-shaped concretions, &c. Many concretions are compact, others are hollow, and their interior is sometimes garnished with crystals forming what is called a *geode,* a little crystal grotto; or sometimes a small concretion is found loose in the hollow interior of the larger one, so as to rattle in it when shaken (*clapperstones*). Some concretions are grouped together like clusters of grapes, or in irregularly kidney-shaped masses. These pass over into the *nodular* or *massive* concretions (Germ. *Steinwulste, Schlangensteine, Lösskindel,* &c.). Others are lenticular in shape, and are called *swellings,* or *septaria.* The latter is the special designation for lenticular concretions irregularly cleft in their interior, and frequently into pentagonal clefts on the outside. The clefts are frequently filled again with new mineral formations such as calcspar, brownspar, or ironspar. If their surface be exposed and much washed away by water, it sometimes occurs that the veins of spar, as being harder than the coating of the concretion, protrude and show a kind of network.

These singular structures have been well described by Ehrenberg, Parrot, and Glocker with engravings. Extracts from the treatises of Ehrenberg are to be found in v. Leonhard und Bronn's Jahrbuch, 1840, pp. 680 and 741. The treatise of Glocker on the Laukasteine appeared in Breslau, 1854.

Stylolites are a very singular formation in certain limestones, dolomites, or marls; they consist of irregular and longitudinally striped cylinders standing at right angles to the rock's stratification, and often ended abruptly. Quenstedt endeavoured to explain their origin by supposing them to consist of spaces left by marine animals which had risen perpendicularly in the rock whilst yet soft, the tubes or spaces so formed being afterwards refilled. (See von L. und B. Jahrbuch, 1837, p. 406.)

Cone in Cone.—Concretions of a conical shape marked with concentric rings, are sometimes to be found in certain marls or marly limestones (in German these concretions are called *Tuten*, and smaller and more pyramidical concretions of the same kind are termed *Nägel*).

No satisfactory explanation of the last three singular forms of concretion has yet been given.

SPECIAL FORMS OF EXTERNAL STRUCTURE.

There are certain other phenomena of rock structure (chiefly of their outward structure) which should not remain entirely unnoticed here. We will, therefore, proceed to mention them, merely premising that they are incapable of systematic arrangement, being individual in their character and unconnected with each other.

Stalactites are formations produced in caverns or vesicular cavities after the manner of icicles, and resembling them in form. They are caused by the dropping of water holding some mineral in solution, and leaving behind a deposit or incrustation thereof. The mineral is usually calc-spar, barytes, aragonite, chalcedony, brown hematite, manganese spar, pyrites, or the like. If the incrustations, on the other hand, have been formed on the floor of the cavern or cavity by the drops when fallen, and have so grown upwards, they are called *Stalagmites*. Both stalactites and stalagmites are frequently met with in caverns of limestone and dolomite, where they are occasionally developed in extraordinary beauty and size. In vesicular cavities they are similarly formed, but of course smaller in size. Their original, normal position is necessarily perpendicular. If they are found in any other, that is the consequence of movement during or subsequent to their formation.

Dendrites (*Dendritic*) are terms applied to certain external crystallisations or deposits, usually arborescent in form, which are found incrusting the surfaces of joints and fissures in many rocks. These dendrites usually consist of oxide of manganese, sometimes of oxide of iron. Their origin appears to resemble that of the flowers of ice on window panes, or the so-called silver trees.

Slickenslides, Friction Surfaces (Germ. *Rutschflächen, Reibungsflächen, Schliffflächen, Spiegelflächen,* or *Harnische*). The surfaces of solid rocks are sometimes found to have been naturally smoothed or polished, and also furrowed or scratched in some one direction. This phenomenon occurs in the most various kinds of rocks, sometimes in the interior of the earth, sometimes on the exposed surface of the rock. When it occurs in the interior of the earth, it has been invariably caused by masses of rock pushing and shoving against each other, and forms one of the clearest proofs of such movements having taken place in the solid crust of the earth. Friction surfaces when met with on the exposed face of a rock may no doubt have been likewise caused in the same manner, and have been laid bare subsequently, but in fact they have very often been caused by the progressive movement of a glacier rubbing over the surface of the rock. These latter friction surfaces may be distinguished from the former kind by the uniform direction of their furrows, always corresponding to the indications of the valley, and further by their never exhibiting protuberant masses between the furrows, as is sometimes the case with the others. They are to be met with in districts where glaciers once existed. Floating ice is said sometimes to produce similar marks on rocky sea-coasts.

Many hard rock surfaces exhibit a peculiar smoothness with at the same time a wavy conformation or a furrowing in one particular direction. It has been observed that sand set in motion by the wind and driven against the surfaces of rocks for very long periods of time, has produced the like singular abrasions. This phenomenon, first described by Naumann (who ascribed it to glacial action), is observable in certain rocks at Wurzen, in Saxony. (See v. L. und B. Jahrb. 1844, pp. 557, 561, 680; 1848, p. 497.)

It is familiar to every one how running water will gradually round off and . eat into the hardest rocks. The singular phenomenon of what are called pot-holes or giant-holes deserve special mention. These circular hollows are formed at waterfalls or rapids by whirlpools carrying sand or pebbles round and round, and so gradually scooping out a smooth round hollow. Basins of this kind are found in river beds from a few inches to many feet in diameter, and even over the height of a man in depth. In places where the origin of these basins is not to be explained by any existing waterfall or stream, we must presume the former existence of such.

Somewhat analogous to the pot holes are the so-called ' *Karren* ' or ' *Karrenfelder*,' which are terms of Swiss geologists for certain rill marks hitherto only observed on limestone and dolomite rocks. They usually only occur in lofty mountain districts, and are very frequent in the Alps. They consist of gutters of from a quarter of an inch to two feet wide, washed out of the face of the rock by the rain, and following the lines of its steepest inclination.

Rocks locally possessing different degrees of hardness when exposed to the weather and the action of rain often present a singular jagged, glandular, or honeycombed appearance from the unequal degree of resistance of their parts. Thus, for instance, the quadersandstone of the Saxon Switzerland, the argillaceous gypsum of the Kiffhauser, &c.

The *traces of raindrops* are not unfrequently found on rock surfaces. These raindrops must have fallen during the formation of the stratum, probably at ebb tide, making small holes surrounded with raised rings. These holes have then been covered by the next stratum, and so preserved for all time, like the ripple- and current-marks, which are also of frequent occurrence on the surfaces of some sedimentary rocks.—Vide Froriep's Neue Notizen, 1839, vol. xi. p. 134; Ann. d. Sc. géol. 1843, p. 61; Compt. rend. 1861, vol. 53, p. 649; Lyell in Royal Institution of Great Britain, 1851–4, Cepr. und Geologie (translated 1858), i. p. 390; i. p. 150.

Animals also take part in the transformation of rock surfaces. Certain kinds of mollusca on the sea coast (*Pholades*) have the peculiar habit of burrowing several inches deep into limestones or dolomite rocks, and even into clays as well as much harder rocks; (as, for instance, mica-schist), so as by degrees to perforate the whole surface. Ancient lines of coast are sometimes to be recognised by means of their appearance.

Rounded Stones, Gravel, Shingle, Pebbles, or Boulders.— These stones have usually been wholly or partially rounded by the action of water. There are, however, such as have been rounded by the motion of glaciers, and some even appear to have been rounded in clefts of rocks, the sides of which have been much agitated.

There are also some special points respecting them which deserve attention. In the first place most pebbles are not spherical, but flattened and lenticular or elongated, egg-shaped, &c. This very universal law is evidently the result of an unequal degree of resistance to waste presented by the stone in the direction of one or more normal axes. In the case of rocks of slaty texture or the like, this phenomenon may be readily conceived; but in the case of compact or granular rocks without a trace of fissile or laminated texture, it is more remarkable, and points to some parallelism of texture or structure which has hitherto escaped observation.

The boulders or pebbles formed by glaciers sometimes exhibit grooves or scratches on their surface.

At the foot of the Alps in the neighbourhood of Vienna, many pebbles and boulders have been formed showing deep grooves and forcible impressions, and some which are partially broken and pieced together again.

In some conglomerates (as in the Nagelflue of St. Gall) pebbles are found partly forced into each other (these are

usually of limestone), and in other conglomerates, for in-
tance at Waldenburg in Silesia, there are pebbles which
have been cleft asunder, their several parts somewhat displaced, and so cemented together again. But perhaps the
most remarkable of these phenomena are the dolomitic
limestone pebbles in a conglomerate at St. Lauretta in
the Leitha mountains, many of which are hollow.

Much has been written on these peculiar forms and
phenomena, as appearing in pebbles. We have referred
to the greater part of such treatises in a former work
(vide Geolog. Fragen, 1858, pp. 198—212), and will only
here add a reference to some later treatises, viz. :

Württenberger in von L. & Br. Jahrb. 1859, p. 153.
Deicke, ibid. 1860, p. 219.
Gurlt, ibid. 1861, p. 225.
Berggeist, 1860, p. 382.
Sorby, On the Direct Correlation of Mechanical and Chemical
Forces.

JOINTED STRUCTURE.

All large masses of rock are internally cleft by fissures or joints, and thereby divided into solids of different
size and form. The general cause of this *jointed structure*
of the mass is evidently contraction which, in the case of
the igneous rocks, in all probability took place during
cooling ; in the case of the sedimentary during the process
of their drying; and in the case of the metamorphic, which
they inherited from the sedimentary, or which was renewed during the process of metamorphism.

In most rocks the jointing is irregular, dividing the
rock into irregular masses; frequently, however, a certain degree of regularity is exhibited—i.e. the dividing
fissures observe one or more prevailing directions, and are
at definite distances from each other, so as to form a
severance into tolerably regular plates, columns, parallelopipeds, or spherical masses.

This so-called jointed structure deserves to be here
described with some particularity, although it has no
connection with the mineralogical composition of the rock,
and solely results from the circumstances attending its
original formation, and especially its solidification.

Tabular Jointing.—The rock's mass is split into parallel
plates or tables, and these, unlike flagstones or strata,

have not been successively deposited one over the other, but were all formed simultaneously and subsequently to the first formation of the rock. This constitutes, indeed, the characteristic distinction between stratification and jointing—the former being the result of successive superposition, the latter of the splitting of a previously formed mass. Tabular jointing occurs most frequently in the igneous rocks, less frequently also in the sedimentary and metamorphic.

A modification of the tabular structure sometimes occurs, consisting in a curvature of the individual plates, which are frequently very thin. This is called in German *Schalige absonderung,* 'conchoidal jointing.'

Columnar, Subcolumnar, Prismatic Jointing. — The rock's mass is split into columns of from 3 to 9 faces, usually 5 or 6 faces, and the thickness of the pillars in each place is tolerably uniform, but in different places varies from a few inches to several feet. The length of the columns is of course unequal. Some are known more than 200 feet long. These columns are, however, usually cross-jointed—i.e. split into shorter blocks by means of cross courses or horizontal fissures at right angles with the first set of joints. This jointing is regular or irregular, it sometimes exhibits rounded surfaces, indicating in that case that the pillars were formed by the joining together of spherical masses (as may be clearly seen, indeed, in some places).

Columnar jointing may be observed with peculiar frequency and beauty in basalt, but it also occurs in diabase, diorite, aphanite, and quartz-porphyry; less frequently in trachyte, granite, or syenite. In all these rocks this jointing is evidently the result of a special process of cooling; moreover, the axes of the columns are for the most part at right angles with the plane of the larger cooling surface. In lava streams, for instance, perpendicular to their surface; in veins or dykes of basalt, perpendicular to the walls of the cleft. If the larger cooling surface has been curviform, the columns at right angles to it will be found bent or radiating.

But sedimentary rocks sometimes exhibit the phenomenon of *columnar jointing.* In them it is probably owing to having dried more rapidly from one side of the mass, and in rare cases, locally, to the effect of heat from contact with igneous rocks.

Parallelopipedic, Cuboidal, or *Rhomboidal Jointing.*— The rocks are severed by joints which traverse them in planes of three different directions, which, if they cross each other at right angles, produce cubes or rectangular parallelopipeds ; if at inclined angles, rhomboidal solids. In sedimentary rocks the direction of one of these planes is frequently determined by the bedding, but in igneous rocks all three sets of joints are independent of such influence.

Spherical, Globular, or *Spheroidal Jointing.*—Some rocks are entirely composed of spherical masses, the interstices or spaces originally existing between them being now filled with a mass of similar substance and composition, but so that the jointing is still apparent. These spherical masses are often formed of concentric layers, and sometimes ranged over each other in columns. In the latter case the globular and columnar jointing may be said to be combined.

A modification of the spherical structure is what is called *ball and socket jointing,* in which single masses with rounded heads more or less approach the globular shape, and seem to fit into a cavity on the other side of the fissure.

This passes over into *irregular or massive jointing,* which occurs more or less distinctly in rocks of the most different description.

All jointing becomes much more distinctly apparent when the rock is weathered, and it sometimes even appears as if the structure were solely caused by decay of the rock. Nevertheless, it is very probable that even in these cases a disposition to the severance previously existed.

STRATIFICATION OF ROCKS.

We have already spoken of the lamination of shaly rocks as consisting of a structure dividing those rocks in planes parallel to their bedding, and originating in the mode in which they were formed—i. e. by successive layers of deposit.

The same phenomenon on a larger scale is called *strati-fication*, and the individual members of the series are termed strata. Page observes in his Adv. Text Book, ' Thus ' (speaking of stratified rocks), ' the terms *stratum* and *bed* are used when the deposit is of considerable thickness ; *layer* or *band* when it is thin, and holds a subordinate place among the other beds ; and *seam* when a rock of a peculiar character occurs at intervals among a series of strata. The miner, for example, speaks of a seam of coal occurring among strata of clay and sand-stone, and of a band of ironstone occurring in a bed of shale.'

The horizontal line on the surface of strata is termed the *strike*, and their steepest inclination towards the hori-zontal plane is termed the *dip*.

Stratification is exhibited more especially and distinctly in the sedimentary rocks, but it is also frequently to be recognised in the metamorphic, and even the igneous rocks may exceptionally be actually stratified, if, for instance, successive streams of lava have overflowed each other, each consolidating separately.

SHAPE AND BEDDING * OF ROCK MASSES.

Both the shape and the mode of bedding of rock masses are dependent on the mode of their original formation.

Igneous rocks neither exhibit any certain shapes nor any uniform bedding in relation to other rocks, whereas in the case of sedimentary rocks and their offspring, the metamorphic, both shape and bedding have some relation to certain general laws.

The form assumed by igneous rocks depends to some extent on the shape and size of the opening by which they forced their passage from the interior of the earth. They accordingly fill clefts more or less regular in form,

---

* The word 'BEDDING' is used indifferently throughout this work in speaking of all rocks, whether stratified or not. It is taken as the equivalent of the German ' *Lagerung*.' We are aware that in England this has not been always usual ; nevertheless, some general word must be adopted. ' Mode of occurrence,' ' position,' 'lie,' &c., are all ex-pressions which fall short of the idea intended to be conveyed.— TRANSLATOR.

or they occupy larger irregular spaces between other rocks, or they have overflowed through craters, and create accumulations after the manner of lava in streams, in plains, or conical heaps.

Where the igneous rock forms a clear and evident filling of a previously existing cleft or fissure, it is termed a *dyke* or *vein*. The latter term is, however, more usually confined by many to such as are metalliferous. The irregular disrupting masses are called in German *Stöcke* (*stehende* or *liegende Stöcke*), for which terms there are no precise equivalents in English nomenclature of very general acceptation. Where igneous rocks are accumulated in great extent, and they appear to have filled greater gaps in the earth's crust, they are spoken of as *ranges, districts*, or *tracts*. These are sometimes of approximately circular or elliptical shape in their horizontal extension, as may be observed on geological maps. From such ranges, again, there frequently run smaller branches in different directions (*ramifications*).

Where igneous rocks in a state of fusion have broken through other rocks and spread themselves over the latter, they are said to be *overlying*. They are either extended longitudinally in one direction in the manner of streams of lava, or they cover broad surfaces, and form extensive fields. In both cases they may afterwards be themselves covered by later rock formations.

The form which the igneous rocks assume above the surface of the ground corresponds little with that of their mass beneath, the geographical outline alone is determined by the latter—not the elevation. Very recent igneous rocks, by reason of their volcanic origin, may be of conical shape, as is the case with many basalts, phonolites, or trachytes; but all the older igneous rocks owe their present shape to the transforming influence of long continued weathering and flooding, so that their present appearance depends much more on their individual power of resistance to those influences than upon the shape in which they first made their appearance on the surface of the globe.

The shape of the sedimentary and metamorphic rocks is always flat, or nearly so. Their material was originally deposited on surfaces more or less even, and if inequalities existed they were filled up, so that at least the upper strata of such deposits are always very regularly flat shaped, or very broadly lenticular. The general shape and extent of these rocks corresponds therefore, more or less, with that of every individual stratum of the same. The conformation of the actual surface in many cases has, however, been much changed by external forces, such as weathering, the action of flood waters, &c.; and, again, the lowest beds of the series may exhibit very great inequalities; even former rents or fissures in underlying rocks may have been filled up by the material of the deposit, so that these fillings of clefts may subsequently assume the shape and character of veins or dykes, in the underlying rock. Such last mentioned cases, however, are rare.

Rents in the earth's crust have come to be filled in very various ways, e. g. by the injection of matter in a state of igneous fusion, by mechanical deposit from above, or by chemical precipitate from solutions. Such fillings are called *dykes, veins,* or *lodes.* The term *lode* is exclusively applied to a metalliferous vein; so also by some geologists is the term *vein,* but this is not the universal practice. The term *dyke* is exclusively applied to such as consist of the same material throughout.

Although the sedimentary rocks, as a rule, form extensive flat-lying systems of stratification, yet there occasionally occur irregular accumulations distinguished from the ordinary flat strata by proportionately greater thickness and less horizontal extent, as well as by irregularity of shape. They may have sometimes arisen by filling of caverns.

The *bedding* of rocks may be divided into the *regular* and *irregular.* The latter is characteristic of the igneous rocks, the former of the sedimentary and metamorphic.

Irregular bedding is in general the consequence of a violent disruption of the pre-consolidated earth's crust. The igneous rocks have forced themselves a path through the existing rocks and filled up the cracks made in the latter by the eruption. These are sometimes, but not always, regularly formed fissures, such as when filled can be called dykes. These violent disruptions are termed *intrusions,* and when they are of unmistakable character we may conclude with certainty that the intruding rock is of more recent formation than the one broken through, but not how much more recent.

Regular Bedding, which, as we have said, chiefly prevails in the sedimentary and metamorphic rocks, corresponds with their internal stratification.

The following are some of the phases of bedding :—

1. *Parallel alternating bedding*, or *uniform bedding*, when two or more rocks alternate with each other in parallel strata, forming a whole system of strata whose general shape is flat or gently swelling.

2. *Divergent bedding.*—When any set of beds incline in different directions, they sometimes incline towards each other (*synclinal*), and sometimes they fall away from each other (*anticlinal*).

3. *Overlapping* (übergreifend), when one set of strata overlaps the edges of another set of strata.

4. A hollow basin-like form (Muldenförmig).

5. *Cloak-like bedding* (Mantelförmig), where the strata or beds surround and nearly envelop a central point from which they dip on all sides (quaquaversal dip).

6. *Subordinate intermediate bedding*, when beds of subordinate size lie in the midst of a larger series of strata.

The originally regular bedding of the sedimentary and metamorphic rocks has very often been more or less disturbed by subsequent processes, such as the intrusion of igneous rocks, subsidence, &c., and even some of the above-named cases are sometimes only the consequence of some such disturbances. The natural or original position of the sedimentary or the metamorphic rocks and their strata is necessarily the horizontal, or nearly so. If we find any very great variations from the horizontal, these are, as a rule, to be considered as the consequence of disturbance, although the original cause of such disturbance may not always be recognised with certainty.

The following are some of the different kinds of disturbance of bedding :—

1. *Uplifting*, by which whole strata or systems of strata frequently appear to have been very strongly inclined from the horizontal direction.

2. *Contortion, foldings, bendings.*

3. *Disruption, breaks* (Zerknickung), where the strata appear to have been uplifted in the centre and broken, the two parts dipping from the place of rupture.

4. *Displacement* or *faults* (Verwerfung) where one portion of the bed has been uplifted or depressed and bodily separated from the remaining portion.

5. *Subversion* (Ueberstürzung), where the bed has been entirely overturned, and its position reversed.

From the bedding of rocks we may often, but not always, determine their relative age. The principles to guide us in this are somewhat as follows:—

1. Overlying rocks as a rule are more recent than those which they cover.

The only exceptions to this rule are created by subversions, or by obliquely upheaved or intruded igneous masses. Such exceptions, however, are usually easily to be recognised by surrounding circumstances.

2. Intruding rocks are always more recent than those which they have penetrated.

The exceptions to this rule can be only apparent; as for instance, if a steep projecting rock has been surrounded by and come to be imbedded in a later deposit and so afterwards possibly been mistaken for an intruder.

3. Rocks which during their formation have created manifest disturbance of the bedding of other rocks are necessarily in every case younger than those.

From this rule also only apparent exceptions can arise, as when the bedding of a rock may have been disturbed by the decay of the underlying stratum, e. g. the dissolution of rock-salt.

4. The level of a rock alone will not enable us to pronounce on its age, for the oldest sedimentary rocks may by upheaval have been shoved up into the highest level; and as regards the igneous rocks, according to their very nature the oldest and the youngest may be met with in any level.

●

CHAPTER IV.

GEOLOGICAL FORMATIONS AND GROUPS OF ROCKS.

ACCORDING to the present state of our geological knowledge, we regard a certain class of rocks as the original
products of the consolidation of parts of the fused mass of
which our planet formerly consisted, and which we still
believe to be the substance of the interior of the globe.
These original products we term *igneous rocks*. All other
rocks are only secondary products arising from their
transmutation, their decomposition, decay or·disintegra-
tion, and reconstruction.

The igneous rocks are subdivided into two principal
groups, the *Volcanic* and the *Plutonic*. The volcanic are
those which, having been ejected from the interior in a
fluid or viscous state, cooled and consolidated at or near
the surface of the earth. The plutonic are those rocks
which have not reached the surface of the earth in a fluid
or viscous state, but solidified at considerable depth,
probably therefore under influences of great heat and
pressure.

The rocks which we have termed secondary products
are likewise divisible into two great classes, the *Sedimentary* and *Metamorphic*. The sedimentary rocks being
formed from the débris of the igneous rocks, and the
metamorphic being the older sedimentary rocks, which, in
process of time, and from various causes, have assumed an
altered character, have undergone 'metamorphosis.' Let
us take a brief review of these principal rock formations :—

1. *Volcanic Formations.*—The active volcanoes of the
present day furnish us with the best instances of
these formations, and the surest data for consider-
ing the phenomena of their origin. First we find
consolidated lavas of various outward form and

internal structure; they assume the shape of narrow streams down the mountain side, they overflow the plains in broad sheets, or filling up previously existing cracks and fissures they form veins or dykes in other rocks, or they form conical mounds on the mountain top. The column of lava which solidifies in the abyss of the crater must frequently assume the shape of a vertical cylinder, which, however, remains inaccessible to observation, unless and until a considerable portion of the whole mountain has decayed and been washed away.

The lavas consist either of basaltic or trachytic rock; their inferior mass is either compact, porphyritic, or crystalline-granular, their exterior frequently vesicular or scoriaceous.

Thus there are many different rocks or varieties entitled to be called lava, and all belonging to one and the same formation. Besides the lavas proper we find at volcanoes various kinds of loose ejected masses, some more and others less decomposed, consisting of large concretions of slag, smaller fragments of lava (lapilli), volcanic sand, and dust-like particles, so-called 'volcanic ash.' These ejectamenta either remain lying loose on the surface of the ground, or they form conical piles 'of slag, or they are washed together by water and are redeposited as volcanic tufa, which thus may be of very various character.

2. *The older Volcanic Formations* differ from the most recent by the entire or almost entire absence of loose ejectamenta, scoria, evident streams of lava, and distinct craters. No doubt all these were once in existence, but in course of time they have decayed and been washed away. We now only find bare conical hills of basalt, dolerite, trachyte, or phonolite (the kernels which have remained of former volcanoes after the decay of the masses which surrounded and covered them), accompanied by veins branching out of those nucleous masses, and by tufa formations or other decomposed forms of volcanic product. So much of the outer vesicular or scorified coating of the original volcanic rocks

as has not been entirely destroyed and washed away has in the course of time been turned to amygdaloid. These older volcanic formations, like the more recent, are partly basaltic and partly trachytic, and they form transition states between the volcanic and plutonic formations.

3. *Upper Plutonic Formations.*—These may be divided into such as are of prevailing *basic* and *acidic* composition, characterised respectively by the greenstones and quartz-porphyries. The Voigtland in Germany presents us with a good example of the basic greenstones, and the north-western district of the Thuringian Forest of the acidic quartz-porphyries.

In the Voigtland, associated with transition rocks, we find various kinds of greenstone, such as diabase and aphanite, granular, compact, porphyritic, fissile, and amygdaloidal, some decayed into wacké, some in the form of tufa, or conglomerate. These greenstones, it would appear, constitute the subterranean portion of a volcanic formation of the Devonian age. We must assume that the upper and perhaps more basaltic portion of this formation has decayed away; loose ejectamenta and genuine volcanic shapes are no longer observable; the conical hills of greenstone are doubtless the result of the superior power of resistance of that rock, just as quartz rocks frequently protrude above masses of a softer rock which formerly enclosed them. It is, nevertheless, remarkable that the tufa and conglomerates which have been preserved imbedded in the transition strata appear to have been originally greenstone and not basalt, whence we might conclude that even the original volcanic portion of these eruptive formations which reached the surface rather resembled greenstone than basalt.

In the Thuringian Forest quartz-porphyries predominate; they are of various kinds, and are associated with mica-porphyrites and greenstones, claystone tufas and conglomerates. The conglomerates contain fragments of rocks belonging unmistakably to the Rothliegende or Dyassic age,

I

so that we must conclude that the eruptions which upheaved these Thuringian porphyries took place during that period or subsequent to it. Every trace of genuine volcanic formation has long since decayed and been swept away; the plutonic part alone has remained, except, indeed, some tufas which have been preserved by superincumbent strata. It need hardly be said that the process of laying bare rocks which lay so deep must have occupied long spaces of time, and therefore plutonic rocks must be very old before they are exposed and rendered accessible to our observation.

4. *Lower Plutonic Formations.*—The most characteristic and strongly marked representatives of these formations are the granites (and syenites). These have consolidated in the earth at great depth. They are for the most part very distinctly crystalline, though their texture is very various.

They are never vesicular, nor do they occur in the form of tufas, for the latter could not possibly be formed in the interior of the earth. On the other hand, they are sometimes accompanied by friction breccias. They branch out into veins traversing other rocks as well as the older masses of the same formation. These branches have frequently cooled more rapidly than the general mass and formed themselves into porphyry. This result has been especially observed where the veins are narrow; but the width of the veins has not been the only determining cause of more rapid cooling; the depth, the temperature of the neighbouring rock, its state of moisture or dryness, must all have operated in hastening or retarding the consolidation of the intruding mass.

Tracts of granite frequently form the back-bone or nucleus of mountain ranges. They occur in larger masses and of more connected range than the upper plutonic formations. It would appear to be the case, as we might *à priori* have supposed, that upon the occasion of every eruption of igneous fluid from the earth's interior the opening made is wider below than at the surface. The eruptive mass when cooled acquires different characters according to the pressure to which it has been subjected during the cooling process; in other words, according to the depth at which it consolidated. The same eruptive mass may be volcanic at the surface, and plutonic below the surface of the earth. The plutonic rocks, in all probability, represent the upper portion of a conical mass, widening towards its base. Thus we may explain the fact that the lower plutonic rocks, when laid bare, occupy a wider area than the upper. It also follows that as a longer time would be requisite for their exposure, the lower plutonic rocks which are exposed to our observation are universally the oldest igneous formations for the time being ; and thus the granites, being those of the plutonic rocks which have consolidated at the greatest depths, are for the most part the oldest of the igneous rocks of the present geological period. This does not however exclude the possibility of newer granite formations being accidentally exposed in some cases, for instance, by very violent local upheavings, or very rapid waste of superincumbent rocks, favoured by numerous fissures. This, in the Alps, has actually taken place. So much of the granite formations as reached the surface at the time of the eruption may perhaps have been of trachytic character, and it may be that the same masses which form the trachyte-lavas of the present time are simultaneously forming granite rocks at great depths below the surface. The fact of the chemical composition of the two rocks being the same is at all events in harmony with such an hypothesis.

These examples may suffice for the igneous rocks. We next proceed to notice the chief sedimentary formations. (The metamorphic rocks being the products of the sedimentary, are consequently later in date of their formation than those.)

5. *Argillaceous Formations.*—These are deposits of clayey mud alternated with marl, lime, or sand, sometimes containing a large proportion of hydrated oxide of iron. These deposits were, in process of time, covered by more recent strata, and produced

clay-slate, argillaceous shale, interstratified with calcareous shale, compact limestone, sandstone, and ironstone.   Such formations have taken place in all geological periods.

6. *Marl Formations.*—These deposits consisted chiefly of marly silt alternating with clay, calcareous mud, sand, and sometimes gypsum or hydrated oxide of iron.   Under the pressure of superimposed strata, these deposits became converted into marl-shale and compact marl, interlaid with strata of argillaceous shale, limestone, gypsum, and ironstone. A very characteristic marl formation of this nature is met with in the German keuper.

7. *Limestone Formations.*—These are the result of the deposit of calcareous silt, invisibly small shells, larger shells, coral reefs (partly dolomitic) or calcareous tufa, alternating with calcareous, argillaceous, or sometimes siliceous strata.   From these under the pressure of superjacent formations, there have resulted beds of limestone and dolomite of many different varieties, earthy and compact, in alternate strata with subordinate beds of marl-shale, clay-slate, argillaceous-shale, ironstone, or flint.   In every geological period these deposits have taken place ; we find them very characteristically developed in Germany in the Jurassic, Muschelkalk, and Zechstein formations.

8. *Sandstone Formations.*—These are deposits of quartz sand (more or less fine-grained) with some clay marl or protoxide of iron.   Pebbles also have been deposited with the sand either locally interspersed or in alternate beds.   The deposited sand when subjected to pressure then became sandstone, and the other ingredients formed themselves into intermediate strata of slate-clay, marl-shale, conglomerate, and the like.   These formations have taken place in all geological periods.   Very characteristic instances are furnished by the Quader-sandstone and variegated sandstone (Buntsandstein) of Germany.

9. *Conglomerate Formations.*—The original deposits were chiefly pebbles, sand, and clay.   From these materials

by pressure, solid conglomerates were formed, consisting of pebbles cemented together by the sand or clay, and interstratified with beds of sand or clay. These deposits have taken place in all periods, but have never attained any great extent at one time or place. Hence the conglomerates play a very subordinate part in the sedimentary formations. In Germany, there is properly speaking but one very characteristic conglomerate formation, which is that of the Rothliegende. The Nagelflue of the Molasse formation is quite subordinate to the sandstone, which is the predominant rock of that formation.

10. *Coal Formations.*—The greater part of these formations originally consisted of peat, or vegetable materials washed together; usually sand and clay were likewise contained in the deposit, and sometimes hydrated oxide of iron or protocarbonate of iron. These deposits, in the course of time, with pressure, were formed into strata of alternate sandstone (usually grey) and slate-clay or shale; and between these strata, beds of brown or black coal or anthracite and clay-ironstone were formed, subordinate, however, in extent and thickness to the sandstone, slate, and shale. Coarse conglomerates, marl, or limestones very rarely occur in these formations.

The Carboniferous period and the Tertiary period furnish the most characteristic examples of these formations; but the carbonaceous deposits of other periods are associated with similar rocks, and are so like the genuine coal formations that, petrographically, they are hardly to be distinguished from them.

11. *Rock-salt Formations.*—Rock-salt is always accompanied by gypsum and anhydrite, and it likewise usually occurs in combination with argillaceous deposits. The rocks of this group are usually imbedded in limestone or dolomite, as in the Muschelkalk of Germany, or in sandstone as in Galicia and Transylvania. In all periods these local deposits appear to have taken place, but

the special conditions and causes of their origin are not yet known with certainty.

If we turn to the rocks which we consider to be of metamorphic origin, the crystalline schists, we find alternating beds analogous to those of the sedimentary rocks, but in an altered state. We, kowever, seldom or never find rock-salt or gypsum, a circumstance which may be explained by the great solubility of those rocks.

The crystalline schist formations may be best described by naming the principal rocks of each. Thus we have :—

12. *Argillaceous Mica-schist Formations*, with subordinate beds of quartz-schist, lydian stone, alum-schist, granular limestone and dolomite, sometimes also hornblende-schist, ironstone, and graphite.
13. *Mica-schist Formations*, with similar subordinate formations to those in the argillaceous mica-schist. In these we include some kinds of gneiss.
14. *Gneiss Formations*, consisting of gneiss of various kinds in parallel and alternating strata, and containing similar subordinate formations to the mica-schists.
15. *Chlorite-schist Formations*, also containing similar subordinate beds of other rocks.

These formations seem to be the result of a special process of transmutation occasioned by the presence of magnesia.

The fact that in the crystalline schists coal, gypsum and anhydrite are much more rarely met with than in the sedimentary formations, and rock-salt almost never, may, as we have already said, be accounted for by the perishable nature of those rocks. It seems remarkable that conglomerates are also very rarely met with. We should not, however, forget that these only play a subordinate part in the sedimentary formations, where they are usually only of local occurrence. They are, moreover, found in some crystalline schists, as, for instance, in Valorsino and in the Upper Rhine Valley, in the west Alpine district, where they occur in the gneiss and mica-schist formations, and pass over by transition into those rocks, their cementing medium having become crystalline, and the pebbles blended with the general mass.

The following is a list of the great geological periods of deposit:—

POST-TERTIARY EPOCH:—
Recent period (human).
Pleistocene period.

TERTIARY EPOCH:—
Pleiocene period.
Meiocene period.
Eocene period.

SECONDARY or MESOZOIC EPOCH:—
Cretaceous period.
Oolitic period.
Triassic period.

PRIMARY or PALÆOZOIC EPOCH:—
Permian period. (Dyas.)
Carboniferous period.
Devonian period.
Silurian period (upper and lower).
Cambrian period.
Præ-cambrian periods.

CHAPTER V.

TRANSITIONS AND TRANSMUTATIONS.

WE have hitherto treated generally of the composition of rocks, their texture, and other outward characteristics, and their formation or origin. It is comparatively easy to describe these phenomena in general terms, but their application to particular rocks in describing and classifying them is a task of great difficulty. One of the principal difficulties of classification is occasioned by the great number of rocks of character varying more or less from the established types. These varieties, in many cases, form series with every shade of divergence from the normal rock until the last member of the series presents a totally different species, coinciding may be with some other normal type. A series of intermediate rocks thus connecting two established types is termed a series of transition; and thus, in the abstract, one type is said to pass into the other; not, however, that any real transition takes place of the actual rock, but merely, as we have said, that two groups are connected together by a chain of rocks partaking partly of the attributes of each.

Transitions of this kind are met with in nature in almost all kinds of rock, in respect alike of their *composition*, their *texture*, and their *origin*. A few instances will suffice for explanation.

1. Transitions in respect of *composition* are said to take place when in a rock of given character a strange mineral ingredient occurs not usual in rocks of that class, or when an essential ingredient of its composition diminishes or altogether disappears.

For instance, in the case of limestone and dolomite, a rock consisting essentially and principally of calc-spar (carbonate of lime) is a limestone, even though it contain some bitter spar or carbonate of magnesia; but if enough of the latter enters into its composition, then the rock will be a dolomite; and an endless variety of rocks are found with very different proportions of those two ingredients, so that it is impossible in many cases confidently to describe them either as limestone or dolomite. These are transition states between those two typical rocks. Again, in the case of gneiss and mica-schist, we find first some, and then more felspar entering into the composition of a mica-schist, until at last we obtain a gneiss; or we find less and less felspar in a gneiss, until at last it is reduced to a mica-schist. These and the like transitions may actually be observed in nature side by side, so that in the same mass we may sometimes find at one end a limestone, at the other a dolomite; at one extremity a gneiss, at the other a mica-schist, &c.; but the term transition is employed in this and other treatises in a wider sense to characterise any rocks of intermediate composition, wherever occurring, by means of which a relationship or connection may be traced between any two species of rock.

2. The same kind of transition takes place between rocks in respect of their *outward characteristics.* The texture of rocks of every kind varies indefinitely from one type to another, without any sharp distinction between the types; thus granite passes over into gneiss in numberless instances where it is more or less foliated in texture; or granite-porphyry passes into porphyritic granite by means of those rocks whose matrix partakes more of the granular than the compact texture; or basalt into dolerite, by those varieties in which the individual minerals are somewhat more separately developed (granular) so as to be partially recognisable.

3. Transitions occur between rocks in respect of their *origin* or *mode of formation.* Certain rocks are only the result of a transmutation of others, and the different stages of such transmutation have been distinguished by separate names. Thus argillaceous shale passes over into clay-slate and argillaceous mica-schist; peat into browncoal;

browncoal into common coal; common coal into anthracite; and anthracite into graphite. Gabbro or granite passes over into serpentine.

These last-mentioned transitions or transmutations are such in the strictest sense of the word, having been occasioned by changes of the rocks' substance in the course of time; whereas the term transition, as applied to the two former classes is only a conventional term for a progressive series of rocks, all of which were from the first different from each other, and remain so.

It need hardly be said that these several transitions and transmutations multiply not a little the difficulties of nomenclature and classification, and frequently render the desired precision and accuracy impossible. We are always driven back to this—that every name applied to a rock can only be considered as establishing an especially characteristic form of its development as a kind of centre point, which, however, in nature is surrounded by numerous varieties and derivative forms of more or less doubtful character.

PART II.

THE ROCKS.

INTRODUCTORY CHAPTER.

CLASSIFICATION.

A SCIENTIFIC classification of rocks is a task of more difficulty than might at first sight appear; as yet, no one has succeeded in producing a perfectly consistent and comprehensive system. Not only do the nature of the subject and our own imperfect knowledge present many serious obstacles to consistent arrangement; but in many cases established usage and nomenclature, too firmly rooted to be lightly disturbed, prevent our changing an old classification even when based on error.

Even were our knowledge far more certain than it is, and were we free to overthrow all previous errors and misconceptions, we could not lay down a logically complete system of classification to embrace all rocks, on any principle, whether of ORIGIN, TEXTURE, or COMPOSITION (chemical or mineralogical). We do not find the mineralogical differences between rocks coincide with those of their chemical composition, nor are either of those dependent on geological position or stratification. There are no rigidly defined classes in nature.

The student must not, therefore, expect too much from any system; but, as we are driven to choose some basis for arrangement of our subject, we consider, on the whole, that the best scheme for our purpose will be one in its general features coinciding, as far as possible, with what we know of the origin of the various rocks, making use, however, of the distinctions arising from differences of texture, composition, or otherwise, for the subdivision of our subject, as the nature of each case may seem to render advisable.

A great number of distinctions have been established by custom between many rock formations, which in truth do not differ from each other very materially. These we shall as far as possible drop, endeavouring to make uniform connected groups, and treating many rocks, which have hitherto been known by different names, as varieties only of one and the same rock. On the same principle, we avoid as far as possible the introduction of new names for rocks. It is impossible, and would be unprofitable, to dignify every slight modification of texture or structure (perhaps only of local occurrence) by a separate name. Even in treating the most important and prevalent rocks, we should seek to confine our nomenclature to their most characteristic forms of development, establishing these as central points of departure, from which manifold transitions are found leading towards other central points in the next group of rocks. One observer may pronounce a doubtful rock to be granite, which another will call a gneiss, without our being able to say that one is right and the other wrong. In cases of this kind there constantly arises the temptation to give new names, but in the interest of science this temptation should be resisted as far as possible.

The following are the general heads under which we have grouped the rocks in this work.

I. IGNEOUS ROCKS* (Eruptive Rocks), all of which are most probably products of igneous fusion.

---

* The term ' IGNEOUS ROCKS ' is used throughout this book as the equivalent of the German ' ERUPTIV-GESTEINE.' The Germans object to the term 'igneous,' as conveying the idea of fire or burning (which could not take place in the absence of air), and also because the metamorphic rocks may have been subjected to heat as well as those we call igneous. Most of our rocks have, however, been named in an imperfect state of knowledge of their origin, and with reference to erroneous ideas; and if we are agreed on the signification of a term, we need not always go back to its derivation. Mr. Jukes objects to the German term ' eruptive,' as applied indiscriminately to these rocks. He thinks that in speaking of the plutonic rocks, we should use the terms, ' irruptive ' or ' intrusive,' &c., as they did not, or are not supposed by us to have reached the surface at the time of their upheaval.

A. Rocks poor in silica, or basic rocks.
(a) *Volcanic.*—Of which the BASALTS are the principal representatives.
(b) *Plutonic.*—Of these the principal representatives are the so-called GREENSTONES (diabase, diorite, &c.).

B. Rocks rich in silica, or acidic rocks.
(a) *Volcanic*, e. g. the TRACHYTES.
(b) *Plutonic*, e. g. the GRANITES.

II. METAMORPHIC CRYSTALLINE SCHISTS.—Most probably the product of the transmutation of sedimentary rocks, but in respect of their mineralogical composition closely allied to the igneous, e. g. GNEISS, MICA-SCHIST, CHLORITE-SCHIST, &c.

III. SEDIMENTARY ROCKS.—The products of deposit.
1. *Argillaceous rocks,* such as CLAY and ARGILLACEOUS SHALE.
2. *Limestone rocks,* such as LIMESTONE and DOLOMITE (including gypsum and anhydrite).
3. *Siliceous rocks,* e. g. SANDSTONES and CONGLOMERATES.
4. *Tufa formations.*
The above are the groups of principal rocks which occur in masses of great extent.

IV. We shall next range those rocks of less frequent occurrence, or which only form subordinate strata or separate beds, and whose origin is in part still doubtful, without attempting in their case a logical classification. To this series belong, for instance, many silicates, the CARBONACEOUS ROCKS, the IRONSTONES, SERPENTINE, &c., and some other rocks of problematical character.

V. Finally we shall instance those rocks which are essentially composed of one mineral, such as QUARTZ, OPAL, &c.
The first book on rocks, at that time a most masterly treatise, was von Leonhard's ' Charakteristik der Felsar-

We have, however, kept to the term *'eruptive'* as a general term for describing the action of all igneous rocks; and any other course would have compelled us to put a construction of our own on the origin of each rock, although not in the mind of our author, and unnecessary for his immediate purpose.—TRANSLATOR.

ten' (1823).   In it is to be found a reprint of Alexander
Brongniart's ' Classification minéralogique des roches
mélangées,' which had appeared in the 34th vol. of the
Journal des Mines.

The following are the most important among the more
recent works on this subject :—

> *Naumann's* Geognosie, vol. i., a second edition of which ap-
> peared in 1858.
> *Senft's* Classification der Felsarten, 1857, in which the rocks
> are arranged with special reference to one or more charac-
> teristic ingredients.
> *Durocher,* Essai de Pétrologie comparée in the Ann. des Mines,
> 1857 ; ii. pp. 217 and 676.   He separates the igneous rocks,
> in the same way that Bunsen did before him, into acidic
> and basic rocks.   He subdivides these again according to the
> degrees of their acidity or basic composition ; these sub-
> divisions nearly correspond with Bunsen's ' Mittelgesteine.'
> *G. Bischof* has examined and pronounced upon a large number
> of rocks from a chemical point of view.   The arrangement
> of the separate treatises in his Lehrbuch der Geologie appears
> to be entirely accidental, and the geological relations of the
> rocks are hardly regarded.*
> *Rammelsberg's* Handwörterbuch der Mineralogie (with sup-
> plements) contains numerous analyses.
> *Roth* has recently attempted to collect all the known analyses
> of rocks and to arrange them according to fixed principles,
> accompanying them with critical remarks.

Having referred the reader to the above-named comprehensive works, we shall abstain from again quoting them
in detail at the mention of each different rock.   In dealing
with the particular views of their several authors we shall
only give the name of the author in question.

On the other hand, we shall have occasion to cite at the
proper places the valuable treatises of Abich, Büntsch,
Bergemann, Blum, Breithaupt, Bunsen, Delesse, Deville,
Ehrenberg, Fischer, Girard, von Hochstetter, Hochmuth,
Jentsch, Knop, List, Naumann, Oppermann, vom Rath,
G. Rose, Freiherr von Richthofen, Scheerer, Söchting,
Stache, Streng, von Walterhausen, &c.

* In the second edition (translated into English) there is much
provement in this respect.

CHAPTER I.

IGNEOUS ROCKS.

WHEN we consider the position and bedding of these rocks, and the disturbances and other changes they have effected in the strata and beds of other rocks, we cannot doubt that they have been forced upwards from the interior of the earth in a fluid or semi-fluid (viscous) state. They have penetrated and overflowed other formations and then become solid, partly in the clefts and partly on the surface of those rocks. The soft state in which they must have existed during their upheaval was in all probability the result of great heat, in other words, it was a state of igneous fusion; hence the term Igneous Rocks. By process of cooling they then passed over into the solid state, assuming (under different circumstances) a crystalline-granular, a porphyritic, a compact or vitreous texture, sometimes vesicular, or sometimes even a fissile texture (schistose or slaty). Amygdaloids and wackés (as we have already seen) were of later origin, i. e. products of transmutation from original formations.

As regards one great division of these rocks, their former state of fusion is capable of direct proof, and may be observed at the present day; we see them in process of formation from the lava of active volcanoes. These are termed *Volcanic Rocks*.

In the case of another class of those which we term Igneous Rocks, their former state of fusion is not so clearly evident; indeed we occasionally find their composition, their bedding, or their relative position with other formations in apparent contradiction to their assumed origin. It is supposed that these became solid at a considerable depth, some of them possibly having been poured out in a state of fusion like lava, but in the interior of the earth without reaching the surface, and consequently that their consolidation took place under very high pressure, and more slowly than in the case of the volcanic rocks. They are therefore termed *Plutonic rocks*, and most geologists are agreed on the nature of their origin. The apparent contradictions to an igneous theory of their formation are to be explained by slow cooling, and the changes produced by time and high pressure.

All igneous rocks consist principally of compounds of some kind of felspar (or leucite and nepheline) with pyroxene, hornblende, mica or quartz, generally also with some magnetic iron-ore and other subordinate minerals.

We divide the igneous rocks, whether volcanic or plutonic, into those poor in silica (*basic*) and those rich in silica (*acidic*).

The first class, the *basic* rocks, are distinguished by their deficiency of quartz; by their felspar being generally poor in silica, and frequently richer in lime than that of the acidic rocks, and being mixed with pyroxene or hornblende; by their texture being frequently vesicular or amygdaloidal, very seldom vitreous; and by their generally prevailing dark colour.

The *acidic* rocks on the other hand are distinguished by a felspar richer in silica; by their frequently containing a large proportion of quartz; by their being rarely vesicular or amygdaloidal, but frequently vitreous; and in general by their lighter colour.

We might add that the *basic* rocks are more frequently compact and porphyritic than distinctly granular; more frequently volcanic than plutonic; more frequently found in small unconnected masses than ranging in great tracts or regions; whereas the *acidic* rocks on the contrary are more frequently distinctly granular and porphyritic than compact; and more frequently extend over vast regions than occur in masses of very circumscribed extent. These data are, however, altogether general in their character, and must be taken with many qualifications.

Bunsen was the first to draw attention to the scientific value of the difference between the basic and acidic rocks, which was previously little known, and had not been carefully investigated. He devoted himself to analysing rock-masses, and from the results of those analyses set up two normal types of composition (see page 364 post). We cannot, however, say that the composition of the individual rocks of each of Bunsen's groups does more than approximately correspond with those normal values. In fact it would be more accurate to describe the individual values as fluctuating between two extremes than approaching any one central type. With this explanation we present the reader with our view of the composition of the two classes of rocks (the basic and acidic) differing somewhat, but not very greatly, from those of Bunsen.

The principal and most important difference between the two groups is that of the quantity of silica, in which respect there really seems to be a kind of leap with most rocks. The basic rocks in general also contain somewhat more lime and magnesia than the acidic.

Average Compositions of the two classes of Igneous Rocks.

	Basic Rocks	Acidic Rocks
Silica	45—55	60—80
Alumina	10—20	8—16
Protoxide } of iron . . Oxide	1—15	1—15
Lime	1—10	1— 5
Magnesia . . .	1— 6	0— 4
Potash	1— 4	1— 6
Soda	1— 5	1— 6
Water	0— 7	0— 8

But the limits which we have above given are sometimes overstepped on each side, and there are igneous rocks which we cannot with mere reference to their chemical composition reckon in either group, and which in fact entirely fill up and annihilate the assumed gap between the two in respect of the content of silica. These rocks of middle character can only be classed with one group or the other by having regard in each case to their geological character or their mineralogical affinities.

If we disregard minor differences, the varieties of igneous rocks are not very numerous; they may be almost reduced to two principal mineral combinations, the other differences consisting chiefly in texture or the presence of accessory or single minerals.

The two principal combinations are as follows :—

(1) Felspar poor in silica (in its stead sometimes nepheline or leucite) combined with pyroxene or hornblende, also mica, magnetic iron-ore, and the like.

K

(2) Felspar rich in silica, combined with quartz, mica, and occasionally amphibole, and the like.

In presenting this broad view, we do not mean to underrate the importance of the minor differences in the igneous rocks. All those differences are the result of varying conditions and circumstances of their original formation, and are therefore deserving of the greatest attention and study.

We will return to this subject in the concluding chapter, and mention some of the theories in respect to the causes of the various development of the different igneous rocks.

BASIC IGNEOUS ROCKS.

These are compounds of felspar (of various species) with augite, pyroxene, hornblende, or dark coloured mica. They frequently also contain magnetic iron-ore, sometimes olivine. In some rocks of this class nepheline or leucite takes the place of the felspar. In most, there is an entire absence of quartz.

Their texture is compact, porphyritic, or crystalline; granular, seldom fissile, more frequently vesicular, or amygdaloidal; they are often found in a wackenitic state (wacké).

According to our arrangement as previously indicated, we divide these rocks into two classes expressive of their origin—viz. the volcanic and the plutonic.

1. Volcanic.

These rocks occur in the form of lava at actual volcanoes of the present day; they are also found in districts where the volcanoes to which they owe their birth have been long extinct. In the latter case they often form isolated conical mountains, or they are found as dykes filling up the rents and fissures of older rocks.

They differ from the plutonic rocks (which have solidified deep down in the earth) by the prevalence of a species of felspar poor in silica, such as labradorite (or in its stead nepheline or leucite); moreover, by the prevalence of augite rather than hornblende; and by the total absence of quartz in their composition. Volcanic rocks also show the traces of their former state of fusion much more distinctly than the plutonic; and they have evidently cooled much more rapidly than them.

All the volcanic rocks hitherto met with are of comparatively recent date, and probably no ancient ones are now existing: for the most part they have decayed away.

BASALTIC ROCKS.

These rocks are mostly compounds of labradorite and augite, with the addition of some magnetic iron-ore. Instead of the labradorite, they sometimes contain oligoclase, nepheline, leucite, or hauyne, and frequently also olivine. In their fresh state they are black or dark-grey.

These rocks have been differently named, partly according to their somewhat varying mineralogical composition, partly in respect of their differing texture. The most usual distinctive designations are the following :—

Dolerite, consisting of labradorite and augite.
Nepheline-dolerite, consisting of nepheline and augite.
Basalt, the same compound in a compact state.
Leucite rock, consisting of leucite and augite.

Besides the above, there occur other, though less frequent combinations, and varieties which have been separately named, or which deserve special notice as frequently recurring. In this category we may place anamesite, tholeite, analcymite, allogovite, hauynophyry.

The basaltic rocks are all much alike in their outward form and bedding. They occur as lava at active or recently extinguished volcanoes. Sometimes they form conical hills, which are to be regarded as the kernels of extinct volcanoes whose outer coating has been washed, or has decayed, away. Again, they frequently form dykes, that is, they fill up clefts in older rocks, but in this case they usually appear to be connected with larger masses of a similar nature from which they have branched out. Where they occur as actual lava we usually find vesicular or scoriaceous varieties and tufa formations of corresponding composition; but not the vitreous state. There can be no doubt that all these rocks are cooled products of igneous fusion, and that the process of their formation is continued at the present day. The proof of this even in the case of the older ones may be found in the effect which they have often produced upon other rocks with which they came into contact while in a state of fusion. Those rocks frequently exhibit transmutations, for which the simplest or only explanation is the effect of heat; such as local vitrefaction, change of their state of oxidation; expulsion of their bitumen, or carbonic acid, change of their texture, or obliteration of their jointed structure. Sometimes also, but less frequently, the stratification of older rocks has been disturbed to a remarkable extent by the eruption of basaltic rocks. Again, the latter very often contain, near their margin, fragments of the rocks which they have broken through, and breccias have been formed in this way.

The basaltic rocks, as purely volcanic, chiefly belong to the most recent geological period. They are nevertheless found in many districts whose former volcanic activity has long since ceased, and where their bedding shows that they are older than some tertiary formations. The original surface of these older basaltic rocks is usually partly or entirely decomposed and washed away, and they partake somewhat of the nature of plutonic rocks, especially resembling certain greenstones of analogous mineral character, and actually forming transitions into the latter from the more genuine basaltic rocks. They appear to have undergone many changes of state through the influence of time and position. Their vesicular cavities have become filled with new mineral substances (amygdaloids), internal decomposition or transmutations have taken place, carbonates, zeolites, and other hydrous minerals (formerly absent) have been formed, and are now intimately blended with, and actually form part of their composition; or else their original fresh condition has become wackenitic. Hence we find that no sharp defining boundary exists between the volcanic and the plutonic rocks. It nevertheless is not a little remarkable that we do not know any rocks of undoubted basaltic character older than tertiary.* The case is the same with the trachytes and other volcanic rocks, and, generally speaking, we find that all the older igneous formations differ materially from the more recent, and more still from the most recent. This fact deserves attention, and seems to require more explanation than it has hitherto received, since we are authorised on other grounds to conclude that

---

* Mr. Jukes believes the Rowley Rag basalt of the South Stafford-shire coalfield to be of Palæozoic age (*Geol. S. Staff. Coalfield, Geol. Survey*).—TRANSLATOR.

volcanic agency has been at work in all periods of the earth's history, much in the same way as at the present time, and has always brought forth like products. What has become of those older products corresponding to the lavas and basalts of the present age? Doubtless a great part may have perished from long exposure to the destroying influence of the atmosphere, or if more deeply buried, has suffered internal change; nevertheless it was to have been expected that here and there (in old conglomerates for instance) we should have discovered some blocks and boulders at least of genuine basalt. Strange to say, none have yet been found, at all events none whose character has been proved with certainty. We are aware that in England some basaltic and phonolitic boulders are said to have been found in Devonian strata, but these statements seem to require further confirmation.*

1. DOLERITE and ANAMESITE.—Mimesite, Nepheline-Dolerite, Trap in part.

DOLERIT und ANAMESIT.—Mimesit, Basaltischer Grünstein, Grünstein, Nephelin-Dolerit. (*Germ.*)
DOLÉRITE, *Haüy*. (*Fr.*)

A crystalline-granular compound of labradorite and augite with some titaniferous magnetic iron-ore. In nepheline-dolerite, nepheline is a substitute for the labradorite.

Spec. grav. . . . . 2·7—2·9
Contains silica . . . . . 42—57 p. c.

The name of Dolerite was given to this rock by Haüy. It is rarely sufficiently coarse-grained to allow of its individual mineral constituents being readily distinguished, but more usually it forms a fine-grained dark grey to black mass, in which we are unable to distinguish

---

* In describing some of the igneous rocks interstratified with the Lower Silurian rocks of Ireland, Mr. Jukes mentions the occurrence of associated beds of conglomerate containing pebbles of vesicular trap, derived probably from the upper surface of the old lava flows (*Student's Manual*, 2nd Edit. p. 82). Some of the traps interstratified with the Carboniferous Limestone of Co. Limerick have the vesicular and quasi-scoriaceous parts of their upper and under surfaces preserved. A similar fact is described by Mr. Geikie in his paper on the trap rocks of Scotland (see *Trans. R. Soc. Edin.* vol. xxii. part 3, p. 641).— TRANSLATOR.

between the labradorite and augite. This fine-grained variety has been specially named by von Leonhard as *Anamesite*.

If the compound is *distinct*, then the labradorite appears in the form of white or light-grey tabular crystals, the augite in black columnar ones. But in such case there is usually also a compact matrix in which the more distinct particles are imbedded. This matrix is a compound of the same ingredients—viz. labradorite and augite, usually with the addition of magnetic iron-ore, and some carbonate of protoxide of iron and carbonate of lime, and is so compact that its several components cannot be recognised with the eye, except that the magnetic iron-ore sometimes appears in distinct octahedrons.

The presence of the carbonates of protoxide of iron and of lime of which we have spoken was first demonstrated by Bergemann, as well as that of a certain silicate of alumina and soda, whose character he could not definitely determine. He showed that almost every dolerite contains one part capable of being decomposed by, and another part which resists the influence of muriatic acid. The first part consists of the carbonates, the magnetic iron-ore, and the undetermined silicate. The latter part consists of augite, and probably also some labradorite, inasmuch as the different kinds of labradorite comport themselves very variously in the presence of muriatic acid, and there is also a material difference according to whether it be heated or not. Most kinds of dolerite contain from 1 to 2 per cent. of water, but this Bergemann regards as accidental, and as not having formed part of the original composition of the rock.

Bergemann made a series of analyses to test the comparative character of two kinds of dolerite, the one at the Meissner Mountain in Hessen, and the other at the Aulgasse in Siegburg in Westphalia, with the following result:—

	Meissner		Aulgasse
Labradorite	47·91	. .	30·06
Augite	9·27	. .	35·43
Magnetic iron-ore	8·97	. .	3·61
Silicate (problematical)	22·21	. .	2·71
Carbonates	11·29	. .	27·75

We thus find two perfectly characteristic varieties of

dolerite differing very widely in their mineralogical composition. In other varieties, in spite of outward uniformity of appearance, other and even greater differences, both of mineral and chemical character, constantly occur.

Besides the above-named more or less essential ingredients of dolerite, it contains a considerable number of accessory ingredients, many of which are only locally found, or in very subordinate quantity. Such, for instance, are nepheline, sodalite, melanite, mica, bronzite, hornblende, olivine, titaniferous iron-ore, and specular iron. In fissures and vesicular cavities there also occur zeolites of various kinds, and distinctly crystallised sparry carbonates.

In some varieties, the proportion of nepheline is very considerable, supplanting the labradorite, and so forming transitions into nepheline-dolerite. Becoming more compact in other varieties, dolerite passes over into basalt, and the different stages of compactness of texture may be typified by the three names of Dolerite, Anamesite, Basalt.

Varieties in Texture.

(a) COMMON DOLERITE.
GEMEINER DOLERIT. (Germ.)
DOLÉRITE LITHOÏDE. (Fr.)
In which the principal ingredients are distinctly visible—Klein-Priesen, near Tetschen, Bohemia.

(b) ANAMESITE.
ANAMESIT, Von Leonhard. (Germ.)
ANAMÉSITE. (Fr.)
Fine-grained, the principal ingredients only barely visible, Steinheim, near Hanau.

(c) PORPHYRITIC DOLERITE.
PORPHYRARTIGER DOLERIT. (Germ.)
DOLÉRITE PORPHYROÏDE. (Fr.)
With crystals of labradorite or augite, rather rare.

(d) VESICULAR or SCORIACEOUS DOLERITE.
BLASIGER (or SCHLACKIGER) DOLERIT. (Germ.)
This texture only occurs in the fine-grained varieties (anamesite); frequent at volcanoes—Steinheim, near Hanau.

(e) AMYGDALOIDAL DOLERITE.
MANDELSTEINARTIGER DOLERIT. (Germ.)
AMYGDALOÏDE, Brongniart. (Fr.)
With filled-up cavities. This variety is rather more rare.

(f) DOLERITE-WACKÉ.
DOLERIT WACKE. (Germ.)
WACKE DOLÉRITIQUE. (Fr.)
Can in general only be recognised as belonging to dolerite by tracing the sequence of transition states, or by its immediate juxtaposition in nature with fresh dolerite.

Variety in Composition.

(g) NEPHELINE-DOLERITE.
NEPHELIN-DOLERIT, Von Leonhard. (Germ.)
NÉPHÉLINITE. (Fr.)
A crystalline granular compound of nepheline and augite with titaniferous magnetic iron-ore.

Spec. grav. . . . . 2·2—2·6
Contains silica . . . 41—51 p. c.

This rock, formerly taken for common dolerite, was first separately described and named by v. Leonhard. It is a dolerite in which nepheline takes the place of labradorite. As accessories we find it to contain thin acicular crystals of apatite, some sanidine, olivine, and titanite. In becoming compact it passes into nepheline-basalt, which is hardly to be distinguished from common basalt.

Subvarieties of Texture.

(a) *Porphyritic Nepheline-dolerite*, the porphyritic texture being created by crystals of nepheline. Katzenbuckel in the Odenwald.

(β) *Vesicular* and *amygdaloidal* and *wackenitic* varieties occur; as also fine-grained ones, answering to anamesite, e.g. in the Löbauer mountains.

Perhaps much of what has hitherto been called dolerite is more properly nepheline-dolerite. The rock is now very distinctly recognisable, e.g. near Meiches in Hessen, at the Löbauer Berg in Upper Lausitz and near Tichlowitz on the Elbe in Bohemia.

Dolerite is found irregularly massive, or of columnar, tabular, or globular jointed structure. It forms lava streams, isolated cones, and veins in other rocks. This rock is so frequent in all countries, especially in volcanic districts, that particular localities need not be further enumerated. We will only add that the doleritic trachytes of G. Rose, which are mentioned in the fourth volume of his ' Kosmos,' as occurring at Etna, Stromboli, &c., appear to be dolerites rather than trachytes.

References.

v. Leonhard, Basaltgebilde, 1832, vol. i. Nepheline in Dolerite, 1822.
Bunsen in Poggendorf's Annalen, vol. lxxxiii. p. 197.
Abich, Vulkanische Erscheinungen, 1841, p. 74.
Bergemann in Karsten's Archiv. 1847, vol. xxi. p. 1 and 41.
Heusser in Poggend. Annalen, 1852, vol. xxxv. p. 299.
G. Rose, On Dolerite, in Neumann's Zeitsch. f. Erdkunde, 1859, vol. vii. p. 265.
Delesse in Ann. des Mines, 1858 [5], vol. xiii. p. 369.
Durocher in Ann. des Mines, 1841 [3], vol. xix. p. 559.'
Hartung, Die Azoren, 1860, p. 97.
v. Rath in the Zeitschr. der deutsch geol. Ges. 1860, vol. xii. p. 40.
Zirkel in the Zeitschr. der deutsch geol. Ges. 1859, vol. xi. p. 530, on Nepheline-Dolerite.
Gumprecht in Poggend. Ann. vol. xlii. p. 177.

G. Rose in Karsten's Archiv. 1840, vol. xiv. p. 261.
Schill in v. L. and Br. Jahrbuch, 1857, p. 43.
Löwe in Poggend. Annalen, 1836, vol. xxxviii. p. 158.
Girard in Poggend. Annalen, 1841, vol. liv. p. 550.
Heideprim in d. Zeitschr. d. d. geol. Ges. 1850, p. 149.
Hesse in Journ. f. prakt. Chem. 1858, vol. lxxv. p. 216.
Mitscherlich, Basalt u. Nephelindolorit am Rhein. Zeitsch. d.
   deutschen geol. Gesellsch. 1863, p. 372.
Otto Prölss, Analysen einiger Dolerite von Tava. Neues Jahrb.
   f. Miner. 1864, p. 426.
v. Rath, Dolerite der Enganeen. Zeitschr. d. deutsch. geolog.
   Gesellsch. 1864, p. 496.
A. Knop, Nephelindolerit von Meiches. Neues Jahrb. f.
   Mineralogie, 1865, pp. 674 and 682.

Appendix.

THOLEITE. Steininger has given the name of Tholeite to a rock
   found at the Schaumberg near Tholei, which he took for a
   compound of albite and titanite. But according to Bergemann's analysis this rock consists of 70 labradorite, 5 augite,
   3 magnetic iron-ore, 11 of undetermined silicate, and 9 of
   carbonate of lime and protoxide of iron. It must therefore from
   its composition be considered a dolerite or basalt unless indeed
   it be considered as plutonic and classed with melaphyre.

ANALCYMITE.   ⎫ Bergemann in Karsten's Archiv. 1847,
   CYCLOPHYRE, *Élie de Beau-* ⎬ vol. xxi. pp. 4, 12. Gemellaro has given
   mont. (*Fr.*)   ⎭ the name of Analcymite to a rock found
   in the Cyclades which appears originally to have been a dolerite
   containing nepheline, but two-thirds of its mass now consist of
   analcime, although the latter chiefly fills clefts and cavities.

   We may here also mention two kinds of volcanic rock which
   might collectively be called

OLIGOCLASE-DOLERITE. We refer to the ANDESITE of L. v. Buch,
   and the TRACHYDOLERITE of Abich.

   Both are compounds of oligoclase, augite, hornblende, magnetic iron and some mica, the latter generally of dark colour.
   But as their silica contents often exceed 60 per cent., and as
   they are frequently found in vitreous state but of trachytic appearance, we have arranged them according to universal custom
   amongst the trachytes; but no doubt they stand on the
   boundary between the trachytic and basaltic rocks, and may be
   considered as transition states between the two.

2. BASALT.—Nepheline Basalt, Trap in part.

BASALT. (*Germ.*)
BASALTE. (*Fr.*)

*A compact rock, nearly or quite black, with dull con-
choidal fracture; an apparently homogeneous compound, of which the essentials are labradorite (or
nepheline), augite, and magnetic iron-ore, frequently*

united with carbonates and zeolitic substances. In the compact mass there often occur prominently distinct grains or even crystals of olivine, labradorite, augite, and magnetic iron-ore.

Spec. grav. . . . . 2·0—3·1
Contains silica . . . . . 40—56 p.c.

The mineral ingredients of basalt are too small and intimately blended to be separately recognised with the naked eye; formerly it was taken to be a simple mineral substance, but it is now shown to be only the compact state of dolerite or nepheline-dolerite. We must, however, observe that olivine and magnetic iron-ore is of much more frequent occurrence in basalt than in the two last-named rocks.

Cordier was the first who, by means of microscopic examination, thought he recognised in basalt a similar composition to dolerite. Hessel confirmed this view by deduction from analysis, and many instances of the gradual transition from basalt into dolerite also coincided. But that basalt was in fact a compound of the above-named minerals was afterwards established beyond doubt by the more accurate analyses of Gmelin, Löwe, Girard, v. Bibra, Gräger, Sinding, Petersen, Ebelmen, Baumann, Rammelsberg, Schmid, and Bergemann.

Gmelin first found that a portion of the mass of basalt was soluble in muriatic acid, and another portion not. The insoluble part he considered must be chiefly augite and olivine, perhaps also labradorite; the soluble part, magnetic iron-ore, a sparry carbonate and zeolitic substance (and sometimes nepheline). The proportion between the two parts (as in the case of dolerite) is very different in different kinds of basalt. The quantity of the soluble portion fluctuates between 36 and 88 per cent. The proportion of the individual mineral constituents, and also that of the elementary ingredients, appear to be equally variable.

Like dolerite, basalt very often contains some carbonate of iron, calcspar, and zeolitic substance (probably arisen from decomposition, and of later date than the rock itself) and some kinds of basalt likewise contain nepheline instead of labradorite. Girard first discovered this composition in the basalt of Wickenstein in Silesia. It is not easy from outward characteristics alone to distinguish

the nepheline-basalt from the ordinary species, unless we
are assisted by finding a transition into a distinct nepheline-dolerite, as is the case, for instance, at the Löbauer
Berg. For this reason it is hardly practicable for the
geologist to separate nepheline-basalt from labradorite-
basalt as a distinct rock, although the difference between
them, in a purely mineralogical point of view, is of more
importance than that between dolerite and basalt, which
are only varieties of texture of the same mass.

Besides the more or less essential ingredients of basalt
(to which we therefore reckon nepheline), other minerals
also very often occur as accessories porphyritically disseminated through the mass. Thus, for instance, basaltic
hornblende, oligoclase, dark brown mica, rubellan, zircon,
(hyacinth), sapphire, apatite, garnet, bronzite, micaceous
iron, titaniferous iron-ore, pyrites, &c. These minerals
may, in consequence of special local circumstances, have
either developed themselves into crystals during the
original cooling of the rocks, or (such as pyrites and
micaceous iron) they may have arisen from later processes
of transmutation. Similar internal transmutations aided
by gases or water have most probably produced the carbonates, zeolites, and water concealed in the compound.
The same influences have, doubtless, also produced the
minerals which have arisen in the vesicular cavities and
narrow fissures of the rock, such as hyalite, chalcedony,
zeolites, sparry carbonates, glauconite, &c.

The essential texture of basalt is compact; if it becomes
crystalline-granular it passes into anamesite and dolerite.
But we frequently find porphyritically disseminated in
the compact base, numerous single crystals or crystalline
grains of augite, hornblende, olivine, magnetic iron-ore, and
the like, or the rock is penetrated with vesicular cavities,
and these are filled with those newer mineral formations of
which we have already spoken. There also often appears
a kind of round-grained or spotted conformation which
seems to be the result of decomposition.

Varieties in Texture.

(*a*) COMMON COMPACT BASALT.
  GEMEINER DICHTER BASALT. | Very frequent, *e.g.*, at Schlossberg,
  (*Germ.*) | near Stolpen, Saxony.
  BASALTE LITHOÏDE. (*Fr.*)

(*b*) PORPHYRITIC BASALT, or BASALTIC PORPHYRY. } Also frequent—Leschtina, near Tetschen, in Bohemia.
BASALTE PORPHYROÏDE. (*Fr.*)
PORPHYRARTIGER BASALT. (*Germ.*)

(*c*) VESICULAR or SCORIACEOUS BASALT. } Often called, *par excellence*, Basaltic Lava, as
SCORIES BASALTIQUES. (*Fr.*)
BLASIGER ODER SCHLACKIGER BASALT. (*Germ.*) this is usually vesicular at the surface—Kammerbühl and Wolfsberg, in Bohemia.

(*d*) AMYGDALOIDAL BASALT, or BASALTIC AMYGDALOID. } Never of recent origin—Schlachenwerth, near Carlsbad.
BASALTE AMYGDALOÏDE. (*Fr.*)
MANDELSTEINARTIGER BASALT. (*Germ.*)

(*e*) SPOTTED AND GRANULAR BASALT (RESEMBLING DOLERITE). } Usually has dark grains in lighter green mass. It is a stage of decomposition. E.g. between Arnsdorf and
KORNIGFLECKIGER ODER DOLERITÄHNLICHER BASALT. (*Germ.*)
Steinschönau, in Bohemia, as Stoppels Kuppe, near Eisenach.

(*f*) BASALT-WACKÉ. } (Werner's Eisenthon) a dark brown or grey, almost earthy mass, in which
WACKE BASALTIQUE. (*Fr.*)
BASALT-WACKE. (*Germ.*) sometimes the textures (*a*) (*b*) (*c*) and (*d*) are distinctly repeated. Pascepole, near Teplitz.

Sometimes, but quite exceptionally, a vitreous state also occurs, which Breithaupt has named Trachylyt, as a separate mineral formation. It is found, e.g. near Dransfeld, in the Vogelsgeberg and skirting basalt-veins in Iceland.

Here may be also fitly mentioned a number of varieties of composition, some of which, if they were always distinguishable, might even be separately classed as distinct rocks.

Varieties in Composition.

(*g*) COMMON (or LABRADORITE) BASALT. } Consisting of labradorite, augite, magnetic iron-
LABRADOR BASALT. (*Germ.*)
ore, and usually also some olivine.

(*h*) NEPHELINE-BASALT. } In which nepheline is substituted for labradorite; according to Girard, it shows traces of a resinous lustre, and thereby differs somewhat from ordinary basalt. But
NEPHELIN-BASALT. (*Germ.*)
BASALTE AVEC NÉPHÉLINE. (*Fr.*)
there must be intermediate gradations or transitions between the two which cannot be distinguished as separate varieties.

(*i*) HAUYNOPHYRY. } Is the name given by Rammelsberg to a rock from Vulture, near Melfi, not far from Naples, which essentially consists of augite and haüyne, with
HAUYNOPHYR, *Rammelsberg.* (*Germ.*)
HAUYNOPHYRE. (*Fr.*)
some olivine, mica, and leucite, in which also the haüyne appears to be the substitute for the labradorite of basalt or dolerite. The simultaneous occurrence of leucite, however, causes it to resemble leucite rock.

The basaltic lava of Niedermendig on the Rhine contains a considerable quantity of haüyne distinctly prominent, but it has been conjectured that this rock according to its composition should belong to the nepheline-basalt.   On account of its vesicular conformation it is well adapted for millstones.

(k) ALLOGOVITE.   ⎱ Is the name given by Winkler to certain
    ALLOGOVIT, *Winkler.* ⎰ dark grey or reddish rocks of the Allgau,
    (*Germ.*)   which according to him are formed of an
intimately blended compound of labradorite with the basalts, although their colour is somewhat different.   This may, however, be the consequence of a slight difference in composition or an incipient decomposition.

Regular jointed structure is very frequent in basalt, usually columnar, sometimes however tabular or spherical, with concentric layers spheroidal, or even irregularly massive.   It forms streams of lava and layers in the basaltic tufa.   It is very characteristically and variously developed in the Bohemian Mittelgebirge; in the columnar form it may be seen with great regularity and beauty at the Giant's Causeway in Ireland, at Staffa, &c. ; but these approach dolerite in their character, and may be more accurately described as transition states between that rock and basalt.

References.

v. Leonhard, Basaltgebilde, 1832, vol. i.
A. Madelung, Metamorphosen von Basalt und Chrysolith. Jahrb. der geol. Reichsanst. 1864, vol. xiv. p. 1.
Abich, Vulkanische Bildungen, 1841.
Bergemann, Analysen in Karsten's Archiv. vol. xxi. p. 88, 1847.
Sartorius v. Waltershausen, Physik. geogr. Skizze v. Island, p. 64.
Schmid, Analysen in der Zeitschrift d. d. geol. Gesellsch. vol. v. p. 230, 1853; and Poggend. Annalen, vol. xcix. p. 291, 1853.
Rammelsberg in der Zeitschrift d. d. geol. Ges. p. 493, 1859; p. 273, 1860; p. 4, 1861, über Hauynophyr.
Schill in v. Leonhard u. Br. Jahrb., p. 44, 1857 (Hegau), and in G. Leonhard's Beitr. z. miner. Kenntn. von Baden, No. 3, p. 43, 1854 (Kaiserstuhl).
Hartung, Die Azoren, p. 97, 1860.
Girard, Ueber Nephelinbasalt in Poggend. Annalen, vol. liv. p. 562, 1841.

3. LEUCITE ROCK.—Leucite - Porphyry, Leucito-
        phyry, Leucilite, Sperone.
LEUCITFELS. (*Germ.*)
LEUCITOPHYRE, *Coquand.* (*Fr.*)

A more or less distinct compound of leucite and augite, with some magnetic iron-ore—porphyritic or compact.

Spec. grav. .   .   .   .   .   2·5—2·9
Contains silica. .   .   .   .   .   45—54 p. c.

Leucite rock may be regarded as a dolerite, in which the labradorite is replaced by leucite. This difference of composition is also usually accompanied by other differences easily to be recognised. The colour of the compact mass or matrix of the rock is more grey or reddish-grey than either dolerite or basalt, and, moreover, the characteristic crystals of leucite are frequently to be found distinctly and prominently developed. It is a distinguishing feature of this mineral in general, that it rarely occurs otherwise than porphyritically imbedded, and not clustered in geodes. Sometimes distinct crystals of augite lie near the leucite in the compact matrix. As accessories leucite rock also contains the following minerals: dark magnesia-mica, sodalite, sanidine, labradorite, nepheline, olivine, haüyne, garnet, and traces of apatite. Zeolites also very frequently occur in the clefts or vesicular cavities of this rock.

Where the proportion of nepheline is greater, a transition takes place into nepheline-dolerite or nepheline-basalt.

Varieties in Texture.

(a) PORPHYRITIC LEUCITE, LEUCITOPHYRY.
LEUCITOPHYRE PORPHYROÏDE. (Fr.)

(b) COMPACT LEUCITE.
LEUCITOPHYRE LITHOÏDE. (Fr.)

(c) VESICULAR or LEUCITE-LAVA.
LEUCITOPHYRE VACUOLAIRE. (Fr.)

(d) AMYGDALOID.
AMYGDALOÏDE. (Fr.)

Leucite rock forms old and recent lavas, e.g. at Monte Somma and at Vesuvius (eruptions of 1828 and 1832); it also occurs at volcanoes long extinct, for instance at Roccamonfina, in the Albanian Mountains, at Rieden, and at Bell near Andernach. Not long since, a leucite-porphyry was discovered at Böhmisch-Wiesenthal, on the highest ridge of the Erzgebirge, with decomposed wackenitic matrix, and crystals of leucite, more than an inch in length, but for the most part changed into orthoclase (or kalioligoclase). This last named occurrence involuntarily suggests the question whether the felspar of many older rocks may not originally have been leucite, whose form has become indistinct or entirely altered so as to be no longer recognised. It certainly is somewhat remarkable that hitherto no ancient leucite rock has been found.

Appendix.

Nosean-Melanite Rock is the name recently given by vom Rath to a rock consisting of a fine-grained compound of nosean, vitreous felspar, and melanite, with some hornblende, augite, and titaniferous iron-ore. Zeitsch. der deutsch. geol. Ges. p. 655, 1862.

Von Fritsch uses the common name of Tephrite to include leucitophyry, hauynophyry, and nepheline rock. Neues Jahrb. f. Mineral. 1865, p. 663.

Dunite is the name given by von Hochstetter to a granular rock which occurs in New Zealand, consisting almost exclusively of olivine. Zeitschr. d. deut. geol. Ges. 1864, p. 341. Sandberger has described a similar rock as occurring in the Tringstein in Nassau. Neues Jahrb. f. Mineral. 1865, p. 449.

References.

Deville in the Bullet. de la Soc. d. Fr. [2] vol. xii. p. 612, 1856.
Dufrenoy, Mem. p. s. à un déscr. géol. d. Fr. vol. iv. p. 308. Compt. rend. vol. xxi. p. 326, 1845.
Wedding in d. Zeitschr. d. d. geol. Ges. vol. x. p. 395, 1858.
v. Rath in d. Zeitschr. d. d. geol. Ges. vol. xii. p. 37 (Zittau), 1860.   Leucitophyr von Rieden : Zeitschr. d. deutschen geol. Gesellsch. 1864, p. 73.
Naumann in v. L. und Br. Jahrbuch, p. 61, 1860 ; p. 59, 1861 (Wiesenthal).
Rammelsberg in d. Zeitschr. d. d. geol. Ges. vol. xi. p. 493, 1859 ; vol. xiii. p. 96, 1861 (Vesuv. and Wiesenthal).

2. Plutonic.

These rocks are compounds of various felspars with pyroxene, hornblende or mica. Besides these essential ingredients they frequently contain some chlorite, nepheline and magnetic iron-ore, quartz only exceptionally; the greater number are free from quartz. Mineralogically as well as chemically, therefore, the composition of these rocks is very similar to that of the basaltic rocks. The chief differences consist in the greater frequency of hornblende as an essential ingredient, and the frequent occurrence of chlorite and the more rare occurrence of quartz as accessories ; and in the development of slaty or schistose texture in many of these plutonic rocks.

All these differences may be accounted for by the greater depth at which these rocks probably attained the solid state, and by their having remained a longer time under the pressure of superincumbent masses. The same causes may have given rise to many transmutations or new formations, such for instance as the formation of chlorite, a characteristic (if not altogether essential) ingredient of the augitic greenstones, and to which they chiefly owe their green colour, and which also usually serves to distinguish them from the basalts.

We divide the plutonic basic rocks into GREENSTONES, MELAPHYRES, PORPHYRITES, MICA-TRAPS and SYENITES. Some of these, however, approach the acidic rocks in the proportion of silica which they contain.

GREENSTONES—(trap in part).

These rocks are compounds of some species of felspar with pyroxene or hornblende as essential ingredients; their prevailing dark green colour they apparently owe partly to hornblende and partly to a small admixture of chlorite.

They are usually divided according to their mineral character into three classes, under the following heads:—

Diabase, consisting of felspar and hypersthene or augite and chlorite.

Gabbro, consisting of felspar and pyroxene.

Diorite, consisting of felspar and hornblende.

Besides these principal divisions, there are several subordinate varieties of composition which have distinguishing names, such as Calc-diabase, Eukrite, Teschinite, Augite-rock, Malakolite-rock, Euphodite, Norite, Hypersthenite, Timazite, Calc-diorite, and Anorthite-diorite. Aphanite is the compact state of greenstone rock in which the several ingredients are not to be distinguished with certainty; and if the compact aphanitic mass contain distinct individual grains or crystals porphyritically disseminated through it, then we employ the names of Calc-aphanite, Labradorite-porphyry, Oligoclase-porphyry, Augite-porphyry, and Uralite-porphyry, for the different varieties.

Greenstones of all kinds occur frequently in subordinate masses, dykes, or stratified veins in the schists or slates of the grey-wacké or transition period, and even alternating with tuff-formations of the same period which contain characteristic fossils, so that we may conclude that many greenstones were contemporaneous with those formations. This association with the transition-forma-

L

tions may be observed in the Voigtland, Fichtelgebirge,
Hartz, and the Rhine district, also in the Silurian district
of Bohemia, in Germany, and many other parts of the
world.   Greenstones are likewise met with which have
broken through and penetrated much more recent formations; the timazite of Hungary and Transylvania for
instance is found to have even penetrated sandstones of
the tertiary period.   But the most recent tertiary formations are nowhere found to have been broken through
by genuine greenstones, although very frequently by
basaltic rocks.   Greenstones are never found in the form
of genuine lava, but always more or less show their
plutonic origin, in which probably consists the whole
difference (not very considerable after all) between them
and the basalts.   It is very possible that the same basic
compound which, consolidating near the surface, has produced the basaltic rocks, when it attained the solid state
at a greater depth formed the greenstones, whose pyroxene and hornblende may have been partly an original
product and partly produced by subsequent transmutation. The basalts and greenstones in general very much
resemble each other both in chemical composition and
mineral character.   The chlorite, by which some of the
augitic greenstones are alone distinguishable from the
basalts, is most usually a product of transmutation.

4. DIABASE.—Hyperite, Scandinavian Trap.

DIABAS. (*Germ.*)
DIABASE, *Brongniart.* (*Fr.*)

*A crystalline-granular compound of oligoclase, labra-
dorite, albite, or anorthite, with pyroxene and some
chlorite—in its fresh state dark green.*

Spec.grav. . . . . . .   2·7—2·9
Contains silica . . . . .   43—56 p. c.

Diabase was first raised to the rank of a separate rock,
and distinguished from other greenstones, by Hausmann.
It is often very fine-grained, and in that case it becomes difficult to determine the species of the felspar or
of the pyroxene, or to recognise the chlorite as such.
The felspar seems in most cases to be a white or greyish-
green, oligoclase or labradorite. The pyroxene is most generally hypersthene, but sometimes common augite. The
green colour of the rock is chiefly owing to its chlorite,

the quantity of which is however small. As accessories the following minerals very frequently occur : magnetic iron-ore, magnetic pyrites, pyrites, sometimes also some chalcopyrite (copper pyrites).

As accessory accompaniments (in clefts, veins, nests and vesicular cavities) are found quartz, actinolite, asbestus, cat's-eye, pistacite, prehnite, axinite, calcspar, brownspar (dolomite), talcspar (magnesite), &c.

The prevailing texture of diabase is fine-grained ; it passes over into the compact (aphanite) ; it is also sometimes porphyritic, slaty, variolitic or amygdaloidal.

Diabase bears a strong relationship to dolerite, the most marked feature of its difference from the latter is its chlorite and its consequent green colour. If this chlorite be a product of transmutation, then all the original difference between diabase and dolerite probably consists in the level or depth of solidification.

The vesicular cavities of diabase (where they occur) are almost always filled up (amygdaloids), and this circumstance may be explained by the rock having long lain in the interior of the earth under modifying hydroplutonic influences.

Varieties in Texture.

(a) GRANULAR DIABASE.
KÖRNIGER DIABAR. (*Germ.*)
DIABASE GRANITOÏDE. (*Fr.*)
Frequent near Berneck, Saalburg, both in the Fichtelgebirge, &c.

(b) FINE-GRAINED (TO COMPACT) DIABASE.
FEINKÖRNIGER BIS DICHTER DIABAS. (*Germ.*)
DIABASE LITHOÏDE. (*Fr.*)
Merging into aphanite, generally occurs with (a).

(c) PORPHYRITIC DIABASE.
PORPHYRARTIGER DIABAR.(*Germ.*)
DIABASE PORPHYROÏDE. (*Fr.*)
In fine-grained base, crystals of labradorite, oligoclase, pyroxene, or uralite appear. If the matrix is compact, then these varieties are also sometimes designated labrador-porphyry, augite-porphyry, or uralite-porphyry (compare with aphanite, post, p. 157).

(d) SCHISTOSE DIABASE, or DIABASE-SCHIST.
DIABAS-SCHIEFER. (*Germ.*)
SCHISTE DIABASIQUE. (*Fr.*)
Indistinctly foliated, going over into aphanite-schist: occurs together with (a) and (b).

(e) AMYGDALOIDAL DIABASE, or DIABASE AMYGDALOID.
DIABAS-MANDELSTEIN. (*Germ.*)
AMYGDALOÏDE. (*Fr.*)
The vesicular cavities are filled with calcspar, chlorite, glauconite, chalcedony and the like. Berneck in Fichtelgebirge.

(f) VARIOLITIC DIABASE (VARIOLITE in part).
VARIOLITISCHER DIABAS. (*Germ.*)
DIABASE VARIOLITIQUE. (*Fr.*)
In the principal mass round concretions occur of a compact or radial-fibrous or concentric felsite (labradorite),

very characteristic near Berneck, where the small felsitic globules have a violet-coloured nucleus and a white ring.

(*g*) WACKENITIC DIABASE, or } Decomposed, discoloured, earthy,
DIABASE WACKÉ.   and can only be determined to be
DIABAS-WACKE. (*Germ.*)   such by its juxtaposition with other
WACKE DIABASIQUE. (*Fr.*)   diabase.

The following rocks are varieties of diabase in respect
of their composition, or are to be classed under the head
of diabase on account of their close approximation.

Varieties in Composition.

(*h*) COMMON DIABASE.

(*i*) CALCAREOUS DIABASE. } In the fine-grained or compact matrix
KALKDIABAS. (*Germ.*)   of diabase rock are found small rounded
DIABASECALCAIRE. (*Fr.*)   grains of calcspar which do not appear
to be the fillings-up of cavities. This somewhat problematical variety has been called calc-trap by Oppermann. By
others it has been called blatterstein, calc-aphanite, diabase,
and amygdaloid, and if somewhat slaty, schalstein. (Loben-
stein in the Fichtelgebirge.)

(*k*) EUKRITE.   } A crystalline-granular compound of anor-
EUKRIT. (*Germ.*)   thite and augite, occasionally with some
olivine, hornblende, and epidote. The latter appears to have
arisen from decomposition.

This rock, according to its mineralogical composition, would
almost appear to be better classed with dolerite than diabase,
but according to Tschermark and Krafft, its geological character is plutonic.

It appears at Gumbelburg near Neutschin in Moravia. Some
meteorites have precisely the same composition.

(*l*) TESCHINITE.   } Is the name given by Hohenegger to a
TESCHINIT, *Hohenegger.*   rock whose mass is chiefly felsitic, and
(*Germ.*)   in which hypersthene forms long black
needles; it sometimes also contains fine needles of apatite.
This rock has broken through chalk formations and even
eocene strata in the neighbourhood of Tetschen, where it sometimes forms irregular masses, sometimes veins. According to
von Hochstetter, hornblende and augite form part of its components, also sometimes augite and labradorite with subordinate admixtures of iron pyrites, magnetic iron-ore, mica, and
chlorite. These therefore are compounds which might partly
be classed with the diorites and partly with diabase, hypersthenite, or even dolerite.

More by way of appendix than as properly inclusive in
this class, we here add :—

(*m*) AUGITE ROCK (LHERZOLITE). } A granular to compact ag-
AUGITFELS, LHERZOLITH. (*Germ.*) gregate, chiefly consisting of
LHERZOLITE. (*Fr.*)   augite, dark-green, brown, or
grey; as accessory components it contains some talc, steatite,

schorl, hornblende, or calcspar. This rock can only be said to be allied to diabase; it forms subordinate masses at the Lake Lherz, near Vicdessos in the Pyrenees. [According to *Damour*, however, this rock of the Lherz is not thus composed, but consists of olivine, eustatite, and diopside. See Neues Jahrb. f. Mineral. 1863, p. 95.]

(*n*) MALAKOLITE. } Found in granular limestone near
MALAKOLITHFELS. (*Germ.*) } Rocklitz at the foot of the Rie-
PYROXÉNITE, *Coquand.* (*Fr.*) } sengebirge, where, according to
Herter and Porth, it forms subordinate masses, containing copper-ore and consisting essentially of compact salite (malakolite).

The diabases and the last mentioned rocks, which are related to them, are either found in indefinite masses or with columnar, spherical, or irregular spheroidal jointings. The genuine diabases are most frequently found in the Devonian, Silurian and Cambrian formations, so for instance in the Voigtland, Fichtelgebirge, and Hartz mountains, where sometimes the immediately adjoining clay-slate is transformed into a kind of hornstone.

References.

G. *Rose* on Greenstones in Poggend. Annalen, 1835, vol. xxxiv. p. 1.
Oppermann, Dissertation über Schalstein und Kalktrapp, 1836.
Hausmann, Ueber die Bildung des Harzgebirges, p. 22.
v. Rosthorn u. Canaval, Kalktrapp oder Schalstein in Kärnthen in v. L. u. Br. Jahrbuch, 1855, p. 584.
Genth on Eukrite in the Annalen der Chemie u. Pharm. 1848, vol. lxvi. p. 17.
Haughton on Eukrite in the Quarterly Journ. of the Geol. Soc. 1856, vol. xii. p. 197.
Tschermack u. Krafft, on Eukrite in the Berichten der Wiener Akademie, pp. 40 and 127.
Hoheneyger on Teschinite in Die geog. Verhältnisse der Nordkarpathen, 1861, p. 43.
v. Hochstetter on the same subject on the Jahrbuch d. geol. Preichsanst, 1853, p. 319.
V. Charpentier on Augite Rock in his Essai sur la const. géol. des Pyrénées, 1823, p. 245.
Marrou on Augite Rock in the Ann. des Mines, 1828 [2] vol. iv. p. 307.
Herter u. Porth on Malakolite in the Jahrbuch der geol. Reichsanst, 1859, p. 10.
Kjerulf (Diabase) in Christiania Silurb. 1855, p. 26.
Delesse (Diabase) in the Ann. des. Mines, 1858 [5] vol. xiii. p. 374.
Madelung, über Teschinit, Neues Jahrb. für Mineral. 1865, p. 345.

5. GABBRO.

GABBRO, *von Buch.* (*Germ.*)
GABBRO. (*Fr.*)

*These rocks are compounds of labradorite or saus-
surite, with diallage, smaragdite, or hypersthene,
and usually some other minerals. They are distinguished by the irregularity of their composition and
texture.*

Spec. grav.   .   .   .   .   .   . 2·8—3·1
Contains silica .   .   .   .   .   . 43—46 p. c.

The Italian name of Gabbro, which L. v. Buch first
applied to a distinct class of rocks, has a broad and a
narrow signification; but as even the narrower meaning
is not very definite, the name is more serviceable in its
comprehensive sense, and in which it is more generally
understood.

Naumann, using the term in its narrower sense, described gabbro as a compound of labradorite or saussurite
with diallage and smaragdite, and he separates from it
hypersthene rock or hyperite, which essentially consists
of labradorite and hypersthene; and there are some very
similar rocks which have received the names of norite and
euphotide.

All these in fact only form varieties of the same rock;
they are very difficult to distinguish from each other
when they occur in a somewhat fine-grained state; and
when they pass over into the quite compact state, as is
often the case, they all become aphanite.

Since the texture of these rocks frequently changes
very rapidly, that is within a small area, from very coarse-
grained to fine-grained, compact, or slaty, their division
into varieties of texture cannot serve any useful purpose.
We shall therefore only enumerate the varieties of composition, which are the following :—

Varieties in Composition.

(*a*) GABBRO, DIALLAGE ROCK, GRANITONE. ⎫ Consists of labra-
GABBRO. (*Germ.*)   ⎬ dorite or saussurite
DIALLAGITE, *Descloizeaux.* (*Fr.*) ⎭ and diallage, or smaragdite irregularly combined, also sometimes of all those minerals together. It is very coarse-grained, fine-grained to
compact, sometimes slaty or spotted (variolitic).

The felspar if in the form of labradorite is coarse-grained to fine-grained; colour—white, grey, or violet. If it be saussurite it is compact and white or greenish. The diallage occurs in white individual crystals of half metallic lustre, grey to green. The smaragdite is grass-green, and has a mother-of-pearl lustre. Small quantities of sparry carbonates are often also contained in the compound frequently; not visible, but recognisable through effervescence with acid: they are probably of secondary origin. The visible accessory ingredients are mica, talc, hornblende (especially at the margins of the diallage), actinolite, garnet, iron pyrites, magnetic iron-ore, titaniferous iron-ore, specular iron, and apatite. Many of these also may be secondary formations. Calcspar and quartz occur in nests or veins.

This rock passes into serpentine by transmutation (as near Siebenlehn in Saxony) into aphanite by becoming compact, and apparently it also even passes into diorite, diabase, granite, and granulite.

The prevailing character of gabbro is massive. It penetrates older rocks and formations in a massive form, or in the form of veins forms apparent parallel strata in such. But it is also frequently penetrated by veins of granite, which in that case generally contain some orthite, as near Rosswein and Böhrigen in Saxony. In the Radauthal in the Hartz, where it may be easily mistaken for diabase, it also contains wollastonite, schillerspar, and rutile, and in fissures also desmine, prehnite, and albite, near La Prese in Upper Italy. It consists, according to Breithaupt, principally of hornblende with metallic pearly lustre (schillerspar), and a felspar of the highest spec. grav. with some brown mica. If the felspars have become much wasted from weathering, then the pyroxenic ingredients often appear above the surface in strong relief.

(b) EUPHOTIDE. The euphotide of French geologists is
EUPHODIT. (*Germ.*) according to Delesse, essentially a com-
EUPHOTIDE, *Haüy.* (*Fr.*) bination of felspar and diallage with titaniferous and chromic magnetic iron-ore, iron pyrites, serpentine and carbonates. The felspar is Saussure's jade, which afterwards Beudant called saussurite. It approaches in character labradorite, also vosgite and anorthite. The diallage often occurs as the variety smaragdite, which, according to Haidinger, properly consists of a combination of hornblende and pyroxene. The talc forms small laminæ, scarcely perceptible, the serpentine minute veins. The carbonates consist of invisible particles of calcspar, dolomite, and iron. As accessories there also occur hornblende, mica, and garnet, especially characteristic in the Alps and in Corsica.

(c) NORITE. The norite of Scheerer (not of Esmark) is a
NORIT, *Scheerer.* compound of hypersthene or diallage, labra-
(*Germ.*) dorite, orthoclase (containing soda), and even some quartz.

The felspathic ingredient of this rock is sometimes so prominent that the whole mass almost appears to be nothing but a granular felspar rock. It occurs on the island Hitteroe, Norway.

(d) HYPERSTHENITE, HYPERITE. } Consists of a coarse-grained to
HYPERSTHENIT, HYPERSTHENSSYENIT, } compact compound of labrado-
SELAGIT. (*Germ.*) } rite and hypersthene.
HYPÉRITE. (*Fr.*) }

Labradorite is the prevailing ingredient, coarse to fine-grained, grey, greenish or bluish. The hypersthene appears dark-brown, to green on its cleavage surfaces, has a metallic pearly lustre, its outer edges sometimes coated with horn-blende. The labradorite is the most strongly affected by weathering, and it decays away, leaving the hypersthene to protrude. The following minerals occur as accessories in this rock :—Titaniferous iron-ore, garnet, hornblende, olivine, brown mica, needles of apatite, iron pyrites, and magnetic iron-ore. It usually is of a massive structure, and forms veins or irregular masses between other rocks. It occurs characteristically in Höllenmühle, near Penig in Saxony, Neurode in Silesia, Isle of Skye, Elfdalen in Sweden.

The monzon-hypersthenite of v. Richthofen differs slightly from the ordinary kind. It consists of a very distinctly crystalline granular compound of dark-green to black hypersthene with greenish-white labradorite. The hypersthene is usually the principal ingredient; sometimes, however, the labradorite is entirely predominant, and in that case distinct crystals of common black augite occur in the mass.

The hypersthenic varieties also sometimes contain the like in small quantities, also dark-brown mica-plates and crystals of titaniferous iron-ore are found. At Monzoni in Southern Tyrol, this rock has broken through genuine syenite (free from quartz) and formed veins in it.

References.

v. *Buch* in the Magaz. d. Gesellsch.-naturforsch.   Freunde zu Berlin, 1810, vol. iv. p. 128.
v. *Rath* in Pogg. Annal. 1855, vol. xcv. p. 535 (Silesia).
Delesse, Bullet. de la Soc. géol. de France, 1849 [2] vol. vi. p. 410, 435, 547, and Ann. des Mines, 1849 [4] vol. xvi. p. 323.
Scheerer in the Gaea Norwegica, vol. ii. p. 313.
v. *Richthofen*, Geogn. Besch. von Süd-Tyrol, 1860, p. 146.
Keibel, Zeitschr. d. d. geol. Ges. 1857, vol. ix. p. 573.
Koch, Jahrb. d. Ver. f. Naturk. in Nassau, 1858, vol. xiii. p. 123.
Kjerulf, Christianias Silurbildungen, 1855, p. 23.
Streng, Zeitschr. d. d. geol. Ges. 1858, vol. x. p. 174 ; Neues Jahrbuch für Mineralogie, 1862, pp. 513 and 932, 1864, p. 257.
Drysdale, London and Edinb. Phil. Journ. 1833, vol. xv. p. 386.
Ebelmen, Ann. des Mines, 1847 [4] vol. xii. p. 629.
Jenzsch has analysed the hypersthenite of Neurode in Silesia, which contains bright shining spots and distinct particles of chlorophœite in dark brown-green matrix, and pronounces both from chemical and microscopic analyses that the matrix consists of about 27 oligoclase and 25 augite, and of 39 vitreous felspar, 5 magnetic iron-ore, 2 chlorophœite and

2 apatite. He found the content of silica very high, viz.
56·5. Poggend. Ann. 1855, vol. xcv. p. 418, and v. L. u.
Br. Jahrb. 1857, p. 436.
Websky, Gabbro von Neurode. Zeitschr. der deutschen geol.
Gesellsch. 1864, p. 530.

6. DIORITE.

DIORIT. (*Germ.*)
DIORITE, *Haüy.* (*Fr.*)

A crystalline-granular compound of felspar and horn-
blende. The felspar is not orthoclase. In fresh state
it is usually dark green.

Spec. grav. . . . . 2·6—2·9
Contains Silica . . . . . . 47—58 p. c.

Diorite was first so named by Haüy. Its texture is
often so fine-grained that it is difficult to determine the
species either of its felspar or hornblende, although the
minute particles of the former in most cases shew the
fine parallel striæ which are characteristic of albite,
oligoclase, anorthite, or labradorite, and which forbid the
idea of orthoclase. Gustav Rose in his first work on
greenstones held the felspar of diorite to be albite. Subsequently he embraced the view that albite never occurs
at all in crystalline rocks. Although this latter opinion
is shared by few, yet all observers now agree that the
felspar in diorite which was formerly taken for albite is
usually oligoclase. Delesse again has recognised labradorite and anorthite as essential ingredients in many
kinds of diorite. Thus the difference in the species
of the felspar constitutes one class of varieties of the
rock. The hornblende is also various : generally it is the
ordinary hornblende; sometimes, however, a variety more
approaching to actinolite, and Breithaupt lately discovered an entirely new species of hornblende as an essential
ingredient in many greenstones of Servia, Transylvania,
and Hungary. It has a black colour and greenish-grey
streaks. He named it *gamsigradite* after the name of the
place where he first found it.

But inasmuch as it is not easy, and in the fine-grained
state of the rock impossible with certainty, to recognise
the different species of felspar and hornblende, it does not
appear to us desirable on their account to dignify these
different varieties of diorite with the character of indi-

vidual rocks, although it is well to distinguish them where possible, since they are somewhat mineralogically different. The gamsigradite variety has been named by Breithaupt *timacite*, from one place where it occurs. This timacite has also a geological importance, as it is found to have broken through the older tertiary strata of Hungary and Transylvania, whereas the greater number of diorites are much more ancient.

All these mineralogical differences are very trifling in a chemical point of view; so that we may well consider them but as the result of somewhat unequal cooling of the same original mass. We do not mean that they should therefore be disregarded, on the contrary we consider that it would be an inquiry of the greatest geological interest to endeavour to trace their causes. Such an inquiry, to be successful, however, would demand a comparison of many special and accurate observations of the rock taken from various localities.

The following minerals sometimes occur in diorite as accessories; mica (brown and black) pyrites, magnetic pyrites, magnetic iron-ore, titaniferous iron-ore, titanite, garnet-pistacite, and quartz. Some of these may be of secondary origin, e.g. the pyrites and the pistacite, which latter appears to have proceeded from the hornblende, and sometimes contributes to the green colour of the rock.

The fine-grained varieties of syenite may be easily mistaken for diorite, the only essential difference between the two being that orthoclase is a necessary ingredient of syenite. The following characteristics may assist in distinguishing the two rocks, although not always to be recognised in them, nor universally to be relied on. Diorite is more frequently fine-grained than syenite, and generally (owing to its hornblende) more green in colour. In diorite the felspar decomposes sooner than the hornblende, and therefore on weathered surfaces the latter often protrudes prominently, whereas syenite weathers more evenly and falls into a kind of sandy grit. Diorite usually contains more pyrites than syenite, and the latter more frequently contains titanite or wöhlerite than the former. Their variations of texture and their outward structure, as well as their place in nature, are usually somewhat different, as will appear from the short account which we shall give of each under their respective heads.

As varieties of texture without regarding varieties of composition, the following kinds of diorite may be distinguished :—

Varieties in Texture.

(a) GRANULAR DIORITE.
KÖRNIGER DIORIT. (*Germ.*)
DIORITE GRANITOÏDE. (*Fr.*)
} The most normal variety, e.g. at the Klumpsen mountain, near Ebersbach, in Oberlausitz.

(b) FINE-GRAINED DIORITE.
FEINKÖRNIGER BIS DICHTER DIORIT. (*Germ.*)
DIORITE LITHOÏDE. (*Fr.*)
} Passing into compact (aphanite) Belmsdorf, near Bischofswerda, in Oberlausitz.

(c) PORPHYRITIC DIORITE, or DIORITE-PORPHYRY.
PORPHYRARTIGER DIORIT. (*Germ.*)
DIORITE PORPHYROÏDE. (*Fr.*)
} With crystals of felspar or amphibole, going over into aphanitic porphyry.

(d) SLATY DIORITE, or DIORITE-SLATE.
DIORIT-SCHIEFER. (*Germ.*)
DIORITE SCHISTOÏDE. (*Fr.*)
} The slaty texture usually imperfect, passing into aphanite slate.

(e) ORBICULAR DIORITE, or NAPOLEONITE.
KUGEL-DIORIT. (*Germ.*)
DIORITE ORBICULAIRE. *Brongniart.* (*Fr.*)
} The globular conformation is only a local appearance in diorite. It occurs very characteristically and beautifully near Sautina and Ajaccio, in Corsica. The rock consists, according to Delesse, of a combination of anorthite, blackish-green hornblende, and some quartz, so that it is a distinct variety in respect of its composition no less than its texture. The constituent minerals form alternating concentric layers round kernels. The kernels themselves consist (almost exclusively) either of the anorthite or hornblende (not of both), and they likewise exhibit a radiated texture. Thus we find balls of from one to three inches in diameter, whose section shews rings of alternate light and dark colour.

At Schemnitz (Stephen-shaft) orbicular timazite occurs, but the spherical masses are not in concentric layers.

(f) AMYGDALOIDAL DIORITE.
MANDELSTEINARTIGER DIORIT. (*Germ.*)
} Only occurs rarely, and with a fine-grained to compact matrix, which passes into the state of aphanite.

(g) WACKENITIC DIORITE, or DIORITE-WACKÉ.
DIORIT-WACKE. (*Germ*).
WACKE DIORITIQUE. (*Fr.*)
} This decomposed discoloured, and somewhat earthy state can only be recognised with certainty as belonging to diorite by tracing its transition from distinct rocks. The foregoing differences of texture are however repeated in it.

Varieties in Composition.

(h) COMMON DIORITE essentially consisting of oligoclase and hornblende, the diorite of the Huhnberge, in the Thuringian Forest, is somewhat differently composed, inasmuch as its felspar contains lithia, and very many small needles of apatite occur disseminated through the whole mass. This rock, which is

sometimes very coarse-grained, has broken through the rothliegende and becomes quite compact near the surfaces of contact.

(*i*) ANORTHITE-DIORITE.   ⎱ In which the oligoclase is partly or
      ANORTHIT-DIORIT. (*Germ.*) ⎰ wholly replaced by anorthite. As for
instance in the orbicular diorite of Corsica, which likewise
contains some quartz.

(*k*) TIMAZITE (TRACHYTIC GREENSTONE). ⎱ Consists, according to
      TIMAZIT, *Breithaupt.* (*Germ.*)   ⎰ Breithaupt, of a grey
or greenish-grey felsitic base, in which are imbedded crystals
of white felspar (albite or mikrokline), black hornblende (gamsigradite), some mica, magnetic iron-ore, and iron pyrites. The
base, which is fine-grained to compact, corresponds most closely
with labradorite.

The cleavage-prism of gamsigradite shews an angle of
124° 26', its hardness is 7, and spec. grav. is 3° 1'; it has a
greenish-grey streak. The mica forms hexagonal brown plates.
The magnetic iron-ore forms very small grains or crystals,
the iron pyrites very small cubes.

According to an analysis by Dr. Rube the timazite of Gam-
sigrad, in Servia, contains about 50 per cent. of silica. We
have already stated that this rock is frequently met with in
Transylvania and Hungary, especially in the mining districts,
and that it has penetrated through the Eocene sandstones. We
have elsewhere described a rock occurring in Borsabánya, in
the Marmaros, in the north of Hungary, which we named
labradorite-rock, because its prevailing base consists of labradorite. According to Breithaupt this is essentially the same
as timazite; but we find from Dr. Rube's analysis that it contains above 63 per cent. of silica, and therefore it belongs to
the acidic rocks. As, according to Delesse, the diorite of Pont
Jean, in the Vosges Mountains, also contains labradorite, it is
very possible that it is a timazite.

(*l*) CALCAREOUS DIORITE.   ⎱ Is the name given by Senft to a dark-
      KALK-DIORIT, *Senft.* (*Germ.*) ⎰ green, more or less distinct compound
      HEMITHRÈNE. (*Fr.*)   of hornblende, oligoclase and mica,
penetrated with calcspar, and which near Ruhla, in the Thuringian Forest, forms a stratum in mica-schist.

The jointed structure of the diorites is usually irregular; but sometimes columnar or globular.

Diorite frequently occurs in subordinate masses, veins,
or dykes in the schistose or slaty rocks of the Silurian or
Devonian age, and (exceptionally) sometimes in much
newer formations; sometimes also in granite, gneiss, or
mica-schist.

Appendix.

The NORITE of Esmark (different from that of Scheerer) very
widely spread in Norway, appears only to be a variety of
diorite containing quartz and mica.

The OPHITE of Palassou is, according to its description, a tolerably compact diorite. The MICA-DIORITE of Delesse on the other hand ought rather to be classed with Syenite than here, on account of its containing orthoclase.

References.

G. Rose on Greenstones in Poggend. Annal. 1835, vol. xxxiv. p. 1.

Keibel, Analysen in d. Zeitschr. d. d. geol. Ges. 1857, vol. ix. p. 575, and v. Leonhard u. Br. Jahrbuch, 1859, p. 445.

Rivière, Bullet. de la Soc. géol. d. Fr. 1844, vol. i. p. 528.

Hunt in Sillim. Amer. Journ. 1859 [2] xxvii. p. 340.

v. Richthofen, Geogn. Beschreibung v. Süd-Tyrol, 1816, p. 111. The diorite at Klausen contains actinolitic hornblende with oligoclase.

Delesse on Orbicular diorite, which was first described in 1785 by Besson, in the Journ. d. Phys., and on the Diorite of the Vosges, Ann. des Mines, 1859, vol. xvi. pp. 160 and 339; 1851, p. 149.

Breithaupt on Timazite, in the Berg- u. Hüttenm. Zeitg. 1861, p. 51. On the Diffusion of Timazite.

Compare *Cotta's* Gangstudien, vol. iv. pp. 28, 56, 65, and 85.

Senft on Calc-diorite. In the Zeitschr. d. d. geol. Ges. 1858, p. 308.

Esmark on Norite in the Magaz. för Naturvidenskabern, vol. i. p. 207.

Charpentier on Ophite, Constit. géol. des Pyrénées, 1823, p. 481.

Dufrenoy on Ophite, Ann. des Mines, 1832 [3] vol. ii. p. 21.

v. Rath. The diorite of Neurode, in Silesia, consists of 56 parts of hornblende, and 44 saussurite. The former has been formed from augite according to *G. Rose*, Pogg. Ann. 1855, vol. xcv. p. 555.

Herm. Vogelgesang, as to globular diorite, Berggeist, 1862, Nos. 90 and 91.

7. APHANITE.—Trap in part, Melaphyre in part.

APHANIT. (*Germ.*)
APHANITE, *Haüy.* (*Fr.*)

A compact, apparently homogeneous mass; usually dark green to black; of about the hardness of felspar; very tough; sometimes porphyritic by reason of crystals of felspar, hornblende, or pyroxene; also vesicular or amygdaloidal.

Spec. grav. . . . . . . 2·6—2·9
Contains silica . . . . 43—58 p. c.

The separate ingredients of the principal mass of this rock are not to be recognised with the naked eye, hence the name of aphanite, given by Haüy. We have already shown that transitions take place into aphanite from diabase, gabbro, or diorite; proving it to be but a compact state of one or other of those rocks, bearing the same relation to them as basalt to dolerite; a view which is entirely confirmed by chemical analysis.

The minuteness and intimate union of the individual constituent ingredients of aphanite when quite compact, no less than their general resemblance to each other, make it impossible with the ordinary aids to discover from the appearance of the rock whether it belongs to diabase, gabbro, or diorite. We can only draw conclusions in this respect from finding it in conjunction with one or other of those rocks. If, however, the aphanite be porphyritic, then the minerals porphyritically enclosed in the compact matrix may give a clue to the composition of the latter; for instance, we frequently find labradorite, oligoclase, pyroxene, or hornblende thus porphyritically imbedded in aphanite. It is dangerous, however, to rely too implicitly on conclusions so drawn, and on every account, therefore, in describing the varieties of aphanite we refrain from the attempt to keep up distinctions corresponding to the three normal rocks of diabase, gabbro, and diorite.

Possibly by careful microscopic observations we might succeed in determining the special mineral character of every aphanite. But such observations are attended with considerable labour, and the appliances are not always within reach; on a journey they would be out of the question. We may, however, state that the microscopic observations which have been made of aphanite entirely confirm what we have already said respecting its nature, and show that even the accessory ingredients of the three normal rocks are represented in its composition. The greater number of aphanites appear to belong to the pyroxenic greenstones, or we might rather say that these latter have more frequently assumed the compact state than the hornblendic varieties. Many varieties of texture and composition which are found in the three granular rocks are likewise repeated in the compact rock.

Varieties in Texture.

(a) COMMON COMPACT APHANITE.
    GEMEINER DICHTER DIORIT. (Germ.)
    APHANITE LITHOÏDE. (Fr.)

(b) PORPHYRITIC APHANITE or   } With crystals of labradorite, oli-
    APHANITE-PORPHYRY.   goclase, hornblende, augite, or
    PORPHYRARTIGER DIORIT. (Germ.) uralite. Accordingly we dis-
    APHANITE PORPHYROÏDE. (Fr.) tinguish labradorite-porphyry,

oligoclase-porphyry, augite-porphyry, or uralite-porphyry, of which we will treat more at large hereafter.

Near Manebach, Herges, and Tabarz, in the Thuringian Forest, there occur aphanitic porphyries whose felspar crystals are not yet accurately determined.

(c) SLATY APHANITE or APHANITE-SLATE.
APHANIT-SCHIEFER. (*Germ.*)
APHANITE SCHISTOÏDE. (*Fr.*)
} Usually only indistinctly slaty, or of thick cleavage.

(d) VESICULAR APHANITE.
BLASIGER APHANIT. (*Germ.*)
APHANITE VACUOLAIRE. (*Fr.*)
} Rather rare; sometimes it would appear that the vesicular cavities have been once filled, and their contents weathered out. We often find them empty at the weathered surface, but still remaining filled in the fresh interior of the rock.

(e) AMYGDALOIDAL APHANITE.
APHANIT-MANDELSTEIN. (*Germ.*)
APHANITE AMYGDALOÏDE. (*Fr.*)
} The vesicular cavities are most usually filled with calcspar or zeolitic substance.

(f) WACKENITIC APHANITE, or APHANITE-WACKÉ.
APHANIT-WACKE. (*Germ.*)
WACKE APHANITIQUE. (*Fr.*)
} Discoloured and earthy through decomposition, its petrographic character only to be determined by its surroundings.

As varieties of composition the following species may be distinguished in addition to the usual quite compact form :—

Varieties in Composition.

(g) CALCAREOUS APHANITE.
KALKAPHANIT, SCHALSTEIN in part. (*Germ.*)
} In the compact and slaty mass are found grains of calcspar or brown spar which are not fillings up of vesicular cavities.

(h) VARIOLITIC APHANITE, VARIOLITE.
VARIOLITHISCHER APHANIT, VARIOLITH. (*Germ.*)
VARIOLITHE, JADEGLANDULEUX, *Brongniart, Élie de Beaumont.* (*Fr.*)
} The compact base contains concretions of greenish or violet grey-ish colour, either of stringy, radiated, or concentric texture from the size of a grain of mustard-seed to that of a walnut, firmly grown in, and not very sharply defined. They consist of a felsite (probably labradorite), but frequently also contain some pistacite in concentric layers. As accessories in the matrix of the rock we find iron pyrites and magnetic iron-ore, in its clefts and cavities quartz, pistacite, calcspar, and chlorite.

Delesse has narrowly investigated and described the variolites of the Durance, and he also mentions those of the Fichtelgebirge, and of Savoy, &c. (Ann. des Mines, 1850, vol. xvii. p. 116.) Their spherical concretions often exhibit a reddish, violet, or grey kernel, round that a lighter coloured rind, and round the latter a green shell of a somewhat lighter colour than the enclosing matrix of the rock. In the latter, with the aid of the microscope, he also discovered small laminæ of felspar.

(i) LABRADORITE-PORPHYRY(BLACK PORPHYRY).
LABRADORPORPHYR. (*Germ.*)
MÉLAPHYRE FELDSPATHIQUE. (*Fr.*)
} The black matrix incloses crystals of labradorite and

small particles of a dark green mineral not yet determined ; spec.
grav. 2·7, content of silica 56–58 p. c. By aid of the magnifying
glass Streng found the apparently compact matrix to be distinctly crystalline, consisting of one mineral of dark-green inclining to black, and another of a lighter green colour. Probably
they are the same as the minerals which also occur in a distinct
form. The crystals of labradorite often shew a dark dull-green
kernel, surrounded by a light and shining margin. The striæ
of twin crystallisation are continued equally through both.
Sometimes the reverse is the case, the kernel is light and
shining, and the margin dull and of a darker colour. As accessories, but rarely, and only in small particles, brownish-black,
mica plates, pyrites, and magnetic iron-ore. Near Elbingerode
at the Hartz, this rock penetrates Devonian slates and limestones.

To this class belong the rocks described by Delesse, found
by him at Belfaly and Ternuay, in the Vosges ; these contain
augite, and are amygdaloidal in part. Also the rock described by
Kjerulf as melaphyre from Barnekjern, near Christiania, as well
as many other so-called melaphyres and porfido-verde-antico.

Streng in v. L. u. Br. Jahrb. 1860, p. 397.
Delesse in Ann. des Mines, 1847 [4] vol. xii. p. 228.
Kjerulf, Christiania Silurbecken, 1855, p. 28.

(*k*) OLIGOCLASE-PORPHYRY. ⎫ Is the name given by G. Rose to a
OLIGOKLASPORPHYR. (*Germ.*) ⎭ diabasic or aphanitic rock in the Ural
Mountains, which has a dark green compact or nearly compact
matrix containing crystals of oligoclase. Much porfido-verde-
antico is of this character; also the rock described by Delesse,
as found by him at Lescines, in Belgium, containing some
pyrites, and some copper pyrites (unless it belongs to mica-
diorite) and several rocks from the neighbourhood of Christiania
described by Kjerulf.

G. Rose, Reise nach dem Ural, vol. ii. p. 571.
Delesse, Bulletin de la Soc. géol. d. Fr. 1849 [2] vol. vi. p.
386 ; 1850 [2] vol. vii. p. 310.
Kjerulf, Christiania Silurbecken, 1855, p. 9.

(*b*) AUGITE-PORPHYRY.   ⎫ (Often called Melaphyre.) A com-
AUGITPORPHYR. (*Germ.*)   ⎬ pact matrix, usually dark green,
MÉLAPHYRE PYROXÉNIQUE. (*Fr.*) ⎭ containing crystals of augite.
Fr. v. Richthofen reckons to this division the most of the
rocks of the Fassa region, which are usually designated as
melaphyres.

These contain crystals of augite and labradorite (or sometimes
oligoclase), inclosed in a matrix resembling basalt. Titaniferous
iron-ore is also disseminated through the mass in small particles. They are very variously developed; most frequently we
find them vesicular and amygdaloidal.

V. Richthofen, Southern Tyrol, 1860, p. 128.

(*m*) URALITE-PORPHYRY.   ⎫ Is the name given by G. Rose to
URALITPORPHYR,*G. Rose.* (*Germ.*) ⎬ rock containing crystals of uralite
PORPHYRE À OURALITE. (*Fr.*)   ⎭ in a compact dark, probably diabasic

matrix. This uralite has the form of augite, and the substance of hornblende.

G. Rose, Reise nach dem Ural, vol. ii. p. 370.

The four last-named varieties may be indifferently termed aphanitic porphyries, or greenstone-porphyries; and they are sometimes classed together under the name of melaphyres. The timazites of Hungary likewise frequently have a compact aphanitic base, for instance, those in the neighbourhood of Schemnitz, in which single crystals or crystalline particles of hornblende (gamsigradite) or felspar may be clearly distinguished.

Aphanite is usually of jointed structure, or very distinctly cleft.; generally the blocks are irregularly massive, sometimes, however, regularly columnar, or regularly or irregularly spherical. The aphanites occur in nature under the same circumstances as diabase, diorite, and gabbro; and very often in their company. We have already suggested that they should be regarded as mere modifications of those rocks, differing from them chiefly in the greater rapidity of their original cooling process. The Saxon Oberlausitz affords striking instances in illustration of this opinion. The granite region there is found to have been broken through by diorite, and accordingly numerous dome-shaped hills of the latter rock protrude from the surface; near to these the same eruptive mass has produced narrower dykes (from 5 to 20 ft. thick), whose texture is fine-grained, nearly compact. Near Belmsdorf, not far from Bischofswerde, we observed a diorite dyke 20 to 30 ft. thick, which in the centre was fine-grained, but almost compact towards the walls of the cleft, where it must have cooled more quickly. The offshoots from the same vein into the granite, and the narrow parts of the principal vein of only two inches thick, consist of a completely compact mass, which might easily be taken for basalt, as it is almost quite black. These differences of texture are there manifestly the consequence of different degrees of rapidity of cooling caused by the different volume or thickness of the mass.

On this subject see Erläuter. z. geog. Karte von Sachsen, 1839. No. 3, p. 24. Also on the subject of aphanite,— *Delesse* in Ann. des Mines, vol. xvi. p. 350.

8. MELAPHYRE.—Augite-Porphyry in part, Trap in part.

MELAPHYR. (*Germ.*)
MÉLAPHYRE, *Brongniart.* (*Fr.*)

The rocks which we include under this name are dark-coloured, greenish, brownish, or black ; compact, porphyritic, vesicular, or amygdaloidal ; always free from quartz.   They are compounds (intimately blended) of felsite, pyroxene, hornblende, and magnetic iron-ore.

Spec. grav. .   .   .   .   .   2·6—3·1
Contains silica .   .   .   .   .   54—62 p. c.

The name melaphyre has ceased to bear a distinct character, having been successively used by different geologists, ever since the time of Brongniart, who first introduced it, for many and various igneous rocks having nothing in common with each other, unless it be a prevalent compact texture, dark colour, and absence of quartz.   Hence the name conveys no definite idea, unless qualified by the name of a particular author, and that is not always sufficient without the name of the locality.

There are many and various rocks of uniform dark colour, of a prevailing compact or amygdaloidal texture, close compounds of some kind of felspar with pyroxene, hornblende, and magnetic iron.   We have already spoken of several such under the heads of basalt and aphanite.   Much of what has been called melaphyre certainly belongs to our basalts and greenstones.   The rocks of which we shall treat under the name of porphyrite have often been called melaphyre, and if we take away all that may be ascribed to basalt, greenstone, and porphyrite, little will be left to which to apply the name of melaphyre.

Under these circumstances the name can only be usefully retained as a sort of provisional term for any basic igneous rocks of prevalent compact texture and dark colour, whose composition is not so definitely marked as to entitle them to be included under any other more distinct species; much in the same way as we are often compelled to use the general name of greenstone for rocks whose mineral character is not sufficiently decided, or has not been sufficiently investigated, to enable us to class them as diorite, gabbro, or diabase.

In dealing thus, for our own part, with the name of melaphyre, we here subjoin a quasi-historical account of the mode in which it has been used by different authors. We think the divergence of their readings will be a sufficient justification, if any be needed, for the way in which we propose that the term should in future be accepted.

(a) *Al. Brongniart*, the inventor of the name melaphyre, described it as ' Pâte noire d'amphibole pétrosiliceux enveloppant des cristaux de feldspath ; ' what is here meant by 'amphibole pétrosiliceux ' is very uncertain, the more so as at that time (1813) the differences between hornblende and pyroxene were not so well established or known as they are at present.

(b) *L. von Buch* first applied Brongniart's name of melaphyre to certain black-coloured rocks of the Fassa Thal and the Seisser Alp (see ante, p. 162). He, however, also called these rocks black porphyries or augitic porphyries, because they contained crystals of augite, and their matrix was also black and rich in augite. He also included under the same designation many rocks of the Hartz and Thuringian Forest, &c., whose composition he presumed to be similar, and which he considered to be the original cause of the upheaval of those mountains. To them he also ascribed the formation of dolomite in several localities. As the principal characteristics of this rock, he enumerated dark colour, great content of augite, and complete absence of quartz. See von Leonhard's Taschenbuch, 1824, vol. ii. pp. 289, 372, 437, and 471.

(c) *Naumann* says on this subject, ' The rocks which Al. Brongniart has introduced under the somewhat singular name of melaphyre are for the most part identical with those which Faujas de Saint Fond collected under the Swedish name of trap, and of which Warmholz, Steiniger and others have made use in the same sense. Werner called them trap-porphyries or trap-amygdaloids; Zobel and v. Carnal, porphyrite. Freiesleben called them pseudo-porphyries; v. Raumer, basaltite ; and in many French writings they are also in part called spilite. Trap and melaphyre are probably the most usual names at the present day; for although the Swedish trap, according to Erdmann is a diabasic rock, whereas the rocks which bear the same name in the Faroe Islands and Iceland are basaltic formations, it nevertheless appears to be most useful to retain (with L. von Buch) the name of melaphyre for the rocks which we are about to treat.' These are then described as compounds of labradorite, and (probably) augite in small or invisible crystals (therefore compact), but alone recognisable, and frequently in the form of scattered crystals, the rock very much inclined to the amygdaloidal in texture. They are further described as always containing magnetic iron-ore, carbonate of protoxide of iron, and carbonate of lime, in invisible particles, as well as some rubellan and mica. Their petrographic difference from the basalts, according to Naumann, is confined to the want of olivine, and to the circumstance that the augite is not to be recognised with certainty. Geognosie, and in v. L. u. Br. Jahrb. 1860, p. 1.

(d) *Von Richthofen* attempted to put an end to the confusion which the name of melaphyre had gradually introduced by restoring the definition of Brongniart, and he believed that he had discovered the identical rock in various places; for instance, at Schneidemüllersberg near Ilmenau, in the Schleusenthal, in the Thuringian Forest, between Landshut and Glatz in Silesia, near Oberstein, and between Botzen and Colmann in the Tyrol. He describes the rock thus :—

Compact matrix, dark-green or brown to black. Fracture uneven, inclining to conchoidal; lustre shining; hardness that of felspar or less; spec. grav. 2·7; contains crystals of felspar (oligoclase or labradorite), other minerals only exceptionally to be recognised. In his large work on the Tyrol he also reckons the rock of which the summit of the Margola is formed to this compound of oligoclase and hornblende, with much oligoclase, labradorite, augite, and hornblende, and partly of a fine-grained species; it consists partly of an intimate compound of oligoclase, and few crystals of augite. This latter variety was termed by v. Klipstein mulatt-porphyr.

From the results of the chemical and microscopic analyses of these rocks, from the minerals which they contain in a distinctly crystalline form, and from their specific gravity, von Richthofen framed conclusions respecting the mineralogical composition of the compact matrix, and pronounced it to consist essentially of oligoclase and hornblende, with subordinate quantities of apatite, titaniferous iron, sometimes also some magnetic iron-ore, and chlorophæite, or magnesia-mica. In it often labradorite crystals lie imbedded exceptionally, perhaps, also similar ones of augite, hornblende, epidote, or mica, but never quartz or olivine.

In vesicular cavities there occur quartz and chalcedony, carbonic spars and zeolites. (Vide Zeitschr. d. d. geol. Ges. 1856, pp. 589 and 593, which gives a very complete catalogue of the literature on this subject; Sitzungsb. d. Wiener Akad. d. Wissensch. 1857, vol. xxvii. p. 293; Remarks upon the distinctions between melaphyre and augite-porphyry, Vienna, 1839, and Geogn. Beschreibung v. Süd-Tyrol, 1860, p. 141.)

(e) *E. Söchting*, on the other hand, attempts to show that Richthofen's definition of the matrix is unfounded; that according to the results of the analyses, it might just as well consist of labradorite and augite, and that Brongniart was not to be depended upon as to the determination of hornblende (Zeitschr. d. d. geol. Ges. 1857, p. 427). Söchting himself had formerly described the so-called melaphyres of the Thuringian Forest as an intimate compound of labradorite and augite in the Zeitschr. d. ges. Naturwissenschaften, 1854, p. 197.

(f) *Girard* starts with the principle that the geological character of rocks is the principal thing to be determined, and that they should always be classed and named accordingly, rather than according to their mineralogical or chemical composition. He combats von Richthofen's view in respect of melaphyre, but seems somewhat to have misunderstood his meaning. For Richthofen merely sought to avoid the uncertainty into which the term melaphyre had fallen by keeping as strictly as possible to Brongniart's first definition, and thereby excluding many rocks which had been called melaphyres. Girard, on the other hand, seeks to show that many of these excluded rocks really contain augite and no hornblende, a fact not disputed by Richthofen, but one which according to him did not entitle them to be called melaphyres. We may, perhaps, think von Richthofen's narrowing of the sense of melaphyre unpractical or inconsistent : unpractical because, being too much opposed to prevailing ideas, it is little likely to be adopted; inconsistent if taken in connection with the enlargement of the meaning of the term trachyte which he himself advocated. Nevertheless it does not follow that it is in itself inaccurate, even if we choose to acknowledge Girard's premised principle to be the right one. Girard himself considers the melaphyre of Ilfeld to be a compound of a mineral containing felspar with augite, the augite forming only one-fifth or one-sixth of the entire mass. Whether the prevailing ingredient be labradorite or oligoclase, he leaves undetermined. Small black grains in the same mass, he takes for magnetic or titaniferous iron. He compares also some other melaphyre with that of Ilfeld. (v. L. u. Br. Jahrb. 1858, p. 173.)

(g) *Streng* distinguishes three kinds of rock in the neighbourhood of Ilfeld by the names of melaphyre, porphyry-melaphyre, and melaphyre-amygdaloid. The first, which should belong to our porphyrite, is a grey or brown-coloured rock with matrix resembling hornstone, and containing small crystals of felspar not longer than the tenth part of an inch, white or greenish with twin striæ (labradorite or oligoclase) associated sometimes with crystals of an undetermined dark-green mineral grown into the felspar crystals; the matrix likewise contains small reddish-brown garnet grains, also a light-green mineral, perhaps only the product of decomposition and very small particles of magnetic iron-ore.

In the melaphyre of Streng the principal mass is of dull appearance, and in its fresh state is blue-black, distinctly crystalline, of wavy lustre and friable—by weathering it becomes greenish-grey or brown. It is probably a compound of felsite and augite or hornblende, or a yet undefined mineral of the nature of diallage and some magnetic iron-ore. In the matrix occur very small crystals of the same diallage-like mineral, also larger columns of the same mineral which exhibit a growth of twin crystals, crossing each other regularly at an angle of 60°, and distinct small plates of rubellan. In a second essay Streng described the diallage-like mineral as a schillerspar which contains alumina.

The melaphyre-amygdaloid of Streng consists of a homo-

geneous brown matrix, of the hardness of 5·6, and contains
small amygdaloidal cavities filled with glauconite, chalcedony,
and carbonate of lime.

The specific gravity of these varieties fluctuates between 2·6
and 2·7. Their content of silica, taking the mean of a considerable number of analyses, is for the melaphyre-porphyry 61·3, for
the melaphyre and melaphyre-amygdaloid 54·4. They form
together a plateau of considerable size between the lower and
upper Rothliegende districts (Zeitschr. d. d. geol. Ges. 1858,
p. 99, and 1859, p. 78). Upon the position and bedding of these
rocks see Bäntsch in Abhandl. d. naturf. Ges. zu Halle, 1858.

(h) G. Rose defined the Ilfeld melaphyre as follows :—a fine-grained
almost compact mass of black or brown colour, sometimes containing small acicular crystals, or greenish-white crystals,
(likewise small). The texture is often vesicular or amygdaloidal. According to the known analyses, both microscopic and
chemical, the matrix most probably consists of an intimately
blended crystalline compound of oligoclase, with augite or
hornblende, magnetic iron-ore, and some apatite; the fine
acicular crystals appear to be augite transformed into schillerspar; the greenish white crystals Rose could not determine.
In local varieties also small crystals of mica occur and irregularly shaped grains of some other mineral.

The vesicular cavities, often very regularly shaped (for instance pearshaped), contain concentric layers of chalcedony and
quartz as well as calcspar.

The following are varieties more especially distinguished by
Rose.

Black melaphyre, from the Raben Klippen, at the Hartz.—A
compact compound in which transparent prismatic crystals are
prevalent; between them lie larger white crystals, very small
grains of magnetic iron-ore.

Black melaphyre from Wiegersdorff.—Matrix under the microscope less distinct than the last-named ; in it lie diallage-like
crystals of augite.

Red melaphyre from Wiegersdorff.—Matrix under the microscope less distinct than the last-named; in it lie diallage-
like crystals of augite.

Red melaphyre from the Birkenhoff.—The matrix reddish-
brown, and containing green acicular crystals of augite.

Rose considers these melaphyres to resemble chiefly those of
Lowenberg, Lähn, and Landshut in Silesia. (Zeitschr. d. d.
geol. Gesellsch. 1859, p. 280.)

(i) THE OBERSTEIN AMYGDALOID. This rock, celebrated for its
beautiful agates, is considered by many geologists to belong to
the melaphyres; thus (e.g.) : von Dechen, Dufrenoy, Élie de
Beaumont, and Naumann. Its principal mass, usually brown or
greenish, no doubt consists chiefly of felsite, and often contains
small crystals of felspar, and amygdaloidal cavities filled with
agate and other minerals; accordingly we should term the rock
a porphyrite. Delesse was the first to give a careful analysis
of it. Its spec. grav. is 2·68. Chemically it contains 51·13

silica, 29·73 alumina and peroxide of iron, 4·73 of lime, 40·73 magnesia and alkali, 3·68 water and carbonic acid. From these data, as well as its mineralogical characteristics, Delesse concludes that the principa. mass essentially consists of labradorite ; in fact, there frequently occur in it a great number of small labradorite crystals, white and translucent : its frequent green colour appears to be owing to an admixture of chlorite. Sometimes some augite is observable, also small flakes of brown mica. Magnetic iron-ore in very finely divided particles appears to be uniformly dispersed through the whole mass.

In the numerous amygdaloidal cavities, whose diameters vary from one-tenth of an inch to a foot, Delesse found agate, opal, quartz, chlorite, calcspar, different kinds of zeolite, hydrated oxides of iron and manganese.

The amygdaloid of Oberstein possesses compact fine-grained and porphyritic varieties, and occurs in the coal formation of that district, sometimes forming dykes and masses of considerable size, sometimes parallel seams. It appears to have been thrust up about the time when the deposit of the rothliegende began. Perhaps its character is the same as that of the rock, previously described under the name of tholeite. (See ante, p. 138.)

(Delesse in Ann. des Mines, [4] vol. xvi. p. 511; Steininger, Geogn. Beschreib. d. Landes. zu Saar. u. Rhein, 1840, p. 110.)

(k) *Senft* designates as melaphyres almost all dark quartzless igneous rocks of the Thuringian Forest; according to him, they consist principally of a compact mass of labradorite, combined with magnetic titaniferous iron-ore, calcspar, ironspar, and iron-chlorite (delessite). He distinguishes several varieties, viz. : in the first place, those resembling greenstones from those resembling basalt or felsite-porphyry, then according to their texture; (1) granular like dolerite, near Schmiedelfeld ; (2) porphyritic (melaporphyry), which he subdivides into labradorite- and melaphyre- (trap-porphyry), mica-porphyry and iron-chlorite (delessite) porphyry ; (3) melaphyre-amygdaloids, and (4) compact or fine-grained melaphyres. Surely these are rocks of very various character.

(Bericht der Naturforscherversammlung zu Wien, 1858, p. 144.)

As regards the so-called spilites of the Western Alps, which are also considered to belong to the melaphyre, compare—

Gueymard, in the Ann. des Mines, 1850, [4] vol. xviii. p. 54, with

Delesse, ibid. 1857, [5] vol. xii. p. 457.

E. E. Schmid on Melaphyre of Mombächler Höfen, between Baumholde and Grumbach in Rheinpfalz, in Pogg. Ann. 1863, vol. cxix. p. 138.

Madelung, Melaphyre des Riesengebirges, Neues Jahrb. f. Miner. 1865, p. 344.

PORPHYRITES.

As the rocks which come under this head are all intimately connected with each other by transition states, and they likewise all assume the same geological position, we shall characterise them as the varieties only of one species, describing them, nevertheless, individually.

9. PORPHYRITE. — Felspar-Porphyry, Quartzless Porphyries, Mica-Porphyry or Hornblende-Porphyry.

PORPHYRIT, *G. Rose.* (*Germ.*)
PORPHYRITE. (*Fr.*)

Contains in a felsitic matrix (usually of dark colour) individual crystals of felspar, mica, or hornblende. The matrix is sometimes also vesicular or amygdaloidal.

Spec. grav.   .   .   .   .   .   2·6—2·7
Contains silica .   .   .   .   .   59—61 p. c.

The term *porphyry*, without addition or qualification, denotes, par excellence, *quartz-porphyry*, a rock with quartz-felsitic base and crystals of felspar and quartz (see p. 214 post, where it is more particularly described). Naumann, therefore, proposed (in his treatise on Ilfeld) to collect all the quartzless porphyries with prevailing felsitic base under the common name of PORPHYRITE, which had already been applied to some of them. This nomenclature has now been pretty generally accepted. It appears to us certainly better than Rose's proposal to designate a part of these quartzless rocks syenitic porphyry (see also post, p. 210, where Rose's divisions are further explained). Many varieties of porphyrite stand on the very margin between the basic and acidic rocks (their silica ranging from 49 to 61 per cent.), but the greater part are basic. Quartz only occurs very exceptionally in their composition.

These rocks, by reason of their prevailing dark colour and their deficiency in quartz, were formerly frequently classed as melaphyres. We have already expressed the opinion that most of the so-called melaphyres are either basalts, greenstones, or porphyrites, so that there is scarcely anything left to which to apply the name of melaphyre distinctively. But as it is often very difficult to determine whether a rock is properly a basalt, a green-stone, or a porphyrite, the name of melaphyre for such doubtful rocks may prove convenient and useful. It might have been more correct to give up the name of porphyrite and use that of melaphyre in its stead, both because the name of porphyrite refers to a texture which is not an es-sential feature of these rocks, and because the porphyrites are not always in fact porphyritic. Such an innovation, which Senft seems really to have intended, was, however, open to the serious objection that the name of melaphyre had already been so much abused as to make it hopeless to attempt now to clothe it with a definite meaning, although it may perhaps be usefully retained for rocks of indefinite character.

The porphyrites may be divided into distinguishable varieties, according to their different composition. They may be best classed according to the distinct minerals which occur in them porphyritically. Thus we shall dis-tinguish *Porphyrite* (proper), with crystals of felspar; *Hornblende-porphyrite*, with crystals of felspar and horn-blende; and *Mica-porphyrite*, with crystals of felspar and mica.

The porphyrites are usually severed by joints into irre-gular masses, or very deeply cleft by fissures; they are more rarely jointed in columnar or tabular form.

In Germany they are not met with of much more re-cent origin than the Rothliegende; this formation is, how-ever, sometimes found pierced by them, and the two are very often contemporaneous. In Southern Tyrol, much more recent porphyrites would appear to occur.

The porphyrites never occupy connected fields of great extent, and in general they are far less widely spread than the quartz-porphyries.

(A) PORPHYRITE (FELSPAR-PORPHYRY).

PORPHYRIT. (*Germ.*)
PORPHYRITE. (*Fr.*)

A felsitic principal mass, usually dark-brown, containing crystals of felspar, oligoclase, or sometimes orthoclase, and occasionally other minerals.

Spec. grav. . . . . 2·6—2·7
Content of silica at Ilfeld on the average
(therefore very high). . . . } 61·3 p. c.

The colour of the matrix varies sometimes into grey, red, violet, or blue, and besides the crystals of felspar, it contains as accessory ingredients an admixture of garnet, titanite, magnetic iron-ore, specular iron, and pyrites, &c. This porphyrite is extensively developed in the South of Norway, where L. von Buch has in part named it 'Rhombenporphyr,' on account of the rhombic section of its felspar crystals. At Elfdalen, in Sweden, it is manufactured into small ornaments. It is also very prevalent in the Lenne-Gebiet in Westphalia, and on the southern border of the Hartz Mountains. As the rock of the last-named locality has been recently very accurately described, we subjoin a short abstract of those descriptions.

Porphyrite (Streng's melaphyre-porphyry, p. 165), found at Ilfeld, near the Hartz Mountains, contains in a dark-brown or grey felsitic matrix, crystals of felspar, also a dark-green mineral, a light-green mineral, red garnet, and small scales of micaceous iron. The matrix, according to Streng, consists chiefly of orthoclase, which Rose, however, doubts.

Rose made a microscopic analysis of this rock. The thin polished plates showed a transparent matrix marked with black spots and streaks, and filled with black grains of irregular shape. According to Streng, the felspar crystals as well as the grains consist of labradorite. Baentsch and Girard hold the dark-green mineral for augite; Rose, on the other hand, considers it to be a product of decomposition of hornblende. According to Streng, black and shining grains of titaniferous iron-ore may be recognised in the weathered state of the rock. At Ilfeld no vesicular or amygdaloidal varieties of this rock appear to occur, unless we regard those amygdaloids as such which have been described as melaphyre—a view which Streng and Naumann disapprove.

This rock is often of columnar jointed structure; it forms an extensive plateau in the region of the Rothliegende, where it also probably ramifies downwards in the form of veins.

Many other porphyrites bear a close resemblance to the Ilfeld rock; for instance: the porphyrite of Korgon in the Altai Mountains, which contains greyish-white laminæ of oligoclase and specular-iron in a reddish-brown matrix; the porphyry of Hainersreuth in the Fichtelgebirge, which has reddish-white crystals of oligoclase, and very little specular iron in a reddish-brown matrix; the porphyrite of the Pentland Hills, near Edinburgh, with crystals of oligoclase, and specular-iron sparkling in a brownish-red matrix; the porphyrite of Ziegenrücken, near Hohenelbe, with crystals of oligoclase, is a dark-coloured matrix, and the porphyrite of Rovigo, near Lugano, also with oligoclase crystals in a dark matrix. The amygdaloids of Oberstein, which we have previously described on Delesse's authority, probably also may belong to this class.

Von Richthofen describes certain porphyritic rocks of Mulatto and Cavalessi, in Southern Tyrol, which contain tabular crystals of felspar in a compact, and for the most part reddish matrix, or which sometimes consist of a fine-grained mass without crystals; others contain liebenerite in the forms of nepheline or orthoclase (pseudomorphous); these last-named rocks form narrow veins, penetrating all the other rocks of that district.

Varieties in Texture.

(a) PORPHYRITIC.
(b) COMPACT.
(c) AMYGDALOIDAL PORPHYRITE or AMYGDALOID.
(d) PORPHYRITE-WACKÉ.   } Somewhat decomposed. At Ma-
ARGILOPHYRE, *Brongniart.* (*Fr.*) rienberg in Saxony, these veins of wacké in the gneiss rock are called 'Kalchgänge.'

References.

Streng, Zeitschr. d. d. geol. Ges. 1858, p. 100; 1801, p. 87.
G. Rose, ibid. 1859, p. 290.
Naumann in v. L. u. Br. Jahrb. 1800, p. 24.
Girard, ibid. 1858, p. 145.
Baentsch, Die Melaphyre des Harzes, 1858.
Von Richthofen, Geogn. Beschr. v. Süd-Tyrol, 1800, p. 149.
Kjerulf, Christiania Silurbecken, 1855, p. 20. The rhomben-porphyr of the Vetta Collen (Kjerulf's melaphyr) contains large crystals of labradorite in a felsitic matrix, which according to him also contains augite.

(B) HORNBLENDE-PORPHYRITE.
HORNBLENDEPORPHYRIT. (*Germ.*)
PORPHYRE SYÉNITIQUE. (*Fr.*)

In a compact felsitic matrix, usually of dark colour, are contained crystals or crystalline particles of hornblende and felspar (oligoclase).

Spec. grav. .   .   .   .   .   .   2·6—2·7
Contains silica (at Potschappel, near Dresden)   59 p. c.

The matrix of this rock usually much preponderates over the porphyritic crystalline parts, and is in its fresh state usually brown, violet-brown, or grey; becomes lighter in weathering. The hornblende forms small columnar or acicular crystals, which become very distinct when the matrix is somewhat weathered or discoloured. The crystals or grains of felspar (oligoclase?) are often very intimately blended with the matrix, and their species is therefore difficult to determine. At Wilsdruff, in Saxony, and in some other localities, some dark-coloured mica occurs, together with the hornblende, forming transitions into mica-porphyrite. The rock contains no quartz. The matrix is sometimes vesicular or amygdaloidal. Didey describes a blue porphyry (probably belonging to this class), and occurring at Chaux, near Trejus, where it passes through the Variegated Sandstone. He states that it contains crystals of hornblende and albite.

This rock is not known to be very extensively developed anywhere. In the Plauenschen-Grund, near Dresden, it occurs in the neighbourhood of syenite; it may possibly represent a more compact state of that rock. It is older in that place than the coal formation, and even the lower strata of that formation contain fragments of it; its jointings show smooth surfaces. The masses are irregular, approaching somewhat to the columnar form.

To this rock belong many antique porphyries, particularly the *porfido-rosso-antico*, which contains white felspar and black acicular crystals of hornblende, and usually some micaceous iron in a red matrix.

A rock occurring at the Hutberg, near Weisig, to the east of Dresden (called by Jenzsch 'amygdalophyre'), seems to belong here, as it contains some hornblende; in any case it belongs to the porphyrite group. It is often amygdaloidal, and contains in its vesicular cavities hornstone, chloraphæite, chalcedony, quartz, pyrites, and sometimes felspar, resembling petalite, which Jenzsch has called *weissigite*.

Varieties of Texture.

(*a*) PORPHYRITIC.
(*b*) COMPACT.
(*c*) AMYGDALOIDAL.
(*d*) WACKENITIC.

References.

Delesse on the antique red porphyries, Bullet. géol. 1850, p. 532; also, in v. L. u. Br. Jahrbuch, 1851, p. 422.
Jenzsch in v. L. u. Br. Jahrb. 1853, p. 386, and in 1854, p. 406.
Naumann, Erläuter. zur geogn. Karte v. Sachsen, 1845, No. 5, p. 202.
Diday, Ann. des Mines, éd. 2, p. 193, von L. u. Br. Jahrb. 1855, p. 784.

(C.) , MICA-PORPHYRITE or MICACEOUS PORPHYRY.

GLIMMERPORPHYRIT. (*Germ.*)
PORPHYRE MICACÉ. (*Fr.*)

A compact felsitic matrix, usually of dark colour, containing crystals or crystalline particles of mica and felspar.

Spec. grav. .   .   .   .   . 2·6—2·8
Contains silica at Meissen .   .   .   59 p. c.

The felsitic matrix when fresh is of a brown or violet-brown colour, but is lighter when weathered. It incloses distinct laminæ of mica of dark colour, and often of hexagonal form; also grains or crystals of felspar, sometimes frequently, sometimes sparingly disseminated.

The felspar appears to be partly oligoclase, partly orthoclase; it is white, greenish, or reddish; sometimes only in thin laminæ. Occasionally hornblende or quartz occurs, developed in distinct crystals; and thus a transition arises into hornblende-porphyrite, or granite-porphyry.

Vesicular and amygdaloidal textures sometimes occur, in which case there are usually fewer crystals porphyritically imbedded. The amygdaloidal cavities contain green-earth, calcspar, and siliceous minerals.

Mica-porphyrite abounds in the Thuringian Forest, where it is usually of irregular massive structure, with perhaps a tendency to columnar jointing. When it occurs with quartz-porphyry in that locality, it is older than it, and older too than the Rothliegende, the conglomerates of which formation contain many fragments of mica-porphyrite. Near Meissen a very characteristic mica-porphyrite is found penetrating the syenite-granite, as well as the granite dykes contained in that rock. The veins of the porphyrite are usually compact without crystals towards their outward edges, or throughout the vein, where the ramifications are narrow. At Zwickau, in Saxony, amygdaloidal varieties occur in conjunction with the compact.

Varieties in Texture.

(*a*) PORPHYRITIC.
(*b*) COMPACT.
(*c*) AMYGDALOID.
(*d*) WACKÉ.

Vide *Cotta* in v. L. u. Br. Jahrbuch, 1845, p. 75.

MICA-TRAP ROCKS.

The name mica-trap originated with Naumann, who first proposed it for certain rocks of the Erzgebirge, being compounds of mica and felspar, but himself afterwards (in his ' Geognosie ') preferred the French name of minette for the same rocks, which no doubt is their older designation. Under these circumstances, it may be admissible to transfer the name of mica-trap to an entire group of similar rocks, whose common attributes are: that they *consist principally of compounds of mica and felspar, without marked porphyritic texture ; and that they contain no quartz, unless quite exceptionally.*

We count in this group the following rocks (although it is uncertain if they are all of igneous origin), viz. Minette, Faidronite, Kersanton, and Kersantite. Until that question is determined in the negative, they may be so classed on account of their petrographic affinity ; and for the same reason they will be most conveniently treated as varieties of the same rock.

10. MICA-TRAP.

GLIMMERTRAPP. (*Germ.*)
TRAPP MICACÉ. (*Fr.*)

A compound of felspar and mica.

Spec. grav. . . . . . 2·5—2·9
Contains silica . . . . 50—65 p. c.

Varieties.

(A) MINETTE.

MINETTE. (*Germ.*)
MINETTE. (*Fr.*)

*A felsitic matrix containing much mica and sometimes distinct
crystals of orthoclase or hornblende : grey colour predominates.*

Spec. grav. . . . . . 2·5—2·9
Contains silica . . . . 50—65 p. c.

The blackish-brown magnesian mica sometimes predominates
so completely as to be alone distinctly visible. As accessories,
there occur hornblende, and sometimes chlorite and magnetic
iron-ore.   Calcspar and sparry iron are probably only of
secondary origin, and quartz is probably never present. It is
sometimes difficult to distinguish minette from mica-porphyry
or from kersantite.

It is found in considerable extent near Framont, in the Vosges
Mountains, where it first received its name from the miners, a
name which Voltz first introduced into science. Near Oederan,
in Saxony, it forms subordinate masses in the Red Gneiss, and
not far from Dippoldiswalde, in Saxony, it penetrates the grey
gneiss of the Weissritzthal in distinct veins.

References.

Voltz, Géognosie de l'Alsace, p. 55.
Naumann, Erläuter. zur geogn. Karte v. Sachsen, 1838, No. 2.
p. 96.
Cotta in v. L. u. Br. Jahrb. 1853, p. 561.
Delesse in the Ann. des Mines, [5] vol. x. p. 317, and Compt.
rend. 1857, vol. xliv. p.766. Ausz. in v. L. u. Br. Jahrb. 1858,
p. 848, and 1860, p. 724.
G. Leonhard, on Minette in the Odenwald Verhandl. d. nat.
med. Vereins zu Heidelberg, vol. ii. p. 7, and v. L. u. Br.
Jahrb. 1861, p. 495.
H. Müller Neues Jahrb. f. Min. 1865, p. 1.
H. Pauly, Neues Jahrb. f. Min. 1863, pp. 257, 418.
Th. Ebray, Minette im Morran. Neues Jahrb. f. Min. 1863,
p. 478, 1865, p. 745.

(B) FRAIDRONITE.

FRAIDRONIT. (*Germ.*)
FRAIDRONITE, *E. Dumas.* (*Fr.*)

A greenish felsitic principal mass combined with a greater or less quantity of mica. Iron pyrites and quartz occur as accessories.

This composition so evidently resembles that of minette that it might well be considered as only a variety of that rock. Lan, however, adheres to the name of fraidronite, which had been already given by Dumas, and from the analyses which he made, pronounces it to contain a considerable admixture of chlorite, which he considered as the cause of its greenish colour. He also found carbonate of iron and lime, which he considered as accessory. Delicate veins of calcspar often pervade the whole mass of the rock. On weathering it crumbles into balls or a kind of grit. In the department of Lozere and in the Cevennes it forms dykes and veins in talc-schist, mica-schist, gneiss, and granite. *Lan* in the Ann. des Mines, [5] vol. vi. p. 412; v. L. u. Br. Jahrb. 1858, p. 609.

(C) KERSANTON.

KERSANTON. (*Germ.*)
KERSANTON. (*Fr.*)

In a greenish-grey felspathic matrix are contained hexagonal tabular crystals of mica, brown to black. Less frequently the matrix is granular, and contains crystals of felspar.

Contains silica about 53 p. c.

In the matrix, felspar usually predominates, which is not orthoclase, but most likely oligoclase. The distinct crystals of felspar are generally oligoclase. The mica is magnesian mica, which is not only an ingredient in the matrix, but sometimes forms a coating round small globular grains (amygdaloids) of calcspar or quartz. Marcasite and magnetic iron-ore occur as accessories. Delicate veins of calcspar often run through the whole rock.

The name of kersanton was first given by Rivière. The rock is evidently closely allied to the mica-porphyrite, minette, and kersantite.

It abounds in the district of Brest, and Quimper in Brittany, where it is applied to building purposes.

References.

Rivière, in the Bullet. de la Soc. géol. de Fr.,1844, [2] vol. i. p. 528.
Dufrenoi, Expl. de la Carte géol. de la France, 1844, vol. i. p. 198.
Delesse, Ann. des Mines, 1851, vol. xix. p. 175.

(D) KERSANTITE.

KERSANTIT. (*Germ.*)
KERSANTITE (OLIGOCLASITE). (*Fr.*)

A fibrous or porphyritic compound of oligoclase and mica, frequently containing some hornblende and quartz.

Contains silica, about 64 p. c.

Oligoclase generally predominates in the compact or fine-grained matrix of the rock, which sometimes is entirely composed of that species of felspar, sometimes of oligoclase and mica. In this mass are enclosed crystals of oligoclase with brown stripings, and of white or greenish colour, or tinged with red by decomposition; dark laminæ of magnesia-mica, some small grains of quartz, and frequently some fibrous hornblende, especially in the narrower veins formed by this rock, and, dispersed through the whole rock, very minute particles of magnetic iron-ore.

Carrière also found some red garnet combined with hornblende in places where the latter was more prevalent and the rock somewhat fissile. At Viesembach, in the Vosges Mountains, where the rock is broken through by metalliferous veins, it contains magnetic iron pyrites and common pyrites. It is amygdaloidal. In some places the amygdaloidal cavities are filled with quartz, chlorite, epidote, and calcspar.

The porphyritic varieties of this rock (which owes its name to Delesse) are evidently closely allied to the porphyrites, or perhaps also to granite-porphyry; in other respects it very nearly corresponds with kersanton, from which it is, perhaps, only to be distinguished by its containing hornblende, and also more quartz than that rock, and by its texture being sometimes fissile.

Near Viesembach and Sainte Marie, in the Vosges, this rock forms subordinate masses and veins in gneiss. The veins are often quite compact at their borders. Fournet observed a similar rock in the granite near Francheville in Brittany.

Reference.

Delesse, in the Ann. des Mines, 1851, vol. xix. p. 165.

SYENITE GROUP.

It has been a frequent practice to include under the name of syenite all granites containing hornblende. But as the genuine syenites contain little or no quartz, we consider it more accurate to exclude the first-named rocks from the syenite group, and range them under the head of granites (syenite-granites), confining the term syenite to those rocks which consist essentially of orthoclase or microcline and hornblende, such as the rock of the Plauenschen-Grund, near Dresden. Nevertheless there is no precise boundary to be drawn between these and the syenite-granites. As accessories, some mica and even quartz may occur in syenite, but they are not essential ingredients. This narrowing of the meaning of the term syenite appears to us the more justifiable, as these genuine quartzless rocks only contain 50–60 per cent. of silica, and therefore can be included in the basic group;

whereas those containing quartz have 60—70 per cent. of silica, and so belong to the acidic group. It so happens that the derivation of the name presents no obstacle to our definition, since it is well known to have originated in the erroneous belief that the antique stones which first received the name of syenite came from Syene in Egypt, which was not the case. Rozière therefore proposed to alter the name to *Sinaite*, from Mount Sinai, where genuine syenite is found, whereas at Syene only granite occurs. Werner, who first introduced the name into scientific petrography, applied it to the quartzless rocks of the Plauenschen-Grund; although afterwards, in his 'Klassification der Gebirgsarten' (1787), he called the same rock a greenstone.

In the syenite group we also include miascite, zircon-syenite, and foyaite, as being closely allied to the genuine syenite.

11. SYENITE.

SYENIT, *Werner.* (*Germ.*)
SYÉNITE. (*Fr.*)

A crystalline granular compound of orthoclase or micro-cline and hornblende, and usually some titanite.

Spec. grav. . . . . . . 2·7—2·9.
Content of silica in the rock of the Plauenschen-Grund, near Dresden, 55—60.

The orthoclase or microcline is usually the principal ingredient, and being in general red, it gives that colour to the whole rock, deepened into a brownish-red by the hornblende. There are, however, syenites whose orthoclase is nearly white, and others containing an admixture of oligoclase. The andesine, which Delesse considered he had found in some syenites of the Vosges, is held by Rose to be a decomposed oligoclase. An indistinct fissile texture is sometimes occasioned by the parallel disposition of the felspar crystals (sometimes twins), and a porphyritic texture by the prominence of separate and larger twin crystals. The hornblende is occasionally developed in separate columnar crystals, but it usually only forms part of the general crystalline granular mass of the rock. Besides these, its two principal ingredients, syenite usually contains some titanite (or wöhlerite), forming minute

N

brown crystals of adamantine lustre, dispersed through
the general mass, often only to be recognised with the
lens.   Some mica, quartz, elæolite (nepheline), zircon,
magnetic iron-ore, and pyrites, are also to be found in
the general mass, but only as accessories and in small
quantity.   Epidote, which also occurs partly in the general mass, and partly in the crevices of the rock, is
probably the product of a decomposition of hornblende ;
and an invisibly small proportion of carbonate of lime,
causing a slight effervescence with acids, is traced by
Bischoff to the same origin.

A larger proportion of mica and quartz occasions transitions into syenite-granite or syenite-gneiss ; an increase of
elæolite and zircon, transitions into miascite and zircon-
syenite.   Again, many syenites contain oligoclase as well
as orthoclase or microcline, opening up a transition into
diorite, which latter is essentially nothing but a syenite
containing oligoclase instead of orthoclase.   This trifling
difference, which is usually connected with a coarser texture of the rock, may possibly only be a consequence of
the different level at which it attained the solid state.   We
find, indeed, syenite in its bedding to be more decidedly
plutonic than diorite.

Varieties in Texture.

(a) COMMON SYENITE.   ⎫ Uniformly granular, as in the Plau-
    GEMEINER SYENIT. (*Germ.*) ⎬ enschen-Grund, near Dresden.
    SYÉNITE COMMUNE. (*Fr.*)   ⎭

(b) PORPHYRITIC SYENITE.   ⎫ With separate and larger crys-
    PORPHYRARTIGER SYENIT. (*Germ.*) ⎬ tals of orthoclase.
    SYÉNITE PORPHYROÏDE. (*Fr.*)   ⎭

   Frh. von Richthofen has given the name of syenite-porphyry
to a rock of this class found in the Visena Valley, near Predazzo,
in Tyrol.   He describes it as consisting of a granular matrix of
orthoclase, with little hornblende, and sometimes oligoclase in
small quantity.   The matrix enclosing twin crystals (three
inches long) of orthoclase.

It would be too much to say that there are no compact,
vesicular, or amygdaloidal varieties of syenite ; we are
only unable directly to trace any rocks of such textures
through transition states from genuine syenite so as to
show a direct connection with it ; and therefore we confine the name to the distinctly granular compound of
felspar and hornblende, as above described.   But amongst
the aphanites there are certainly compact and vesicular

rocks, whose chemical composition, at least, is so exactly that of syenite, that under a slower and more plutonic process of cooling, they might well have become syenite. They bear the same relation to it as petrosilex to granite. That these compact rocks do not occur in geological connection with syenite may be owing to the thoroughly plutonic origin of the latter, causing it always and everywhere to have cooled uniformly and very slowly. The same observation applies to granite.

Properly speaking, there are no varieties of composition to adduce, unless we consider as such those transitions into granite and diorite which are occasioned by the occurrence of mica, quartz, and oligoclase. The zircon-syenite is rather a variety of miascite than of syenite proper. But this seems a fitting place in which to introduce the rock which Delesse has termed

MICA-DIORITE.
GLIMMERDIORIT. (*Germ.*)
DIORITE MICACÉ, *Delesse.*
(*Fr.*)

It consists of a crystalline granular compound of hornblende, orthoclase, oligoclase, mica, and very little quartz, generally of a dark colour, almost black. Content of silica only 48. From this composition we may regard this rock as something between diorite, syenite, and granite. In the Vosges it occurs in dykes in granite.

Syenite is usually jointed into large irregular or thick tabular masses; it forms entire mountains and occupies extensive regions; only seldom forms distinct veins or dykes in other rocks, but is not unfrequently traversed by granitic veins, or it often contains granitic concretions. It is often associated with great tracts of granite, and then passes over into syenite-granite, and finally into granite. The syenite of the Plauenschen-Grund, near Dresden, is eminently characteristic. Near Ditro, in Transylvania, instead of titanite it contains much wöhlerite.

References.

Naumann on the Saxon Syenite, Erläuterung zur geog. Karte von Sachsen, 1845, No. 5, p. 110.

L. von Buch on the Monzon-syenite in v. Leonhard's Taschenbuch, 1824, p. 345.

von Richthofen on Monzon-syenite, in Geogn. Beschr. v. Süd-Tyrol, 1860, p. 144, which contains, besides orthoclase and hornblende, some oligoclase, mica, and pyrites; ibid. p. 150.

Zirkel, Syenit des Plauenschen-Grundes. Poggendorf's Ann. vol. cxxii. p. 621.

Delesse on Mica-diorite, in which he also includes rocks from the Kuhlenberg, near Harzburg, (gabbro ?) and from the Felsberg, near Darmstadt, in the Ann. des Mines, 1851, [4] vol. xix. p. 150. Karsten's Archiv. 1851, vol. xxiv. p. 280. Bullet. de la Soc. géol. de Fr. 1850, vol. vii. p. 524. The *syénite rose d'Égypte* here described is granite, Ann. des Mines, 1847, [4] vol. xii. p. 268; 1848, [4] vol. xiii. p. 685; 1852, [5] vol. iii. p. 384; 1858, [5] vol. xiii. p. 389. On Vogesensyenit in v. L. u. Br. Jahrb. 1848, p. 769.

The following works on Syenite relate partly to rocks rich in quartz, which we class under the head of syenite-granite, viz.:—

v. Dechen in v. L. u. Br. Jahrbuch, 1858, p. 339.
v. Rath in v. L. u. Br. Jahrbuch, 1858, p. 339.
Streng in Poggend. Ann. 1853, vol. xc. p. 132.
Kjerulf, Christiania Silurbecken, 1855, pp. 8, 12, and 15.

12. MIASCITE.

Miascit.   (*Germ.*)
Miascite.   (*Fr.*)

A crystalline compound of orthoclase, nepheline, sodalite, and black mica; coarse-grained to fine-grained (in the different varieties other minerals also occur).

This rock was first discovered by G. Rose in the Ural Mountains. Its orthoclase is Breithaupt's Mikrokline, and is white or grey; the nepheline is yellowish-white (elæolite); lustre only slightly resinous; the sodalite is grey or a fine blue; the black mica is nearly unaxial. Besides these principal ingredients, the following occur, but frequently only as accessories: davyne, wöhlerite, zircon, magnetic iron-ore, pyrites, pyrochlore, cancrinite, apatite, monazite, even quartz, hornblende, &c. By means of these minerals, transitions take place into granite, syenite, and especially zircon-syenite. At Miask the texture of this rock is sometimes fissile; at Ditro, in Transylvania, where miascite occurs at the margin between syenite and mica-schist, and intimately blended with the former, the blue sodalite is frequently arranged in layers, and the texture is generally very unequal, sometimes quite coarse, sometimes fine-grained.

References.

G. Rose, Reise nach dem Ural, vol. ii. pp. 47, 93, and 535, and Poggend. Ann. vol. xlvii. p. 375.

Breithaupt, Berg- u. Hüttenm. Zeit. 1861, p. 493.
Cotta, ibid. 1862, p. 73.

Varieties in Composition.

A. ZIRCON-SYENITE.

ZIRKONSYENIT, *Von Buch.* (*Germ.*)
SYÉNITE ZIRCONIENNE. (*Fr.*)

A crystalline-granular compound of orthoclase, nepheline (elæolite), zircon, and usually only little hornblende.

This rock is closely allied to miascite, both in respect of its essential and accessory ingredients. However, its composition varies so much in different places, that it is frequently difficult to decide what are essential and what accessory ingredients. The principal place where it occurs is the district of Laurvig and Brevig, in Norway; here there also occur eukolite and eudialite as accessory ingredients.

References.

L. v. Buch, Reise nach Norwegen, vol. i. p. 133.
Haussmann, Reise nach Skandinavien, vol. ii. p. 103, and vol. x. p. 235.

B. FOYAITE.

FOYAIT. (*Germ.*)

A crystalline granular compound of orthoclase-nepheline (elæolite), and hornblende.

Spec. grav. . . . . 2·6.

The orthoclase is white or greyish-white, forms long tabular crystals with twin growth (but not very perfectly developed), and is decidedly predominant. The reddish elæolite of greasy lustre occurs in single hexagonal crystals.

The greenish-black hornblende forms columnar crystals or small grains and parts of grains. The varieties of texture are the coarse-grained, fine-grained, compact, and porphyritic; the latter contain crystals of orthoclase and elæolite in a fine-grained matrix. The orthoclase crystals themselves some-times contain elæolite and hornblende. The texture often changes very rapidly, as in gabbro. As accessories there occur titanite and magnetic iron-ore (very frequent), hexagonal brown laminæ of mica, and iron-pyrites.

This rock forms the mountains Foya and Picota in the pro-vince of Algarve in Portugal, where it is jointed in irregular masses. Blum has named it after the first mountain.

Blum in von Leonhard's Jahrbuch, 1861, p. 426.

ACIDIC IGNEOUS ROCKS.

These rocks are compounds of orthoclase, sanidine, or oligoclase, with quartz, mica, or hornblende.

They also contain many other minerals as accessories. Their proportion of silica is almost always above 60 per cent., and extends in some cases to upwards of 80 per cent.

Their texture is generally granular or porphyritic, but sometimes compact or vitreous, seldom vesicular, and never amygdaloidal. Frequently they have a somewhat fissile or foliated structure, and so they even form transitions into certain of the crystalline schists.

Like the basic rocks, they are divisible into the volcanic and the plutonic.

1. Volcanic.

In the rocks of this division the prevailing species of felspar is sanidine or oligoclase; the labradorite (rich in lime), so often found with pyroxene in the basic rocks, is very rare in the acidic. The felspar is combined with some hornblende, and more rarely also with quartz, yet the rock always contains a large proportion of silica; augite is only an accessory ingredient.

The volcanic acidic rocks fall into two principal groups; the *trachytes* and *phonolites*. The trachytic group, however, contains many varieties both of composition and texture, and hence a great number of separate names, such as pearlstone, obsidian, &c. The trachytes occur as lava at active volcanoes of the present day, which is rarely, if ever, the case with the phonolites. Perhaps the latter are, to a certain extent, products of transmutation from compact or porphyritic trachytes.

Although the trachytes, when characteristically developed, differ very widely from the basalt, so that these two may be called the extreme products of volcanic agency, yet there are many volcanic rocks of intermediate character, which, to a certain extent, form transitions between the two groups, and prevent any very definite line of distinction between them. In many individual cases it is, in fact, difficult to distinguish trachytic from basaltic rocks.

THE TRACHYTE GROUP.

The term trachyte, signifying rough stone, was first introduced by Haüy, to denote a crystalline granular compound, in which sanidine, as the predominant ingredient, is combined with some other felspar, with hornblende (or augite), mica, or even quartz, in subordinate quantities. The principal mass is sometimes fine-grained, or even compact, with distinct minerals porphyritically prominent.

Soon after Haüy had first called attention to this rock, many other rocks came to be observed, having the same mineral composition, differing somewhat from it in texture, but connected with the normal trachyte by intermediate transition states. These were called trachytic rocks, without being reckoned as actual trachytes; thus, for instance, trachyte-porphyry, pearlstone, obsidian, pumice-stone, and many compact as well as porous trachyte-lavas.

Then it was discovered that many of the rocks which, without accurate mineralogical investigation, had been taken for trachyte of the prescribed composition, contained an oligoclase-felspar instead of the sanidine formerly considered so essential an ingredient; but in other respects their trachytic character was preserved. Accordingly, the trachytes came to be divided into *sanidine-trachyte* and *oligoclase-trachyte*; these two varieties are, however, connected with each other by many transition states, and their geological position and character are identical. In compact or fine-grained states the difference between them is scarcely to be recognised; the varieties of texture appear likewise to be essentially the same in both.

It may be useful, before going on to the description of the individual trachytic rocks, to take a general survey of what have been described under that name, and the mode in which different writers have dealt with the different varieties.

Before the difference as to the species of felspar was recognised or known, the following varieties of the rock were distinguished by *Beudant* (in his Voyage en Hongrie), and by *Burat* (in his Description des Terrains volc. de la France centr. 1833), and also by *Naumann*.

(*a*) TRACHYTES.

Trachyte granitoïde (granitic trachyte), e. g. at Handerlo, near Schemnitz.

Fibrous or *gneiss-like Trachyte*, e. g. on the Pontellaria.

Trachyte schistoïde (schistous trachyte), e. g. at the Pas de Compain, department of Cantal in France.

Trachyte à gros crystaux, a trachyte rich in felspar, at Drachenfels, near Bonn.

Trachyte amphibolique, a trachyte rich in hornblende, e. g. near Schemnitz (perhaps the same as Breithaupt's timazite).

Trachyte micacé (micaceous trachyte), Monte Catini, in Tuscany.

Domite, or *Trachyte terreux* (domite or claystone-like trachyte), e. g. at the Puy de Dôme.

Trachyte porphyroïde (porphyritic trachyte), Schemnitz and Kremnitz in Hungary.

Trachyte homogène (simple trachyte), frequently resembling phonolite, Monts Dorés in Vélay.

Trachyte semi-vitreux (semi-vitreous trachyte), Tokay in Hungary; Iceland.

Masenga, according to Naumann, the genuine trachyte of the Euganean Hills in Lombardy.

Nenfro of Brocchi, according to Naumann, genuine trachytes of the Cimini Mountains.

Nekrolite of Brocchi, according to Naumann, trachyte from Viterbo and Tolfa.

(*b*) TRACHYTE-PORPHYRIES CONTAINING QUARTZ.

Perlite-like Trachyte-porphyry. Hungary.

Porous Trachyte-porphyry. Hungary.

Vesicular Trachyte-porphyry (with globular cavities). Hungary.

Millstone porphyry, or cavernous trachyte-porphyry. Mühlensteinporphyr, or cavernöser Trachytporphyr. — Porphyre meulier. Illiniker valley, in Hungary.

Claystone-like Trachyte-porphyry. Thonsteinähnlicher Trachytporphyr, Ponza Islands.

(*c*) QUARTZLESS TRACHYTE-PORPHYRIES.

Perlite-like Trachyte-porphyry, without quartz. Hungary.

Claystone-like Trachyte-porphyry, without quartz. Hungary.

Pumice-stone-like Trachyte-porphyry, without quartz. Hungary.

Slaty Trachyte-porphyry, without quartz. Ponza Islands.

(*d*) PERLITES AND PEARLSTONE-PORPHYRIES.

Perlite testacé (granular shelly perlite). Telkebanya in Hungary.

Spherolitic perlite or spherolite rock. Schemnitz in Hungary.

Perlite retinitique (pitchstone-like perlite); Ofen in Hungary. Lipari Islands.

Perlite porphyrique (perlite porphyry), Hungary.
Perlite lithoïde compacte (claystone-like perlite), Hungary.
Perlite ponceaux (perlite pumice-stone), Hungary.

(e) PURE OBSIDIAN.
  Porphyritic Obsidian, or obsidian-porphyry, spherulitic obsidian.

(f) PUMICE-STONE.
  Obsidian pumice-stone.
  Perlite pumice-stone.
  Trachyte pumice-stone.

(g) ANDESITE.

(h) TRACHYTE-DOLERITE.
  In the decomposed states of trachyte, and especially in the so-called alumstone, we can of course not recognise the fresh state of the rock.

The first thing which strikes us with reference to the foregoing catalogue is the great number and variety of rocks which may be included under the head of trachyte in its more extended signification. All the distinctions which have been made are, however, not equally important. Some varieties occur only in one locality, and some scarcely belong to the trachytes at all. In investigating a particular district, we should, of course, notice the smallest modifications in the nature of the rocks which come under our observation; but for the purposes of definition in a general treatise like the present it is impossible, and would be undesirable, to record every trifling variety of texture and composition.

G. Rose, in the 4th vol. of the 'Kosmos,' has proposed to subdivide all trachytic rocks into the six following groups:—

1. A rock whose principal mass consists entirely of crystals of vitreous felspar, which are tabular and usually large. Little or no hornblende and mica are contained in its composition, and are quite non-essential as ingredients—Campi Phelegräi, Ischia, La Tolfa, &c. Augite shows itself in small crystals in the Mont Doré, but very rarely. In the Campi Phelegräi, where there is hornblende there is no augite, also no leucite, but of this last mineral Hoffman discovered some specimens at the Lake of Averno, and G. Rose on the cliffs of the Monte Nuovo.

2. A rock whose principal mass contains single vitreous felspar crystals and a great number of small snow-white oligoclase crystals. The latter are frequently regular, and grown into the vitreous felspar, and form a covering round it. Sometimes a small proportion of hornblende and mica, and in some varieties augite, are found in it.
  The trachytes of Drachenfels and the Perlenhardt in the

Siebengebirge, and many varieties in the Mont Doré and Cantal, belong to this subdivision.

3. These are dioritic trachytes whose principal mass contains many small oligoclase crystals with black hornblende and brown magnesian mica. To this species belong the trachytes of Ægina, the Kozelniker valley near Schemnitz, Nagyag in Transylvania, and Montabaur in Nassau, Stenzelberg and Wolkenburg in the Siebengebirge, Puy de Chaumont, near Clermont, and Liorant in Cantal. The Kasbegk in the Caucasus, the Mexican volcanoes of Toluca and Orizaba, also the domites of L. v. Buch, belong to this subdivision. In the white fine-grained matrix of the trachytes of the Puy de Dôme are enclosed vitreous crystals which have always been considered to be felspar, by which term Rose implies orthoclase, but the cleavage surfaces of which always show striæ, and are, therefore, in fact, oligoclase. (The above-named examples from Hungary and Transylvania belong to Breithaupt's timazite.)

4. The principal mass contains augite and oligoclase. The peak of Teneriffe, the Mexican volcanoes, Popocatapetl and Colima, the South American volcanoes, Tolima, Purace near Popayan, Pasto, and Cumbal Ruca Pichincha, Antisana, Cotopaxi, Chimborazo, Tunguragua. In Tunguragua, associated with the augite crystals, there occur small independent crystals of uralite of blackish-green colour (diabase or dolerite ?).

5. A combination of labradorite and augite, a doleritic trachyte, Ætna, Stromboli, &c. (Why should not these rocks be genuine dolerites ?)

6. A rock whose matrix is usually grey, in which crystals of leucite and augite are enclosed, with some olivine (very little). Vesuvius and Somma ; also the extinct volcanoes Vulture, Rocca Monfina ; the Albanian Mountains and Borghetto. (This is the same as our leucite rock.)

It will be seen that Rose's idea of trachyte is much more extended than is at all usual : it embraces almost all the volcanic rocks.

More recently Freiherr v. Richthofen has divided the trachyte formations of Transylvania and Hungary into two classes—the rhyolitic and trachytic. The latter are almost exclusively rocks containing hornblende and oligoclase as their essential constituents. Sanidine is not the predominant felspar except in certain rocks of the most recent and subordinate eruptions ; so that, speaking generally, according to von Richthofen, by far the greater proportion of the whole group of trachytes (proper) consists of oligoclase, and not of sanidine rocks. The silica is never so abundant as to develope distinct crystals of quartz.

Von Richthofen subdivides the trachytes again into 'greenstone trachytes' and 'grey trachytes.' The former (our timazite) often correspond exactly with the oldest diorites and dioritic porphyries. The latter, on the other hand, consist principally of oligoclase and hornblende, with the occasional addition of some augite.

Under the term *rhyolite*, Richthofen embraces all the most acidic (richest in silica) amongst the recent igneous rocks. He especially instances in Hungary the trachyte-porphyries, perlites, &c. (Vide L. u. B. Jahrb. 1859, p. 304, and 1861, p. 98 ; Jahrbuch d. geol. Reichsanst. 1860, Sitzungsber. p. 92.)

These two groups of trachytes *proper* and rhyolites certainly appear of general geological importance; they bear the same relation to each other, within the acidic group, as the acidic rocks bear to the basic; and although in Hungary they both belong to one and the same great tertiary eruptive period, the rhyolites always appear the more recent of the two.

We find similar phenomena in the rocks of all eruptive periods, the plutonic as well as the volcanic. Where syenites and granites occur together, the granite (rich in silica) is usually the most recent; in the same way we often find veins of granite intersecting the gabbro (poor in silica). In the Thuringian Forest the quartz-porphyries are in general of more recent origin than the mica-porphyrites (poor in silica), although they both belong to the same great period. In the Bohemian Mittelge-birge, whose conical mountains consist partly of basalt and partly of phonolite, both of which appear to have been formed during the tertiary period, the phonolite (somewhat the richer of the two in silica) is found throughout as the most recent; so that putting all these facts together, we are almost justified in holding it for a universal law, that wherever igneous rocks rich in silica occur together with basic igneous rocks of the same great period of eruption, the former are of somewhat later origin than the latter. Basalt, nevertheless, sometimes forms an exception to this rule, as in Hungary, where it penetrates the trachytes; but it is questionable whether the basalt in these cases may not belong to a separate period more recent still than the trachytes.

If we find it impossible to define a precise boundary
between the acidic and basic volcanic rocks, any more
than between the volcanic and plutonic groups themselves,
there can hardly be matter for surprise; we should, on
the contrary, be at a loss to explain any such sharp distinction if it existed. We find rocks of character' so
undecided, that we may with almost equal justice group
them with the greenstones as the trachytes. Such, for
instance, is timazite. With others it may appear doubtful
whether we should attach them to basalt or trachyte. Such
are trachydolerite and andesite. The latter was in the first
instance, without much inquiry, grouped with the trachytes
because of its geological position and its rough texture.
Subsequently the prevailing felspar species was taken for
albite, and L. von Buch called the rock andesite from the
Andes, where it occurs in great extent, to distinguish it
from ordinary trachyte; and although it has lately been
discovered that the felspar is not albite but oligoclase,
that does not seem to us to furnish a sufficient reason for
changing the name of the rock (as proposed in ' Kosmos'),
if we wish to preserve any individuality for it at all. It
may, however, remain questionable how the rock should
be grouped. If we find with the oligoclase, pyroxene
and hornblende occurring as essential and important ingredients; if the rock contains no quartz, but occasionally
dark magnesia-mica, olivine, and titanite (and always
magnetic iron-ore), then it may certainly be that andesite,
if a volcanic product, should be assigned to the basalts;
or if plutonic, to the greenstones. Whilst, on the other
hand, its somewhat high proportion of silica (59—67 per
cent.), as well as its sometimes vitreous state, is opposed
to this grouping, and gives the rock a more trachytic
character. It is for these reasons a rock of middle character, of which there are many such. Roth even distinguishes a pyroxene-andesite and an amphibole-andesite.
With the first he classes many volcanic rocks of Iceland
and Teneriffe; with the latter, the so-called trachytes of
Wolkenburg, and of Stenzelberg in the Siebengebirge, the
domite of the Puy de Dôme, and many lavas of Ætna.

The trachytes often form an essential part of the products of active volcanoes, and form actual lava streams.
They are also frequently found at so-called extinct

volcanoes; and form single conical hills or connected groups of mountains in districts where, since the tertiary period, no eruptions have taken place. These last-mentioned older trachytes approach in character the plutonic rocks. We are, however, unacquainted with any trachytes which are certainly older than the Tertiary period.

We propose, with Von Richthofen, to divide all the trachytic rocks into two separate sub-groups (trachytes and rhyolites), the differences between which are more marked than those of the several varieties of mere texture and composition. These latter differences are, however, important enough to deserve a more special notice than the corresponding varieties of many other rocks; and we shall, therefore, accord them a full description, merely premising in general that they are apt to run one into the other by gradual transitions occasioned by the preponderance or the reverse of a principal ingredient.

13. TRACHYTE.

TRACHYT. (*Germ.*)
TRACHYTE, *Haüy*. (*Fr.*)

A compound of sanidine, oligoclase (or even albite and labradorite), with some hornblende or augite and dark-coloured mica. A rough principal mass in which, as matrix, some of its mineral constituents are frequently distinctly and separately developed and imbedded.

Spec. grav. . . . . . 2·4—2·8
Contains silica . . . . 50—67 p. c.

As a rule, in all trachytes the felspar is predominant. The detailed grouping of their different mineral ingredients will appear from the description which we give below of the several varieties in composition.

Varieties in Texture.

(*a*) GRANULAR TRACHYTE.
KÖRNIGER TRACHYT. (*Germ.*)
TRACHYTE GRANITOÏDE. (*Fr.*)

(*b*) PORPHYRITIC TRACHYTE.
PORPHYRARTIGER TRACHYT. (*Germ.*) } With large felspar crystals.
TRACHYTE PORPHYROÏDE. (*Fr.*)

(*c*) COMPACT TRACHYTE.
ZIEMLICH DICHTER TRACHYT. (*Germ.*) } (Or of a state very nearly approaching the compact.)
TRACHYTE LITHOÏDE. (*Fr.*) } Also somewhat porphyritic.

(d) VESICULAR TRACHYTE.   } Often, par excellence, called *Tra-*
　　BLASIGER TRACHYT. (*Germ.*) } *chyte lava.*
　　TRACHYTE VACUOLAIRE. (*Fr.*) }

(e) DECOMPOSED TRACHYTE.   } Many decomposed varieties are
　　ZERSETZTER TRACHYT. (*Germ.*)} called *Alumstone,* on account of
　　TRACHYTE DÉCOMPOSÉ. (*Fr.*) } their containing alum.

Varieties in Composition.

(A) SANIDINE-TRACHYTE.

　　SANIDIN-TRACHYT.   (*Germ.*)

An aggregate of sanidine crystals, with some hornblende or mica as subordinate ingredients. Texture coarse or fine-grained to compact.

　　Spec. grav. . . . . . 2·4—2·6
　　Contains silica . . . . . 59—60 p. c.

In this compound, principally consisting of sanidine, hornblende, and magnesia-mica, occur, as accessory ingredients, magnetic iron-ore, sodalite, olivine, titanite, and augite or quartz. It further appears probable, from the frequent preponderance of the proportion of soda over the potash in the whole rock, that the compact matrix which permeates the whole mass, cementing the distinct and recognisable minerals, contains, in addition to those we have mentioned, some mineral rich in soda, such as oligoclase, sodalite, or nepheline. The sanidine often occurs in a porphyritic form. The colour of the rock fluctuates between greyish-white and dark-brown grey. In most cases the texture is porphyritic, with granular or sometimes compact matrix; some varieties are vesicular, and at the surface even scoriaceous, but not amygdaloidal. By decomposition a state is produced, not wackenitic, but more resembling claystone. The mass then appears almost white, whereas, in fresh condition, it is often very dark-coloured. The rock is generally of irregularly jointed structure.

To this species belong, according to Roth, the trachytes of Rabertshausen, in the Grand Duchy of Hessen; of Kappellenberg (which contains some pyrope); of Mondhalde and Silberbrunnen, at the Kaiserstuhl; of Gleichenberg, in Styria; of Monte Olibano, near Pozzuoli. Likewise the lavas found at Monte Nuovo, and those of the Azores, &c.

The grey porous sanidine-trachyte, which occurs at the Laager lake, contains a good deal of haüyne.

(B) SANIDINE-OLIGOCLASE-TRACHYTE (DRACHENFELS TRACHYTE).

　　SANIDIN-OLIGOKLASTRACHYT.   (*Germ.*)

A crystalline compound of sanidine and oligoclase with magnesia-mica and hornblende, also some augite, magnetic iron-ore, and titanite.

　　Spec. grav. . . . . . 2·6—2·7
　　Contains silica . . . . 60—67 p. c.

This very characteristic rock of the Drachenfels, near Bonn, with its large sanidine crystals porphyritically enclosed in granular matrix, served a long time as the principal type of the trachytes, and all the felspar in that rock was assumed to be sanidine. Now, however, it appears, from the very considerable quantity of soda contained in the matrix (up to 5 per cent.), that the latter probably consists principally of oligoclase. It is especially worthy of remark that in this porphyritic trachyte the large sanidine crystals frequently assume a parallel position to each other; they are also sometimes broken in two, but both pieces still lie close together imbedded in the matrix. According to Roth, to this class belong the trachytes of Kühlsbrunnen, in the Siebengebirge, and Freienhäuschen, in the Eifel; also, according to Richthofen, many trachytes of Hungary and Transylvania.

(C) OLIGOCLASE-TRACHYTE (DOMITE).

OLIGOKLAS-TRACHYT. (*Germ.*)

DOMITE. (*Fr.*)

In this rock oligoclase is the only recognisable felspar, as it contains no sanidine. The oligoclase is combined with some hornblende or augite and dark-coloured mica.

These trachytes have been the least accurately analysed of any. They contain many other accessory minerals. If the quantity of hornblende be above the average, then they pass into greenstones, e.g. into the greenstone-trachyte of Richthofen, or the timazite of Breithaupt. Whether andesite and trachydolerite should be included here may be doubtful. We prefer to treat them separately. This variety occurs in a tolerably fresh state at Stenzelberg, and at Wolkenburg, in the Siebengebirge. At the Puy de Dôme, on the other hand, it is much decomposed, rough, almost crumbly, and is there called domite. It would be hazardous to attempt to distinguish varieties of texture.

At Stenzelberg this rock exhibits a singular cylindrical jointed structure, in so-called 'outliers,' which consist of round columns, composed of concentric layers. Usually its structure is massive.

(D) ANDESITE.

ANDESIT. (*Germ.*)

ANDÉSITE. (*Fr.*)

A fine-grained or compact, and sometimes vitreous matrix, usually of dark-grey to black colour; contains crystals which, according to G. Rose, are oligoclase and augite. According to Abich, on the other hand, they are albite or oligoclase; and Abich adds, that some sanidine and hornblende, and always magnetic iron-ore, are likewise found in the rock. Dark-coloured mica frequently also occurs.

Spec. grav. . . . . . . 2·6—2·7
Contains silica . . . . . 50—67 p. c.

Roth distinguishes an amphibole-andesite and a pyroxene-andesite, but as the latter likewise contains some hornblende, this distinction would be difficult to maintain. To the amphibole-andesites, according to him, the localities which we have

above given under the head of 'oligoclase-trachyte' apply;
to the pyroxene-andesite, many volcanic rocks of Iceland and
Teneriffe.

This rock was first named by L. v. Buch, and its felspar was
taken to be entirely albite. G. Rose could only discover oligoclase in it. Doubts have also arisen respecting the other ingredients. The matrix is sometimes easily to be reduced to
powder. Known localities of its occurrence are: Pinchincha,
Chimborazo, Antisana, and Cotopaxi; according to Abich, also
the Caucasus and Mount Ararat.

(E) TRACHYDOLERITE.

    TRACHYDOLERIT.   (*Germ.*)
    TRACHY-DOLÉRITE.   (*Fr.*)

A compound of oligoclase (or labradorite) with hornblende or
augite, some magnetic iron-ore, and frequently also mica. These
minerals lie imbedded in a grey or brown matrix.

    Spec. grav. .   .   .   .   . 2·7—2·8
    Contains silica .   .   .   .   . 54—61 p. c.

We may here distinguish the varieties which contain hornblende from those which contain augite; the latter are very
nearly related to dolerite.

Vesicular varieties also occur. Abich, who first distinguished
this rock and gave it its name, designates the following places
where it is found :—The Peak of Teneriffe, the Schivelutsch in
Kamtschatka, the island of Liscanera, near Stromboli, and the
older lavas of Ætna, for the varieties which contain hornblende;
and the top of the crater of Stromboli, and the central cone of
the Rocca Monfina, for those containing augite.

Deiters recognised in the rock of the Löwenburg, in the
Siebengebirge, a complete transition grade between trachyte
and dolerite. Under the microscope its principal mass appears
to consist of crystalline felspar (either oligoclase or labradorite),
imbedded in which lie scattered crystals of striated felspar,
of hornblende, augite, magnetic iron-ore, and even some olivine.
The content of silica here diminishes to 52 per cent.

References.

Beudant, Voyage en Hongrie, translated (into German) by
    Kleinschrod, 1825.
Abich, Vulkanische Erscheinungen, 1841; Vulkanische Bil-
    dungen, 1849; Natur des armenischen Hochlandes, 1843,
    p. 25; and Poggendorf's Annalen, 1840, vol. l. p. 345.
Bunsen, in Poggendorf's Annalen, vol. lxxxiii. p. 197.
Sartorius v. Walterhausen, Die vulk. Gesteine in Sicilien und
    Island, 1853.
Schill, in G. Leonhard's Beitr. z. mineral. Kenntn. von Baden,
    1854, No. 3, p. 46.
Deville, Sur le Trachytisme d. Roches, in Compt. rend. 1859,
    vol. xlviii. p. 16.
Engelbach, in der Erläuter. d. geogn. Karte von Hessen. Sect.
    Schotten. Darmst. 1859, p. 43.

Rammelsberg, in Zeitschr. d. d. geol. Ges. 1859, vol. xi. p. 434.
Zirkel, Die trachytischen Gesteine der Eifel, in Zeitschr. d. d.
geol. Ges. 1859, vol. xi. p. 507.
L. v. Buch on Andesite, in Poggendorf's Ann. vol. xxxvii. p. 189.
v. Dechen gives eight divisions of trachyte in his Geogn. Beschr.
des Siebengebirges (Verhandl. d. nat. Ver. d. Rheinlande,
1852). He appears, however, to have abandoned these in
his more recent 'Geogn. Führer durch d. Siebengebirge.'
Zehler observed, in 1837, as many as forty different trachyte
varieties in his ' Siebengebirge.'
Vom Rath, in his treatise, 'Die Trachyte des Siebengebirges,'
1860, makes the following divisions:—

1. *Drachenfels trachyte*, whose white or grey matrix contains crystals of vitreous felspar and oligoclase, and some
magnesia-mica and hornblende; accessorily, titanite, magnetic iron-ore, augite, and apatite. Content of silica, 65—66.

2. *Wolkenburg trachyte*. The colour of the matrix from grey
to black, or sometimes reddish. It contains crystals of oligoclase, no vitreous felspar, but some hornblende and magnesia-
mica. Accessorily, augite, olivine, magnetic iron-ore, pyrites,
and perhaps some quartz. Content of silica, 59—62 per cent.

3. *Trachyte of Rosenau* (not in connected rocks, only found
in blocks). The base contains crystals of vitreous felspar,
no oligoclase, more rarely some magnesia-mica, hornblende,
sphene, and magnetic iron-ore. Content of silica, 78·8.

The matrix appears in all these three varieties to be principally felsitic. Acid produces a weak effervescence, which
may well be owing to carbonates of later origin than the
rock itself, and the small quantity of zeolite which occurs is
in all probability the result of decomposition.

Vom Rath, Ueber Trachyt d. Enganeen. Zeitschr. d. deutschen
geol. Ges. 1864, pp. 254–498.
Deiters, Die Trachytdolerite des Siebengebirges, in Zeitschr.
d. d. geol. Ges. 1861, p. 99.
v. Richthofen, in the Jahrbuch d. geol. Reichsanst. 1860, Sitzungsber. p. 92; extract in von L. u. Br. Jahrbuch, 1859,
p. 304, and 1861, p. 98 ; Jahrb. d. geol. Reichsanst. 1864, p. 7.
Stache has given the name of DACIT to a quartzose trachyte of
Transylvania. Geogn. Beschr. von Siebenbürgen.

14. RHYOLITE.

RHYOLITH. (*Germ.*)

*A compact, enamel-like, or vitreous matrix enclosing
grains or crystals of sanidine, oligoclase, mica, or
even quartz.*

Spec. grav.	.	.	.	.	2·3—2·6
Contains silica .	.	.	.	.	67—82 p. c.

The matrix, which should, strictly speaking, always be
of a prevailing felsitic character, varies however from the

O

simple compact to the vitreous state.   It is distinguished
from that of the trachyte proper by its larger proportion
of silica; and the same difference in the proportion of
silica is found to obtain between the trachytes and rhyolites in the collective analysis of each rock in its entirety.
Hence in rhyolite free quartz appears much more frequently than in genuine trachyte; on the other hand, the
former contains no hornblende or augite, or, at least,
those minerals are much more rarely found in it than in
trachyte.

Under the common name of rhyolite we comprehend
the following principal varieties:—*Trachyte-porphyry*,
perlite, obsidian, and *pumice-stone*, all of which possess
sub-varieties.

A. TRACHYTE-PORPHYRY.—Liparite.

TRACHYTPORPHYR, LITHOIDIT in part.   (*Germ.*)
PORPHYRE TRACHYTIQUE.   (*Fr.*)

A compact felsitic matrix containing crystals of felspar,
and sometimes also mica or quartz.   But as this
general definition essentially agrees with that of
many porphyrites and quartz-porphyries, it is perhaps better to say: *Trachyte-porphyry is the name*
given to those rocks (prevalently felsitic and porphy-
ritic with a compact matrix) which are geologically
allied to the trachytes.

Spec. grav.   .   .   .   .   .   .   2·4—2·6
Contains silica .   .   .   .   .   .   67—81 p. c.

The trachyte-porphyries are, as a rule, much richer in
silica than the trachytes proper which we have described
above.   Their matrix is of prevalent felsitic composition
and character, scarcely to be distinguished from that
of the quartz-porphyries, and it only very rarely and
exceptionally contains some traces of hornblende.

Some trachyte-porphyries even contain grains or crystals of quartz or mica, or of both those minerals together,
and thereby their resemblance to quartz-porphyry, granite-porphyry, or mica-porphyrite, becomes still greater,
and in fact so great, that occasionally, in the form of
single specimens, it is impossible to tell the difference.
In these cases, the only real difference consists in their
geological connection with genuine trachytes or their

petrographical transition into perlite or pumice-stone. The felspar of the distinctly developed crystals in trachyte-porphyry is most usually oligoclase, but sometimes also sanidine; both of these also occur in quartz-porphyries.

The most important varieties in texture, but which may almost all be divided into those with, and those without, quartz, are:—

(a) COMMON TRACHYTE-PORPHYRY. } Its felsitic matrix is compact
    GEMEINER TRACHYTPORPHYR. (*Germ.*) } in fresh fracture, and frequently somewhat shining; usually light-coloured, containing (more or less plentifully dispersed) crystals of sanidine or oligoclase, mica, or sometimes quartz. At the Schlossberg of Neusohl the matrix is of greenish colour, compact, with crystals of felspar, mica, and quartz. In the Hliniker valley, near Schemnitz, the matrix is yellowish, and especially distinguished for its crystals of mica.

(b) PERLITE-LIKE TRACHYTE-PORPHYRY. } The matrix is often
    PERLITÄHNLICHER TRACHYTPORPHYR. (*Germ.*) } somewhat enamel-like, and contains, besides those crystals which we have mentioned, small compact balls of felspar (spherulites), frequently with radial fibrous texture, sometimes also grains of quartz and mica. These rocks pass over by transition into perlite.

(c) ARGILO-TRACHYTE-PORPHYRY. } The matrix is dull
    THONSTEINÄHNLICHER TRACHYTPORPHYR. (*Germ.*) } or earthy, and usually penetrated with firm veins or nests of harder texture. Bereghasz in Hungary.

(d) VESICULAR or CAVERNOUS TRACHYTE-} The matrix contains
    PORPHYRY, MILLSTONE PORPHYRY. } round vesicular cavi-
    BLASIGER oder CAVERNÖSER TRACHYTPOR- } ties, or is entirely pene-
    PHYR, MÜHLSTEINPORPHYR. (*Germ.*) } trated with small irregularly shaped cavities, whose sides are sometimes partly coated with chalcedony or quartz.

These cavities, however, are never entirely filled, so as to form genuine amygdaloids. Hliniker valley near Schemnitz.

(e) PUMICEOUS TRACHYTE-PORPHYRY. } Forms a transition
    BIMSTEINÄHNLICHER TRACHYTPORPHYR. (*Germ.*) } from the vesicular variety into pumice-stone.

(f) SLATY TRACHYTE-PORPHYRY. } The slaty texture is pro-
    SCHIEFRIGER TRACHYTPORPHYR. (*Germ.*) } duced by the manifold alternation of their layers of somewhat differing composition.

Forchhammer has designated certain varieties of trachyte-porphyry which occur in Iceland by the special names of Krablite and Baulite. According to Bunsen, these are compounds of orthoclase and quartz.

All these varieties abound in certain trachyte regions, as, for instance, in the neighbourhood of Schemnitz in Hungary, in the Euganean Hills, on the Ponza Islands and the Lipari Islands. They are usually irregularly cleft into angular masses, with columnar or tabular jointed structure.

References.

Beudant, Voyage en Hongrie, 1822, in many places.
Poulet Scrope, Ponza Islands, in Transact. of the Geol. Soc. [2]
    vol. ii. p. 195.
Abich, Vulkanische Bildungen, 1849, p. 23. Vulkanische Er-
    scheinungen, 1841, p. 20; Geol. N. d. armenischen Hoch-
    landes, 1843, p. 44.
K. v. Hauer, Jahrbuch d. Geol. Reichsanst. 1859, p. 466.
Forchhammer, in the Journ. f. prakt. Chemie, 1843, p. 390.
Bunsen, in Poggend. Annalen, 1851, vol. lxxxiii. p. 201.

B. PERLITE.—Pearlstone, Pearlstone-porphyry.

PERLIT.   (*Germ.*)
PERLITE.   (*Fr.*)

*An enamel-like matrix containing round grains, several
of which are constructed with concentric layers.*

Spec. grav.   .   .   .   .   .   .   2·3—2·4
Contains silica .   :   .   .   .   .   · 70—77 p. c.

The whole mass of the rock perlite is of the same composition as that of trachyte-porphyry, except that, on an
average, it is somewhat more rich in silica.   The state,
however, of this compound, which is distinguished as
perlite, often alternates with the simple compact obsidian
state, or that other state which has become porphyritic
by the occurrence of sanidine crystals.   It also forms
transition states into pumice-stone.   Occasionally there
occur, in addition to the sanidine crystals, some small
mica flakes, red garnets, and even crystals of quartz.
According to texture, Beudant distinguishes the following varieties :—

(*a*) GRANULAR SHELLY PERLITE.
    KÖRNIGSCHALIGER PERLIT.   (*Germ.*)
    TRACHYTE TESTACÉ.   (*Fr.*)

(*b*) SPHÆRULITIC PERLITE.   } With compact or radial striped
    SPHÄROLITISCHER PERLIT. (*Germ.*) } felsite balls.
    PERLITE GLOBULAIRE.   (*Fr.*)

(*c*) PERLITE-PORPHYRY.
    PERLITPORPHYR.   (*Germ.*)
    PERLITE PORPHYROÏDE. (*Fr.*)

(*d*) VITREOUS, WITH RESINOUS LUSTRE.
    PECHSTEINARTIGER PERLIT.   (*Germ.*)

(*e*) ARGILLACEOUS PERLITE.
    THONSTEINARTIGER PERLIT.   (*Germ.*)

(*f*) PUMICEOUS PERLITE.
    PERLITBIMSTEIN.   (*Germ.*)

All these varieties are found (for instance) in the trachytic regions
of Hungary, near Schemnitz, Tokay, Telkebanya, &c., near Zimapan
in Mexico, on the Lipari Islands, &c.

References.

Beudant, Voyage en Hongrie, vol. ii. p. 363.
v. Pettko, in Haidinger's Abhandlungen, 1847, vol. i. p. 298;
and as to Schemnitz, in the Abhandlung. d. geol. Reichstanst.
1853, vol. ii. No. 1. He names the variety with felsite balls
'Spherolite rock.'
Erdmann, Journ. f. tech. Chemie, 1832, vol. xv. p. 38.
Delesse, Bullet. de la Soc. géol. 1854, [2] vol. xi. p. 100; v. L.
u. Br. Jahrb. 1856, p. 105.

C. OBSIDIAN and PUMICE-STONE.

OBSIDIAN und BIMSTEIN. (*Germ.*)
OBSIDIENNE et PONCE. (*Fr.*)

*Obsidian is a volcanic glass, sometimes porphyritic by
reason of sanidine crystals; this glass, however, when
it becomes vesicular, passes over into the most exquisite
foam-like pumice-stone.*

Spec. grav. . . . . . . 2·3—2·5
Contains silica . . . . . . 71—82 p. c.

This glassy or frothy texture belongs only to the rocks
of the trachyte group, and more especially to the trachyte-porphyries or rhyolites. Their colour is (in the
case of obsidian) usually dark—black, brown, or greenish;
in the case of pumice-stone, on the other hand, white or
yellowish-grey. According to differences of texture, we
may distinguish:—

(*a*) COMMON OBSIDIAN.
GEMEINER OBSIDIAN. (*Germ.*) } A mere glass.
OBSIDIENNE COMMUNE LITHOÏDE. (*Fr.*)

(*b*) OBSIDIAN-PORPHYRY } With sanidine crystals, or some-
OBSIDIANPORPHYR. (*Germ.*) } times also mica plates.
OBSIDIENNE PORPHYROÏDE. (*Fr.*)

(*c*) SPHÆRULITIC OBSIDIAN. } With felsite balls, passing
SPHÄROLITISCHER OBSIDIAN. (*Germ.*) } over into perlite.
OBSIDIENNE GLOBULAIRE. (*Fr.*)

(*d*) VESICULAR OBSIDIAN, PUMICE-STONE. } This rock is often of
BLASIGER OBSIDIAN (BIMSTEIN). (*Germ.*) } such long fibre and so
OBSIDIENNE VACUOLAIRE. (*Fr.*) } porous that it will even
} float on water.

These species of volcanic glass are only found in trachytic volcanic
regions. They are very characteristically developed at the Peak of
Teneriffe, the Lipari Islands, in Iceland, in Mexico, &c.

References.

Beudant, Voyage en Hongrie, vol. iii. p. 389.
Erdmann, Journ. f. techn. Chem. 1832, vol. xv. p. 36.
K. v. Hauer, Jahrb. d. g. Reichsanst. 1854, p. 868.
Damour, Poggend. Ann. 1844, vol. lxii. p. 287.

Mundoch, Phil. Mag. and Journ. 1844, [2] vol. xxv. p. 495.
v. d. Boon-Meesch, Pogg. Ann. 1828, vol. xii. p. 616.
Herter, Perlstein. Zeitschr. d. deutschen geol. Gesellsch. vol. xv.
    p. 459.

PHONOLITE GROUP.

15. PHONOLITE, CLINKSTONE.

PHONOLITH, KLINGSTEIN, PORPHYRSCHIEFER. (*Germ.*)
PHONOLITHE. (*Fr.*)

*A compact base or matrix, in its fresh state dark
greenish-grey, showing here and there single cleavage
surfaces of a vitreous felspar.   The mass is as a rule
somewhat slaty or schistose in texture, or of thinly
tabular jointed structure—gives a clear sound when
struck by the hammer; on weathering a sharply
defined white crust is formed.*

Spec. grav. .   .   .   .   .   .   2·4—2·6
Contains silica .   .   .   .   .   .   50—62 p. c.

Klaproth proposed the name of phonolite for this rock,
as having a more scientific air than that of klingstein,
previously in use, of which it is the translation, and
the new name has been very generally accepted.   The
peculiar properties of the rock had long been recognised,
its difference from basalt, trachyte, felsite rock, &c., but its
exact ingredients had not been investigated.   Gmelin first
drew attention to its analysis by muriatic acid, in which it
is partly soluble and partly insoluble.   The soluble part was
considered to be a zeolitic substance, the latter a felspar,
and the whole was considered to be an intimately blended
compound of zeolite and felspar (sanidine).

By the more exact microscopic and chemical investigations of later times, however, it has appeared that the
composition of the phonolite mass is not so simple, and is
in some part wholly different from what was supposed.
It is even questionable whether in its fresh state it contains any zeolitic substance at all; certain is it that the
nepheline crystals which both Breithaupt and Rose early
recognised in phonolite, as well as the mineral forming
part of the matrix which Rammelsberg also judged to be
nepheline, have frequently been mistaken for zeolite.

G. Jenzsch ventures to give the following as the mineralogical composition of this rock, after investigating microscopically and chemically several very characteristic
phonolites of Bohemia :—

	Per cent.
Sanidine, estimated at	53·55
Nepheline, do.	31·76
Hornblende (arvendsonite)	9·34
Titanite	3·67
Pyrites	0·04

These proportional values must, of course, vary greatly with locality.

As accessories, the following minerals occur, and are sometimes distinctly to be recognised in the rock ; viz. oligoclase, augite, magnetic iron-ore, olivine, haüyne, brown mica, leucite, and nosean ; the last two minerals are the least frequent. It is possible that the zeolite (natrolite) which sometimes fills the crevices of the rock may also occur in the principal mass, but if so, it is probably the result of decomposition.

In respect of the proportion of silica contained in phonolite, we might equally well group it with the basic as the acidic igneous rocks ; it forms one of the intermediate links between the two. As it never contains quartz distinctly and separately developed, it might seem to be more allied mineralogically to the basic rocks ; but geologically its character is nearer that of the trachytes than the basalts. Where it occurs together with the latter, as is very frequently the case, it seems to play the same part as the trachytes under similar circumstances.

Its small content of water (0·6—0·8 per cent.) appears to be (at least in part) a secondary product, the result of a commencing decomposition ; and in the same manner the occurrence of many accessory minerals in the mass, more especially those appearing in the clefts and vesicular cavities.

Phonolite often acquires a porphyritic texture from the prominence of distinct crystals of sanidine and acicular hornblende. The most marked porphyritic varieties are as a rule little slaty and somewhat decomposed. As decomposition progresses, the crystals become more prominent, and even the titanite then is frequently to be easily recognised. Many phonolites are dark-spotted, or they contain round grains of peculiar composition and colour ; these, however, as in the case of basalt, appear chiefly to arise from commencing decomposition. Many are entirely decomposed (kaolinised), and show an earthy fracture, with a light colour. Whole mountains of phonolite have, apparently at least, decayed in this manner, with scarcely a trace of slaty texture remaining. Naumann calls this variety *Trachytic phonolite*; it is almost the only variety in which vesicular and amygdaloidal texture is found; it never occurs in the fresh, dark, and slaty kinds. Jenzsch is even of opinion that the apparent vesicular and amyg- daloidal cavities of the phonolite are not genuine bubbles of the original rock, but have arisen subsequently by a kind of corrosive process of decay. This view certainly agrees with the absence of cavities in the perfectly fresh rock. Yet in some few phonolites are found very decided vesicular cavities. These cavities, as also the clefts and fissures, most usually contain zeolites; especially apo- phyllite, chabasite, comptonite, desmine, natrolite, anal- cime, or calcspar and hyalite.

Varieties in Texture.

(*a*) COMMON PHONOLITE. Dark-coloured, compact, schistose,
GEMEINER PHONOLITH.(*Germ.*) or imperfect slaty cleavage, and
PHONOLITHE COMMUNE. (*Fr.*) with ringing sound when struck by
the hammer. Mileschauer in Bohemia; Milzburg on the Rhön Mountain.

(*b*) PORPHYRITIC PHONOLITE. The same mass with dis-
PORPHYRARTIGER PHONOLITH. (*Germ.*) tinct crystals of hornblende,
PHONOLITHE PORPHYROÏDE. (*Fr.*) augite, or sanidine. Aussig
and Jakuben, near Tetschen in Bohemia.

(*c*) TRACHYTIC PHONOLITE. Not slaty, not clinking,
TRACHYTÄHNLICHER PHONOLITH. (*Germ.*) rough, of a rather light-
grey colour; frequently porphyritic, geodic, or amygdaloidal. Aussig, in Bohemia.

(*d*) SPOTTED PHONOLITE. Luschwitz, near Aussig, in Bo-
GEFLECKTER PHONOLITH. (*Germ.*) hemia.
PHONOLITHE TACHETÉE. (*Fr.*)

(*e*) VESICULAR PHONOLITE. Blattendorf, near Haida, in Bo-
BLASIGER PHONOLITH. (*Germ.*) hemia.
PHONOLITHE VACUOLAIRE. (*Fr.*)

(*f*) AMYGDALOIDAL PHONOLITE. Marienberg, near Aus-
MANDELSTEINARTIGER PHONOLITH. (*Germ.*) sig, in Bohemia.
PHONOLITHE AMYGDALOÏDE. (*Fr.*)

The slaty or schistose phonolites are those which are most usually of tabular or columnar jointed structure. Those which are not slaty are usually only irregularly massive.

This rock forms isolated conical hills, even more per- fectly than basalt, especially so in the Bohemian Mittel- gebirge and in the Oberlausitz. Much more rarely does it form great connected mountain ranges, and it is more rarely found in the form of dykes than basalt. On the continent of Europe, phonolite is only known as of tertiary or of still more recent origin, and never as a genuine plutonic rock. It is, on the other hand, also unknown as actual lava at active volcanoes, and from this it would appear that its state must be more or less the result of cooling under pressure or of transmutation. In favour of the latter supposition (of transmutation) is the presence of zeolite, which is, however, not a constant ingredient.

Lyell, in his Geology, has instanced the occurrence of a phonolite of the Devonian period in Forfarshire. If this be a genuine phonolite, it is the only recorded instance of such being found of earlier than tertiary origin, but as the notice is quite incidental, and has reference to a different subject, and is moreover very brief, we cannot, without further explanation, accept it as authority in contravention of a law which otherwise appears universal.

References.

Gmelin, in Poggend. Ann. 1828, vol. xiv. p. 250.
Struve, in Poggend. Ann. 1826, vol. vii. p. 348.
Meyer, in Poggend. Ann. 1839, vol. xlvii. p. 192.
Redtenbacher, in Poggend. Ann. 1839, vol. xlviii. p. 494.
Schill, in G. Leonhard's Beitr. z. miner. Kenntn. von Baden, 1854, vol. iii. p. 59.
Schmid, in Poggend. Ann. 1853, vol. lxxxix. p. 205 ; v. L. u. Br. Jahrb. 1856, p. 845.
Jenzsch, in the Zeitschr. d. d. geol. Ges. 1856, p. 167 ; and Poggend. Ann. vol. xcix. p. 417.
v. Rath, in the Zeitschr. d. d. geol. Ges. 1856, p. 291, and 1860, p. 29.
Engelbach, in the Erl. z. geogn. Karte v. Hessen, Sect. Schotten, 1859, p. 45.
Fischer, Die Trachyte u. Phonolithe des Höhganes, v. L. Jahrb. 1862, p. 356.
Rammelsburg, Analysen von Phonolithen, Zeitschr. der d. geol. Ges. 1862, vol. xiv. p. 750.
v. Fritsch has lately set up a distinction between nepheline-phonolite, nosean-phonolite, leucite-phonolite, and felspar-phonolite, Neues Jahrb. für Mineral. 1865, p. 663.

2. Plutonic.

Granite is the principal rock of the plutonic division of the acidic igneous rocks, as trachyte is of the volcanic division of the same rocks.

The other plutonic rocks rich in silica may all be classed with granite as subordinate varieties of the same compound. The principal of these are quartz-porphyry, felsite rock, and pitchstone, all of which may be almost regarded but as different states of the same substance, bearing somewhat the same relation to granite as the rhyolites to the trachytic rocks. We therefore describe them all as granitic igneous rocks, although the idea of a granular texture is usually conveyed by the name of granite.

In the composition of all these rocks, orthoclase, or an orthoclastic substance, is predominant (frequently associated with other felspars), and is combined with quartz, mica, chlorite, talc, some hornblende, &c.; never with augite.

The various combinations of these mineral ingredients give the following specially named rocks each with their subordinate varieties.

1. *Granite.* A compound of felspar, quartz, and mica; granular, and sometimes also porphyritic, or other variety of texture. The following are varieties in composition:— protogine, syenite-granite, schorl-granite, adularia-granite, granitite, ferruginous granite, graphite-granite, beresite, aplite.

2. *Granitic porphyry* and (so-called) *syenitic porphyry.* A rock containing the same ingredients as granite. The matrix is usually compact, enclosing distinct crystals or grains of felspar, quartz, and mica, or chlorite.

3. *Quartz-porphyry.* A compact matrix of the same chemical composition as granite, with separate individual crystals of felspar and quartz.

4. *Felsite rock,* or *petrosilex.* The matrix of quartz-porphyry without its crystals.

5. *Pitchstone* and *pitchstone-porphyry.* The same substance as the above in a vitreous state, sometimes with crystals of felspar and quartz.

It may appear to be inconsistent to treat the four last-mentioned rocks as distinct species, instead of mere varieties of the same species, as in the case of the rhyolites in the trachytic group. Our only reason for a different treatment is, that in general they are capable of being more easily distinguished from each other.

16. GRANITE.

GRANIT. (*Germ.*)
GRANITE. (*Fr.*)

A crystalline granular compound of felspar, quartz, and mica. In certain varieties there occur chlorite, talc, hornblende, and schorl.

Spec. grav. . . . . . . 2·6—2·7
Contains silica . . . . . . 62—81 p. c.

The several mineral grains or particles are firmly knit together by their crystalline surfaces, without any uniting medium. They are of a size to be individually recognised, but their size is very various, and the rock is accordingly coarse-grained, fine-grained, or medium-grained. The so-called giant granites have grains larger than a walnut, other varieties not larger than mustard-seed. If the grains are so small as to become indistinct, and the rock assumes a compact texture, then it is no longer granite according to the usual meaning of the term.

We shall treat of these compact states hereafter under the names of felsite rock and petrosilex; they form states of transition between granite and other rocks.

The felspar is usually the predominant ingredient, and the mica occupies the smallest place in granite.

The felspar is chiefly orthoclase, very often accompanied by some oligoclase. Oligoclase alone has not yet been observed with certainty. It is also uncertain if albite or labradorite ever occur in the granitic compound.

The orthoclase is somewhat various; it is usually the common opaque species of yellowish-white or reddish colour; more rarely grey or greenish. At many places (as, for instance, in the central chain of the Alps), it is principally that transparent vitreous variety, frequently split and cracked, which is termed *adularia*. The orthoclase of granite is most readily to be distinguished from the oligoclase by its fresher state, its mother-of-pearl lustre, and simple twin growth; whereas the oligoclase is somewhat of resinous lustre, and has delicate parallel striæ arising from multiform twin growths, or it is more decomposed, dull, paled in colour, or even transmuted into a totally different substance resembling steatite. Sometimes a thin coating of oligoclase is found incrusted round the grains of orthoclase.

Orthoclase not only occurs as an ingredient in the normal granitic compound, but sometimes prominently in distinct twin crystals imbedded in the granitic mass, in which case the rock is termed *porphyritic granite*. These crystals are sometimes several inches long, and they enclose particles of quartz and mica, so as to form inside the crystal small kernels or parallel streaks of fine-grained granite. In the granite of the Fichtelgebirge, very large twin crystals of orthoclase are sometimes found broken, their several parts lying imbedded close together, just as in the case of the sanidine crystals of the Drachenfels trachyte.

The quartz in granite is seldom in the form of perfect crystals; it usually forms grains of irregular shape, or masses grown in with the other mineral ingredients of the granite, chiefly with the felspar. It is tolerably transparent and colourless or white, dark-grey, vitreous, most easily recognisable by its hardness. The granite of Rumburg in Bohemia contains a dark-blue variety of quartz. It is remarkable that this, the most difficult of fusion of all the ingredients of granite, is often found hemmed in between the felspar and mica, and to have received impressions from the felspar at least; whence it follows that the quartz must have solidified somewhat later than it.

The mica of granite occurs in the form of thin laminæ or small hexagonal plates, whose cleavage-planes lie in various directions, and therefore do not occasion a foliated texture. Sometimes they are clustered in small bunches; or sometimes long continuous rays of mica run through the whole rock. Most usually it is potash-mica or magnesia-mica; sometimes margarodite; or lithia-mica, white, grey, brown, black, more rarely yellow or green in colour. Occasionally different coloured micas occur in the same rock, or a narrow border of white potash-mica envelopes the dark magnesia mica. But it is often difficult accurately to determine the species of mica in these thin laminæ; the easiest test is generally the optical. It is worthy of remark that potash-mica and tourmaline (schorl) appear only to occur (as original products) in plutonic-igneous or metamorphic rocks, and in plutonic dyke formations; never in volcanic rocks.

The ingredients which we consider as essential for granite are nevertheless sometimes replaced by others.

This species of substitution occasions varieties in composition which will be more particularly described below. It occurs especially with the mica, whose substitutes are, *talc*, *chlorite* (in protogine), *schorl* (in schorl-granite), *graphite* (in graphite-granite), *micaceous iron* (ferruginous granite). Sometimes a fourth ingredient appears in local but characteristic varieties of granite; e.g. hornblende (in syenitic granite) or pyrites (in beresite).

The following minerals occasionally occur in granite, but only as accessories; viz., tourmaline, garnet (always in the form of trapezohedra), andalusite, topaz, beryl, pinite, apatite, fluorspar, pistacite, corundum, zircon, titanite, gadolinite, orthite, pyrorthite, allanite, cordierite, magnetic iron-ore, tin-ore, mispickel, molybdenite, and native gold.

We find many transitions from granite into other rocks. These are partly occasioned by variations of composition, and partly by variations of texture. The accession of talc, chorite, schorl, or hornblende to the granitic compound occasions transitions into *protogine, schorl rock*, or *syenite*. If the felspar of granite disappears, we obtain *griessen*, or if the quartz disappears, *mica-trap* (*minette*), or if the mica disappears, *aplite*, and a kind of *granulite*. If the laminæ of mica assume a parallel direction, then the texture becomes foliated, and *gneiss* is the result. If the matrix of a porphyritic granite becomes very fine-grained to compact, then we have a transition to *granitic porphyry*; and if in that case the mica also disappears, then the rock becomes *quartz-porphyry*. Finally, if the whole granitic compound becomes very fine-grained to compact, then the rock is *felstone*.

Varieties in Texture.

(*a*) COMMON GRANITE. | Coarse, medium, or fine-grained, pro-
GEMEINER GRANIT. (*Germ.*) | bably the most extensively diffused of
GRANITE COMMUN. (*Fr.*) | all igneous rocks. If the texture be
very coarse, it is sometimes called *giant granite*. Trebendorf, near Eger. Very fine-grained varieties, on the other hand, occur at Kerbersdorf, near Eger, in Bohemia, at Welsau, near Redwitz, and in the Vienna paving-stone.

(*b*) PORPHYRITIC GRANITE. | The porphyritic texture is usually
GEBIRGS-GRANIT, *v. Leonhard.* | caused by large orthoclase crys-
(*Germ.*) | tals, more rarely by quartz crys-
GRANITE PORPHYROÏDE. (*Fr.*) | tals. The principal mass is
granular. Carlsbad and Ellenbogen, Ochsenkopf and Göpfersgrün in the Fichtelgebirge, &c. As a subvariety of this class, we may cite the *rappakivi* of Finland, the principal mass

of which is usually much decomposed; it encloses rounded masses of red felspar often half an inch across, enclosed by orbicular envelopes of green oligoclase a quarter of an inch in diameter.

(c) GNEISSIC GRANITE.

GNEISSGRANIT. (*Germ.*)
GRANITE GNEISSIQUE. (*Fr.*)

A granite with foliated texture. In a geological point of view, much of what latterly has been called *red gneiss* (gneissite), and which appears to be eruptive, must be here included. Perhaps some grey gneiss too.

(d) GRAPHIC GRANITE.

SCHRIFTGRANIT. (*Germ.*)
GRANITE GRAPHIQUE. (*Fr.*)

The orthoclase is altogether predomi- nant in large crystals, and is penetrated by the quartz according to a singular crystallographic law, so that in certain cleavage-planes it pro- duces figures resembling writing. The mica (usually white) is accumulated separately in groups. This remarkable variety usually only forms subordinate masses or dykes of small extent in the ordinary granite or in gneiss or mica-schist, but such dykes are very frequent, e. g. in the Schloitzbachthal, near Tharand, in Saxony.

(e) PEGMATITE.

PECHMATIT, *Naumann.* (*Germ.*)
PEGMATITE, *Haüy.* (*Fr.*)

This rock Naumann separates from the graphic granite, and he understands by it a variety, very coarsely and irregu- larly constituted, of orthoclase, quartz, and silvery-white mica. It often contains tourmaline, and occurs under the same conditions as the graphic granite, and frequently together with it.

This seems the proper place for certain other granites of irregular composition very rich in felspar. Some are traversed by dark continuous rays of mica, in others the felspar assumes a form resembling flowering stalks (*Blumengranit*).

In the granite of Ballybrack, near Dublin, the mica (Marga- rodite) assumes this *plumose* form, occurring in branches of Prince of Wales' feathers, one inch across and several inches long.—*Jukes.*

The granites of this class are all of very small extent, and their particular character is probably owing to special circum- stances. They all usually contain many accessory minerals, such as albite, tourmaline, topaz, beryl, garnet, gadolinite, orthite, &c.

They are sometimes so imbedded between strata of crystalline schist that they can scarcely be regarded as of eruptive origin.

(f) MIAROLITE.

MIAROLITH. (*Germ.*)
MIAROLITE, *Fournet.* (*Fr.*)

Is the name given by Fournet to a geodic granite, rich in oligoclase, in the neighbourhood of Lyons, and at Baveno in the Alps.

The following are varieties in composition; in them we find many of the varieties in texture repeated.

(g) PROTOGINE.

PROTOGIN. (*Germ.*)
PROTOGINE, *Jurine.* (*Fr.*)

A granite which contains talc or chlorite or decomposed mica instead of the usual mica. It is very extensively developed in the Western Alps. In the Erzgebirge much of the granite lying between Schneeberg and Eibenstock contains no mica, but in its stead siskin-green talc, which combined with flesh-red felspar and white quartz gives that rock a singular appearance.

(*h*) SYENITIC GRANITE, granite with hornblende. If the quartz and mica gradually diminish and finally disappear from the granitic compound, then the rock passes over into a syenite. Syenitic granite is often porphyritic, owing to the presence of large crystals of orthoclase. It is very abundant near Moritzburg and Meissen, in Saxony. The greater part of what is usually called syenite properly belongs to this class, especially those syenites which contain quartz or mica as characteristic ingredients. But there is no definite boundary between syenitic granite and syenite.

(*i*) SCHORLACEOUS GRANITE. Granite with schorl in the place of mica,
SCHÖRLGRANIT. (*Germ.*) usually fine-grained, and forms veins in
LUXULLIANITE, *Pisani*. other granite; as, for instance, near Heidelberg and near Predazzo in Tyrol (very characteristic): the latter is a compound of orthoclase, quartz, and schorl.

The name Luxullianite has been proposed by M. Pisani for a porphyroidal granite, in which the mica is replaced by tourmaline, 'because it is found in the parish of Luxullian,' in Cornwall.

(*k*) ADULARIA GRANITE and ADULARIA PROTOGINE. With adularia
ADULARGRANIT und ADULARPROTOGIN. (*Germ.*) in the place of
the ordinary felspar; very extensively developed in the Alps.

(*l*) GRANITITE. Is the name proposed by G. Rose for all
GRANITIT. (*Germ.*) granites containing much oligoclase with red orthoclase, quartz, blackish-green magnesia-mica in small quantity, and no white mica. This rock forms the principal material of the Riesen Gebirge; it occurs in the Brocken of the Hartz Mountains, Brixen in the Tyrol, &c. In composition it is identical with the mariolite of Fournet.

(*m*) RUMBURG GRANITE. With blue quartz, occurs at Rumburg in Bohemia, also at Pic Blanc
RUMBURGER GRANIT. (*Germ.*) burg in Bohemia, also at Pic Blanc in the Monte Rosa chain.

(*n*) GRAPHITIC GRANITE. With graphite in the place of mica,
GRAPHITGRANIT. (*Germ.*) e. g. near Passau, on the Danube.

(*o*) FERRUGINOUS GRANITE. With micaceous iron instead of the
EISENGRANIT. (*Germ.*) ordinary mica. Occurs at several places in the Fichtelgebirge, also in iron-mines near Dossenheim in the Odenwald.

(*p*) BERESITE. A granite containing pyrites and very little
BERESIT. (*Germ.*) mica; forms considerable dykes in the clay-slate near Beresowsk in the Ural. These dykes are themselves traversed by quartz veins containing gold.

(*q*) APLITE or SEMI-GRANITE. Is the name given to a variety
APLIT oder HALBGRANIT. (*Germ.*) of very subordinate extent, consisting only of quartz and orthoclase, and therefore mineralogically allied to granitite.

GREISEN might also be reckoned as a variety of granite without felspar. It does actually pass over into granite. Its special geological character seems, however, to entitle it to be mentioned as a separate rock. (See post, No. 50.)

(*r*) TONALITE. The name given by Vom Rath to the
TONALIT, *Vom Rath*. (*Germ.*) rock which forms the principal mass of the Adamello group of mountains in Southern Tyrol, and

which has hitherto always been described as granite. It is a crystalline granular compound of triclinic felspar with quartz, magnesia-mica, and hornblende. The triclinic felspar belongs to an entirely new species not yet named. The quartz forms at least one-third of the whole mass. It contains as accessories, orthoclase, orthite, titanite, and magnetic iron-ore. It contains 67 per cent. of silica. Many dark-coloured concretions are contained in the rock. In Tyrol this rock has broken through the mica-schist. (Zeitschr. d. deutsch. geol. Ges. 1864, p. 240.)

All the varieties of granite are most commonly of *irregularly massive* or else of *thick tabular* jointed structure. By weathering, elliptical bodies are sometimes formed which fall off in concentric layers, the interior remaining fresh and firm. Granite is often found in large blocks and boulders on the surface of the ground.

Granite is unquestionably one of the most extensively prevalent of rocks, and its mineral compound, which is also that of gneiss, is without doubt the most important and frequent of all the rock substances of the earth. Moreover, we find granite in all regions of the globe assume the same or analogous bedding in relation to other rocks. It frequently occupies extensive tracts, and sometimes forms the backbone of whole mountain regions. It also frequently forms dykes, and these sometimes penetrate the larger granite masses (from which they may be distinguished by their texture); sometimes the crystalline schists or older sedimentary formations : granite dykes having been exceptionally found as late as the Jurassic formations, e. g. in the Alps. The greater part of the granites accessible to observation appear, however, to be older than the coal formation, and to be of deep plutonic origin. These granitic dykes are occasionally accompanied by so-called contact formations; such as friction breccias; silicification of the neighbouring rock ; chiastolite-schist ; nodular schist (see post, p. 257); granulation of limestone, &c.

The usual bedding* of granite, and its relation to the bedding of adjoining rocks, unmistakably prove its eruptive character, except, perhaps, in some special cases. Some doubts, however, which deserve our notice, have been raised as to its former state of igneous fusion.

* The term 'bedding' applied to igneous rocks, especially to granitic rocks, must be taken as equivalent to 'mode of occurrence;' and 'eruptive' as only meaning 'intrusive' or 'irruptive.'—TRANSLATOR.

These rest chiefly upon the fact of the quartz having solidified later than the felspar and mica, and on the want of distinct traces of the effect of heat on the rocks which the granite appears to have broken through. These objections, it appears to us, may be satisfactorily answered by supposing the granite always to have consolidated at great depth, and under genuine plutonic influences, perhaps even with the aid of water. The great resemblance which granite bears to the trachytic rocks speaks, at all events, for a similar process of formation for both.

That there are no new granites of volcanic origin is a necessary consequence of the assumed fact that the granitic compound can only have originated in the depths of the earth. We must likewise assume that great periods have elapsed in every instance from the time of the formation of granite rocks before they have become exposed to view. We may well assume that the trachytes represent the volcanic part of the same igneous formation which gave birth to the granites.

The name of granite (according to Emmerling's Lehrb. d. Mineralogie) was first applied to rocks by Tournefort in the year 1698. But according to Breislack's Lehrb. d. Geologie, it had been used by Caesalpinus as early as 1596. For a long time it was, doubtless, used to designate every coarse-grained compound rock. The meaning of the term was first more definitely fixed by Werner. It has from the first been felt to be a geological necessity to group with granite many other rocks bearing a close affinity to it, but it has always been no less difficult to say where the line should be drawn.

In 1849, G. Rose proposed the following new division and grouping of granitic rocks (see Zeitschr. d. d. geol. Ges. p. 352):—

1. *Granite* (proper), essentially consisting of orthoclase, white (potash-) mica, black (magnesia-) mica, and oligoclase ; as accessories, hornblende, orthite, titanite, apatite, and iron pyrites.

2. *Granitite*, essentially consisting of orthoclase, oligoclase, quartz, and magnesia-mica ; as accessories, hornblende, orthite, zircon, titanite, pyrites, chalcopyrite, and molybdenite.
    Now as Rose himself subdivides his granite (proper) into several varieties whose composition differs as much from each other as granitite from granite, no sufficient reason appears for this violent division and new nomenclature.

3. *Syenite*, essentially consisting of orthoclase, oligoclase, hornblende,

P

magnesia-mica, and quartz; as accessories, titanite, apatite, magnetic iron-ore, &c.

The difference between this and the granitite also consists in the greater frequency of the hornblende, in its being named as an essential instead of an accessory ingredient. This is our syenitic granite. The genuine syenite of the Plauenschen-Grund does not agree with this definition because it seldom contains mica and, perhaps, contains no quartz at all. Therefore Rose sets up varieties of composition differing, however, more from each other than his syenite from granite.

4. *Porphyry*, essentially consisting of orthoclase, oligoclase, quartz, and magnesia-mica; as accessories, cordierite, garnet, orthite, and pyrites, its essential difference from his granite or granitite consisting only in texture.

Now, as oligoclase and mica entirely fail in many rocks which Rose reckons as porphyries, he has been driven again to make varieties which differ almost more from each other than his porphyries from the other granitic rocks.

5. *Syenitic Porphyry*, with a matrix enclosing crystals of orthoclase, oligoclase, magnesia-mica, and hornblende; as accessories, garnet, nepheline, titanite, quartz, magnetic iron-ore, specular iron, and pyrites.

This is a very different rock from that which has received the name of syenitic porphyry ever since Werner's time. It is our *porphyrite*, which as we have seen may be divided into (A) a rock essentially felspathic, (B) containing felspar and hornblende, and (C) containing felspar and mica.

The literature respecting granite is, as we might expect, a very rich one—we will only cite a few treatises on the more special phenomena.

References.

G. Rose, On the Granitite of the Riesengebirge, Zeitschr. d. d. geol. Ges. 1857, p. 513.

Cotta, On the Rumburg Granite with blue Quartz. Erläuter. z. geogn. Karte v. Sachsen, 1839, No. 3, p. 14.

Fournet, On Miarolit, Mém. sur la Géol. des Alpes, part. 2, p. 24, and Bullet. de la Soc. géol., [2] vol. ii. p. 495.

Böthlinkg, On Rappakivi—a granite which, however, often contains no quartz, and then is very similar to mica-trap. v. L. u. Br. Jahrb. 1840, p. 613.

v. Rosthorn and Canaval, On Albite-granite and Tourmalin-granite in the Alps. v. L. u. Br. Jahrb. 1855, p. 584.

v. Richthofen, On Granitite, Tourmalin-granite, and Tourmalin-syenite, Geogn. Beschr. von Süd-Tyrol, 1860, pp. 108 and 148.

Axel-Gadolin distinguished two kinds of granite dykes in the gneiss of Ladoga Lake, viz.: older dykes, with albite from two of more recent formation, containing much oligoclase. Verhandl. der k. russ. mineral. Ges. zu Petersburg, 1857-8, p. 85.

Svanberg comes to the conclusion from analysis that besides orthoclase other orthoclastic felspars occur in granite. Journ. f. prakt. Chem. 1844, vol. xxxi. p. 101.
Delesse distinguishes in the Vosges Mountains protogine from 'Granite syénitique des Ballons.' Bullet. de la Soc. géol. 1852, [2] vol. xi. p. 464.
   Also, 'Granite des Ballons,' 'Granites des Vosges,' and 'Filons de Granite.' Ann. des Mines [5] vol. iii. p. 309.
   On the Pegmatite with Tourmalin of Saint Étienne in the Vosges. Ann. des Mines, 1849, [4] vol. xvi. On Pegmatite of Ireland. Bullet. de la Soc. géol. 1853 [2] vol. x. p. 568.
Haughton, Quart. Journ. Geol. Soc. 1856, vol. xii. p. 177; and 1858, vol. xiv. p. 300. Address delivered before the Geol. Soc. of Dublin, 1862.
R. Scott, The Granites of Donegal. Journ. of the Geol. Soc. of Dublin, vol. ix. p. 285.
Scheerer, Granite Tyrols. Jahrb. f. Min. 1864, p. 385.
Sir W. E. Logan, Classification of Eruptive Rocks. Rep. Geol. Surv. Canada to 1863, p. 645.
G. Leonhard distinguishes between older and newer granite veins in the Heidelberg mountain granite. Gegend um Heidelberg, 1844.
Bunsen, On Granite formation. Zeitschr. d. d. geol. Ges. 1861, p. 96.
C. Röthe, über die krystallinischen Gesteine des Ries. Jahrb. für Mineralogie, 1863, p. 109, contains many new analyses of granite.
v. Helmersen has described the *Rappakivi* of Finland, of which the Alexander column of St. Petersburg is formed, as a porphyritic granite with a flesh-red felspar predominant.
Bryson treats of the supposed neptunic origin of granite in the Edinb. New Philos. Journal, 1861, vol. xiv. p. 149.
Fuchs on the granite of the Hartz in the Jahrb. für Mineralogie, 1862, pp. 769, 807.
H. C. Sorby. On the Microscopical Structure of Mount Sorrel Granite: Proc. Geol. and Polytech. Soc. W. Riding of Yorksh., 1863-4, pp. 301-4. On the Microscopical Structure of Crystals, indicating the Origin of Minerals and Rocks: Quart. Journ. Geol. Soc. 1858, vol. xiv. p. 453.

Sorby and (later) Zirkel have made interesting discoveries by microscopic analysis of granites and several other igneous rocks.

The quartz and the felspar of *Granite* are found to enclose numerous very small vesicles filled with water and air, and also many minute particles of glass. The quartz also contains some very minute crystals of felspar. The microscopic structure of the *Trachytes* very closely resembles that of the granites; their compact matrix Zirkel recognised as a compound of felspar and quartz. In the compact mass of fresh *Basalt* he recognised a compound of felspar and magnetic iron-ore with very little olivine, and traces only of augite. The vitreous mass of *Pitchstone* resolved itself under the microscope into a confused compound of very delicate acicular crystals. The same thing with *Obsidian.* Even the newest *Lavas* exhibited in their mass very minute pores filled with water.

17. GRANITIC PORPHYRY and SYENITIC PORPHYRY.

GRANITPORPHYR und SYENITPORPHYR. (*Germ.*)

A compact or fine-grained felsitic base, enclosing crystals or crystalline grains of felspar, quartz, and mica, or chlorite.

Spec. grav. . . . . . . 2·6—2·7
Contains silica . . . . . 61—64 p. c.

The matrix is yellowish, brownish, or dark green. When not quite compact, its material may be recognised as consisting principally of felspar, combined with quartz, mica, or chlorite in small proportion. The presence of chlorite occasions transitions into porphyritic granite or protogine; but in distinguishing and naming these transition rocks, their geological relations must always, to some extent, be taken into account.

The distinct crystals of felspar are very numerous in this rock, and are usually of large size. They are for the most part twin crystals of orthoclase, and these are often coated with a different species of felspar, probably oligoclase, crystallographically combined (grown together) with the orthoclase. There sometimes occur also separate and smaller felspar crystals and grains; these latter, as well as the crust of the larger crystals, show delicate stripings, and therefore both, probably, consist of oligoclase.

The quartz most usually forms small grains or crystals of a smoke-grey colour, often, however, larger diplohedrons (which were formerly mistaken for double pyramids) very distinct and prominent.

The dark mica usually only occurs in small delicate flakes or thin hexagonal plates. If the rock contains chlorite instead of mica, as in the variety termed syenitic porphyry, the chlorite forms small dark green scaly grains, or else it is intimately blended with the matrix, to which it imparts a green colour.

The above-mentioned modifications give rise to several varieties of the rock.

Varieties in Texture.

(a) COMMON GRANITE-PORPHYRY. The matrix is compact throughout; often dark-coloured. It contains separate crystals, grains, or laminæ of orthoclase (and sometimes oligoclase), quartz, and mica. If the mica fails, the rock passes into ordinary quartz-porphyry. Frequent in the Thuringian Forest, e.g. near Schmiedefeld, and in the Drusenthal, where it forms dykes of great thickness.

(b) GRANITIC GRANITE-PORPHYRY. } The matrix resembles
    GRANITÄHNLICHER GRANITPORPHYR. (*Germ.*) } in part a fine-grained granite, but distinct crystals of orthoclase, and large grains of quartz, and also laminæ of mica, are separately and prominently developed. Frequent in the neighbourhood of Schellerhau and Bärenburg in the Erzgebirge. The composition of this rock is very similar to that of *porphyritic granite*. The geological character in these doubtful cases should determine the nomenclature of each particular case.

At Niederschöna, near Freiberg, where a rock belonging to this class forms a vein in gneiss, it contains large light-coloured twin crystals of orthoclase, whose exterior appears fresh, but inside each crystal is a decomposed nucleus frequently changed into a greenish substance like lithomarge. It would almost seem as if the nucleus of the orthoclase crystal had originally consisted of oligoclase or a compound of oligoclase and quartz. The magnificent columnar granite-porphyry of Altenhain, near Frankenberg, in the Erzgebirge, is a rock of the same class, but the orthoclase crystals do not exhibit the same phenomenon as those of Niederschöna.

Near Liebenstein in the Thuringian Forest, a granitic porphyry traverses and forms dykes in the ordinary granite. It possesses a very fine granitic matrix, and very distinct white crystals of orthoclase, with brown edges; also dark spots or fragments (which are still compact) of greenstone which the porphyry has broken through.

(c) MICACEOUS GRANITE-PORPHYRY. } This rock, which Kit-
    GLIMMERREICHER GRANITPORPHYR. (*Germ.*) } tel first described under the name of granitic porphyry, and which occurs at Aschaffenburg, interposed between syenite rocks, consists of a fine-grained to compact felsitic mass rich in mica (a kind of minette) in which numerous grains or crystals of quartz and somewhat fewer, but much larger crystals of felspar are imbedded. According to Kittel, the quartz crystals often show prismatic surfaces. The orthoclase crystals are partly single, partly twins, very fresh, without marginal crust, and have well-defined edges, but strange to say, completely rounded off, so that their cross-section always appears elliptical.

(d) CHLORITIC GRANITE-PORPHYRY. } Often called *syenitic por-*
    CHLORITISCHER GRANITPORPHYR. (*Germ.*) } *phyry*, probably because

the particles of chlorite which it contains have been mistaken for hornblende; but in some places the rock appears actually to contain some hornblende as an accessory. The matrix is compact or fine-grained, brown or dark green, often very rich in quartz, and contains chlorite, and sometimes mica also. The chlorite forms little flakes or grains, the quartz is in the form of diplohedrons, and the twin crystals of orthoclase are sometimes more than an inch long. In the syenitic porphyries of the Erzgebirge (the rocks originally so named by Werner) these orthoclase crystals are often enveloped in an outer coating of oligoclase, of about one-tenth of an inch thick, showing distinct twin stripings. The oligoclase is sometimes lighter in colour than the orthoclase (greenish-yellow) sometimes darker (brown), and it is generally more decomposed than it. This rock near Frauenstein and Altenberg has broken through gneiss, mica-schist, granite, and quartz-porphyry, and forms very important and extensive dykes in those rocks many miles in length. Near Frauenstein it contains, according to Rube, about 64 p. c. of silica.

Naumann has described a rock of somewhat different character under the name of green porphyry. It occurs in the neighbourhood of Wurzen in Saxony, where it forms small rocky hills. Its matrix is dark-green, probably from chlorite, and it also contains some magnetic iron-ore.

Dr. Rube determined its proportion of silica at about 61 p. c. This rock is likewise more recent than the quartz-porphyry of the same district.

(e) THE BASE or MOTHER ROCK of these Porphyries occasionally occurs free from crystals (towards the outer margin of the rock), and it then assumes very much the character of a fine-grained granite, poor in mica and rich in chlorite.

All the above-named varieties are most usually massive, but sometimes of columnar-jointed structure. They form great mountain masses or thick dykes. There are no vesicular or amygdaloidal varieties, or tufa formations of rocks belonging to this group.

References.

Zirkel, Geogn. Verh. d. Umg. von Aschaffenburg, 1840, p. 30.
Naumann, Erläuter. zur geogn. Karte von Sachsen, 1836, No. 1, p. 139.

18. QUARTZ-PORPHYRY, ELVANITE.

QUARZPORPHYR. (*Germ.*)
PORPHYRE QUARTZIFÈRE, ELVAN. (*Fr.*)

A compact felsitic mass as matrix, enclosing crystals or crystalline grains of felspar and quartz.

Spec. grav. . . . . . . 2·5—2·6
Contains silica . . . . . 70—81 p. c.

The compact matrix of the quartz-porphyries consists principally, if not altogether, of felspar; this is sufficiently proved by its hardness, weight, colour, as well as by chemical analysis; and from its compactness, its large proportion of silica and the crystals of orthoclase which are imbedded in it, we conclude that it most probably consists of orthoclase. Its proportion of silica is, however, too high even for orthoclase, and it is therefore probable that some quartz is intimately combined with the felspar. If this be the case, it would not alter the fusibility of the rock before the blowpipe. An intimate compound of felspar and quartz melts almost as readily as felspar alone. The colour of the matrix generally varies between yellowish and reddish, but sometimes goes over into brown and grey, and even to white. Exceptionally, also, violet and green varieties occur.

The state or texture of the matrix varies somewhat, and the differences are partly original, partly occasioned by decomposition and weathering. Sometimes it is quite compact like hornstone, with a smooth conchoidal fracture; most usually it is compact with uneven dull fracture, which appears to be the sign of transition towards a crystalline state; finally, it is sometimes rough and dull, almost earthy, which is a sign of commencing decomposition (kaolinising of the felspar). Owing to these differences of texture or state, the substance of the rock itself was formerly regarded as varying essentially, and it has been so described, whence the names of *hornstone-porphyry*, *felstone-porphyry*, and *claystone-porphyry*, or even *clay-porphyry*. The differences, no doubt, exist, but they are only of a different arrangement of particles, or of decomposition of one and the same substance. This matrix of the quartz-porphyries, which sometimes occurs as a separate rock without crystals, has received separate names, such as *felsite* or *felsite rock, eurite, petrosilex*, and *hälleflinta*, hence also the names of *felsite-porphyry* and *eurite-porphyry*. It is seldom or never of vesicular or amygdaloidal texture.

In genuine quartz-porphyry, felspar and quartz are the only crystals which are porphyritically developed. If mica or chlorite occur in addition they constitute a transition into granitic porphyry. The felspar is usually

orthoclase, and from its twin growth is usually very distinctly to be recognised; sometimes, also, oligoclase or
sanidine occur.   All these felspars where they occur porphyritically are very distinctly and sharply developed,
and are easily distinguished from the matrix.

The crystals of quartz are white, grey, or almost black,
but withal frequently transparent; they are small, seldom
larger than the size of a pea; they form either sharp-
edged diplohedrons (without a trace of prismatic surface),
or they are more or less rounded off at the edges and
angles, or finally they form mere rounded grains without
crystal surfaces.   The rounding of these crystals is sometimes so remarkable that it has given rise to the idea of
their having been actually rounded by friction, which in
genuine porphyries can hardly be the case.   The number
and proportion of the quartz crystals contained in the
matrix, as also that of the felspar crystals, is very variable,
and sometimes diminishes even to total disappearance, so
that transitions take place into the quartzless-porphyrite or
into felsite rock; but quartz-porphyry, although poor in
quartz, is nevertheless always to be distinguished from
genuine porphyrite by its far greater proportion of silica.
The quartz-porphyries on an average have more silica
even than the granite, just as the rhyolitic division of the
trachytes contains more silica than the trachytic.   There
is scarcely any petrographic difference between many
quartz-porphyries (especially if they contain sanidine or
oligoclase) and some kinds of trachyte-porphyry.   They
are sometimes so much alike as not to be distinguished
from each other in ordinary hand specimens.   In such
cases the character of a given rock can only be determined
geologically, and ascribed to the granitic or the trachytic
group respectively, according as it occurs in a granite or
trachyte district, or from its relation to some rock of more
distinct character to which it may be traced by transitions.

Smaller crystals or particles of quartz, but large enough
to be discovered by the eye or with an ordinary lens, are
often interspersed in the matrix between the larger and
more distinct crystals of this rock.

The quartz-porphyries seldom contain any accessory
ingredients properly so called, and where such do occur
they are probably only of secondary origin, products of

transformation, or new formation; thus, for instance, pinite, talc, lithomarge, chlorite, pinguite, pyrites, and specular iron. But in veins or in clefts, nests or concretions in the rock, many minerals are frequently found, such for instance as quartz, hornstone, chalcedony, agate, opal, lithomarge, calc-spar, brown-spar, fluor-spar, barytes, specular iron, and dendritic pencillings of oxides of iron and manganese — all which appear to be secondary formations caused by secretion from the rock's mass, or by infiltrated solutions.

The porphyritic texture of the rock is sometimes united with a fissile or fine laminated structure (riband-porphyry, band-porphyry); also sometimes with geodic structure (millstone-porphyry), or else with spotted texture—or there lie dispersed through the rock's mass smaller or larger felsite balls (pyromeride).

Varieties in Texture.

(a) COMMON QUARTZ-PORPHYRY.   } With compact matrix and
    GEMEINER QUARZPORPHYR. (*Germ.*)   } crystals of felspar and quartz.
    PORPHYRE QUARTZIFÈRE COMMUN. (*Fr.*)

    (α) *Hornstone-porphyry* (Hornsteinporphyr, *Germ.*; Elvan, *Fr.*).

    (β) *Felstone-porphyry* (Feldsteinporphyr, *Germ.*; Pétrosilex, *Fr.*).

    (γ) *Claystone-porphyry* or *Argillophry* (Thonsteinporphyr oder Thonporphyr, *Germ.*; Argilophyre, *Fr.*).

    All frequent, in the Thuringian Forest and near Meissen, and near Tharand in Saxony.

(b) STRIPED PORPHYRY (SLATY } Composed of thin layers of
    PORPHYRY).   } somewhat dissimilar texture or
    SCHIEFRIGER PORPHYR, SCHALEN- } colour; hence the fracture ap-
    oder BANDPORPHYR. (*Germ.*) } pears to be striped like a riband,
    PÉTROSILEX RUBANÉ. (*Fr.*) } and the rock splits more easily
in the direction of the layers than straight across. The layers are often much bent and twisted. Mohorn near Freiberg; Winterstein in the Thuringian Forest, Wachenberg in the Odenwald.

(c) SPOTTED PORPHYRY.   } Contains worm-shaped spots of dif-
    FLECKENPORPHYR. (*Germ.*) } ferent colour and texture from the
matrix. This variety has also been called Kattun-porphyry. Leukersdorf near Chemnitz, Saxony.

(d) POROUS, CAVERNOUS, OR } A rock penetrated by numerous
    MILLSTONE PORPHYRY.   } small irregular cavities or geodes,
    PORÖSER, DRUSIGER, oder MÜHL- } which are seldom vesicular, more
    STEINPORPHYR. (*Germ.*) } usually the result of weathering.
Tannebergsthal in the Erzgebirge, Regenberg near Friedrichsroda, in the Thuringian Forest, where it is combined with pyromeride.

(*e*) PYROMERIDE (BALL-PORPHYRY). } This rock in addition to the
    KUGELPORPHYR oder PYROMERID.   usual quartz crystals, contains
    (*Germ.*)   balls of felsite (either small
    PYROMÉRIDE, *Monteiro*. (*Fr.*)   and numerous, or large and
isolated. The small balls are frequently marked internally
with radial streaks. The interiors of the larger ones are usually
split after the manner of septaria, or they contain a geodic
cavity. The clefts or cavities in the balls are wholly or
partly filled with hornstone, chalcedony, agate, quartz, amethyst, calc-spar, fluor-spar, micaceous iron, &c. These balls, as
we have already mentioned, frequently occur in combination
with a geodic structure of the matrix. Regenberg and Schnee-
kopf in the Thuringian Forest, the island of Corsica.

(*f*) PORPHYRY WITH } Forms a transition into felsite rock
    FEW CRYSTALS.   (petrosilex) or into porphyrite. The
    KRYSTALLARMER POR-   matrix alone, without crystals, is some-
    PHYR. (*Germ.*)   times found towards the outer margin of
masses of very distinct quartz-porphyries—thus e.*g*. at the
Weissritz, close above Dippoldiswalde in Saxony. The Freiberg porphyry dykes are also mostly very poor in crystals of
felspar and quartz, but they often contain, in their stead, small
cubic crystals of pyrites.

Varieties in Composition.

(*g*) ORTHOCLASE-QUARTZ-PORPHYRY. } With orthoclase and quartz
    ORTHOKLAS-QUARZPORPHYR. (*Germ.*)   crystals only—very frequent.

(*h*) OLIGOCLASE-QUARTZ-PORPHYRY. } The rock contains crystals of
    OLIGOKLAS-QUARZPORPHYR. (*Germ.*)   oligoclase in addition to the
orthoclase and the quartz. The oligoclase is distinguishable by
its twin stripings, its different colour, or more advanced decomposition. Under this head we include, for instance, the brown
porphyry of Manebach, in the Thuringian Forest, with its
distinct orthoclase twin crystals of an inch long, containing, in
addition to these, numerous smaller crystals of oligoclase, much
decomposed. Frequently the oligoclase is transformed into a
yellowish-green substance resembling steatite. Hermsdorf and
Schönfeld in the Erzgebirge.

Von Richthofen discovered certain porphyries at the Trost-
burg and Monte Bocche, near Botzen in Tyrol, which, in addition
to their quartz, only contain crystals of oligoclase, and (usually)
some black mica, in a dark matrix. In the same neighbourhood some porphyries contain quartz and orthoclase alone
(at Bronzell and Pelegrin); others quartz, orthoclase, and some
oligoclase (Castelruth, Blumau, Hoch-Eppen). Perhaps the
beautiful brown porphyries of Lehnau near Kemnath, and of
Kronberg near Erbendorf, are rocks containing oligoclase only.
Their felspar crystals are all decomposed, although the matrix
is unusually fresh.

(*i*) SANIDINE-QUARTZ-PORPHYRY. } Is a name given by Jenzsch to a
    SANIDIN-QUARZPORPHYR. (*Germ.*)   variety occurring at Zwickau in
Saxony, containing sanidine and quartz. To the west of Oederan

near Freiberg, there occurs a porphyry containing crystals of orthoclase, sanidine, and quartz.

It would be impossible to instance here all local differences, many of which only result from transmutation, or are to be regarded but as accessory phenomena. Of this kind is the change of the felspar crystals into a greenish substance resembling steatite, occurring in a quartz-porphyry rock at the Raubschlösschen, near Weinheim. Again, in a porphyry of Manebach, near Ilmenau, rich in orthoclase, all the quartz crystals are encrusted with a greenish-blue coating, probably containing copper; and in the gold-containing porphyry of Csetatye in Transylvania, the large diplohedrons of quartz are very much rounded off, and the matrix very rich in quartz, &c.

Quartz-porphyries are usually much rent by fissures, but sometimes are found of very regular columnar or of tabular-jointed structure. They are probably never gnarled or irregularly spherical. They sometimes occupy connected regions of great extent, but in that case are by no means of uniform structure, consisting usually of many different varieties which penetrate and traverse each other in all directions, as in the Thuringian Forest, and near Botzen. They sometimes again form isolated dykes in granite, gneiss, &c., as near Freiberg. It is very rarely that they are found to have penetrated any more recent formations than the Devonian or Silurian. In Waldenburg in Silesia, however, they traverse the coal formations, and in the Thuringian Forest the Rothliegende, but these are exceptional cases. Their comportment in this respect is similar to that of granite, and with the difference of their containing throughout a somewhat higher proportion of silica, they would appear to represent but the porphyritic state of that rock, since they actually contain the elements of mica in small quantity. The compact state of their principal mass may to some extent be owing to their greater quantity of silica, but in all probability chiefly to their having originally cooled down more rapidly than granite, as is more especially likely to have been the case with the frequent isolated dykes and small masses of this rock. Quartz-porphyry as a rule, when found with granite, is more recent than the latter, bearing much the same relation to it as the trachyte-porphyries to the trachytes. Thus in Cornwall we find the quartz-porphyry or elvanite to have broken through the granite, and to form dykes or veins in that rock.

References.

G. *Leonhard,* Die quarzführenden Porphyre, 1851.

Naumann in the 5th No. of the Erläuter. zur geogn. Karte von Sachsen, 1845.

Laspeyres on careful microscopic examination of the quartz-porphyries of Halle found the compact base to consist of felspar, quartz, and some mica. The crystals of felspar, according to him, had originally been sanidine, and are only in part transmuted to orthoclase. Zeitschr. d. deut. geol. Ges. vol. xvi. p. 367.

Delesse, Porphyry from Lescines in Belgium, Bullet. de la Soc. Géol. 1850 [2] vol. vii. p. 310.

Jenzsch, on Sanidine-quartz-porphyry, Zeitschr. d. d. geol. Ges. 1858, p. 49.

v. *Richthofen* in the Zeitschr. d. d. geol. Ges. 1826, vol. viii. p. 644; v. L. u. Br. Jahrb. 1859, p. 312; and geogn. Beschr. von Süd-Tyrol, 1860, p. 112.

Hochmuth, the Porphyries of Halle in the Bergwerksfreund, 1847, vol. xi. p. 450.

Streng in v. L. u. Br. Jahrb. 1860, pp. 129 and 257.

H. *Vogelsang* on the Pyromerides of Corsica (Berggeist), 1862, Nos. 90 and 19; Jahrb. für Mineralogie, 1863, p. 102.

19. FELSTONE, FELSITE-ROCK AND FELSITE-SCHIST, PETROSILEX,* EURITE, HÄLLEFLINTA.

FELSITFELS UND FELSITSCHIEFER. (*Germ.*)

A rock of compact texture, about the hardness of felspar, with dull or smooth conchoidal or fissile fracture; colour yellowish, reddish, grey, greenish, or bluish, weathering white.

Spec. grav. .   .   .   .   .   2·5—2·7
Contains silica   .   .   .   .   71—81 p. c.

Gerhard was the first to discover that this rock, which we have already noticed as being identical with the matrix of the quartz-porphyries, consists chiefly of felspar, and he accordingly gave it the name of felsite. Some years later, Dolomieu surmised that it contained the essential ingredients of granite in a compact state, and

---

* The name of petrosilex was first proposed by Brongniart, who applied it to felsite rocks, believing them to be identical with hornstone. The name has stuck to these rocks in spite of the original error, and cannot well now be ignored. Some authors, wishing probably to correct the original misconception, have, however, applied the name of petrosilex to hornstone, but this is simply to create unnecessary confusion—better drop the name altogether.—TRANSLATOR.

Daubisson proved it to consist of an intimate compound of felspar and quartz, and gave it the name *eurite* on account of its fusibility. The same substance has also received the names of *petrosilex*, and in Scandinavia *hälleflinta*, which are of earlier date than the names of felsite and felstone. All the later analyses of this rock have confirmed the fact that it contains both felspar and quartz, and besides these the elementary ingredients of some mica.

In 1845, Durocher showed, by comparing the various analyses, that felstone, or petrosilex, is of the average chemical composition of granite, even quantitatively; and it may therefore be regarded as a granite in compact state, something in the same way as basalt and aphanite respectively represent the compact states of the dolerites and the granular greenstones. Now, this fact is of importance with respect to the process of granite formations, since we know that felsite rock, although it contains quartz, is as easily fusible as felspar alone. For we gather from it that the quartz of granite, when in combination with its other ingredients, might remain in a fluid state quite as long as the felspar and mica, so that the process of crystallisation of all might be contemporaneous, and it would then depend on the individual crystallizing force of each, which mineral would first develop its form. Quartz-porphyry, granitic-porphyry, and granite, with all their several varieties, are therefore products of essentially the same mineral dough, and probably they only differ by reason of slower or more rapid cooling or slight variations in the proportion of the several ingredients. That this igneous compound has most usually resulted in granite, especially in great connected regions of its development, probably proceeds from the fact of deep plutonic solidification; or we may reverse the proposition and say, that wherever this igneous mass attained the solid state deep in the interior of the earth, granite, or a granitic rock, has been the result; on the other hand, when it became solid at or nearer to the earth's surface, then trachyte (rhyolite) and trachytic lavas were its products.

Felstone may be divided into two principal varieties, the massive and the schistose. It goes over on the one hand very frequently into quartz-porphyry, or less usually into granitic porphyry; and on the other, it is con-

nected by stages of transition with granulite and gneiss.
The rock called *Wernerite* we reckon to the first of these
two divisions: it has the character of an eruptive rock,
whilst the foliated varieties of felsite are more closely
connected with the metamorphic crystalline schists, and
may be regarded as compact granulite or gneiss.

Varieties.

(a) FELSTONE PROPER, or PETROSILEX. PETROSILEX. (*Germ.*) PÉTROSILEX, *Dolomieu.* (*Fr.*) Not fissile, usually of massive jointed structure, or very much divided by clefts and fissures. It is frequently found continuous with porphyry, but sometimes forming independent dykes in the same way as porphyry. Dippoldiswalde in Saxony, Bellmannsloos, near Tharand.

(b) WERNERITE ROCK. WERNERITFELS. (*Germ.*) SKAPOLIT-FELS. (*Fr.*) Is the name given by Jasche to a compact compound of common felspar and scapolite (wernerite), with accessory admixtures of graphite, magnetic pyrites, and iron pyrites. It traverses the ironstone beds of Buchenberg at the Hartz. A similar rock, according to Axel Gadolin, occurs on the island of Pusu in the Ladoga Lake.

(c) HÄLLEFLINTA, or FELSITE-SCHIST. HÄLLEFLINTA, oder FELSITSCHIEFER. (*Germ.*) HÄLLEFLINTA. (*Fr.*) Foliated or unevenly laminated. Sometimes contains an admixture of chlorite intimately blended in its mass, and occasionally some mica. This rock is almost always found in parallel bedding with granulite or gneiss, into which it goes over by transition states. It is most frequently found in Sweden, and therefore, for the most part, should be considered as belonging to the metamorphic schistous rocks, but it is not always possible distinctly to separate its different forms of development according to origin.

The schistous as well as the massive varieties of felstone are very frequent among some of the older formations in the British Islands, making up whole mountain masses.

It is most probable that the felsitic matrix of the quartz-containing porphyries of the granite group, is somewhat different in composition from that of the porphyrites which are free from quartz. The former will always contain more silica than that of the porphyrite, and its felsitic constituent will partake of the nature of orthoclase. This is our petrosilex. To outward appearance this difference is often scarcely appreciable, although the matrix of the porphyrites is usually (not always) darker in colour than that of the quartz-porphyries and granitic porphyries.

References.

Gerhard, Abhandl. d. k. Akad. d. Wissensch. zu Berlin, 1814 and 1815, p. 12.
Daubuisson, Traité de Géognosie, 1st ed. 1819, vol. i. p. 112.
Durocher, Compt. rend. 1845, vol. xx. p. 1277.
Schweitzer, in Poggend. Ann. 1840, vol. li. p. 287.
Kersten, in Poggend. Ann. 1843, vol. liii. p. 130.
Wolff, Journ. f. prakt. Chemie, vol. xxxiv. p. 193, and vol. xxxvi. p. 412.
Svanberg, Vet. Akad. Handl. 1850, p. 9.
Haughton, Journ. of the Geol. Soc. of Dublin, 1857, [7] p. 283; and Phil. Mag. 1857, [4] vol. xiv. p. 40.
Jasche, on Wernerite rock, Mineralogische Studien, 1838, p. 4.
A. Gadolin, on Wernerite rock, in the Verh. d. k. Russ. mineral. Ges. at St. Petersburg, 1857–58, p. 85.

20. PITCHSTONE and PITCHSTONE-PORPHYRY.

PECHSTEIN und PECHSTEINPORPHYR. (*Germ.*)
RÉTINITE. (*Fr.*)

The principal mass is homogeneous; of vitreous pitch-like appearance; conchoidal fracture; resinous lustre, translucent at the edges; very variously coloured, viz., yellow, red, brown, black, and green; it sometimes encloses (porphyritically) small crystals of vitreous felspar, grains of quartz, and laminæ of mica; frequently also balls of felsite.

Spec. grav. . . . . . . 2·2—2·3
Contains silica . . . . . 63—75 p. c.

Pitchstone is evidently to be regarded only as a vitreous state of felsite rock, quartz-porphyry, or granite—its chemical composition being essentially the same as that of these rocks, except that it contains more water than they, sometimes as much as 6 p. c. This may be one cause of its vitreous state. Its colour is dependent on the relative proportions which it contains of the peroxide or the protoxide of iron and protoxide of manganese. The first of these gives the rock a red or yellow colour, the latter green, grey, and black. In spite of its large proportion of silica, thin splinters of pitchstone melt easily before the blowpipe to a white vesicular glass without intumescence. Formerly pitchstone was regarded as an independent mineral, but it is clearly nothing but a close compound of felspar and quartz, with which the elements of mica are also combined.   Recently it has been even doubted whether this compound is really an amorphous vitreous mass, or only a very intimately blended crystal-line aggregate.   It may be that this opinion has arisen from some few fine crystalline particles which swim in the prevailing vitreous mass.

Crystals of sanidine are sometimes found porphyritically imbedded in the rock; they are small, but usually quite fresh, and are frequently coated with a thin light-red crust, evidently caused by oxide of iron; grains of quartz and laminæ of mica are also found, but more rarely, and are often similarly coated.   Instead of these crystals, or in addition to them, there also very frequently occur nodules or balls of felsite, very various in size and struc-ture.   In the pitchstone-porphyry at Spechtshausen, near Tharand in Saxony, such are found varying from one-tenth of an inch to six inches diameter, consisting of compact felsite, and some of the very small balls of shining sani-dine.   The larger ones occasionally contain veins of chal-cedony in their interior; the grey pitchstone of Planitz, near Zwickau, contains balls of from one to five inches diameter veined inside in the manner of septaria, the veins narrowing towards the periphery and filled with chalcedony and quartz.   At the Fichtenmühle, near Meissen, a yellowish-brown pitchstone contains irregular nodules, whose size extends even to ten feet diameter, consisting of quartz-porphyry, with a matrix resembling hornstone.   It would almost seem as if these were frag-ments torn from the adjoining quartz-porphyry (which is here traversed and disturbed by the pitchstone) and then rounded off in the convulsion.   Near Corbitz, in the neighbourhood of Meissen, there is a pitchstone rock very much weathered, containing nodules from a quarter to three feet diameter; these nodules consist of a compact felsitic mass, which itself contains other more compact and dark-coloured ball-shaped concretions of the same sub-stance.   Similar phenomena with many modifications re-peatedly occur in the pitchstone of other localities.   These nodules appear to answer to those in the pearlstone (sphe-rulites), which are smaller in size; they are frequently coated with a deep-red crust or their surfaces much weathered.

The pitchstone of Planitz in Saxony is found to contain in some places small fragments of (so-called) mineral charcoal (a coal of woody texture without bitumen, and containing much silica) which indicate that the pitchstone has broken through the coal formation of that district.

Scarcely any other minerals than those we have named are known to be similarly enclosed in pitchstone.

This rock passes over into obsidian and pearlstone. By decomposition it becomes a kind of claystone rock, which variety Naumann called *Pechthonstein* (pitch-clay-stone).

Varieties in Texture.

(a) COMMON PITCHSTONE.
GEMEINER PECHSTEIN. (*Germ.*)
RÉTINITE LITHOÏDE. (*Fr.*) } Very variously coloured. Ex. g. Triebisch Thal, near Meissen.

(b) PITCHSTONE-PORPHYRY.
PECHSTEINPORPHYR. (*Germ.*)
RÉTINITE PORPHYROÏDE. (*Fr.*) } With sanidine crystals. Mohorn and Spechtshausen, between Freiberg and Dresden.

A rock of this description is met with at Castelruth in Southern Tyrol; it contains a felspar resembling sanidine and round grains of quartz, and v. Richthofen describes it as a quartz-porphyry.

(c) ARGILLACEOUS PITCHSTONE.
PECHTHONSTEIN, *Naumann.* (*Germ.*)
ARGILORÉTINITE. (*Fr.*) } The Pitch-claystone of Naumann, a stage of decomposition not unfrequent near Meissen.

Pitchstone is for the most part of irregular massive structure. It usually occurs associated with quartz-porphyries, and traverses them in dykes; probably, however, its geological age is not very different from that of the quartz-porphyries, and it would seem to bear somewhat the same relation to the porphyries as perlite and obsidian to the trachyte porphyries.

The vitreous state of pitchstone is somewhat enigmatical, inasmuch as that rock usually occurs with rocks of decidedly plutonic origin, and moreover contains a large proportion of water: Bischof and Jenzsch consider the glassy texture to be the consequence of transmutation by aqueous process, and only to be apparently vitreous. But it is very possible that under special circumstances in the interior of the earth, eruptive igneous masses may have cooled very rapidly, perhaps in consequence of the sudden accession of a large quantity of water, and so have become converted into a vitreous state containing water.

Q

References.

Knox discovered a bituminous substance in pitchstone. Transact. of the Geol. Soc. 1811, vol. i. p. 278, and Ann. d. Phys., et Chem. 1823, vol. xxii. p. 44.

Necker de Saussure. Voyages en Écosse et aux Îles Hébrides, vol. ii. p. 455. The pitchstone of the Hebrides exhibits under the lens a fine granular texture resembling basalt.

Macculloch, Descr. of the Western Islands, vol. i. p. 520, on the pitchstone of the Hebrides.

v. Oeynhausen and *v. Decken,* on the Pitchstone of the Hebrides, in Karsten's Archiv. vol. i. p. 50.

Haughton concludes from his analysis of pitchstone, that it consists of a combination of about 62 felspar, 30 stibite, and 7 quartz.

Naumann, on Pitchstone and Pitch-claystone from Meissen, in the Erläuter. zur. geogn. Karte v. Sachsen, 1844, No. 5, p. 184.

Cotta, on the Pitchstone of Meissen and Tharand, Geognostiche Wanderungen, 1836, vol. i. pp. 40 and 104.

Scheerer, Analysen u. Folgerungen in the Art. Pechstein in Liebig's Handwörterbuch der Chemie, 1854, vol. vi. p. 105, and in v. L. u. Br. Jahrbuch, 1855, p. 60.

Jenzsch considers pitchstone to be fine crystalline, and a product of transmutation and the balls of felsite in it, for remains of porphyry not yet transformed. Zeitsch. d. d. geol. Ges. 1856, p. 257.

Rentzsch, Die Pechsteine, 1860.

H. Fischer, on Pitchstone and Pearlstone, Zeitschr. der deutsch. geol. Ges. 1862, vol. xiv. p. 312.

CHAPTER II.

METAMORPHIC CRYSTALLINE SCHISTS.

THE term *Metamorphic* as applied to these rocks implies that they are the product of the metamorphosis of rocks originally sedimentary, and, although several gneiss rocks may have had another origin, they cannot be lithologically separated from those of undoubted metamorphic character. The designation of *Crystalline Schist* on the other hand rests solely on petrographical characteristics.

The mineral composition of these rocks most resembles that of the plutonic division of the acidic igneous rocks, i.e. they consist (like those) chiefly of compounds of felspar, quartz, mica, talc, chlorite, and hornblende, and do not essentially contain pyroxene. We might indeed have anticipated the resemblance of the metamorphic rocks to the plutonic rather than the volcanic division of igneous rocks (whether basic or acidic) as their transmutation has probably taken place deep in the interior of the earth, therefore under plutonic influences; and the fact that they contain more silica and less lime and magnesia on the average than the basic igneous rocks, is accounted for by the *separate* beds of carbonate of lime and magnesia (limestones and dolomites) which interlie the metamorphic rocks, whence we should expect to find the last mentioned rocks somewhat deficient in those bases. But we shall find that some of the crystalline schists are in fact rich in lime and magnesia, and therefore are more allied to the basic rocks. Those of prevailing acidic character are principally *granulite, gneiss, mica-schist, quartz-schist, itacolumite* and *argillaceous mica-schist.* The basic on the other hand are: *chlorite-schist, talc-schist,* and *hornblende-schist,* and others.

All the rocks of this class are to be distinguished from the igneous by their foliated texture, and yet more by their alternate bedding in parallel layers or strata, and the traces which they often very distinctly show of internal stratification. These phenomena it is true are sometimes exceptionally met with in the igneous rocks, but in them they are the reverse of characteristic; their foliated texture, when it occurs, is usually to be explained by local pressure, their stratification by successive overflows of fused matter; as a general rule the igneous rocks also differ very widely in the character of their bedding from the metamorphic schists. Nevertheless there are actual petrographic transitions between the two, and in some individual cases where the nature of the bedding is not very distinctly marked it is difficult to decide the character of a given rock.

The properties which the crystalline schists have in common with the sedimentary rocks are stratification, fissile texture, and parallel alternating bedding; on the other hand the schists are wanting in organic remains (fossils) and in mechanical aggregates. In their composition they differ from the sedimentary rocks by the crystalline state of their mineral ingredients. There is, however, no very definite boundary between the two; on the contrary there are series of distinct transitions from one to the other just as we might expect to find if the crystalline were really as we suppose them to be, the offspring of the sedimentary rocks. We moreover find that the greater part of the sedimentary rocks, and especially the older ones, are no longer in their original state but are somewhat changed, doubtless by the identical influences which at last have transmuted them into crystalline rocks and which are probably still in operation, viz. heat and pressure.

The term Metamorphic, however, is in practice only applied to the extreme products of this slow process of transmutation, such as by assuming a crystalline state have entirely departed from that of their original deposit, although their connection with it may still be traced through stages of transition. This is simply a matter of usage, for looking to the meaning of the term, we might just as well call every clay-slate or firm sandstone metamorphic (transmuted) since they were not originally formed in the state in which we find them at the present day.

For these and other reasons it is difficult to prescribe

a definite and consistent limit to metamorphic rocks. From a geological point of view we ought to include in that term most granular limestone, serpentine, graphite, magnetic iron-ore, &c., and reject many kinds of gneiss and granulite as being irruptive; but in a system of lithology this treatment, however logically correct, would lead to so many inconveniences and difficulties as to render it impossible in practice.

For these reasons we have not made use of the general designation *Metamorphic rocks* as the title for this chapter, but chosen the more restricted term of *Metamorphic crystalline schists.* These for the most part are compounds rich in silica, which, in their chemical composition approach Bunsen's formula for the normal trachytic rocks. Some few, however, are poor in silica and resemble the basic igneous rocks in composition. We do not propose to divide the metamorphic schists into basic and acidic groups; we prefer to group them according to their leading mineral ingredients without attempting a strict scientific arrangement, except that we begin with those which in their mineral character bear the greatest resemblance to the granite rocks and place those last which approach most in character to the unchanged sedimentary rocks.

CRYSTALLINE SCHISTS, RICH IN FELSPAR.
(Granulite and Gneiss.)

21. GRANULITE, LEPTYNITE.

GRANULIT, WEISSSTEIN. (*Germ.*)
LEPTYNITE, *Haüy.* (*Fr.*)

A fine-grained to compact fissile compound of felspar and quartz, usually with some mica.

Spec. grav.	.	.	.	.	2·6—2·7
Contains silica	.	.	.	.	70—80 p. c.

This rock, on account of its frequent white or light-yellowish colour, was formerly called weissstein (white stone); but as the same mineral compound also occurs of a dark colour, Weiss proposed to substitute the name of granulite, which has now been generally adopted. Its mineral composition is for the most part that of a granite or gneiss (a red gneiss), with very little mica. Its characteristic varieties are nevertheless easily to be distinguished from granite and gneiss, as will appear from a more special description of the rock. Intermediate grades of uncertain character and transitions are, however, frequent, and if these occur in the midst of gneiss or granite, we reckon them without hesitation, to those rocks, and call them granulitic gneiss, or granulitic granite; but if found in granulitic regions the same rocks would be properly termed gneissic granulite, and reckoned to the granulites.

The felspar of granulite is mostly orthoclase; sometimes, however, in part oligoclase. It is intimately blended with the quartz, which is less in quantity, or at all events is less apparent, than in granite or gneiss. The free quartz forms few and very thin separate layers, or flat lenticular grains, which are to be most distinctly seen when the rock is weathered. The mica appears in small scattered laminæ, disposed in parallel planes, or if sometimes found connected, scaly seams entirely dividing the rock, which otherwise is an intimate compound of felspar and quartz. In both cases the mica increases the fissile texture of the rock. It is usually a white variety of mica—seldom black. The felspar, which is always predominant, is usually white, yellowish, or light-red; and these are, therefore, the prevailing colours of the rock. The quartz is never dark-coloured, seldom transparent, and usually white. In a section of the rock the seams of mica sometimes produce riband stripings of dark colour. There are, however, varieties of granulite in which the whole mass is of a blackish-green to almost quite black colour (owing perhaps to protoxide of iron); for these the old name of weissstein is inappropriate.

We repeat, then, that the essential constituents of the rock are its felspar and quartz, and a small proportion of mica. In addition to these, red garnets often appear disseminated through the mass in small grains or crystals; where little or no mica is present, then these garnets are especially frequent, and this is the most characteristic composition of granulite. Where much mica is found, the garnets appear to fail, and varieties of this latter kind form the transitions into gneiss. Another characteristic accessory ingredient of granulite, though but sparingly distributed, is blue disthene (kyanite). Schorl and horn-blende also occur, but more locally.

This rock forms transitions into granite by assuming a more distinctly granular, and less fissile texture, into gneiss, by the increase of its mica, and into felsite-schist, when its mica disappears and the mass becomes quite compact.

Varieties in Texture.

(a) COMMON GRANULITE.
GEMEINER GRANULIT. (*Germ.*)
LEPTYNITE COMMUN. (*Fr.*)
} White, yellowish, or flesh-red, with little or no mica, contains small garnets, and frequently some disthene. It is more laminated than properly speaking foliated or slaty. Rosswein in Saxony.

(b) RIBAND-STRIPED GRANULITE.
BANDSTREIFIGER GRANULIT. (*Germ.*)
LEPTYNITE RUBANÉ. (*Fr.*)
} Striped by parallel seams of mica, interlying the main mass of felspar and quartz.
On the Zschopau between Sachsenburg and Schönborn in Saxony.

(c) MICACEOUS GRANULITE or GNEISS-GRANULITE.
GLIMMERREICHEN oder GNEISSGRANULIT. (*Germ.*)
LEPTYNITE MICACÉ. (*Fr.*)
} With few or no garnets. Mitt-weida in Saxony.

(d) GRANITIC GRANULITE.
GRANITGRANULIT. (*Germ.*)
LEPTYNITE GRENU. (*Fr.*)
} More granular than fissile. This variety passes into a kind of granite which contains little mica, and where it occurs in the form of dykes or veins, it may be considered as a granite. Neighbourhood of Herrnhut in Saxony.

(e) BLACK GRANULITE.
SCHWARZER GRANULIT. (*Germ.*)
LEPTYNITE NOIR. (*Fr.*)
} Probably coloured by protoxide of iron. Penig in Saxony.

(f) SPOTTED GRANULITE.
GEFLECKTER oder FORELLEN-GRANULIT. (*Germ.*)
} With dark spots caused by horn-blende. Glocknitzer Schlossberg, Wiener Neustadt.

(g) SCHORLACEOUS GRANULITE.
TOURMALINGRANULIT. (*Germ.*)
LEPTYNITE TOURMALINIFÈRE. (*Fr.*)
} With considerable quantity of schorl in its composition. According to v. Hochstetter, it occurs near Krummau in Bohemia.

Granulite is usually of very regular tabular-jointed structure, disposed parallel to the foliation or lamination of the rock; but besides this more or less horizontal jointing, it is also usually intersected at right angles by cross joints, somewhat crooked, but whose surfaces are smooth. This latter jointing is characteristic of granulite, which by its means may sometimes be distinguished from gneiss at a considerable distance.

In Saxony, Bohemia, and Moravia, this rock fills con-siderable regions of elliptical shape, surrounded by other

crystalline schists.   The granulite region of Mittweida
in Saxony is surrounded and overlayed with mica-schist
and dichroite-gneiss, of which latter it contains large fragments.   It is also penetrated in all directions by numerous
often very distinct, but narrow dykes or veins of granite.
Naumann considers this region to be of eruptive origin.
Metamorphic rocks may possibly in some cases have
become eruptive here.

References.

Engelbrecht, Kurze Beschreibung des Weisssteins, 1802.
Weiss, Neue Schriften naturf. Freunde in Berlin, vol. iv.
    p. 350.
Hornig, Analysen des Kremser Granulits, in den Sitzungs-
    berichten der k. k. Akademie zu Wien, 1851, vol. vii. p. 586.
v. Hochstetter, Granulit von Krummau, in Jahrb. d. geol.
    Reichsanst. 1854, vol. v. p. 11, and the Corresp.-Bl. d. geol.
    mineral. Ver. zu Regensburg, 1853, p. 157.
Naumann, in Erläuter. z. geogn. Karte v. Sachsen, No. 1,
    p. 9, and 1838, No. 2, p. 19; Karsten's Archiv, 1832, vol. v.
    p. 393, and Jahrb. d. geol. Reichsanst. 1856, p. 766.
Zirkel, Granulit-analysen, in Poggendorff's Annalen, vol. cxxii.
    p. 624.

22. GNEISS.

GNEISS, GNEUSS.   (*Germ.*)
GNEISS.   (*Fr.*)

*A crystalline-granular compound of quartz, felspar, and
mica; texture foliated.*

Spec. grav.   .   .   .   .   .   2·6—2·7
Contains silica .   .   .   .   .   64—76 p. c.

The mineral composition of gneiss is precisely the same
as that of granite; the only petrographic difference between the two rocks consists in the foliated texture of the
former.   We may, therefore, say that gneiss is the name
given to schistose granite.   The term gneiss originated
with the Freiberg miners, who from ancient times have
used it to designate the rock in which their veins of silver
ore were found, and more especially such parts of the
rock as were much decomposed.

The felspar of gneiss is usually orthoclase, sometimes
with oligoclase, and perhaps even albite.   The orthoclase
is white, grey, yellow, or reddish, and on fresh cleavage
surfaces has mother-of-pearl lustre.   Usually it occurs

only in small grains, sometimes larger crystals or lentil-shaped masses so called, swellings or eyes (Schwielen, Augen), with the regular twin growth peculiar to ortho-clase (porphyritic gneiss, augen-gneiss). The oligoclase which occurs with and subordinate to the orthoclase or (more rarely) as its substitute may usually be recognised by its twin stripings, more resinous lustre, or more advanced decomposition.

The quartz forms small white or grey lentil-shaped grains or irregular excrescences upon the felspar; more-over it often appears in separate larger and irregular masses.

The mica is usually potash-mica (more rarely magnesia-mica), brown, black, white, or dark-green; and some-times in the same gneiss different coloured micas occur together.

Gneiss occasionally contains accessory ingredients of various kinds, such as chlorite, talc, graphite, micaceous iron, dichroite, garnet, tourmaline, andalusite, pistacite, zircon, disthene, rutile, titanite, pyrites, magnetic iron-ore, &c.

Sometimes one or other of these minerals is abundant, and assume the character of an essential ingredient; thus, for instance, the prevalence of hornblende occasions a tran-sition from ordinary gneiss into syenite-gneiss, the presence of chlorite or talc into protogine-gneiss, &c. These different varieties in composition are easy of recognition.

It is more difficult in many cases to recognise the perhaps more important difference between the so-called 'red' and 'grey' gneiss. It was formerly considered that all gneiss was of metamorphic origin, but it has of late years been established beyond a doubt that many kinds of gneiss are irruptive, and some geologists have gone so far as to regard all gneiss as of igneous origin.

In the mining districts of the Erzgebirge it had been observed that the veins in the red varieties of gneiss were usually non-metalliferous, although within a short distance the same veins traversing grey gneiss were rich in ore.

Previously to the year 1844, we ourselves had observed red gneiss of a distinctly eruptive character, forming veins in the grey gneiss, which latter is the prevalent rock of the mining districts of the Erzgebirge; the result of these observations we published in von Leonhard's Almanack. (Vide v. L. u. Br. Jahrb. 1844, p. 681.)

Subsequently Professor Scheerer received a commission from the Saxon mining authorities, to analyse several kinds of gneiss, with a view to discover the cause of the superior richness of the metalliferous veins in the grey gneiss; and he found amongst other chemical differences that the red gneiss usually, if not always, contained a considerably larger proportion of silica than the grey.

Accordingly the gneiss of the Erzgebirge came to be divided into two principal classes of distinct mineralogical as well as chemical characters, termed respectively red gneiss and grey gneiss.

The red gneiss is not, however, always to be easily distinguished from the grey gneiss, as the colours of the two distinct classes do not in every case correspond with the names that have been given to them, and some so-called grey gneiss is of red colour, and *vice versâ*; and although in several instances the bedding of the red gneiss shows it to be of distinctly irruptive character, yet the bedding of both kinds of gneiss is frequently indistinct and uncertain, or might be capable of various interpretations, and therefore would not alone serve the purposes of lithological distinction. The recognised and only reliable distinction consists in the proportion of silica, only to be arrived at by chemical analysis of the rock. These considerations compel us, regardless of origin, to retain the usual classification for all gneissic rocks, and notwithstanding the irruptive character of some varieties, to treat them collectively in this place amongst the metamorphic rocks.

We proceed to define these two principal classes of gneiss, and (to avoid attaching an undue importance to their mere colour) we propose the name of gneissite for the variety formerly known as the red gneiss:—

A. GNEISSITE, or RED GNEISS. (Rother Gneiss oder Gneissit. *Germ.*)—The felspar of the compound appears to be always orthoclase, and to be the predominant ingredient. The mica is always white, or at all events not dark-coloured, not abundant in quantity, but usually scattered through the mass in thin straight laminæ.

The rock contains 74—76 per cent. of silica.

According to Scheerer, it is an acidic compound, a sesqui-silicate. Its extreme varieties are easily to be recognised, and may be better distinguished from the grey gneiss than gneiss from many varieties of granulite. Its felspar is usually reddish, exceptionally, however, white or greyish.

In the Erzgebirge this gneissite is found in irregular tracts, and sometimes forming distinct dykes or veins in the ordinary gneiss, of which it frequently encloses fragments. We may therefore say that there it comports itself as an eruptive igneous rock towards the common gneiss, and geologically speaking should perhaps properly be considered a granite. But as its bedding is frequently indistinct and the character of single specimens is often not to be recognised with certainty, and as some kinds of gneissite may very possibly be of metamorphic origin, we cannot usefully separate it lithologically from every other gneiss by taking it out of the class of the crystalline schists.

B. GREY GNEISS. (Grauer Gneiss. *Germ.*) — The felspar of the compound is principally orthoclase, sometimes, however, with the orthoclase some oligoclase or albite is associated. The mica is partly dark-coloured (ferruginous and more basic than that of the gneissite), it is moreover abundant, whence the rock usually assumes a dark or grey colour.

The rock contains 64—67 per cent. of silica.

According to Scheerer, it is a neutral silicate. The normal Freiberg variety is granular, scaly, and unevenly foliated. The felspar is usually white or grey, but sometimes of a reddish colour. The mica is mostly dark-coloured, but some white. Mica occasionally occurs in the compound. Accordingly, the differences between these two normal varieties (the gneissite and the grey gneiss) may be stated as follows : —

Gneissite, or Red Gneiss.	*Ordinary, or Grey Gneiss.*
Content of silica, 74—76 p. c.	Content of silica, 64—67 p. c.
Felspar—orthoclase only.	Felspar—orthoclase and sometimes oligoclase.
Mica — in small quantity and light-coloured.	Mica—abundant and dark-coloured.
Approximate proportion of mineral ingredients.	Approximate proportion of mineral ingredients.
30 quartz	25 quartz
60 felspar	45 felspar
10 mica	30 mica

The mica (both of the gneissite and grey gneiss) usually contains about 4 per cent. water, and this water Scheerer regards as an original ingredient of the mineral entering into its chemical composition, as a base to the silicic acid.

Besides these two extreme kinds of gneiss, it appears that many intermediate grades exist, which may be collectively designated as—

C. MEDIUM GNEISS. (Mittelgneiss, *Germ.*) — Gneiss containing an intermediate proportion of silica between that of the gneissite and the grey gneiss. The mineral character sometimes resembles the one and sometimes the other of those two extremes.

Scheerer has endeavoured to show that, chemically speaking, this medium gneiss C forms an independent rock or variety, whose proportion of silica is constant between 69 and 70 per cent., and that it therefore uniformly and essentially differs from the varieties A and B. (Vide Scheerer über die Gneusse des Erzgebirges in the Zeitschrift der deutschen geol. Ges. vol. xiv.; also published separately, Berlin, 1862.)

Later analyses have, however, shown the existence of gneisses varying in their composition, and especially in the proportion of silica which they contain, as much from the normal medium gneiss as from the two extreme varieties of red and grey gneiss. Therefore we must guard ourselves against expecting any sharply defined chemical character in the different varieties which come under our notice.

We must remember that it is only of late years that attention has been called to this subject, and with the utmost chemical industry but few analyses, comparatively speaking, have yet been made with the special object of distinguishing different species of gneiss. These analyses have chiefly been conducted at Freiberg, and mainly with a view to ascertain and discover whether any and what differences of rock coincide with the richness of metalliferous veins in the Erzgebirge. It appears to be an established fact that the grey gneiss is more favourable for the yield of rich veins than the gneissite or red gneiss.

This is a very interesting fact, which deserves the

attention of geologists. At present we are not aware of any thoroughly satisfactory explanation of it, unless we adopt Scheerer's theory that the iron of the mica in the grey gneiss is the cause of its advantage in this important respect. He has shewn that the mica is invariably decomposed for some distance on each side of the metalliferous veins.

The gneiss of the Erzgebirge is undoubtedly partly irruptive and partly metamorphic; and we believe that its character in this respect must always be determined rather from observation of the bedding than from the chemical composition of each individual rock; at all events, the analyses which have hitherto been made do not justify the conclusion that rocks of a definite proportion of silica are confined to any particular geological origin, or *vice versâ* that rocks of the same geological origin are uniformly of one chemical character.

It would, indeed, be somewhat remarkable if it were found that the collective elementary ingredients of a rock like gneiss, consisting of three separate minerals, were combined in such uniform proportions as to be capable of being expressed by a simple chemical formula; we should rather expect that from a mass so constituted a homogeneous rather than a compound rock would have resulted. We are, however, ready to admit that the strangeness of a phenomenon to our preconceived ideas is no valid argument against its truth.

In the present state of our chemical investigations, therefore, we can only seek approximately to range all known gneisses under one or other of the three heads we have named. If geologists in different parts of the world will assist in this work, there is room for hope that some general law may be discovered which shall advance the state of science with respect both to the origin of gneiss and the causes which have influenced the superior richness of the metalliferous veins in some rocks to the exclusion of others.

Independently of the division into gneissite, grey gneiss and medium gneiss, which, however important geologically, depends mainly on chemical, and only partly on mineralogical, differences, we have the following varieties in texture and composition.

Varieties in Texture.

(*a*) COMMON FREIBERG GNEISS.   } Belongs to the class of grey
     FREIBERGER NORMALGNEISS. (*Germ.*) } gneiss. The flakes or laminæ
     GNEISS COMMUN ou NORMAL. (*Fr.*) } of mica are distributed in
parallel planes through the granular compound of felspar and
quartz. The rock has often a folded or wavy texture. In the
immediate neighbourhood of metalliferous veins, near Freiberg,
it is impregnated with pyrites, sometimes with arsenical pyrites,
galena or blende, by which latter its decomposition is much
accelerated.

(*b*) PORPHYRITIC GNEISS.   } In the otherwise uniform schis-
     AUGENGNEISS oder PORPHYR- } tose mass there occur at in-
     ARTIGER GNEISS. (*Germ.*) } tervals large egg-shaped crystals
     GNEISS PORPHYROÏDE. (*Fr.*) } of orthoclase (usually they are
twin crystals, sometimes they are amorphous), round which
the foliated texture bends itself with a wavy sweep. This is
very characteristically developed near Schwartzenberg in the
Erzgebirge, Redwitz in the Fichtelgebirge.

(*c*) STANGEL GNEISS, COARSELY FIBROUS GNEISS. } The ingredients
     STÄNGELGNEISS oder HOLZGNEISS. (*Germ.*) } are disposed in
a fibrous manner towards one direction, so that a peculiar
linear parallel conformation is produced. The stalks or fibres
may consist of felspar and quartz, or of stripes of mica. In
the extreme development of this texture a wood-like conformation is produced, which almost supersedes the schistose
texture. Lippersdorf, Lengefeld, Weissenborn, and Weig-
mannsdorf, near Freiberg, Saxony, Sonnenberg in Bohemia.

(*d*) VERY FINE SLATY GNEISS } All the mineral parts small; the
     or SLATE-GNEISS. } numerous parallel flakes of mica
     SCHIEFERGNEISS. (*Germ.*) } occasion very distinct slaty texture.
In the cleavage, mica alone is usually seen.

(*e*) VERY FINE-GRAINED, ALMOST } With only indistinct foliated tex-
     COMPACT GNEISS. } ture. Radegrube, near Freiberg,
     GNEISS À GRAINS FINS. (*Fr.*) } Radeberg, near Dresden.

(*f*) LAGEN GNEISS.   } Quartz and felspar on the one hand, and
     LAGENGNEISS. (*Germ.*) } the mica on the other, form thin parallel
     GNEISS RUBANÉ. (*Fr.*) } and mutually alternating seams or layers,
which, in the cross section, occasion a ribbon striping.

(*g*) GRANITE-GNEISS or GRANITIC GNEISS.   } With very
     GRANITGNEISS oder GRANITÄHNLICHER GNEISS. (*Germ.*) } granular and
only indistinctly foliated texture, forming a transition state
between gneiss and granite. Sageritz near Grossenhain, Boxdorf
near Moritzburg, Brambach in the Voigtland, Höfles near Eiger.

Naumann has collected into one class, under the name of
'CORNUBIATES,' several exceptional varieties of gneiss, some
compact, or of very indistinctly compound texture, others of
contorted foliated texture. They occur variously, usually as
contact formations at the margins of more recent igneous rocks.
Saussure called them 'PALAIOPÊTRE,' Boase 'PROTEOLITE.'
Properly speaking they belong only geologically, and not petrographically to gneiss, and they can only be classed as gneiss
where their position and bedding give them that character.

Varieties in Composition.

(*h*) GRANULITE-GNEISS. } With very little mica, and that usually
GRANULITGNEISS. (*Germ.*) } white. Felspar predominates, and is
often intimately combined with quartz. Always belongs to
the gneissite or red gneiss. Grosswaltersdorf near Freiberg,
Lauterbach near Marienberg, Mautern near Mölk, Poppenreut
near Münchberg. Hochberg near Eger;—and a variety with
dark-coloured mica, Fahrnleiten, near the Schneeberg, in the
Fichtelgebirge.

(*i*) MICACEOUS GNEISS. } Forming a transition state into mica-
GLIMMERGNEISS. (*Germ.*) } schist, with much mica, chiefly dark-
coloured, and little felspar; usually of a fine foliated texture.
Near Rabenau and Dippoldiswalde in Saxony, where it occurs
between strata of ordinary gneiss; also, in like manner, at
Gastein in the Alps.

(*k*) GNEISS VERY RICH IN QUARTZ, and going over into a kind of
quartz-schist.

(*l*) SYENITIC GNEISS. } With characteristic admixture of horn-
SYENITGNEISS. (*Germ.*) } blende. Neighbourhood of Aschaffen-
GNEISS AMPHIBOLIQUE. (*Fr.*) } burg, Salzburg Alps, Gefrees in the
Fichtelgebirge.

(*m*) PROTOGINE-GNEISS. } With chlorite or talc instead of mica.
PROTOGINGNEISS. (*Germ.*) } Oberhasli and Mont Blanc in the Alps.
GNEISS TALQUEUX. (*Fr.*) } At the Goldberg near Bernek, in the
Fichtelgebirge, a somewhat indistinct protogine-gneiss encloses
fragments of clay-slate, and from this would appear to be of
igneous (irruptive) character.

(*n*) ADULARIA-GNEISS. } With adularia in the place of the usual
ADULARGNEISS. (*Germ.*) } orthoclase. Very widely spread in the
Alps, e.g. St. Gotthard.

(*o*) OLIGOCLASE-GNEISS. } With oligoclase in the place of ortho-
OLIGOKLASGNEISS. (*Germ.*) } clase. According to v. Hochstetter, the
lofty Adam's Peak of Ceylon (7,000 ft.) consists of this rock.
It contains many garnets, and is found in alternate layers with
syenite-gneiss, granulite-gneiss, granulite, and hornblende-slate.

(*p*) GNEISS WITH TWO KINDS OF MICA, white and black, occurs very
frequently. Seerenbach near Tharand, Lauenstein in the Erzgebirge, Steingrün near Eger.

(*q*) DICHROITE-GNEISS. } With dichroite in the place of mica.
DICHROITGNEISS. (*Germ.*) } Found in the margin of the Saxon
GNEISS AVEC DICHROITE. (*Fr.*) } granulite region. E. g. near Wech-
selburg.

(*r*) MICACEOUS IRON GNEISS. } With micaceous iron instead of com-
EISENGLIMMERGNEISS. (*Germ.*) } mon mica. In the southern Fichtelgebirge.

(*s*) GRAPHITE-GNEISS. } With graphite in the place of the mica.
GRAPHITGNEISS. (*Germ.*) } Near Passau, on the Danube.

(*t*) ALPINITE. } Is a name given by Simler to a schistose com-
ALPINIT, *Simler.* } pound of quartz, felspar (oligoclase), and a
(*Germ.*) } flaky green mineral, probably belonging to the
mica species, but certainly not chlorite or talc (über die Petro-
geneses; Berne, 1862). Very frequent in the Alps.

The above are the principal varieties of this very important rock; it would neither be possible nor desirable to enumerate every modification of differing texture and composition.

Gneiss, in addition to those of its accessory ingredients which have been already mentioned, sometimes contains irregular concretions or minute veins of quartz, felspar, or a kind of granite resembling the graphic granite.

The foliated texture of gneiss is a universal characteristic. Gneiss is also usually stratified or jointed in a direction parallel to its texture. At all events a divergence from this direction has not been hitherto observed. Besides this *tabular jointing* there is sometimes a tolerably regular oblique *parallelopipedic jointing* dividing the rock into irregular rhombs, two of whose faces correspond with the stratification of the rock.

Gneiss is found in extensive regions in many mountain districts. The mountains which it forms are of very various shapes, according to the position and direction of the foliated texture. If this be horizontal then we have flat undulating table-lands where valleys appear like cuts in the otherwise uniform surface. If, however, the bedding of the rock has been upheaved so that the parallel planes of the texture assume a vertical position, then it forms jagged alpine heights. Both the bedding and the texture are frequently very much contorted.

Gneiss, wherever we can approximately determine its geological age, is found to be of high antiquity. It occurs with granite rocks usually lying above them, but often penetrated and traversed by them. The oldest sedimentary rocks usually overlie the gneiss, but there are some exceptions where, as in the Alps and the Fichtelgebirge, the gneiss is found uppermost; these exceptions are capable of being explained by disturbances of the original bedding.

References.

Scheerer, Chemische Untersuchungen des Gneisses im Jahrb. d. k. sächs. Bergakademie z. Freiberg, 1858, p. 210, 1861, p. 252, 1862, p. 188; Berg- u. Hüttenm. Zeitung, 1861, p. 188; and v. L. u. Br. Jahrb. 1861, p. 613; Zeitsch. d. d. geol. Gesells. 1862; also separately published under the title of ' Die Gneusse des Erzgebirges.'

Naumann, Erläuter. z. geogn. Karto v. Sachsen, No. 2, p. 265, and No. 5, p. 51.
Cotta, Rother u. Grauer Gneiss, in v. L. u. Br. Jahrb. 1844, p. 681, and 1854, p. 39.
Credner, Syenitgneiss, in v. L. u. Br. Jahrb. 1850, p. 549.
Peters, Syenitgneiss, in Jahrb. d. geol. Reichsaust. 1853, p. 236.
Kittel, Syenitgneiss, Umgegend v. Aschaffenburg, 1840, pp. 11 and 27.
v. Rath, Gneiss in Graubündten, Zeltschr. d. d. geol. Ges. 1858, p. 199.
Fournet, Gneiss der Alpen, Mém. sur la Géol. de la part des Alpes, p. 29.
Boase, Transact. of the Geol. Soc. of Cornwall, vol. vi. p. 390.
Quincke, Schönfeld and *Roscoe*, Analysen in Ann. der Chem. u. Pharm. 1854, vol.xci. p. 306, and 1856, vol. xcix. p. 239 ; v. L. u. Br. Jahrb. 1855, p. 453.
v. Hochstetter, Oligoklasgneiss, Novarra-Reise, 1861, Th. i. p. 324.

CRYSTALLINE SCHISTS RICH IN QUARTZ.
(Mica-schist, Quartz-schist, Itacolumite.)

23. MICA-SCHIST.

GLIMMERSCHIEFER. (*Germ.*)
MICASCHISTE, *Brongniart.* (*Fr.*)

A crystalline schistose compound of mica and quartz.

Spec. grav.	2·7—3·1
Contains silica	69—82 p. c.

Its texture is always foliated, but with many varieties of modification. Its composition varies between two extremes ; one consisting almost entirely of mica, the other (quartz-schist) almost entirely of quartz.

The mica is most usually the optically biaxial potash-mica, but sometimes dark magnesia-mica, damourite, or paragonite. Two different kinds of mica occasionally occur together in the same rock. Usually the laminæ, whether large or small, all lie in planes approximately parallel to each other, and thereby occasion the foliated texture of the rock; it is rare to find them in diverging directions.

The mode in which the mica and quartz are united is somewhat various. In those varieties which contain the most mica the small grains or lenticular particles of quartz usually lie hidden in it, and the rock appears almost exclusively to consist of mica. If the quantity of quartz be greater, then its larger lenticular masses are distinctly prominent amongst the mica in a cross fracture of

R

the rock. Again, these lenticular bodies extend and are elongated into thin parallel layers of granular composition, and sometimes themselves enclose small flakes of mica of divergent direction. Those varieties which are very rich in quartz consist almost entirely of that mineral, and only receive a foliated texture from the thin parallel layers of mica imbedded in the quartz.

Sometimes (and even in varieties very rich in mica) in addition to the quartz contained in the main mass of the rock, irregularly swollen-shaped masses and veins of quartz occur, round which the foliated texture bends itself, or there are found actual seams of quartz in the rock. Garnets frequently occur in such abundance as to be characteristic for certain varieties. They are red or brown, and occur porphyritically as isolated crystals, unusually rhombic dodecahedrons, from the size of a scarcely visible grain to that of an apple. In each individual rock, however, these are usually nearly of a uniform size. The flakes of mica bend round these crystals as if they had been pushed on one side during the process of their formation. Near Fahlun, in Sweden, there is a magnesian variety of mica-schist containing very large dodecahedrons of garnet, which are sometimes split into two parts which have become joined together again in a displaced position.

Mica-schist also frequently contains some or other of the following as accessory ingredients: schorl, staurolite, disthene, andalusite, hornblende, chiastolite, beryl, chlorite, talc, and felspar less frequently, also graphite, micaceous iron, cordierite, pyrites, or cinnabar, &c.

Some of these accessory ingredients are characteristic for certain varieties of mica-schist, and they also occasion transitions from mica-schist into other rocks. Thus the presence of chlorite occasions a transition into chlorite-schist, of talc into talc-schist, of felspar into gneiss, of schorl into schorl-schist, of graphite into graphite-schist, of micaceous iron into ferruginous mica-schist. If the mass becomes compact, and especially if the mica should become indistinctly blended with the other ingredients, then the rock passes over into argillaceous mica-schist, and finally into clay-slate, so that we have thus a complete series of transitions from the most distinct gneiss through mica-schist into clay-slate. But we know of no transition from mica-schist into the granular greisen, although the composition of those two rocks is mineralogically the same.

Varieties in Texture.

(a) COMMON MICA-SCHIST.
GEMEINER GLIMMERSCHIEFER. (SCHUPPEN-
GLIMMERSCHIEFER.) (*Germ.*)
MICASCHISTE COMMUN ou NORMAL. (*Fr.*)
Somewhat unevenly foliated, of a scaly appearance with very much mica, but the quartz nevertheless distinct. Of very frequent occurrence.

(b) MICA-SCHIST, VERY FINE AND EVEN IN TEXTURE.
PLANGLIMMERSCHIEFER. (*Germ.*)
Also frequent.

(c) MICA-SCHIST OF WAVY TEXTURE.
FALTENGLIMMERSCHIEFER. (*Germ.*)
À TEXTURE ONDULÉE. (*Fr.*)
A delicate wave-like texture, occasions a very distinct linear parallelism.
Sometimes there occur larger and more irregular foldings, windings, and contortions of the texture, but these are frequently very parallel in their main direction. E. g. at Schwarzenbach, near Hof in the Fichtelgebirge.

(d) MICA-SCHIST WITH WOOD-LIKE OR COARSELY FIBROUS TEXTURE.
GESTRECKTER GLIMMERSCHIEFER oder HOLZGLIMMERSCHIEFER. (*Germ.*)
Or as if the different particles had been elongated by stretching. This peculiar texture is caused by a special conformation of the quartz stripped into thin and long strips or stalks.

(e) MICA-SCHIST WITH CONTORTED AND IRREGULAR TEXTURE.
VERWORRENSCHIEFRIGER oder WULST-GLIMMERSCHIEFER. (*Germ.*)
À TEXTURE FROISSÉE ou PLISSÉE. (*Fr.*)
The disturbances of the parallel texture are partly occasioned by external forces, and partly by many tuberous swellings of the quartz contained in the rock. Very frequent.

(f) STRATIFIED MICA-SCHIST.
LAGENGLIMMERSCHIEFER. (*Germ.*)
Thin seams of mica with slaty cleavage, alternate with fine-grained layers of quartz, in which last are sometimes disseminated flakes of mica not parallel to the stratification. This rock is very characteristically developed near Eger, in Bohemia, and between Korbach and Gefrees in the Fichtelgebirge.

(g) MICA-SCHIST OF KNOTTY TEXTURE.
KNOTENGLIMMERSCHIEFER. (*Germ.*)
Small nodules or concretions pervade the mass and occasion a knotty texture, disturbing the otherwise parallel layers of the mica. Occurs in the Fichtelgebirge, between Walpenreuth and Hühnerhof.

Varieties in Composition.

(h) GARNETIFEROUS MICA-SCHIST.
GRANATGLIMMERSCHIEFER. (*Germ.*)
MICASCHISTE GRENATIFÈRE. (*Fr.*)
Rich in garnets. Of very frequent occurrence.

(i) GNEISSIC MICA-SCHIST.
GNEISSGLIMMERSCHIEFER. (*Germ.*)
With some felspar in the compound; forms a transition state between gneiss and mica-schist. Frequent in the Erzgebirge.

(*k*) CHLORITIC MICA-SCHIST. CHLORITGLIMMERSCHIEFER. (*Germ.*) MICASCHISTE AVEC CHLORITE. (*Fr.*) } With some admixture of chlorite ; forms a transition into chlorite-schist. Frequent in the Alps.

(*l*) TALCOSE MICA-SCHIST. TALKGLIMMERSCHIEFER. (*Germ.*) MICASCHISTE AVEC TALC. (*Fr.*) } With an admixture of some talc; forms a transition into talc-schist. Occurs in the Alps.

(*m*) MICA-SCHIST WITH TWO KINDS OF MICA (dark and light-coloured). Zschopau in Saxony.

(*n*) GRAPHITIC MICA-SCHIST. GRAPHITGLIMMERSCHIEFER. (*Germ.*) MICASCHISTE AVEC GRAPHITE. (*Fr.*) } With admixture of graphite; forms a transition into graphite-schist.

(*o*) MICACEOUS IRON-SCHIST. EISENGLIMMERHALTIGER GLIMMERSCHIEFER. (*Germ.*) } Forms a transition into ferruginous schist.

(*p*) SCHORLACEOUS MICA-SCHIST. SCHORLGLIMMERSCHIEFER. (*Germ.*) MICASCHISTE AVEC TOURMALINE. (*Fr.*) } Forming a transition into schorl-schist. Eibenstock in Saxony.

(*q*) HORNBLENDIC MICA-SCHIST. HORNBLENDEGLIMMERSCHIEFER. (*Germ.*) MICASCHISTE AVEC HORNBLENDE. (*Fr.*) } Forming a transition into hornblende-schist. E. g. between Goldmühl and Brandholz, near Berneck in the Fichtelgebirge.

(*r*) QUARTZOSE MICA-SCHIST, forming a transition into quartz-schist.

(*s*) CALCAREOUS MICA-SCHIST. KALKGLIMMERSCHIEFER, BLAU-SCHIEFER. (*Germ.*) } This is either a granular limestone, very rich in mica, and therefore of fissile texture (cipolline), as it, for instance, occurs in the limestone beds in the neighbourhood of Zaunhaus in the Erzgebirge, or it is a rock composed of thin alternate layers of mica-schist and granular limestone, as is frequently found in the Eastern Alps.

The following varieties differ in the species of their mica :—

(*t*) PARAGONITE-SCHIST. PARAGONITSCHIEFER, *Schafthäutl.* (*Germ.*) } The name given by Schafthäutl to certain mica-schist of the Alps in which the ordinary mica is replaced by paragonite or damourite. To this belongs, e. g., the beautiful variety found at St. Gotthard, and is distinguished by its containing many cyanites and staurolites.

(*u*) AMPHILOGITE-SCHIST. AMPHILOGITSCHIEFER, *Schafthäutl.* (*Germ.*) } The name given by Schafthäutl to the delicate flaky and somewhat greenish-white mica-slate of Zillerthal in the Tyrol, which only contains 40 p. c. silica.

(*v*) NACRITIDE. NACRITID, *Schill.* (*Germ.*) } The name given by Schill to a schist occurring at Pike's Peak in Kansas, consisting of quartz with black and white mica. Perhaps it is the same as the Saxon variety described ante (*m*).

Mica-schist is usually more or less stratified or laminated independently of and more or less parallel to its schistose or foliated texture. Sometimes many different varieties alternate and are stratified in thin beds or layers one above the other.

Mica-schist is extensively developed in many mountain districts, and there it is usually accompanied by gneiss or talc, and chlorite-schist; it frequently also contains subordinate intermediate layers of quartz-schist, hornblende-schist, granular limestone, or dolomite, ironstone, or even graphite. The distinctly sedimentary formations usually overlie the mica-schist, but to this rule there are exceptions, as in the case of gneiss. From its bedding and the rocks with which it is usually associated, we must conclude that mica-schist has chiefly been formed by transmutation from very ancient argillaceous and arenaceous deposits. During this process the quartz has undergone the least change, the clay has for the most part become mica, the superfluous substances in the sedimentary rock appearing, as accessory minerals in the mica-schist. A clay-slate very poor in quartz might produce a mica-schist very rich in mica; and a clay-slate very rich in quartz (or very sandy) might produce a mica-schist very rich in quartz. An argillaceous sandstone might perhaps produce that variety of mica-schist which forms a transition into quartz-schist. If the original rock contained lime, then garnet, hornblende, and other minerals might also be formed. If the original rock contained subordinate strata or layers of limestone, ironstone, coal, or the like, these would be changed into granular limestone, ferruginous mica-schist, graphite, &c.

We must assume that these processes of transmutation have always taken place deep in the earth under the influence of great pressure, high temperature, and perhaps that they have been aided by the presence of water —in other words, that they were plutonic or hydro-plutonic processes. If there were sufficient alkali in the argillaceous deposit, or if alkalies happened to be within reach (possibly in a state of solution), then gneiss and not mica-schist would be the result. If these hypotheses are well founded, they explain the possible mode of formation of some mica-schists, which appear to be of considerably more recent origin than the greater part of those rocks. The process of transmutation may have been hastened in these exceptional cases by an extraordinary degree of pressure. Cases of this kind are met with in the Alps, where between strata of mica-schist certain beds of a sandy calcareous composition occur containing distinct remains of Belemnites.

Although mica-schist has been very frequently analysed and described, there are but few treatises which make it their principal subject. The following describe certain special forms of this rock.

References.

Beudant and *Naumann* (the former in Hungary, the latter in Scandinavia) have both observed apparent pebbles of quartz in mica-schist—a circumstance which forcibly suggests a mechanical origin (Naumann's Geognosie, 2nd. ed. vol. i. p. 527, Anm.). We have also ourselves observed distinct pebbles of quartz in beds of limestone lying between parallel beds of mica-schist at Jakobeni in the Bukowina. Jahrb. d. geol. Reichsanst. 1855, p. 7.

Schafthäutl, on the peculiar varieties of the Alps, Ann. d. Chem. u. Pharm. 1843, p. 733. (*Schönfeld* and *Roscoe,* ibid. 1854, vol. xci. p. 305.)

Schill, on Nacritide, Ann. d. Chem. u. Pharm. 1857, vol. ciii. p. 119.

24. QUARTZ-SCHIST.

QUARZSCHIEFER. (*Germ.*)
QUARTZ SCHISTEUX. (*Fr.*)

A rock chiefly consisting of quartz, but usually containing some mica.

We regard this rock as more or less belonging to the mica-schists. It is found to pass over into genuine mica-schist through the transition grade of quartzose mica-schist.

Mineralogically, this rock has greater affinity to the siliceous or quartz rocks. Geologically, however, it undoubtedly belongs to the metamorphic crystalline schists, with which it is usually interstratified in parallel but subordinate beds; and, like the other crystalline schists, appears to have originated in metamorphosis of sedimentary rocks (probably sandstone).

We ought, perhaps, on the same principle to include some other rocks in the metamorphic series (granular limestone, for instance); calcspar, however, does not occur as an essential ingredient of any crystalline schists, whereas quartz is contained in most, and we must constantly remind our readers that a logically consistent system of classification is impossible with rocks. We shall again allude to this rock under the head of quartz rocks, No. 69 post.

Varieties in Texture.

(a) COMMON QUARTZ-SCHIST. ⎫ Consists principally of com-
· GEMEINER QUARZSCHIEFER. (*Germ.*) ⎬ pact, imperfectly - foliated
QUARTZ SCHISTEUX COMMUN. (*Fr.*) ⎭ white quartz, containing only little mica; sometimes with very distinct parallel elongations. Occurs in the gneiss of Freiberg.

(b) GRANULAR QUARTZ-SCHIST, ⎫ Fine-grained, resembling sand-
or QUARTZITE. ⎬ stone.
QUARZIT. (*Germ.*) ⎪ Jukes says, 'Quartz rock or
QUARTZITE. (*Fr.*) ⎭ quartzite is a compact fine-grained but distinctly granular rock, very hard, frequently brittle, and often so divided by joints as to split in all directions into small angular, but more or less cuboidal, fragments. The colours are generally some shade of yellow, passing occasionally into red, and at other times into green. When examined with a lens it may be seen to be made of grains, which appear some-times as if they had been slightly fused together at their edges or surfaces, and sometimes as if imbedded in a purely siliceous cement. This cementation or semi-fusion of the grains shows at once that it is a sandstone which has been altered and in-durated by the action either of heat alone or of heat and water.'

25. ITACOLUMITE.

ITAKOLUMIT. (*Germ.*)
ITACOLUMITE. (*Fr.*)

A fine-grained and at the same time schistose compound of quartz with some mica, talc, or chlorite. In thin plates it is sometimes flexible.

This rock first received its name from Von Eschwege. Its principal mass consists of grains of quartz, and re-sembles a sandstone. The grains of quartz, however, are bound together by thin crystalline laminæ of mica, chlorite, or talc, and these often assume a parallel arrange-ment and form thin seams through the rock. Thus its foliated texture is occasioned, and the somewhat elastic properties of the mica, chlorite, or talc occasionally give a flexibility to thin layers or plates of the rock. But not all varieties of itacolumite are flexible. The prevailing colour of the rock is yellowish; sometimes, however, it has a white-reddish or bluish-grey colour.

As subordinate ingredients, there occur in it micaceous iron, magnetic iron-ore, martite, native gold, and even diamond. The quartz also occurs locally in the form of rounded stones or pebbles enclosed in the rock's mass, showing clearly the mechanical arenaceous or conglomeratic origin of the rock. If the specular or magnetic iron-ores occur in considerable quantity, then a transition takes place into ferruginous mica-schist or itabirite (vide post, No. 62 *k*); and if the quartz be altogether predominant, into quartz-schist (No. 24).

We may take it as proof of the variable character of this rock that it has received many different names. Alexander von Humboldt called it *itacolumite* or *quartz chloriteux*; Clausen termed it *gres rouge, micaschiste quartzeux*, and *grès itacolumite*; Von Martius, *elastischer Sandstein* (elastic sandstone), *Quartz-schist* and *Gelenkquarz* (articulated quartz); Walchner, *quartzose talcschist*; Jacquemont, *grès schisteux*; Shepard includes it under the head of *mica-schist*; Toumey terms it *quartz rock* or the '*quartz of the mica slate*,' and indicates that it may be a hornstone; Van Uxem even appears to have considered it in South Carolina as a variety of Greissen.

Jukes describes Itacolumite as being a genuine unaltered sandstone, more or less micaceous like other sandstones, but the mica in worn spangles, not in connected flakes.

Varieties.

(*a*) COMMON ITACOLUMITE. — GEMEINER ITAKOLUMIT. (*Germ.*) ITACOLUMITE COMMUN. (*Fr.*) — Firm, not flexible, resembling a firm and somewhat fissile sandstone.

(*b*) FLEXIBLE ITACOLUMITE. — BIEGSAMER ITAKOLUMIT. (*Germ.*) ITACOLUMITE FLEXIBLE. (*Fr.*) — Usually very fine-grained, and in thin layers or plates—very flexible.

(*c*) CONGLOMERATIC ITACOLUMITE. — CONGLOMERATARTIGER ITAKOLUMIT. (*Germ.*) ITACOLUMITE GRENU. (*Fr.*) — Enclosing rounded pebbles of quartz.

Von Eschwege informs us that in the Brazils itacolumite forms whole systems of strata of great thickness, extending for several hundred miles in length. The mountain Itacolumi, near Villa Rica (5,400 feet high), consists almost entirely of this rock. Shepard and Lieber found it very extensively developed in North and South Carolina, where it generally lies between lime-

stone and clay-slate, and contains subordinate layers or
beds of talc-schist, ferruginous mica-schist, itabirite, ca-
tawbarite, and fine-grained limestone. Von Helmersen
and Hofmann also found the rock in the Ural Mountains; Von Eschwege in Portugal; Schulz in Spain;
Gergens in the slate region of the Rhine.

References.

v. Eschwege, Beitr. z. Gebirgskunde von Brasilien, 1832, p. 174.
O. Lieber, Gangstudien, vol. iii. p. 323.
Shepard, Report of South Carolina, 1854.
Schulz, Bullet. de la Soc. géol. de la France, 1834, p. 416.
Gergens, in v. L. u. Br. Jahrb. 1841, p. 566.
Lucas (as early as 1815) found diamonds in it in the Brazils.
    Nouveau dictionnaire d'hist. nat., art. Diamant. The same
    fact was confirmed by *Heusser* and *Claraz*, in the Zeitschr.
    d. d. geol. Ges. 1850, vol. xi. p. 448.
v. Humboldt, Gisement des Roches dans les deux Hémisphères,
    p. 80.
v. Martius, Reise in Brasilien, vol. ii.
Clausen, Bullet. de l'Acad. de Bruxelles, 1841.
Walchner, Handbuch d. Geognosie, p. 38.
Toumey, Report on the Geology of South Carolina, 1848, p. 6.
Jacquemont, Voyage dans l'Inde.

CHLORITE, TALC, AND HORNBLENDE GROUP.

These rocks have been severally termed *Chlorite-schist,*
Talc-schist, and *Hornblende-schist,* from the prevalence of
those respective minerals in their composition.

In their chemical composition they resemble the basic
rather than the acidic igneous rocks; that is, they contain
more magnesia and lime, and, for the most part, less silica
than the acidic rocks.

They occur as subordinate beds in the mica-schist, or
they entirely take the place of mica-schist in some formations.

Serpentine might also be included in this group, by
reason of its chemical and frequently also its geological
character. Nevertheless, inasmuch as serpentine often
occurs under other and very different geological relations (appearing as the product of igneous rocks), we
prefer to class that rock separately amongst the *special*
rock formations.

By introducing this group of rocks between the mica-
schists and the argillaceous mica-schists, we interrupt a

connected series of transition between those two groups, but such interruption only represents similar interruptions actually occurring in nature.

26. CHLORITE-SCHIST and POTSTONE.

CHLORITSCHIEFER und TOPFSTEIN. (*Germ.*)
SCHISTE CHLORITIQUE. (*Fr.*)

A schistose aggregate of chlorite, usually combined with quartz, sometimes also with felspar, mica, and talc. It has a greenish colour and scaly appearance.

Spec. grav. . . . . . . 2·7—2·8
Contains silica . . . . 31—42 p. c.

The principal mass of this rock is composed of chlorite of green or blackish-green colour and greyish-green streak. It is usually of coarsely foliated texture and soft. The quartz sometimes transfuses the whole mass, and so makes the rock hard; sometimes it only occurs in the form of thin scattered laminæ, lenticular or irregular swellings; sometimes again it traverses the rock in thin veins. Felspar, mica, or talc are only occasionally to be distinctly recognised as ingredients; many other minerals are, however, found as accessories, and often in very perfectly formed crystals; the most frequent of these are magnetic iron-ore, garnet, talcspar, actinolite, and tourmaline.

This rock forms transitions into talc-schist, protogine gneiss, mica-schist, clay-mica-schist, and slaty serpentine, and it often lies in alternate strata with these rocks. It is widely spread in the central chain of the Alps, is very characteristically developed in the Fichtelgebirge, near Schwarzbach, Wiersberg, &c., and also in the Eastern Carpathians. It very often contains subordinate beds or layers of magnetic iron-ore, ferruginous mica-schist, copper and iron pyrites, granular limestone, quartz, &c. It is usually very distinctly stratified.

Chlorite-schist can scarcely be divided into separate varieties, which have not found a place under other heads, but some analogous rocks may be annexed to it, and may almost take the place of varieties.

(*a*) THE CHLORITE-SCHIST OF HARTHAU (near Chemnitz). The principal mass of this rock consists of an imperfectly foliated chlorite-schist of dark-green colour, traversed by many layers and veins of quartz. Numerous very distinct yellow spots appear prominently arranged in certain zones. These were for a long time taken to be flakes of talc. A. Knop has, however, analysed this rock more narrowly, and discovered that the spots do not consist of talc, but mostly of a yellowish-green micaceous substance, a kind of pinite, which, however, itself appears to be a product of transmutation from oligoclase (or labradorite), and in many places has preserved its crystalline form and distinct cleavage. Strange to say, these felspar crystals, in the process of their transmutation into aggregates of mica, have even changed their outward shape, and accommodated themselves somewhat to the foliated texture of the rock. This rock frequently contains some pyrites, brownspar, and titanic iron as accessories. It divides into plates or wood-like fibres. It forms subordinate beds in the clay-mica-schist of the same district.

(b) CHLORITOID SCHIST is the name given by Hunt to a certain dark-coloured schist, very extensively developed in Canada, principally consisting of chloritoid, a mineral closely allied to chlorite, and also to ottrelite.

(c) POTSTONE.   ⎫ Consists of a felt-like web of chlorite;
TOPFSTEIN, LAVEZSTEIN, ⎪ it is only rarely foliated. Specific gra-
GILTSTEIN. (Germ.) ⎬ vity, 2·8 (?); content of silica, 30—60
PIERRE OLLAIRE. (Fr.) ⎭ p. c. (?) The mass is greenish-grey to
blackish; its streak greenish-white. It is soft, sectile, and quite infusible. It sometimes contains mica, calcspar, dolomite, and magnetic iron-ore or iron pyrites scattered through its mass, and hence it sometimes effervesces on the application of acid. In fire it loses 7·21 per cent. of its weight, probably in consequence of the large quantity of water which it contains (sometimes as much as 11 per cent.).

This rock is easily manufactured into firebricks and fireproof utensils. It is found in very characteristic form in the Alps, together with serpentine as a subordinate stratum in chlorite-schist, and it forms transition states into serpentine—Chiavenna, Drontheim in Norway (?), Boston in Massachusetts, Potton in Canada.

References.

Varrentrapp, Poggend. Annalen, 1849, vol. xlviii. p. 189.
Knop, Progr. der Chemnitzer Gewerbschule, 1856. (?) Neues Jahrb. f. Min. 1863, p. 808.
Brush, on Chloritoid Slate, v. Leonhard's Jahrbuch, 1861, p. 574.
Delesse (Potstone), Bullet. de la Soc. géol. de France, 1857, [2] vol. xiv. p. 281.
Studer (Potstone), Bibl. univers. de Genève, 1856, [4] p. 213.

27. TALC-SCHIST.

TALKSCHIEFER. (*Germ.*)
TALCSCHISTE (STÉASCHISTE, *Brongniart*). (*Fr.*)

A schistose aggregate of talc, usually combined with some quartz or sometimes with felspar, yellowish or greenish colour and soft greasy feel.

Spec. grav.   .   .   .   .   .   .   2·6—2·8
Contains silica 50—57 p. c.; at Zebernick, in Hungary, only 27·6; at Hinterbrühl, even 62·1.

The principal mass of these rocks consists of talc, of light-yellow, yellowish-green, or greenish-grey colour, with a mother-of-pearl varying to resinous lustre. As it contains less silica than the mineral talc (which has 64 per cent.), we may infer that some chlorite enters into its composition.

It contains little quartz ; and only in grains, flat lenticular particles, laminæ, or irregularly shaped masses, or irregular veins, all subordinate as to size and quantity.

Felspar is only to be seen in delicate particles scattered here and there ; it is not more frequent than several of the following accessory minerals :—chlorite, mica, talcspar, garnet, actinolite, asbestos, magnetic iron-ore, and iron pyrites. This rock forms transitions into chlorite-schist, clay-slate, mica-schist, and protogine-gneiss.

Varieties.

(a) COMMON TALC-SCHIST.   Not unusual in the Alps. At
    GEMEINER TALKSCHIEFER. (*Germ.*)   Ochsenkopf, near Schwarzen-
    TALCSCHISTE COMMUN. (*Fr.*)   berg in the Erzgebirge, a
variety (with corundum) occurs imbedded between strata of mica-schist.

(b) LISTWENITE is the name which has been given to a variety in the Ural Mountains, which contains much quartz combined with talcspar or calcspar, and from that combination assumes a somewhat granular slaty texture. The same rock, at Beresowsk is displaced and penetrated by veins of Beresite, which are again penetrated with quartz veins containing some gold.

(c) DOLERINE is the name given by Jurine to a talc-schist with essential ingredients of felspar and chlorite, and according to Favre this rock is extensively spread in the Pennine Alps.

Talc-schist is almost always stratified, and forms alternating beds with other crystalline schists.

References.

G. Rose, on Liswänit, Reise n. d. Ural, vol. ii. p. 537.
Jurine, on Dolerine, in the Journ. des Mines, vol. xix. p. 374.
Favre, on Dolerine, in v. L. u. Br. Jahrb. 1849, p. 41.
Scheerer, Analyse des Talksch. von Fahlun, in Poggend. Ann. 1851, vol. lxxxiv. p. 345.
Richter, Anal. d. Talksch. von Gastein, in Poggend. Ann. 1851, vol. lxxxiv. p. 368.

Ferjentsik, Anal d. Talksch. v. Zebernick, in Jahrb. d. geol.
Reichsanst. 1850, p. 807.
Ragsky, Anal. d. Talksch. v. Hinterbrühl, in Jahrb. d. geol.
Reichsanst. 1854, p. 642.

28. HORNBLENDE-SCHIST and HORNBLENDE ROCK.

HORNBLENDESCHIEFER und HORNBLENDEFELS, AMPHIBOLIT.
(*Germ.*)
SCHISTE AMPHIBOLIQUE et AMPHIBOLITHE, *Brongniart.* (*Fr.*)

A schistose or fine-grained to compact rock, consisting chiefly of hornblende, combined with small quantities of felspar, quartz, or brown mica. Always dark-green to black.

Spec. grav. . . . . . . 3—3·1
Contains silica . . . . . 48—54 p. c.

This rock is most usually of foliated texture. Its principal mass is granular and sometimes also fibrous, and consists of common dark-green hornblende as its principal ingredient, with which some felspar, quartz, or mica is usually combined. If the latter are present in considerable quantity, then transitions take place into diorite (6), diorite-schist (No. 6 *a*), or syenite-gneiss (No. 22). As accessories there also occur garnet, pistacite, iron pyrites, magnetic iron-ore, &c.

The varieties of prevailing schistose character are usually imbedded between strata of other crystalline schists, to which they clearly belong, and into which they pass over by grades of transition.

They also sometimes pass into rocks not of a fissile texture, such as hardly can be classed with the argillaceous schists, and which may perhaps be of igneous (eruptive) origin, especially as they form transitions into diorite.

Varieties of Texture.

(*a*) HORNBLENDE-SCHIST.
HORNBLENDESCHIEFER. (*Germ.*)
SCHISTE AMPHIBOLIQUE. (*Fr.*)
} Usually thickly foliated, and at the same time fibrous; this texture being occasioned by the parallel position of fibres of hornblende of various thickness. Quartz and felspar occur as a part of the compound of the principal rock, but also in nests or veins. This rock is often found (subordinate) in strata of gneiss, mica-schist, and chlorite-schist; e. g., Miltitz, near Meissen, and the district of Münchberg in the Fichtelgebirge.

At Hanover in North America hornblende-schist is found, containing large dodecahedrons of garnet.

(*b*) HORNBLENDE ROCK.　　　 ⎫ Without fissile texture. E. g. in
　HORNBLENDEFELS. (*Germ.*)　⎬ the district of Hof in the Fichtel-
　AMPHIBOLITHE. (*Fr.*)　　　 ⎭ gebirge.

Variety in Composition.

(*c*) ACTINOLITE-SCHIST.　　　　　 ⎫ Chiefly consisting of actinolite, and
　STRAHLSTEIN oder ACTINO-　⎬ therefore entirely fibrous, otherwise
　LITHSCHIEFER. (*Germ.*)　　 ⎭ just like hornblende-schist. Found to
the south of Oberwiesenthal in the Erzgebirge; also at Clausen in the Tyrol.

We might also include eklogite (No. 44) under this head, but as it is at least doubtful if its origin be that of the metamorphic schists, and as it belongs to the rocks of exceptional character, and by reason of its richness in garnets may be conveniently placed with the other garnet rocks, we have so classed it.

References.

Bischof's Geologie (1st edition) contains almost the only detailed account of hornblende-schist. See II. p. 130.
On actinolite-schist, see *Reuss* in v. L. u. Br. Jahrb. 1840, p. 41.

SCHISTS INDISTINCTLY CRYSTALLINE.

These form the connecting link between the extreme metamorphic crystalline schists (especially gneiss and the mica-schists) and the clay-slate and slate-clay rocks, which latter being much less changed are still distinctly sedimentary. We therefore term them argillaceous mica-schists.

29. ARGILLACEOUS MICA-SCHIST, PHYLLITE.

THONGLIMMERSCHIEFER, PHYLLIT, URTHONSCHIEFER. (*Germ.*)
PHYLLADE, *D'Aubuisson.* (*Fr.*)

A schistose aggregate in which mica is usually to be recognised as the chief ingredient, or in which the peculiar structure of mica rocks is apparent. Sometimes the whole mass appears homogeneous, differing only from clay-slate by its superior lustre.

Spec. grav. .　.　.　.　.　.　2·6—2·8
Contains silica　.　.　.　.　.　45—74 p. c.

Argillaceous mica-schist is but a transition state between

mica-schist and clay-slate, as is apparent from its passing over into both these rocks. We might term it an imperfect mica-schist or a very much transformed and somewhat crystallised clay-slate. Its chemical analysis also agrees with this definition. But its chemical composition varies as much as that of mica-schist or clay-slate. Its principal ingredients are always quartz and mica (or some mineral of the same character as mica), but the quantitative proportions of these ingredients are very different in different rocks. With these principal ingredients are associated chlorite, talc, felspar, hornblende, garnet, &c., which occasion transitions into chlorite-schist, talc-schist, hornblende-schist, and gneiss.

The colour of these rocks is usually grey, greenish, or bluish-grey, but sometimes yellowish, reddish, brownish, and violet. Their lustre varies between the mother-of-pearl, the silky, and the half metallic. They always have a distinctly fissile texture, but not by any means a perfect cleavage. Sometimes they show fine parallel foldings, or sometimes there occurs a second fissile texture obliquely traversing the principal direction, occasioning a rough fibrous cleavage. When the slaty cleavage is perfect, it is usually not parallel to the stratification.

In the apparently homogeneous principal mass, we discover grains or irregular lenticular swellings or masses of quartz, or else veins of quartz or flakes of mica (or sericite), chlorite, talc, hornblende, felspar, chiastolite, andalusite, iron pyrites, magnetic iron-ore, or graphite. When these minerals are considerable in quantity, there arise varieties in composition. But these varieties are not peculiar to this rock; they are necessarily repeated in mica-schist, as well as in clay-slate.

Varieties in Texture.

(a) COMMON ARGILLACEOUS MICA-SCHIST.
GEMEINER THONGLIMMERSCHIEFER. (*Germ.*)
PHYLLADE COMMUN (SATINÉ). (*Fr.*)

(b) FOLDED OR CONTORTED.
GEFÄLTETER THONGLIMMERSCHIEFER. (*Germ.*)

(c) FIBROUS OR WOODY TEXTURE.
HOLZARTIGER THONGLIMMERSCHIEFER. (*Germ.*)

(d) VERY MUCH CONTORTED.
SEHR VERWORREN SCHIEFRIGER oder WULSTIGER THONGLIMMERSCHIEFER. (*Germ.*)
PLISSÉ, FROISSÉ. (*Fr.*)

(e) NODULAR SCHIST.
   KNOTENSCHIEFER. *(Germ.)* } Which we also enumerate below, as
   SCHISTE NODULEUX. *(Fr.)* } a variety in composition.

Varieties in Composition.

(f) RICH IN MICA.
   GLIMMERREICHER THONGLIM-
      MERSCHIEFER. *(Germ.)* } Transition into mica-schist.
   MICACÉ. *(Fr.)*

(g) RICH IN QUARTZ.
   QUARZREICHER THONGLIMMER-
      SCHIEFER. *(Germ.)* } Forms transitions into quartz-
   QUARTZEUX. *(Fr.)* } schist.

(h) CHLORITIC.
   CHLORITISCHER THONGLIMMER-
      SCHIEFER. *(Germ.)* } Forming transitions into chloritic
   CHLORITIQUE. *(Fr.)* } schists.

(i) TALCOSE.
   TALKIGER THONGLIMMER-
      SCHIEFER. *(Germ.)* } Forming a transition into talc-schist.
   TALQUEUX. *(Fr.)*

(k) A VARIETY CONTAINING HORNBLENDE.
   HORNBLENDEHALTIGER THONGLIMMERSCHIEFER. *(Germ.)*

(l) A VARIETY CONTAINING FELSPAR.
   FELSPATHHALTIGER THONGLIMMERSCHIEFER. } Forming a transition
      (Germ.) } into gneiss.

(m) A VARIETY CONTAINING GARNETS.
   GRANATHALTIGER THONGLIMMERSCHIEFER. } Forming a transition
      (Germ.) } into garnet-mica-schist.
   GRENATIFÈRE. *(Fr.)*

(n) SERICITE-SCHIST. } The name given by List to a variety
   SERICITSCHIEFER. *(Germ.)* } whose principal mass consists of seri-
   SCHISTE À SÉRICITE. *(Fr.)* } cite (a green micaceous mineral, re-
sembling damourite, with a silky lustre, see *ante*, p. 23), and
which usually also contains quartz and felspar (albite according
to List). The colour of this rock in the Taunus, where it is
very extensively developed, is greenish with green and yellow
spots, or violet. It is often penetrated by veins which contain
quartz and albite. The very considerable quantity of alkalies
which it contains, especially of potash, is remarkable. List
further distinguishes three sub-varieties, according to their
colour.

   (a) *Violet*, very soft, with thin slaty cleavage. Spec. grav.
      2·88.

   (β) *Green*, harder, with thick slaty cleavage (folded), with
      little albite, and a microscopic quantity of magnetic
      iron-ore. Spec. grav. 2·79.

   (γ) *Spotted*, soft; often decomposed; with much albite and
      quartz. Spec. grav. 2·68.

(o) OTTRELITE-SCHIST. } The principal mass foliated, and usually
   OTTRELITSCHIEFER. *(Germ.)* } grey. It contains greenish laminæ of
   SCHISTE À OTTRÉLITE. *(Fr.)* } ottrelite. This variety is frequently
found in the Ardennes. It has also been discovered by Güm-
bel in the district of Ebnat in Bavaria.

(p) CHIASTOLITE-SCHIST. } The mass is slaty, and usually
   CHIASTOLITHSCHIEFER. *(Germ.)* } dark-coloured. It contains many
   SCHISTE MACLIFÈRE. *(Fr.)* } crystals of chiastolite disseminated

through it in the most opposite directions. The chiastolite-schist (which also forms a variety of clay-slate) is found on the contact margins of plutonic igneous rocks, e. g. next to granite. Near Gefrees in the Fichtelgebirge. Also abundant about Skiddaw, Cumberland.

(q) NODULAR or SPOTTED SCHIST.⎫ This schist contains small con-
KNOTENSCHIEFER, FLECK- oder ⎪ cretions of different structure,
FRUCHTSCHIEFER. (*Germ.*) ⎪ hardness, and colour to that of
SCHISTE NODULEUX ou RUBANÉ. ⎬ the general mass. They are, for
(*Fr.*) ⎭

the most part, harder and darker, and they either form small knots or only spots with indistinct margin; sometimes they resemble the currants in a fruit-pudding, hence their different names. Their composition has not yet been determined with accuracy by the various mineralogical chemical analyses which they have undergone, according to which they have been successively taken for a kind of fahlunite, for hornblende, serpentine, chiastolite, or andalusite. It is very possible that at different places they are somewhat differently composed. In reference to their origin, it is of special interest that according to the careful investigations of Carius, the schist with nodules does not differ in the quality or proportionate quantity of its ingredients from the same schist without nodules farther removed from the contact, so that no new substance appears to have been added to form those concretions, but they appear rather to have arisen from a new arrangement of the previously existing ingredients. At the margin of the granite in the Western Erzgebirge and Voigtland, these nodular schists are very frequent, and are observed there just as much in the clay-mica-schist as in the ordinary clay-slate. A similar appearance occurs at Wechselburg in Saxony, in a rock which is decidedly mica-schist.

(r) ALUM-SCHIST.⎫ This schist contains much carbon, and
ALAUNSCHIEFER. (*Germ.*) ⎬ is thereby rendered black. Pyrites is
SCHISTE ALUMINEUX. (*Fr.*) ⎭ always mixed with it in fine particles,

through whose decomposition alum and iron-vitriol are formed. In the case of this variety, we can only decide from the bedding whether it belongs to argillaceous mica-schist or to clay-slate, for the carbon which it contains thoroughly obliterates the slender landmarks by which the difference might otherwise be established. It is characteristic of most of the alum-schists, that they are of very much contorted or displaced texture, and are frequently pervaded by irregular swollen-shaped fragments of quartz and lustrous but bent laminæ (mica), and sometimes also lenticular concretions of bituminous limestone or anthraconite. Reichenbach in Voigtland.

(s) CARBONACEOUS SCHIST, BLACK CHALK.⎫ In the case of this
ZEICHENSCHIEFER, SCHWARZE KREIDE. (*Germ.*) ⎬ variety, very rich in
SCHISTE HOUILLER. (*Fr.*) ⎭ carbon, we can only

determine by its bedding whether it belongs to argillaceous mica-schist or to clay-slate. It is a quartzless and very soft slate, which, from admixture of carbon, is of a black colour, and also imparts a black streak, so that it may be used for drawing or writing. Ludwigstadt in the Thuringian Forest, where it belongs to clay-slate.

All the above-mentioned varieties in composition are equally applicable to the ordinary clay-slate as to the argillaceous mica-schist, and we shall therefore have to enumerate them again when we come to consider that rock, but our previous descriptions will suffice for both.

Argillaceous mica-schist is usually also distinctly stratified in addition to its foliated texture, which, as already said, is not parallel to the stratification; otherwise, as to its bedding and extent, it exactly resembles mica-schist, with this only difference, that it more usually than that rock is interstratified with the oldest sedimentary and distinctly fossiliferous rocks.

By the name of argillaceous mica-schist we do but seek to establish a stage of transmutation between clay-slate proper and mica-schist.

References.

Frick, Pleischl, Sauvage, and *Kjerulf* have contributed various analyses to Poggend. Ann. 1835, vol. xxxv. p. 188; in the Journ. f. prakt. Chemie, 1844, vol. xxxi. p. 45; and 1855, vol. lxv. p. 192.

List, on Sericitschiefer, in the Jahrb. d. Vereins f. Naturk. in the Duchy of Nassau, 1850, No. 6, p. 128.

Lipold, on Sericitschiefer in the Alps, Jahrb. d. geol. Reichsanst. 1854, pp. 201 and 359.

Gümbel, on Ottrelitschiefer, in Corresp.-Bl. d. zool. mineral. Ver. z. Regensburg, 1853, p. 53, and on Phyllit, in the same, 1854, p. 12.

Naumann, on Knotenschiefer, Erläuter. z. geogn. Karte v. Sachsen, 1838, No. II. p. 204, and 1845, No. V. p. 50.

Kersten, on Knotenschiefer, in Journ. f. prakt. Chemie, vol. xxxi. p. 108.

Carius, on Knotenschiefer, in the Annalen d. Chemie. u. Pharm. 1855, vol. xciv. p. 45; and in v. L. u. Br. Jahrb. 1856, p. 595.

Müller, on Knotenschiefer, in the Berg- u. Hüttenm. Zeitung, 1858, p. 107.

Durocher, on Chiastolith and Knotenschiefer, in Bullet. de la Soc. géol. de la France, 1846, vol. iii. p. 546.

CHAPTER III.

SEDIMENTARY AND FRAGMENTAL ROCKS.

ALL sedimentary rocks are stratified; or at least, their beds lie one above the other in parallel planes. The greater part consists of the débris of older rocks mechanically washed together and deposited from a state of suspension in water. A few only are the result of chemical precipitate of mineral substances. Many contain organic remains (fossils) more or less distinct; some consist entirely of such.

As a consequence of their origin, the sedimentary rocks are rarely of genuine crystalline conformation. Some, however, which appear to be actual chemical precipitates from aqueous solutions, such as gypsum and rock-salt, usually possess a crystalline structure.

Following the different origin of these rocks, we may divide them into

(a) Mechanical deposits.
(b) Chemical precipitates.
(c) Rocks resulting from organic processes.

(α) *Phytogenic*, caused by the accumulation of vegetable matter.
(β) *Zoogenic*, caused by the accumulation of animal remains.

The minerals which chiefly predominate in sedimentary rocks are not the same as those which are most abundant in the igneous and the metamorphic rocks. We find in the sedimentary rocks little or no felspar, hornblende, or pyroxene. The following are those which occur with greatest frequency:—Quartz, which in general terms we may call the most abundant mineral of the earth; clay (itself, however, a compound rather than a distinct mineral); carbonates of lime and magnesia, as calcspar (limestone) and dolomite; sulphate of lime, as gypsum and anhydrite; chloride of sodium, as rock-salt; finally, coal and iron-ores.

Gypsum (or anhydrite), salt, coal, and iron, usually form distinct and separate beds of comparatively small

s 2

extent: the principal and most important sedimentary rocks are composed chiefly of the first-named of the above minerals, quartz, clay, and carbonate of lime (or magnesia). They may be accordingly divided into argillaceous rocks, calcareous rocks, and quartzose rocks. The marl rocks occupy an intermediate place between the calcareous and argillaceous. The quartzose rocks may be divided into the arenaceous or sandstones, and the conglomerates, to which we may add certain other fragmental rocks containing less quartz, usually termed *tufa* or *tuff*.

The material for all these several rocks was mostly derived from the disintegration of more ancient previously existing rocks. The igneous rocks, by the decay of their felspar, hornblende, augite, and mica, have supplied the following substances towards the formation of the sedimentary rocks:—argillaceous mud, and weak solutions of lime, magnesia, silica, potash, soda, oxide of iron; their quartz has furnished grains of sand; in some cases their mica has remained undecomposed, and is found as mica in minute laminæ in the sedimentary rocks. The older sedimentary rocks have also in process of time become disintegrated, and have furnished similar materials to form the more recent, and every solid rock has at times furnished pebbles, and other fragments for the formation of conglomerates.

The several sedimentary deposits have been divided into so-called formations, according to the order of their superposition, and consequently of their age, and these again have been gathered into groups, which answer to longer periods of deposit.

It may therefore be useful here to present the following

TABLE OF GEOLOGICAL PERIODS.*

Post-Tertiary.

Recent Formations of every kind.
> Mud, sand, gravel, calcareous and volcanic tuff, coral reefs, bog iron-ore, turf, peat, &c., guano, infusorial beds.

Pleistocene, or Post-Pliocene Formation.
> Diluvial or glacial deposits, loam and breccias of bone-caverns, brick-earth and fluviatile loam or loess, valley gravels, bog iron-ore, calcareous tuff, coral-reefs, &c.

* In different countries these are somewhat differently divided and named.

ENGLAND.	GERMANY.

Terfiary or Cáinozoic.

Pleiocene Formations.
Red and coralline crag. — Aralo-Caspian deposits.

Miocene Formations.

Absent in England. — Molasse formation of the Alps —Tegel, near Vienna. Browncoal formation in North Germany.

Eocene Formations.
Fluvio-marine strata of Isle of Wight and Hampshire. } Nummuliten formation.
Bagshot series. — Flysch formation.
London clay and Bognor beds.
Plastic clay or Woolwich and Reading beds.
Thanet beds. •

Secondary or Mesozoic.

Cretaceous Formations.
White chalk with flints.
White chalk without flints. — Maestricht beds.
Chalk marl. — Turonien, quadersand, pläner.
Upper greensand. — Cenomanien.
Gault. — Albien, aptien.
{ Lower greensand or neocomian. — Hils-formation.
{ Speeton clay.
Wealden beds, weald clay, and Hastings sand. — Deister formation.

Oolitic or Jurassic Formations.
Purbeck beds. — White Jura.
Portland beds.
Kimeridge clay. — Lithographic slate of Solenhofen.

Coral rag.
Oxford clay.
Cornbrash. — Brown Jura.
Forest marble and Great or Bath oolite.
Fullers' earth.
Inferior oolite.
Upper lias sand and clay.
Marlstone or middle lias. — Black Jura.
Lower lias clay and limestone.

Triassic Formations.

Penarth or Rhætic beds. — Keuper.
Dolomitic conglomerate. — Kœssen or Upper St. Cassian beds.
Red marls with rock-salt and gypsum.
White and brown sandstones (waterstones).
Red and mottled sandstones, pebble-beds of conglomerate. — Muschelkalk (absent in England.
Buntsandstein.

Primary or Palæozoic.

	ENGLAND.	GERMANY.
	Dyas or Permian Formations.	
	Red marls and magnesian limestone.	Zechstein formation.
		Kupferschiefer.
	Lower sandstone.	Rothliegendes.
	Carboniferous Formations.	
	Coal-measures.	
	Millstone grit.	Steinkohlen formation.
	Carboniferous limestone	Flötzleerer sandstein.
	Lower limestone shale.	Kohlenkalkstein.
		Kohlen formation of Hainichen, or kulm.
	Devonian Formations (Old Red Sandstone).	
	Dartmouth slate group.	Cypridinenschiefer, or Kramenzelstein.
	Plymouth group.	
	Liskeard or Ashburton group.	Stringocephalen-Kalk.
		Calceolaschiefer.
	Old red sandstone.	Spiriferen-Sandstein and Schiefer.
	Silurian Formations.	
	Ludlow group ⎫	
	Wenlock group ⎬	
	May hill group ⎭	
	Lower Llandovery beds	
	Caradoc sandstone and Bala beds ⎫	
	Llandeilo flags ⎬	
	Lingula flags ⎭	
	Cambrian Formations.	
	Gritstone, sandstone, and slate, with few or no organic remains.	

Laurentian rocks of Canada and the north-west of Scotland.

Below the sedimentary rocks are usually found the crystalline schists.

The entire series of formations is, however, never to be found in any one locality.

The mere geological age of deposit does not inform us of the nature of the rock, nor can we, on the other hand, from the petrographic character arrive at its geological age. Both attributes are to a certain extent independent of each other. No kind of rock is restricted to any particular period, and although there exist some very general differences between the rocks of recent and ancient deposit, yet even these do not prevail universally.

ARGILLACEOUS GROUP.

The argillaceous rocks were originally nothing but sediments of clayey mud, with some admixture of fine quartz-sand, flakes of mica, hydrated oxide of iron, and organic remains. These materials, by a slow process of transmutation and mechanical consolidation, have ultimately become solid rocks, some of them carboniferous or bituminous.

The principal rocks of this group are clay-slate, argillaceous shale, claystone, clay, and mud or silt (loess), with their several varieties. To these we must also add the marl rocks.

To arrange these rocks according to the order of their origin and development, we should begin with the clay and loess, from which (perhaps by the simple agency of pressure) claystone, argillaceous shale, and clay-slate have been successively formed; the several varieties of these rocks being occasioned by the accessory admixtures contained in the original compound.

In the present treatise the order is inverted, and the metamorphic rocks having been already described, we most naturally pass first to those of the sedimentary rocks which are nearest to them, i.e., the most changed, taking the newer formations last.

We cannot draw a sharp distinction between argillaceous mica-schist, clay-slate, and argillaceous shale, but the extreme or ideal development of each of these stages of transmutation has a marked character, distinct from the others. Characteristic argillaceous mica-schist is still somewhat crystalline; clay-slate is not crystalline, and in fracture it is dull, but yet firm, and has a perfect slaty cleavage; characteristic argillaceous shale, on the other hand, is soft or flexible, separates along the lamination instead of by slaty cleavage, and is more obviously an earthy aggregate. Argillaceous mica-schist frequently contains various crystalline accessory minerals, but genuine clay-slate much more rarely, and of fewer kinds; argillaceous shale at the most only occasionally contains some pyrites.

30. CLAY-SLATE.

THONSCHIEFER. (*Germ.*)
SCHISTE ARGILEUX, SCHISTE ARDOISIER. (*Fr.*)

A compact fissile rock of a dull blue-grey, bright red, purple, green, or black colour ; consists chiefly of clay ; sometimes with accessory admixtures of quartz, mica, and other minerals.

The slaty cleavage is usually very perfect, and only occasionally coincides with the original lamination of the rock.

Spec. grav. . . . . 2·5—2·8
Contains silica . . . . 40—75

The characteristic feature of clay-slate as distinguished from other rocks of the argillaceous group is that its slaty cleavage, frequently very perfect, is altogether independent of its original bedding, although in some instances (which we may regard as accidental) it coincides with the original lamination. Whether this slaty cleavage is due to pressure, or to some agency resembling the crystallising force which has acted on smaller mineral masses, has been a subject of debate since the time of Sedgwick, who first called attention to this important phenomenon. It is a question which is still unsettled, and which must probably so remain for some time longer.

Varieties in Texture.

(*a*) COMMON CLAY-SLATE. GEMEINER THONSCHIEFER. (*Germ.*) SCHISTE ARGILEUX COMMUN. (*Fr.*) With perfect or imperfect cleavage, very variously coloured, and often rich in accessory minerals. It contains, e. g., quartz, in irregular masses (or swellings), or lenticular masses, or in veins ; pyrites, in crystals or nodules, &c. Sometimes its slaty cleavage is much distorted. It is very frequent in all districts of the transition period (greywacké) in Germany.

(*b*) ROOFING SLATE. DACHSCHIEFER und TAFEL-SCHIEFER. (*Germ.*) SCHISTE ARDOISIER. (*Fr.*) The name given to the purest varieties of clay-slate, whose cleavage is very perfect and smooth, allowing of their being split into very thin plates, which nevertheless retain a high degree of firmness and solidity. A dark-coloured variety, containing an admixture of carbon, is termed in Germany Tafelschiefer.

Roofing slate, with a view to its fitness for the purpose its name indicates, should be free from accessory crystallised ingredients. North Wales, Lehsten in the Thuringian Forest, &c.

(*c*) PENCIL-SLATE, PINSILL or PENCIL. GRIFFELSCHIEFER. (*Germ.*) AMPÉLITE GRAPHIQUE. (*Fr.*) A clay-slate of pure composition, soft, but withal firm ; separated or separable into pencils (the slaty cleavage crossing the planes of lamination), and used for writing on slate. Found in North Wales, Sonnerberg in the Thuringian Forest, and other slate districts.

Varieties in Composition.

(d) WHETSLATE, WHETSTONE, HONE, OILSTONE, NOVACULITE. WETZSCHIEFER. *Germ.* SCHISTE SILICEUX (NOVACULAIRE), *De Charpentier.* (*Fr.*) } This is a very highly siliceous clay-slate, perfectly compact and homogeneous. Usually only indistinctly of slaty cleavage, and its fracture often conchoidal and even splintery. Used for sharpening knives and other instruments. E. g. Wales, Devonshire, Katzhütte in the Thuringian Forest.

(e) CARBONACEOUS CLAY-SLATE. KOHLENREICHER THONSCHIEFER. (*Germ.*) SCHISTE HOUILLER. (*Fr.*) } Passes into alum-schist and black chalk (Zeichnenschiefer), see p. 257, ante.

(f) ARENACEOUS CLAY-SLATE. SANDIGER THONSCHIEFER (GRAU-WACKENSCHIEFER). (*Germ.*) } Passes into argillaceous sandstone. By the Germans it is frequently termed greywacké-slate, from its occurrence in the transition or greywacké formations.

(g) MICACEOUS CLAY-SLATE. GLIMMERREICHER THONSCHIEFER. (*Germ.*) SCHISTE MICACÉ (PAILLETÉ). (*Fr.*) } Differing from clay-mica-schist, in that the flakes of mica are evidently only mechanically dispersed. This variety also passes in Germany under the name of greywacké-slate.

(h) CALCAREOUS CLAY-SLATE. KALKKNOTIGER THONSCHIEFER (KRA-MENZELSTEIN). (*Germ.*) } Containing numerous lenticular or irregular nodules of limestone (which frequently owe their origin to fossils); passes over into nodular limestone.

The varieties which we have already described under the head of argillaceous mica-schist we find repeated in the clay-slate, and accordingly we have :—chlorite-slate, talc-slate, sericite-slate, ottrelite-slate, chiastolite-slate, nodular and spotted or mottled slate, alum-slate, and carbonaceous slate.

Clay-slates are usually very distinctly stratified, although their slaty cleavage does not in general correspond with the planes of their stratification.

Clay-slates aré not confined to one geological period of formation; the genuine clay-slates, however, usually only occur in the older formations, viz. the transition or greywacké. In the newer formations shales are usually found. Nevertheless there are exceptions to this rule; in the Alps there occur genuine roofing slates, also common arenaceous and micaceous clay-slates (Grauwackenschiefer) belonging to the Chalk and even to the Tertiary periods.

Geological Varieties.

(1) GLARUS SLATE.
 MATTERERSCHIEFER, *Heer.* (*Germ.*)
 SCHISTE SATINÉ (LUISANT). (*Fr.*)
} A genuine clay-slate, in part a roofing-slate, occurring in Switzerland, belonging to one of the Tertiary periods.

(2) CYPRIS SLATE.
 CYPRIDINERSCHIEFER. (*Germ.*)
 SCHISTE À CYPRIDINE. (*Fr.*)
} A clay-slate with *Cypridinæ*, the upper member of the Devonian formation at the Rhine and Hartz.

(3) WISSENBACH SLATE.
 WISSENBACHERSCHIEFER. (*Germ.*)
 SCHISTE DE WISSENBACH. (*Fr.*)
} A clay-slate of the Devonian formation at the Hartz.

(4) CALCEOLA SLATE.
 CALCEOLASCHIEFER. (*Germ.*)
 SCHISTE À CALCÉOLES. (*Fr.*)
} A black and sometimes calcareous clay-slate of the Devonian formation at the Hartz.

(5) GREYWACKÉ-SLATE.
 GRAUWACKENSCHIEFER. (*Germ.*)
 GRAUWACKE SCHISTEUSE. (*Fr.*)
} An arenaceous and usually micaceous clay-slate of the transition periods.

(6) GRAPTOLITE SLATE.
 GRAPTOLITENSCHIEFER. (*Germ.*)
 SCHISTE À GRAPTOLITES. (*Fr.*)
} A clay-slate, or sometimes a siliceous slate (lydian-stone) with Graptolites, belonging to the Silurian formation.

31. ARGILLACEOUS SHALE, SHALE.

SCHIEFERTHON. (*Germ.*)
ARGILE SCHISTEUSE. (*Fr.*)

A laminated clay-rock whose fissile texture is due to its original stratification and not to slaty cleavage. In other respects, similar to clay-slate. Shale and clay-slate pass into each other, and many shales show a tendency more or less decided towards a slaty cleavage. Shales are usually more recent, geologically speaking, than the genuine clay-slates.

Varieties in Texture.

(*a*) COMMON ARGILLACEOUS SHALE.
 GEMEINER SCHIEFERTHON. (*Germ.*)
 ARGILE SCHISTEUSE COMMUNE. (*Fr.*)
} Is only a softer, less firm, and more earthy variety of clay-slate without its cleavage, but laminated according to the plane of its original deposition. It is often mixed with quartz grains and with flakes of mica.

(*b*) SCHIEFERLETTEN (of German geologists) is a modification of the usual argillaceous shale in which the clay is still somewhat moist, and the rock therefore is somewhat plastic and greasy.

Varieties in Composition.

(c) BITUMINOUS SHALE.
BITUMINÖSER SCHIEFERTHON. (*Germ.*)
SCHISTE BITUMINEUX. (*Fr.*)
} Of dark-brown colour, passing into Brandschiefer.

(d) CARBONACEOUS SHALE, CARBONIFEROUS SHALE (BATT or BASS, KELVE).
KOHLENSCHIEFER. (*Germ.*)
SCHISTE HOUILLER. (*Fr.*)
} Dark-grey to black, from admixture of carbonaceous matter; frequently arenaceous or micaceous. When many fossil plants occur in the rock, it is sometimes called in Germany Kräuterschiefer. This rock especially belongs to the Coal formation.

(e) VARIEGATED SHALE.
BUNTER SCHIEFERTHON oder SCHIEFERLETTEN. (*Germ.*)
SCHISTE BIGARRÉ. (*Fr.*)
} Yellow, red, violet, or green, according to the different degrees of oxidation of the iron which it contains.

(f) ARENACEOUS SHALE.
SANDIGER SCHIEFERTHON. (*Germ.*)
SCHISTE SABLEUX. (*Fr.*)
} Passing into argillaceous sandstone.

(g) MICACEOUS SHALE.
GLIMMERREICHER SCHIEFERTHON. (*Germ.*)
SCHISTE MICACÉ. (*Fr.*)
} Corresponding with micaceous clay-slate.

(h) CALCAREOUS SHALE.
MERGELIGER SCHIEFERTHON. (*Germ.*)
SCHISTE MARNEUX. (*Fr.*)
} Slightly effervescing with acid; passing into calcareous slate.*

Geological Varieties.

(1) FLYSCH, an arenaceous and micaceous shale, sometimes approaching the state of a clay-slate. Eocene in the Alps.

(2) FUCOIDAL SHALE
FUCOIDENSCHIEFER. (*Germ.*)
SCHISTE À FUCOÏDES. (*Fr.*)
} With remains of Fucoids. Eocene and older in the Alps and Carpathians.

(3) ROETH, a term employed by the German geologists for a variegated arenaceous shale, which occurs imbedded between the Muschelkalk and variegated sandstone (Thuringia).

---

* 'The colliers' and quarrymen's terms for shale are bind, blue-bind, metal, plate, &c.; when very fine and containing a large proportion of carbonaceous matter, the collier calls it batt or bass, the geologist carbonaceous (or bituminous) shale, and the coal merchant often slate. In Scotland the collier's term for shale appears to be blaes or blues, the shale being often bluish-grey; when lumpy they are called lipey blaes. Black argillaceous shales or "batts" are called "dauks." Fekes or grey fekes seem to be sandy shales such as would be called rockbinds in South Staffordshire (see Williams' "Mineral Kingdom.") In the South of Ireland, carbonaceous shale is called kilve, and indurated slaty shale is termed "pinsill" or "pencil," as it is often used for slate pencils.'—*Jukes.*

(4) WERFNER SCHIEFER, a shale, usually arenaceous and micaceous, occurs in the Alps in strata, which there represent the variegated sandstone formation.

(5) CARBONIFEROUS SHALE or SLATE. } This is a geological
    KOHLENSCHIEFER (KRAUTENSCHIEFER). (*Germ.*) } designation applied
    SCHISTE ET ARGILE CARBONIFÈRES. (*Fr.*) } to all shales of the
Coal formation, whether or not they actually contain carbon (see ante, *e*).

(6) POSIDONOMYA SHALE. } A dark-coloured shale of the
    POSIDONOMYENSCHIEFER. (*Germ.*) } Carboniferous formation (that
    SCHISTE À POSIDONOMYES. (*Fr.*); } of the Lias formation is a bituminous marl-slate).

(7) WENLOCK SHALE. Silurian formation, England.

The following relate chiefly to chemical analysis of clay-slates and argillaceous shales.

References.

O. L. Erdmann, Thonschiefer in Thüringen, Journ. f. techn. Chem. 1832, vol. xiii. p. 114.

Frick, Thonsch. in Thür. am Harz in Westphalen, Poggend. Ann. 1835, vol. xxxv. p. 193.

Pleischl, Thonsch. in Böhmen, Journal f. prakt. Chemie, 1844, vol. xxxi. p. 45.

Delesse, Thonsch. in den Vogesen, Ann. des Mines, 1847, [4] vol. xii. p. 303; 1853, [5] vol. iii. p. 747; and Bullet. de la Soc. géol., [2] vol. x. p. 562.

Forchhammer, Thonsch. v. Christiania, Oversigt over det K. Danske Vidensk Silesk Forhandlinger, 1844, p. 91. Journ. f. prakt. Chem. 1845, vol. xxxvi. p. 394; and on Bornholm, Berzelius, Jahresber. 1844, [25] p. 405.

Dahl, Thonsch. bei Christiania, Nyt. Mag. f. Naturv. 1848, [5] p. 317.

Kjerulf, Thonsch. bei Christiania, in Christianias Silurb. 1855, p. 34.

Jwanhow, Thonsch. bei Christiania, Mém. Acad. de St. Pétersb. 1859, [6] p. 325.

Wilson, Thonsch. in Schweden, Phil. Mag. 1855, [4] p. 114; p. 417.

K. v. Hauer, Thonsch. in Steiermark, Jahrb. d. geol. Reichsanst. 1854, pp. 362 and 869.

Ferjenstik, Werfner Schiefer, Jahrb. d. geol. Reichs. 1855, p. 852.

Sauvage, Ardennenschiefer, Ann. des Mines, 1845, [4] vol. vii. p. 420.

List, Tannusschiefer, Ann. d. Chem. u. Pharm. 1852, vol. lxxxi. pp. 192 to 260.

Kayser, Thonsch. von Clausthal, v. L. u. Br. Jahrbuch, 1850, p. 682.

Schnabel, Amelung and *v. d. Mark,* in den Verhandl. d. naturh. Ver. d. pr. Rheinlande, 1851, pp. 10, 56, and 127; 1853, p. 127; and 1855, p. 122.

Risse, Geol. Beschr. d. Gegend von Baden, 1861, p. 47.

32. CLAY and LOAM.

THON und LEHM. (*Germ.*)
ARGILE. (*Fr.*)

*These are earthy deposits chiefly consisting of clay, and
when moist are more or less plastic.*

Loam or lehm is a word of German origin; between it
and clay there is no sharp distinction. The purest and
therefore the most plastic varieties are called clay (also
potter's clay or pipe-clay). They are usually white or
greyish-blue, but sometimes yellow, red, or greenish,
or (if containing carbon) even black. Those varieties
which contain much fine sand and hydrated oxide of iron
are called loam (in Germany, Lehm), and the iron usually
gives them a yellow or brownish colour.

Varieties in Composition.

(*a*) CLAY.   The purest varieties are white or light-bluish
THON. (*Germ.*) grey, and are very plastic. These are called
ARGILE (*Fr.*)   potter's clay or pipe-clay. Those containing
much silica or fine sand are called fire-clay; those containing
bitumen, bituminous clay; some are variously coloured by
different oxides of iron, and are then termed variegated clay.

(*b*) LOAM.   Contains more or less sand, flakes of mica, and
LEHM. (*Germ.*) such like admixtures; is coloured by hydrated
oxide of iron, and is therefore less plastic than clay, almost
earthy and yellow or brown in colour. It sometimes even contains small crystals of felspar (Glasurlehm of the Germans);
or it contains particles of lime, marly loam (Mergellehm); or
nodules of marl (Lösskindeln); nodules of pyrites (Kiesknollen);
microscopic shells, &c. If it contains a very large proportion
of hydrated oxide of iron, then it passes over into yellow ochre
(Gelberde), which is used as a colouring matter.

(*c*) SALIFEROUS CLAY.   A clay containing chloride of sodium,
SALZTHON. (*Germ.*) sometimes with distinct grains or crys-
ARGILE SALIFÈRE. (*Fr.*) tals of this salt; usually occurs together
with rock-salt.

The following are the geological terms of certain
clays:—

(1) LOESS, or DILUVIAL LOAM. Frequently somewhat calcareous
Löss. (*Germ.*)
Löss, LIMON DILUVIEN. (*Fr.*) with marly nodules (Lösskindeln).

(2) TILE OR BRICK EARTH. A Miocene or Neogene deposit of clay
TEGEL. (*Germ.*) in the Vienna basin.

(3) BROWNCOAL CLAY. Usually white. Miocene in North-
BRAUNKOHLENTHON. (*Germ.*) ern Germany.

(4) SEPTARIAN CLAY. } Containing septaria of lime, in North-
  SEPTARIENTHON. *(Germ.)* } ern Germany Miocene (or Eocene).
(5) BARTON CLAY. Hampshire, Eocene.
(6) BOGNOR CLAY. Eocene of the Hampshire basin.
(7) LONDON CLAY. Eocene in the London basin.
(8) PLASTIC CLAY. } Eocene in the Paris basin.
  ARGILE PLASTIQUE. *(Fr.)* }
(9) HILS CLAY. } In the Hils formation (Wealden) of West-
  HILSTHON. *(Germ.)* } phalia.
(10) SPEETON CLAY, in the Lower Greensand formation of England.
(11) WEALD CLAY. } In the Wealden formation of Sussex.
  ARGILE WEALDIENNE. *(Fr.)* }
(12) ORNATEN-THON. *(Germ.)* With *Ammonites ornatus* in the Jura formation of Swabia.
(13) OPALINUS-THON. *(Germ.)* With *Ammonites opalinus* in the Brown Jura of Swabia.
(14) KIMERIDGE CLAY. } In the Jura formation of England.
  ARGILE KIMMÉRIDIENNE. *(Fr.)* }
(15) OXFORD CLAY. } In the Jura formation of England.
  ARGILE OXFORDIENNE. *(Fr.)* }
(16) AMALTHEEN-THON. *(Germ.)* With *Ammonites amaltheus*, in the Lias formation of Swabia.
(17) TURNERI-THON. *(Germ.)* In the Lias formation of Swabia.
(18) MIACYTEN-THON. *(Germ.)* Containing *Myacites*, and frequently also remains of plants, the lowest branch of the Keuper formation in Thuringia.

As clay loses its plasticity when subjected to a strong pressure, especially if accompanied by high temperature, the plastic clays are chiefly confined to the recent formations : the older clays have doubtless been converted into argillaceous shale, clay-slate, or claystone. There can be no doubt that all these rocks originally were mud deposits.

Literary references on the subject of clay and loam appear unnecessary.

33. CLAYSTONE and HARDENED CLAY.

THONSTEIN, oder VERHÄRTETER THON. *(Germ.)*

A compact and tolerably solid mass, chiefly consisting of clay, not slaty ; its fracture earthy ; very variously coloured.

The rock designated by this name is not always an actual sediment, but sometimes a product of the disintegration of felsitic rock. The nature of its origin is generally only to be determined by its geological position and surroundings. The sedimentary claystones are always stratified sometimes in very thin layers, white, yellowish grey, red-brown, greenish, or brownish, sometimes with variegated stripes or spotted. They sometimes contain nodules of pyrites, flakes of mica, impressions of plants, or petrified parts of plants.

We have already said that the distinction between the sedimentary claystones and certain weathered felsitic rocks is sometimes difficult. In like manner it is frequently difficult to distinguish the former from certain tuff rocks, e. g. from porphyry-tuff, which indeed is very often called claystone, especially in England; but the genuine sedimentary clay rock seems to have at least as good a title to the name.

MARLS.

These are closely allied to the clays, standing between them and the limestones. They are in fact compounds of clay and carbonate of lime, and also sometimes contain carbonate of magnesia; they likewise frequently contain fine particles of quartz, flakes of mica, oxide of iron, bitumen, or carbon. According to their state or texture, they may be divided into the slaty, the compact, and the earthy varieties; according to the predominance of one or other of their ingredients, they may be further divided into the calcareous, dolomitic, arenaceous, micaceous, ferruginous, and bituminous. Of carbon they only contain very subordinate quantities, serving as a dark colouring matter.

The original state of these rocks, like that of the clays, was a muddy sediment somewhat more various in its character than in the case of those rocks. The same process of pressure has consolidated them into firm, rocky, slaty, or sometimes bituminous masses.

The processes of animal and vegetable life have even participated in the formation of some of these rocks to the extent of contributing their calcareous and bituminous ingredients. The calcareous ingredients often show traces with the microscope of organic remains. Marls as well as clays occur in the deposits of almost every geological period; and as to the difference between those of different periods, we can only in general terms say that the older varieties are usually slaty or fissile, whereas in the more recent deposits earthy varieties more frequently occur, but this is by no means a rule without exception.

34. MARL.

MERGEL. (*Germ.*)
MARNE. (*Fr.*)

A compound of clay and lime, earthy, compact, or fissile, usually soft; crumbles on exposure to air, effervesces with acid.

Marl is a compound of clay and lime or dolomite, but its ingredients are blended together and cannot be distinguished except by chemical agents. The proportion of lime or dolomite varies from 10 to about 50 per cent. Outside of these limits the rock ceases to be marl, and does not crumble on exposure to the air. It will then either be a clay or a limestone.

The most frequent colour is grey, but marl is sometimes yellow, brown, red, violet, bluish, or greenish.

Varieties in Texture.

(*a*) MARL-SHALE.　　　　In fresh state very similar to argil-
　　MERGELSCHIEFER. (*Germ.*)　laceous shale, but crumbles on ex-
　　SCHISTE MARNEUX. (*Fr.*)　posure to the air; frequently con-
tains much quartz, sand, mica, or bitumen.

(*b*) COMPACT MARL, or MARLSTONE.　　Without distinct fissile
　　DICHTER MERGEL, VERHÄRTETER MERGEL,　slaty structure, similar to
　　　STEINMERGEL, oder MERGELSTEIN.　claystone, but falls to
　　　(*Germ.*)
　　MARNE COMPACTE. (*Fr.*)　pieces on exposure to the
air. Admixtures of quartz and mica or bitumen similar to marl-shale. A modification of compact marl, separates into small conical concretions (*cone in cone*). Germ. *Tuten-Mergel.*

(*c*) EARTHY MARL.　　　In its dry state resembles clay, but
　　ERDIGER MERGEL. (*Germ.*)　is not plastic when wet. Its ingredients are the same as those of the other marls.

Varieties in Composition.

(*d*) CALCAREOUS MARL.　　With much carbonate of lime in its
　　KALKMERGEL. (*Germ.*)　composition.
　　MARNE CALCAIRE.(*Fr.*)

(*e*) DOLOMITIC MARL.　　　With dolomite, and usually also
　　DOLOMITMERGEL. (*Germ.*)　with carbonate of lime. The dif-
　　MARNE MAGNÉSIENNE. (*Fr.*)　ferences between (*d*) and (*e*) can
only be determined by chemical analysis.

(*f*) ARGILLACEOUS MARL. } With little carbonate of lime or dolo-
THONMERGEL. (*Germ.*) mite ; forms transitions into clay, clay-
MARNE ARGILEUSE. (*Fr.*) stone, or argillaceous shale.

(*g*) ARENACEOUS MARL.
SANDMERGEL. (*Germ.*) } With much sand.
MARNE SABLEUSE. (*Fr.*)

(*h*) MICACEOUS MARL.
GLIMMERMERGEL. (*Germ.*) } Contains much mica.
MARNE MICACÉE. (*Fr.*)

(*i*) BITUMINOUS MARL. } Usually in the form of shale, al-
BITUMINÖSER MERGEL. (*Germ.*) ways dark-coloured by reason
MARNE BITUMINEUSE. (*Fr.*) of the bitumen, sometimes even
black. To this belong the so-called Oelschiefer (oil-slate) and
Kupferschiefer (cupiferous slate) of the Germans ; the latter is
distinguished by the quantity of copper which it contains.

(*k*) GLAUCONITE MARL. } With much glauconite in its compo-
GLAUKONITMERGEL. (*Germ.*) sition, and by it coloured green. The
MARNE GLAUCONIEUSE. (*Fr.*) small grains, when examined under
the microscope, appear mostly to proceed from the shells of
microscopic Foraminiferæ.

(*l*) GYPSEOUS MARL. } A marl penetrated by stringy veins of
GYPSMERGEL. (*Germ.*) gypsum, or thin laminæ of the same.
MARNE GYPSEUSE. (*Fr.*)

Besides the above-mentioned varieties of composition,
some marls have been named according to their geological
position ; e. g.:—

(1) SUB-APENNINE MARL.
SUBAPENNINEN-MERGEL. (*Germ.*) } Pliocene in Upper Italy.
MARNE SUBAPENNINE. (*Fr.*)

(2) CYRENIAN MARL. } With many *Cyrenes*; Miocene, in
CYRENEN-MERGEL. (*Germ.*) the Mayence basin.
MARNE À CYRÈNES. (*Fr.*)

(3) CHALK MARL. } In the Chalk formations of England
KREIDEMERGEL. (*Germ.*) and Westphalia.
CRAIE MARNEUSE. (*Fr.*)

(4) PLÄNER MARL. } In the Quadersandstone formations of
PLÄNERMERGEL. (*Germ.*) Saxony and Bohemia.

(5) FOLKESTONE MARL. } In the Gault formation of England.
MARNE DU GAULT. (*Fr.*)

(6) SPEETON MARL, belonging to the Lower Greensand formation of
England.

(7) FOREST MARL. } In the Lias formation of England.
CALCAIRE MARNEUX. (*Fr.*)

(8) LIAS SLATE. } A bituminous marl-slate of the Lias
LIASSCHIEFER. (*Germ.*) formation, sometimes called Oel-
SCHISTE LIASIQUE. (*Fr.*) schiefer.

(9) JURENSIS MARL. } With *Ammonites jurensis*, in the
JURENSIS-MERGEL. (*Germ.*) Lias formation of Swabia.

(10) POSIDONOMYA SLATE. } A dark bituminous marl-slate
POSIDONOMYEN-SCHIEFER. (*Germ.*) of the Lias formation of Swa-
SCHISTE À POSIDONIES. (*Fr.*) bia, with many *Posidonomya*.

T

(11) NUMMISMALIA MARL. } With *Terebratula nummismalis*,
    NUMMISMALIS-MERGEL. (*Germ.*) } in the Lias formation of Swabia.

(12) BELEMNITE MARL. } A dark bituminous marl-slate in
    BELEMNITENSCHIEFER. (*Germ.*) } the Lias formation of Swabia,
    MARNE À BELEMNITES. (*Fr.*) } with many *Belemnites*.

(13) SPOTTED MARL, or ALGÄU SLATE. } In the formation
    FLECKENMERGEL, oder ALGÄUSCHIEFER. (*Germ.*) } of the Northern
    Alps answering to the uppermost Lias.

(14) KEUPER MARL. } Chiefly variegated in colour, fre-
    KEUPERMERGEL. (*Germ.*) } quently with gypsum.
    MARNES IRISÉES. (*Fr.*) }

(15) PARTNACH SLATE, or BACTRILLIAN SLATE. } A marl formation
    PARTNACHSCHIEFER oder BACTRILLIENSCHIEFER. } with thick slaty
    (*Germ.*) } cleavage, which in
    the Northern Alps is found in part answering to the Keuper
    formation.

(16) BITUMINOUS MARL-SLATE. } Of the Zechstein forma-
    BITUMINÖSER MERGELSCHIEFER. (*Germ.*) } tion of Thuringia.

(17) COPPER SLATE. } Is a bituminous marl-slate of the
    KUPFERSCHIEFER. (*Germ.*) } Zechstein formation of Thuringia, in
    which various sulphurous compounds of metals are contained.
    These sulphur compounds, besides their copper, contain iron,
    silver, lead, cobalt, nickel, &c.

It will hardly be necessary to add anything respecting
the occurrence of marl in nature, nor to refer to literature
on the subject.

LIMESTONE GROUP.

(Limestone, Dolomite, Gypsum, Anhydrite.)

Pure limestone is an aggregate of particles of calcspar:
it therefore consists of carbonate of lime. Pure dolomite
or magnesian limestone is an aggregate of particles of the
mineral dolomite or bitter-spar: it is therefore a carbonate of lime and of magnesia. Gypsum is a sulphate
of lime combined with water; anhydrite is gypsum without water.

Rocks consisting of pure limestone or dolomite rarely
occur in nature. What we chiefly find are rocks of intermediate character, which we may regard as transitions
between the two extremes; in other words, all limestones
are more or less magnesian, probably consisting of an
intimate compound of the two minerals, calcspar and
bitterspar.

These rocks likewise usually contain other admixtures
in small quantities; e. g. clay, silica, oxides of iron, or
bitumen. The presence of such minerals occasions many

varieties in colour as well as composition; there are also many modifications in texture, so that the limestones present us with many very dissimilar rocks.

It is not always easy or possible without analysis to distinguish limestone from dolomite, even if pure, still less to determine the various rocks of intermediate character. Many rocks have been long held to be limestone which later chemical analysis has shown to be dolomite. Nevertheless, the distinction is important enough to be preserved, although it may be difficult always to apply it.* We are compelled to create an arbitrary boundary by determining how great a percentage of magnesia should entitle a rock to be called a dolomite. The mineral dolomite contains about 45·7 per cent. carbonate of magnesia to 54·3 per cent. carbonate of lime. We may therefore halve the 45·7 per cent., and say that all rocks containing more than 23 per cent. carbonate of magnesia should be called dolomites, and those containing less than that amount retain the name of limestones. Some such division must be agreed on for purposes of classification, although otherwise of little scientific value.

The general difference between characteristic forms of the two rocks may be briefly stated as follows :—

LIMESTONE.	DOLOMITE.
Hardness . . 3·	Hardness . . . . 3·5
Spec. grav. . 2·6—2·8	Spec. grav. . . . . 2·8—2·9
Crystalline-granular limestone seldom occurs except between strata of crystalline schists.	The crystalline-granular and saccharoid varieties of dolomite occur in sedimentary formations, as well as between strata of crystalline schists.
Many beds of limestone of silurian and carboniferous age are coarsely crystalline; as are, also, the limestone of some coral reefs and some stalagmites.	Sometimes these varieties pulverise to a crystalline sand.
Very often compact.	Seldom quite compact.
Frequently oolitic.	Probably never oolitic.
Lustre, when crystalline, vitreous.	Lustre, when crystalline, vitreous to pearly.

---

* The quicksilver mines of Idria are in dolomite rock, which adjoins and is intersected by limestone in many places; and the difference between the two rocks is there very important, as the ore is confined to the dolomite, none being ever found in the limestone.— TRANSLATOR.

T 2

LIMESTONE.	DOLOMITE.
Effervesces strongly with acid.	Solid portions of the rock do not effervesce with acid. The powder effervesces, especially if heated.
Its powder, when heated before the blowpipe on platinum foil, adheres together.	When its powder is heated on platinum foil, before the blowpipe, it tumefies and does not gelatinise.

The circumstances under which these two rocks occur in nature are very similar. They both occur in a crystalline-granular state, imbedded between strata of metamorphic schists; they both form strata in formations of various geological periods; but in the sedimentary formations the dolomites are frequently also found in a crystalline-granular state, whereas the limestones, though often crystalline, are almost always compact, earthy, or oolitic. Deposits of genuine dolomites are never formed by springs, but limestones frequently. Limestones, again, are more frequently fossiliferous, and they are also more usually distinctly stratified than dolomites.

Gypsum and anhydrite are not so extensively developed as limestone and dolomite; they are prevalent only in distinctly sedimentary formations, and are usually crystalline, seldom distinctly stratified, seldom fossiliferous. They are often accompanied by rock-salt. In general they are much more free from foreign ingredients than either limestone or dolomite.

35. LIMESTONE.

KALKSTEIN. (*Germ.*)
CALCAIRE. (*Fr.*)

A crystalline-granular, compact, earthy, or oolitic aggregate of calcspar; effervesces strongly with acid; easily scratched with the knife.

Spec. grav. . . . . . . 2·6—2·8.

Pure limestone consists of 56 per cent. lime and 44 per cent. carbonic acid. It seldom occurs so pure in nature, but is usually more or less intimately combined with dolomite, alumina, silica, peroxide and protoxide of iron, bitumen, or carbon. By these ingredients its properties undergo alteration, and there arise distinct varieties in composition when their quantity is considerable. The texture of the limestone rocks is likewise various, and gives rise to other varieties, to many of which separate names attach. Many limestones consist entirely, and others partially, of the calcareous shells of animals ; and it is very possible that this is the case with several whose original structure is no longer apparent. There are other limestones which are undoubtedly the product of chemical precipitate of carbonate of lime from aqueous solutions ; and some that are the result of consolidation of calcareous mud proceeding from the mechanical disintegration of older limestones.

In appearance, many limestones and dolomites much resemble some siliceous rocks, or compact felsitic rocks, or gypsum. But from these they may easily be distinguished by the difference of their hardness, and by their effervescence with acids.

Varieties in Texture.

(a) GRANULAR LIMESTONE. Including marble. A granular
KÖRNIGER KALKSTEIN. (Germ.) aggregate of distinct individual
CALCAIRE SACCHAROÏDE. (Fr.) crystalline particles of calcspar.
The grains vary in size from the almost invisibly small (fine-grained compact varieties) to the size of a nut (coarse-grained). Most usually the colour is white, but sometimes yellowish-grey, reddish, greenish, bluish, and even black. By admixture of dolomite it passes into magnesian limestone and dolomite. Granular limestone also contains other admixtures, especially in its crystalline state, and these are then porphyritically disposed, as, for instance, mica, chlorite, talc, hornblende, pyroxene, garnet, vesuvian, felspar, chondrodite, couzeranite, chiastolite, epidote, zircon, titanite, spinel, corundum, quartz, fluor-spar, apatite, magnetic iron-ore, iron pyrites, zinc-blende, galena, copper pyrites, anthracite, and graphite. The rock also contains geodes, nests, or veins, with fully developed crystals of calcspar, aragonite, bitter-spar (dolomite), asbestus, serpentine, &c.

The following special varieties of granular limestone are occasioned by the occurrence of some of the above minerals in considerable quantity and characteristic form.

(α) CIPOLLINO. A granular limestone rich in
CIPOLLIN. (Germ.) mica, by which a slaty texture is
CIPOLIN. (Fr.) sometimes occasioned; goes over
into calcareous mica-schist. Zaunhaus, near Altenberg in Saxony.

(β) ANTHRACONITE. The name given by v. Moll to
ANTHRAKONIT, Von certain carbonaceous black granu-
Moll. (Germ.) lar limestones, which are usually
only found in the form of nests, lentils, or veins in other rocks. To this class belongs the Lucullite of the ancients.

(γ) OPHICALCITE.

OPHICALCIT. (*Germ.*)
OPHICALCE, *Brongniart.*
(*Fr.*)

} The name given by Brongniart to a compound of limestone and serpentine; its texture granular to compact.

This is the Verde Antique of archæologists.

(δ) CALCIPHYRE.

CALCIPHYR. (*Germ.*)
CALCIPHYRE, *Brongniart.*
(*Fr.*)

} The name given by Brongniart to a compound of granular limestone with garnet, pyroxene, or felspar, usually porphyritic.

(ε) HEMITRENE.

HEMITREN. (*Germ.*)
HEMITHRÈNE, *Brongniart.*
(*Fr.*)

} A granular compound of limestone, hornblende, and grammatite. The varieties (γ), (δ), and (ε) are probably always contact formations.

(ζ) HISLOPITE.

HISLOPIT. (*Germ.*)

} The name given by Samuel Haughton to a granular limestone occurring at Takli in the East Indies.

Granular limestone is of irregular massive structure; it likewise usually shows distinct traces of stratification, sometimes also a fissile texture; it most usually occurs in subordinate beds between strata of crystalline schists, and is frequently itself the product of metamorphosis from compact sedimentary deposits of limestone. The form of its beds is sometimes very irregular, they assume a swollen shape, or resemble the dykes or veins of igneous rocks. It would seem as if the limestone, in the process of transmutation, had become softer than the surrounding schist, and that its mass had consequently been squeezed into the breaches and clefts of the latter. This appearance may be observed at Miltitz near Meissen, and at Auerbach near Heidelberg.

In England and Ireland beds of crystalline limestone occur variously interstratified with the compact limestones of the carboniferous limestone series through a thickness of from 2,000 to 3,000 feet.

Granular limestone is also found at the margin of those igneous rocks which have broken through the compact or earthy limestones. Such may be observed at the Kaiserstuhl in Breisgau, in County Antrim and Island of Rathlin, Ireland.

(*b*) COMPACT LIMESTONE.

DICHTER KALKSTEIN. (*Germ.*)
CALCAIRE COMPACTE. (*Fr.*)

} The particles of calcspar are invisibly small, and the mass therefore appears to be compact. Its fracture is conchoidal, or splintery, or dull. Its prevailing colour is grey or yellowish; it varies, however, to white, blue, green, red, brown, and even black. Some varieties are variegated, spotted, or veined, like marble. The following accessory ingredients are usually intimately blended with the general mass, viz., dolomite, clay, silica, oxide of iron, bitumen, or carbon. If these only occur in small quantity, they can hardly be recognised, but if their quantity be considerable, then distinct varieties of the rock are occasioned, such as the following:—

(α) DOLOMITIC.
DOLOMITISCHER DICHTER KALKSTEIN. (*Germ.*)
MAGNÉSIEN. (*Fr.*)

(β) BITUMINOUS. } Fetid limestone, swine-
STINKSTEIN, STINKKALK. (*Germ.*) } stones, always dark-
CALCAIRE BITUMINEUX. (*Fr.*) } coloured, and emitting
a bituminous smell when rubbed.

(γ) ARGILLACEOUS or MARLY LIMESTONE. } With consider-
MERGELKALKSTEIN, (*Germ.*) } able admixture
CALCAIRE ARGILEUX ou MARNEUX. (*Fr.*) } of clay; usually
grey, and in fracture dull, almost earthy.

(δ) FERRUGINOUS LIMESTONE. } Very rich in hydrated
EISENKALKSTEIN. (*Germ.*) } oxide of iron, which im-
CALCAIRE FERRUGINEUX. (*Fr.*) } parts a brown colour to
the rock.

(ε) CHERTY LIMESTONE, or SILICEOUS } Combined with si-
LIMESTONE. } lica, and therefore
KIESELKALKSTEIN. (*Germ.*) } harder than ordi-
CALCAIRE SILICIEUX. (*Fr.*) } nary limestone.

Very frequently traversed by veins of chert or hornstone.

In all the varieties of these compact limestones there occur,
occasionally, veins, seams, nodules, or nests of calcspar, hornstone (chert), or flint.

Jukes remarks, 'Almost all large masses of limestone have
ther flints or siliceous concretions. These are frequently called
chert, as in the carboniferous limestone (see post, p. 351), where
the nodules and layers of chert exactly resemble the flints in
chalk. Even the tertiary limestones round Paris have their
flints the menilite of that locality being nothing but a siliceous
concretion (see post, p. 340), found in the calcaire St. Ouen, and
possibly other places. Pure siliceous concretions occur even in
the freshwater limestones and gypsum beds of Montmartre.
This invariable, or nearly invariable, accompaniment of limestone and siliceous deposits, those siliceous parts having a
chemical and not a mechanical formation, strengthens the hypothesis of the organic origin of both, as previously described.
The silica diffused through the calcareous mud, of which the
limestone was composed, has sometimes remained so diffused
instead of separating as nodules or layers, producing a cherty or
siliceouslimestone.'

Page says, 'To the percolation of water charged with carbonic acid, we owe the production of rottenstone from beds
of siliceous limestone, the carbonated waters dissolving the
limy portion, and leaving the light porous siliceous residuum
which forms the rottenstone of commerce.'

The compact limestones are usually distinctly stratified, and
are found associated with other sedimentary rocks of almost
every age

(c) EARTHY LIMESTONES. } Chalk (in part). Rough to the
ERDIGER KALKSTEIN. (*Germ.*) } feel; friable; the white chalk
CALCAIRE GRAYEUX. (*Fr.*) } readily imparting its colour to any
body against which it is rubbed. In chalk the particles consist

of very minute shells of Foraminifera, Polythalamiæ, &c., which may be recognised under the microscope.

These minute shells constitute a fine earthy mass, in which larger fossils are likewise found, as well as nodules and layers of flint or chert, grains of glauconite, or of sand and other mineral substances. The following subvarieties may be named:—

(α) WHITE CHALK.
   WEISSE KREIDE. (*Germ.*)
   CRAIE BLANCHE. (*Fr.*)

(β) GLAUCONITIC CHALK.
   GLAUKONITISCHE KREIDE. (*Germ.*)
   CRAIE GLAUCONIEUSE. (*Fr.*)

(γ) ARENACEOUS SANDSTONE.) Consisting of remains of
   SANDIGER KALKSTEIN. (*Germ.*) } shells. These earthy and
   CALCAIRE ARÉNACÉ. (*Fr.*)) distinctly zoogenic rocks
are more frequent in recent than in old formations. We may presume that in the older formations they have been metamorphosed into compact limestone.

(d) OOLITIC LIMESTONE, OOLITE, ROESTONE,) This variety is en-
   PEASTONE, or PISOLITE.   } tirely composed of
   OOLITHISCHER KALKSTEIN, OOLITH, ROGENSTEIN, } small and almost
   ERBSENSTEIN, oder PISOLITH. (*Germ.*)   } spherical grains, from
   CALCAIRE OOLITHIQUE, CALCAIRE PISOLITHIQUE.) the size of a millet-
   (*Fr.*)
seed to that of a pea or larger. This granular texture is very different from the crystalline granular. The single round grains usually lie close together, but this is not always the case; they are sometimes wide apart, connected by a compact matrix—indeed they are always held together by a matrix. The individual grains are often of compact structure, more usually, however, of radial texture; sometimes both radial and concentric in alternate coats, with a nucleus of foreign substance, such as a grain of sand; sometimes they are nothing but fossils. The geological position of these oolites is identical with that of the compact limestones. The genuine peastone is, however, an exception. It is (e, g. Carlsbad) evidently a formation from a spring of water holding in solution carbonate of lime (see p. 94), and it moreover consists of aragonite and not calcspar. Jukes remarks, 'Its peculiar structure gives to oolite the character of a freestone, working easily in any direction, whence its value as a building stone. Bath stone, Portland stone, Caen stone are well-known examples of oolitic limestone.'

The pea-grit of Cheltenham is a marine formation, one of the oolites, only the spherical nodules are somewhat irregular and elliptical in shape.

(e) NODULAR LIMESTONE.) This variety consists entirely of
   KNOTENKALKSTEIN. (*Germ.*) } small compact nodules or irregular
   CALCAIRE NODULEUX. (*Fr.*)) swellings, united and bound to-
gether by a compact limestone mass, or by a matrix of marl or clay-slate. Its composition, as well as its texture, therefore, presents varieties:—

(α) NODULES OF LIMESTONE IN LIME-) At Partenkirchen
   STONE or MARL MATRIX.   } in Bavaria.
   KALKKNOTEN IN KALK oder MERGEL.)
   (*Germ.*)

(β) KRAMENZELSTEIN. } Nodules of lime in a matrix
KRAMENZELSTEIN. (*Germ.*) of clay-slate, hence the rock itself is somewhat slaty. These nodules sometimes are nothing else than indistinct fossils. Polwand, near Saalfeld.

(*f*) SLATY LIMESTONE. } This is, however, usually not
SCHIEFRIGER KALKSTEIN. (*Germ.*) of genuine slaty texture or
CALCAIRE SCHISTEUX. (*Fr.*) cleavage, but only a thin stratification (lamination) presenting a slaty appearance; thus, e. g., at Solenhofen in Bavaria, where a finely laminated limestone is even used for roof-slating.

(*g*) POROUS LIMESTONE. }
PORÖSER KALKSTEIN. (*Germ.*) We here distinguish between—
CALCAIRE CAVERNEUX. (*Fr.*)

   (*n*) SPONGY LIMESTONE, APHRITE. } Very extensively de-
SCHAUMKALK oder MEHLBATZEN. veloped in the Mu-
(*Germ.*) schelkalk formation of
Thuringia, and

   (β) LIMESTONE TUFF, CALCA- } A deposit from springs,
REOUS TUFF. usually porous by reason of
KALKTUFF. (*Germ.*) its origin as an incrustation
TUF CALCAIRE. (*Fr.*) of plants.

(*h*) GEODIC LIMESTONE. } With numerous sparry ca-
DRUSIGER KALKSTEIN. (*Germ.*) vities of crystallised calcspar,
CALCAIRE GÉODIQUE. (*Fr.*) brownspar, and the like.

(*i*) CELLULAR LIMESTONE, or ROUGH } With numerous angular
LIMESTONE. cells or holes. These latter
ZELLENKALK oder RAUHKALK. (*Germ.*) are sometimes occasioned
CALCAIRE CELLULEUX. (*Fr.*) by the decay or weakening
of fragments enclosed in the rocks, in which case the porosity of the rock is only at the surface.

(*k*) BRECCIA-LIMESTONE, or LIMESTONE } Fragments of limestone
BRECCIA. cemented together by
BRECCIENKALK oder KALKBRECCIE; TRÜM- limestone. The partial
MER und RUINEN-MARMOR. (*Germ.*) weakening or decay of
BRÈCHE CALCAIRE. (*Fr.*) these fragments some-
times causes a cellular tissue on the surface of the rock.

(*l*) STYLOLITE LIMESTONE. } Names given by Ger-
STYLOLITHENKALK und NAGELKALK. (*Germ.*) man geologists to cer-
CALCAIRE À STYLOLITES. (*Fr.*) tain compact limestones
which show peculiar striped jointings, so-called stylolites, or are made up of small conical or wedge-shaped pieces.

(*m*) FIBROUS LIMESTONE } To this variety we may reckon
FASERIGER KALKSTEIN, FASER- the calc-sinter and aragonite-
KALK. (*Germ.*) sinter, formed by the dripping of
CALCAIRE FIBREUX. (*Fr.*) water containing lime in solution,
e. g. at Carlsbad in Bohemia. There also occur seams or layers of fibrous limestone between beds of marl, which have clearly some other origin. Stalactitic calc-sinter is frequently sparry and not fibrous, but as it is a subordinate formation we include it here because of its origin.

Over and above the varieties in texture and composi-

tion which we have enumerated, limestone is very various
in its geological character, and especially in the nature of
the fossils which it contains. The geological varieties are
not of distinct lithological character, but they nevertheless deserve a brief enumeration, as they sometimes
acquire local importance. They are only to be distinguished with certainty by means of their fossils; we will
arrange them as nearly as possible according to their
respective ages.

Geological Varieties.

(1) LIMESTONE TUFF, CAL- } Usually a porous friable deposit from
    CAREOUS TUFF.   } springs, and containing many remains
    KALKTUFF. *(Germ.)* } of plants and animals.
    TUF CALCAIRE. *(Fr.)*

(2) TRAVERTINE.   } A formation in Italy similar to calc-tuff,
    TRAVERTIN. *(Germ.)* } 'but usually more compact, hard, and
    TRAVERTIN. *(Fr.)* } semi-crystalline.' See Bristow's Glossary.

(3) CORAL REEFS.   }
    KORALLENRIFFE. *(Germ.)* } In tropical seas.
    CALCAIRE CORALLIEN. *(Fr.)*

(4) FRESHWATER LIMESTONE. } Containing   freshwater   shells.
    SÜSSWASSERKALK. *(Germ.)* } 'Freshwater limestones have com-
    CALCAIRE D'EAU DOUCE (LA- } monly a peculiarity of aspect from
    CUSTRE). *(Fr.)*
which their origin may sometimes be suspected, even before
examining their palæontological contents or petrological relations. They are generally of a very smooth texture, and either
dull white or pale grey; their fracture only slightly conchoidal,
rarely splintery, but often soft and earthy.'—*Jukes.*

(5) STEPPE LIMESTONE. } A very recent semi-marine brackish
    STEPPENKALK. *(Germ.)* } limestone deposit. In Southern Russia.

(6) LEITHA LIMESTONE. } A tertiary limestone in the Leitha Moun-
    LEITHAKALK. *(Germ.)* } tains, with corals and marine shells.

(7) LITORINELLA LIMESTONE. } In the Mayence basin, con-
    LITTORINELLENKALK. *(Germ.)* } taining numerous *Paludinæ,*
    CALCAIRE À LITTORINELLES. *(Fr.)* } *Litorinellæ.*

(8) CERITHIUM LIMESTONE. } In the Mayence basin, with many
    CERITHIENKALK. *(Germ.)* } *Cerithia.*
    CALCAIRE À CÉRITES. *(Fr.)*

(9) CALCAIRE GROSSIER (Grobkalk), sandy, and full of fossil shells.
Eocene in the Paris basin.

(10) NUMMULITIC LIMESTONE. } Consisting almost exclusively
    NUMMULITENKALK. *(Germ.)* } of Nummulites. Eocene; very
    CALCAIRE À NUMMULITES. *(Fr.)* } extensively developed in the
                               South of Europe.

'The nummulitic formation, with its characteristic fossils,
plays a far more conspicuous part than any other tertiary group
in the solid framework of the earthy crust, whether in Europe,
Asia, or Africa. It often attains a thickness of many thousand
feet, and extends from the Alps to the Carpathians, and is in
full force in the North of Africa, as, for example, in Algeria

and Morocco. It has also been traced from Egypt, where it was largely quarried of old for the building of the Pyramids, into Asia Minor, and across Persia, by Bagdad, to the mouths of the Indus. It occurs not only in Cutch, but in the mountain ranges which separate Scinde from Persia, and which form the principal passes to Cabul; and it has been followed still farther eastward into India, as far as Eastern Bengal and the frontiers of China.'—*Page.*

(11) ORBITOIDAL LIMESTONE.   } 'As the nummulitic limestone
    CALCAIRE À ORBITOLITES. (*Fr.*) } seems characteristic of the old world, so the orbitoidal limestone seems characteristic of the new, mountain masses full 300 feet in thickness, and almost wholly made up of Orbitoides, occurring near Suggsville, in North America, and apparently in the same, or nearly the same, geological horizon.'—*Page.*

(12) MAJOLICA, a white compact limestone.

(13) SCAGLIA, a red limestone, in the Alps.

(14) OSTRÆA LIMESTONE.   } Full of *Ostreæ.* Eocene; occurs
    OSTREENKALK. (*Germ.*)   } to the north of Kusstein, in Tyrol.
    CALCAIRE À OSTRACÉES. (*Fr.*) }

(15) UPPER AND LOWER CHALK. } Nearly white. The upper and
    KREIDEKALK, KREIDE. (*Germ.*) } principal branch of the Chalk formation in England, containing many flints.

'Chalk flints occur as rounded nodular masses of very irregular and sometimes fantastic shape, and of all sizes, up to a foot in diameter. They are commonly white outside, but internally are of various shades of black or brown, sometimes passing into white. They have sometimes concentric bands of black and white colours internally, and exhibit markings derived from organic bodies, round which they have often been formed. Flint occurs in chalk, not only in nodules, but also in seams or layers, sometimes short and irregular, sometimes regular over a distance of several yards. These seams vary from half an inch to two inches in thickness, and are commonly black in colour.' *Jukes.*

(16) HIPPURITIDEA, or HIPPURITE } Full of Hippuritidea; equiva-
    LIMESTONE.   } lent to the Lower Chalk for-
    HIPPURITENKALK. (*Germ.*)   } mation in Europe, Northern
    CALCAIRE À HIPPURITES. (*Fr.*) } Africa, and America.

(17) RUDISTENKALK, oder HIEROGLYPHEN- } Equivalent to the Lower
    KALK. (*Germ.*)   } Chalk formations.
    CRAIE À RUDISTES. (*Fr.*)

(18) SPATANGUS LIMESTONE.   } Containing many *Spatangidæ*;
    SPATANGENKALK. (*Germ.*)   } belonging to the Chalk group in
    CALCAIRE À SPATANGUES. (*Fr.*) } the Alps.

(19) APTYCHUS LIMESTONE.   } Containing many *Aptychi*; there
    APTYCHENKALK. (*Germ.*)   } are two species of this fossil, one
    CALCAIRE À APTYCHUS. (*Fr.*) } belonging to the Chalk, and the
other to the Jura formation.

(20) PLÄNER LIMESTONE. } Thinly stratified, usually somewhat
    PLÄNERKALK. (*Germ.*) } marly, occurs with the Quadersandstein in Saxony.

(21) SERPULITE LIMESTONE.　　　Full of fossil Serpulæ of the Deister
　　　SERPULIT. *(Germ.)*　　　　　or Wealden formation of West-
　　　CALCAIRE À SERPULES. *(Fr.)*　phalia.

(22) PORTLAND STONE AND OOLITE.　A limestone belonging to the
　　　PORTLAND-OOLITH. *(Germ.)*　　upper Jura of England, fre-
　　　CALCAIRE PORTLANDIEN. *(Fr.)*　quently Oolitic.

‘ A well-known group of the upper Oolite as developed in
the South of England. It consists of shelly freestones of
variable texture underlaid by thick beds of sand, and derives its
name from the Isle of Portland in Dorsetshire, where certain
of the freestones have for centuries been largely quarried for
architectural purposes. The Portland beds abound in fossil
shells, bones of saurians, and drift coniferous wood.’

(23) ASTARTE LIMESTONE.　　　Containing many *Astartidæ* be-
　　　ASTARTENKALK. *(Germ.)*　　longing to the upper Jura forma-
　　　CALCAIRE À ASTARTES. *(Fr.)*　tion.

(24) DICERAS LIMESTONE.　　　Containing *Diceræ*, and belonging
　　　DICERASKALK. *(Germ.)*　　to the upper Jura formation.
　　　CALCAIRE À DICÉRATES. *(Fr.)*

(25) CORAL RAG.　　　　　　　Frequent in the Jura forma-
　　　KORALLENKALK, POLYPENKALK, oder　tion, the upper member of
　　　MADREPORENKALK. *(Germ.)*　the Middle Oolite in England.
　　　CALCAIRE CORALLIEN. *(Fr.)*

(26) NERINEA LIMESTONE.　　　Full of *Nerineæ* of the Jura for-
　　　NERINEENKALK. *(Germ.)*　　mation.
　　　CALCAIRE À NÉRINÉES. *(Fr.)*

(27) AMMONITE LIMESTONE.　　Full of Ammonites of the Jura or
　　　AMMONITENKALK. *(Germ.)*　Lias formation.
　　　CALCAIRE AMMONITIFÈRE. *(Fr.)*

(28) JURA LIMESTONE.
　　　JURAKALK. *(Germ.)*　　　　Usually white, yellowish, or grey.
　　　CALCAIRE JURASSIQUE. *(Fr.)*

(29) OXFORD OOLITE.　　　　　Belonging to the Jura or Oolite for-
　　　OXFORD-OOLITH. *(Germ.)*　mation of England.
　　　OOLITHE D'OXFORD. *(Fr.)*

(30) CORNBRASH.
　　　PLASSENKALK. *(Germ.)*　　The same formation.
　　　CORNBRASH. *(Fr.)*

(31) BATH OOLITE.
　　　GRAND OOLITHE, OOLITHE　The like.
　　　DE BATH. *(Fr.)*

(32) INFERIOR OOLITE.
　　　VILZER KALK. *(Germ.)*　　The like.
　　　OOLITHE INFÉRIEUR. *(Fr.)*

(33) LIAS LIMESTONE.
　　　LEIAS-KALK. *(Germ.)*　　Usually dark-coloured and bituminous.
　　　CALCAIRE LIASIQUE. *(Fr.)*

(34) GRYPHITE LIMESTONE.　　Containing numerous *Gryphæ*, the
　　　GRYPHITENKALK. *(Germ.)*　former designation for the Lias
　　　CALCAIRE À GRYPHITES. *(Fr.)*　limestone.

(35) BELEMNITE LIMESTONE.　　Containing numerous Belemnites,
　　　BELEMNITENKALK. *(Germ.)*　and belonging to the Lias for-
　　　CALCAIRE À BÉLEMNITES. *(Fr.)*　mation.

(36) DACHSTEINKALK *(Germ.)*, a limestone of the Northern Alps,
corresponding with the Lias formation in other parts of Europe.

(37) KLIPPENKALK *(Germ.)*, a limestone occurring in the Carpathians,
its age not to be determined with certainty.

(38) HALLSTÄTTER LIMESTONE.　A limestone of the Alps correspond-
　　　HALLSTÄTTERKALK. *(Germ.)*　ing with the Keuper of Germany.

(39) MUSCHELKALK (SHELL LIMESTONE). MUSCHELKALK. (*Germ.*) CALCAIRE CONCHYLIEN. (*Fr.*) } The middle member of the Trias in Germany, usually grey, and very extensively developed in Western Germany.

(40) WELLENKALK (*Germ.*), stratified in thin wavy layers, or with nodular concretions, the lower member of the Muschelkalk in Germany.

(41) GUTTENSTEINER KALK (*Germ.*), a limestone of the Alps answering to the Muschelkalk of Germany.

(42) ENCRINAL or ENCRINITAL LIMESTONE. ENCRINITEN- oder TROCHITEN-KALK. (*Germ.*) CALCAIRE À ENCRINES. (*Fr.*) • } Full of remains of Encrinites, an upper member of the Muschelkalk formation of Germany.

'The internal calcareous skeletons of the encrinites (in scattered joints and fragments) are so abundant in some Carboniferous limestones as to compose the greater part of the mass, hence the term encrinal or encrinital limestone. The minuter joints of the fingers and rays are usually termed entrochi or wheelstones, and these when abounding in certain limestones confer on them the title *entrochal limestones*. The stalk having been perforated by a canal which kept the whole in vital union, the separated joints present a beadlike appearance: hence such familiar terms as "St. Cuthbert's beads" and "wheelstones" for the solid pieces, and "pulley stones" and "screw stones" for their hollow casts in limestones.'—*Page.*

(43) TEREBRATULA LIMESTONE. TEREBRATULAKALK. (*Germ.*) CALCAIRE À TÉRÉBRATULES. (*Fr.*) } Almost entirely consisting of *Terebratula vulgaris*. Frequent in the Muschelkalk of Northern Germany.

(44) ROESTONE. ROGENSTEIN. (*Germ.*) } A rock occurring in the sandstone of Northern Germany.

(45) MAGNESIAN LIMESTONE (DOLOMITIC). ZECHSTEINKALK. (*Germ.*) CALCAIRE DU ZECHSTEIN. (*Fr.*) } The term Zechstein literally translated signifies mine-stone, so called because it has to be mined or cut through to reach the copper-slate which lies immediately beneath it; usually dark-coloured and bituminous. The chief member of the Zechstein formation of Germany.

(46) CARBONIFEROUS LIMESTONE, or MOUNTAIN LIMESTONE. KOHLENKALK, oder BERGKALK. (*Germ.*) CALCAIRE CARBONIFÈRE. (*Fr.*) } Chief member of the Carboniferous limestone formation in England; when it contains metal, it is called metalliferous limestone; when it contains much hornstone or chert, it is called chert-limestone.

(47) SCAR LIMESTONE, a lower member of the Carboniferous limestone in Westmoreland and Cumberland.

(48) TRANSITION or GREYWACKÉ LIMESTONE. GRAUWACKENKALK, oder UEBERGANGSKALK. (*Germ.*) GRAUWACKE CALCAIRE. (*Fr.*) } A limestone of the transition period, usually compact, solid, and grey.

(49) STRINGOCEPHALUS LIMESTONE. STRINGOCEPHALENKALK. (*Germ.*) } Containing many *Stringocephalus Burtini* in the Devonian formation of Germany.

(50) EIFEL LIMESTONE.   } Lying immediately under the pre-
    EIFLER KALK. (*Germ.*)   } ceding.

(51) ORTHOCERAS LIMESTONE.   } Full of remains of Orthocera-
    ORTHOCERATITENKALK. (*Germ.*)   } tites belonging to the Silurian
    CALCAIRE À ORTHOCÈRES. (*Fr.*)   } formation, e.g. in Scandinavia.

(52) URKALK (aboriginal or primitive limestone) is a general name,
formerly very frequently applied in Germany to denote all
granular limestones, especially those associated with the crystalline schists.

Limestones, as we have already remarked, are of various
origin. A few only are direct chemical precipitates from
aqueous solutions; the greater part are probably the
product of certain animals. Some have been occasioned by
the washing together of lime mud. The crystalline limestones owe their state chiefly to a plutonic process of
transmutation.

As to their bedding in relation to that of other rocks, we
have nothing to add to what has previously been stated.

We only adduce a few leading references on the subject of limestones. It would serve no useful purposes
to cite all treatises respecting their local occurrence.

[References.'

Ehrenberg, on the Animal Origin of many Limestones, Die
fossilen Infusorien, 1837, Mikrogeologie, and v. L. u. Br.
Jahrb. 1861, p. 785.

Darwin, on the Formation of Coral Limestones in his 'Coral
Islands.'

G. Rose, on the heteromorphic State of Carbonate of Lime in the
Abhandl. d. k. Akad. d. Wissenschaft zu Berlin, 1856–1858.

Haughton, on Hislopite in the Philos. Mag. 1859, [17] p. 66.

Delesse, on Hislopite in the Ann. des Mines, 1861, vol. xx. p. 435.

L. Cordier gives his views on the formation of limestones in an
article published in the Compt. rend. 1862, vol. lxiv. p. 293.
He takes them to be principally chemical precipitates from
the sea, which formerly held much greater quantities of salts
of lime and magnesia in solution than at present.

Leymerie expounded similar views in his Éléments de Miné-
ralogie et de Géologie, 1861, p. 358.

Chemical analyses of limestone exist in great variety; but they are only of local importance, serving
to decide the character of any given rock: for instance,
whether it be a limestone or a dolomite, or whether it be
fitted for building or other practical use.

As to the formation of oolite, see pp. 94–5, ante.

36. DOLOMITE, MAGNESIAN LIMESTONE.

DOLOMIT. (*Germ.*)
DOLOMIE. (*Fr.*)

A granular, compact, or earthy aggregate of bitter-spar (dolomite), usually combined with some calcspar; does not effervesce, or only slightly effervesces with acid; is easily scratched with the knife.

Spec. grav. . . . . . . 2·8—2·9.

Pure dolomite, or bitter-spar, is a mineral, which we have already described as such in the earlier part of this work; chemically it consists of 54 carbonate of lime to 46 carbonate of magnesia. It is very seldom that the rock occurs in this pure state; it usually contains a much larger proportion of carbonate of lime, and most probably in such case consists of an intimate compound of bitter-spar and calcspar. It usually also contains small quantities of several other substances, such as clay, silica, oxides of iron, bitumen, and the like. The chief differences between limestone and dolomite, and the mode of distinguishing the two rocks, have been explained (p. 275, ante). In general terms, we may say that the dolomites closely resemble the limestones as regards their bedding and their other attributes, except that they are more frequently crystalline than the limestones, and sometimes even are entirely made up of small rhombohedrons.

It was long supposed that all dolomites had been formed by process of transmutation from limestone. It is, however, much more probable that dolomites and magnesian limestones were for the most part formed by sedimentary deposit, in the same manner as the limestones proper. Many coralline structures, and probably many marine shells, contain some magnesia, and therefore may likewise yield magnesian limestones; some dolomites again have very probably resulted from chemical precipitate from aqueous solutions. Nevertheless the origin of many dolomites still remains very problematical, and it is by no means impossible that transmutations of limestone into dolomite may have taken place and may still take place in the interior of the earth. We know that magnesia plays an important part in the transmutation of several rocks, in proof of which we need only instance chlorite-schist, talc-schist, serpentine, steatite, &c. The magnesia would appear in such cases to have penetrated in a state of solution into the pores of the rocks, whose character it has changed, displacing other substances. Haidinger has suggested that sulphate of magnesia might in very high temperature, and under great pressure, decompose carbonate of lime, converting it into dolomite and gypsum; and Von Morlot has in some measure confirmed this suggestion by experiment.

Dolomite, like limestone, has many varieties, most of which are analogous to those of limestone, and resemble them also in their geological relations; we may therefore treat them briefly. (See Sterry Hunt, in Report of Brit. Association for 1860.)

Varieties in Texture.

(*a*) GRANULAR DOLOMITE.
KÖRNIGER DOLOMIT. (*Germ.*)
DOLOMIE SACCHAROÏDE. (*Fr.*)
Closely resembles granular limestones, sometimes however saccharoid, consisting of small rhombohedrons, sometimes crumbling into dolomite sand; usually more porous than limestone. Frequently penetrated by geodes and cavities. Its accessory ingredients are similar to those of limestone, perhaps more abundant and multifarious.

Granular dolomites are more frequently associated with distinctly sedimentary rocks than are the granular limestones.

(*b*) COMPACT DOLOMITE.
DICHTER DOLOMIT. (*Germ.*)
DOLOMIE COMPACTE. (*Fr.*)
Difficult to distinguish from compact limestone, perhaps more rare. Accessory admixtures and varieties of composition are probably the same.

(*c*) EARTHY DOLOMITE.
ERDIGER DOLOMIT. (*Germ.*)
DOLOMIE GROSSIÈRE. (*Fr.*)
Usually rougher to the feel than earthy limestone, probably owing to its microscopically small rhombohedral crystals. If it be grey, which is sometimes the case, by reason of its accessory ingredients, then it is sometimes called dolomitic sand.

(*d*) POROUS DOLOMITE.
PORÖSER DOLOMIT. (*Germ.*)

(*e*) CELLULAR DOLOMITE.
ZELLIGER DOLOMIT (RAUHWACKE). (*Germ.*)
CARGNEULE. (*Fr.*)
With angular cavities.

(*f*) BRECCIAN DOLOMITE, or
DOLOMITE BRECCIA.
DOLOMITBRECCIE. (*Germ.*)
BRÈCHE DOLOMITIQUE. (*Fr.*)
Corresponds with limestone breccia (p. 281, ante).

(*g*) CONCRETIONARY DOLOMITE.
DOLOMIE CONCRÉTIONNÉE. (*Fr.*)
Consisting of a number of balls touching each other either like bunches of grapes (when it is called botryoidal), or like musket-balls, or great piles of cannonshot. Many of these balls when broken open are found to have a radiated structure. But

they have been produced subsequently to the deposition of the mass, as is shown by the fact of the lines of stratification proceeding through them regularly. (Jukes.)

Dolomite is seldom oolitic, slaty, fibrous, or stylolotic, or at all events, such varieties are much more rare than in limestone.

The calcareous dolomite is very similar to the dolomitic limestone. The two may be said to meet half way. The argillaceous, bituminous, micaceous, siliceous, arenaceous, ferruginous, and carbonaceous varieties, correspond with the similar varieties of limestone.

Three crystalline varieties of dolomite must, however, be mentioned.

Varieties in Composition.

(*h*) CHROMIC DOLOMITE. CHROM DOLOMIT. (*Germ.*) Is the name given by Breithaupt to a compound of dolomite, chromite, and oxide of chromium, occurring at Nischne-Tagilk in the Ural, and valued as a marble on account of its beautiful green colour. The chromite appears in the form of delicate grains or crystals, the green oxide of chromium appears to form thin laminæ. This beautiful rock also contains some iron pyrites and native gold, and appears to be penetrated by manifold veins of quartz.

(*i*) DOLOMITE OF THE BINNEN THAL (ALPS). This dolomite occurs with very rich combination of various minerals. According to Hugard, it is somewhat phosphorescent in the dark. It contains the following minerals—pyrites, quartz, much mica, orthoclase, tourmaline, tremolite, chiastolite, garnet, ruby, realgar, orpiment, blende, antimony-glance, dufrénite, binnite, celestine, barytes, and calcspar. (Compt. rend. 1858, vol. xlvi. p. 1261; v. L. u. Br. Jahrb. 1858, p. 591.)

(*k*) PREDAZZITE (*from Predazzo, in Tyrol*). PREDAZZIT. (*Germ.*) PREDAZZITE. (*Fr.*) Is the name given by Petzold to a dolomite occurring at Predazzo, in South Tyrol. It adjoins syenite-granite, of which it is a metamorphic product. It is white and crystalline-granular, resembling the most beautiful marble. Besides carbonate of lime and magnesia, it contains some siliceous clay and some water. Hence Petzold called it a special mineral: probably it is a compound of dolomite and brucite. (v. L. u. Br. Jahrb. 1848, p. 583.)

Geological Varieties.

(1) CORALLINE DOLOMITE. KORALLENDOLOMIT. (*Germ.*) DOLOMIE CORALLIENNE. (*Fr.*) Jura formation in England and Germany.

(2) ALPINE DOLOMITE. DOLOMIE ALPINE (CARGNEULES). (*Fr.*) Chief dolomite of the Northern Alps, corresponding with the lower part of the Lias formation.

(3) KEUPER DOLOMITE. KEUPERDOLOMIT. (*Germ.*) In the Keuper of Germany.

(4) FLAMMEN DOLOMITE. FLAMMENDOLOMIT. (*Germ.*) DOLOMIE ROUGE. (*Fr.*) In the Keuper of Swabia.

U

(5) MYOPHORIA DOLOMITE. } In the lower division of the
    MYOPHORIEN-DOLOMIT. (*Germ.*) Keuper formation.

(6) MALBSTEIN or NAGELFELS (*Germ.*). A dolomite of the upper
    division of the Muschelkalk, in Swabia.

(7) WELLENDOLOMIT (wavy dolomite), belonging to the lower divi-
    sion of the Muschelkalk, in Germany.

(8) MAGNESIAN LIMESTONE. } A dolomite limestone of the Per-
    CALCAIRE MAGNÉSIEN. (*Fr.*) mian formation in England.

(9) ZECHSTEIN DOLOMITE. } In Thuringia and
    ZECHSTEIN-DOLOMIT, RAUHWACKE. (*Germ*). Franken.

(10) DOLOMITIC SAND. } In the Zechstein of Thuringia.
     DOLOMIT-ASCHE. (*Germ.*)

Many different varieties of dolomite are known in the Carboniferous system, or occur in the Cambrian, Silurian, Devonian, and Permian formations. The dolomite of Derbyshire,
Durham, and Yorkshire in the latter formation furnishes the
well-known building-stone of which the Houses of Parliament
are built. In the more recent formations, dolomite would
appear to be less frequent, unless it be that many compact dolomites are still mistaken for limestones.

Much has been written on the formation of dolomites since
the first celebrated treatise on that subject of L. v. Buch, in
Leonhard's Almanack, 1824. Of the various arguments in
favour of the transmutation of limestone into dolomite, perhaps
the most deserving attention is the hypothesis developed by
Haidinger and v. Morlot, according to which the conversion
was effected by means of solutions of sulphate of magnesia
(Epsom salt), and gypsum was produced at the same time.
In many cases this is very probable. (Haidinger's Naturw.
Abhandl. vol. i.) To us it appears very probable that many
dolomites have been formed by crystallisation of coral-reefs, as
v. Richthofen has ably proved in the case of some of the
dolomites of Southern Tyrol. Vide MM. Seemann and Guyerdot,
Bullet. de la Soc. géol. de France, (n. s.) vol. xix. p. 095, 1862.

GYPSUM AND ANHYDRITE.

Gypsum is a combination of sulphate of lime with
water. Anhydrite is sulphate of lime without water.

Gypsum as a rock is much more frequent than anhydrite—at least we seldom find anhydrite on the surface
of the earth—a circumstance which is explained by its
readiness to absorb water, and consequent conversion into
gypsum. For the rest, the geological position of the two
is very similar. ·

37. GYPSUM.

GYPS. (*Germ.*)
GYPSE. (*Fr.*)

*An aggregate of sulphate of lime, usually crystalline,
sometimes compact or fibrous; soft, and usually white.*

Spec. grav. . . . : . . . . 2·3.

Pure gypsum consists of 46·5 per cent. sulphuric acid, 32·5 lime, and 21 water. It is so soft that it may be scratched with the nail, and only gives a dead sound when struck with the hammer. By these properties it may be most easily distinguished from white granular limestone, to which it bears great resemblance. Its texture is most usually fine-grained (alabaster), sometimes also porphyritic, containing large shining crystals of selenite. It is only rarely quite compact; in thin layers or narrow veins it is frequently fibrous or sparry. Its original snow-white colour is sometimes tinged grey by admixture of bitumen or clay, or red by oxide of iron. The mass sometimes (though rarely) contains as accessories some mica, talc, quartz, boracite, pyrites, copper pyrites, grey copper, zincblende, and sulphur.

Moreover, in gypsum rock are sometimes found nests or veins of aphrite, anhydrite, rock-salt, sulphur, and chert.

The weathered surfaces of gypsum (owing to its solubility in water) are usually much worn or eaten into.

Varieties in Texture.

(a) GRANULAR GYPSUM or ALABASTER. KÖNNIGER GYPS oder ALABASTER. (*Germ.*) GYPSE SACCHAROÏDE. (*Fr.*) } Almost always white, somewhat translucent.

(b) PORPHYRITIC GYPSUM. PORPHYRARTIGER GYPS. (*Germ.*) } With crystals of gypsum in a fine-grained gypsum matrix.

(c) COMPACT GYPSUM. DICHTER GYPS. (*Germ.*) GYPSE COMPACTE. (*Fr.*) } Rare, usually mixed with clay or bitumen, which impart a grey colour to the rock.

(d) FIBROUS GYPSUM. FASERGYPS. (*Germ.*) GYPSE FIBREUX. (*Fr.*) } Usually only in the form of thin veins or seams occurring in other gypsum, or in argillaceous shale or marl.

(e) SPATHIC or SPARRY GYPSUM, or SELENITE. SPÄTHIGER GYPS oder BLÄTTERGYPS. (*Germ.*). GYPSE LAMINAIRE. (*Fr.*) } Occurs in similar manner to the fibrous variety.

(f) TRIPESTONE. GEKRÖSESTEIN. (*Germ.*) PIERRE DE TRIPES. (*Fr.*) } Is a variety both of texture and composition. It is formed of thin layers of pure white gypsum, alternating with grey argillaceous gypsum, the whole twisted or crumpled to resemble a ruff, whence the German name.

Varieties in Composition.

(g) ARGILLACEOUS GYPSUM. THONGYPS. (*Germ.*) MARNE GYPSEUSE. (*Fr.*) } Grey, spotted, or striped, by reason of an admixture of clay.

(*h*) BITUMINOUS GYPSUM.   ⎫ Difficult to distinguish from the
    BITUMINÖSER GYPS. (*Germ.*) ⎬ last-named variety.
    GYPSE BITUMINEUX. (*Fr.*)   ⎭
(*i*) MICACEOUS GYPSUM.   ⎫ Mixed with mica or talc; analogous to
    GLIMMERGYPS. (*Germ.*)   ⎬ micaceous limestone; of rare occur-
    GYPSE NIVIFORME. (*Fr.*)   ⎭ rence, and only in strata of crystalline
    schists, as (e.g.) on the south slope of the St. Gotthard.

Gypsum is rarely distinctly stratified or fossiliferous; both facts are in all probability connected with the mode of its original formation, pointing to a chemical rather than mechanical origin. It is contained in deposits of the most different periods, and exceptionally in the crystalline schist formations. It seldom forms extensive beds parallel to the other strata, but rather flat lenticular or irregular masses or accumulations in connection with anhydrite, rock-salt, and clay, or sometimes with dolomite. Sometimes it even occurs in abnormal bedding between other sedimentary rocks. From the circumstances under which it is found to occur, it has been inferred that gypsum must be a product of the local conversion of limestone. Chemically, no doubt, this would be possible, if the requisite sulphuric acid were present, but such origin on a large scale is not capable of demonstration from any known facts. Some gypsum rocks may be actually shown to have been formed by deposit from aqueous solution of sulphate of lime; others by the decomposition of pyrites in the immediate neighbourhood of calcspar; others, again, by the absorption of water into anhydrite. Haidinger and Von Morlot have also shown that gypsum and dolomite may together be formed by the operation of solutions of sulphate of magnesia (Epsom salt) on limestone; nevertheless all these different facts or theories of possible formation hardly suffice to account satisfactorily for the origin of the great masses of gypsum (frequently combined with rock-salt and anhydrite) which occur in the flotz or secondary series. The supposed origin of gypsum from anhydrite leaves the greater difficulty unsolved of the original deposit of anhydrous sulphate of lime.

The exceptional nature of the bedding of gypsum rocks, as well as the frequent disturbances which appear in the adjoining strata, are best explained by the action of water in partially washing away the original deposit of gypsum, and also the rock-salt with which it is usually accompanied. The first consequences of such process would be to form great cavities; after a time the roofs of these cavities would break down and cause disruption in the super-incumbent rocks. This is to us the most probable mode of accounting for the existing phenomena. Certain it is that these disturbances of the neighbouring strata are not of a nature to authorise us to infer an eruptive origin of the gypsum rock.

The gypsum beds of different geological periods have not received different names, as they are not petrographically to be distinguished from each other. It may nevertheless be of interest to compare the different places of their occurrence in the European geological series. These are chiefly as follows:—

(1) In Miocene deposits, with remains of plants at Paris, in Italy—with sulphur and rock-salt in Sicily.
(2) In Eocene deposits, with bones of animals, in the Paris basin.
(3) In the Triassic formations of the French and Swiss Alps with rock-salt and cargneule (*Lory, Favre,* &c.)
(4) In the Keuper of Germany, sometimes with rock-salt, but without fossils.
(5) In the Muschelkalk of Germany, with anhydrite and rock-salt, without fossils.
(6) In the Upper Variegated Sandstone of Germany and the Alps, with rock-salt and anhydrite, without fossils.
(7) In the New Red Sandstone of England, with rock-salt, without fossils.
(8) In the Zechstein of Germany, with rock-salt and anhydrite, without fossils.
(9) In the Permian formations of Russia, with rock-salt.
(10) In the clay-mica-schist of Herren-Grund, in Hungary (of undoubted antiquity), with fahlerz and copper pyrites.
(11) In the crystalline schists of the Alps at St. Gotthard, with mica; at Bugg, in Switzerland, with mica and talc.

References.

Hausmann, Bemerkungen über Gyps und Karstenit, 1847.
Karsten, über Gyps und Karstenit in his Archiv, 1848, vol. xxii. pp. 545 and 578.

38. ANHYDRITE, MURIACITE, KARSTENITE.

ANHYDRIT, MURIACIT, KARSTENIT. (*Germ.*)
ANHYDRITE. (*Fr.*)

A granular or compact aggregate of anhydrous sulphate of lime ; harder than gypsum ; white, grey, or blue.

Spec. grav. . . . . 2·8—2·9.

Pure anhydrite is white, and may easily be mistaken for gypsum or dolomite. It may, however, be easily distinguished from dolomite by its not effervescing with acid even when pulverised and heated; and it is much harder than gypsum. The colour of the grey or blue varieties is caused by the admixture of clay or bitumen in small quantities. There are scarcely any distinct varieties of texture. It occurs in nature under similar relations to gypsum, except that it is scarcely ever met with on the surface of the ground, because there, by the absorption of water, it is converted into gypsum.

For literary references refer to those under the head of gypsum.

FRAGMENTAL ROCKS.

These rocks are composed of the fragments of older rocks, which have been broken up by mechanical forces, and their parts deposited and reunited or cemented together into a solid mass; they are therefore termed fragmental rocks.

A somewhat similar origin may no doubt be ascribed to the argillaceous rocks, marls, and some limestones, but in this case the parent rocks have undergone chemical decomposition, as well as mechanical disintegration, and the disintegrated parts have been resolved into very fine mud before the work of reconstruction commenced, so that the connection of the new rocks thus formed with those from which they spring is not so evident or easily traceable as in the fragmental rocks proper.

SANDSTONES consist of grains of some mineral (usually quartz) compacted together; CONGLOMERATES of rounded stones or pebbles cemented together; BRECCIAS of angular fragments likewise bound.

Uncompacted SAND, GRAVEL, SHINGLE, and HEAPS OF RUBBISH belong to this division of the materials of which the earth's crust is composed.

TUFA rocks are conglomerates, more or less firmly united, of fragments thrown from volcanoes of the present or an earlier time.

39. SANDSTONE and GRITSTONE.

SANDSTEIN, PSAMMIT. (*Germ.*)
GRÈS. (*Fr.*)

Small grains of some mineral, usually of quartz, are cemented together by some mineral substance.

The process of the original formation of all sandstones has consisted jn the washing together of small grains of some solid mineral, usually quartz, and these were afterwards bound together into a solid rock by some cementing medium, or perhaps by simple pressure. In other words, these rocks were formed from sand, into which they may be resolved again. The grains are usually rounded off, and only exceptionally exhibit faces and edges of crystals.

Quartz being the most abundant mineral of the earth, and at the same time very hard and difficult of decomposition, furnishes the material for the most sandstones ; these, however, also contain particles of felspar, flakes of mica, fragments of shells, and grains of glauconite. The binding medium of these grains usually consists of clay, marl, or hydrated oxide of iron ; less usually of silica, carbonate of lime, kaolin, talc, or asphalte. Sandstones often contain as accessories concretions of hydrated oxide of iron, frequently in the form of balls (eagle stones *) or irregular masses, nodules of pyrites, rounded pieces of amber, coal, and the like.

As all sandstones are mechanical aqueous deposits, they are always stratified. They frequently are interstratified with other rocks in alternate beds, such, for instance, as clay-slate, argillaceous shale, marl, &c. They belong to no exclusive geological period, but are found in those of most various age.

Varieties in Texture.

(*a*) COMMON SANDSTONE. } With grains about the size of a
   GEMEINER SANDSTEIN. (*Germ.*) } mustard-seed.

---

* ' " Eagle stone," the Ætites lapis of the ancients, fabled to have been laid in the nest of the eagle. A variety of nodular argillaceous iron-ore, having a concentric structure and occasionally so decomposed within as to have a loose kernel which rattles on being shaken. This kernel was known by the name of Callimus, and was supposed to be the young in the womb of the parent nodule ; hence the fable of the ætites bringing forth young. When there is no internal kernel the nodule becomes a geode.'—*Page.*

(b) COARSE-GRAINED SANDSTONE.
GROBKÖRNIGER SANDSTEIN. (Germ.)
GRÈS À GROS GRAINS. (Fr.)
} Passing into conglomerate.

(c) FINE-GRAINED SANDSTONE.
FEINKÖRNIGER SANDSTEIN oder
FEINSANDSTEIN. (Germ.)
GRÈS À GRAINS FINS. (Fr.)
} Or fine sandstone, passing into an apparently compact state.

(d) CRYSTALLISED SANDSTONE.
KRYSTALLSANDSTEIN. (Germ.)
GRÈS CRISTALLIN. (Fr.)
} With grains of quartz-crystals on which the crystalline faces may be recognised.

In all these sandstones the texture varies not only in respect of the size of the grains, but in respect of their quantity or abundance compared with that of the cementing medium. Some sandstones, owing to the predominance of the latter, pass into rocks of a totally different character, such as marl, claystone, &c.

(e) FISSILE SANDSTONE.
SCHIEFRIGER SANDSTEIN oder
SANDSTEINSCHIEFER. (Germ.)
GRÈS FISSILE. (Fr.)
} Flagstone in part; usually owes its texture to a plentiful admixture of mica.

(f) GLOBULAR SANDSTONE.
KUGELSANDSTEIN. (Germ.)
GRÈS NODULEUX. (Fr.)
} With ball-shaped concretions of compact or firm sandstone in a matrix of more friable structure. In Transylvania very extensively developed.

According to differences in the nature of the cementing material, we have the following varieties :—

(g) ARGILLACEOUS SANDSTONE.
THONIGER SANDSTEIN oder THON-
SANDSTEIN. (Germ.)
GRÈS ARGILEUX. (Fr.)
} The most frequent variety. If the clay predominates, it passes into arenaceous clay, argillaceous shale, or clay-shale.

(h) MARLY SANDSTONE.
MERGELIGER SANDSTEIN oder
MERGELSANDSTEIN. (Germ.)
GRÈS MARNEUX. (Fr.)
} The next most frequent variety. If the marl predominates, then it passes into arenaceous marl or marl-shale.

(i) CALCAREOUS SANDSTONE.
KALKIGER SANDSTEIN oder KALK-
SANDSTEIN. (Germ.)
GRÈS CALCARIFÈRE. (Fr.)
} With a calcareous cementing medium; somewhat rare; passes into arenaceous limestone.

(k) SILICEOUS SANDSTONE.
KIESELSANDSTEIN. (Germ.)
GRÈS SILICEUX. (Fr.)
} With a very solid hornstone-like cementing material, in which the individual grains of quartz are finely imbedded and are frequently not to be distinctly recognised. When these grains are intimately blended with the matrix, then this variety of sandstone passes into quartzite, quartz-rock, or a kind of hornstone.

(l) FERRUGINOUS SANDSTONE.
EISENSANDSTEIN oder EISENSCHÜSSIGER
SANDSTEIN. (Germ.)
GRÈS FERRUGINEUX. (Fr.)
} A sandstone with hydrated oxide of iron, or peroxide of iron, as its cementing material, which always gives the rock a red or brown colour. Sometimes it is spotted or

striped from the unequal distribution of the iron (Tiger Sand-stein, *Germ.*; Tiger sandstone, *Engl.*). If the hydrated oxide of iron should become predominant, as is sometimes the case, then we even find transitions into brown hæmatite.

(*m*) KAOLIN SANDSTONE.   } With kaolin as cementing medium;
KAOLINSANDSTEIN. (*Germ.*) } almost always white. Occurs, e. g., at Wissenfels in Thuringia. If sandstones of this description contain only quartz and kaolin, they form very fine fire-proof stones, and may be used for lining furnaces; e. g. Steinhaide, in the Thuringian Forest.

(*n*) TALCOSE SANDSTONE.   } With a talcose cementing medium.
TALKSANDSTEIN. (*Germ.*) } This variety approaches in character
GRÈS TALQUEUX. (*Fr.*) } to itacolumite, which, as we have already seen, is a kind of sandstone (vide p. 247, ante).

(*o*) ASPHALTIC SANDSTONE.   } With asphalte as cementing me-
ASPHALTSANDSTEIN. (*Germ.*) } dium, a variety only of exceptional
GRÈS BITUMINEUX. (*Fr.*) } occurrence.

NOTE. — It is frequently very difficult to determine the exact nature of the cementing medium, especially as two or more kinds often occur together in the same rock.

According to differences in the nature and substance of which the grains themselves are composed, we have the following varieties :—

(*p*) QUARTZ-SANDSTONE. QUARTZ- } (The quartz-psammit of Nau-
PSAMMIT. QUARTZ-GRIT. } mann.) With grains of quartz.
QUARZSANDSTEIN. (*Germ.*) } This is the most frequent of
GRÈS QUARTZEUX. (*Fr.*) } all sandstones.

(*q*) MICACEOUS SANDSTONE. MICACEOUS GRIT. } (The mico-psammit
GLIMMERSANDSTEIN. MICO-PSAMMIT, *Naumann.* } of Naumann.) Con-
(*Germ.*) } taining flakes of
PSAMMITE (GRÈS MICACÉ), *Brongniart.* (*Fr.*) } mica with the grains of quartz.

(*r*) ARKOSE or FELSPATHIC SANDSTONE. } With grains of felspar as
ARKOSE. (*Germ.*) } well as quartz, combined
ARKOSE. (*Fr.*) } in some cases with flakes of mica. This rock thus resembles granite in its composition, and is therefore sometimes called Regenerated granite.

(*s*) GREEN SANDSTONE (GREENSAND). } Containing grains of glauco-
GRÜNSANDSTEIN. (*Germ.*) } nite with quartz, imparting
GRÈS VERT. (*Fr.*) } a more or less green colour to the whole rock, sometimes even a dark-green colour. According to Ehrenberg's microscopic analysis, these glauconite grains usually consist of the fossils of very minute Testacea.

(*t*) SHELL-SANDSTONE. } Coral sandstone: the grains are fragments
MUSCHELSANDSTEIN. } of shells or coral; the cementing mate-
(*Germ.*) } rial carbonate of lime. Rare.
GRÈS COQUILLIER. (*Fr.*) }

The difference between sandstone and gritstone is a vague and undeterminable one, as must necessarily be the case where the things themselves are so various and capricious in composition and texture. The term gritstone is, perhaps, most applicable to the harder sandstones, which consist most entirely of grains of quartz, most firmly compacted together by the most purely siliceous cement. The angularity of the particles cannot be taken as a character, since the rock commonly called 'millstone grit' is generally composed of perfectly round grains, sometimes as large as peas and even larger; the stone then commencing to pass into a conglomerate.'— *Jukes.*

Jukes gives the following local terms for sandstone:—

Rock, used generally in South Staffordshire to denote any hard sandstone.

. Rotche or *Roche,* generally used for a softer and more friable stone.

Rubble means either loose angular gravel, or a slightly compacted brecciated sandstone.

Hazel is a North of England term for a hard grit.

Post is a similar term for any bed of firm rock, and is usually applied to sandstone.

Peldon is a South Staffordshire term for a hard, smooth, flinty grit.

Calliard or *Galliard* is a northern term for a similar rock.

Freestone is a term in general use which is often applied to sandstones, but sometimes to limestones and even to granite, as in the counties of Dublin and Wicklow. It means any stone which works equally freely in any direction, or has no tendency to split in one direction more than another.

Flagstone (see ante, p. 296), on the contrary, means a stone which splits more freely in one direction than any other, that direction being along the lines of the original deposition of the rock. These stones are ordinarily sandstones, though often very argillaceous, and some flagstones are perhaps rather indurated clay in their beds than sandstone.

Thin-bedded limestones may also be flagstones.

Independently of the different petrographic varieties of sandstone, we have numerous geological varieties. These must always be determined by their bedding or by their fossils; and they are frequently only local in their character.

(1) THE MOST RECENT MARINE SANDSTONE. NEUESTER MEERESSANDSTEIN. (*Germ.*) } Which on some coasts is still in process of formation.

(2) BLÄTTERSANDSTEIN (*Germ.*), containing impressions of leaves of trees; occurs in the Mayence Tertiary basin.

(3) MOLASSE SANDSTONE. | A sandstone of the Molasse forma-
MOLASSESANDSTEIN. (*Germ.*) | tion on the northern margin of the
GRÈS MOLASSE. (*Fr.*) | Alps; usually grey.

(4) BROWNCOAL SANDSTONE. | Sandstone of the Browncoal
BRAUNKOHLENSANDSTEIN. (*Germ.*) | formation in Bohemia and
Northern Germany. Miocene, Frequently siliceous sandstone.

(5) BAGSHOT SAND, in England. Eocene.

(6) THANET SAND, in England. Eocene.

(7) VIENNA SAND. | Partly Eocene, partly older.
WIENER SANDSTEIN. (*Germ.*)

(8) CARPATHIAN SANDSTONE. | Partly Eocene, partly older.
KARPATHENSANDSTEIN. (*Germ.*)

(9) FUCOIDAL SANDSTONE. | With remains of Fucoids.
FUCOIDENSANDSTEIN. (*Germ.*) |
GRÈS À FUCOÏDES. (*Fr.*)

(10) NUMMULITIC SANDSTONE. | Containing remains of Num-
NUMMULITENSANDSTEIN. (*Germ.*) | mulites.
GRÈS NUMMULITHIQUE. (*Fr.*)

(11) RALLIGSANDSTEIN (*Germ.*). A sandstone of Switzerland. Eocene.

(12) TAVIGLIANAZ SANDSTONE. | The like. Eocene.
TAVIGLIANAZ-SANDSTEIN. (*Germ.*)

(13) MACIGNO. | In North Italy. Eocene, or older.
MACIGNO. (*Germ.*) |
MACIGNO. (*Fr.*)

(14) QUADER SANDSTONE. | So called on account of its rectan-
QUADERSANDSTEIN. (*Germ.*) | gular jointings. In conjunction with
the pläner limestone, with which it is associated and interstratified, it forms a part of the Chalk group in Saxony and
Bohemia.

(15) GREENSAND (UPPER AND LOWER). | These constitute two di-
GRÜNSAND. (*Germ.*) | visions of the cretaceous
GRÈS VERT (SUPÉRIEUR ET INFÉRIEUR). | group in England.
(*Fr.*)

(16) HILS SANDSTONE. | The lowest member of the Chalk group
HILSSANDSTEIN. (*Germ.*) | in Westphalia.

(17) TASELLO. | A sandstone of the Chalk period in Istria.
TASELLO. (*Germ.*)

(18) DEISTER SANDSTONE. | Westphalia, belonging to the Weal-
DEISTERSANDSTEIN. (*Germ.*) | den formation.

(19) HASTINGS SAND, England. Wealden formation.

(20) PORTLAND SAND. Upper Oolite formation of England.

(21) DOGGER (*Germ.*). A coarse-grained sandstone, brown, sometimes very argillaceous. Whitby, Yorkshire. Westphalia.
Jura formation.

(22) LIAS SANDSTONE AND SAND. | Usually light-yellow and fine-
LEIASANDSTEIN. (*Germ.*) | grained. A lower member of
GRÈS LIASIQUE. (*Fr.*) | the Lias, at Gotha. An upper
member of the Lias of England.

(23) CARDINIA SANDSTONE. | Containing many Thalassites
THALASSITEN-SANDSTEIN. [(*Germ.*) | (*Cardinia*).

(24) KEUPER SANDSTONE. | Germany, frequent.
KEUPERSANDSTEIN. (*Germ.*)

(25) SCHILF SANDSTONE. | A member of the Upper Keuper in
SCHILFSANDSTEIN. (*Germ.*) | Swabia.

(26) VARIEGATED SANDSTONE. So called on account of its being
BUNTSANDSTEIN. (*Germ.*) frequently particoloured. It is,
GRÈS BIGARRÉ. (*Fr.*) however, sometimes of one uniform
colour (white, yellow, or red). It constitutes the chief member of the Buntsandstein formation of Germany.

(27) VOSGES SANDSTONE. Lower division of the Sandstone
VOGESENSANDSTEIN. (*Germ.*) formation of the Vosges Mountains.
GRÈS VOSGIEN. (*Fr.*)

(28) RED SANDSTONE OF THE ALPS Corresponds with the Varie-
(VERRUCANO). gated Sandstone of Germany
ROTHER ALPENSANDSTEIN. (*Germ.*) and the New Red Sandstone
GRÈS ROUGE DES ALPES. (*Fr.*) of England.

(29) NEW RED SANDSTONE. Name applied in England to the whole
series of strata lying between the Lias and the Permian rocks.

(30) NEWENT SANDSTONE. A member of the Keuper series of
Gloucestershire.

(31) WEISS- oder GRAULIEGENDES. (*Germ.*) A White or Grey
Sandstone (frequently conglomeratic), forming the lowest member of the Zechstein in Thuringia, and sometimes containing
copper-ore (Sanderz).

(32) CUPRIFEROUS SANDSTONE. A member of the Permian forma-
KUPFERSANDSTEIN. (*Germ.*) tion in Russia. Old Red Sand-
GRÈS CUPRIFÈRE. (*Fr.*) stone of south of Ireland.

(33) ROTHER SANDSTEIN. (*Germ.*) Former designation for the Rothliegende formation, containing arkose and other sandstones,
usually of red colour.

(34) CARBONIFEROUS SANDSTONE. White, brown, yellow, grey,
KOHLENSANDSTEIN. (*Germ.*) or almost black, in which case
GRÈS HOUILLER. (*Fr.*) it contains carbon. Frequent
in the Carboniferous strata of old countries.

(35) MILLSTONE GRIT. Lowest member of the Coal
FLÖTZLEERER SANDSTEIN. (*Germ.*) formation sometimes.
MEULIÈRE. (*Fr.*)

(36) GREYWACKÉ SANDSTONE. Usually very firm, with ar-
GRAUWACKEN-SANDSTEIN, oder KÖR- gillaceous cementing medium.
NIGE GRAUWACKE. (*Germ.*) When very fine-grained, or
VIEUX GRÈS ROUGE. (*Fr.*) almost thick, it has been
called grauwacké or quartzite; sometimes it is very coarse-
grained, even conglomeratic. If the clay medium should
become slaty, then it goes over into greywacké-schist. It is
frequent in Devonian formations. Delesse, however, appears
to have understood something different in the Vosges under
the term of greywacké, since he says that it consists almost
entirely of albite, forming a felspathic matrix, containing
quartz, hornblende, several kinds of mica, chlorite, and occasionally some carbonates. Ann. des Mines, vol. iii. p. 747;
v. L. u. Br. Jahrb. 1856, p. 359.

(37) BAGGY POINT SANDSTONE (*Page*). Upper Devonian.

(38) DURA-DEN SANDSTONES, Fifeshire (*Page*), with *Holoptychii*
and *Pterichthys*. Upper Devonian.

(39) DUNSE SANDSTONES, Scotland (*Page*). Red and white. Upper
Devonian.

(40) FLAGSTONES OF FORFAR, with *Cephalaspis*, *Cheiracanthus*, and
Pterygotus. Lower Devonian.

(41) LUDLOW SANDSTONE, micaceous, grey. Upper Silurian.
(42) WENLOCK SANDSTONE, Upper Llandovery; gritty. Upper Silurian.
(43) CARADOC SANDSTONE, frequently quartzite. Lower Silurian.
(44) LLANDEILO and LINGULA FLAGS, laminated sandstone, rich in mica. Lower Silurian.
(45) STIPER STONES, Shropshire; siliceous sandstones, passing into quartz rock. Cambrian.

We will cite a few treatises only as to sandstone, relating to special varieties.

References.

Gerhard draws attention to the fact that the grains of quartz are angular and transparent in many sandstones. Abhandl. d. berl. Akad. 1816–17, p. 13.

Schafthäutl found grains of amorphous silica in sandstone. v. Leonhard's Jahrb. 1846, p. 648.

Zeuschner, Schafthäutl, and *v. Hauer,* on Carbonate of Lime and Magnesia as connecting Media. v. Leonhard's Jahrb. 1843, p. 166; 1846, p. 665; and Jahrb. d. geol. Reichsanst. vol. v. p. 880.

Gutberlet published a treatise on the crystalline sandstones formed between the Vogelsgebirge and the Rhön, in v. Leonhard's u. Br. Jahrb. 1811, p. 860.

Ehrenberg, on Greensand, Berlin, 1856, in v. L. u. Br. Jahrb. 1855, p. 469; and 1857, p. 91.

Bischof considers the mica of the sandstone as a recent formation. Geologie, vol. ii. p. 1450.

Appendix.

This seems the most appropriate place in which to introduce the mention of loose sand, which consists of incoherent grains of quartz, or other mineral, and to a certain extent is a necessary preliminary state to the formation of all sandstone.

SAND.

SAND. (*Germ.*)
SABLE. (*Fr.*)

Usually grains of quartz, sometimes, however, of other minerals, e. g. felspar, dolomite, calcspar, mica, and the like; without binding medium.

These loose aggregates of mineral grains need no further description, although they may vary considerably in the size as well as the substance of their individual particles. A certain coarse sand is called grit.

Sand sometimes derives a special importance from admixture of metallic grains or precious stones; these, however, only occur locally, and are subordinate in quantity; thus, for instance,

sand is found to contain grains of gold, platinum, tin-ore, magnetic iron-ore, diamond, zircon, hyacinth, topaz, emerald, garnet,
pyrope, &c. It is worthy of remark that such admixtures are
almost unknown, except in the newest incoherent aggregates
of sand or clay (stream beds), very seldom in solid sandstone.
It may be, however, that solid sandstones do contain similar
ingredients, and only that .they have been less subjected to investigation than the loose superficial sand. Traces of gold
have been actually found, e.g. in the Molasse sandstone of
Switzerland, and again, some tin-ore has been discovered in a
sandstone of Brittany.

CONGLOMERATES.

40. CONGLOMERATE, PUDDINGSTONE.

Conglomerat, Pouddingstein. (*Germ.*)
Conglomérat, Poudingue. (*Fr.*)

*Pebbles or rounded stones of any mineral or rock firmly
cemented together by media of various kinds.*

Conglomerates are of very various composition. Almost the only restriction to the nature of their materials is
that pebbles can only consist of a very firm substance
capable of resisting decomposing influences. Their binding medium usually consists of some of the most frequent
and abundant of the earth's materials, such as clay, sand,
quartz, or oxide of iron. The pebbles chiefly consist of
quartz, lydian-stone, granite, gneiss, mica-schist, quartz-
porphyry, greenstone, basalt, compact limestone, and the
like; much more rarely of sandstone, clay-slate, argillaceous shale, coal, and the like.

A special geological importance attaches to conglomerates, from the fact that they must in every case be more
recent than the rocks whence their pebbles were derived.
Thus they often serve to determine the relative age of
individual rocks. By noting the position of the parent
rocks, the geologist is often enabled to draw conclusions
as to the course and direction of former watercourses.
Again, they often present interesting phenomena pointing
to certain special processes in their formation. For
instance, the pebbles are sometimes broken or dislocated,
their parts remaining imbedded close together; or the
pebbles are found marked with grooves and scratches;
or they are sometimes indented and forced one into

another (which latter case is the most difficult of explanation). There is a conglomerate at St. Loretta in the Leitha Mountains, of exceptional character, containing hollow limestone pebbles, the inside cavities of which are concentric with the outside surface.

It is difficult to classify conglomerates, on account of their manifold variety. We can, of course, speak of more or less coarse textures—we may also designate them according to the nature of their principal pebbles, or the character of their binding medium. Some examples will suffice to explain how such a mode of nomenclature might be adapted to individual cases. Taking the nature of the pebbles as the distinguishing feature, we may speak of quartz-conglomerate, porphyry-conglomerate, gneiss-conglomerate, or miscellaneous conglomerate; or, according to the character of the matrix, we may call the rock argillaceous, siliceous, ferruginous, &c.

The following are conglomerates which have been specially named from their bedding or geological position :—

(1) NAGELFLUE. *NAGELFLUHE. (Germ.) CONGLOMÉRAT ALPIN. (Fr.)* A conglomerate of the Molasse formation on the northern margin of the Alps, the pebbles chiefly consisting of Alpine limestone, but partly of quartz, lydite, granite, gneiss, &c.

(2) PLÄNERCONGLOMERAT (*Germ.*) in Saxony belongs to the Quadersandstone, with pebbles of granite, syenite, or quartz-porphyry bound together by sandstone cement.

(3) HILSCONGLOMERAT (*Germ.*), with limestone and ironstone pebbles, and likewise many remains of shells, occurring in the lower division of the Hils formation of Westphalia.

(4) VOSGES CONGLOMERATE. *CONGLOMÉRAT VOSGIEN. (Fr.)* Lower division of the variegated sandstone of the Vosges, with many pebbles of quartz and lydite.

(5) CONGLOMERATE OF THE WEISSLIEGENDE. *CONGLOMERAT DES WEISSLIEGENDEN. (Germ.),* In Thuringia, the lowest member of the Zechstein formation, with numerous pebbles of quartz, lydite, and clay-slate.

(6) CONGLOMERATE OF THE ROTHLIEGENDE. *CONGLOMERAT DES ROTHLIEGENDEN. (Germ.)* In Germany, with pebbles of quartz, lydite, granite, gneiss, mica-schist, and quartz-porphyry, and a cementing medium of ferruginous sand.

(7) GREY CONGLOMERATE. *GRAUES CONGLOMERAT. (Germ.)* Lowest member of the Rothliegende, in Saxony.

(8) CONGLOMERATE OF HAINICHEN. *CONGLOMERAT VON HAINICHEN. (Germ.)* In Saxony, answering to the Carboniferous Limestone formation; containing clay-slate, mica-schist, gneiss,

granulite, granite, and greenstone ; binding medium arenaceous and of brown colour.

(9) GREYWACKÉ CONGLOMERATE.   } At the Hartz, in Thuringia,
    GRAUWACKEN-CONGLOMERAT. *(Germ.)* } in Bohemia, and other places,
    GRAUWACKE GROSSIÈRE. *(Fr.)*   partly Devonian, partly Si-
lurian, with pebbles of quartz, lydite, clay-slate, granite, &c.
Binding medium argillaceous, or arenaceous, and of grey colour.

We should state that there are some so-called pudding-stones which have altogether the appearance of conglomerates, but, in fact, are not such, as they do not consist of pebbles cemented together, but they contain rounded concretions of some siliceous or calcareous substance.

We shall confine our references to some treatises containing mention of special phenomena.

References.

Haidinger, on the Lauretta Conglomerate, in Ber. d. k. k. Akad. d. Wissensch. zu Wien, 1856, July 15.

Lartet, on Pebbles showing Indentations, in v. L. u. Br. Jahrb. 1836, p. 196.

Blum, on the same, ibid. 1840, p. 525.

Daubrée, on the same, in Compt. rend. vol. xliv. p. 823.

Cotta, on the same, Geol. Fragen, 1858, p. 204, and on Ver-worfene Geschiebe in the same account, p. 212.

Würtenberger, on the same subject, in v. L. u. Br. Jahrb. 1859, p. 153.

Deicke, on the same subject, ibid. 1860, p. 219.

Gurlt, on the same subject, ibid. 1861, p. 225.

Appendix.

BOULDERS and PEBBLES.

GESCHIEBE und GERÖLLE. *(Germ.)*

These may consist of very various materials; and when united by a cementing medium, they form a conglomerate rock.

Erratic Blocks and *Boulders* are of especial geological importance ; they are sometimes only partially rounded, and they are dispersed over the earth's surface, far from their parent rocks.

They consist of very different kinds of rock, and have for the most part been transported to their present position by means of glaciers or of drift-ice.

41. BRECCIA.

BRECCIE. *(Germ.)*
BRÈCHE, BRECCIOLA, *Brongniart. (Fr.)*

A rock composed of angular fragments of minerals or solid rocks cemented or bound together by some matrix or binding medium. [BRECCIOLA *when the fragments are small.*]

Breccias, like conglomerates, may consist of the most various substances, both in their fragmental ingredients and their connecting medium, whence a similar richness in the number of varieties, which are too numerous and manifold to admit of classification. They must in each case be named according to the character of their ingredients—thus, quartz-breccia, gneiss-breccia, limestone-breccia, &c.—or according to the nature of their matrix, as in the case of conglomerates.

Breccias are geologically important, because in every case the fragmental parts must be of greater age than that of the rock itself; also because they indicate violent disruption of the rocks in their immediate neighbourhood, and from the circumstance that very angular fragments can never have travelled very far from the place of their original bedding.

The following kinds of breccia are noteworthy on geological grounds.

Geological Varieties.

(1) FRICTION BRECCIAS.
    REIBUNGSBRECCIEN. (*Germ.*)
    BRÊCHES DE FILON (DE FROTTEMENT). (*Fr.*)

These are breccias formed at the margin of eruptive igneous rocks at the time of their eruption; the matrix of the breccia consisting of the substance of the igneous rock, and the enclosed fragments being pieces of the rocks broken through. These breccias are very frequently found at the margin of porphyries, greenstones, basalts, trachytes, &c., and may be designated accordingly.

Simler has given the name of Metamixite to these contact formations. (Ueber Petrogenese, 1802.)

(2) QUARTZ-BRECCIA.
    QUARZBROCKENFELS. (*Germ.*)
    BRÊCHE SILICEUSE. (*Fr.*)

Consisting of fragments of quartz bound together by quartz or by ferruginous quartz. It very frequently occurs as the filling up of wide gaps or clefts in the crystalline schists, e.g. at Schwarzenfels in the Erzgebirge.

(3) BONE BRECCIA.
    KNOCHENBRECCIE. (*Germ.*)
    BRÊCHE À OSSEMENTS. (*Fr.*)

A breccia whose fragmental portions chiefly consist of fossil bones, frequently found in clefts and cavities of limestones, and, as it would appear, always of very recent origin.

(4) HASELGEBIRGE (*Germ.*) is the name given to certain breccia-like rocks occurring in connection with the rock-salt formations of the Northern Alps. They consist of clay as matrix, and contain very various fragments of the neighbouring rocks. They have probably arisen from the breaking in of the roof of cavities caused by partial washing away of the rock-salt.

x

TOPAZ ROCK.
TOPASFELS. (*Germ.*)
TOPAZOLITHE, TOPAZOGÈME,
Brongniart. (*Fr.*)

} This rock may be treated as a breccia, and is therefore placed here. We shall also notice it again as a separate rock (page 324, *post*).

Cotta, on Breccia formation, in Geolog. Fragen, 1858, p. 186.

Appendix.

ACCUMULATIONS OR HEAPS OF LOOSE FRAGMENTS OF STONES OR RUBBISH.

These may be naturally or artificially formed, e.g. naturally by the fall of a rock or mountain, or artificially by the 'tipping' of stones at the mouth of a mine or elsewhere.

42. TUFA or TUFF.

TUFFBILDUNGEN. (*Germ.*)
TUF. (*Fr.*)

Accumulations of lapilli, fragments, ash, or other substances, ejected from volcanoes, and more or less firmly compacted together.

We can hardly, within reasonable limits, give a more definite description of these rocks, on account of their great variety both of state and composition. They may be best understood by a description of the mode of their origin; volcanoes during their eruptions cast out masses or lumps of lava, usually scoriaceous—so-called 'bombs' —which are for the most part rounded, and vary in size from the size of a man's fist to that of a human head and larger; but besides these bombs, volcanoes also emit what is termed 'volcanic sand,' and even dust-like particles of lava or 'volcanic ash,' often accompanied by non-volcanic fragments which have been torn away from the sides of the crater.

In still weather all such products fall on the slopes, or in the immediate neighbourhood of the volcano; but in storms of wind they are often borne to a considerable distance, and so become separated according to their size and weight. If the volcano be in the neighbourhood of the sea, or of a freshwater lake, then they often fall into these.

They are likewise frequently washed down by floods of rain from the steeper slopes of the volcano, and are so accumulated in one or more separate localities. By such means they cover the land with a loose stratum, or with the assistance of water they become more or less regularly

stratified, form deposits of various thickness; and sometimes trunks of trees or other substances become imbedded
with them. Again, if these volcanic products are deposited in considerable quantity, either in the sea or
freshwater basins, then they envelope such remains of
coral, shells, fishes, and the like, as may happen to come
in their way, these latter being in such case converted
into fossils.

Such is the origin of volcanic tufa, which may therefore
either be a land formation, or a freshwater, or marine
formation. At some very lofty volcanoes, especially some
near Quito, there occur streams of mud, which are occasioned by the rapid melting of the mountain snow or
the bursting of some internal reservoir of water. The
violent rush of water carries with it all loose materials
with which it comes into contact, converting them into
mud, which is deposited where the mountain slopes are
most gradual. The mass thus formed is called Moja. It
is, however, nothing but a kind of volcanic tufa.

Tufas sometimes contain fragments of various kinds,
large and small, angular and rounded, confusedly mingled
together; sometimes the fragments have become sorted
according to size and weight, so that we find some tufas
consisting entirely of fine dust resembling claystone;
others of small grains resembling sandstone; and others,
again, of only coarse fragments resembling conglomerate.

It would be impossible to distinguish and arrange the
manifold varieties of tufa systematically; we can only in
some measure indicate the local designations for particular
varieties, commencing with those belonging to active
volcanoes, then instancing those associated with the older
volcanoes, or even, as sometimes happens, with plutonic
igneous rocks. A genuine plutonic, i.e. subterranean,
formation of tufa, is not to be imagined as possible.
Therefore, as we nevertheless sometimes find tufas connected with and belonging to plutonic rocks, for instance
with greenstones and quartz-porphyries, we must assume
that these greenstones and quartz-porphyries formerly
had an upper volcanic portion to which the tuff formations
properly belonged, but which has since been destroyed
and washed away, whilst a part of the tufas have been
preserved, being perhaps protected by other deposits.

We have no tufa formations belonging to the granites, because they never reached the surface in their melted state, and tufas and breccias are the result of eruptions which have taken place at the surface of the earth, or beneath the waters of shallow seas.

(A) VOLCANIC TUFAS, BASALTIC AND TRACHYTIC.

The materials of which they consist are slags, lapilli, ash, fragments of pumice, or lava mixed with other substances. Their structures are rough, earthy to compact, arenaceous, conglomeritic, or breccian.

(*a*) PEPERINO.
PEPERIN. (*Germ.*)
PEPERINO. (*Fr.*)
Grey wackenitic matrix, enclosing laminæ of black mica and grains or crystals of augite, leucite, and magnetic iron-ore; sometimes with angular fragments of basalt, leucite rock, limestone, and the like. In the Albanian Mountains it occurs in extensive beds of great thickness.

(*b*) BASALT-TUFA, and BASALT-CONGLOMERATE, or BRECCIA.
BASALTTUFF und BASALT-CONGLOMERAT oder BRECCIE. (*Germ.*)
TUF BASALTIQUE, CONGLOMÉRAT BASALTIQUE. (*Fr.*)
Fragments of basalt of very various sizes, joined together by pulverised particles of basalt or by clay, or some other decomposed rocky matter. This kind of tufa often likewise contains fragments or pebbles of other rocks, pieces of augite, hornblende, olivine, mica, and magnetic iron-ore, grains of glauconite, &c. It is occasionally penetrated by nests and veins of calcspar, aragonite, or sparry iron-ore. It frequently contains fossils.

(*c*) PALAGONITE-TUFA.
PALAGONITTUFF. (*Germ.*)
PALAGONITE. (*Fr.*)
This is the name given by Sartorius v. Waltershausen to a variety of basalt tufa, first observed by him near Palagonia in Sicily. It is probably the product of transmutation from ordinary basalt tufa, taken place under water. The principal mass of this rock consists of a peculiar mineral formation termed palagonite, which shapes itself into compact masses, or into aggregates of small grains; and it encloses fresh pieces of basalt, dolerite, or basaltic amygdaloid. Palagonite itself is amorphous, resembling pitch, with a yellow to blackish-brown colour, vitreous to greasy lustre, conchoidal or splintery fracture. H. 4·5. Spec. grav. 2·4—2·6. It is a hydrous silicate of iron, alumina, lime, and magnesia, with little potash or soda.

(*d*) PUZZULANA.
PUZZULAN. (*Germ.*)
POUZZOLANE. (*Fr.*)
A loosely coherent deposit of volcanic sand, very useful in the construction of hydraulic mortars.

(*e*) TRACHYTE-TUFA, TRACHYTE-CONGLOMERATE, TRACHYTE-BRECCIA.
TRACHYTTUFF, TRACHYT-BRECCIE und CONGLOMERAT. (*Germ.*)
TUF TRACHYTIQUE, CONGLOMÉRAT TRACHYTIQUE. (*Fr.*)
Fragments or pebbles of trachyte are more or less firmly cemented together by finely pulverised particles of the same material. Or the matrix occurs alone as a compact fine earth mass of a white, yellow, or even green colour. Sometimes it contains pieces of sanidine

hornblende, or magnetic iron-ore in a better state of preservation. In clefts and fissures of the tuff an opal-like stone has found itself at Kaschau in Hungary; for instance, precious opal. Here and there it contains impressions of plants and other fossils.

(*f*) PUMICEOUS TUFA, PUMICEOUS SAND and CONGLOMERATE.
BIMSTEINTUFF, BIMSTEIN-SAND und CONGLO-MERAT. (*Germ.*)
TUF PONCEUX, CONGLOMÉRAT PONCEUX. (*Fr.*)
} White, yellow, or grey; its texture earthy to compact, very rough to the feel. It consists of an aggregate of pulverised particles of pumice-stone, frequently enclosing fragments of the same or of trachyte. As accessory ingredients, it also contains laminæ of mica, crystals of felspar, grains of magnetic iron-ore, less frequently quartz and garnet. The fine pumiceous tufa has sometimes formed itself into small concentric globules (pisolites), as happens at the present day when rain occurs during a volcanic shower of ash.

(*g*) TRASS (Rhine), PAUSILIPPO TUFA (Sicily), TOSCA (Teneriffe).
TRASS (DUCKSTEIN), PAUSILIPPTUFF, TOSCA. (*Germ.*)
TRASS, TUF DU PAUSILIPPE. (*Fr.*)
} Are only local varieties of pumiceous tufa which sometimes contain carbonised trunks of trees and other organic remains, and usually are well adapted to the construction of hydraulic mortars. Much of this pumiceous tufa seems to be the product of volcanic mud-streams, and therefore to answer to the moja of South America.

(*h*) ALUM-STONE, ALUM ROCK (Tolfa).
ALAUNSTEIN, ALAUNFELS, TOLFA. (*Germ.*)
ALUNITE DE LA TOLFA. (*Fr.*)
} Is the name given to a certain argilo-trachytic tufa, containing alum, occurring at Bereghsacz, in Hungary, and at La Tolfa, in Italy, &c. But much of what has received this name is probably only decomposed trachytic rock, and therefore not a genuine tufa.

(*i*) PHONOLITE-TUFA, and CONGLOMERATE.
PHONOLITTUFF und CONGLOMERAT. (*Germ.*)
TUF PHONOLITHIQUE, CONGLOMÉRAT PHONOLITHIQUE. (*Fr.*)
} Fragments or pebbles of phonolite are united together by an aggregate compound of ashy particles, and of earthy to compact texture, sometimes containing sanidine, hornblende, augite, &c. It is found, e.g., in Högau and at the southern foot of the Erzgebirge.

(B) TUFF FORMATIONS OF PLUTONIC ROCKS.

(*k*) PORPHYRY-TUFF, or FELSITE-TUFF (FELSPATHIC ASH), *Jukes.*
PORPHYRTUFF oder FELSITTUFF. (*Germ.*)
TUF PORPHYRIQUE ou FELSPATHIQUE. (*Fr.*)
} Sometimes called claystone; a compact aggregate of felsitic parts, somewhat decomposed, fracture earthy, often variegated in colour, seldom distinctly stratified, but sometimes containing fossil plants, especially trunks of trees. At Chemnitz, in Saxony, where this tufa occurs as the lowest member of the Rothliegende, it is supposed to belong to the quartz-porphyries of that district. It is, however, very difficult to distinguish these rocks in themselves from ordinary claystones, or from certain products of decomposition of compact or porphyritic felsitic rocks.

Porphyry-tuff sometimes encloses fragments and pebbles of quartz-porphyry, and thereby passes over into a kind of porphyry-breccia or conglomerate. At Flöha, in Saxony, there occurs a porphyry-breccia of this description, the matrix consisting of crystalline particles of felspar.

(*l*) GREENSTONE-TUFF, and GREENSTONE-CONGLO- ⎫ A compact ag-
    MERATE (GREENSTONE-ASH). ⎪ gregate of pul-
    GRÜNSTEINTUFF und GRÜNSTEINCONGLOMERAT. (*Germ.*) ⎬ verised or sand-
    TUF DIORITIQUE et CONGLOMÉRAT DIORITIQUE. (*Fr.*) ⎪ like particles of
greenstone; fracture earthy; colour grey or brownish-green, sometimes enclosing fragments or pebbles of greenstone, and frequently organic remains.

At Planschwitz, in Saxony, greenstone-tufa is imbedded between strata of greywacké slate, and contains many fossils of the Devonian formation. Probably much of what in Nassau has been called schalstein belongs to greenstone-tufa. On account of the indistinct character attached to the name schalstein, we have preferred to treat it separately.

In Southern Tyrol, in the Fassa district, Von Richthofen has lately made distinctions between eruptive tufas, sedimentary tuffs, and regenerated tuffs, but they all belong to augite rocks, and take their geological rank amongst the deposits of more recent Trias formations.

References.

Naumann, on Porphyry-tufa, in the Erläuter. z. geogn. Karte v. Sachsen, 1838, No. 2, p. 434.

Grüner, Porphyry-tufa with Mica Crystals in the Dep. of the Loire, Ann. des Mines, 1841, [3] vol. xix. pp. 98 and 122.

Beudant, Voyage min. et géol. en Hongrie, vol. ii. p. 416.

v. Oeynhausen, on Trass, in the Erläuter. z. geogn. Karte des Laachner Sees, 1847.

Brongniart has given the name of Brecciole to certain basalt-tufas of an arenaceous texture, in the Mém. sur les terr. des sédim. sup. du Vincentin. Paris, 1823.

Sartorius v. Waltershausen, on Palagonittuff: Die submarinen Ausbr. des Val di Noto, 1846, p. 34; Skizze von Island, 1847, p. 76; Vulk. Gest. in Sicilien und Island, 1853, pp. 179 and 215.

Darwin, Palagonittuff on Chatham Island, in Geol. obs. on the volc. islands, 1844, p. 98.

Sandberger, Palagonittuff at Limburg in Nassau, in Geol. Verh. d. Herzgoth. Nassau, 1847, p. 81.

Girard, Palagonittuff near Montpellier, in v. L. u. Br. Jahrb. 1853, p. 568.

v. Richthofen, Geogn. Beschr. v. Süd-Tyrol, 1861.

W. Evas, Felsittuff von Chemnitz Analyse, v. Leonh. u. Br. Jahrb. 1861, p. 643.

Mitscherlich, über den Alaunstein, Zeitschr. der geol. Ges. 1862, p. 253.

Appendix.

Some part at least of what has been called schalstein belongs to the tufa formations; we therefore propose here to treat of all the rocks to which this name has been applied, and we shall subjoin a few observations on the so-called laterite.

43. SCHALSTEIN.

SCHALSTEIN. (*Germ.*)

So many rocks have been described under this name, that we can only say in general that by it is understood a laminated rock interspersed with small particles of calcspar. We must distinguish them according to their localities and the authors who have described them.

(A) SCHALSTEIN, or BLATTERSTEIN-SHALE. In Nassau. This SCHALSTEIN oder BLATTERSTEINSCHIEFER. (*Germ.*) rock was certainly first to receive the name, but it varies greatly in its character. The base or matrix appears here to be a very fine somewhat laminated greenstone-tufa, which contains calcspar in grains or thin layers of green, grey, or variegated spotted colour. In some places, however, this rock partakes of the character of breccia, or is porphyritic by reason of crystals of labradorite, or it is amygdaloidal, or is even penetrated by clay-slate and chlorite-schist. In the Rhenish grauwacke district it usually occurs in company with greenstone (diabase)—a circumstance which confirms its origin as a tufa formation.

Sandberger distinguishes the following varieties of schalstein in Nassau:—

(*a*) NORMAL SCHALSTEIN.
(*b*) CALCAREOUS SCHALSTEIN, with much calcspar.
(*c*) SCHALSTEIN-BRECCIA, with calcspar as the cementing medium.
(*d*) SCHALSTEIN-CONGLOMERATE.
(*e*) SCHALSTEIN-AMYGDALOID.
(*f*) PORPHYRITIC SCHALSTEIN, with crystals of labradorite.

These are therefore varieties consisting of what under other circumstances we should perhaps consider quite dissimilar rocks, and which here are only classed together because of their occurring together or under similar circumstances in the Devonian formation.

(B) SCHALSTEIN, or CALC-TRAP, which is a somewhat slaty diabase or aphanite, containing grains of calcspar, and therefore may be classed among those greenstones (see pp. 148, 159).

(C) SCHALSTEIN OF ZELLE, NEAR NOSSEN. Is only a variety of SCHALSTEIN VON ZELLE BEI NOSSEN, oder SCHAL- clay-slate containing STEINÄHNLICHER THONSCHIEFER. (*Germ.*) grains or amygda- loids of calcareous spar.

The name of schalstein has been used, or abused, for many other kinds of rock, and hence we find a tolerably rich literature on the subject.

References.

Stifft, in v. Leonhard's Zeitschr. f. Min. 1825, vol. i. pp. 147 and 236; also in Geogn. Beschr. d. Herzogth. Nassau, 1831, p. 468.
Oppermann, Dissert. über den Schalstein und Kalktrapp, 1836.
Dollfus and *Neubauer*, Analyses of Schalstein in the Journ. f. Prakt. Chemie, 1855, vol. lxv. p. 109.
Eglinger, Analyses, in the Jahrbuch des Ver. f. Naturk. in Nassau, 1856, No. 11, p. 205.
Murchison and *Sandberger*, Transact. of the Geol. Soc., second series, vol. vi. p. 249.
v. *Dechen*, in Nöggerath's Rheinland Westphalen, 1822, vol. ii. p. 71; and in Archiv f. Miner. Geogn. &c., vol. xix. p. 516.
Hausmann, on the Formation of the Harz Mountains, 1842, p. 23.
Sandberger, Uebers. der geol. Verh. des Herzogth. Nassau, 1847, p. 33.
Gumprecht, in v. L. u. Br. Jahrb. 1842, p. 825.
Naumann, Erläuter. d. geogn. Karte v. Sachsen, 1836, No. 1, p. 60.

Appendix.

We shall here append a rock of somewhat doubtful character.

LATERITE. This is the name given by English geologists to certain rocks of East India, which in part are red traps, very much resembling brick, but others are the products of the decomposition of crystalline schists. Upon such uncertain data, of course, no definite character can be established for a rock.

References.

Gumprecht's Zeitschr. f. Erdkunde, vol. v. p. 160.
According to v. *Richthofen*, the laterite of Ceylon is decomposed calcareous gneiss: v. Leonhard's Jahrb. 1862, p. 739.

CHAPTER IV.

ROCKS OF SPECIAL CHARACTER OR BEDDING.

WE propose under this general head to gather together several formations of very various character, but subordinate extent—in point of comparative bulk hardly important enough to be considered altogether essential ingredients of the earth's crust. Several of the rocks we have classed under previous heads are likewise comparatively insignificant in point of their extent, but they form part of larger connected groups, and so enter into the family of the great rock formations of the globe. In this chapter we have to deal with more separate and disconnected formations, frequently of local character only, and which we rather force into groups for the sake of convenience than in conformity with the nature of their origin, which is very various and in many cases doubtful. Some are of igneous, some of sedimentary or metamorphic origin, but others, in their bedding and composition, differ so much from the greater part of the rocks of each of those three classes, that we are compelled to regard them, for the present at least, as problematical formations, although we may account for several by supposing a concurrence of extraordinary and exceptional circumstances at their first origin or during their mutations.

We have not, therefore, attempted to classify these special rocks according to origin; but have arranged them somewhat arbitrarily in groups in the following order :—

1. Serpentine rocks.
2. Garnet rocks.
3. Greisen and schorl rocks.
4. Coal and carbonaceous rocks.
5. Ironstone rocks.
6. Various minerals as rocks.

These are rocks, probably, of very various original character, but which have all undergone the same special transmutation. This process has not been one of increase of crystallisation, nor of actual decomposition: it seems to have simply consisted in the absorption of magnesia, just as we know has happened in the case of many and various minerals. These have been converted from their original state into serpentine, steatite, or other magnesian compounds, and are pseudomorphs retaining the form of their original crystallisation.

44. SERPENTINE, OPHIOLITE.

SERPENTIN, OPHIOLITH. (*Germ.*)
SERPENTINE. (*Fr.*)

A compact rock, dull in fresh fracture, soft, with greasy feel, usually dark-green or brown.

Spec. grav.   .   .   .   .   .   .   2·5—2·7.

It may be doubted whether serpentine exists as an original and independent mineral; for the crystals with amorphous fracture, which some mineralogists call serpentine, according to others are nothing more than pseudomorphs of chrysolite or some other mineral. If, however, the existence of serpentine as an independent mineral were established, the question still remains whether the rock which we term serpentine is to be regarded as consisting of such mineral, because, although its composition is similar, in many cases it may be distinctly shown that the rock has been derived by transmutation from other rocks. We know of undoubted pseudomorphs of hornblende, felspar, augite, &c., consisting of a substance bearing at least a very close resemblance to serpentine, and actually so called. We will not pursue this mineralogical question further, but proceed to the description of the rock.

Serpentine rock consists of two-thirds silicate of magnesia combined with 12—21 per cent. of water. It also contains some protoxide of iron, and this, as well as the water, enters into combination with the silica, supplanting a part of the magnesia: the proportion of silica varies from 38 to 43 per cent.; the magnesia from 34 to 44; lime, clay, manganese, bitumen, and carbon are only present in small quantity. The mass is so soft and tractable, and yet so tough, that it admits of being cut into various shapes or turned with the lathe. Its unctuous feel is a very characteristic property of serpentine, and is caused by the great quantity of magnesia which it contains. Probably the numerous friction surfaces which often divide the rock in all directions are also owing to the presence of magnesia. These surfaces have a resinous lustre and are sometimes striped. The rock is usually of a dark-green colour, but some varieties are light-green, grey-green, brown, reddish-brown, or almost black, and the rock sometimes presents rapid alternation of colour, causing spots, flames, or vein-like markings.

The principal mass of serpentine often porphyritically encloses many minerals of various kinds. The most frequent are pyrope, or magnesia-garnet, sometimes accompanied by talc, less frequently bronzite, schiller-spar, chlorite, mica, magnetic iron-ore, pyrites, mispickel, chromic iron-ore, and very rarely (in the Ural) native platinum. The quantity of magnetic iron-ore is exceptionally so considerable, as to influence the magnetic needle; for instance, in the Fichtelgebirge, where, however, the rock is not a very characteristic serpentine. The mass of serpentine rock is frequently penetrated by veins consisting of fibrous serpentine (asbestus), chrysotile, chlorite, or picrolite.

Somewhat more rarely there occur veins or nests of calcspar, calcareous magnesian spar, magnesite, saponite, pyknotrope, dermatine, talc, brucite, völknerite, hornblende, strahlstein, quartz, chalcedony, jasper, chrysoprase, opal, pyrites, chalcopyrite, chromic iron-ore, magnetic iron-ore, and native copper.

Varieties in Texture.

(*a*) COMMON COMPACT SERPENTINE.
DICHTER SERPENTIN. (*Germ.*)
SERPENTINE COMPACTE. (*Fr.*)

(*b*) PORPHYRITIC SERPENTINE. } Often with crystals of py-
PORPHYRARTIGER SERPENTIN. (*Germ.*) } rope.
SERPENTINE PORPHYROIDE. (*Fr.*)

(*c*) SLATY SERPENTINE.
SCHIEFRIGER SERPENTIN. (*Germ.*) } Of imperfect thick cleavage.
SERPENTINE SCHISTEUSE. (*Fr.*)

(*d*) VEINED SERPENTINE.
GEADERTER SERPENTIN. (*Germ.*)
SERPENTINE BRÉCHIFORME, OPHIOLITHE, *Brongniart.* (*Fr.*)

Inasmuch as all serpentine is probably the product of the metamorphosis of some other rock, it need hardly be said that transition states of this metamorphosis are found which differ not only from the extreme result of the process of change—the genuine serpentine—but from each other. If, however, this theory of the origin of serpentine be well founded, we cannot always succeed in determining with certainty the character of the original rock ; perhaps in these cases the whole of the rock's mass has undergone change, and if bordered by other rocks of a different character, no trace is left of its original composition.

Several of the transition states of serpentine have received specific names.

(e) FORELLENSTEIN (*Germ.*) or TROUT-STONE, at Neurode, in Silesia. A compact labradorite mass, speckled with spots of serpentine, which are frequently of angular form, and which Von Rath believes to have formerly been crystals of labradorite now converted into serpentine.

(f) RENSLAERITE is the name given by Emmons, in his American Geology, 1855, to a serpentine-like rock, somewhat more crystalline than ordinary serpentine. Its colour ranges from greyish white to green or black. Specific gravity, 2·87 ; composition, 59·2 silica, 32·9 magnesia, 3·4 protoxide of iron, 1 lime, and only 2·8 water.

(g) SCHILLER ROCK. } The name given to a compound of
    SCHILLERFELS. (*Germ.*) } schillerspar and serpentine, which goes
    BASTITE. (*Fr.*) } over into ordinary serpentine. It occurs at the Baste in the Hartz Mountains. It has a serpentine matrix enclosing crystals of schillerspar of considerable size. It also contains labradorite, augite, mica, chlorite, and pyrites.

Cocchi proposes that serpentine rocks should be designated according to the particular rocks from which they sprang ; e.g. diallage-serpentine, diorite-serpentine, granite-serpentine, &c. This may be very advisable where it is possible.

Serpentine for the most part is jointed into irregular, massive, or gnarled masses. Exceptionally it is of columnar structure, but not unfrequently it shows a kind of stratification or tabular jointing. This latter may have been occasioned by actual stratification, since serpentine may well have arisen from stratified rocks. It is most frequently found in irregular and subordinate beds between strata of crystalline schist, but it also occurs in uncrystalline rocks both in the massive form and in veins. The surface of the little round-topped hills which it often forms usually shows a very scanty vegetation.

In some places, as already said, its transmutation from other rocks is very evident, as, for instance, from gabbro at Siebenlehn, near Freiberg; from dykes of granite traversing serpentine rocks near Böhrigen and Waldheim in Saxony, where the main serpentine rock itself is not improbably a transmuted granulite; from chlorite-schist at Zell, in the Fichtelgebirge, where the change does not · appear to be yet complete; and from gneiss (probably), or an eklogite rock in the gneiss, at Zöblitz, in the Erzgebirge. The processes and causes of the metamorphosis of serpentine are doubtless very different to those of the crystalline schists. When serpentine occurs in strata of crystalline schist, it is usually of later origin than those, and its conversion may have been occasioned by the continued infiltration of water, holding magnesia in solution, during long periods of time. We are therefore unable to class this rock with the crystalline schists any more than we can with the igneous or sedimentary rocks. According to Jukes, many serpentines are metamorphosed magnesian limestone. In the Engadine, a serpentine rock has been lately found to contain a considerable proportion of phosphate, so that it is proposed to use it as manure.

Serpentine has been recently discovered by Sir William Logan in the Laurentian limestones of Canada, replacing the remains of the foraminiferal organism, *Eozoön Canadense*.

References.

Scheerer, Mineral Serpentine, Poggend. Ann. 1854, voL xcii. p. 287.

Haughton, Philos. Mag. 1855, vol. x. p. 253.

Websky, Krystallstructur des Serpentins, Zeitschr. d. d. geol. Ges. 1858, p. 277.

T. Sterry Hunt, on the Serpentines of Canada and their associated Rocks, Lond. Edin. and Dubl. PhiL Mag. vol. xiv. p. 388, 1857. Quart. Jour. Geol. Soc. vol. xxi. p. 67.

v. Rath, Forellenstein, Poggend. Ann. vol. xcv. p. 552.

Cocchi, in v. L. u. Br. Jahrb. 1857, p. 600.

Emmons, in Americ. Journ. of Sc. 1843, vol. xlv. p. 122.

A. Streng, Serpentin in Gabbro von Neurode, v. Leonh. u. Br. Jahrb. 1864, p. 257.

C. W. Fuchs, Schillerfels bei Schriestheim, v. Leonh. u. Br. Jahrb. 1864, p. 326.

GARNET GROUP.

The one property which these rocks possess in common is, that they all contain garnet as an essential, sometimes a predominant, constituent. The minerals with which the garnet is cómbined are various, such as amphibole, pyroxene, felspar, mica, dichroite, &c. Garnet rocks frequently occur in subordinate masses, often of irregular shape and doubtful origin, in strata of crystalline schists, or in granitic rocks. We include in this group the following rocks:—Eklogite, Disthene rock, Eulisite, Garnet rock, Kinzigite, and Dichroite rock.

45. EKLOGITE, OMPHACITE ROCK, SMARAGDITE ROCK, DISTHENE ROCK.

EKLOGIT, OMPHACITFELS, SMARAGDITFELS, DISTHENFELS. (*Germ.*)
ECLOGITE, OMPHAZITE, *Haüy.* (*Fr.*)

A compound of green smaragdite and red garnet. The smaragdite forms a finely crystallised matrix, usually somewhat slaty or fibrous, in which the crystals of garnet are porphyritically enclosed.

This rock, to which Haüy gave the name of eklogite, is usually very firm and coherent, difficult to break with the hammer. Its fresh fracture presents a peculiarly beautiful appearance, from the red garnets sparkling in a light-green matrix. Its accessory ingredients cause it to vary somewhat in different localities. The beautiful eklogites of the district of Münchberg, in the Fichtelgebirge, sometimes contain mica; more rarely they contain zoisite or some other variety of epidote, quartz, pyrites, and magnetic iron-ore. In the eklogite of the Sau-Alp mountain in Styria, zoisite and actinolite are almost its predominant constituents, and it contains in addition to the crystals of garnet some quartz, corinthine, and disthene. On the island of Syra, the common eklogite is found in layers or strata, alternating with a rock consisting of a compound of disthene-garnet and mica of a silvery white colour: this latter rock has been termed by Virlet disthene rock; we might, however, with equal propriety, call it a variety of eklogite. A rock occurring at Haslau, near Eger, which has been sometimes called eklogite, consists principally or in great part of idocrase (so-called Egeran).

Eklogite most frequently occurs irregularly imbedded in strata of crystalline schist, as, for instance, at Münchberg, in the gneiss district of that locality. The direction of its slaty texture there is in conformity with that of the prevailing foliation of the schist, and we may therefore doubt whether it should be regarded as a contemporaneous formation with the gneiss, or as having forced its way into the latter at a subsequent period. Owing to its greater power of resistance to the decomposing influences of the atmosphere, this rock usually forms prominent knolls or rocks.

Virlet, in the Bullet. de la Soc. géol. 1833, vol. iii. p. 201.

46. EULISITE.

EULISIT. (*Germ.*)
EULISITE. (*Fr.*)

A compound composed of protoxide of iron, resembling olivine, green pyroxene, and brownish-red garnet.

This name was given by A. Erdmann to a rock which forms a bed of great thickness in the gneiss at Tunaberg, in Sweden.

Erdmann, Försök till en geogn. mineral Beskrifing öfver Tunabergs Socken, 1849, p. 11.

47. GARNET ROCK.

GRANATFELS. (*Germ.*)
GRÉNATITE, *Cordier.* (*Fr.*)

A crystalline granular compound of garnet and hornblende, usually with some magnetic iron-ore.

Sometimes the brown or yellowish garnet (aplome) predominates, so that the mass almost entirely consists of a granular aggregate of that mineral; sometimes, again, the rock contains many other minerals besides the hornblende and magnetic iron.

This rock only occurs in subordinate matter; e. g. in the mica-schist on the Teufelsstein and Klobenstein, near Schwarzenberg, in Saxony, where it forms small projecting rocks.

Cotta, Erläuter. z. geogn. Karte von Sachsen, No. 2, p. 225; v. L. u. Br. Jahrb. 1844, p. 413.

48. KINZIGITE.

KINZIGIT. (*Germ.*)
KINZIGITE. (*Fr.*)

A crystalline compound of black mica, garnet, oligoclase, sometimes passing over into the compact state.

This is a rock which was discovered at Wittichen, at the Kinzig in the Black Forest. It was formerly considered to be a garnet rock and so designated, but H. Fischer pointed out its individual properties, and gave it a separate name. He afterwards found the same rock at Gadernheim and Auerbach, in the Odenwald, and certain rocks occurring at Bodenmais in Bavaria and at Cabo de Gata in Spain are considered by him to be closely allied to it.

In some of the above-named rocks, cordierite, fibrolite, and mikrocline occur, the last as a substitute for oligoclase.

Fischer, in v. L. u. Br. Jahrbuch, 1860, p. 796; and 1861, p. 641.

49. DICHROITE ROCK.

DICHROITFELS. (*Germ.*)

An irregular compound of felspar, dichroite, garnet, and mica (the latter in small quantity); firm, dark-coloured.

This rock is allied to dichroite-gneiss. It is found (e.g.) forming a dyke in the granite of the Erlbachgrund, near Kriebstein, in Saxony.

Naumann, Erläuter. d. geogn. Karte v. Sachsen, No. 2, p. 13.

GREISEN AND SCHORL GROUP.

The rocks of this little group are distinguished by their consisting principally of quartz, frequently impregnated with fine particles of tin-ore, or else associated with beds or veins containing tin-ore. In addition to the quartz, there occur in these rocks white mica, chlorite, or schorl as essential ingredients, and wolfram, specular iron, and topaz as accessories.

The following are the rocks included in this group:—

1. Greisen, a compound of quartz and mica.

2. Zwitter rock, consisting of quartz, chlorite, specular iron- and tin-ore.

3. Schorl rock, a compound of quartz and schorl.

4. Topaz rock, a breccian variety of schorl rock, with topaz.

50. GREISEN.

GREISEN. (*Germ.*)
HYALOMICTE, *Brongniart.* (*Fr.*)

A crystalline granular compound of quartz and mica.

This, therefore, is granite without felspar, or we may say it is the substance of mica-schist, without its foliated texture and conformation. It is of somewhat rare occurrence. It actually passes into granite; that is to say, some felspar, or at least kaolin, occasionally enters into its composition. But no transitions into mica-schist are known; in other words, it shows no disposition to a fissile texture; it is always distinctly granular (coarse or fine-grained).

The mica of greisen is chiefly lithia-mica. Some tin-ore likewise occurs as an accessory ingredient, and the rock is frequently penetrated with or associated with veins of tin-ore, as at Zinnwald, in the Erzgebirge, where this rock occurs very characteristically. Less characteristically it also occurs near Ober-Pöbel, to the west of Altenberg.

Greisen is of massive structure, without a trace of stratification. Its constant association with beds and veins of tin-ore, in the granite districts of Schlaggenwald, Cornwall, &c., and its resemblance to the zwitter, lead us to the conclusion that special circumstances have led to its formation from granite by decomposition of its felspar, although in the coarse varieties it is difficult to conceive how and by what substance the felspar has been replaced. In this view we might regard greisen but as a variety of granite. We have separately classed it and the other tin-bearing rocks in a distinct group, because they probably all owe their peculiar properties to special and analogous causes, although these have not yet been satisfactorily ascertained.

Y

51. ZWITTER ROCK.

ZWITTERGESTEIN, STOCKWERKSPORPHYR. (*Germ.*)

A dark-grey aggregate, rich in quartz, texture fine-grained to compact; its other ingredients are not to be distinguished by the naked eye.

By help of the lens, we may recognise in the fine-grained mass of this rock subordinate quantities of chlorite, tin-ore, arsenical pyrites, and also some micaceous iron combined with the quartz. To these the dark colour of the rock is probably owing.

The tin-ore in Altenberg (the only locality where the rock is known to occur characteristically) is called zwitter, and the rock therefore was called Zwitter rock by the miners there. The unsuitable name of *Stockwerksporphyr* is another miners' term, given under the erroneous belief that greisen belonged to the porphyries, although it has no trace of porphyritic texture,

The celebrated 'pinge' of Altenberg is a large crater-like hollow, formed by the falling in of extensive mining works in this rock, which is worked for its tin-ore. At the margin of this pinge may be observed the gradual transition from fine-grained granite into zwitter rock. The granite is first found to be penetrated by numerous and very irregular cracks or fissures filled with quartz, and on each side of the quartz there is usually a dark stripe of from one quarter to one inch thick and upwards. These stripes, on closer investigation, are found to be zwitter rock, containing no felspar, although they merge gradually into the surrounding granite, which is of the common kind. The stripes are evidently the result of influences proceeding from the fissures, and towards the principal mine they become broader and broader, so that very little unconverted granite is left between the numerous clefts. At length the last remnant of the granite disappears, the whole mass having been converted into zwitter rock, in which, however, the quartz veins still remain distinctly perceptible. It would appear that the transmutation must have been caused by some solution or vapour impregnated with tin penetrating the granite through its many fissures.

Dr. Rube has carefully analysed several specimens of the unchanged granite, of the dark stripes near the quartz, and of the entirely converted zwitter rock. From these analyses it has appeared that the composition of the dark stripes and of the genuine zwitter rock were identical. They each contain 3 p. c. silica and 2 p. c. potash less than the granite. On the other hand, they contain 4 p. c. protoxide of iron, 2 p. c. alumina, 0·6 oxide of tin, and 0·5 — 1·0 lime more than the granite. It follows, therefore, that in addition to the ingredients which we have above mentioned as being recognisable in the zwitter rock it must also contain a silicate of alumina. The penetrating solution appears to have decomposed the felspar and mica, and in their stead to have formed micaceous iron-ore, chlorite, tin-ore, a silicate of alumina, and also to have left a deposit of lime. The potash must have been carried away in solution; the silica was probably concentrated, at least in part, in the cleft of the rock, forming the veins of quartz which we now see.

Cotta, in Berg- u. Hüttenm. Zeitung, 1860, No. 1, and 1862, p. 74.

52. SCHORLACEOUS SCHIST and SCHORL ROCK.

Schörlschiefer und Schörlfels. (*Germ.*)
Hyalotourmalithe, *Daubrée*. (*Fr.*)

A crystalline compound of schorl and quartz, foliated or granular to compact.

The schistose varieties are most prevalent, and we have therefore placed them foremost; the compact varieties are rare, and in the absence of transition states they are difficult of recognition. As accessory ingredients, this rock contains mica, chlorite, felspar, tin-ore, arsenical pyrites, and exceptionally, in some places, topaz. These schorl rocks are (like griesen) almost always accompanied by or associated with beds containing tin-ore. The proportion of silica which they contain is very unequal, and depends on the prevalence of their quartz.

Varieties in Texture.

(*a*) Schorlaceous Schist. Its somewhat indistinct foliated texture is owing to the parallel disposition or distribution of the acicular particles of schorl. The quartz sometimes forms itself into contorted layers quite independent of the schistose texture. This rock occurs (e.g.) in subordinate beds, alternating with mica-schist at Eibenstock, in Saxony, where it is traversed by veins of tin-ore.

(b) GRANULAR SCHORL ROCK. This is either a tolerably uniform compound (fine or coarse-grained) of schorl and quartz; or it consists principally of quartz, with small separate columnar particles of schorl, which are frequently broken.

(c) COMPACT SCHORL ROCK. A blackish-grey mass, in which the ingredients are too intimately blended to be distinguished, as, for instance, in the tin mining district of Cornwall.

Varieties in Composition.

(d) TOPAZ ROCK. ⎫ Hitherto only known at the Schneck-
TOPASFELS, *Werner.* (*Germ.*) ⎬ enstein, in the Voigtland, where it
TOPAZOSÈME, *Brongniart.* ⎪
(*Fr.*) ⎭ forms a dyke of considerable thickness in the mica-schist. The composition of the rock is singular; large fragments of schorl-schist (containing topaz), with quartz, lithomarge, and geodes of topaz, are cemented together to a kind of geodic breccia. The rock likewise contains tin-ore, apatite, malachite, and azurite as accessories.

Von Eschwege has given the name of *Carvoeira* to a quartz rock containing schorl, found in the Brazils.

References.

Freiesleben, Geogn. Arbeiten, vol. iv. p. 1.
Breithaupt, Paragenesis, in v. Leonhard's Jahrb. 1854, p. 787.
Boase, Transact. of the Geol. Soc. of Cornwall, 1832, vol. iv. pp. 240 and 373.
Naumann, Erläuter. d. geogn. Karte v. Sachsen, No. 2, p. 201.
Daubrée (Hyalotourmalite), Ann. des Mines, 1841, 3e sér. vol. xx. p. 84.

CARBONACEOUS GROUP.

In these rocks carbon is the principal ingredient. They are always of dark colour, varying between brown and black. They are usually, but not always, combustible. They are all of organic origin, and for the most part products of vegetable accumulation; some (exceptionally) perhaps are the result of the accumulation of animal matter. The differences now exhibited are doubtless chiefly owing to the degree of metamorphosis of the original organic substance. If we start with this assumption, we may class these rocks as follows, beginning with those whose state is the least changed, and proceeding up to those which are most completely metamorphosed:—

1. *Peat.*—The vegetable substance has undergone little change. We are not authorised to conclude that all coal has been formed from peat-mosses. On the contrary, we know of much coal which is the undoubted product of trunks and leaves of trees, and various other vegetable substances.

2. *Browncoal* or *Lignite,* containing much bitumen.

3. *Common coal* (German, Schwarzkohle), containing much less bitumen.

4. *Anthracite,* containing very little bitumen.

5. *Graphite,* without any bitumen, and not combustible.

Some other differences result from foreign admixtures.

We observe from the above series that the first process of change (from the peat to the browncoal) was accompanied by a development of bitumen, which in the subsequent stages of metamorphosis has again gradually disappeared, and become lost in all probability by evaporation. The relative geological ages of the different coals in general correspond with and confirm this view; and the only exceptions of which we are aware are capable of explanation from special local causes. We may therefore say that the varying proportion of bitumen contained in the carbonaceous rocks furnishes us with a series which at the same time is expressive of their geological age.

In addition to the above, and in some measure the complement of the series, we have—

6. *Mineral pitch* (including asphalte, elastic bitumen, and mineral oil) consisting of the bitumen which has been volatilised or distilled from bituminous coal. It is sometimes found separately bedded as a distinct rock, sometimes as an impregnation of other rocks, such as limestone, shale, &c.

The following rocks we add by way of appendix to the coal group, as bearing an affinity with it in respect of their origin, or otherwise.

7. *Bituminous shale* (Brandschiefer), an argillaceous shale containing very much bitumen, and frequently carbon. Also,

8. *Kohlenbrandgesteine* (burnt clay rocks), which are not carbonaceous, but are the result of burning coal upon clay rocks.

9. *Guano and coprolite beds.* The product of local accumulations of animal excrement.

We have already stated that the usual and normal bedding of the different kinds of coal entirely corresponds with the theory of their origin and of the causes of their different composition and structure. The individual exceptions only serve to prove the rule; they may all be explained by special circumstances, and when so explained are in fact necessary consequences of our assumed theory.

The following review of the most important coal formations will best explain our meaning:—

Age.	Usual Coal-beds.	Exceptional Coal-beds.
Post Tertiary.	Peat-mosses and beds of turf in many places.	
Tertiary.	Browncoal in North Germany, Bohemia, Hessen, &c.	Anthracite (with basalt) at the Meissner, in Hessen.
	Browncoal containing little bitumen near Häring, in Tyrol (Eocene).	Ordinary pit-coal or 'black coal' at Silthal, in Transylvania.
Chalk period.	Browncoal poor in bitumen of the Gosau formation in the Alps.	Ordinary black coal at Ruszkberg, in the Banat.
Oolite or Jura period.	Bituminous shale and coal of the Jura and Lias formations in Germany and England.	Ordinary black coal at Fünfkirchen in Hungary, and at Steierdorf in the Banat.
Trias period.	Lettenkohle, an impure browncoal, containing little bitumen, belonging to the Keuper formation in Germany.	
Coal period.	Common black coal of the Coal and Culm formations in England, Germany, and France.	Anthracite at Schönfeld, Zaunhaus and Brandau, in the Erzgebirge, in the State of Ohio, adjoining the porphyry at Waldenberg, &c.
Transition or Greywacké period.	Anthracite in Scotland and in Ireland.	
Still older.	Graphite in the crystalline schists at Passau in Bavaria, &c.	

We see from the foregoing that in every geological period in which any sedimentary deposits have taken place, there have been accumulations of vegetable matter, and that these have (occasionally at least) formed beds,

and have afterwards become coal. But it is very remarkable that as far as those countries which have hitherto
been geologically explored extend, the principal coal
formations are confined to two of the great geological
periods, viz., the Tertiary, to which the browncoals belong, and the Carboniferous. This would be a fact very
difficult to explain, if it were proved to be true for the
whole globe; but as only about one-twelfth part of the
surface of the earth has been hitherto explored, we may
be permitted to doubt whether coal may not yet be found
in large quantity in other formations than those at present
known. In the interior of Africa, Asia, and Australia,
and South America, as well as under the ocean, very
extensive beds of coal may exist, which, together with
those we already know of the Chalk, Oolite, Trias, and
transition periods, would fill up all the apparent gaps, and
furnish as uniform a result with reference to the deposit
in all ages of material for coal-beds, as of that for any
other rock.

According to our present experience, we are authorised
to believe that the deposit of material for coal formation
has taken place in a similar manner and under like conditions in every period. We accordingly find a certain
petrographic uniformity or mutual relationship in the coals
of all ages. The coal-beds are almost universally found
interstratified and alternating with beds of argillaceous
rocks and sandstones, usually of grey colour (never red),
frequently with spherosiderite, or so-called clay-ironstone (Blackband) very seldom with limestone. The state
of these argillaceous and arenaceous rocks has undergone
a change corresponding to that of the coal. Their greater
compactness, solidity, and their laminated texture, almost
always correspond with the degree in which the bitumen
has been expelled from the coal, or, in other words, with
the geological age of the latter.

53. PEAT, TURF, BOG.

TORF, DARG. (*Germ.*)
TOURBE. (*Fr.*)

*An aggregate of vegetable growth, interwoven and more
or less compressed and decomposed, of yellow, brown,
or black colour.*

The plants whose remains are usually found in peat are of marshy origin, and in Germany usually spring from *Sphagnum.* The moss is more or less compacted, felt-like, or almost compact. Sometimes there are found imbedded in it trunks of trees, or their branches, roots, leaves, hard fruits, and the like; some of which have undergone little or no change. Besides these vegetable ingredients, peat frequently contains earthy admixtures, also red ochre, nodules of ' kieselguhr' (an aggregate of fossil infusoria), crystallised gypsum and pyrites, or earthy particles of vivianite.

The following varieties are sometimes distinguished, though they cannot be definitely characterised and separated:—

(*a*) PEAT-MOSS.
  FILZ- oder MOOSTORF. (*Germ.*) } Loose and felt-like.
  TOURBE FIBREUSE. (*Fr.*)
(*b*) HEATH-TURF.
  HAIDETORF. (*Germ.*)
(*c*) GRASS-TURF.
  RASENTORF. (*Germ.*)
(*d*) LEAF-TURF.
  PAPIERTORF oder BLÄTTERTORF. (*Germ.*)
(*e*) MUD-TURF.
  BAGGERTORF. (*Germ.*) } Very wet, and thereby mud-like.
(*f*) PITCH-TURF.
  PECHTORF. (*Germ.*) } Very compact and solid, the vege-
  TOURBE COMPACTE (LIMO-   table matter having been much com-
  NEUSE). (*Fr.*)   pressed and transformed.

Beds of peat and turf are formed or grow before our eyes at the present day; in marshy places we may observe the mosses springing and growing out of the graves of their predecessors. The beds of moss are found of great depth as well as extent; but they are only known on the surface of the earth, and as belonging to the most recent geological period. The older beds have been converted into coal more or less bituminous, only very exceptionally, as, for instance, at Mühlhausen, in Thuringia, do we find peat of an older date, covered there by diluvial loam, not having lost its original character.

References.

Wigmann, über Entstehung, Bildung, and Wesen des Torfes, 1837.

Winkler, über Zusammensetzung der Torfsorten des Erzgebirges, 1840.

Papius, die Lehre vom Torf, 1845.
Kast, die Entstehung, Gewinnung u. Nutzung des Torfes, 1847.
Griesbach, Bildung des Torfes in den Ensmoosen, 1846.
Lutteroth, Umgegend von Mühlhausen, 1848, p. 25.
Gaudin, Diluvialtorf bei Biarritz, in v. Leonhard's Jahrb. 1857, p. 84.

54. BROWNCOAL or LIGNITE.

BRAUNKOHLE und LIGNIT. (*Germ.*)
LIGNITE. (*Fr.*)

A compact or earthy mass, very inflammable, brown or black ; streak invariably brown.

Spec. grav. . . . . 1·2—1·5.

Browncoal essentially differs from ordinary black coal in containing a much greater proportion of bitumen, or the elements which with carbon form bitumen. Hence its brown colour and streak, its greater inflammability than ordinary coal, and likewise its burning with more smoke and smell. Even when very dark-coloured, its difference from the ordinary coal may be made to appear by boiling its powder with potash-ley, which it will colour brown.

Browncoal contains 55 to 75 p. c. of carbon, with hydrogen, oxygen, and nitrogen, and earthy admixtures in very various proportions. Some varieties contain proportionally little bitumen, and so form transition states between brown and black coal.

The following minerals sometimes occur as accessories : —amber, mellite, asphalte, gypsum, calcspar, pyrites, and lenticular particles of clay-ironstone.

Varieties in Texture.

(a) COMMON BROWNCOAL.
GEMEINE DICHTE BRAUNKOHLE, STÜCKKOHLE. (*Germ.*) LIGNITE COMPACTE, *Fayet.* (*Fr.*) } Compact with dull fracture and brown colour.

(b) EARTHY BROWNCOAL.
ERDIGE BRAUNKOHLE, STREICH-KOHLE. (*Germ.*) LIGNITE TERREUX. (*Fr.*) } Easily pulverised to a brown powder.

(c) RESINOUS BROWNCOAL.
PECHBRAUNKOHLE. (*Germ.*) LIGNITE RÉSINEUX. (*Fr.*) } Very compact and dark, almost black, and its fracture shining like pitch.

(d) LIGNITE, BITUMINOUS WOOD.
LIGNIT, BITUMINÖSES HOLZ. (*Germ.*) LIGNITE, BITUMINEUX. (*Fr.*) } Retaining the texture of the original wood from which it was derived.

(e) LEAF COAL or DYSODILE.   ⎫ Laminated in consequence
 BLÄTTERKOHLE, PAPIERKOHLE, oder ⎬ of its origin from leaves of
  DYSODIL. (*Germ.*)   ⎪ trees, or of strong pressure
 LIGNITE SCHISTOÏDE, ou DYSODIL. (*Fr.*)⎭ of its vegetable particles
 causing a similar effect.

(f) MOOR COAL.   ⎫
 MOORKOHLE, STREICHKOHLE. ⎬ Felt-like and resembling turf.
  (*Germ.*)   ⎪
 LIGNITE PICIFORME. (*Fr.*) ⎭

Varieties in Composition.

(g) COMMON BROWNCOAL.

(h) BROWNCOAL WITH LITTLE BITUMEN, to which many of the browncoals of the Alps belong; e.g. the Molasse coal of Miesbach and
Tölz, and the Eocene coals of Häring in the Tyrol. Their appearance is very like that of the ordinary black coal, even the
powder of their streak is very dark, and they only impart a
weak colour to caustic ley.

(i) IMPURE BROWNCOAL combined with much earthy matter, passing
over into bituminous shale. To this class belongs, for instance,
the so-called Lettenkohle in the lowest division of the Keuper
formation.

(k) ALUM EARTH.   ⎫ An earthy impure browncoal which con-
 ALAUNERDE. (*Germ.*) ⎬ tains pyrites; and has a tendency to
 TERRE ALUMINEUSE. ⎭ decompose into alum and vitriol.
  (*Fr.*)

Browncoal is frequently found in Tertiary deposits,
exceptionally, however, in older ones; even in the Tertiary strata it is sometimes found to have been transmuted
into anthracite by the influence of heat from adjoining and
more recent igneous rocks; as, for instance, at the Meissner,
in Hessen, where it is found in contact with basalt, or it
assumes a character very similar to the ordinary black
coal, as in many Tertiary browncoal beds of the Alps.

Browncoal may be clearly proved to have had its origin in accumulated remains of plants. Some browncoal
is the product of the conversion of beds of peat and turf,
some of more distinctly separate plants and parts of plants
washed together by floods. Subjected to pressure, a slow
chemical change took place in the mass (the formation of
bitumen). In some places, under special circumstances,
this change has proceeded more rapidly than ordinary, and
thus even in Tertiary strata we find it assuming a character approaching to the state of the ordinary black coal.

It is hardly necessary to instance localities from
amongst the very many where browncoal is found in
Germany and elsewhere.

References.

Zincken, Die Braunkohle und ihre Verwerthung. Hanover, 1805.

Gümbel, Analysen von Alpenkohlen, v. Leonh. Jahrb. f. Min. 1864, p. 52.

55. COMMON COAL, BLACK COAL, or PIT-COAL.

SCHWARZKOHLE oder STEINKOHLE. (*Germ.*)

HOUILLE. (*Fr.*)

A compact black mass, in fresh fracture usually of resinous lustre ; streak black, usually friable ; not so inflammable as browncoal, but, like it, burns with flame, smoke, and smell.

Spec. grav. . . . . . . 1·3—1·5.

The substance of coal is principally carbon. It has less of the elements of bitumen (oxygen, hydrogen, and nitrogen) than browncoal, but more than anthracite. It forms a transition state between browncoal and anthracite, and occasionally goes over into each. Like browncoal and peat, it contains more or less earthy matter, by which its value is depreciated. The following minerals occur as accessories in coal :—Pyrites, clay-ironstone (in nodules or septaria), gypsum and calcspar ; frequently also clumps of fibrous anthracite, stone-coal (Werner's 'mineral charcoal').

Jukes observes : ' In many ordinary coals little flakes of mineral charcoal occur, retaining that part of the vegetable structure called the vascular tissue. They are called "mother of coal" by the colliers, in some places. It is frequently seen in the form of a thin silky coating, covering some of the surfaces of the coal. Its powder is black, and if boiled with caustic ley, it scarcely colours the latter.'

In coal districts a very great number of different kinds of coal are distinguished according to their special values for use—' indeed their varieties are often as numerous as the different seams of a coal-field, and even the different beds of a compound seam are readily distinguished from each other by the colliers, who give particular names to them ; and even small blocks of these varieties can be recognised by them and identified with the seam or part of a seam from which they are derived. Neither are these distinctions, which are only to be perceived after long practice, unimportant, since these varieties have distinct qualities; some of them being better adapted to smelting, and said to be " good furnace-coal;" some of them to blacksmith's work, or " good shop-coal;" others to various uses; while only a few comparatively are best fitted for domestic purposes, and are brought to market by the coal-merchant.'—*Jukes*.

' Some idea of the immense varieties of coal may be gained from an inspection of the Admiralty Coal Investigation (Mem. Geol. Survey, vol. i.), as well as from the varying qualities of those we are in the habit of using daily in our houses. As many as seventy denominations of coal are said to be imported into London alone.

' All these minute varieties are commonly included under four principal heads:—1. *Caking Coal*; 2. *Splint* or *Hard Coal*; 3. *Cherry* or *Soft Coal*; and 4. *Cannel* or *Parrot Coal*.

' *Caking Coal* is so named from its fusing or running together on the fire so as to form clinkers, requiring frequent stirring to prevent the whole mass being welded together. It breaks commonly into small fragments, with a short uneven fracture. The Newcastle coal, and many others from different localities, are caking coals. They leave many cinders, and a dark dirty ash.

' *Splint* or *Hard Coal* is well known in the Glasgow coal-field. It is not easily broken, nor is it easily kindled, though when lighted it affords a clear, lasting fire. It can be got in much larger blocks than the caking coals.

' *Cherry* or *Soft Coal* is an abundant and beautiful variety, velvet black in colour, with a slight admixture of grey. It has a splendid or shining resinous lustre, does not cake when heated, has a clear shaly fracture, is easily frangible, and readily catches fire. It leaves comparatively few cinders, and its ash is white and light. It requires little stirring, and gives out a cheerful flame and heat. The Staffordshire coals principally belong to this variety.

' *Cannel* or *Parrot Coal* is called cannel, from its burning with a clear flame like a candle; and parrot, in Scotland, from its crackling or chattering when burnt. Cannel coal varies much in appearance from a dull earthy to a brilliant, shining, and waxy lustre. It is always compact, and does not soil the fingers. Its fracture is sometimes shaly, sometimes compact. The bright shining varieties often burn away like wood, leaving scarcely any cinders and only a little white ash. The duller and more earthy kinds leave a white ash, retaining nearly the same size and shape as the original lumps of coal. Cannel coal often takes a good polish, and can be worked into boxes and other articles. *Jet* is an extreme variety of cannel coal in one direction, as *batt* or carbonaceous shale is in another.'—*Jukes.*

In Germany the varieties have been thus classed:—

(*a*) GEMEINE STEINKOHLE, or common Black Coal, compact with resinous lustre.
(*b*) PECHKOHLE (or Pitch-coal), compact with resinous lustre.
(*c*) KÄNNELKOHLE (GAGAT), Cannel coal.
(*d*) SCHIEFERKOHLE, a bituminous shale, sometimes composed of alternate layers of common coal and anthracite.
(*e*) RUSSKOHLE (Sooty Coal), an earthy variety, dirty to the touch, apparently consisting of a compound of common coal and anthracite. •

The origin of coal as a product of vegetable substances is well established. The texture of the original plants may sometimes be discovered under the microscope. Beds of turf or parts of plants accumulated by flood-water have furnished the material. Geinitz has even endeavoured to explain the different structure of many coal-beds by the differences of their original vegetable substance. At Zwickau, in Saxony, and a few other places, he has distinguished the following varieties:—

(*a*) FARNENKOHLE (Fern-coal), formed principally of ferns. To this class belong the four uppermost flötz of resinous coal (Pechkohle), at Oberhohndorf, many coals of Wettin, Löbejün and Ilmenau in Germany.
(*β*) CALAMITENKOHLE (Calamitan Coal). To this the Russkohle of Zwickau belongs, also the so-called mineral charcoal. It is always very anthracitic and siliceous.
(*γ*) SIGILLARIENKOHLE (Sigillarian Coal). To this belong the Planitzflötz, and the deep 'Pechkohle' near Zwickau.
(*ι*) SAGENNARIENKOHLE (Sagennarian Coal). To this belong, e.g., the older coals of Hainichen and Ebersdorf, in Saxony.

The following are the principal typical varieties in France, according to Leplay:—

(A) Houille sèche.
(B) Houille maréchale.
(C) Houille grasse.　(Caking coal.)
(D) Houille maigre.

Coal chiefly occurs in separate beds or subordinate strata in the sandstone and argillaceous shale of the Coal formation. It occurs, however, with very similar rocks in somewhat older and in much younger formations. Thus, for instance, at Hainichen in the Kulm formation, near Fünfkirchen, in Hungary, and Steindorf, in the Banat, in the Lias formation; at Ruszkberg, in the Banat, between strata of the Chalk formation; and in Silthal, in the southern boundary of Transylvania, even in Tertiary strata. The existence of black coal in these more recent formations is to be accounted for by exceptional geological circumstances, which have accelerated the process of transmutation. The character of the plants themselves may also have contributed to this result. We find that the remains of Calamites have usually been converted into siliceous anthracite; and it is very possible that the particular nature of the original plant-substance may have affected the character of the coal in many other respects. In certain localities again, the eruption of recent igneous rocks have occasioned special phenomena of transmutation; as, for instance, at Waldenburg, in Silesia, where the porphyries have locally converted ordinary black coal into native coke or anthracite.

Jukes observes: ' Microscopical examination exhibits not only the vascular, but the cellular tissue of plants in the substance of many coals, as was shown by Mr. Witham in his work on the structure of fossil plants, and by many observers since. All coals have a peculiar structure, which bears a slight analogy to crystallisation. They break or split, not only along the bedding, but across it, along two sets of planes at right angles to the bedding and to each other. The smooth clean faces produced by one of those cleavage planes are more marked and regular than that produced by the other, as may be seen by examining any lump of coal. The principal of these division planes are called by the colliers the *face* of the coal, the other being called the *back*, or *end*, of the coal. They preserve their parallelism sometimes over very wide areas; and the mode of working or getting the coal, and the direction of the galleries, is governed by the direction of the face.

' It is a structure which is probably the result of the mineralising process undergone in passing from an organic to an inorganic state, and may be likened perhaps to the " cleavage " of a mineral rather than to either the true " slaty cleavage" of rocks, or to their " foliation" or " jointing." '—*Jukes*, p, 134.

References.

Tenney has contributed numerous analyses to the New York Mining Magazine, 1856, p. 15.

Dawson, über die Pflanzenstructur der Steinkohle, in v. L. u. Br. Jahrb. 1860, p. 571.

Newberry, Entstehung der Cannelkohle, in v. L. u. Br. Jahrb. 1858, p. 852.

Geinitz, Die Versteinerungen der Steinkohlenformation in Sachsen, 1855, and Geogn. Darst. der Steinkohlenformation in Sachsen, 1856. Geologie der Steinkohlen Europas, München, 1865.

Göppert, über die Bildung der Steinkohle, im 4. Deel xx. Tweede Verzammling von naturkundige Verhandlingen von de Hollandische Maatschappij d. Wetenschappen te Haarlem.

v. Leonhard in the deuts. Vierteljahresschrift, 1838.

Stein, Untersuchung der Steinkohlen Sachsens, 1857.

Ronald and *Richardson*, Chemical Technology, vol. i. p. 30, &c.

Lovetz, Mineralien in fossilen Brennstoffen, v. Leonh. Jahrb. 1863, p. 654.

56. ANTHRACITE.

ANTHRACIT oder GLANZKOHLE. (*Germ.*)
ANTHRACITE. (*Fr.*)

Black with vitreous to half-metallic lustre, friable, streak black, not easily ignited, and burns almost without smoke and smell.

Spec. grav. . . . . . . 1·5—1·7.

Anthracite consists almost entirely of carbon, and contains very little hydrogen, oxygen, or nitrogen; that is to say, it is almost free from bitumen—a native compact coke. It contains earthy admixtures in various quantity, as is the case with other coal. It also contains the following accessory ingredients :—pyrites, clay-ironstone, gypsum, or calcspar in clefts.

There are scarcely any special varieties of anthracite to

describe, unless we consider as such the transition states
between anthracite and common coal and the compounds
of the two with each other.

Extensive beds of anthracite are only met with in the
formations of the Greywacké (transition) and Carboniferous periods. Locally, anthracite is sometimes associated with browncoal. As a rule, beds of anthracite are
never met with in the Coal formation except in localities
where it appears to have been exposed to special plutonic
influences, as at Zaunhaus, Schönfeld, and Brandau in the
Erzgebirge, Sablé and Beaulieu in Marne (France), at
the Stangen Alp in Styria, at Osnabruck, and in the
Alleghany Mountains. The normal position of anthracite
appears to be in the transition formations.

> We are not aware of any treatises or works specially devoted
> to the subject of anthracite. Much, however, respecting it will
> be found in those cited under the head of coal.

57. GRAPHITE, PLUMBAGO.

GRAPHIT. (*Germ.*)
GRAPHITE. (*Fr.*)

*A greyish-black aggregate, consisting of graphite; texture
varying from flaky to compact; soft, gives a black
streak (like lead pencil), greasy feel, not inflammable,
on the contrary capable of resisting fire.*

Spec. grav   .   .   .   .   .   .   1·9—2·2.

Graphite or plumbago is carbon in a state nearly pure,
but differing very widely from that of the diamond. As
a rock, graphite contains admixtures of silica, clay, oxide
of iron, or sometimes small crystalline grains of other
minerals. By these admixtures its properties are, however, only slightly altered.

Graphite is the last member of the series of transmutation of the carbonaceous rocks, and is therefore principally
(and normally) found in subordinate beds in strata of
crystalline slate-rocks or as a local admixture in the same
rocks;—at Passau in Bavaria, in Bohemia, at Borrowdale in England, &c. It occurs exceptionally in granite,
and is even found to fill fissures in that and other rocks.

We might theoretically regard the diamond as a still
more perfect, that is to say more crystalline and purer
product of transmutation of the carboniferous series. Its
occurrence is however so rare, and so subordinate, that
we cannot here notice it further.

References.

Prinsep, Graphite, Calcutta Gleanings of Science. Edin. Phil. Journ. 1832, vol. xxvi. p. 346.
Glocker, Graphit, Erdmann's Journ. f. Chem. vol. vi. p. 330.
Regnault, Graphite, Ann. des Mines, 3e Sér. vol. xii. p. 161.
Herter, Graphitschiefer mit Pflanzenresten, Zeitsch. d. deut. geol. Ges. vol. xv. p. 459.
Respecting the localities of the occurrence of Graphite, refer to v. L. u. Br. Jahrb. 1833, p. 552; 1836, p. 595; 1838, p. 427; 1839, p. 448; Journ. d. Phys. vol. xliv. p. 301; Correspondenzbl. des zool. mineral. Vereins zu Regensburg, 1827, p. 20, and 1848, p. 158.

58. BITUMEN and MINERAL PITCH.

BITUMEN und ERDPECH, ASPHALT. (*Germ.*)
BITUME, MALTHE, ASPHALTE. (*Fr.*)

A pitch-like mass, colour varying from dark-brown to black, softens with heat.

Spec. grav. bitumen . . . . . . 0·7—0·9
Mineral pitch . . . . 1·1—1·2

This bituminous mass consists of 80·82 carbon, 9—10 hydrogen, and 8·9 oxygen and nitrogen.

Bitumen is very seldom found in mass in the interior of the earth, but frequently as an accessory admixture in calcareous, marly, or argillaceous rocks. On the surface of the earth it occasionally forms small pitch lakes, as at the Dead Sea, and in the island of Trinidad. To this class belongs the petroleum, or rock-oil, which in North America has been recently found streaming in great abundance from the earth.

The origin of bitumen may be, and probably is, twofold. Bitumen or the gaseous elements of bitumen must of necessity be disengaged where bituminous coals undergo transmutation into coals of a less bituminous character, or into anthracite. This bitumen may either permeate the neighbouring rocks and make them bituminous, or it may rise to the surface of the earth and become a separate deposit of a fluid or semi-fluid substance. Again, bitumen will be formed wherever animal remains—gasteropods, fishes, and the like—have been enclosed by stratified beds of rock, and have become transmuted. And thus some limestones, marls, or clay-rocks may have become bituminous (being converted into oil-slate, stinkstein, &c.). Or the bitumen contained in

z

such rocks may, under the influence of heat or other causes, again escape and become deposited elsewhere.

The occurrence of bitumen in nature, taken in connection with the animal and vegetable fossils found in coal, completes the evidence in support of the established view of the origin of coal.

> Mayer's Asphalt des Val de Travers, 1839, is the only separate treatise on bitumen known to us. On rock-oil springs in North America, vide *Petermann's* Mittheilungen, 1861, vol. iv. p. 151; and *Kone's* Zeitschrift d. Erdkunde, 1862, vol. xii. p. 279.

59. PYROSCHIST (*Hunt*), BITUMINOUS SHALE.

BRANDSCHIEFER. (*Germ.*)
SCHISTE BITUMINEUX, MARNOLITE, *Cordier.* (*Fr.*)

Is the name given to very bituminous and thereby dark-brown or black-coloured argillaceous shale, which, although it burns in fire, yet, owing to its containing so much clay, cannot itself be used as fuel.

These are best classed with the carbonaceous rocks, together with which they frequently appear, and for which they have sometimes even been mistaken. Their streak is of resinous lustre; they often contain distinct remains of plants or fishes; sometimes bitumen may be extracted from them, and they are then sometimes called oil-slate (*Oelschiefer,* Germ.; *Schiste oléifère,* Fr.).

Bituminous shales of this class are found in Germany, especially in the lower Rothliegende, e.g. at Oschatz, in the Lias of Würtemburg, and in the chain of the Weser, and in the Brown-coal formation at many places.

> *Sterry Hunt,* Bitumen and Brandschiefer (Pyroschist), Silliman and Dana's American Journal, vol. xxxv. p. 157.

Appendix.

We may here add the burnt clays and the beds of guano or coprolites. The first because they have originated from the burning of coal-beds, the latter as accumulations of organic matter.

60. BURNT CLAYS.

GEBRANNTE THONE, KOHLENBRANDGESTEINE, ERDSCHLACKEN und PORZELLANJASPIS. (*Germ.*)
THERMANTIDE, *Cordier.* (*Fr.*)

These are local products of transmutation from clay rocks produced by burning coal-beds. They are too unlike in character to admit of a common definition. We, therefore, separately describe a few principal varieties.

(*a*) BURNT ARGILLACEOUS SHALE. } Hard, and resembling
GEBRANNTEN SCHIEFERTHON. (*Germ.*) } buck-colour, yellow,
ARGILE SCHISTEUSE MÉTAMORPHIQUE. (*Fr.*) } brown, or even violet;
nevertheless, still exhibiting the original laminated texture, and impressions of plants of the slate-clay. At Planitz, near Zwickau, in the Coal formation, and at Zittau in Saxony, in the Browncoal formation.

(*b*) ROCKSLAG. } By reason of greater heat the lami-
ERDSCHLACKE, KOHLENBRAND- } nated texture has been destroyed,
SCHLACKE. (*Germ.*) } and a scoriaceous slag-like texture
GLAISE. (*Fr.*) } arisen. Colours similar to the
burnt argillaceous shale. Found in the same localities.

(*c*) PORCELAIN JASPER, PORCELANITE. } The clay mass is half vi-
PORZELLANJASPIS. (*Germ.*) } trefied, porcelain-like, of
THERMANTIDE, *Cordier.* (*Fr.*) } greasy lustre, pearl-grey,
bluish-grey, lavender-blue, or brown. The same localities.

61. GUANO and other COPROLITE BEDS.

GUANO und andere KOPROLITHENLAGER. (*Germ.*)
GUANO. (*Fr.*)

These deposits must also be enumerated amongst rocks. In some localities they occupy a considerable place in the earth's crust.

(*a*) GUANO. } Forms earthy white, grey, or yellowish-
GUANO. (*Germ.*) } brown accumulations of very disagreeable
GUANO. (*Fr.*) } smell. It is chiefly known as a deposit
upon certain rocky islands of tropical climates. It consists chiefly of the excrement of birds, and contains, according to Boussingault, about 50—53 organic matter and ammonia-salts, 19—20 phosphate of lime, 3 phosphoric acid, 7 alkali, 1—2 silica and sand, and 15—16 water. These accumulations attain a depth of more than 100 feet, and frequently contain many other organic remains of recent date.

References.

v. Etzel, in Gumprecht's Zeitschr. f. Erdkunde, vol. v. pp. 326 and 425, vol. vi. p. 152.
Behm, in Petermann's Geogn. Mittheilungen, 1859, p. 173.
Boussingault, in Compt. rend. 1860, vol. li. p. 844; v. L. u. Br. Jahrb. 1861, p. 206.
Sandberger, Sombrero Phosphat (Guano), v. Leonh. Jahrb. 1864, p. 631.
Jenisch, Guano verschiedener Länder, v. Leonh. Jahrb. 1864, p. 866.

(*b*) COPROLITE BEDS. ⎱ Composed of excrements of fishes, reptiles,
    KOPROLITHENLAGER. ⎰ and mammalia which inhabited caverns,
      (*Germ.*)   some portions entirely petrified, but yet
containing much phosphoric acid. Found in many sedimentary
strata, also in caverns.

(*c*) BLACK EARTH. ⎱ May also be enumerated in this place,
    SCHWARZERDE, TSCHOR- ⎰ although the 6—9 per cent. of organic
     NOSEM. (*Germ.*)   admixtures contained in this black
clayey earth do not altogether appear to have been derived from
excrement. In Southern Russia this formation covers a great
extent, and lies on the surface of the earth. It attains a maxi-
mum depth of twenty feet. If subjected to the strong pressure of
overlying strata, it might possibly turn into bituminous shale.

References.

Murchison, Geology of Russia, 1845, p. 547.
Schmid, in v. L. u. Br. Jahrb. 1850, p. 350.
Wangenheim v. Qualen, ibid. 1856, p. 75.

IRONSTONE GROUP.

These are rocks principally consisting of minerals rich
in iron, so called iron-ores; these ores contain hydrated
oxide of iron, peroxide of iron, protoxide of iron, or carbonate of protoxide of iron, and accordingly are respectively termed *brown hematite, red hematite, magnetic
iron,* and *spathose* or *sparry iron.* Of these varieties there
are many modifications both of structure and composition.
We append to this group pea-iron-ore (Bohnerz) a pisi-
form spherosiderite which consists of a silicate of protoxide
of iron.

These different ironstones occur in the form of strata
or layers, veins or irregular masses, imbedded between
other rocks of various geological antiquity. The different
ironstones themselves, however, have a certain difference
of geological character which may be expressed somewhat
as follows :—

Hydrated Oxide of Iron, or   Is sometimes an original formation and
  Brown Hematite,   sometimes a secondary product. It
                             occurs in the form of layers, veins, or
                             irregular masses in formations or rocks
                             of every age.

Peroxide of Iron. Red He-   Is in most cases undoubtedly a secon-
  matite.   dary product. It occurs in the form of
                             veins, layers, or irregular masses, but
                             usually only in the older formations
                             and rocks.

Peroxide and Protoxide of Iron (combined) or Magnetic Iron-ore.	Forms layers, veins, or irregular masses; these only in the crystalline schists and plutonic igneous rocks. Frequently occurs also as an impregnation in the volcanic rocks.
Carbonate of Protoxide of Iron, or Spathose Iron.	As clay-ironstone, it forms layers or concretions, principally in the Coal formations; as spathic iron, it forms veins and irregular masses in various different rocks.
Pea-iron ore (Bohnerz).	Fills cavities and depressions in limestones.

62. BROWN HEMATITE.

BRAUNEISENSTEIN. (*Germ.*)
LIMONITE, *Beudant.* (*Fr.*)

A compact earthy, porous, or fibrous aggregate of brown iron-ore (limonite), yellowish-brown to black with brown streak.

Brown hematite consists entirely, or at least essentially, of hydrated oxide of iron ($\ddot{Fe}^2\overset{..}{H}^3$) containing 85·6 per cent. oxide of iron and 14·4 water. It sometimes, however, contains admixtures of oxide of manganese, silica, clay, or lime.

Varieties in Texture.

(*a*) COMPACT BROWN HEMATITE.
GEMEINER DICHTER BRAUNEISENSTEIN. (*Germ.*)
LIMONITE COMPACTE. (*Fr.*)

(*b*) SCALY AND OCHRY BROWN IRON-ORE, YELLOW OCHRE.
ERDIGER BRAUNEISENSTEIN, oder EISENOCKER. (*Germ.*)
OCHRE JAUNE. (*Fr.*)

(*c*) FIBROUS BROWN IRON-ORE, or GLASKOPF.
FASRIGER BRAUNEISENSTEIN, oder GLASKOPF. (*Germ.*)
HÉMATITE BRUNE CONCRÉTIONNÉE FIBREUSE. (*Fr.*)
} Occurs only in subordinate quantities, as stalactite.

(*d*) RENIFORM IRON-ORE.
NIERENERZ, REINERZ, STOCKERZ. (*Germ.*)
} Rounded concretions of brown iron-ore, chiefly found in clay, and usually occurring in combination with

(*e*) PEA-ORE.
BOHNERZ. (*Germ.*)
MINERAI EN GRAINS. (*Fr.*)
} Made up of globules (about the size of peas), mostly of concentric structure, imbedded in a mass of clay, iron-ochre, or limestone.

(*f*) OOLITIC BROWN ORE.
OOLITHISCHER BRAUNEISENSTEIN. (*Germ.*)
MINERAI BRUN OOLITHIQUE. (*Fr.*)
} Occurs in the form of layers in many formations.

(*g*) Bog-ore.

RASENEISENSTEIN, SUMPFERZ, QUELL-
ERZ, MORASTERZ, WIESENERZ, LI-
MONIT. (*Germ.*)
MINERAIS DE MARAIS, LIMONITE.
(*Fr.*)

Which likewise differs in the mode of its occurrence from other varieties. It is a porous arenaceous deposit of brown iron-ore on the earth's surface, and is created by springs or stagnant water. Frequently contains some phosphoric acid.

Varieties in Composition.

(*h*) A VARIETY RICH IN MANGANESE, BLACK IRONSTONE.

MANGANREICHER BRAUNEISENSTEIN,
SCHWARZEISENSTEIN. (*Germ.*)
LIMONITE MANGANÉSIFÈRE. (*Fr.*)

Frequently quite black, therefore sometimes called black ironstone.

(*i*) AN ARGILLACEOUS VARIETY (BROWN OR YELLOW CLAY-IRON-STONE).

THONREICHER BRAUNEISENSTEIN, THONEISENSTEIN. (*Germ.*)

(*k*) A SILICEOUS VARIETY, PASSING INTO BROWN FERRUGINOUS QUARTZ.

KIESELREICHER BRAUNEISENSTEIN. (*Germ.*)
HÉMATITE BRUNE SILICEUSE (JASPOIDE). (*Fr.*)

All these different varieties (with the exception of bog-ore, which only occurs on the surface of the ground) frequently form subordinate beds or veins filling up clefts in other rocks. Sometimes, but more rarely, they form local massive and irregular accumulations especially at the contact of two different rocks (contact formations).

Bog-ore is formed at the present day as a chemical precipitate from water holding salts of iron in solution; this process is occasioned or accompanied by decomposition of organic substances. If we suppose similar deposits of brown hematite to have taken place in former periods, and then to have been covered by other sedimentary formations, we may easily conceive how in process of time the thin compact layers of iron-ore which we find imbedded in other strata would have arisen. Sometimes brown hematite is evidently a product of transmutation from spathic iron, or even magnetic iron-ore.

63. RED HEMATITE.

ROTHEISENSTEIN. (*Germ.*)
HÉMATITE ROUGE. (*Fr.*)

A compact, earthy, or fibrous, or sometimes crystalline, slaty, aggregate of red iron-ore; colour red to black; streak red.

Spec. grav. . . . . 4—5.

Red hematite consists entirely or essentially of peroxide

of iron (70 p. c. iron + 30 p. c. oxygen), sometimes intimately combined with oxide of manganese, silica, or clay. Its crystalline state is termed specular iron (Eisenglanz), or micaceous iron (Eisenglimmer).

Varieties in Texture.

(*a*) COMMON RED HEMATITE.
GEMEINER DICHTER ROTHEISENSTEIN. (*Germ.*) } Compact.
HÉMATITE ROUGE COMPACTE. (*Fr.*)

(*b*) EARTHY HEMATITE, or RED IRON-MOULD.
ERDIGER ROTHEISENSTEIN, oder ROTHER EISENMULM. (*Germ.*)

(*c*) FIBROUS HEMATITE, REDDLE.
FASRIGER ROTHEISENSTEIN, RÖTHEL oder ROTHER GLASKOPF. (*Germ.*)
HÉMATITE ROUGE FIBREUSE. (*Fr.*)

(*d*) OOLITIC HEMATITE, or FERRUGINOUS OOLITE.
OOLITHISCHER ROTHEISENSTEIN, oder EISENOOLITH. (*Germ.*)
HÉMATITE ROUGE OOLITHIQUE. (*Fr.*)

(*e*) MICACEOUS IRON-SCHIST. } Consisting of a schis
EISENGLIMMERSCHIEFER. (*Germ.*) } tose aggregate of mica
FER OLIGISTE ÉCAILLEUX ou MICACÉ. (*Fr.*) } ceous iron, e.g. on the
Görgeleu in Marmaros, in Hungary, where it is imbedded between strata of chlorite-schist and limestone.

(*f*) SPECULAR IRON. } As rock, an aggregate of specular
EISENGLANZGESTEIN. (*Germ.*) } iron (iron-glance), usually combined
FER SPÉCULAIRE. (*Fr.*) } with some quartz. Of rare occurrence as a rock; e.g. on the Island of Elba, and at Picton-nob, in North America.

Varieties in Composition.

(*g*) A VARIETY RICH IN MANGANESE { Whence its black
(BLACK HEMATITE). { colour; sometimes
MANGANREICHER ROTHEISENSTEIN (SCHWARZ- { called black hematite
EISENSTEIN). (*Germ.*) { (Schwarzeisenstein).
HÉMATITE MANGANÉSIFÈRE. (*Fr.*) {

(*h*) RED CLAY-IRONSTONE, RED OCHRE. }
THONREICHER ROTHEISENSTEIN (THON- } An argillaceous variety.
EISENSTEIN). (*Germ.*) }
OCRE ROUGE. (*Fr.*) }

(*i*) SILICEOUS HEMATITE. }
KIESELREICHER ROTHEISEN- } Passing into red ferruginous quartz.
STEIN. (*Germ.*) }
HÉMATITE ROUGE SILICEUSE }
(JASPOÏDE). (*Fr.*) }

(*k*) ITABIRITE. } A compound of specular iron, micaceous
ITABIRIT. (*Germ.*) } iron, magnetic iron-ore, and some quartz;
ITABIRITE. (*Fr.*) } granular, schistose, or compact. As accessories, it contains talc, chlorite, actinolite, and native gold. Found at Itabira, in Brazil (v. Eschwege, ' Brasilien ').

(*l*) TOPANHOACANGA (MOORSHEAD ROCK). This rock consists of angular or somewhat rounded fragments of specular iron, micaceous iron, and magnetic iron-ore, cemented together by a ferruginous compound. Sometimes it also contains fragments of quartz, itacolumite, clay-slate, &c., rarely also, grains of native gold. At Itabira, Villa Rica, and Marianna, in Brazil, it forms a crust on the surface of the ground of from four to twelve feet thick.

Most of the above-mentioned varieties of red hematite occur in stratifications or veins, like the brown hematite; and they are also (though more rarely) found irregularly massed between other rocks, usually of the transition or crystalline schist formations—never those of very recent origin.

We may, perhaps, be justified in regarding the red hematites as products of catogenic transmutation from brown hematite; yet it would appear that they have some-times been formed from spathic iron under special circumstances. Certain it is from their anhydrous state we may safely say that they are never original deposits from aqueous solution, although they sometimes contain distinct fossils.

Specular iron, or iron-glance (as a mineral), is some-times found in the clefts or fissures of volcanoes, where it is a product of sublimation.

64. MAGNETIC IRONSTONE, MAGNETITE.

MAGNETEISENSTEIN. (*Germ.*)
MAGNÉTITE, FER OXYDULÉ, *Haüy* and *Dufrénoy*. (*Fr.*)

A granular or compact aggregate of magnetic iron-ore; black; streak black; metallic lustre; influences the magnetic needle.

Spec. grav. .   .   .   .   .   .   4·5—5·2.

Pure magnetic iron-ore consists of 69 to 75 per cent. peroxide of iron, and 31 to 25 per cent. protoxide of iron (therefore it contains about 72 per cent. iron). As a rock it occurs mixed with specular iron, chlorite, chromic iron-ore, titanic iron-ore, pyrites, chalcopyrite, quartz, horn-blende, augite, garnet, or felspar, &c.

Varieties in Texture.

(*a*) GRANULAR.
(*b*) COMPACT.
(*c*) SCHISTOSE. The foliation is occasioned by admixture of foreign minerals.

Varieties in Composition.

(*d*) PURE MAGNETIC IRON-ORE.
(*e*) CHLORITIC MAGNETIC IRONSTONE.
(*f*) CHROMIC IRONSTONE, in which chromic iron predominates or forms the only ingredient.
(*g*) GARNETIFEROUS IRONSTONE, passing over into garnet rock.

(*h*) PYRITO-MAGNETIC IRONSTONE.

(*i*) CATAWBIRITE is the name given by O. Lieber to a rock found by him in South Carolina, occurring there in great abundance. It consists of a compound of talc and magnetic iron, intimately blended together.

Magnetic ironstone forms subordinate beds or veins in the crystalline schists. It is very extensively developed at Schmiedefeld, in the Thuringian Forest, at Arendal in Norway, at Danemora in Sweden, as a stratum in the clay-slate at Berggieshübel in Saxony. Chromic ironstone is usually associated with serpentine.

65. SPATHIC IRON, SIDERITE.

SPATHEISENSTEIN. (*Germ.*)

FER CARBONATÉ, *Haüy* ; SIDÉROSE, *Beudant.* (*Fr.*)

A granular or compact aggregate of spathic iron; yellowish-white, grey, or yellowish-brown; streak white; effervesces with acid.

Spec. grav. . . . . . . 3·7—3·9.

Spathic iron is carbonate of protoxide of iron (62 per cent. protoxide of iron, and 38 carbonic acid); where it occurs as a rock it is sometimes mixed with ankerite, calc-spar, clay, specular iron, copper pyrites, &c., in small quantities.

Varieties in Texture.

(*a*) GRANULAR.

(*b*) VERY FINE-GRAINED.

(*c*) COMPACT SPHEROSIDERITE (CLAY-IRONSTONE). } So called from its occurring in the form of spheroidal concretions or septaria.
DICHTER SPATHEISENSTEIN, SPHÄROSIDERIT. (*Germ.*)
SIDÉROSE COMPACTE. (*Fr.*)

(*d*) A SHALY VARIETY OF SPHEROSIDERITE, or CARBONIFEROUS IRONSTONE (BLACKBAND).
SCHIEFRIGER SPHÄROSIDERIT, oder KOHLENEISENSTEIN. (*Germ.*)

Varieties in Composition.

(*e*) ROHWAND (*Germ.*). A granular spathic ironstone, mixed with much ankerite or calcspar.

(*f*) ARGILLACEOUS SPHEROSIDERITE, or CLAY IRONSTONE. } Also called clay carbonate of iron.
THONREICHER SPHÄROSIDERIT, oder THONEISENSTEIN. (*Germ.*)
SEPTARIA ARGILEUX. (*Fr.*)

(*g*) CARBONIFEROUS IRONSTONE, BLACKBAND. } Dark-coloured by reason of admixture of coal; usually a
KOHLENEISENSTEIN. (*Germ.*)
MINERAI DE FER DES HOUILLÈRES. (*Fr.*)

slaty spherosiderite or clay ironstone (*d*).

This is the black band of Scotland. 'This natural admixture of coaly matter confers on these rocks their special value, the raw stone being readily calcined, in fact igniting and slagging itself without the expensive admixture of coal, as is the case with the ordinary clay ironstones and hematites.'—*Page.*

Mushet makes a distinction between *Blackband* and *Clayband*, Berg- u. Huttenm. Zeit. 1863, p. 295.

The crystalline varieties occur as subordinate strata, veins or regular masses, in the crystalline schists or the older sedimentary formations. The compact spherosiderites are most usually found with beds of coal. The origin of these stratified beds and irregular masses of spathic iron has not hitherto been satisfactorily explained, since a carbonate of protoxide of iron could not be deposited under atmospheric influences. Probably the carbonic acid may have supervened at a later period. On the other hand, the influence of the air will quickly change spathic iron into brown hematite, and hence it is that we find the surface of spherosiderite usually coated with a brown crust, and many entire beds of brown hematite appear to have been formed in this manner. A different process of mutation may, perhaps, in some cases, have produced red hematite and magnetic iron-ore.

Appendix.

66. DISILICATE OF PROTOXIDE OF IRON.

HALBKIESELSAURES EISENOXYDUL. (*Germ.*)
CHAMOISITE (Chamoison, Valais). (*Fr.*)

This compound sometimes occurs in the form of pea-iron-ore contained in ferruginous clay, together with nodules of jasper, as, for instance, at Kandern, on the western margin of the Schwarzwald in Germany.

Deffner, zur Erklärung der Bohnerzgebilde, Stuttgart, 1859.

67. SILICEOUS SPHEROSIDERITE.

KIESELIGER SPHÄROSIDERIT. (*Germ.*)
CARBONATE DE FER SILICEUX. (*Fr.*)

This is a rock, described by Naumann, of a peculiar and fine arenaceous character, consisting essentially of spherosiderite (containing manganese) and siliceous earth or quartz-sand. It forms a stratum (very rich in fossils) in the Nummulite formation of the Bavarian Alps between Traunstein and Sonthofen.

Schafthäutl, in v. L. u. Br. Jahrbuch, 1846, p. 604.

CHAPTER V.

MINERALS AS ROCKS.

WE have in the first three chapters treated of those rocks which, by reason of their great extent and volume, may be regarded as the principal ingredients of the earth's crust. We have seen that they are mostly of compound character, although some few are essentially simple mineral substances.

In this place we propose to enumerate those simple minerals which appear as local accumulations in different parts of the globe, forming essential members of particular formations, sometimes as stratified beds, sometimes as veins or dykes, or irregular masses; their volume being just sufficient to entitle them to be considered as members of the rock family, taking an independent part in the structure of the solid crust of the earth, although in comparison with the other rock-formations which we have hitherto treated, their bulk is for the most part very inconsiderable.

A description of the formation, texture, &c., of these mineral rocks will, in most cases, be unnecessary, as they must be mineralogically determined and recognised. We shall, therefore, in each case only give the name of the mineral, adding some short remarks as to its exceptional lithological character.

68. ICE.

EIS. (*Germ.*)
GLACE. (*Fr.*)

Sometimes compact, sometimes granular, fibrous or laminated.

We need not here describe the properties of ice, but it is not unimportant to consider the conditions under which perpetual ice occurring in large masses forms part of the solid crust of the earth.

The snow which falls in the polar regions, and in

mountain districts above the snow-line, only partially thaws in summer; the remainder accumulates year by year. The successive falls of snow form a series of super-jacent strata, the fleecy mass becomes consolidated by pressure, and grains of ice are formed which unite into a stratified granular ice; this in the Alps is called *firn* or *névé*. The masses of névé thus formed glide gradually down over the mountain slopes and precipices into the ravines and valleys. In the course of their downward movement their stratification becomes much contorted and otherwise disturbed; they are, moreover, transformed from distinctly granular névé into indistinctly granular ice, or so-called glaciers.

The glacier continues to glide with a slow movement down the valley. Its lower extremity, thus arrived in warmer regions, thaws more rapidly and equalises the accumulation of snow pressing down in fresh masses from above. Hence the general extent and size of the glacier usually remains much the same, although the individual parts are constantly changing their position. By the mo-tion of the glacier the traces of original stratification be-come more and more contorted and effaced. The glacier, moreover, becomes rent with frequent fissures (crevasses), and in these the water arising from occasional thawing accumulates and freezes during night or winter into new ice, which may be distinguished from the genuine glacier ice by its more compact structure.

All these phenomena are very instructive, and afford many analogies to other rock formations and transfor-mations. From loose accumulations, by means of pressure and consolidation, masses are formed which become firmer and more solid, and at last tolerably compact. Strata are bent, pushed out of place, and overturned. The mass is torn by cracks and fissures, which are filled by water rendered fluid by heat. This freezes and constructs ice veins in ice, somewhat like granite veins in granite, only that these latter were probably filled from below, and under a much higher temperature. By a kind of weather-ing process even the compact venous ice in its turn be-comes granular or separates into thin columnar parts, and all these changes take place before our eyes in compara-tively short spaces of time.

Very similar phenomena occur on a much larger scale in the polar regions; only they are less accessible, and therefore more difficult of observation.

Besides these permanent masses of ice lying on the surface of the earth, there occur in the northern plains of Siberia extensive underground ice strata of great thickness, sometimes interstratified with beds of sand, or they contain sand mixed with the ice, and occasionally these strata are covered with a surface layer of soil, which during the short summer of Siberia supports vegetation.

69. OPAL.

OPAL. (*Germ.*)
OPALE. (*Fr.*)

As a rock, usually only forms very subordinate masses, e.g. the so-called vitrite, which occurs at Meronitz, in Bohemia, and contains numerous pyropes.

If, however, we reckon under the name of opal all the various amorphous silicates enumerated by Naumann, we find amongst them several very important rocks:—

Varieties.

(*a*) SILICEOUS SINTER, or SILICEOUS TUFF. Stratified incrustations and porous masses; found as a deposit of hot springs in Iceland and Kamtschatka, and, according to Hochstetter, still more frequently in New Zealand. (*Novarareise*, 1862, vol. iii. p. 165.)
KIESELSINTER oder KIESELTUFF. (*Germ.*)
TUF SILICEUX, GEYSÉRITE. (*Fr.*)

(*b*) SEMI-OPAL. Forms independent deposits, e. g. at Bilin, in Bohemia; also irregular fillings of clefts in basaltic rocks, e. g. at Ilanau on the Maine, in the dolerite.
HALBOPAL. (*Germ.*)
SEMI-OPALE. (*Fr.*)

(*c*) MENILITE. Menilite occurs in the Paris basin in clumps and beds. It is found there in gypsum and in marl (Eocene); in Auvergne, in freshwater marl (Miocene).
MENILIT. (*Germ.*)
MÉNILITE. (*Fr.*)

(*d*) POLISHING SLATE, TRIPOLI. Consists of small shell-shaped particles of silica of a peculiar form, only to be distinguished with the aid of the microscope, so-called siliceous armour of Diatomaceæ or Infusoria; Naumann therefore calls it *Diatomeenpelit*. Ehrenberg reckoned that the polishing slate of Bilin in Bohemia contained in a cubic inch 41,000 millions siliceous shells of *Gaillonella*. Each individual is invisible to the naked eye, so that when used for polishing metallic surfaces it produces only fine invisible scratches. Distinction is made in Bohemia between
POLIRSCHIEFER, SAUGSCHIEFER, KLEBSCHIEFER, TRIPPEL. (*Germ.*)
TRIPOLI. (*Fr.*)

the polirschiefer (soft, friable, not adhering to the tongue) and saugschiefer (adhering to the tongue and more solid, probably because it is impregnated with opal substance). Both are only known in very recent deposits; the older ones have probably been transmuted into hornstein or lydian stone. (*Ehrenberg*, Fossil Infusoria, Berlin, 1837, and Mikrogeologie.)

(*e*) KIESELGUHR. } The same substance as polishing slate,
KIESELGUHR. (*Germ.*) } but more dust-like, earthy, generally
SILICE PULVÉRULENTE, } white or yellow. Found in beds many
RANDANITE. (*Fr.*) } feet thick in the turf deposits at Soos,
near Franzensbad, Bohemia. The rock called RANDANITE by Salvetat belongs to this species; it consists of a white powder. (v. L. u. Br. Jahrb. 1848, p. 124.)

70. QUARTZ.

QUARZ. (*Germ.*)
QUARTZ. (*Fr.*)

Occurs as an essential ingredient in many rocks, but it also occurs as an independent rock in many varieties, some of which are of considerable extent. We repeat the mention in this place of several quartz rocks which we have already noticed and included in other groups.

Varieties.

(*a*) ROCK CRYSTAL and AMETHYST. } Sometimes the essential
BERGKRYSTALL und AMETHYST. (*Germ.*) } ingredient of veins and
CRYSTAL DE ROCHE et AMÉTHYSTE. (*Fr.*) } dykes.

(*b*) COMMON QUARTZ. } Forms independent bed-veins or irre-
QUARTZ COMMUN. (*Fr.*) } gular masses. Quartz-schist, see p. 246, ante; Quartz-breccia, p. 305; Quartz-sandstones (siliceous sandstone), p. 296. Millstone-quartz, freshwater-quartz, or lemon-quartz, are porous varieties resembling chert, which, . according to the fossils occasionally found in them, have been deposited by fresh water, as, e. g., the celebrated millstones of the Paris basin (Quartz meulier).

(*c*) FERRUGINOUS QUARTZ. } Yellow, red-brown, or black; forms
EISENKIESEL. (*Germ.*) } transition states into jasper. Its
QUARTZ FERRUGINEUX. (*Fr.*) } mode of occurrence in nature is the
same as that of ordinary quartz.

(*d*) HORNSTONE, CHERT. } Compact, forms independent beds,
HORNSTEIN, HORNFELS. (*Germ.*) } veins, and masses. In Germany
AMAS SILICEUX. (*Fr.*) } the name of Hornfels is given to
certain rocks, the product of transmutation of argillaceous deposits, and found adjoining to plutonic rocks, to which they probably owe the change they have undergone.

(*e*) LYDIAN STONE, or LYDITE, BLACK } Contains carbon which
CHERT. } gives it a greyish colour
KIESELSCHIEFER oder LYDIT. (*Germ.*) } inclining to black;
QUARTZ LYDIEN. (*Fr.*) } usually stratified in thin
laminæ, and hence of a laminated texture; generally penetrated by numerous white veins of quartz; much rent by

angular fissures, sometimes containing lenticular concretions, and also sometimes containing laminæ of clay-slate. In fissures it contains wavellite, calaite, variscite. It occurs with tolerable frequency as a subordinate stratum in clay-slate, slate-clay, or even mica-schist.

(*f*) JASPER. | Compact, variegated, frequently striped or
JASPIS. (*Germ.*) } flamed (riband-jasper, agate-jasper). Much
JASPE. (*Fr.*)) has been called jasper which properly belongs to the felsitic rocks, even to the felsitic tuffs. It forms subordinate layers imbedded in other rocks, and nodular concretions. Jasper may be readily distinguished from petrosilex (which it otherwise sometimes resembles) by the fusibility of the latter.

(*g*) AGATE. | The name given to certain combinations of
ACHAT. (*Germ.*) } chalcedony, carnelian, amethyst, and quartz.
AGATE. (*Fr.*)) There are many varieties :—banded agate, fortification-agate, coral-agate, &c. It frequently forms veins or fills cavities in other rocks.

(*h*) FLINT. | Very similar to hornstone, but half amor-
FEUERSTEIN. (*Germ.*) } phous, chiefly yellow, brown, grey, or
SILEX. (*Fr.*)) black. Forms nodules, and then are frequently disposed in layers; very frequent, e.g. in chalk.

71. CORUNDUM.

KORUND oder SCHMIRGEL. (*Germ.*)
CORINDON. (*Fr.*)

Forms fine-grained subordinate layers imbedded in crystalline schists, frequently accompanied by magnetic iron-ore. Ochsenkopff, in the Erzgebirge; Gumuchdagh, in Asia Minor; Naxos; Chester, Massachusetts.

72. FLUOR-SPAR.

FLUSSSPATH. (*Germ.*)
FLUORINE, SPATHFLUOR. (*Fr.*)

Frequently an essential ingredient in metalliferous veins. A compact aggregate of fluor-spar forms a rock at Rottleberode and Strassberg in the Hartz Mountains.

73. ROCK-SALT.

STEINSALZ. (*Germ.*)
SEL GEMME. (*Fr.*)

Chloride of sodium occurring as a rock is usually crystalline-granular, white, translucent or transparent, easily soluble in water, and possesses a saline taste.

Spec. grav. . . . . . . 2·1—2·2.

Pure chloride of sodium consists of 60 per cent. chlorine to 40 per cent. sodium. In nature, however, it almost always contains sulphate of lime, chloride of calcium, chloride of magnesium, and other salts; frequently admixtures of bitumen, clay, or boracite. Salt itself sometimes only forms an ingredient of some clays (Salzthon, saliferous clay).

The colour of rock-salt is variable; it is sometimes yellow, red, bluish, or greenish, by reason of small admixtures of oxide of iron.

Varieties.

(*a*) GRANULAR ROCK-SALT.
KÖRNIGES STEINSALZ. (*Germ.*)
SEL GEMME GRANULAIRE. (*Fr.*)
(*b*) SPARRY ROCK-SALT.
BLÄTTRIGES STEINSALZ. (*Germ.*)
SEL GEMME LAMINAIRE (SPATHIQUE). (*Fr.*)
(*c*) FIBROUS ROCK-SALT.
FASRIGES STEINSALZ. (*Germ.*)
SEL GEMME FIBREUX. (*Fr.*)
(*d*) KNISTERSALZ. (*Germ.*)
(*e*) GRÜNSALZ, SPIZASALZ, SZYBIKER SALZ. (*Germ.*)

Reference.

The origin of the rock-salt of Strassfurt, near Magdeburg, has been lately treated in a masterly manner by *F. Bischof*, Die Steinsalzwerke zu Strassfurt, 1864.

74. TRONA.

TRONA. (*Germ.*)
SESQUI-CARBONATE DE SOUDE. (*Fr.*)

Occurs in Fezzan, in North Africa, forming a rock which is even used for building purposes.

75. ALUNITE, or ALUM STONE.

ALUNIT, oder ALAUNSTEIN. (*Germ.*)
ALUNITE. (*Fr.*)

Forms a rock in the neighbourhood of Tolfa, near Civita Vecchia. (See p. 185.)

76. BARYTES, or HEAVY SPAR.

BARYT, oder SCHWERSPATH. (*Germ.*)
BARYTINE, ou SPATH PESANT. (*Fr.*)

This mineral, which forms an essential part of many metalliferous veins, was discovered by Von Dechen, as constituting a compact rock forming a bed some ten feet in thickness, in the clay-slate of Meggen in the Lennethal. Its colour was dark-grey.

Karsten's Archiv, 1845, vol. xix. p. 748; see also v. *Hoiningen*, Verh. der naturh. Ver. d. pr. Rheinl. 1856, vol. xiii. p. 300; *Sandberger*, geol. Verh. d. H. Nassau, p. 11; and *Zimmermann*, Harzgebirge, 1834, vol. i. p. 151.

77. BORACITE, or STASSFURTITE.

BORACIT, STASSFURTIT. (*Germ.*)
BORACITE, STASSFURTITE. (*Fr.*)

Forms irregular layers imbedded in the rock-salt of Stasfurt.

Zeitschr. d. d. geol. Ges. 1856, vol. viii. p. 156.

78. PHOSPHORITE.

PHOSPHORIT. (*Germ.*)
CHAUX PHOSPHATÉE, APATITE. (*Fr.*)

Sometimes forms compact spheroidal masses, or subordinate layers, and even dykes or veins. Kragerÿe in Norway.

79. CRYOLITE.

KRYOLITH. (*Germ.*)
CRYOLITE. (*Fr.*)

Forms considerable veins in the granitic gneiss at Evigtok, in Greenland. (Journ. of Geol. Soc.)

80. ARAGONITE.

ARAGONIT. (*Germ.*)
ARAGONITE. (*Fr.*)

Many so-called calcareous sinters and peastones consist, properly speaking, not of calcspar, but aragonite. (See p. 281.)

81. ANKERITE.

ANKERIT. (*Germ.*)
ANKÉRITE. (*Fr.*)

This is most frequently found mixed in subordinate quantities with spathic iron (vide p. 345, ante); and is sometimes found separately as an independent rock.

82. MAGNESITE.

MAGNESIT. (*Germ.*)
MAGNÉSIE CARBONATÉE. (*Fr.*)

Frequently forms compact masses, but of subordinate size and extent.

A A

83. DIALLOGITE, CARBONATE OF MANGA-NESE.

MANGANSPATH. (*Germ.*)
DIALLOGITE. (*Fr.*)

Frequently forms the principal constituent of metal-liferous veins, e. g. at Kapnik, in Hungary.

84. MALACHITE.

MALACHIT. (*Germ.*)
MALACHITE. (*Fr.*)

Sometimes forms great clumps or masses in beds of copper-ore in Russia.

85. TALC, or STEATITE.

TALK oder SPECKSTEIN. (*Germ.*)
TALC ou STÉATITE. (*Fr.*)

Forms independent compact beds, e.g. at Göpfers-Grün, in the Fichtelgebirge, where it forms a rock which can-not be classed as a talc-schist.

86. MEERSCHAUM.

MEERSCHAUM. (*Germ.*)
ÉCUME DE MER, MAGNÉSITE. (*Fr.*)

Forms separate beds in Natolia, Negroponte, Crimea, &c.

87. AGALMATOLITE, or FIGURE-STONE.

AGALMATOLITH oder BILDSTEIN. (*Germ.*)
AGALMATOLITHE. (*Fr.*)

The principal member of a dyke or vein at Dilln, near Schemnitz. Also in China.

88. KAOLIN, or PORCELAIN CLAY.

KAOLIN oder PORZELLANERDE. (*Germ.*)
KAOLIN. (*Fr.*)

This is probably everywhere merely a product of the decomposition of rocks very rich in felspar. Aue, in Saxony, where it is a decomposed granite. In some places a slight change has converted it into clay.

89. LITHOMARGE.

STEINMARK. (*Germ.*)
LITHOMARGE. (*Fr.*)

Is found in very subordinate quantity between other rocks.

90. ORTHOCLASE.

ORTHOKLAS. (*Germ.*)
ORTHOSE. (*Fr.*)

Sometimes forms independent dykes and accumulations, e. g. in the granite at Carlsbad.

91. PYCNITE.

PYKNIT. (*Germ.*)
PYCNITE. (*Fr.*)

Forms concretions and dykes in the Zwitter rock, at Altenberg, in Saxony.

92. EPIDOSITE, or PISTACITE ROCK.

EPIDOSIT oder PISTAZITFELS. (*Germ.*)
ÉPIDOSITE. (*Fr.*)

Epidote usually combined with some quartz. A subordinate formation in the Island of Elba.

93. LEPIDOLITE, or LITHIA-MICA.

LEPIDOLITH oder LITHIONGLIMMER. (*Germ.*)
LÉPIDOLITE (MICA À LITHINE). (*Fr.*)

Forms an independent rock of fine-grained and foliated texture, e. g. at Rozena, in Moravia.

94. ROCK SOAP.

BERGSEIFE. (*Germ.*)
PIERRE DE SAVON. (*Fr.*)

Occurs in masses of subordinate extent, e. g. at Bilin, in Bohemia.

95. BOLE.

BOL. (*Germ.*)
BOLE. (*Fr.*)

Occurs in masses of subordinate size in many limestone rocks.

96. FULLERS' EARTH.

WALKERDE. (*Germ.*)
TERRE À FOULON. (*Fr.*)

A substance resembling clay, somewhat greasy, but not in the smallest degree plastic, but falling to pieces in water, usually of yellowish green colour; is probably a product of the decomposition of basic igneous rocks. Cilli in Styria; Nutfield, near Reigate.

97. FERREO-LITHOMARGE.

EISENSTEINMARK. (*Germ.*)
TÉRATOLITE. (*Fr.*)

Occurs in subordinate masses at Zwickau, in Saxony.

98. YELLOW EARTH, or MELINITE.

$$\ddot{A}l\ddot{S}i + 2\ddot{F}e\ddot{S}i + 6\ddot{H}.$$

GELBERDE. (*Germ.*)

Occurs in small accumulations at Amberg, and other places.

99. GALMEY, CARBONATE OF ZINC (in part).

GALMEI. (*Germ.*)
CALAMINE. (*Fr.*)

This name is indifferently applied to both the principal zinc-ores: the silicate of zinc and the carbonate of zinc. They occur together, and they form aggregates of considerable size in the dolomite limestones of Tarnowitz, Iserlohn, Aix-la-Chapelle, &c.

100. RHODONITE (in part), MANGANESE SPAR (Bisilicate of Manganese).

KIESELMANGAN oder MANGANKIESEL. (*Germ.*)
RHODONITE (MANGANÈSE SILICATÉ). (*Fr.*)

Occurs (e. g.) in subordinate beds at Rosenau, in Hungary; Cummington, Massachusetts, U.S.

101. LIEVRITE, or ILVAITE.

LIÈVRIT. (*Germ.*)
ILVAITE. (*Fr.*)

Occurs (e. g.) in subordinate beds in the mica-schist of the Island of Elba.

102. MANGANESE-ORES.

MANGANERZE. (*Germ.*)
MINERAIS DE MANGANÈSE. (*Fr.*)

One or more of these form veins of considerable thickness, or beds of irregular shape, at Ilmenau, Ilfeld, Kleinlinden, Warwickshire, &c.

103. RED ZINC-ORE.

ROTHZINKERZ. (*Germ.*)
MINERAI ROUGE DE ZINC (FRANKLINITE). (*Fr.*)

Combined with Franklinite forms a bed of very considerable thickness at Franklin, in New Jersey.

104. GALENA.

BLEIGLANZ. (*Germ.*)
GALÈNE. (*Fr.*)

Usually associated with blende and sulphurets; forms veins of considerable extent and thickness, and occurs otherwise in separate beds..

105. ANTIMONY-GLANCE.

ANTIMONGLANZ. (*Germ.*)
ANTIMOINE. (*Fr.*)

Forms veins of considerable thickness, e. g. at Magurka, in Hungary.

106. ARSENICAL PYRITES.

ARSENKIES. (*Germ.*)
PYRITES ARSÉNICALES. (*Fr.*)

Usually associated with other sulphurets; occurs in separate formations of considerable thickness.

107. MARCASITE, or HYDROUS PYRITES.

MARKASIT oder WASSERKIES. (*Germ.*)
MARCASSITE. (*Fr.*)

Forms subordinate layers imbedded in other rocks, e. g. in the Browncoal formation at Littmitz, in Bohemia.

108. PYRITES.

SCHWEFELKIES, PYRIT. (*Germ.*)
PYRITES. (*Fr.*)

Usually associated with some chalcopyrite; forms beds,

veins, or irregular masses of considerable size, e.g. at Domokos in Transylvania, Rio Tinto in Spain, Schmöllnitz in Hungary, Goslar at the Hartz, Fahlun in Sweden, Agordo in the Alps.

109. CINNABAR.

ZINNOBER. (*Germ.*)
CINABRE. (*Fr.*)

Occurs but rarely in beds of considerable size or thickness, e.g. at Almaden in Spain, Idria, California.

110. SULPHUR.

SCHWEFEL. (*Germ.*)
SOUFRE. (*Fr.*)

Forms rounded concretions and layers, in marl formations, e.g. at Radoboj in Croatia, Sicily, Perticara in Umbria.

PART III.

OBSERVATIONS ON THE PROCESSES OF ROCK FORMATION IN NATURE.

THE NATURAL PROCESSES by which rocks have been formed and are still in course of formation are partly indicated in the foregoing pages. The following are those known to us from actual observation:—

1. CONSOLIDATION OF SUBSTANCES FROM A STATE OF IGNEOUS FUSION BY PROCESS OF COOLING. This is the process which all lavas undergo, and by which, probably, all igneous rocks have been formed. We must assume that a first crust of the earth was likewise so formed, but we cannot with certainty point to any of the rocks remaining to us at the present day as representing this primeval formation.

2. DEPOSIT OF SUBSTANCES FROM A STATE OF SUSPENSION IN WATER, AND OF SUBSTANCES FALLEN THROUGH THE AIR. Thus are formed the sedimentary rocks, under which general designation every kind of deposit is included.

They may be divided as follows:—

(a) *Mechanical deposits* (actual sediments).—To this class belong deposits of mud, sand, and pebbles of every kind, which by process of condensation and cementation produce argillaceous shale, clay-slate, limestone, sandstone, conglomerate, and other similar rocks.

From the atmosphere are deposited particles of dust and sand. These are frequently held in a state of suspension for a considerable time, and transported by the wind to great distances. Volcanoes vomit detached substances or fine particles of dust, which with the aid of water form volcanic tufas of various kinds.

(*b*) *Chemical precipitates* from aqueous solutions.— By chemical agency many kinds of deposit are formed. For instance, calc-tuff, siliceous tuff, bog iron-ore, incrustations of salt, and many mineral formations in clefts and cavities of rocks. The crystalline particles of ice which fall from the air in the form of snow may be considered as a chemical precipitate. Snow, as we have seen, forms the névé and glaciers of high mountain regions.

(*c*) *Zoogenic deposits* are products of animal agency. Their massive accumulation is partly a mechanical process. Thus we have rocks formed entirely of siliceous infusoria, also the chalks, banks of shells, coral-reefs, guano and coprolite beds, &c.

From the condensation of these rocks, hornstone, lydian-stone, limestone, &c., may have resulted.

(*d*) *Phytogenic deposits* are such as consist chiefly of vegetable substances; these have either grown *in situ*, or have been washed together. From these deposits, by process of consolidation and subsequent conversion, the different coal formations have resulted.

The above-mentioned processes of rock-formation are those which admit of direct observation. There are others at whose nature we only arrive by reasoning from the results. Such are :—

3. METAMORPHOSIS, OR TRANSMUTATION OF PRE-VIOUSLY EXISTING ROCKS. This is a process constantly at work—it has even begun to affect most of the distinctly sedimentary rocks. Few of these but have undergone some change. Thus the changes from argillaceous mud to shale and then to clay-slate, from sand to sandstone, from loose stones to conglomerate, from calcareous silt to limestone, from peat-moss to browncoal, or ordinary black coal, &c., are, properly speaking, all cases of metamorphosis, although the rocks we have just named are not usually termed metamorphic. That term is reserved for the further stages of transmutation, where the change is so complete that the first state of the rock can no longer be easily or with certainty recognised by mere observa-

tion. The genuine metamorphic rocks are mica-schist, gneiss, and the other crystalline schists, whose identity with their originals can only be proved by deduction from a variety of collateral circumstances.

The foregoing, are the only processes of rock-formation known to us by observation, or which can be ascertained by deduction from known facts. These processes are, however, undoubted and indisputable, and our chief difficulty consists in determining in each instance to which mode of formation a rock owes its origin. Here many difficulties and justifiable doubts present themselves. Let us therefore attempt the application of these experiences and their consequences to the several groups of rocks which we have described in the preceding pages.

IGNEOUS ROCKS. (*Eruptiv-Gesteine.*)

No unprejudiced observer of geological phenomena can doubt that those which we have classed and named as igneous rocks were once in a fluid or viscous state, and that whilst in that state they broke through pre-existing rocks, overflowed them, and afterwards consolidated. Ample proofs of these operations of nature are found in the relation of the bedding of the igneous to those of their surrounding rocks, the disturbances which they have frequently (but not invariably) caused in the rocks broken through, the fragments of the latter which they enclose, and the veins or branches which they have thrust into those adjoining. These general conditions established, there still remain many special phenomena of formation to be explained and accounted for, which we propose briefly to consider in this place.

The great mutual resemblance of all igneous rocks both chemically and mineralogically bespeaks a like process of formation for all, i.e. they were all forced upwards from the interior towards the surface of the earth in a molten state, like the lavas (which are evidently igneous products) from the active volcanoes of the present-day. But although the composition and mode of occurrence of all these rocks is, generally speaking, of a very uniform character, yet special differences show that a great part of those which are now exposed to our view did not originally reach the surface and overflow at the time of their upheaval in the manner of genuine lavas, but became solid at a considerable depth underground, where they still were covered by or imbedded between other rocks; and we must assume that their present appearance on the face of the earth is owing to subsequent destruction and washing away of the superincumbent rocks. Hence we distinguish between *volcanic* and *plutonic* rocks. The volcanic (as we have seen) are those which are known, or supposed, to have consolidated at or near the surface; and the plutonic those which are presumed to have solidified at a considerable depth in the interior of the earth. There is no definite depth of measurement which we can fix as a boundary between these two kinds of formation; the question of such depth must remain a subject for entirely speculative estimate. Nor is the division of rocks into volcanic and plutonic dependent on their mere age, although in most cases it corresponds to a certain extent in fact with their relative antiquity, because most of the older volcanic formations have decayed away and disappeared, whilst the newer plutonic formations have not yet been laid bare, and are therefore inaccessible to our view. The deeper in the earth that any rock was formed, the longer would be (*cæteris paribus*) the time necessary for its denudation; and therefore the older will it be when we meet with it at the surface.

Recent chemical analysis (as we have already had occasion to remark) shows a great uniformity of elementary composition in all classes of igneous rocks. We have seen that they all consist of silica, alumina, peroxide or protoxide of iron, lime, magnesia, potash, and soda, and frequently some water. Their other ingredients are but subordinate in quantity, and can only be regarded as accessory; such are protoxide of manganese, titanic acid, carbonic acid, phosphoric acid, sulphuric acid, oxide of chromium, oxide of copper, baryta, lithia, sulphur, &c.

The quantitative proportions of the essential elements vary considerably in different rocks, but this variation is almost as great between different kinds of the same rock as between the different rocks themselves; and no igneous rock is of so invariable or marked a chemical character as to be distinguishable from the rest by it alone.

Taking the whole range of the igneous rocks, the average values of their chemical constituents may be stated somewhat as follows :—

	Extreme actual values.	*Ideal average.*
Silica	50—80	45
Alumina	10—25	15
Peroxide and Protoxide of Iron	1—25	10
Lime	0—15	6
Magnesia	0—12	5
Potash	0—10	4
Soda	0— 7	4
Water	0— 5	2

Where the extreme values, as above given, are found to be exceeded on the one side or the other, the excess or deficiency appears invariably to have been the result of change, decomposition, or some similar process subsequent to the formation of the rock, which, therefore, is no longer in its original state.

We have already indicated the division of the igneous rocks, in respect of their chemical composition, into two principal groups.

1. Poor in silica, or *basic.*

2. Rich in silica, or *acidic* igneous rocks.

The distinction between these two groups is deserving of considerable attention, for they also differ to some extent both mineralogically and geologically, although they cannot be very rigidly separated from each other; and certain rocks of each group vary so greatly in their composition as actually to graduate into the opposite group.

The following proportions may be stated as an approximate average of the analysis for the two groups :—

	Basic.	Acidic.
Silica	45—60	55—80
Alumina	10—25	10—15
Iron (Peroxide or Protoxide)	1—25	1—15
Lime	1—15	0— 8
Magnesia	1—12	0— 4
Potash	1— 9	1—11
Soda	1— 7	2— 8
Water	0— 4	0— 6

These two groups nearly correspond with the *pyroxenic* and *trachytic* groups of Bunsen, for which he calculated certain ideal or normal average values of their elementary constituents.* (See Poggend. Ann. 1851, vol. lxxxiii.)

Without, therefore, being able to fix any very precise standard, the distinguishing feature of the basic rocks is, that they contain less silica, more alumina, iron, lime, and magnesia, and less alkali than the acidic rocks. Within the limits of each group we find no constant differences of chemical composition between the several species. These only differ in their mineral development, their texture, or the mode and accidents of their occurrence in nature.

We may, therefore, say in general terms that all igneous rocks consist of one or other of two compounds normally differing in the proportions of their elementary constituents, but that several intermediate gradations exist between the two extremes. Each of these two compounds has produced many different species and modifications of rock which have received different names. The differences are partly those of texture, partly of mineral composition. The first may in most cases be very simply accounted for by the particular circumstances of

---

* Bunsen's values of the different elements were as follows :—

	Pyroxenic.	Trachytic.
Silica	48·47	76·67
Alumina and Protoxide of Iron	30·16	14·23
Lime	11·87	1·44
Magnesia	6·89	0·28
Soda	1·06	3·20
Potash	0·65	4·18
	100·00	100·00

cooling. The quicker the cooling process, the more compact or even vitreous the product would be; and the
slower the process, the more crystalline and coarse-
grained would the rock become. Inequality in the crystallising power of the different ingredients would give a
porphyritic texture; parallel arrangement of certain of
the ingredients would give a slaty or schistose texture;
development of gases during the cooling would give a
vesicular or slag-like texture.

The differences of mineral composition are not great.
In most cases the elementary substances are the same;
and the differences of proportion in which they are combined are so small as to appear unimportant. We are
unable satisfactorily to explain in any particular case why,
with differences of composition so trifling, one particular
species of felspar, of hornblende or pyroxene, or of mica
was produced rather than another, or why, under apparently similar conditions in another rock, other minerals, such as nepheline, leucite, talc, chlorite, &c., were
formed in their stead. A part only of these differences
can be traced to have any distinct relation to the quantitative proportions of the chemical composition of the
whole rock. Other differences consist in the presence of
various accessory minerals. These we may presume to
represent a surplus or residuum of certain elementary
substances remaining uncombined after the crystallisation
of the essential mineral ingredients. Many accessory
minerals are, however, evidently the result of later processes of transmutation.

If we disregard the specific but minor differences between those similar minerals, which, to a certain extent,
occur as substitutes for each other in rocks, we find a
certain correspondence in the mineralogical with the chemical phenomena, and that, speaking generally, there are
two principal kinds of rock essentially differing from each
other in the aggregate of their mineral composition,
if only in their normal states of development—one a
basic, and the other an acidic compound. These are again
subdivided, according to their texture and recognisable
mineral differences, into rocks of several species, as indicated in the following tabular statement.

Granular	Porphyritic	Compact	Vitreous, vesicular, or amygdaloidal	Slaty-achistose (chiefly metamorphic)
Acidic Rocks. Granite Syenitic- granite Protogine Trachyte (Greisen)	Granitic- porphyry Quartz- porphyry Trachyte- porphyry	Felsite rock Petrosilex	Pitchstone Pearlstone Obsidian Pumice-stone	Granulite Gneiss Protogine- gneiss Felsite-schist (Mica-schist)
Basic Rocks. Syenite Diorite Diabase Timacite Dolerite Nepheline- dolerite Gabbro Miascite Mica-trap	Hornblende- porphyry Mica-por- phyry Porphyrite Aphanite- porphyry Melaphyre	Melaphyre Aphanite Basalt	Vesicular rocks and amygdaloids	Hornblende- schists Chlorite-schist Talcose schist

As already stated, the mineral differences in the igneous rocks do not appear to have been all original, but to have been partly produced at a later period by process of transmutation. In individual cases this has been very well shown to be the fact by Bischof and Rose, although both of those distinguished men may, perhaps, have gone too far in their hypotheses on this subject. The extent to which such transmutations have taken place is not yet established by proof, and we may say generally that it is impossible to be too cautious in admitting the process of transmutation as a sufficient explanation of differences between rocks, unless we are willing to be content with mere convenient hypotheses.

We have already observed that the causes are not yet satisfactorily ascertained why, from compounds chemically very similar, in one rock orthoclase has resulted, in others sanidine, oligoclase, labradorite, anorthite, &c. ; in one rock a hornblende, in another a pyroxene.

The exact causes of these phenomena can never be ascertained with certainty. One cause, however, of different forms of mineral development may be well conceived, viz. the different depths at which cooling and solidification have taken place in rock masses. It cannot be doubted that the conditions under which substances have combined to form minerals were very different at a depth of 10,000 feet from those which prevailed at a depth of 10 or 100 feet only from the surface. In the former case the masses have been subjected to far higher pressure—were shut out from the atmosphere—they were probably exposed in some degree to the action of water, but their cooling must, in masses of equal bulk, have been on the average a much slower process than would have obtained near the surface. Again, not only the depth of the formation, but the geological period of the earth's development may have had considerable influence in determining the character of minerals. For if the theory is correct that the earth has cooled into a solid from a previous molten state, its average temperature in former periods, even at the surface, must have been higher, and the atmosphere more dense and heavy than at present. Each cooling process under such circumstances would be slower, and would take place under a different degree of pressure than now. Thus we have one recognised general cause for the differences we observe; but the definite proof of what its precise effects have been under different circumstances is wanting.

The cause for a division of the igneous rocks into those poor in silica and rich in silica remains a great problem for solution. *A priori* we should expect to find all igneous rocks of the same composition. Bunsen's theory of the existence of two separate volcanic furnaces in the interior of the earth is a mere hypothesis, which, no doubt, might, if it were true, suffice to explain the existing differences, but which in itself is very improbable. Such furnaces, if they existed at all, must have been in existence through all geological time ; in almost every part of the globe they must have been placed side by side or one above the other, and yet have remained distinct and unmixed. No circumstance, unless it be the very difference which we are endeavouring to explain, speaks for such an assumption. Even if the cooling and solidifying of the fluid mass of the globe should have proceeded contemporaneously equally from the centre and surface towards a middle plane, as Bunsen supposes, so that at last only an intermediate stratum of fluid matter

will remain between the two, the existence of separate
basic and acidic basins of lava will not by this assume
greater probability. For the present we must confess
that the cause of the differences between these two chief
groups of igneous rocks has not yet been satisfactorily
explained.

It has been very ingeniously suggested that a cause
might be sought in the different specific gravity of the
several rock masses, starting with the assumption that in
the former molten state of the earth the ingredients must
have arranged themselves in some measure according to
their specific gravity; so that the heaviest substances
would be accumulated towards the centre, and the lighter
towards the surface. If the cooling process began with
the outside of the globe proceeding inwards, then it
follows that the specifically lighter bodies would first
attain the solid state, and these we actually find to be
richest in silica; and that the heavier bodies, which are
at the same time the most basic, would only cool at a
later period. This law, it was considered, must prevail
alike in an incrustation formed under quiet circumstances, as in the case of eruptive rocks necessarily emer-
ging from a great and ever increasing depth; so that the
oldest would be the lightest and most acidic; the recent
the heaviest and most basic. This theory, which Petz-
bold (in his *Geologie*, 1840) pushed to the utmost extreme, i. e. to the formation of mineral veins, has been
lately attempted to be applied in a narrower sense by
Von Richthofen (Geol. Beschreib. von Süd-Tyrol, 1861,
p. 308). It evidently has a great appearance of theoretical probability in its favour. But when we come to
test this theory by comparison with ascertained facts, we
at once find it untenable, at least in part, and undoubtedly
altogether insufficient satisfactorily to explain those facts.
Every geological age has produced acidic as well as
basic, specifically light and specifically heavy, igneous
rocks. Where syenite and granite occur together, it is
even most usually the case that the basic syenite is older
than the acidic granite. The basic porphyries in the
Thuringian Forest and the Erzgebirge are on the
average older than the acidic quartz-porphyries which
belong to the same great period. The trachyte-por-

phyries belong to the most acidic and yet frequently to the most recent eruptive rocks. According to von Richthofen's own investigations, they are, on an average, of more recent formation than the trachytes, which contain less silica and are also somewhat heavier. Therefore, von Richthofen himself, to support his theory, was compelled to have recourse to various hypotheses, such as a second fusion and new eruption of old igneous rocks, &c., which in themselves are neither probable nor sufficient to solve all the difficulties of the case. We have yet to seek the true solution of many important problems relating to this subject. Nevertheless, we are not of opinion that the theory of an arrangement of substances according to their specific gravity should be disregarded as entirely unworthy of serious attention. Specific gravity may, and probably has had, a certain influence in the first arrangement of rock masses; and if we are unable now to trace a consistent arrangement deducible from the laws of specific gravity, it may be only because those traces have to a great extent been subsequently effaced by other circumstances which we have not yet discovered. A primary crust formed by cooling and the first sedimentary deposits, resulting from the decay of that first crust, may well have been pre-eminently rich in silica; more especially if at the time of those sedimentary deposits animal life had not begun to act on the calcareous waters, and so cause a redeposit of the dissolved lime in large masses. If this primary portion of the earth's crust should at a later date have been subjected to a second process of fusion under high pressure, at a considerable depth, it may have become partially eruptive, and have produced recent rocks very rich in silica and of very uniform chemical composition. We may, in fact, reasoning from analogy to the meteoric stones, which represent to us the small planetary bodies of our solar system, believe the aggregate of the earth's mass to be far more strongly basic than that part of it which is open to our observation.

Taking into account *composition*, on the one hand, and *geological character*, on the other, we come to distinguish four great groups of igneous rocks, which groups are, however, not divided from each other by exact boundaries. Each may be characterised by some typical rock;

and each may be also connected with the other groups by means of other rocks of intermediate character. We may represent these groups somewhat as follows :

BASIC . . $\left\{\begin{array}{l} Volcanic : \text{Basalt} \\ Plutonic : \text{Diorite} \end{array}\right\}$ Diabase, Porphyrite, Melaphyre

ACIDIC . . $\left\{\begin{array}{l} Volcanic : \text{Trachyte} \\ Plutonic : \text{Granite} \end{array}\right\}$ Trachyte-porphyry Quartz-porphyry

or :—

VOLCANIC . $\left\{\begin{array}{l} Basic : \text{Basalt} \\ Acidic : \text{Trachyte} \end{array}\right\}$ Trachydolerite, Andesite, Porphyrite

PLUTONIC . $\left\{\begin{array}{l} Basic : \text{Diorite} \\ Acidic : \text{Granite} \end{array}\right\}$ Syenite

We must not omit to remark that some considerations entitled to attention have been started against the igneous character of certain of the rocks so named, and chiefly those which contain quartz.

Granite is the principal representative of these rocks. In the case of this rock, so universally spread over the surface of the globe, it has been objected that, looking to the mode in which its essential ingredients, felspar, quartz, and mica are joined together, and fitted one into the other, those minerals could not have been formed in the order of their respective degrees of rapidity of solidification from a state of fusion, i.e. first the quartz, then the felspar, and last the mica; but, on the contrary, that it very often appears distinctly that the quartz, which is the most difficult of fusion, has been formed the last. It has been further objected that in granite, as well as in many other, even in certain basic igneous rocks, there sometimes occur accessory minerals whose formation by igneous means can scarcely be conceived as possible, or at least is contradicted by all experience. For instance, pyrites, apatite, pyrochlore, carbonate of lime, carbonate of magnesia, protocarbonate of iron, &c. These are found side by side with silicates, and yet without forming chemical combinations with the latter. Finally, it has been objected that many so-called igneous rocks contain some water, and according to the analyses of Delesse, even small quantities of nitrogen. (Ann. des. Mines, 1860, vol. xviii.)

Now, as regards the first objection—the solidification of

the quartz subsequently to the felspar—Durocher has long since shown (Compt. rend. 1845, p. 1275), that in fusing the compact rock petrosilex, whose composition is often precisely the same as that of granite, the quartz which it contains being associated with the other ingredients of the rock, is quite as readily fusible as felspar alone ; and hence we may conclude that upon the cooling of such a mass the quartz would not necessarily separate itself from the rest of the compound by solidifying sooner than the felspar.   If this be so, in the case of a granitic mass it might depend on some circumstance, which for want of a better term we may call accident, whether the quartz or the felspar should first happen to complete the process of its crystallisation, and whichever of those two minerals first crystallised would necessarily determine the form of the other.   Now the felspar in granite appears to have been the first to crystallise, and has determined the form of the quartz in many cases.   Bunsen has lately thrown much light on this question (vide Zeitsch. d. geol. Ges. 1861, p. 61); he has shown that the melting and solidifying points of a mineral, when taken singly, by no means determine those of an intimate compound or alloy of such mineral with other mineral or minerals.   In a letter to Streng, which appeared in the Berggeist (1862, p. 1), Bunsen, in illustration of the same law, adduces instances of aqueous solutions, where heat is necessary to the solution.   The so-called *Pattinson's process* is the result of a similar experience.   It is found that pure lead crystallises sooner than lead containing a proportion of silver; and accordingly when the liquid mass of mixed lead and silver is subjected to a process of slow cooling, the pure lead congeals first, leaving the richer metal still in a fluid state (termed ' mother water'). Moreover, high pressure and water (chemically combined) may have exercised many important modifying influences upon the process of the formation of the granitic rocks.

The second suggestion referring to the presence of certain minerals as accessory ingredients in so-called igneous rocks which appear incompatible with their igneous origin, loses much of its force from our likewise finding some of the same minerals in genuine lavas, whose origin is undoubted.   Moreover, those minerals or substances may

not have been actually present in the rocks in question at
the period of their first formation, but have originated in
them at a later date. As to the water contained in rocks,
Scheerer has clearly proved that water forms a basic ingredient of many minerals (e.g. many kinds of mica),
entering into combination with silica and other acids in
precisely the same way as any other basic oxide. Daubrée has established the same fact synthetically, showing
that under great pressure at a high degree of temperature,
water may be made chemically to combine with mineral
matter. Whether the very small quantity of nitrogen
contained in many igneous rocks was there originally, or
whether it only insinuated itself into them at a later
period, may, for the present, remain an open question; all
minor difficulties like this will probably find a satisfactory solution in time. On the other hand, as regards
the carbonates of lime, magnesia, and iron contained in
igneous rocks, they appear to be invariably the result of
change or transmutation subsequent to the formation of
the rock. Hence we never find them in very recent lavas,
but only in those igneous rocks which have been long
and continuously exposed to the action of chemical influences, calculated to bring forth those minerals, and
therefore we find them more frequently in the plutonic
than the volcanic rocks. Pyrites, magnetic pyrites, chlorite, and talc, all likewise appear to have been the result
of such transmutations, even if we cannot as yet satisfactorily so explain every single case of the occurrence
of a particular mineral. These considerations prevent us
from attaching much weight to the objections raised to
the igneous origin of granite—an origin which on other
grounds appears so conclusively established.

The differences between the volanic and plutonic rocks
of both principal groups, the basic and acidic (although
smaller and more filled up by transition states than
those between the two groups themselves), deserve a
full share of our attention, and require some explanation. We have already more than once adverted to one
general cause of difference, namely, the unequal conditions under which the cooling and solidification first took
place, whether under simple or multiplied atmospheric
pressure; and whether on the surface of the globe, or in
a closed space, where water probably had access.

Besides these original causes of difference, there are also the many changes which appear to have taken place in the state as well as composition of all rocks, subsequently to their first formation, chiefly no doubt under the influence of water and gas penetrating and permeating them.

In the present state of science it is impossible everywhere separately to specify and define the results of all these different causes, yet we will attempt by contrasting the characteristic attributes of the two principal groups to present some general views applicable to the subject.

The original differences may shortly be stated as follows :—

In Volcanic Rocks.	*In Plutonic Rocks.*
Prevalent compact, porphyritic, vesicular, or vitreous states. Seldom or never slaty or schistose texture.	Prevalent crystalline - granular and porphyritic, sometimes also schistose or slaty texture; seldom vitreous or vesicular.
Small content of water.	Greater content of water.
Seldom crystallised quartz.	More frequently crystals of quartz.
Frequent tufa formations.	Seldom tufa formations.

The differences occasioned by gradual metamorphosis are as follows :—

In Volcanic Rocks.	*In Plutonic Rocks.*
There is little or no change.	The formation of amygdaloids, by the filling up of previously existing vesicular cavities with newly-formed minerals.
	The new formation or transformation of certain minerals in the interior of the mass, e.g. pyrites, carbonates, zeolites, apatite, chlorite, talc, serpentine, &c. The absorption of more water. Decomposed wackenitic states; possibly even many formations of quartz.

To sum up these observations : It appears that in the present state of science we cannot but regard all the so-called igneous rocks as parts of the earth's interior mass, thrust out whilst in a state of fusion, without being able as yet satisfactorily to explain their division into the two principal groups of acidic and basic composition respectively, the minor differences inside of these groups being capable of explanation by the different circumstances under which the several rocks attained the solid state or by subsequent process of their transmutation.

In addition to the works cited in the text we will here only notice the following :—

Delesse, on the origin of igneous rocks, in Compt. rend. 1859, vol. xlviii. p. 955 ; v. L. u. Br. Jahrb. 1859, p. 459 ; and Ann. des Mines, 1858, vol. xv. p. 459. *Delesse* distinguishes between Igneous rocks (trachyte, dolerite), Pseudo-Igneous rocks (trap), and Non-Igneous rocks (granite, diorite, &c.). If we wish for extreme precision of nomenclature, the term Igneous is altogether inappropriate, even for the volcanic rocks, which have but consolidated from a state of liquid fusion, without any fire or burning in the ordinary acceptation of the word fire. Hence in Germany the Igneous rocks are termed Eruptive rocks. One name is as good as another for practical purposes, if we do not seek to attach theory too closely to nomenclature.

Daubrée, Sur le Métamorphisme et sur la Formation des Roches Cristallines, 1860.

Scheerer, über den Astrophyllit und sein Verhältniss zu Augit und Glimmer und Zirconsyenit nebst Bemerkungen über die plutonische Entstehung solcher Gebilde, 1864.

See also *Cotta's* Geologische Fragen, 1858. The argument against the igneous origin of granite which has been built on the score of the specific gravity of the quartz falls to the ground if we believe that it became solid under high pressure.

SEDIMENTARY ROCKS.

The general character of the processes by which these rocks were formed is well known and evident. They are deposits of fallen substances, chiefly precipitated from water—a small part from the atmosphere. This, their origin, is proved in a variety of ways, by their composition, their stratification and bedding, and the fossils which they enclose.

A few words as to their composition may not be out of place here.

If the views now prevalent respecting the earth's history are correct, the igneous rocks must be regarded as the most original, or rather the only original formations. Should it appear that any part of the first crust produced by the original cooling of the earth's surface remains undisturbed at the present day, it will properly belong to the igneous rocks, although not like the other igneous rocks, eruptive. If we take all the igneous rocks together, we have products of the eruptions of all geological periods. To these products we must, therefore, chiefly look for information as to the nature of the substances contained in the interior earth's mass. They may represent a part only of that mass, but they constitute our only evidence on the subject. The nucleus of the earth may possibly be differently composed, but we possess no means of investigating it.

In the aggregate composition of the sedimentary rocks, which we assume to be but the product of decomposition, re-deposition, and transmutation of the original and first consolidated igneous rocks, we should expect to find the same ingredients as in the igneous rocks, and in somewhat similar proportions. Therefore we should look for silica as the predominant ingredient, and alumina, oxides of iron, lime, magnesia, potash, and soda in smaller quantities. We do, indeed, find these to constitute the substance of the stratified rocks (although not grouped in the same manner as in the igneous rocks). We likewise find other ingredients such as compounds of carbon, sulphur, and chlorine; but these we infer have been derived from the atmosphere or from water. It is doubtless very difficult to form a sound opinion, whether in point of fact, the quantitative proportions of the ingredients we have first named are in the aggregate about the same in the sedimentary as in the igneous rocks, since the combinations are for the most part very different in the two classes. In the sedimentary rocks the lime and magnesia have united with carbonic acid to form the limestones and dolomites, or with sulphuric acid to form gypsum and anhydrite; silica has produced quartzite rocks and the sandstones; alumina has combined with silica to form the argillaceous rocks; oxides of iron, the ironstones (iron is also much disseminated in other rocks); potash and soda have become very much distributed amongst many kinds of sedimentary rock; soda, again, has united with muriatic acid to form rock-salt; carbon (concentrated by process of vegetation) has formed coal-beds.

At a cursory glance it might appear as if the sedimentary rocks in the aggregate contained more lime and less potash than the igneous. We must, however, remember that some lime is contained in almost all igneous rocks (especially the basic rocks), but by no means in all sedimentary rocks; again, that the sulphuric acid and water make up a very considerable part of the bulk of the limestones, dolomites, and gypsums; which bulk we may moreover easily be led to overrate as they are apt to stand out very conspicuously and prominently amongst the other sedimentary rocks in separate and exceptionally compact masses. Taking all these circumstances into account we should probably find that the proportion of lime in the aggregate of the stratified rocks does not essentially differ from that in the aggregate of the igneous rocks. As regards the potash we must recollect that its quantity in the igneous rocks only reaches about 4 per cent. as an approximate average, that the greater part of the sedimentary rocks contain some potash, and several a very considerable quantity. Great quantities of soda have been converted into rock-salt. We have, therefore, no sufficient reason to doubt that the aggregate ingredients of the igneous and the sedimentary rocks are equally balanced.

In the case of all sandstones, stratified conglomerates, tuff formations, compact and slaty argillaceous rocks, as well as the greater part of the marls, limestones, dolomites, and coals, their sedimentary origin is so apparent that nobody will doubt it. The matter is less clear in the case of many granular limestones and dolomites, also in that of the massive accumulations of rock-salt and gypsum, although the sedimentary origin of these latter is now generally admitted. It is most difficult to distinguish the sedimentary from the igneous rocks in those cases where the two are found interlying each other in parallel beds as sometimes happens, the igneous perhaps indistinctly composite or even somewhat decomposed.

Whilst we thus find no difficulty in pronouncing on the origin of the sedimentary rocks in general, it is somewhat difficult to determine what rocks we should reckon as sedimentary, and in what cases we should apply the term 'metamorphic.'

The expression 'metamorphic' will best serve a useful purpose of distinction if it be reserved for cases where a rock originally sedimentary (according to our previous definition) is so essentially changed in its mineral character as not to be capable of recognition without the evidence of collateral circumstances to identify it with the original formation. From the nature of the case, however, no distinct division between the sedimentary and the metamorphic rocks is possible; on the contrary, gradual transitions take place from one to the other, and the extremes alone are distinctly different in their character.

There remains much for investigation as to the particular circumstances under which the several kinds of sedimentary rock came to be deposited.

We cannot lay down any general law applicable to all sedimentary rocks as to the conditions under which their first deposit took place. The case of each rock has to be separately considered with reference to its bedding, and the organic remains which it contains. The most that we can say as a general proposition is, that many of these rocks have been deposited by the sea—some on the coasts, some at a great distance from the shore; others have been deposited in freshwater lakes by means of rivers or springs. The greater part consist of matter washed together by floods; some consist of the ejectamenta of volcanoes; some are crystalline precipitates, and some are the result of processes of animal and vegetable life.

Nor can we in general terms describe the mechanical forces which have acted on the materials of the sedimentary rocks to fit them for union, the mode of that union, the separation or combination of the chemical ingredients, the nature of the substances which have been introduced or become changed subsequently to the first deposit, the alterations of level which have taken place in the beds of those rocks by depression or upheaval, &c. All these are of great moment to be determined, but they can only be subjects of separate consideration in each individual case.

The oldest rocks which are capable of being recognised at the present day as distinctly sedimentary, are those of the transition period. Now as these rocks still contain a considerable number and variety of organic remains, it is reasonable to conclude that there have been many of yet more ancient date, for, according to the igneous theory of the earth's structure there must necessarily have existed a long period of time in which deposits took place before any organic remains existed. These oldest deposits would be the lowest sedimentary formations, and would contain few or no fossil remains. It is probable that they have been changed into, and now form the principal bulk of the metamorphic schists. If we would speculate on their former probable structure, we should expect their composition to have been very uniform, because at the time of their deposit there were fewer causes for difference in rock formation than in later periods;—many of such causes having arisen subsequently, such for instance as organic life, the origin of many calcareous, and all the carboniferous strata. Reasoning backwards, if we believe the crystalline schists to have chiefly sprung from the oldest sedimentary rocks, we may thus account for their very rarely enclosing calcareous or carboniferous beds (limestone and graphite). That the composition of these crystalline schists should much resemble that of the first igneous rocks, would seem to be but a natural consequence of their transmutation from the earliest sedimentary rocks, which themselves were the products of the disintegration of those first igneous rocks. But these speculations should be indulged in with caution, as they may easily lead us too far into the regions of unfounded hypothesis.

METAMORPHIC CRYSTALLINE SCHISTS.

Notwithstanding what we have had occasion to remark in describing the sedimentary rocks, the true interpretation of the crystalline schists remains one of the most difficult problems for the geologist, since the process of their formation can only be subject of theory, and not of direct observation.

Various theories as to the nature of their origin have been advanced. They have been taken for the original deposits of a so-called antediluvian age; for the first cooled igneous products of the earth; a part for rocks of eruptive character ; and finally for sedimentary rocks very greatly changed or transmuted. These different views have been put forward at different times, have been more or less accepted, but all except the last have been very generally abandoned.

Nobody now holds that the crystalline schists were deposited in their present state and condition. A few at most may have been formed by the first cooling of the earth's crust—perhaps some gneiss districts, if any such can be found entirely free from subordinate interlying beds. It is improbable that such origin can ever be satis-factorily proved, and it remains for the present at best an hypothesis which is possible for certain cases. Some gneiss certainly appears to be of igneous (eruptive) origin, but a very large proportion of the known gneiss forma-tions admit of no such explanation, nor is it applicable to any of the other crystalline schists. From a geological point of view we shall therefore do well to consider the eruptive gneiss as a schistose variety of granite, and every other (for the present at least) as metamorphic. Hence, according to the present state of our scientific knowledge, the only explanation left for by far the greater part of the crystalline slates is that of transmutation from sedimentary formations.

The following are some of the principal reasons which appear clearly to speak for such transmutation, without, however, giving us certain information as to the manner of the process :—

1. Those rocks the traces of whose sedimentary origin are evident and distinct, present us with numerous series of transitions tending towards or rendering possible further transitions into crystalline schist, or corresponding with the subordinate beds which are found interlying those schists. We will give a few instances of such series of transmutation :—

(a) Clay-mud successively passes into (or becomes) argillaceous shale, clay-slate, argillaceous mica-schist, and mica-schist. If this be so we should expect in the final products of this series of transmutations to find indications of the special composition of the dif-ferent original clays influencing the character of each rock, which accordingly should vary with the varying

quantities of sand, lime, magnesia, potash, or soda contained in the original clay. And to such differences of
original composition we do in fact attribute the different
varieties of mica-schist, or the formation in its stead of
gneiss, hornblende-schist, chlorite-schist, or talc-schist
(although the special character of the two latter is probably in some measure owing to the later accession of
solutions of magnesia).

(*b*) Sand passes into (or becomes) sandstone, quartzite, quartz-schist, or itacolumite, according to the
character of the substances originally mixed with the
sand, or which have subsequently come to it. A mica-
schist rich in quartz, or a gneiss, might also result from
the transmutation of a sandstone having a copious combining medium.

(*c*) Calcareous mud, consisting of microscopically
small shells, passes into (or has actually become) chalk;
chalk (probably by means of pressure) has turned
to compact limestone. Chalk or compact limestone
under pressure, by means of a high degree of temperature, may have been transmuted into granular limestone, beds of which frequently occur in subordinate
layers between the strata of crystalline schists.

(*d*) Browncoal, coal, anthracite, and graphite have
without doubt resulted from peat or other vegetable
accumulations. Anthracite and graphite we again find
as subordinate formations imbedded between strata of
crystalline schists.

(*e*) Hydrated oxide of iron forms a deposit in the
form of bog-ore or brown hematite, and these under
the pressure of thickly overlying masses appear to have
parted with their water, and become converted into red
iron-ore, or red hematite. Further, by the absorption
of one part of oxygen, red iron-ore is converted into
magnetic iron-ore. The latter is found in subordinate
layers between beds of crystalline schists. But in each
of these cases the transmutations are sometimes found
to have been reversed, and other processes have taken
place which have somewhat complicated the actual
phenomena.

2. The several kinds of crystalline schist and their
different varieties are found imbedded in manifold parallel

alternating layers or strata. Between these lie subordinate layers of granular limestone, dolomite, quartzite, ironstone, graphite, &c., and the whole series are found stratified in a parallel direction. This alternate bedding and imbedding correspond exactly with that of the sedimentary rocks—their state only is changed, being usually crystalline. The bedding and stratification of the crystalline schists therefore furnishes a second and most important argument for their metamorphic origin; in no other way can the existing phenomena be accounted for.

3. The usual or normal bedding of the crystalline schists is lower than that of all sedimentary rocks, and complete gradual transitions between the two are frequently to be observed. These outward indicia alone are strong evidences of metamorphic origin.

4. Finally, we may bring certain more rare or exceptional phenomena in proof of the theory of transmutation, e.g. the occurrence in strata of crystalline schist of beds containing certain still recognisable fossils; as for instance the limestone-slate with remains of belemnites between the mica-schist and gneiss of the Alps, at the Furca and Pass of Nufenen. At the last-named locality more recent formations are also found exceptionally very much changed, but not entirely transmuted.

Taking all these facts together they appear to us to furnish as complete a chain of indirect evidence in favour of the transmutation of a very large proportion of the crystalline schists as we could well expect to find where from the nature of the case direct observation is unattainable.

The causes and manner of the transmutation, however, constitute a different question.

The first theory of geologists upon this matter was that the crystalline schists had been formed out of the sedimentary by the operation of great eruptive masses of igneous rocks thrusting themselves through, over, and by the side of the sedimentary rocks—therefore by the effect of contact; and it was also supposed that the felspar of the gneiss was only forced into it from granitic compounds. The frequent occurrence of granite in the immediate neighbourhood of gneiss, the fact that granite districts are frequently entirely surrounded by gneiss, which latter

gradually merges into mica-schist towards its external
boundary (as for instance, in many parts of the Erzgebirge); all these and like phenomena might no doubt
be cited in favour of such an hypothesis. But on the
other hand, no possible explanation could be afforded on
this assumption for the uniform distribution of the felspar
in the gneiss, nor for the extent of the supposed effect
of the contact without a regular diminution of force corresponding with the distance from the transforming cause.
Very frequently the observable mass of eruptive rock
(which according to the theory should be the cause of
the transmutation) bears no adequate proportion to the
extent of the crystalline schist (which has become transmuted). Many large districts of crystalline schist are,
moreover, entirely free from granitic or other eruptive
intrusions; and it would, to say the least, be hazardous in
such cases always to presume the existence of a substratum
of granite which had failed to penetrate to the surface.
Again, many considerable granite districts are not surrounded by gneiss or other crystalline schists, but on the
contrary are immediately in contact with distinctly sedimentary rocks, which latter have remained almost entirely
unchanged by the contact, or at all events are not changed
into crystalline schists, although their bedding shows
clearly enough that they have been actually broken
through by the granite. The Hartz and Saxon Voigtland afford remarkable instances of this kind. Thus we
find clay-slate formations of different ages broken through
by great masses of granite; at the margin of the granite,
however, we find no trace of gneiss or mica-schist formations, but only the ordinary clay-slate changed for a
relatively small distance into hornstone, nodular schist
(Knotenschiefer), or chiastolite-schist—changes which no
doubt have been caused by contact with the granite,
but which bear no resemblance to gneiss-formations, and
are probably the consequence more of a hydroplutonic
operation than of the high temperature of the granite
alone.

We are aware that Credner (in v. L. u. Br. Jahrb.
1849, p. 8) has described an occurrence at Glasbach on
the Schwarza, in the Thuringian Forest, where it really
appears as if the clay-slate, broken through by a very

considerable dyke of granite, has been transmuted into gneiss for some short distance from the granite. Under special circumstances, and if we find the clay-slate to contain the same elements as the gneiss, we may well admit the possibility of such an effect of the contact of granite without our being authorised therefore to conclude that all gneiss has arisen from the same or similar transmuting causes. We should rather regard such an instance as proving that in particular cases special causes have been competent to supply those more universal conditions and processes of transmutation by which the greater part of gneiss rocks have been formed; just as in the neighbourhood of basaltic rocks and porphyries exceptional formations of anthracite have taken place.

From all these considerations we gather that no effect which could be produced by the contact of eruptive igneous rocks would be sufficient to have caused the formation of the great mass of the crystalline schists, but that we should rather look for causes much more general in their operation. These are most probably no other than pressure and heat. We accordingly hold that not only the crystalline schists but also the subordinate masses imbedded in them are nothing more than the latest result of that very general process of transmutation which all sedimentary deposits have undergone and are still undergoing from the moment that they begin to be covered more or less thickly with other more recent deposits.

Now a very thick covering with recent deposits can only be the consequence of a previous depression. But by the combined effect of depression and the weight of fresh deposits the underlying strata are subjected not only to an increased pressure but also an increased temperature.

In the earliest periods of the earth's development, there probably was also an increased pressure from a denser and more heavily laden atmosphere, and besides the increase of heat with the depth from the surface, there was doubtless a generally higher temperature of the whole globe, so that the difference which now exists between older and more recent igneous rocks, and between volcanic and plutonic rocks, would at that time be much smaller, all volcanic formations partaking more or less of the nature of the plutonic.

Therefore, pressure and heat, with the addition, perhaps, of water (which has either penetrated the earth to
a considerable depth or which chemically formed a part of
its original composition), appear to have worked together
through great periods of time to produce the final result
of the transmutation into crystalline schist; and those
crystalline schists which are now to be seen on the earth's
surface must also have been lifted and partially deprived
of their superincumbent masses. But as each process of
covering, of transmutation, of raising and re-exposure,
must have occupied extensive periods of time, it follows
that all crystalline slates which are now accessible to observation are of very ancient formation. In general language, they may be said to represent the oldest deposits
in a metamorphosed state. Exceptions to this character
can only be attributed to special circumstances. In the
Alps, such exceptions do appear to have taken place. The
deposits of the Jurassic, the Chalk, and the Tertiary periods
exhibit there an extraordinary thickness of development,
and, consequently, belemnitic strata (of the oldest deposits
of the Jurassic period) appear in certain places to have been
so thickly covered as to have been changed into crystalline schist; and very energetic upliftings have also at
a later period exposed them.

In general we may say of the Alps, that the process of
metamorphosis has been there pushed up higher in the
scale of the earth's history than elsewhere is usual. The
Eocene deposits contain firm clay-slate, which is used for
roofing purposes; the Miocene browncoals of the Molasse formation appear already to have almost become
ordinary black coal, &c. On the other hand, we find the
converse of this state of things in the low lands of Russia,
where the oldest Silurian formations are still partially in
the state of plastic clay and friable sandstone, probably
because they have never been thickly covered.

The temperature to which the lowest deposits have been
subjected, under very great pressure of thicklying superincumbent masses, may even have reached so great a
degree that some or all of the rocks composing such strata
have been softened or perhaps partially fused. In this way,
for instance, we may explain the otherwise singular phenomenon of layers of granular limestone which sometimes

lie between beds of crystalline schist; yea, even siliceous rocks may have been softened by this means, entirely losing their slaty texture and stratification.

No doubt, we may be easily led by such speculations into regions of unfounded hypothesis, but the causes to which we have referred afford a possible explanation of many bedding relations between granulite and gneiss, which cannot be accounted for by simple transmutation from a sedimentary formation.

Now, granted that we are able to explain the special state of the crystalline schists by such general plutonic influences as pressure and heat, there yet remains the important question whether their chemical composition also corresponds with this theory of their transmutation; in other words, whether the sedimentary rocks originally contained, or could have subsequently absorbed, those ingredients which were necessary to the formation of the crystalline schists. In many of the sedimentary rocks this is most certainly the case. We need only compare the ingredients of the crystalline schists with those of the as yet uncrystalline slates as given in the tables, p. 86, ante, in order to perceive that, even without the accession of new ingredients or parting with any which they now contain, many a clay-slate might be changed into a mica-schist, and others into a gneiss, if their ingredients could be so disposed as to combine into crystalline mineral aggregates. The elements are there; the opportunity of assuming a new shape is the only thing wanting. The composition of different clay-slates, several of which also contain some lime and magnesia, corresponds with that of many different varieties of gneiss, mica-schist, and hornblende-schist. Doubtless an additional quantity of magnesia would be necessary to the formation of the chlorite and talcose schists, but the possibility of the accession of solutions of magnesia is proved beyond doubt by the existence of numerous pseudomorphs of certain well-known minerals. With reference to the formation of these magnesian rocks (to which serpentine also belongs), certain special conditions would appear to have been necessary in their case in addition to the general causes which contributed to the formation of the great mass of the other crystalline schists.

C C

Our hypothesis (to which, however, we lay no personal claim) by no means excludes the possibility of water as an auxiliary agent in such transmutations as we have described. The comparatively recent experiments of Daubrée have established that water will remain in combination with other substances, such as silicates, under high atmospheric pressure, even at a white heat; and that in such cases it even materially affects the fusing point of substances; and Scheerer has proved that the water contained in the mica of gneiss was a part of its original composition. This water may have caused many phenomena in the interior of the earth, which as yet we are not able accurately to explain or prove.

What thickness of superlying strata should be assumed as sufficient to produce the transmutation which has resulted, we are unable to say; and we have fewer data for any computation, as, according to the igneous theory of the earth's formation, the average temperature of the whole globe, including the surface, must formerly have been much higher, and the atmosphere more compact and dense, therefore the pressure much greater, than at the present day. Moreover, in all geological phenomena the duration of a particular influence will to some extent supply any deficiency in its energy; and, as we have no standard by which to measure the time of geological processes, we have free scope to assume any duration of time that appears necessary to explain their operation.

The crystalline schists, if we take their principal representatives, gneiss and mica-schist, are more closely allied to the acidic than the basic igneous rocks. The cause of this is easily explained. In the igneous rocks, the two principal bases, whose greater or less proportion chiefly creates the distinction between the acidic and basic groups, are lime and magnesia. Now, on the decomposition or disintegration of the igneous rocks, their lime and magnesia having first been taken up in solution (for the most part in combination with carbonic acid), have then been separately deposited in the form of independent beds of limestone and dolomite. The aluminous and quartzose ingredients of the igneous rocks have formed the more mechanical deposits of clay and sand, free from lime, and appear to have produced the greater part of the crystalline schists; and as the calcareous and magnesian deposits were originally formed between the strata of clay and sand, so we again meet with limestone and dolomite rocks imbedded between the acidic crystalline schists; and we may assume that they represent the collective amount of lime and magnesia in which the average of the crystalline schists is deficient as compared with the average of the igneous rocks. This separate development of the lime and magnesia may likewise be the reason why combinations of hornblende, pyroxene, and labradorite are, generally speaking, far less frequent in the crystalline schists than in the igneous rocks.

The crystalline schists, according to our theory, must represent the most ancient or undermost deposits of the world's history. They are the oldest rocks of which we have knowledge, since we find them overlaid by all the sedimentary rocks, and broken through by every kind of igneous rock. But the question arises, upon what foundation can these deposits have first rested, if no other rocks were previously in existence? Doubtless there must have previously existed a firm foundation or floor of deposit separating the fused mass of the interior from the covering of water and air, by whose means alone deposits could be formed. If, therefore, we acknowledge the fused state of the whole earth as its most ancient geological condition, we are necessarily led to assume the existence of a very thick first crust, caused by the cooling of the surface of this molten matter before it would be possible for any sedimentary or eruptive rocks to form. Now what has become of this first crust, unless it be represented by the crystalline schists? It is certainly difficult categorically to answer a question of this nature, referring to ages and circumstances long since passed; but one thing is certain, viz. that such gneiss, mica-schist, or argillaceous mica-schist, as contain parallel subordinate interlying beds of limestone, dolomite, hornblende-schist, quartz-schist, ironstone, or graphite, and the like, cannot have been formed by the first cooling of the earth's mass. No doubt where such interlying beds are entirely absent, as, for instance, in some gneiss, it is possible that such districts may be the remains of a first crust of the earth. Further, it is not certain that all granite is of eruptive origin; indeed, there are many circumstances that point to a contrary assumption in certain districts. Here, therefore, we have something which may possibly date from the first cooling of the earth's surface. But uniform districts of gneiss containing no foreign subordinate beds, and granite districts without recognisable traces of eruptive origin, are phenomena so rare to our present geological experience, that they evidently do not suffice to represent a great primeval crust of the earth. Under these circumstances, there seems nothing left for us in the present state of our knowledge but to assume that the greater part of the first crust, having become very thickly covered with deposits, has been gradually remelted and become eruptive, perhaps in the form of granite. There is, indeed, no reason why the same fate should not have been shared by the oldest rocks of deposit; and thus it may be that the chronological starting-point of geological development has frequently been effaced, and become altogether uncertain.

In what we have said above, we have endeavoured to develope the plutonic theory of the origin of crystalline schists. Recently, however, other explanations of the origin of those rocks have been started, not so much by geologists as by chemists, who also assume their origin by transmutation from sedimentary rocks, and differ from the geologist chiefly in denying all plutonic agency, only acknowledging the efficacy of such chemical processes as might have taken place under the conditions existing at the surface of the globe.

We have already more than once shown, in the course of this work, that plutonic processes do not exclude the combined action of water as an auxiliary agent; and thus may deserve the name of HYDROPLUTONIC; but, according to the more recent views of some chemists, water alone is said to suffice, under circumstances of ordinary pressure and temperature, to have brought about these transmutations in the course of time.

We do not venture to pronounce upon such theories from a chemical, but only from a geological point of view, and in this respect they do not satisfy our mind, chiefly because they disregard the effect and influence of very thick overlying strata, therefore of high pressure and increased temperature ; because they do not explain why, for instance, in the Alps, very recent deposits are greatly altered in character, whereas in other countries very old deposits where they have remained uncovered are scarcely changed at all (as, for instance, in Northern Russia); and finally, because they leave the phenomena of contemporaneous mechanical changes, such as condensation, slaty structure, &c., entirely unexplained. Assuming it to be the fact that by the agency of water alone, under circumstances of ordinary pressure and temperature, mica-schist or gneiss, hornblende-schist, &c., might be produced from clay (argillaceous shale or clay-slate), it would still be difficult to believe that by such agency proceeding from the surface, whole complicated systems of strata should not have been more locally influenced, and very differently affected at different depths, instead of having been almost everywhere equally and uniformly influenced by the transforming cause. Again, if all these important changes and transmutations were entirely or chiefly due to water, it would be very extraordinary if we did not find that they had been occasionally modified by the increase of temperature and of pressure to which they must have been subjected, since we cannot shut our eyes to the existence of such influences in the interior of the earth, and numerous geological facts sufficiently prove that many rocks which once were very thickly covered have been subsequently laid bare by processes of uplifting and denudation.

If we adopt the pure chemical hypothesis, then we must abandon the idea of that relationship existing between bedding and transmutation which, according to the plutonic theory, is an invariable law. It is indeed somewhat suspicious that the supporters of the chemical theory, in order to make the plutonic appear improbable, almost entirely dispute as a fact the operation of pressure and increased temperature in the interior of the earth, whereas every unprejudiced person acquainted with the rudiments of physics must admit these forces to exist inevitably under the given circumstances. The same persons are even in the habit of disputing the eruptive character of the greater number of igneous rocks, from which we infer that they are deficiently acquainted with geological facts from personal observation. We purposely use the word eruptive (not igneous) because the eruptive cha-' racter of the rock is unmistakably proved by the form of its mass, even if occasional doubts should arise as to the actual state of some few rocks at the time of their intrusion.

In other words, we do not regard those chemists very competent guides in pure geological questions, who fail adequately to regard the external phenomena of form and bedding no less than the elementary composition of rocks.

We would not be understood to depreciate the careful experiments and researches which we owe to G. Bischof and others on the effect of water in the processes of formation and transmutation of minerals. These are highly instructive, and they are more especially valuable as clearing up and explaining very scientifically what was previously only matter of surmise respecting the nature of the process of formation of mineral deposits in vesicular cavities and fissures of some rocks, and respecting the special formation and transmutation of minerals in the interior of other rocks, by which latter process, for instance, serpentine, chlorite-schist, talcose schist, &c., may in many instances have resulted.

In the course of these observations mention has been made of transmutation by means of contact; i. e. of such transmutations as are found at the margin or in the neighbourhood of eruptive igneous rocks which have broken through sedimentary rocks. That such exist cannot be doubted; as a rule, however, they extend to only a very limited distance from the eruptive rock. They may be divided into such as are purely plutonic or hydroplutonic, and such as are volcanic processes. To the plutonic processes belong the formations of hornstone, nodular schist (Knotenschiefer), and chiastolite-slate on the contact-margins of granite or greenstone. To the volcanic processes belong special induration, slacking, vitrefaction, coking and columnar jointing of argilla-. ceous sandy or carboniferous rocks on the margins of basalt, trachyte, or porphyry. These latter cases appear to be simply the result of greatly increased temperature and subsequent rapid cooling without water. The plutonic processes, on the other hand, admit of the combined agency of water and heat.

Transmutations occasioned by the burning of beds of coal (as the burnt clays, described p. 338, ante) are processes of entirely local character, and there may be many other such which it is unnecessary further to describe for our present purpose.

The transmutations of which we have hitherto spoken are chiefly such as have taken place in the interior of the earth with exclusion of atmospheric air. For these Haidinger has proposed the term *catogenic* in contradistinction to the *anogenic* transmutations which proceed from the exterior towards the interior, under the influences of air and water. These latter correspond in part with the very general process of weathering the rocks; they do not, however, always consist in the decomposition or disintegration of the masses affected, but sometimes rather in the formation of hydrates. To this belong the coalescing of the felspathic rocks, the formation of wackés by means of compounds containing augite or hornblende, the formation of gypsum from anhydrite, &c. These *anogenic* transmutations likewise play an important part in the chain. of processes by which in nature matter circulates through its various forms.

The most striking of the contrasts between the *catogenic* and *anogenic* transmutations may be stated somewhat in the following manner:—

Catogenic.	*Anogenic.*
Condensation and induration.	Disintegration.
Crystallisation.	Frequent destruction of the crystalline state.
Deoxidation.	Oxidation.
Loss of water (to a certain extent).	Formation of hydrates.
Formation of slaty schistose or texture.	

The following recent works may be here cited as especially noteworthy upon the metamorphosis of rocks :—

St. Claire Deville, the Operation of Chlorides and Sulphates upon the Metamorphism of the Sedimentary Rocks, Compt. rend. 1858, vol. xlvii. p. 89.

A. Gages, on the Study of some Metamorphic Rocks, Philos. Mag. 1859, March, p. 169.

O. Lieber, Critique on the Views of Bischof and Naumann on the Subject of Metamorphism, in Mining Mag. vol. i. December 1859.

Delesse, Études sur le Métamorphisme des Roches, Paris, 1861:
v. L. u. Br. Jahrb. 1858, pp. 335 and 727, 1859, pp. 222 and
223; l'Institut, 1861, p. 276.

Daubrée, Études sur le Métamorphisme et sur la Formation des
Roches Cristallines, Paris, 1860.

MINERAL VEINS AND VEINS OF ORE.

These almost form a special group of rocks, and would
be entitled to an equal place by the side of the three
other groups, if the extent of space which they occupy in
nature were not so small. They but fill up narrow fissures in other rocks. Their origin appears, almost without exception, to have been hydroplutonic. They are, for
the most part, chemical precipitates from aqueous solutions formed in the interior of the earth under very different circumstances of pressure and heat than those
which prevail upon the surface.

Having treated these formations, which occupy so subordinate a space in the composition of the earth's crust,
at length in our book on 'Erzlagerstätten,' we shall not
devote further space to them here.

CONCLUSION.

BEARING in mind the facts and considerations above stated, if we take a general review of the various formations and transformations of rocks, we shall discover in them a perpetual process of circulation or rotation of substances, and of their different states. The substances remain, but the forms in which they appear and the mode of their combinations vary.

Disregarding for the moment the first solid products of cooling on the earth's surface, as not being capable of identification at the present day, we may most conveniently enter the circle of transmutations with the eruptive igneous rocks, as approaching most nearly to original formations. These then are constantly attacked and decomposed by chemical and mechanical forces acting from their surface inwards, and from their cracks and fissures outwards.

The products of this decay are deposited either in the form of chemical precipitates or mechanical aggregates. By chemical process of precipitation cavities and fissures in rocks become filled up (*amygdaloids* and *veins*), deposits are made at the mouths of springs of *limestone-tuff, siliceous tuff, bog-ore,* &c. ; or else, other crystalline rocks are formed, such as *gypsum* or *rock-salt.* By mechanical agency, on the other hand (partly aided by organic processes), there arise the much more important and extensive deposits of *clay, sand, pebbles, marl, limestone,* and *dolomite* ; and during the process of deposit, *carbon* (in the form of carbonic acid from the atmosphere), *water, chlorine,* and some other substances are added to the previously existing materials.

But, like the eruptive masses, all these deposited masses in their turn are partly decomposed and washed away by external forces, and in other part they become greatly changed internally by pressure and the action of heat.

By means of heat and pressure acting during long periods,
parts which thus in the first instance were only mechanically bound together, enter into new chemical combinations with each other, and assume a crystalline state
more or less analogous to that of the crystalline mineral
aggregates of the eruptive rocks. It is even probable in many cases that the substance of these derivative rocks has been fused and become eruptive a second
time.

Thus the process of destruction and new formation of
rocks, be it ever so slow, and therefore difficult of observation, has never, at any time of the earth's history,
been interrupted, but continues at the present day; and
not only is this true of the original formations, but the
new products of consolidation, of deposit, and of transmutation have always been equally subjected, and are still
subject, to the same processes.

This is the perpetual circulation of matter in the world
of rocks.

In the course of such various and renewed working up
and transformation of the same substances, with the addition of those others furnished by the air and water, it
cannot be matter of wonder that the variety of their
groups has been always somewhat on the increase; for, if
certain processes in this rotation are altogether universal
in their character, recurring in the same way, everywhere
and in every age, yet in consequence of the general mul-
tiplication of conditions and circumstances, and the increasing aggregate of their results, special combinations
of the same processes have constantly arisen in later times
and brought about special formations of rocks which were
not previously in existence, or which do not belong to
the normal phenomena of nature.

This increase in variety of the products of later times
is not confined to geological and mineral substances; a
greater and more rapid increase has taken place in the
organic world, where the forms of life have multiplied in
an ever ascending ratio (partly in consequence of the
change and increase of the conditions of existence from
geological causes).

The processes of change, to which the outward conformation of the globe's surface is subject, likewise mul-

tiply more rapidly than mere strictly geological phenomena.

Reasoning, therefore, from the past and from analogy
with other kingdoms, we must expect the species of rocks
and kinds of rock-formation to go on increasing indefinitely for the future, as they have been increasing con-
tinually ever since the first solidification of our earth's
crust.

INDEX OF LOCALITIES.

GENERAL INDEX.

E E

LONDON

PRINTED BY SPOTTISWOODE AND CO.

NEW-STREET SQUARE

In crown 8vo. with 486 Figures on Wood, price 12s. cloth,

A GLOSSARY OF MINERALOGY.

By HENRY WILLIAM BRISTOW, F.G.S.

OF THE GEOLOGICAL SURVEY OF GREAT BRITAIN.

OPINIONS of the PRESS.

'This is really a handy book. A concise account of all known minerals is given in alphabetical order, and references are added to the cases in which specimens may be found in the British Museum and the Museum of Practical Geology. There is also a useful introduction on the characters, properties, and chemical composition of minerals.'

MEDICAL TIMES and GAZETTE.

'We can recommend Mr. BRISTOW'S *Glossary of Mineralogy* to all geologists, as well as to mining students, and the cadets of Sandhurst and Woolwich. It is a real handy book; the arrangement, being alphabetical, is suited to everyone's capacity.....As a work of general utility, this book is the best of its class, and the only one we should ever think of opening by way of amusement. We refer to such articles as arsenolite, amber, asbestos, asphalt, avanturine, &c., or to that on the diamond.'

CRITIC.

'The student in physical science has long desired a book combining facility of reference with a concise and familiar account of all the known minerals. This want is now fully supplied by the present work, which is not a mere glossary, as its title would imply, but is intermediate between it and a manual. The first fifty pages contain a description of the general characters of minerals, their various properties, composition, and classification; whilst the Glossary professes to give information upon every known mineral substance, and this information is as complete as the present state of our knowledge will allow.....The Author's task has been ably executed, and his work will be much in request.'

LANCET.

'There has been hitherto no work in English at all answering to this *Glossary* of Mr. BRISTOW. It is a Dictionary of Mineralogy of the most complete kind, and yet in the most portable form, and must become a *sine quâ non* to every practical mineralogist. Unincumbered with any system of classification, it describes every mineral species or variety alphabetically, with references to synonymes, English, French, and German. The description of the minerals is at once concise and yet sufficient for practical purposes. It includes their crystalline and physical characteristics, chemical composition (shewn both by formula and analyses), behaviour before the blowpipe, and their principal localities and uses. It need scarcely be said that Mr. BRISTOW, having the resources of the Jermyn Street Museum at his hand, as well as the assistance of so eminent a mineralogist as Mr. WARINGTON SMITH, has had great opportunities of turning out a good book. And he has certainly done so.....Notwithstanding the great body of information it contains, this little volume has the advantage of extreme clearness of type and great portability. For tourists and practical men interested in mineralogy it will be indispensable; among the former we expect Mr. BRISTOW'S green book will be seen often side by side with Mr. MURRAY'S red volumes.'

MINING and SMELTING MAGAZINE.

London: LONGMANS, GREEN, and CO. Paternoster Row.

In course of publication periodically, to be completed in 12 PARTS, each containing 240 pages, price 5s. forming THREE VOLUMES, medium 8vo. price 21s. each, VOLS. I. *and* II. now ready.

A DICTIONARY

OF

SCIENCE, LITERATURE, AND ART

COMPRISING

THE DEFINITIONS AND DERIVATIONS OF THE SCIENTIFIC TERMS IN GENERAL USE, TOGETHER WITH THE HISTORY AND DESCRIPTIONS OF THE SCIENTIFIC PRINCIPLES OF NEARLY EVERY BRANCH OF HUMAN KNOWLEDGE.

EDITED BY THE LATE

W. T. BRANDE, D.C.L. F.R.S.L. & E.

Of Her Majesty's Mint, Honorary Prof. of Chemistry in the Royal Institution of Great Britain.

AND THE

REV. GEORGE W. COX, M.A.

Late Scholar of Trinity College, Oxford;

ASSISTED BY GENTLEMEN OF EMINENT SCIENTIFIC AND LITERARY ACQUIREMENTS.

LIST OF CONTRIBUTORS.

General Editor .... W. T. BRANDE, F.R.S. &c. late of Her Majesty's Mint, and Honorary Professor of Chemistry in the Royal Institution of Great Britain.

Joint-Editor .... The Rev. GEORGE W. COX, M.A. late Scholar of Trinity College, Oxford.

Agriculture .... JOHN CHALMERS MORTON, Editor of the 'Agricultural Gazette,' &c.

Architecture, History, Language, Mythology, and General Literature .... The Rev. GEORGE W. COX, M.A.

Astronomy, Observational and Descriptive, and Meteorology .... E. FRANKLAND, Ph.D. F.R.S. Prof. of Chem. in the R. Inst. of Great Britain ; and J. N. LOCKYER, Esq.

Biological Sciences, comprising Anatomy, Physiology, Zoology, and Palæontology .... Professor RICHARD OWEN, F.R.S. LL.D. D.C.L. Superintendent of the Nat. Hist. Depts. Brit. Mus. ; and C. CARTER BLAKE, Ph.D. F.G.S. For. Assoc. of the Anthropol. Soc. of Paris.

Botany and Gardening .... JOHN LINDLEY, F.R.S. F.L.S. late Emeritus Professor of Bot. in Univ. Coll. London ; and THOMAS MOORE, F.L.S. Curator of the Botanic Garden, Chelsea.

Building and Engineering ...... G. R. BURNELL, Architect and Civil Engineer, F.R.I.B.A. F.G.S. F.S.A. ; and JOHN BOURNE, Civil Engineer.

General Chemistry and Physics .. W. T. BRANDE, D.C.L. F.R.S.L. & E. ; E. FRANKLAND, Ph.D. F.R.S. ; JOHN ATTFIELD, Ph.D. F.C.S. Director of the Laboratories of the Pharmaceutical Soc. of Great Britain ; JOHN BROUGHTON, B.S. ; W. F. BARRETT ; and HERBERT McLEOD.

Geology, Physical Geography, and Hydrology .... D. T. ANSTED, M.A. F.R.S. F.G.S. &c. Hon. Fellow of King's Coll. London.

Law, History, and General Literature .... HERMAN MERIVALE, M.A. C.B. late Fellow of Balliol College, Oxford.

Law .... ARTHUR P. WHATELY, M.A. of Lincoln's Inn, Barrister-at-Law ; late Student of Christ Church, Oxford.

Mathematics, Pure and Applied .. T. A. HIRST, Ph.D. F.R.S. Prof. of Mathematical Physics in Univ. Coll. London.

Military Subjects .... Lieut. H. BRACKENBURY, R.A. F.S.A. Assistant-Instructor in Artillery, R.M. Academy, Woolwich.

Mineralogy .... HENRY WILLIAM BRISTOW, F.R.S. F.G.S. Hon. Fell. of King's Coll. Lond. of the Geol. Survey of Great Britain.

Music .... Prof. W. POLE, F.R.S. Mus. Bac. Oxon.

Naval Subjects .... DENHAM ROBINSON.

Navigation .... H. W. JEANS, F.R.A.S. R.N. Coll. Portsmouth.

Painting and the Fine Arts .... RALPH N. WORNUM, Keeper and Secretary of the National Gallery.

Political Economy .... JAMES E. THOROLD ROGERS, M.A. Professor of Political Econ. Tooke Professor of Economic Science and Statistics in King's Coll. London.

Printing, Bibliography, &c. .... R. J. COURTNEY, Superintendent at Messrs. Spottiswoode and Co.'s Printing Office.

Theology and Ecclesiastical Literature .... C. MERIVALE, B.D. Chaplain to the Speaker of the House of Commons.

London: LONGMANS, GREEN, and CO. Paternoster Row.

[APRIL 1869]

GENERAL LIST OF WORKS

PUBLISHED BY

MESSRS. LONGMANS, GREEN, AND CO.

PATERNOSTER ROW, LONDON.

~~~~~~~~~~

Historical Works.

LORD MACAULAY'S WORKS. Complete and Uniform Library Edition. Edited by his Sister, Lady TREVELYAN. 8 vols. 8vo. with Portrait, price £5 5s. cloth, or £8 8s. bound in tree-calf by Rivière.

The **HISTORY of ENGLAND** from the Fall of Wolsey to the Death of Elizabeth. By JAMES ANTHONY FROUDE, M.A. late Fellow of Exeter College, Oxford. VOLS. I. to X. in 8vo. price £7 2s. cloth.

VOLS. I. to IV. the Reign of Henry VIII. Fourth Edition, 54s.

VOLS. V. and VI. the Reigns of Edward VI. and Mary. Third Edition, 28s.

VOLS. VII. and VIII. the Reign of Elizabeth, VOLS. I. and II. Fourth Edition, 28s.

VOLS. IX. and X. the Reign of Elizabeth, VOLS. III. and IV. 32s.

The **HISTORY of ENGLAND** from the Accession of James II. Lord MACAULAY.

LIBRARY EDITION, 5 vols. 8vo. £4.

CABINET EDITION, 8 vols. post 8vo. 48s.

PEOPLE'S EDITION, 4 vols. crown 8vo. 16s.

An **ESSAY on the HISTORY of the ENGLISH GOVERNMENT** and Constitution, from the Reign of Henry VII. to the Present Time. By JOHN EARL RUSSELL. Fourth Edition, revised. Crown 8vo. 6s.

On **PARLIAMENTARY GOVERNMENT in ENGLAND**: Its Origin, Development, and Practical Operation. By ALPHEUS TODD, Librarian of the Legislative Assembly of Canada. In Two Volumes. VOL. I. 8vo. 16s.

HISTORY of the REFORM BILLS of 1866 and 1867. By HOMERSHAM COX, M.A. Barrister-at-Law. 8vo. 7s. 6d.

Antient Parliamentary Elections, a History shewing how Parliaments were Constituted, and Representatives of the People Elected, in Ancient Times. By the same Author. 8vo. 8s. 6d.

Whig and Tory Administrations during the Last Thirteen Years. By the same Author. 8vo. 5s.

A

The HISTORY of ENGLAND during the Reign of George the Third. By the Right Hon. W. N. Massey. Cabinet Edition. 4 vols. post 8vo. 24s.

The CONSTITUTIONAL HISTORY of ENGLAND, since the Accession of George III. 1760—1860. By Sir Thomas Erskine May, C.B. Second Edition. 2 vols. 8vo. 33s.

HISTORICAL STUDIES. By Herman Merivale, M.A. 8vo. price 12s. 6d.

The OXFORD REFORMERS of 1498; being a History of the Fellow-work of John Colet, Erasmus, and Thomas More. By Frederic Seebohm. 8vo. 12s.

LECTURES on the HISTORY of ENGLAND, from the earliest Times to the Death of King Edward II. By William Longman. With Maps and Illustrations. 8vo. 15s.

The HISTORY of the LIFE and TIMES of EDWARD the THIRD. By William Longman. With 9 Maps, 8 Plates, and 16 Woodcuts. 2 vols. 8vo. 28s.

HISTORY of CIVILISATION in England and France, Spain and Scotland. By Henry Thomas Buckle. Fifth Edition of the entire Work, with a complete Index. 3 vols. crown 8vo. 24s.

WATERLOO LECTURES: a Study of the Campaign of 1815. By Colonel Charles C. Chesney, R.E. late Professor of Military Art and History in the Staff College. 8vo. with Map, 10s. 6d.

HISTORY of GRANT'S CAMPAIGN for the CAPTURE of RICHMOND, 1864—1865: with an Outline of the Previous Course of the American Civil War. By John Cannon. Post 8vo. 12s. 6d.

DEMOCRACY in AMERICA. By Alexis De Tocqueville. Translated by Henry Reeve. 2 vols. 8vo. 21s.

HISTORY of the REFORMATION in EUROPE in the Time of Calvin. By J. H. Merle D'Aubigné. D.D. Vols. I. and II. 8vo. 28s. Vol. III. 12s. Vol. IV. 16s. Vol. V. price 16s.

HISTORY of FRANCE, from Clovis and Charlemagne to the Accession of Napoléon III. By Eyre Evans Crowe. 5 vols. 8vo. £4 13s.

The HISTORY of GREECE. By C. Thirlwall, D.D. Lord Bishop of St. David's. 8 vols. fcp. 8vo. price 28s.

The TALE of the GREAT PERSIAN WAR, from the Histories of Herodotus. By George W. Cox, M.A. New Edition. Fcp. 3s. 6d.

GREEK HISTORY from Themistocles to Alexander, in a Series of Lives from Plutarch. Revised and arranged by A. H. Clough. Fcp. with 44 Woodcuts, 6s.

CRITICAL HISTORY of the LANGUAGE and LITERATURE of Ancient Greece. By William Mure, of Caldwell. 5 vols. 8vo. £3 9s.

HISTORY of the LITERATURE of ANCIENT GREECE. By Professor K. O. Müller. Translated by the Right Hon. Sir George Cornewall Lewis, Bart. and by J. W. Donaldson, D.D. 3 vols. 8vo. 21s.

HISTORY of the CITY of ROME from its Foundation to the Sixteenth Century of the Christian Era. By Thomas H. Dyer, LL.D. 8vo. with 2 Maps, 15s.

HISTORY of the ROMANS under the EMPIRE. By the Rev. C. MERIVALE, LL.D. 8 vols. post 8vo. 48s.

The FALL of the ROMAN REPUBLIC: a Short History of the Last Century of the Commonwealth. By the same Author. 12mo. 7s. 6d.

The HISTORY of INDIA, from the Earliest Period to the close of Lord Dalhousie's Administration. By JOHN CLARK MARSHMAN. 3 vols. crown 8vo. 22s. 6d.

INDIAN POLITY: a View of the System of Administration in India. By Major GEORGE CHESNEY, Fellow of the University of Calcutta. 8vo. with Map, 21s.

HISTORY of the FRENCH in INDIA, from the Founding of Pondichery in 1674 to its Capture in 1761. By Lieutenant-Colonel G. B. MALLESON, Bengal Staff Corps. 8vo. 16s.

REALITIES of IRISH LIFE. By W. STEUART TRENCH, Land Agent in Ireland to the Marquess of Lansdowne, the Marquess of Bath, and Lord Digby. With Illustrations from Drawings by the Author's Son, J. TOWNSEND TRENCH. Third Edition, with 30 Plates. 8vo. 21s.

JOURNALS, CONVERSATIONS, and ESSAYS relating to IRELAND. By NASSAU WILLIAM SENIOR. 2 vols. post 8vo. 21s.

MODERN IRELAND; its Vital Questions, Secret Societies, and Government. By an ULSTERMAN. Post 8vo. 6s.

IRELAND in 1868 the BATTLE-FIELD for ENGLISH PARTY STRIFE: its Grievances, Real and Factitious; Remedies, Abortive or Mischievous. By GERALD FITZGIBBON. Second Edition. 8vo. 8s. 6d.

AN ILLUSTRATED HISTORY of IRELAND, from the Earliest Period to the Year of Catholic Emancipation. By MARY F. CUSACK. Second Edition, revised and enlarged. 8vo. 18s. 6d.

CRITICAL and HISTORICAL ESSAYS contributed to the *Edinburgh Review.* By the Right Hon. LORD MACAULAY.

> LIBRARY EDITION, 3 vols. 8vo. 36s.
>
> CABINET EDITION, 4 vols. post 8vo. 24s.
>
> TRAVELLER'S EDITION, in One Volume, square crown 8vo. 21s.
>
> PEOPLE'S EDITION, 2 vols. crown 8vo. 8s.

GOD in HISTORY; or, the Progress of Man's Faith in the Moral Order of the World. By the late Baron BUNSEN. Translated from the German by SUSANNA WINKWORTH; with a Preface by Dean STANLEY. In Three Volumes. VOLS. I. and II. 8vo. 30s.

HISTORY of EUROPEAN MORALS, from Augustus to Charlemagne. By W. E. H. LECKY, M.A. 2 vols. 8vo. price 28s.

HISTORY of the RISE and INFLUENCE of the SPIRIT of RATIONALISM in EUROPE. By W. E. H. LECKY, M.A. Third Edition, revised. 2 vols. 8vo. 25s.

The HISTORY of PHILOSOPHY, from Thales to Comte. By GEORGE HENRY LEWES. Third Edition. 2 vols. 8vo. 30s.

EGYPT'S PLACE in UNIVERSAL HISTORY; an Historical Investigation. By Baron BUNSEN, D.C.L. Translated by C. H. COTTRELL, M.A. With Additions by S. BIRCH, LL.D. 5 vols. 8vo. price £8 14s. 6d.

MAUNDER'S HISTORICAL TREASURY; comprising a General Introductory Outline of Universal History, and a series of Separate Histories. Latest Edition, revised and brought down to the Present Time by the Rev. G. W. Cox, M.A. late Scholar of Trinity College, Oxford. Fcp. 10s. 6d.

HISTORY of the NORMAN KINGS of ENGLAND. Drawn from a New Collation of the Contemporary Chronicles, by Thomas Cobbe, of the Inner Temple, Barrister-at-Law. 1 vol. 8vo. [Nearly ready.

HISTORY of the CHRISTIAN CHURCH, from the Ascension of Christ to the Conversion of Constantine. By E. Burton, D.D. late Prof. of Divinity in the Univ. of Oxford. Eighth Edition. Fcp. 3s. 6d.

SKETCH of the HISTORY of the CHURCH of ENGLAND to the Revolution of 1688. By the Right Rev. T. V. Short, D.D. Lord Bishop of St. Asaph. Seventh Edition. Crown 8vo. 10s. 6d.

HISTORY of the EARLY CHURCH, from the First Preaching of the Gospel to the Council of Nicæa, A.D. 325. By Elizabeth M. Sewell, Author of 'Amy Herbert.' Fcp. 4s. 6d.

The ENGLISH REFORMATION. By 'F. C. Massingberd, M.A. Chancellor of Lincoln and Rector of South Ormsby. Fourth Edition, revised. Fcp. 8vo. 7s. 6d.

Biography and Memoirs.

DICTIONARY of GENERAL BIOGRAPHY; containing Concise Memoirs and Notices of the most Eminent Persons of all Countries, from the Earliest Ages to the Present Time. Edited by W. L. R. Cates. 8vo. 21s.

LIVES of the TUDOR PRINCESSES, including Lady Jane Grey and her Sisters. By Agnes Strickland, Author of 'Lives of the Queens of England.' Post 8vo. with Portrait, &c. 12s. 6d.

MEMOIRS of BARON BUNSEN. Drawn chiefly from Family Papers by his Widow, Frances Baroness Bunsen. Second Edition, abridged; with 2 Portraits and 4 Woodcuts. 2 vols. post 8vo. 21s.

LIFE and CORRESPONDENCE of RICHARD WHATELY, D.D. late Archbishop of Dublin. By E. Jane Whately. Popular Edition, with Additions and Omissions. Crown 8vo. with Portrait, 7s. 6d.

LIFE of the DUKE of WELLINGTON. By the Rev. G. R. Gleig, M.A. Popular Edition, carefully revised; with copious Additions. Crown 8vo. with Portrait, 5s.

HISTORY of MY RELIGIOUS OPINIONS. By J. H. Newman, D.D. Being the Substance of Apologia pro Vitâ Suâ. Post 8vo. 6s.

FATHER MATHEW: a Biography. By John Francis Maguire, M.P. for Cork. Popular Edition, with Portrait. Crown 8vo. 3s. 6d.

THE LIFE of FRANZ SCHUBERT. Translated from the German of K. Von Hellborn, by A. D. Coleridge, M.A. late Fellow of King's College, Cambridge. With an Appendix by G. Grove. 2 vols. post 8vo. with Portrait, 21s.

REMINISCENCES of FELIX MENDELSSOHN-BARTHOLDY; a Social and Artistic Biography. By ELISE POLKO. Translated from the German by Lady WALLACE. With additional Letters addressed to English Correspondents. Post 8vo. with Portrait and View, 10s. 6d.

FELIX MENDELSSOHN'S LETTERS from *Italy and Switzerland,* and *Letters from* 1833 *to* 1847, translated by Lady WALLACE. New Edition, with Portrait. 2 vols. crown 8vo. 5s. each.

FARADAY as a DISCOVERER. By JOHN TYNDALL, LL.D. F.R.S. Professor of Natural Philosophy in the Royal Institution of Great Britain. With Two Portraits. Crown 8vo. 6s.

MEMOIRS of SIR HENRY HAVELOCK, K.C.B. By JOHN CLARK MARSHMAN. Cabinet Edition, with Portrait. Crown 8vo. price 5s.

CAPTAIN COOK'S LIFE, VOYAGES, and DISCOVERIES. 18mo. Woodcuts, 2s. 6d.

LIFE of Sir JOHN RICHARDSON, C.B. sometime Inspector of Naval Hospitals and Fleets. By the Rev. JOHN MCILRAITH. Fcp. 8vo. with Portrait, 5s.

LIFE of PASTOR FLIEDNER, Founder of the Deaconesses' Institution at Kaiserswerth. Translated from the German by CATHERINE WINKWORTH. Fcp. 8vo. with Portrait, 3s. 6d.

VICISSITUDES of FAMILIES. By Sir J. BERNARD BURKE, C.B. Ulster King of Arms. New Edition, remodelled and enlarged. 2 vols. crown 8vo. 21s.

THE EARLS of GRANARD: a Memoir of the Noble Family of Forbes. Written by Admiral the Hon. JOHN FORBES, and edited by GEORGE ARTHUR HASTINGS, present Earl of Granard, K.P. 8vo. 10s.

GEORGE PETRIE, LL.D. M.R.I.A. &c. formerly President of the Royal Hibernian Academy; his Life and Labours in Art and Archæology. By WILLIAM STOKES, M.D. &c. Physician-in-Ordinary to the Queen in Ireland. 8vo. 12s. 6d.

ESSAYS in ECCLESIASTICAL BIOGRAPHY. By the Right Hon. Sir J. STEPHEN, LL.D. Cabinet Edition (being the Fifth). Crown 8vo. 7s. 6d.

ESSAYS on EDUCATIONAL REFORMERS: the Jesuits, Locke, J. J. Rousseau, Pestalozzi, Jacotot, &c. By the Rev. R. H. QUICK, M.A. Trin. Coll. Cantab. Post 8vo. 7s. 6d.

ESSAYS, BIOGRAPHICAL and CRITICAL. By A. L. MEISSNER, Ph.D. Professor of Modern Languages in Queen's College, Belfast, and in the Queen's University in Ireland.   [*Nearly ready.*

MAUNDER'S BIOGRAPHICAL TREASURY. Thirteenth Edition, reconstructed, thoroughly revised, and in great part rewritten; with about 1,000 additional Memoirs and Notices, by W. L. R. CATES. Fcp. 10s. 6d.

LETTERS and LIFE of FRANCIS BACON, including all his Occasional Works. Collected and edited, with a Commentary, by J. SPEDDING, Trin. Coll. Cantab. VOLS. I. and II. 8vo. 24s. VOLS. III. and IV. price 24s.

Criticism, Philosophy, Polity, &c.

The INSTITUTES of JUSTINIAN; with English Introduction, Translation, and Notes. By T. C. SANDARS, M.A. Barrister, late Fellow of Oriel Coll. Oxon. Fourth Edition. 8vo. 15s.

SOCRATES and the SOCRATIC SCHOOLS. Translated from the German of Dr. E. ZELLER, with the Author's approval, by the Rev. OSWALD J. REICHEL, B.C.L. and M.A. Crown 8vo. 8s. 6d.

The ETHICS of ARISTOTLE, illustrated with Essays and Notes. By Sir A. GRANT, Bart. M.A. LL.D. Second Edition, revised and completed. 2 vols. 8vo. price 28s.

ELEMENTS of LOGIC. By R. WHATELY, D.D. late Archbishop of Dublin. Ninth Edition. 8vo. 10s. 6d. crown 8vo. 4s. 6d.

Elements of Rhetoric. By the same Author. Seventh Edition. 8vo. 10s. 6d. crown 8vo. 4s. 6d.

English Synonymes. By E. JANE WHATELY. Edited by Archbishop WHATELY. 5th Edition. Fcp. 3s.

BACON'S ESSAYS with ANNOTATIONS. By R. WHATELY, D.D. late Archbishop of Dublin. Sixth Edition. 8vo. 10s. 6d.

LORD BACON'S WORKS, collected and edited by R. L. ELLIS, M.A. J. SPEDDING, M.A. and D. D. HEATH. Vols. I. to V. *Philosophical Works*, 5 vols. 8vo. £4 6s. VOLS. VI. and VII. *Literary and Professional Works*, 2 vols. £1 16s.

On REPRESENTATIVE GOVERNMENT. By JOHN STUART MILL. Third Edition. 8vo. 9s. Crown 8vo. 2s.

On LIBERTY. By JOHN STUART MILL. Fourth Edition. Post 8vo. 7s. 6d. Crown 8vo. 1s. 4d.

Principles of Political Economy. By the same Author. Sixth Edition. 2 vols. 8vo. 30s. Or in 1 vol. crown 8vo. 5s.

A System of Logic, Ratiocinative and Inductive. By the same Author. Seventh Edition. Two vols. 8vo. 25s.

ANALYSIS of MR. MILL'S SYSTEM of LOGIC. By W. STEBBING, M.A. Fellow of Worcester College, Oxford. Second Edition. 12mo. 3s. 6d.

UTILITARIANISM. By JOHN STUART MILL. Third Edition. 8vo. 5s.

Dissertations and Discussions, Political, Philosophical, and Historical. By the same Author. Second Edition, revised. 3 vols. 8vo. 36s.

Examination of Sir W. Hamilton's Philosophy, and of the Principal Philosophical Questions discussed in his Writings. By the same Author. Third Edition. 8vo. 16s.

An OUTLINE of the NECESSARY LAWS of THOUGHT: a Treatise on Pure and Applied Logic. By the Most Rev. WILLIAM, Lord Archbishop of York, D.D. F.R.S. Ninth Thousand. Crown 8vo. 5s. 6d.

The **ELEMENTS** of **POLITICAL ECONOMY**. By HENRY DUNNING MACLEOD, M.A. Barrister-at-Law. 8vo. 16s.

A **Dictionary** of **Political Economy**; Biographical, Bibliographical, Historical, and Practical. By the same Author. VOL. I. royal 8vo. 30s.

The **ELECTION** of **REPRESENTATIVES**, Parliamentary and Municipal; a Treatise. By THOMAS HARE, Barrister-at-Law. Third Edition, with Additions. Crown 8vo. 6s.

SPEECHES of the **RIGHT HON. LORD MACAULAY**, corrected by Himself. Library Edition, 8vo. 12s. People's Edition, crown 8vo. 3s. 6d.

LORD MACAULAY'S SPEECHES on **PARLIAMENTARY REFORM** in 1831 and 1832. 16mo. 1s.

INAUGURAL ADDRESS delivered to the University of St. Andrews. By JOHN STUART MILL. 8vo. 5s. People's Edition, crown 8vo. 1s.

A **DICTIONARY** of the **ENGLISH LANGUAGE**. By R. G. LATHAM, M.A. M.D. F.R.S. Founded on the Dictionary of Dr. SAMUEL JOHNSON, as edited by the Rev. H. J. TODD, with numerous Emendations and Additions. In Two Volumes. VOL. I. 4to. in Two Parts, price £3 10s. In course of publication, also, in 36 Parts, price 3s. 6d. each.

THESAURUS of **ENGLISH WORDS** and **PHRASES**, classified and arranged so as to facilitate the Expression of Ideas, and assist in Literary Composition. By P. M. ROGET, M.D. New Edition. Crown 8vo. 10s. 6d.

LECTURES on the **SCIENCE** of **LANGUAGE**, delivered at the Royal Institution. By MAX MÜLLER, M.A. Fellow of All Souls College, Oxford. 2 vols. 8vo. FIRST SERIES, Fifth Edition, 12s. SECOND SERIES, Second Edition, 18s.

CHAPTERS on **LANGUAGE**. By FREDERIC W. FARRAR, F.R.S. late Fellow of Trin. Coll. Cambridge. Crown 8vo. 8s. 6d.

WORD-GOSSIP; a Series of Familiar Essays on Words and their Peculiarities. By the Rev. W. L. BLACKLEY, M.A. Fcp. 8vo. 5s.

A **BOOK ABOUT WORDS**. By G. F. GRAHAM, Author of ' English, or the Art of Composition,' ' English Synonymes,' ' English Grammar Practice, ' English Style,' &c. Fcp. 8vo. [Nearly ready.

The **DEBATER**; a Series of Complete Debates, Outlines of Debates, and Questions for Discussion. By F. ROWTON. Fcp. 6s.

MANUAL of **ENGLISH LITERATURE**, Historical and Critical. By THOMAS ARNOLD, M.A. Second Edition. Crown 8vo. price 7s. 6d.

SOUTHEY'S DOCTOR, complete in One Volume. Edited by the Rev. J. W. WARTER, B.D. Square crown 8vo. 12s. 6d.

HISTORICAL and **CRITICAL COMMENTARY** on the **OLD TESTAMENT**; with a New Translation. By M. M. KALISCH, Ph.D. VOL. I. Genesis, 8vo. 18s. or adapted for the General Reader, 12s. VOL. II. Exodus, 15s. or adapted for the General Reader, 12s. VOL. III. Leviticus, PART I. 15s. or adapted for the General Reader, 8s.

A **Hebrew Grammar**, with Exercises. By the same Author. PART I. Outlines with Exercises, 8vo. 12s. 6d. KEY, 5s. PART II. Exceptional Forms and Constructions, 12s. 6d.

A LATIN-ENGLISH DICTIONARY. By J. T. WHITE, D.D. of
Corpus Christi College, and J. E. RIDDLE, M.A. of St. Edmund Hall, Oxford.
2 vols. 4to. pp. 2,128, price 42s. cloth.

White's College Latin-English Dictionary (Intermediate Size),
abridged for the use of University Students from the Parent Work (as
above). Medium 8vo. pp. 1,048, price 18s. cloth.

White's Junior Student's College Latin-English and English-Latin
Dictionary. Square 12mo. pp. 1,058, price 12s.

Separately { The ENGLISH-LATIN DICTIONARY, price 5s. 6d.
{ The LATIN-ENGLISH DICTIONARY, price 7s. 6d.

An ENGLISH-GREEK LEXICON, containing all the Greek Words
used by Writers of good authority. By C. D. YONGE, B.A. New Edition. 4to. 21s.

Mr. YONGE'S NEW LEXICON, English and Greek, abridged from
his larger work (as above). Revised Edition. Square 12mo. 8s. 6d.

A GREEK-ENGLISH LEXICON. Compiled by H. G. LIDDELL, D.D.
Dean of Christ Church, and R. SCOTT, D.D. Master of Balliol. Fifth Edition.
Crown 4to. 31s. 6d.

A Lexicon, Greek and English, abridged from LIDDELL and SCOTT'S
Greek-English Lexicon. Twelfth Edition. Square 12mo. 7s. 6d.

A SANSKRIT-ENGLISH DICTIONARY, the Sanskrit words printed
both in the original Devanagari and in Roman Letters. Compiled by
T. BENFEY, Prof. in the Univ. of Göttingen. 8vo. 52s. 6d.

WALKER'S PRONOUNCING DICTIONARY of the ENGLISH LAN-
GUAGE. Thoroughly revised Editions, by B. H. SMART. 8vo. 12s. 16mo. 6s.

A PRACTICAL DICTIONARY of the FRENCH and ENGLISH LAN-
GUAGES. By L. CONTANSEAU. Thirteenth Edition. Post 8vo. 10s. 6d.

Contanseau's Pocket Dictionary, French and English, abridged from
the above by the Author. New Edition, revised. Square 18mo. 3s. 6d.

NEW PRACTICAL DICTIONARY of the GERMAN LANGUAGE;
German–English and English-German. By the Rev. W. L. BLACKLEY, M.A.
and Dr. CARL MARTIN FRIEDLÄNDER. Post 8vo. 7s. 6d.

Miscellaneous Works and *Popular Metaphysics.*

The ESSAYS and CONTRIBUTIONS of A. K. H. B., Author of ' The
Recreations of a Country Parson.' Uniform Editions:—

Recreations of a Country Parson. FIRST and SECOND SERIES, crown
8vo. 3s. 6d. each.

The Common-place Philosopher in Town and Country. Crown 8vo.
3s. 6d.

Leisure Hours in Town; Essays Consolatory, Æsthetical, Moral,
Social, and Domestic. Crown 8vo. 3s. 6d.

The Autumn Holidays of a Country Parson; Essays contributed
to *Fraser's Magazine* and to *Good Words*. Crown 8vo. 3*s*. 6*d*.

The Graver Thoughts of a Country Parson.   FIRST and SECOND
SERIES, crown 8vo. 3*s*. 6*d*. each.

Critical Essays of a Country Parson. Selected from Essays contributed to *Fraser's Magazine*. Crown 8vo. 3*s*. 6*d*.

Sunday Afternoons at the Parish Church of a Scottish University
City. Crown 8vo. 3*s*. 6*d*.

Lessons of Middle Age, with some Account of various Cities and
Men. By A. K. H. B. Author of 'The Recreations of a Country Parson.'
Crown 8vo. 3*s*. 6*d*.

Counsel and Comfort spoken from a City Pulpit.   Crown 8vo. 3*s*. 6*d*.

Changed Aspects of Unchanged Truths : Memorials of St. Andrews
Sundays. Crown 8vo. 3*s*. 6*d*.

SHORT STUDIES on GREAT SUBJECTS.   By JAMES ANTHONY
FROUDE, M.A. late Fellow of Exeter Coll. Oxford. Third Edition. 8vo. 12*s*.

LORD MACAULAY'S MISCELLANEOUS WRITINGS :—
LIBRARY EDITION. 2 vols. 8vo. Portrait, 21*s*.
PEOPLE'S EDITION. 1 vol. crown 8vo. 4*s*. 6*d*.

The REV. SYDNEY SMITH'S MISCELLANEOUS WORKS ; includ-
ing his Contributions to the *Edinburgh Review*. 2 vols. crown 8vo. 8*s*.

The Wit and Wisdom of the Rev. Sydney Smith. a Selection of
the most memorable Passages in his Writings and Conversation. 16mo. 5*s*.

EPIGRAMS, Ancient and Modern ; Humorous, Witty, Satirical, Moral,
and Panegyrical. Edited by Rev. JOHN BOOTH, B.A. Cambridge. Second
Edition, revised and enlarged. Fcp. 7*s*. 6*d*.

The PEDIGREE of the ENGLISH PEOPLE; an Argument, Historical and Scientific, on the *Ethnology* of the English. By THOMAS
NICHOLAS, M.A. Ph.D. 8vo. 16*s*.

The ENGLISH and THEIR ORIGIN : a Prologue to authentic English
History. By LUKE OWEN PIKE, M.A. Barrister-at-Law. 8vo. 9*s*.

ESSAYS selected from CONTRIBUTIONS to the *Edinburgh Review*.
By HENRY ROGERS. Second Edition. 3 vols. fcp. 21*s*.

Reason and Faith, their Claims and Conflicts. By the same Author.
New Edition, accompanied by several other Essays. Crown 8vo. 6*s*. 6*d*.

The Eclipse of Faith ; or, a Visit to a Religious Sceptic. By the
same Author. Twelfth Edition. Fcp. 5*s*.

Defence of the Eclipse of Faith, by its Author ; a rejoinder to Dr.
Newman's *Reply*. Third Edition. Fcp. 3*s*. 6*d*.

Selections from the Correspondence of R. E. H. Greyson. By the
same Author. Third Edition. Crown 8vo. 7*s*. 6*d*.

B

CHIPS from a GERMAN WORKSHOP; being Essays on the Science of Religion, and on Mythology, Traditions, and Customs. By MAX MÜLLER, M.A. Fellow of All Souls College, Oxford. Second Edition, revised, with an Index. 2 vols. 8vo. 24s.

ANALYSIS of the PHENOMENA of the HUMAN MIND. By JAMES MILL. A New Edition, with Notes, Illustrative and Critical, by ALEXANDER BAIN, ANDREW FINDLATER, and GEORGE GROTE. Edited, with additional Notes, by JOHN STUART MILL. 2 vols. 8vo. price 28s.

An INTRODUCTION to MENTAL PHILOSOPHY, on the Inductive Method. By. J. D. MORELL, M.A. LL.D. 8vo. 12s.

Elements of Psychology, containing the Analysis of the Intellectual Powers. By the same Author. Post 8vo. 7s. 6d.

The SECRET of HEGEL: being the Hegelian System in Origin, Principle, Form, and Matter. By J. H. STIRLING. 2 vols. 8vo. 28s.

The SENSES and the INTELLECT. By ALEXANDER BAIN, M.A. Professor of Logic in the University of Aberdeen. Third Edition. 8vo. 15s.

The EMOTIONS and the WILL. By the same Author. Second Edition. 8vo. 15s.

On the STUDY of CHARACTER, including an Estimate of Phrenology. By the same Author. 8vo. 9s.

MENTAL and MORAL SCIENCE: a Compendium of Psychology and Ethics. By the same Author. Second Edition. Crown 8vo. 10s. 6d.

The PHILOSOPHY of NECESSITY; or, Natural Law as applicable to Mental, Moral, and Social Science. By CHARLES BRAY. Second Edition. 8vo. 9s.

The Education of the Feelings and Affections. By the same Author. Third Edition. 8vo. 3s. 6d.

On Force, its Mental and Moral Correlates. By the same Author. 8vo. 5s.

The FOLK-LORE of the NORTHERN COUNTIES of ENGLAND and the Borders. By WILLIAM HENDERSON. With an Appendix on Household Stories by the Rev. S. BARING-GOULD, M.A. Post 8vo. 9s. 6d.

Astronomy, Meteorology, Popular Geography, &c.

OUTLINES of ASTRONOMY. By Sir J. F. W. HERSCHEL, Bart. M.A. Ninth Edition, revised ; with Plates and Woodcuts. 8vo. 18s.

SATURN and its SYSTEM. By RICHARD A. PROCTOR, B.A. late Scholar of St John's Coll. Camb. 8vo. with 14 Plates, 14s.

Handbook of the Stars. By the same Author. With 3 Maps. Square fcp. 5s.

CELESTIAL OBJECTS for COMMON TELESCOPES. By the Rev. T. W. WEBB, M.A. F.R.A.S. Second Edition, revised, with a large Map of the Moon, and several Woodcuts. 16mo. 7s. 6d.

NAVIGATION and NAUTICAL ASTRONOMY (Practical, Theoretical, Scientific) for the use of Students and Practical Men. By J. MERRIFIELD, F.R.A.S and H. EVERS. 8vo. 14s.

DOVE'S LAW of STORMS, considered in connexion with the Ordinary Movements of the Atmosphere. Translated by R. H. SCOTT, M.A. T.C.D. 8vo. 10s. 6d.

PHYSICAL GEOGRAPHY for **SCHOOLS** and **GENERAL READERS**. By M. F. MAURY, LL.D. Fcp. with 2 Charts, 2s. 6d.

A TREATISE on the **ACTION of VIS INERTIÆ in the OCEAN**; with Remarks on the Abstract Nature of the Forces of Vis Inertiæ 'and Gravitation, and a New Theory of the Tides. By WILLIAM LEIGHTON JORDAN, F.R.G.S. With 12 Charts and Diagrams. 8vo. 14s.

M'CULLOCH'S DICTIONARY, Geographical, Statistical, and Historical, of the various Countries, Places, and Principal Natural Objects in the World. New Edition, with the Statistical Information brought up to the latest returns by F. MARTIN. 4 vols. 8vo. with coloured Maps, £4 4s.

A GENERAL DICTIONARY of GEOGRAPHY, Descriptive, Physical, Statistical, and Historical; forming a complete Gazetteer of the World. By A. KEITH JOHNSTON, LL.D F.R.G.S. Revised Edition. 8vo. 31s. 6d.

A MANUAL of GEOGRAPHY, Physical, Industrial, and Political. By W. HUGHES, F.R.G.S. With 6 Maps. Fcp. 7s. 6d.

The STATES of the RIVER PLATE: their Industries and Commerce. By WILFRID LATHAM, Buenos Ayres. Second Edition, revised. 8vo. 12s.

MAUNDER'S TREASURY of GEOGRAPHY, Physical, Historical, Descriptive, and Political. Edited by W. HUGHES, F.R.G.S. With 7 Maps and 16 Plates. Fcp. 10s. 6d.

Natural History and Popular Science.

ELEMENTARY TREATISE on PHYSICS, Experimental and Applied. Translated and edited from GANOT's *Eléments de Physique* (with the Author's sanction) by E. ATKINSON, Ph. D. F.C.S. New Edition, revised and enlarged; with a Coloured Plate and 620 Woodcuts. Post 8vo. 15s.

The ELEMENTS of PHYSICS or NATURAL PHILOSOPHY. By NEIL ARNOTT, M.D. F.R.S. Physician Extraordinary to the Queen. Sixth Edition, rewritten and completed. Two Parts, 8vo. 21s.

SOUND: a Course of Eight Lectures delivered at the Royal Institution of Great Britain. By JOHN TYNDALL, LL.D. F.R.S. Crown 8vo. with Portrait of M. Chladni and 169 Woodcuts, price 9s.

HEAT CONSIDERED as a MODE of MOTION. By Professor JOHN TYNDALL, LL.D. F.R.S. Third Edition. Crown 8vo. with Woodcuts, 10s. 6d.

LIGHT: Its Influence on Life and Health. By FORBES WINSLOW, M.D. D.C.L. Oxon. (Hon.). Fcp. 8vo. 6s.

An ESSAY on DEW, and several Appearances connected with it. By W. C. WELLS. Edited, with Annotations, by L. P. CASELLA, F.R.A.S. and an Appendix by R. STRACHAN, F.M.S. 8vo. 5s.

A TREATISE on ELECTRICITY, in Theory and Practice. By A. DE LA RIVE, Prof. in the Academy of Geneva. Translated by C. V. WALKER, F.R.S. 3 vols. 8vo. with Woodcuts, £3 13s.

The **CORRELATION of PHYSICAL FORCES.** By W. R. Grove, Q.C. V.P.R.S. Fifth Edition, revised, and followed by a Discourse on Continuity. 8vo. 10s. 6d. The *Discourse on Continuity*, separately, 2s. 6d.

MANUAL of GEOLOGY. By S. Haughton, M.D. F.R.S. Revised Edition, with 66 Woodcuts. Fcp. 7s. 6d.

A GUIDE to GEOLOGY. By J. Phillips, M.A. Professor of Geology in the University of Oxford. Fifth Edition, with Plates. Fcp. 4s.

The **STUDENT'S MANUAL of ZOOLOGY and COMPARATIVE PHYSIOLOGY.** By J. Burney Yeo, M.B. Resident Medical Tutor and Lecturer on Animal Physiology in King's College, London. [*Nearly ready.*

VAN DER HOEVEN'S HANDBOOK of ZOOLOGY. Translated from the Second Dutch Edition by the Rev. W. Clark, M.D. F.R.S. 2 vols. 8vo. with 24 Plates of Figures, 60s.

Professor **OWEN'S LECTURES** on the **COMPARATIVE ANATOMY** and Physiology of the Invertebrate Animals. Second Edition, with 235 Woodcuts. 8vo. 21s.

The **COMPARATIVE ANATOMY and PHYSIOLOGY of the VERTE-** brate Animals. By Richard Owen, F.R.S. D.C.L. With 1,472 Woodcuts. 3 vols. 8vo. £3 13s. 6d.

The **FIRST MAN and HIS PLACE in CREATION,** considered on the Principles of Common Sense from a Christian Point of View. By George Moore, M.D. Post 8vo. 8s. 6d.

The **PRIMITIVE INHABITANTS of SCANDINAVIA:** containing a Description of the Implements, Dwellings, Tombs, and Mode of Living of the Savages in the North of Europe during the Stone Age. By Sven Nilsson. Translated from the Third Edition; with an Introduction by Sir J. Lubbock. With 16 Plates of Figures and 3 Woodcuts. 8vo. 18s.

BIBLE ANIMALS; being an Account of the various Birds, Beasts, Fishes, and other Animals mentioned in the Holy Scriptures. By the Rev. J. G. Wood, M.A. F.L.S. Copiously illustrated with Original Designs, made under the Author's superintendence and engraved on Wood. In course of publication monthly, to be completed in 20 Parts, price 1s. each, forming One Volume, uniform with 'Homes without Hands.'

HOMES WITHOUT HANDS: a Description of the Habitations of Animals, classed according to their Principle of Construction. By Rev. J. G. Wood, M.A. F.L.S. With about 140 Vignettes on Wood (20 full size of page). New Edition. 8vo. 21s.

MANUAL of CORALS and SEA JELLIES. By J. R. Greene, B.A. Edited by Joseph A. Galbraith, M.A. and Samuel Haughton, M.D. Fcp. with 39 Woodcuts, 5s.

Manual of Sponges and Animalculæ; with a General Introduction on the Principles of Zoology. By the same Author and Editors. Fcp. with 16 Woodcuts, 2s.

Manual of the Metalloids. By J. Apjohn, M.D. F.R.S. and the same Editors. Revised Edition. Fcp. with 38 Woodcuts, 7s. 6d.

A FAMILIAR HISTORY of BIRDS. By E. Stanley, D.D. F.R.S. late Lord Bishop of Norwich. Seventh Edition, with Woodcuts. Fcp. 3s. 6d.

The **HARMONIES of NATURE and UNITY of CREATION.** By Dr.
GEORGE HARTWIG. 8vo. with numerous Illustrations, 18s.

The **Sea and its Living Wonders.** By the same Author. Third
(English) Edition. 8vo. with many Illustrations, 21s.

The **Tropical World.** By the same Author. With 8 Chromoxylographs and 172 Woodcuts. 8vo. 21s.

The **POLAR WORLD**; a Popular Description of Man and Nature in the
Arctic and Antarctic Regions of the Globe. By Dr. GEORGE HARTWIG.
With 8 Chromoxylographs, 3 Maps, and 85 Woodcuts. 8vo. 21s.

CEYLON. By Sir J. EMERSON TENNENT, K.C.S. LL.D. Fifth Edition;
with Maps, &c. and 90 Wood Engravings. 2 vols. 8vo. £2 10s.

KIRBY and SPENCE'S INTRODUCTION to ENTOMOLOGY, or
Elements of the Natural History of Insects. 7th Edition. Crown 8vo. 5s.

MAUNDER'S TREASURY of NATURAL HISTORY, or Popular
Dictionary of Zoology. Revised and corrected by T. S. COBBOLD, M.D.
Fcp. with 900 Woodcuts. 10s. 6d.

The **TREASURY of BOTANY,** or Popular Dictionary of the Vegetable
Kingdom; including a Glossary of Botanical Terms. Edited by J. LINDLEY,
F.R.S. and T. MOORE, F.L.S. assisted by eminent Contributors. Pp. 1,274,
with 274 Woodcuts and 20 Steel Plates. 2 Parts, fcp. 20s.

The **ELEMENTS of BOTANY for FAMILIES and SCHOOLS.**
Tenth Edition, revised by THOMAS MOORE, F.L.S. Fcp. with 154 Woodcuts, 2s. 6d.

The **ROSE AMATEUR'S GUIDE.** By THOMAS RIVERS. Twelfth
Edition. Fcp. 4s.

The **BRITISH FLORA**; comprising the Phænogamous or Flowering
Plants and the Ferns. By Sir W. J. HOOKER, K.H. and G. A. WALKER-
ARNOTT, LL.D. 12mo. with 12 Plates, 14s. or coloured, 21s.

LOUDON'S ENCYCLOPÆDIA of PLANTS; comprising the Specific
Character, Description, Culture, History, &c. of all the Plants found in
Great Britain. With upwards of 12,000 Woodcuts. 8vo. 42s.

MAUNDER'S SCIENTIFIC and LITERARY TREASURY. New
Edition, thoroughly revised and in great part re-written, with above 1,000
new Articles, by J. Y. JOHNSON, Corr. M.Z.S. Fcp. 10s. 6d.

A **DICTIONARY of SCIENCE, LITERATURE, and ART.** Fourth
Edition, re-edited by W. T. BRANDE (the Author), and GEORGE W. COX, M.A.
assisted by contributors of eminent Scientific and Literary Acquirements.
3 vols. medium 8vo. price 63s. cloth.

The **QUARTERLY JOURNAL of SCIENCE.** Edited by JAMES
SAMUELSON and WILLIAM CROOKES, F.R.S. Published quarterly in
January, April, July, and October. 8vo. with Illustrations, price 5s. each
Number.

Chemistry, Medicine, Surgery, and the *Allied Sciences.*

A **DICTIONARY of CHEMISTRY** and the Allied Branches of other
Sciences. By HENRY WATTS, F.R.S. assisted by eminent Contributors.
Complete in 5 vols. medium 8vo. £7 3s.

ELEMENTS of CHEMISTRY, Theoretical and Practical. By WILLIAM A. MILLER, M.D. LL.D. F.R.S. F.G.S. Prof. of Chemistry, King's Coll. London. 3 vols. 8vo. £3. PART I. CHEMICAL PHYSICS, 15*s.* PART II. INORGANIC CHEMISTRY, 21*s.* PART III. ORGANIC CHEMISTRY, 24*s.*

A MANUAL of CHEMISTRY, Descriptive and Theoretical. By WILLIAM ODLING, M.B. F.R.S. PART I. 8vo. 9*s.* PART II. *just ready.*

A Course of Practical Chemistry, for the use of Medical Students. By the same Author. New Edition, with 70 Woodcuts. Crown 8vo. 7*s.* 6*d.*

Lectures on Animal Chemistry, delivered at the Royal College of Physicians in 1865. By the same Author. Crown 8vo. 4*s.* 6*d.*

HANDBOOK of CHEMICAL ANALYSIS, adapted to the UNITARY *System* of Notation. By F. T. CONINGTON, M.A. F.C.S. Post 8vo. 7*s.* 6*d.* —CONINGTON'S *Tables of Qualitative Analysis,* price 2*s.* 6*d.*

The DIAGNOSIS, PATHOLOGY, and TREATMENT of DISEASES of Women; including the Diagnosis of Pregnancy. By GRAILY HEWITT, M.D. Second Edition, enlarged; with 116 Woodcut Illustrations. 8vo. 24*s.*

LECTURES on the DISEASES of INFANCY and CHILDHOOD. By CHARLES WEST, M.D. &c. Fifth Edition, revised and enlarged. 8vo. 16*s.*

A SYSTEM of SURGERY, Theoretical and Practical. In Treatises by Various Authors. Edited by T. HOLMES, M.A. &c. Surgeon and Lecturer on Surgery at St. George's Hospital, and Surgeon-in-Chief to the Metropolitan Police. 4 vols. 8vo. £4 13*s.*

The SURGICAL TREATMENT of CHILDREN'S DISEASES. By T. HOLMES, M.A. &c. late Surgeon to the Hospital for Sick Children. Second Edition, with 9 Plates and 112 Woodcuts. 8vo. 21*s.*

LECTURES on the PRINCIPLES and PRACTICE of PHYSIC. By Sir THOMAS WATSON, Bart. M.D. New Edition in preparation.

LECTURES on SURGICAL PATHOLOGY. By J. PAGET, F.R.S. Edited by W. TURNER, M.B. New Edition in preparation.

On CHRONIC BRONCHITIS, especially as connected with GOUT, EMPHYSEMA, and DISEASES of the HEART. By E. HEADLAM GREENHOW, M.D. F.R.C.P. &c. 8vo. 7*s.* 6*d.*

A TREATISE on the CONTINUED FEVERS of GREAT BRITAIN. By C. MURCHISON, M.D. New Edition in preparation.

CLINICAL LECTURES on DISEASES of the LIVER, JAUNDICE, and ABDOMINAL DROPSY. By CHARLES MURCHISON, M.D. Post 8vo. with 25 Woodcuts, 10*s.* 6*d.*

ANATOMY, DESCRIPTIVE and SURGICAL. By HENRY GRAY, F.R.S. With 410 Wood Engravings from Dissections. New Edition, by T. HOLMES, M.A. Cantab. Royal 8vo. 28*s.*

The THEORY of OCULAR DEFECTS and of SPECTACLES. Translated from the German of Dr. H. SCHEFFLER by R. B. CARTER, F.R.C.S. With Prefatory Notes and a Chapter of Practical Instructions. Post 8vo. 7*s.* 6*d.*

OUTLINES of PHYSIOLOGY, Human and Comparative. By JOHN MARSHALL, F.R.C.S. Surgeon to the University College Hospital. 2 vols. crown 8vo. with 122 Woodcuts, 32*s.*

ESSAYS on PHYSIOLOGICAL SUBJECTS. By GILBERT W. CHILD, M.D. F.L.S. F.C.S. of Exeter College, Oxford. 8vo. 5s.

PHYSIOLOGICAL ANATOMY and PHYSIOLOGY of MAN. By the late R. B. TODD, M.D. F.R.S. and W. BOWMAN, F.R.S. of King's College. With numerous Illustrations. VOL. II. 8vo. 25s.
VOL. I. New Edition by Dr. LIONEL S. BEALE, F.R.S. in course of publication; PART I. with 8 Plates, 7s. 6d.

COPLAND'S DICTIONARY of PRACTICAL MEDICINE, abridged from the larger work and throughout brought down to the present State of Medical Science. 8vo. 36s.

The WORKS of SIR B. C. BRODIE, Bart. collected and arranged by CHARLES HAWKINS, F.R.C.S.E. 3 vols. 8vo. with Medallion and Facsimile. 48s.

On ANILINE and its DERIVATIVES: a Treatise on the Manufacture of Aniline and Aniline Colours. By M. REIMANN, Ph.D. L.A.M. To which is added the Report on the Colouring Matters derived from Coal Tar shewn at the French Exhibition of 1867. Edited by WILLIAM CROOKES, F.R.S. With 5 Woodcuts. 8vo. 10s. 6d.

A MANUAL of MATERIA MEDICA and THERAPEUTICS, abridged from Dr. PEREIRA'S Elements by F. J. FARRE, M.D. assisted by R. BENTLEY, M.R.C.S. and by R. WARINGTON, F.R.S. 8vo. with 90 Woodcuts, 21s.

THOMSON'S CONSPECTUS of the BRITISH PHARMACOPŒIA. 25th Edition, corrected by E. LLOYD BIRKETT, M.D. 18mo. price 6s.

MANUAL of the DOMESTIC PRACTICE of MEDICINE. By W. B. KESTEVEN, F.R.C.S.E. Third Edition, revised, with Additions. Fcp. 5s.

GYMNASTS and GYMNASTICS. By JOHN H. HOWARD, late Professor of Gymnastics, Comm. Coll. Rippenden. Second Edition, revised and enlarged, with 135 Woodcuts. Crown 8vo. 10s. 6d.

The Fine Arts, and Illustrated Editions.

MATERIALS for a HISTORY of OIL PAINTING. By Sir CHARLES LOCKE EASTLAKE, sometime President of the Royal Academy. VOL. II. 8vo. 14s.

HALF-HOUR LECTURES on the HISTORY and PRACTICE of the Fine and Ornamental Arts. By WILLIAM B. SCOTT. New Edition, revised by the Author; with 50 Woodcuts. Crown 8vo. 8s. 6d.

LECTURES on the HISTORY of MODERN MUSIC, delivered at the Royal Institution. By JOHN HULLAH. FIRST COURSE, with Chronological Tables, post 8vo. 6s. 6d. SECOND COURSE, on the Transition Period, with 40 Specimens, 8vo. 16s.

SIX LECTURES on HARMONY, delivered at the Royal Institution of Great Britain in the Year 1867. By G. A. MACFARREN. With numerous engraved Musical Examples and Specimens. 8vo. 10s. 6d.

The CHORALE BOOK for ENGLAND: the Hymns translated by Miss C. WINKWORTH; the tunes arranged by Prof. W. S. BENNETT and OTTO GOLDSCHMIDT. Fcp. 4to. 12s. 6d.

Congregational Edition. Fcp. 2s.

SACRED MUSIC for FAMILY USE; a Selection of Pieces for One, Two, or more Voices, from the best Composers, Foreign and English. Edited by JOHN HULLAH. 1 vol. music folio, price 21s.

The NEW TESTAMENT, illustrated with Wood Engravings after the Early Masters, chiefly of the Italian School. Crown 4to. 63s. cloth, gilt top ; or £5 5s. elegantly bound in morocco.

LYRA GERMANICA ; the Christian Year. Translated by CATHERINE WINKWORTH; with 125 Illustrations on Wood drawn by J. LEIGHTON, F.S.A. 4to. 21s.

LYRA GERMANICA ; the Christian Life. Translated by CATHERINE WINKWORTH; with about 200 Woodcut Illustrations by J. LEIGHTON, F.S.A. and other Artists. 4to. 21s.

The LIFE of MAN SYMBOLISED by the MONTHS of the YEAR. Text selected by R. PIGOT ; Illustrations on Wood from Original Designs by J. LEIGHTON, F.S.A. 4to. 42s.

CATS' and FARLIE'S MORAL EMBLEMS ; with Aphorisms, Adages, and Proverbs of all Nations. 121 Illustrations on Wood by J. LEIGHTON, F.S.A. Text selected by R. PIGOT. Imperial 8vo. 31s. 6d.

SHAKESPEARE'S MIDSUMMER NIGHT'S DREAM, illustrated with 24 Silhouettes or Shadow-Pictures by P. KONEWKA, engraved on Wood by A. VOGEL. Folio. 31s. 6d.

SHAKSPEARE'S SENTIMENTS and SIMILES, printed in Black and Gold, and Illuminated in the Missal Style by HENRY NOEL HUMPHREYS. Square post 8vo. 21s.

SACRED and LEGENDARY ART. By Mrs. JAMESON.

Legends of the Saints and Martyrs. Fifth Edition, with 19 Etchings and 187 Woodcuts. 2 vols. square crown 8vo. 31s. 6d.

Legends of the Monastic Orders. Third Edition, with 11 Etchings and 88 Woodcuts. 1 vol. square crown 8vo. 21s.

Legends of the Madonna. Third Edition, with 27 Etchings and 165 Woodcuts. 1 vol. square crown 8vo. 21s.

The History of Our Lord, with that of his Types and Precursors. Completed by Lady EASTLAKE. Revised Edition, with 31 Etchings and 281 Woodcuts. 2 vols. square crown 8vo. 42s.

Arts, Manufactures, &c.

DRAWING from NATURE. By GEORGE BARNARD, Professor of Drawing at Rugby School. With 18 Lithographic Plates, and 108 Wood Engravings. Imperial 8vo. price 25s. Or in Three Parts, royal 8vo. 7s. 6d. each.

GWILT'S ENCYCLOPÆDIA of ARCHITECTURE, with above 1,100 Engravings on Wood. Fifth Edition, revised and enlarged by WYATT PAPWORTH. Additionally illustrated with nearly 400 Wood Engravings by O. Jewitt, and more than 100 other new Woodcuts. 8vo. 52s. 6d.

ITALIAN SCULPTORS ; being a History of Sculpture in Northern, Southern, and Eastern Italy. By C. C. PERKINS. With 30 Etchings and 13 Wood Engravings. Imperial 8vo. 42s.

TUSCAN SCULPTORS, their Lives, Works, and Times. With 45 Etchings and 28 Woodcuts from Original Drawings and Photographs. By the same Author. 2 vols. Imperial 8vo. 63s.

ORIGINAL DESIGNS for WOOD-CARVING, with PRACTICAL INstructions in the Art. By A. F. B. With 20 Plates of Illustrations engraved on Wood. 4to. 18s.

HINTS on HOUSEHOLD TASTE in FURNITURE, UPHOLSTERY, and other Details. By CHARLES L. EASTLAKE, Architect. With about 90 Illustrations. Square crown 8vo. 18s.

The ENGINEER'S HANDBOOK; explaining the Principles which should guide the Young Engineer in the Construction of Machinery. By C. S. LOWNDES. Post 8vo. 5s.

The ELEMENTS of MECHANISM. By T. M. GOODEVE, M.A. Professor of Mechanics at the R. M. Acad. Woolwich. Second Edition, with 217 Woodcuts. Post 8vo. 6s. 6d.

LATHES and TURNING, Simple, Mechanical, and ORNAMENTAL. By W. HENRY NORTHCOTT. With about 240 Illustrations on Steel and Wood. 8vo. 18s.

URE'S DICTIONARY of ARTS, MANUFACTURES, and MINES. Sixth Edition, chiefly rewritten and greatly enlarged by ROBERT HUNT, F.R.S. assisted by numerous Contributors eminent in Science and the Arts, and familiar with Manufactures. With above 2,000 Woodcuts. 3 vols. medium 8vo. price £4 14s. 6d.

HANDBOOK of PRACTICAL TELEGRAPHY, published with the sanction of the Chairman and Directors of the Electric and International Telegraph Company, and adopted by the Department of Telegraphs for India. By R. S. CULLEY. Third Edition. 8vo. 12s. 6d.

ENCYCLOPÆDIA of CIVIL ENGINEERING, Historical, Theoretical, and Practical. By E. CRESY, C.E. With above 3,000 Woodcuts. 8vo. 42s.

TREATISE on MILLS and MILLWORK. By W. FAIRBAIRN, C.E. Second Edition, with 18 Plates and 322 Woodcuts. 2 vols. 8vo. 32s.

Useful Information for Engineers. By the same Author. FIRST, SECOND, and THIRD SERIES, with many Plates and Woodcuts. 3 vols. crown 8vo. 10s. 6d. each.

The Application of Cast and Wrought Iron to Building Purposes. By the same Author. Third Edition, with 6 Plates and 118 Woodcuts. 8vo. 16s.

IRON SHIP BUILDING, its History and Progress, as comprised in a Series of Experimental Researches. By the same Author. With 4 Plates and 130 Woodcuts. 8vo. 18s.

A TREATISE on the STEAM ENGINE, in its various Applications to Mines, Mills, Steam Navigation, Railways and Agriculture. By J. BOURNE, C.E. Eighth Edition: with Portrait, 37 Plates, and 546 Woodcuts. 4to. 42s.

Catechism of the Steam Engine, in its various Applications to Mines, Mills, Steam Navigation, Railways, and Agriculture. By the same Author. With 89 Woodcuts. Fcp. 6s.

Handbook of the Steam Engine. By the same Author, forming a KEY to the Catechism of the Steam Engine, with 67 Woodcuts. Fcp. 9s.

C

A TREATISE on the SCREW PROPELLER, SCREW VESSELS, and
Screw Engines, as adapted for purposes of Peace and War; with Notices
of other Methods of Propulsion, Tables of the Dimensions and Performance
of Screw Steamers, and detailed Specifications of Ships and Engines. By
J. BOURNE, C.E. Third Edition, with 54 Plates and 287 Woodcuts. 4to. 63s.

EXAMPLES of MODERN STEAM, AIR, and GAS ENGINES of
the most Approved Types, as employed for Pumping, for Driving Machinery,
for Locomotion, and for Agriculture, minutely and practically described.
Illustrated by Working Drawings, and embodying a Critical Account of all
Projects of Recent Improvement in Furnaces, Boilers, and Engines. By
the same Author. In course of publication monthly, to be completed in 24
Parts, price 2s. 6d. each, forming One volume 4to. with about 50 Plates and
400 Woodcuts.

A HISTORY of the MACHINE-WROUGHT HOSIERY and LACE
Manufactures. By WILLIAM FELKIN, F.L.S. F.S.S. Royal 8vo. 21s.

PRACTICAL TREATISE on METALLURGY, adapted from the last
German Edition of Professor KERL'S *Metallurgy* by W. CROOKES, F.R.S. &c.
and E. RÖHRIG, Ph.D. M.E. VOL. I. comprising *Lead, Silver, Zinc,
Cadmium, Tin, Mercury, Bismuth, Antimony, Nickel, Arsenic, Gold,
Platinum*, and *Sulphur*. 8vo. with 207 Woodcuts, 31s. 6d.

MITCHELL'S MANUAL of PRACTICAL ASSAYING. Third Edi-
tion, for the most part re-written, with all the recent Discoveries incor-
porated, by W. CROOKES, F.R.S. With 188 Woodcuts. 8vo. 28s.

The ART of PERFUMERY; the History and Theory of Odours, and
the Methods of Extracting the Aromas of Plants. By Dr. PIESSE, F.C.S.
Third Edition, with 53 Woodcuts. Crown 8vo. 10s. 6d.

Chemical, Natural, and Physical Magic, for Juveniles during the
Holidays. By the same Author. Third Edition, with 38 Woodcuts. Fcp. 6s.

LOUDON'S ENCYCLOPÆDIA of AGRICULTURE: comprising the
Laying-out, Improvement, and Management of Landed Property, and the
Cultivation and Economy of the Productions of Agriculture. With 1,100
Woodcuts. 8vo. 31s. 6d.

Loudon's Encylopædia of Gardening: comprising the Theory and
Practice of Horticulture, Floriculture, Arboriculture, and Landscape Gardening. With 1,000 Woodcuts. 8vo. 31s. 6d.

BAYLDON'S ART of VALUING RENTS and TILLAGES, and Claims
of Tenants upon Quitting Farms, both at Michaelmas and Lady-Day.
Eighth Edition, revised by J. C. MORTON. 8vo. 10s. 6d.

Religious and *Moral* *Works.*

An EXPOSITION of the 39 ARTICLES, Historical and Doctrinal.
By E. HAROLD BROWNE, D.D. Lord Bishop of Ely. Seventh Edit. 8vo. 16s.

ARCHBISHOP LEIGHTON'S SERMONS and CHARGES. With
Additions and Corrections from MSS. and with Historical and other Illustrative Notes by WILLIAM WEST, Incumbent of S. Columba's, Nairn.
8vo. 15s.

The ACTS of the APOSTLES; with a Commentary, and Practical and
Devotional Suggestions for Readers and Students of the English Bible. By
the Rev. F. C. COOK, M.A. Canon of Exeter, &c. New Edition. 8vo. 12s. 6d.

The LIFE and EPISTLES of ST. PAUL. By W. J. CONYBEARE, M.A. late Fellow of Trin. Coll.Cantab. and the Very Rev. J. S. HOWSON, D.D. Dean of Chester.

LIBRARY EDITION, with all the Original Illustrations, Maps, Landscapes on Steel, Woodcuts, &c. 2 vols. 4to. 48s.

INTERMEDIATE EDITION, with a Selection of Maps, Plates, and Woodcuts. 2 vols. square crown 8vo. 31s. 6d.

PEOPLE'S EDITION, revised and condensed, with 46 Illustrations and Maps. 2 vols. crown 8vo. 12s.

The VOYAGE and SHIPWRECK of ST. PAUL; with Dissertations on the Life and Writings of St. Luke and the Ships and Navigation of the Ancients. By JAMES SMITH, F.R.S. Third Edition. Crown 8vo. 10s. 6d.

The NATIONAL CHURCH; HISTORY and PRINCIPLES of the CHURCH POLITY of ENGLAND. By D. MOUNTFIELD, M.A. Rector of Newport, Salop. Crown 8vo. 4s.

EVIDENCE of the TRUTH of the CHRISTIAN RELIGION derived from the Literal Fulfilment of Prophecy. By ALEXANDER KEITH, D.D. 37th Edition, with numerous Plates, in square 8vo. 12s. 6d.; also the 39th Edition, in post 8vo. with 5 Plates, 6s.

The HISTORY and DESTINY of the WORLD and of the CHURCH. according to Scripture. By the same Author. Square 8vo. with 40 Illustrations, 10s.

A CRITICAL and GRAMMATICAL COMMENTARY on ST. PAUL'S Epistles. By C. J. ELLICOTT, D.D. Lord Bishop of Gloucester & Bristol. 8vo.

Galatians, Fourth Edition, 8s. 6d.

Ephesians, Fourth Edition, 8s. 6d.

Pastoral Epistles, Fourth Edition, 10s. 6d.

Philippians, Colossians, and Philemon, Third Edition, 10s. 6d.

Thessalonians, Third Edition, 7s. 6d.

Historical Lectures on the Life of our Lord Jesus Christ: being the Hulsean Lectures for 1859. By the same Author. Fourth Edition. 8vo, price 10s. 6d.

An INTRODUCTION to the STUDY of the NEW TESTAMENT, Critical, Exegetical, and Theological. By the Rev. S. DAVIDSON, D.D. LL.D. 2 vols. 8vo. 30s.

Rev. T. H. HORNE'S INTRODUCTION to the CRITICAL STUDY and Knowledge of the Holy Scriptures. Twelfth Edition, as last revised throughout and brought up to the existing state of Biblical Knowledge under careful Editorial revision. With 4 Maps and 22 Woodcuts and Facsimiles. 4 vols. 8vo. 42s.

Rev. T. H. Horne's Compendious Introduction to the Study of the Bible, being an Analysis of the larger work by the same Author. Re-edited by the Rev. JOHN AYRE, M.A. With Maps, &c. Post 8vo. 6s.

EWALD'S HISTORY of ISRAEL to the DEATH of MOSES. Translated from the German. Edited, with a Preface and an Appendix, by RUSSELL MARTINEAU, M.A. Prof. of Hebrew in Manchester New Coll. London. Second Edition, continued to the commencement of the Monarchy. 2 vols. 8vo. 24s. VOL. II. comprising Joshua and Judges, for Purchasers of the First Edition, 9s.

The TREASURY of BIBLE KNOWLEDGE; being a Dictionary of the Books, Persons, Places, Events, and other matters of which mention is made in Holy Scripture. By Rev. J. AYRE, M.A. With Maps, 16 Plates, and numerous Woodcuts. Fcp. 10s. 6d.

The GREEK TESTAMENT; with Notes, Grammatical and Exegetical. By the Rev. W. WEBSTER, M.A. and the Rev. W. F. WILKINSON, M.A. 2 vols. 8vo. £2 4s.

VOL. I. the Gospels and Acts, 20s.

VOL. II. the Epistles and Apocalypse, 24s.

The CHURCHMAN'S DAILY REMEMBRANCER of DOCTRINE and DUTY: consisting of Meditations taken from the Writings of Standard Divines from the Early Days of Christianity to the Present Time; with a Preface by W. R. FREMANTLE, M.A. New Edition. Fcp. 8vo. 6s.

EVERY-DAY SCRIPTURE DIFFICULTIES explained and illustrated. By J. E. PRESCOTT, M.A. VOL. I. *Matthew* and *Mark*; VOL. II. *Luke* and *John.* 2 vols. 8vo. 9s. each.

The PENTATEUCH and BOOK of JOSHUA CRITICALLY EXAMINED. By the Right Rev. J. W. COLENSO, D.D. Lord Bishop of Natal. People's Edition, in 1 vol. crown 8vo. 6s. or in 5 Parts, 1s. each.

The CHURCH and the WORLD: Three Series of Essays on Questions of the Day. By Various Writers. Edited by the Rev. ORBY SHIPLEY, M.A. FIRST SERIES, Third Edition, 15s. SECOND SERIES, Second Edition, 15s. THIRD SERIES, 1868, price 15s. 3 vols. 8vo. 45s.

The FORMATION of CHRISTENDOM. By T. W. ALLIES. PARTS I. and II. 8vo. price 12s. each Part.

ENGLAND and CHRISTENDOM. By ARCHBISHOP MANNING, D.D. Post 8vo. price 10s. 6d.

CHRISTENDOM'S DIVISIONS, PART I., a Philosophical Sketch of the Divisions of the Christian Family in East and West. By EDMUND S. FFOULKES. Post 8vo. price 7s. 6d.

Christendom's Divisions, PART II. Greeks and Latins, being a History of their Dissensions and Overtures for Peace down to the Reformation. By the same Author. Post 8vo. 15s.

The WOMAN BLESSED by ALL GENERATIONS; or, Mary the Object of Veneration, Confidence, and Imitation to all Christians. By the Rev. R. MELIA, D.D. P.S.M. With 78 Illustrations. 8vo. 15s.

LIFE of the BLESSED VIRGIN; the FEMALE GLORY. By ANTHONY STAFFORD. Together with the Apology of the Author, and an Essay on the Cultus of the Blessed Virgin Mary. Fourth Edition, with Facsimiles of the 5 Original Illustrations. Edited by the Rev. ORBY SHIPLEY, M.A. Fcp. 8vo. 10s. 6d.

CELEBRATED SANCTUARIES of the MADONNA. By the Rev. J. SPENCER NORTHCOTE, D.D. Post 8vo. 6s. 6d.

The HIDDEN WISDOM of CHRIST and the KEY of KNOWLEDGE; or, History of the Apocrypha. By ERNEST DE BUNSEN. 2 vols. 8vo. 28s.

The KEYS of ST. PETER; or, the House of Rechab, connected with the History of Symbolism and Idolatry. By the same Author. 8vo. 14s.

The TYPES of GENESIS, briefly considered as Revealing the Development of Human Nature. By ANDREW JUKES. Second Edition. Crown 8vo. 7s. 6d.

The Second Death and the Restitution of All Things, with some Preliminary Remarks on the Nature and Inspiration of Holy Scripture. By the same Author. Second Edition. Crown 8vo. 3s. 6d.

ESSAYS and REVIEWS. By the Rev. W. TEMPLE, D.D. the Rev. R. WILLIAMS, B.D. the Rev. B. POWELL, M.A. the Rev. H. B. WILSON, B.D. C. W. GOODWIN, M.A. the Rev. M. PATTISON, B.D. and the Rev. B. JOWETT, M.A. Twelfth Edition. Fcp. 8vo. 5s.

The POWER of the SOUL over the BODY. By GEORGE MOORE, M.D. M.R.C.P.L. &c. Sixth Edition. Crown 8vo. 8s. 6d.

PASSING THOUGHTS on RELIGION. By ELIZABETH M. SEWELL, Author of 'Amy Herbert.' New Edition. Fcp. 8vo. 5s.

Self-Examination before Confirmation. By the same Author. 32mo. price 1s. 6d.

Readings for a Month Preparatory to Confirmation, from Writers of the Early and English Church. By the same Author. Fcp. 4s.

Readings for Every Day in Lent, compiled from the Writings of Bishop JEREMY TAYLOR. By the same Author. Fcp. 5s.

Preparation for the Holy Communion; the Devotions chiefly from the works of JEREMY TAYLOR. By the same. 32mo. 3s.

PRINCIPLES of EDUCATION Drawn from Nature and Revelation, and applied to Female Education in the Upper Classes. By the Author of 'Amy Herbert.' 2 vols. fcp. 12s. 6d.

The WIFE'S MANUAL; or, Prayers, Thoughts, and Songs on Several Occasions of a Matron's Life. By the Rev. W. CALVERT, M.A. Crown 8vo. price 10s. 6d.

SINGERS and SONGS of the CHURCH : being Biographical Sketches of the Hymn-Writers in all the principal Collections; with Notes on their Psalms and Hymns. By JOSIAH MILLER, M.A. New Edition, enlarged. Crown 8vo. [Nearly ready.

'SPIRITUAL SONGS' for the SUNDAYS and HOLIDAYS throughout the Year. By J. S. B. MONSELL, LL.D. Vicar of Egham and Rural Dean. Fourth Edition, Sixth Thousand. Fcp. 4s. 6d.

The Beatitudes: Abasement before God ; Sorrow for Sin ; Meekness of Spirit; Desire for Holiness; Gentleness; Purity of Heart; the Peacemakers; Sufferings for Christ. By the same. Third Edition. Fcp. 3s. 6d.

His PRESENCE—not his MEMORY, 1855. By the same Author, in Memory of his SON. Sixth Edition. 16mo. 1s.

LYRA DOMESTICA; Christian Songs for Domestic Edification. Translated from the Psaltery and Harp of C. J. P. SPITTA, and from other sources, by RICHARD MASSIE. FIRST and SECOND SERIES, fcp. 4s. 6d. each.

LYRA GERMANICA, translated from the German by Miss C. WINKWORTH. FIRST SERIES, Hymns for the Sundays and Chief Festivals. SECOND SERIES, the Christian Life. Fcp. 3s. 6d. each SERIES.

LYRA EUCHARISTICA; Hymns and Verses on the Holy Communion, Ancient and Modern: with other Poems. Edited by the Rev. ORBY SHIPLEY, M.A. Second Edition. Fcp. 7s. 6d.

Lyra Messianica; Hymns and Verses on the Life of Christ, Ancient and Modern; with other Poems. By the same Editor. Second Edition, altered and enlarged. Fcp. 7s. 6d.

Lyra Mystica; Hymns and Verses on Sacred Subjects, Ancient and Modern. By the same Editor. Fcp. 7s. 6d.

ENDEAVOURS after the **CHRISTIAN LIFE**: Discourses. By JAMES MARTINEAU. Fourth and cheaper Edition, carefully revised; the Two Series complete in One Volume. Post 8vo. 7s. 6d.

WHATELY'S Introductory Lessons on the Christian Evidences. 18mo. 6d.

INTRODUCTORY LESSONS on the **HISTORY of RELIGIOUS** Worship; being a Sequel to the 'Lessons on Christian Evidences.' By RICHARD WHATELY, D.D. New Edition. 18mo. 2s. 6d.

BISHOP JEREMY TAYLOR'S ENTIRE WORKS. With Life by BISHOP HEBER. Revised and corrected by the Rev. C. P. EDEN, 10 vols. price £5 5s.

Travels, Voyages, &c.

SIX MONTHS in **INDIA.** By MARY CARPENTER. 2 vols. post 8vo. with Portrait, 18s.

NARRATIVE of the **EUPHRATES EXPEDITION** carried on by Order of the British Government during the years 1835, 1836, and 1837. By General F. R. CHESNEY, F.R.S. With 2 Maps, 45 Plates, and 16 Woodcuts. 8vo. 24s.

The **NORTH-WEST PENINSULA of ICELAND**; being the Journal of a Tour in Iceland in the Summer of 1862. By C. W. SHEPHERD, M.A. F.Z.S. With a Map and Two Illustrations. Fcp. 8vo. 7s. 6d.

PICTURES in **TYROL** and **Elsewhere.** From a Family Sketch-Book. By the Authoress of 'A Voyage en Zigzag,' &c. Second Edition. Small 4to. with numerous Illustrations, 21s.

HOW WE SPENT the SUMMER; or, a Voyage en Zigzag in Switzerland and Tyrol with some Members of the ALPINE CLUB. From the Sketch-Book of one of the Party. In oblong 4to. with 300 Illustrations, 15s.

BEATEN TRACKS; or, Pen and Pencil Sketches in Italy. By the Authoress of 'A Voyage en Zigzag.' With 42 Plates, containing about 200 Sketches from Drawings made on the Spot. 8vo. 16s.

MAP of the **CHAIN** of **MONT BLANC**, from an actual Survey in 1863—1864. By A. ADAMS-REILLY, F.R.G.S. M.A.C. Published under the Authority of the Alpine Club. In Chromolithography on extra stout drawing-paper 28in. × 17in. price 10s. or mounted on canvas in a folding case, 12s. 6d.

HISTORY of **DISCOVERY** in our **AUSTRALASIAN COLONIES,** Australia, Tasmania, and New Zealand, from the Earliest Date to the Present Day. By WILLIAM HOWITT. 2 vols. 8vo. with 3 Maps, 20s.

The **CAPITAL** of the **TYCOON**; a Narrative of a Three Years' Residence in Japan. By Sir RUTHERFORD ALCOCK, K.C.B. 2 vols. 8vo. with numerous Illustrations, 42s.

The **DOLOMITE MOUNTAINS**; Excursions through Tyrol, Carinthia, Carniola, and Friuli, 1861-1863. By J. GILBERT and G. C CHURCHILL, F.R.G.S. With numerous Illustrations. Square crown 8vo. 21s.

GUIDE to the **PYRENEES**, for the use of Mountaineers. By CHARLES PACKE. 2d Edition, with Map and Illustrations. Cr. 8vo. 7s. 6d.

The **ALPINE GUIDE.** By JOHN BALL, M.R.I.A. late President of the Alpine Club. 3 vols. post 8vo. with Maps and other Illustrations:—

Guide to the Eastern Alps, price 10s. 6d.

Guide to the Western Alps, including Mont Blanc, Monte Rosa, Zermatt, &c. Price 6s. 6d.

Guide to the Central Alps, including all the Oberland District. 7s. 6d.

Introduction on Alpine Travelling in General, and on the Geology of the Alps, price 1s. Each of the Three Volumes or Parts of the *Alpine Guide* may be had with this INTRODUCTION prefixed, price 1s. extra.

NARRATIVES of **SHIPWRECKS** of the **ROYAL NAVY** between 1793 and 1857, compiled from Official Documents in the Admiralty by W. O. S. GILLY; with a Preface by W. S. GILLY, D.D. Third Edition. Fcp. 5s.

TRAVELS in **ABYSSINIA** and the **GALLA COUNTRY**; with an Account of a Mission to Ras Ali in 1848. From the MSS. of the late WALTER CHICHELE PLOWDEN, Her Britannic Majesty's Consul in Abyssinia. Edited by his Brother TREVOR CHICHELE PLOWDEN. With Two Maps. 8vo. 18s.

MEMORIALS of **LONDON** and **LONDON LIFE** in the 13th, 14th, and 15th Centuries; being a Series of Extracts, Local, Social, and Political, from tho Archives of the City of London. A.D. 1276-1419. Selected, translated, and edited by H. T. RILEY, M.A. Royal 8vo. 21s.

COMMENTARIES on the **HISTORY, CONSTITUTION**, and **CHARTERED FRANCHISES** of the CITY of LONDON. By GEORGE NORTON, formerly one of the Common Pleaders of the City of London. Third Edition. 8vo. 14s.

CURIOSITIES of **LONDON**; exhibiting the most Rare and Remarkable Objects of Interest in the Metropolis; with nearly Sixty Years' Personal Recollections. By JOHN TIMBS, F.S.A. New Edition, corrected and enlarged. 8vo. with Portrait, 21s.

The **NORTHERN HEIGHTS** of **LONDON**; or, Historical Associations of Hampstead, Highgate, Muswell Hill, Hornsey, and Islington. By WILLIAM HOWITT. With about 40 Woodcuts. Square crown 8vo. 21s.

VISITS to **REMARKABLE PLACES**: Old Halls, Battle-Fields, and Scenes Illustrative of Striking Passages in English History and Poetry. By WILLIAM HOWITT. 2 vols. square crown 8vo. with Woodcuts, 25s.

The **RURAL LIFE** of **ENGLAND.** By the same Author. With Woodcuts by Bewick and Williams. Medium 8vo. 12s. 6d.

The **IRISH** in **AMERICA.** By JOHN FRANCIS MAGUIRE, M.P. for Cork. Post 8vo. 12s. 6d.

ROMA SOTTERRANEA; or, an Account of the Roman Catacombs, and especially of the Cemetery of St. Callixtus. Compiled from the Works of Commendatore G. B. DE ROSSI, with the consent of the Author, by the Rev. J. S. NORTHCOTE, D.D. and the Rev. W. R. BROWNLOW. With numerous Engravings on Wood, 10 Lithographs, 10 Plates in Chromolithography, and an Atlas of Plans, all executed in Rome under the Author's superintendence for this Translation. 1 vol. 8vo.   [*Nearly ready.*

Works of Fiction.

The **WARDEN**: a Novel. By ANTHONY TROLLOPE. Crown 8vo. 2s. 6d.

Barchester Towers : a Sequel to 'The Warden.' Crown 8vo. 3s. 6d.

STORIES and TALES by ELIZABETH M. SEWELL, Author of 'Amy Herbert,' uniform Edition, each Tale or Story complete in a single Volume.

AMY HERBERT, 2s. 6d.	IVORS, 3s. 6d.
GERTRUDE, 2s. 6d.	KATHARINE ASHTON, 3s. 6d.
EARL'S DAUGHTER, 2s. 6d.	MARGARET PERCIVAL, 5s.
EXPERIENCE OF LIFE, 2s. 6d.	LANETON PARSONAGE, 4s. 6d.
CLEVE HALL, 3s. 6d.	URSULA, 4s. 6d.

A Glimpse of the World. By the Author of 'Amy Herbert.' Fcp. 7s. 6d.

The Journal of a Home Life. By the same Author. Post 8vo. 9s. 6d.

After Life; a Sequel to 'The Journal of a Home Life.' Price 10s. 6d.

UNCLE PETER'S FAIRY TALE for the **XIX CENTURY.** Edited by E. M. SEWELL, Author of 'Amy Herbert,' &c. Fcp. 8vo. 7s. 6d.

BECKER'S GALLUS; or, Roman Scenes of the Time of Augustus : with Notes and Excursuses. New Edition. Post 8vo. 7s. 6d.

BECKER'S CHARICLES; a Tale illustrative of Private Life among the Ancient Greeks: with Notes and Excursuses. New Edition. Post 8vo. 7s. 6d.

NOVELS and TALES by G. J. WHYTE MELVILLE :—

The GLADIATORS, 5s.	HOLMBY HOUSE, 5s.
DIGBY GRAND, 5s.	GOOD FOR NOTHING, 6s.
KATE COVENTRY, 5s.	The QUEEN'S MARIES, 6s.
GENERAL BOUNCE, 5s.	The INTERPRETER, 5s.

TALES of ANCIENT GREECE. By GEORGE W. COX, M.A. late Scholar of Trin. Coll. Oxon. Being a Collective Edition of the Author's Classical Stories and Tales, complete in One Volume. Crown 8vo. 6s. 6d.

A MANUAL of MYTHOLOGY, in the form of Question and Answer. By the same Author. Fcp. 3s.

Poetry and The Drama.

THOMAS MOORE'S POETICAL WORKS, the only Editions containing the Author's last Copyright Additions :—

SHAMROCK EDITION, crown 8vo. price 3s. 6d.
RUBY EDITION, crown 8vo. with Portrait, price 6s.
PEOPLE'S EDITION, square crown 8vo. with Portrait, &c. 12s. 6d.
LIBRARY EDITION, medium 8vo. Portrait and Vignette, 14s.
CABINET EDITION, 10 vols. fcp. 8vo. price 35s.

MOORE'S IRISH MELODIES, Maclise's Edition, with 161 Steel Plates from Original Drawings. Super-royal 8vo. 31s. 6d.

Miniature Edition of Moore's Irish Melodies with Maclise's De- signs (as above) reduced in Lithography. Imp. 16mo. 10s. 6d.

MOORE'S LALLA ROOKH. Tenniel's Edition, with 68 Wood Engravings from original Drawings and other Illustrations. Fcp. 4to. 21s.

SOUTHEY'S POETICAL WORKS, with the Author's last Corrections and copyright Additions. Library Edition, in 1 vol. medium 8vo. with Portrait and Vignette, 14s. or in 10 vols. fcp. 3s. 6d. each.

LAYS of ANCIENT ROME; with *Ivry* **and the** *Armada.* **By the** Right Hon. LORD MACAULAY. 16mo. 4s. 6d.

Lord Macaulay's Lays of Ancient Rome. With 90 Illustrations on Wood, from the Antique, from Drawings by G. SCHARF. Fcp. 4to. 21s.

Miniature Edition of Lord Macaulay's Lays of Ancient Rome, with the Illustrations (as above) reduced in Lithography. Imp. 16mo. 10s. 6d.

GOLDSMITH'S POETICAL WORKS, with Wood Engravings from Designs by Members of the ETCHING CLUB. Imperial 16mo. 7s. 6d.

MEMORIES of some CONTEMPORARY POETS; with Selections from their Writings. By EMILY TAYLOR. Royal 18mo. 5s.

POEMS. By JEAN INGELOW. Thirteenth Edition. Fcp. 8vo. 5s.

POEMS by Jean Ingelow. With nearly 100 Illustrations by Eminent Artists, engraved on Wood by the Brothers DALZIEL. Fcp. 4to. 21s.

A STORY of DOOM, and other Poems. By JEAN INGELOW. Fcp. 5s.

POETICAL WORKS of LETITIA ELIZABETH LANDON (L.E.L.). 2 vols. 16mo. 10s.

BOWDLER'S FAMILY SHAKSPEARE, cheaper Genuine Edition, complete in 1 vol. large type, with 36 Woodcut Illustrations, price 14s. or with the same ILLUSTRATIONS, in 6 pocket vols. 3s. 6d. each.

HORATII OPERA, Pocket Edition, with carefully corrected Text, Marginal References, and Introduction. Edited by the Rev. J. E. YONGE, M.A. Square 18mo. 4s. 6d.

HORATII OPERA. Library Edition, with Marginal References and English Notes. Edited by the Rev. J. E. YONGE. 8vo. 21s.

The ÆNEID of VIRGIL Translated into English Verse. By JOHN CONINGTON, M.A. Crown 8vo. 9s.

ARUNDINES CAMI, sive Musarum Cantabrigiensium Lusus canori. Collegit atque edidit H. DRURY, M.A. Editio Sexta, curavit H. J. HODGSON, M.A. Crown 8vo. 7s. 6d.

EIGHT COMEDIES of ARISTOPHANES, viz. the Acharnians, Knights, Clouds, Wasps, Peace, Birds, Frogs, and Plutus. Translated into Rhymed Metres by LEONARD HAMPSON RUDD, M.A. 8vo. 15s.

PLAYTIME with the POETS : a Selection of the best English Poetry for the use of Children. By a LADY. Revised Edition. Crown 8vo. 5s.

The HOLY CHILD : a Poem in Four Cantos; also an Ode to Silence, and other Poems. By STEPHEN JENNER, M.A. Fcp. 8vo. 5s.

D

The **ILIAD** of **HOMER** **TRANSLATED** into **BLANK VERSE**. By ICHABOD CHARLES WRIGHT, M.A. 2 vols. crown 8vo. 21s.

The **ILIAD** of **HOMER** in **ENGLISH HEXAMETER VERSE**. By J. HENRY DART, M.A. of Exeter Coll. Oxford. Square crown 8vo. 21s.

The **ODYSSEY of HOMER**. Translated into Blank Verse by G. W. EDGINTON, Licentiate in Medicine. Dedicated by permission to Edward Earl of Derby. VOL. I. 8vo. with Map, 10s. 6d.

DANTE'S DIVINE COMEDY, translated in English Terza Rima by JOHN DAYMAN, M.A. [With the Italian Text, after *Brunetti*, interpaged.] 8vo. 21s.

HUNTING SONGS and MISCELLANEOUS VERSES. By R. E. EGERTON WARBURTON. Second Edition. Fcp. 8vo. 5s.

An **OLD STORY**, and other Poems. By ELIZABETH D. CROSS. Second Edition. Fcp. 8vo. 3s. 6d.

The **THREE FOUNTAINS**, a Fäery Epic of Euboea; with other Verses. By the Author of 'The Afterglow.' Fcp. 8vo. 3s. 6d.

The **Afterglow**; Songs and Sonnets for my Friends. By the Author of 'The Three Fountains.' Second Edition. Fcp. 8vo. 5s.

The **SILVER STORE** collected from Mediæval Christian and Jewish Mines. By the Rev. SABINE BARING-GOULD, M.A. Crown 8vo. 6s.

Rural Sports, &c.

BLAINE'S ENCYCLOPÆDIA of RURAL SPORTS; Hunting, Shooting, Fishing, Racing, &c. With above 600 Woodcuts (20 from Designs by JOHN LEECH). 8vo. 42s.

Col. HAWKER'S INSTRUCTIONS to YOUNG SPORTSMEN in all that relates to Guns and Shooting. Revised by the Author's SON. Square crown 8vo. with Illustrations, 18s.

The **DEAD SHOT**, or Sportsman's Complete Guide; a Treatise on the Use of the Gun, Dog-breaking, Pigeon-shooting, &c. By MARKSMAN. Revised Edition. Fcp. 8vo. with Plates, 5s.

The **FLY-FISHER'S ENTOMOLOGY.** By ALFRED RONALDS. With coloured Representations of the Natural and Artificial Insect. Sixth Edition; with 20 coloured Plates. 8vo. 14s.

A **BOOK on ANGLING**; a complete Treatise on the Art of Angling in every branch. By FRANCIS FRANCIS. Second Edition, with Portrait and 15 other Plates, plain and coloured. Post 8vo. 15s.

HANDBOOK of ANGLING : Teaching Fly-fishing, Trolling, Bottom-fishing, Salmon-fishing; with the Natural History of River Fish, and the best modes of Catching them. By EPHEMERA. Fcp. Woodcuts, 5s.

WILCOCKS'S SEA-FISHERMAN; comprising the Chief Methods of Hook and Line Fishing in the British and other Seas, a Glance at Nets, and Remarks on Boats and Boating. Second Edition, enlarged; with 80 Woodcuts. Post 8vo. 12s. 6d.

The **CRICKET FIELD**; or, the History and the Science of the Game of Cricket. By JAMES PYCROFT, B.A. Fourth Edition. Fcp. 5s.

HORSE and MAN. By C. S. MARCH PHILLIPPS, Author of 'Jurisprudence,' &c. Fcp. 8vo. 2s. 6d.

The HORSE'S FOOT, and HOW to KEEP IT SOUND. By W. MILES, Esq. Ninth Edition, with Illustrations. Imperial 8vo. 12s. 6d.

A Plain Treatise on Horse-Shoeing. By the same Author. Sixth Edition. Post 8vo. with Illustrations, 2s. 6d.

Stables and Stable-Fittings. By the same. Imp. 8vo. with 13 Plates, 15s.

Remarks on Horses' Teeth, addressed to Purchasers. By the same. Post 8vo. 1s. 6d.

ROBBINS'S CAVALRY CATECHISM, or Instructions on Cavalry Exercise and Field Movements, Brigade Movements, Out-post Duty, Cavalry supporting Artillery, Artillery attached to Cavalry. 12mo. 5s.

BLAINE'S VETERINARY ART; a Treatise on the Anatomy, Physiology, and Curative Treatment of the Diseases of the Horse, Neat Cattle and Sheep. Seventh Edition, revised and enlarged by C. STEEL, M.R.C.V.S.L. 8vo. with Plates and Woodcuts, 18s.

The HORSE: with a Treatise on Draught. By WILLIAM YOUATT. New Edition, revised and enlarged. 8vo. with numerous Woodcuts, 12s. 6d.

The Dog. By the same Author. 8vo. with numerous Woodcuts, 6s.

The DOG in HEALTH and DISEASE. By STONEHENGE. With 70 Wood Engravings. Square crown 8vo. 10s. 6d.

The GREYHOUND. By STONEHENGE. Revised Edition, with 24 Portraits of Greyhounds. Square crown 8vo. 10s. 6d.

The OX; his Diseases and their Treatment: with an Essay on Parturition in the Cow. By J. R. DOBSON. Crown 8vo. with Illustrations. 7s. 6d.

Commerce, Navigation, and Mercantile Affairs.

BANKING, CURRENCY, and the EXCHANGES; a Practical Treatise. By ARTHUR CRUMP. Post 8vo. 6s.

The ELEMENTS of BANKING. By HENRY DUNNING MACLEOD, M.A. Barrister-at-Law. Post 8vo. [Nearly ready.

The THEORY and PRACTICE of BANKING. By the same Author. Second Edition, entirely remodelled. 2 vols. 8vo. 30s.

PRACTICAL GUIDE for BRITISH SHIPMASTERS to UNITED States Ports. By PIERREPONT EDWARDS. Post 8vo. 8s. 6d.

A DICTIONARY, Practical, Theoretical, and Historical, of Commerce and Commercial Navigation. By J. R. M'CULLOCH, Esq. New and thoroughly revised Edition. 8vo. price 63s. cloth, or 70s. half-bd. in russia.

The LAW of NATIONS Considered as Independent Political Communities. By Sir TRAVERS TWISS, D.C.L. 2 vols. 8vo. 30s. or separately, PART I. Peace, 12s. PART II. War, 18s.

Works of Utility and *General Information.*

MODERN COOKERY for **PRIVATE FAMILIES**, reduced to a System of Easy Practice in a Series of carefully-tested Receipts. By ELIZA ACTON. Newly revised and enlarged Edition; with 8 Plates of Figures and 150 Woodcuts. Fcp. 6*s.*

On FOOD and its DIGESTION; an Introduction to Dietetics. By W. BRINTON, M.D. With 48 Woodcuts. Post 8vo. 12*s.*

WINE, the VINE, and the CELLAR. By THOMAS G. SHAW. Second Edition, revised and enlarged, with 32 Illustrations. 8vo. 16*s.*

A PRACTICAL TREATISE on BREWING; with Formulæ for Public Brewers, and Instructions for Private Families. By W. BLACK. 8vo. 10*s.* 6*d.*

SHORT WHIST. By MAJOR A. A thoroughly revised Edition, with an Essay on the Theory of the Modern Scientific Game by PROF. P. Fcp. 3*s.* 6*d.*

WHIST, WHAT TO LEAD. By CAM. Fourth Edition. 32mo. 1*s.*

A HANDBOOK for READERS at the BRITISH MUSEUM. By THOMAS NICHOLS. Post 8vo. 6*s.*

The CABINET LAWYER; a Popular Digest of the Laws of England, Civil, Criminal, and Constitutional. Twenty-fourth Edition, brought down to the close of the Parliamentary Session of 1868. Fcp. 10*s.* 6*d.*

The PHILOSOPHY of HEALTH; or, an Exposition of the Physiological and Sanitary Conditions conducive to Human Longevity and Happiness. By SOUTHWOOD SMITH. M.D. Eleventh Edition, revised and enlarged; with 113 Woodcuts. 8vo. 7*s.* 6*d.*

HINTS to MOTHERS on the MANAGEMENT of their HEALTH during the Period of Pregnancy and in the Lying-in Room. By T. BULL, M.D. Fcp. 5*s.*

The Maternal Management of Children in Health and Disease. By the same Author. Fcp. 5*s.*

The LAW RELATING to BENEFIT BUILDING SOCIETIES; with Practical Observations on the Act and all the Cases decided thereon; also a Form of Rules and Forms of Mortgages. By W. TIDD PRATT, Barrister. Second Edition. Fcp. 3*s.* 6*d.*

NOTES on HOSPITALS. By FLORENCE NIGHTINGALE. Third Edition, enlarged; with 13 Plans. Post 4to. 18*s.*

COULTHART'S DECIMAL INTEREST TABLES at 24 Different Rates not exceeding 5 per Cent. Calculated for the use of Bankers. To which are added Commission Tables at One-Eighth and One-Fourth per Cent. 8vo. price 15*s.*

MAUNDER'S TREASURY of KNOWLEDGE and LIBRARY of Reference: comprising an English Dictionary and Grammar, Universal Gazetteer, Classical Dictionary, Chronology, Law Dictionary, a Synopsis of the Peerage, useful Tables, &c. Revised Edition. Fcp. 10*s.* 6*d.*

INDEX.

LONDON: PRINTED BY
SPOTTISWOODE AND CO., NEW-STREET SQUARE
AND PARLIAMENT STREET

www.ingramcontent.com/pod-product-compliance
Lightning Source LLC
Chambersburg PA
CBHW052347110726

47901CB00005B/1398